JANE SEYMOUR, QUEEN OF ENGLAND.
FROM AN OLD PRINT

ANNALS OF THE SEYMOURS

BY

H. S^T MAUR

**BEING A HISTORY OF THE SEYMOUR FAMILY,
FROM EARLY TIMES TO WITHIN A FEW YEARS
OF THE PRESENT**

CHARLOTTE, DAUGHTER OF THE DUKE OF
HAMILTON AND BRANDON, DUCHESS OF SOMERSET

LONDON :
KEGAN PAUL, TRENCH, TRÜBNER & CO., LTD.,
PATERNOSTER HOUSE, CHARING CROSS ROAD, W.C.
MCMII.

PREFACE.

By the above lines I do not intend to convey an impression that we should look upon any of the lives recorded in the following pages as being sublime, but merely that, by studying the characters of men of a bygone time, and seeing in what manner they met the difficulties and temptations that come to every one, I think we are likely ourselves to receive much benefit, and our thoughts, when absorbed by such study, are likely to turn from the trivial trials and annoyances of every-day life into a wider, deeper, and perhaps nobler, channel.

Biographies, if they are complete and truthful, afford much interesting and beneficial food for reflection, and, though I have not attempted to give anything like a full account of any person in this book, yet I hope and believe that the short biographies (if I may presume to call them such) contained in it will be found to provide matters of interest, worthy, perhaps, of a few moments' reflection. The annals may seem dry and prosy, but, should the

A

reader find them so, I would beg him to forgive me, remembering always that it is not an easy task to construct amusing or readable matter out of plain facts without adding to them by drawing on the imagination, a thing I have carefully refrained from doing—truth being the great essential to make a biography of any value.

Some members of the Seymour family have, as we all know, become famous in history, and their names frequently recur in various works, but only in a fragmentary manner, scattered here and there throughout the many pages of England's history.   Such accounts are necessarily incomplete (for no individual, however great, is of a sufficient importance as to receive more than passing mention in the history of a great country), and from their brevity are frequently apt to leave upon the reader's mind an erroneous or at least inaccurate impression of the character of the person thus briefly alluded to.   There are but few of the Seymours who stand out with any great prominence or are of any general interest, but the lives of these few are certainly deserving of some fuller record than they have hitherto received,* and it has seemed to me that, even were such record made, something would yet be wanting for the proper understanding of their characters—something that would show in what relation these greater figures stood to each other, something that would complete the links between them and perhaps help to explain, to a certain degree, the motives that led them to certain actions.   This something, I fancied, might be supplied by filling in the gaps, by

* In saying this, I must make an exception of the Protector Somerset whose political life has been fully dealt with by Mr. A. F. Pollard in his essay " England under Protector Somerset," pub. 1901.

inserting the lesser figures, which, of little interest though
they may be in themselves, serve to complete the chain.
And this is what I have attempted to do in these annals.

In this I have been greatly assisted by the discovery
in my library of a great mass of MS. notes, in the
handwriting of the 11th Duke of Somerset, who appears
at one time to have intended writing a complete account
of the family, a task for which he was especially fitted,
being much esteemed by Professor Playfair (who often
sought his advice) for the accuracy and depth of his
researches into history. Many of these notes were drawn
from original documents, letters, and papers in his possession, as well as from papers in the possession of other
families. The material to be found relating to the Seymour family, however, is very considerable, and I have
not attempted to make use of it all. I have merely
stated, in as few words as possible, the more interesting
particulars of what the successive Seymours did, and have
not attempted to give an account of the various phases of
the times in which they lived, or of the political situations
in which the country stood. Such an account would have
become a history of England.

Few people, in these days of ever-increasing hurry and
competition, have anything but a very superficial knowledge of their family history, and I am in hopes that
perhaps these pages may serve, not only to pass away a
few idle hours, but to encourage others to glance back
into the annals of the past and see if the history of their
ancestors, full as they will find it of their family's own
peculiarities of temper and character, will not teach them
at the least one useful lesson. I think that a perusal of
these particular annals will reveal the fact that a prominent

feature in the character of the Seymour family has been a
great, often predominant, pride. Whether this pride
should be accounted a virtue or a fault in them in the
past it would be difficult to judge, but I think in many
cases it has been a pride of the better kind, acting as a
powerful force to urge them on to do their duty to their
country, and spurring them to great and noble deeds. In
some instances it has perhaps acted more in the way of
a stumbling-block, spoiling careers that otherwise might
have been brilliant. A great pride is apt to become a
dangerous possession ; it may degenerate into a mere
foolish conceit in personal antiquity of rank or station.
When this happens, and no doubt it happens often and to
all families, then the purer and nobler objects of life are
lost sight of, and the family's pride degenerates into a
vulgar conceit, which soon becomes the object of a well-
deserved ridicule.

A man may justly be proud of his particular family, not
because of its antiquity or for the reason that some member in former times purchased or even won a title, but on
account of there having been good and upright men in it—
men who, regardless of personal loss of favour, popularity, or property, have throughout done what they
honestly conceived to be their duty to their Sovereign and
to their country, who have, if ever so slightly, helped on
the great cause of Liberty and Progress, and to whom, in
return, posterity owes some measure of gratitude. A man
who is proud of his family for this reason only will feel
the force of former example ; he will feel that to him is
left the responsibility of upholding the honour of the
great men who have preceded him ; that it becomes his duty
to try and climb one rung or two higher on the ladder of

merit ; that it would bring infamy and dishonour to them, and to himself if he did not at least retain his position ; he will realise that the higher his family has already been raised, the greater are the things expected of him, and the more necessary is it for him to do them ; he will know, and may be proud of the knowledge, that it becomes his duty to work harder than other men in utilising to the best advantage such gifts of mind as he may be endowed with in order to retain the respect and esteem hitherto accorded to his name. His pride will act as an incentive, ever urging him to just and noble actions, and ever acting as a check to prevent him straying from the path of integrity and honour.

Such, I venture to say, is the pride that has belonged to many of the Seymours in the past. How, I wonder, will it act in the future ? Will it be the means of lulling them into a false sense of their own importance, of letting them imagine that nothing more is required of them, that the deeds of their forefathers have wiped out their debt and obligation to their country ; that they need now but rest and amuse themselves, secure in the mistaken belief that the brightness of their former renown needs no further care to keep off the tarnish that, without it, inevitably dims the lustre of the brightest object ? Or will it, as I hope, be the means of rousing them again to a noble ambition—an ambition to do good ; to become once more great for the service of their Sovereign and their country, and for the furtherance and security of their religion, of which in its troublous infancy they were the mainstay and the head ; and to help on the cause of Liberty and Justice to which already the family has always been attached, and for which some also have suffered ? Who can tell ?

THE author wishes to acknowledge his most grateful thanks to Mr. A. F. Pollard, whose admirable essay "England under Protector Somerset" has been of the greatest assistance to him, and to the Lady Gwendolen Ramsden and Mr. W. H. Mallock for the "Letters and Memoirs of the 12th Duke of Somerset" and the "Letters of Earl St. Maur and Lord Edward St. Maur," which have also been of the greatest use. He wishes also to acknowledge his indebtedness to the late Lord Leconfield and to Lady Leconfield, to the Lady Gwendolen Ramsden, the Lady Ulrica Thynne, and to Mrs. Alfred Seymour and Miss Seymour, of Knoyle, for their kind permission to reproduce some of their pictures, several of which have never been published before. He also wishes to express his obligation to all other authors and others who have directly or indirectly assisted him in his work.

LIST OF ILLUSTRATIONS.

ERRATA.

Page 254, line 5, *omit* reference to Note 86.
Page 258, line 15, *for* Note 85 *read* Note 84.
Page 258, line 30, *for* Note 86 *read* Note 85.
Page 261, line 5, *for* Note 87 *read* Note 86.
Page 263, line 9, *for* Note 88 *read* Note 87.
Page 263, line 27, *for* Note 88A *read* Note 88.

Sir John Seymour,
d. unmarried,
1552.

Sir Edward Seymour,
of Berry Pomeroy, *m.*
Jane, d. of John Walsh, Esq.,
b. 1529, *d.* 1593.

Ed eymour,
ur,
eymour.

ORIGIN AND EARLY DAYS

OF THE

ST. MAUR OR SEYMOUR FAMILY.

THE origin of every family, of no matter how great importance, can scarcely be traced without considerable difficulty to the time when it first became of sufficient greatness to obtain even the slightest mention in such few chronicles as were kept in the obscure and stormy days of European history preceding the Norman Conquest. Even such writings as remain in old and almost undecipherable manuscripts, can hardly be considered as affording reliable and trustworthy information. Most of them were written by the monks of old who, in the seclusion of their monasteries, could only write on hearsay evidence of the events passing around them. Such stories as thus came to their knowledge had already, we may be sure, passed through many repetitions, and were certain to have become inaccurate and distorted. One cannot, therefore, look upon them without a certain amount of suspicion.

In endeavouring to discover early traces of the St. Maur family, a further difficulty is encountered in the fact that, after William the Conqueror's arrival in England, accompanied, as will presently be seen, by a Seigneur de Saint Maur, no mention is made of the family for a considerable time (that is, no mention of their doings, though the name is to be met with in deeds and charters of the time), not in fact until they once again reach sufficient prominence to be noticed by the chroniclers. This has, not unnatu-

B

rally, cast a doubt in the minds of historians as to their
real origin, which the majority do not attempt to trace
beyond the St. Maurs of Penhow, in Monmouth, whom,
however, they generally agree to have been without doubt
of Norman origin, and to have come to this country either
with, or shortly after, the Conqueror.

In a history of this kind it is of course necessary to
start as far back as possible, and it is my intention to
begin with the first mention of the name.   At the same
time I must caution the reader that I can obtain no
authentic data earlier than the year 1000, and that although
I commence at an earlier date, I myself can only look
upon it as little better than a legend, drawn from unreliable sources.

There is in France a small but very ancient village
named " Saint Maur-sur-Loire."   It is supposed to have
been named thus on account of a black hermit, famous
for his goodness and piety,* who is said to have lived in
the 7th century, and to have been an Abyssinian prince,
descended from the royal race of Solomon and (sad to
relate) the Queen of Sheba, but who had been obliged to
leave his country during some insurrection in which his
father and his nearest relatives had been massacred.

710.   In the year 710 this village is said to have been
in the possession of the family of St. Maur, who
no doubt must have taken their name from the place, from
being the most important owners there, for it is beyond
the bounds of possibility that they can have been the
issue of the hermit.   The head of the family is supposed
to have been Richard de St. Maur, and he is said
679.   to have been mentioned in a grant to the royal
Abbey of Villers, founded by Queen Frédégonde.

In addition to Richard, a Guy de St. Maur is said

---

* There undoubtedly was a famous saint called St. Maur, to
whom churches were dedicated and whose feast days were held,
but it is doubtful whether there was any connection between the
hermit and the saint, who, I believe, during his lifetime, was an
abbot.

701. to have performed his fealty and homage at the same Abbey in 701, and a Ludo de St. Maur is
919. said to have been mentioned in a list in 919.

Even legend, however, does not supply us with any account of these or their descendants, and it is necessary to go on to Goscelin de Ste. Maur or Maure, surnamed Peitazinua, probably on account of some voyage, pilgrimage, or exploit, that he performed in Aquitaine. This Goscelin de Ste. Maur is mentioned :—

1000. 1. In a charter of Foulque Martel, Comte d'Anjou, in the year 1000.
2. In the foundation of the Abbey of Beaulieu, with Suhard de Craon, and other gentlemen.

He is always styled " Castri Sanctæ Mauræ dei gratiâ jure hereditario possessor et dominus." Pope Gregory VII wrote him a letter (the 22nd in the second volume of his letters) which is reproduced in "l'Histoire de Sablé," p. 254.

1009. Goscelin de Ste. Maur married Aremburge in the year 1009, and by her had four sons, viz., Josbert, Guillaume, Hugues, Goscelin. Of these the latter had a son Guillaume who died s.p., and Hugues married Alner de Berlay de Montreuil by whom he had several children, only one of whom, Hugues (1087 to 1105), however, left any issue. This was a son Gautier, whose son Guillaume left an only daughter who married the Seigneur de Pressigny in Tourraine, who took the name of the heiress and founded the second house of Ste. Maur.* The above Guillaume is mentioned in 1198 as being in Normandy.†

Of Goscelin's two elder sons one appears to have been a priest. This must have been Josbert, for the second son

---

* For the above statements, see La Chenaye des Bois. It does not, however, mention where Goscelin de Ste. Maur came from, but mentions the walls of Ste.-Maur, near which was the priory of Mesmin.
† See The Norman People.

Guillaume seems to have had a son Wido de Ste.
1066. Maur who came to England during the Norman
        invasion.   It is of course impossible to show any
proof as to who did or did not actually accompany the
Conqueror, as there is no list of names in which the
least reliance can be placed.   In an account of the Battle
Abbey Roll (the inaccuracy of which is, I believe, generally admitted) in Fuller's Church History by Brewer,
where the lists in Holinshed and Stow's Chronicle are
compared, the name appears in both.   In Holinshed,
p. 5, as Sent More and in Stow, p. 107, as Seint More.
The difference in spelling has probably caused the name
to be overlooked, but I feel confident that it is intended
for Saint Maur.   This name indeed has undergone very
many changes of spelling and even pronunciation.   In
Latin deeds it generally became de Sancto Mauro, but we
also find Saynt-Mor, Sayn-Maur, Seyne-More, Senne-
Maur, Seyne-Maure, Semor, Semore, Seimour, and
finally Seymour.   Even in Queen Elizabeth's time I
have found it spelt Seymaur, and in Queen Anne's reign
Seimour, whilst in these days of education I frequently
receive letters addressed Saint Mor, St. Mor, St. More,
and even St. Muyre.

Wido de St. Maur, as we have seen, came over to
        England in 1066.   He died before 1086, leaving
1086. a son William Fitz-Wido who held a barony in
        Somerset, Wilts, and Gloucester, and ten manors
in Somerset.*   Most of this property he no doubt inherited from his father, who must have received them from
the Conqueror, as there is no mention of either marrying
an heiress.   We may therefore conclude that Wido must
have rendered some service to the Conqueror to merit
such a reward.

During the period immediately following the Conquest,
when the country was still far from being settled down,
very few records appear to have been kept or, if they

* See The Norman People.

were, they have for the most part been lost. It is not surprising, therefore, that we should find but little mention of a private family. There appears, however, to 1100. have been a Roger de St. Maur living in the year 1100,* a son, apparently, of William Fitz-Wido, and in 1129 he appears as a witness to a charter of Richard de Cormeil to the Priory of Monmouth.†

1129. This deed has no date, but it must have been signed in that year, for Baderon, Lord of Monmouth, and Rohesia his wife, who were married in 1128, also signed it as witnesses, and it was made prior to the death of Prior Godfrey which occurred in 1130.† This Roger had therefore some connection with the county of Monmouth, and it may not be unreasonable to suppose that he had settled at Penhow, for we find the family owning that place not many years after. He is stated to have been the founder of two families, but there is some confusion in tracing them.* An Almericus de Sancto Mauro is mentioned as being master of the order of Knights Templars,* and also a Bartholemew de Sancto 1170. Mauro who witnessed a charter of William, Earl of Gloucester, to Keynsham Abbey about 1170.† This Bartholemew seems without doubt to have been a son of Roger, and father of William de Sancto Mauro, one of the King's esquires in 1175.‡ This 1217. William apparently had a son, Milo, for in 1217 we find a Milo de St. Maur who is stated to have been without doubt a direct descendant of Roger.§ But little is known about him, except that he took part with the rebellious Barons against King John, on the occasion when the latter was forced to sign the Magna Charta, and that he left two sons, Geffrey and William.‖

* Complete Peerage, by Rev. A. Jacob, 1766.
† Notes on Penhow Castle, by O. Morgan and J. Wakeman, 1867.
‡ Notes on Penhow Castle (Pipe Roll, 21 Henry II).
§ Dugdale's Baronage ; also Complete Peerage (Jacob).
‖ Dugdale's Baronage ; also Complete Peerage (Jacob). (Among

In the Wiltshire Archæological Magazine, vol. xv, p. 142, we see Mr. J. R. Planché (Brit. Archæol. Journ., 1856, p. 325) says : " There are two families of St. Maur. The St. Maurs or Seymours of Kingston Seymour, in Somersetshire, who trace their pedigree to Milo de Sancto Mauro, who with his wife Agnes, is named in a fine roll of King John ; and the St. Maurs or Seymours of Penhow, Monmouthshire, from which the present ducal house of Somerset descends. All our genealogists, from Dugdale downwards, are scrupulous in observing that there is no connection whatever between the two families, who bore different arms and settled in different counties, and I freely admit there is no connection to be traced between them from the earliest date to which they have proved their pedigree ; but that fact by no means satisfies me that they did not branch from the same Norman stock. We have no proof that there were two St. Maurs who came over with the Conqueror (probably from St. Maure-sur-Loire in la Haute Touraine), nor can we assert that if there were two or more they were not, as in many similar instances, near kinsmen . . . . That their arms should be different is no proof at all, for, although a similarity in their bearings would be strong evidence in favour of some connection, it is one of the most common things in the world to find, in those early days of heraldry, the son bearing a coat quite distinct from that of his father, as he frequently did a perfectly different name." The St. Maurs of Kingston bore Argent, two chevrons gules, a label of five points. The St. Maurs of Penhow, Gules, a pair of wings conjoined in lure, or.

It would appear, therefore, according to Dugdale and others, that the two families were entirely distinct, but I am more inclined to agree with Mr. Planché's reasoning and even to go further and assert that, as far as probabilities can be made to take the place of evidence, these probabilities all tend to show that the two families were

the signatures we find an Aymer de Sancto Mauro, Master of the Temple.—Cott. MS., Aug. 11, 106.)

connected, though, for some reason or other, they were neither of them inclined to acknowledge the fact. To begin with, we must notice that the St. Maur family obtained lands in Wilts and Somerset through Wido de St. Maur. Afterwards, Roger de St. Maur obtained additional lands in Monmouth. Milo de St. Maur undoubtedly held these lands in Monmouth as well as those in Wilts and Somerset yet, immediately after him, we are told that the St. Maurs holding the Monmouthshire property and the St. Maurs holding the Somerset and Wilts property are separate families, having absolutely no connection. And yet Milo left two sons ! There is, however, no record of whom he married, and it is possible that the sons were by different wives, or even that one of them may have been a natural son, which might account for their disclaiming each other. It would be futile to enter into any long argument either for or against the descent of the Seymour family from Milo de St. Maur in the absence of any proofs which could prove or disprove it. The reader must draw his own conclusions from the slender materials here produced, always remembering that Dugdale is by no means an authority to be absolutely relied on, and that many later genealogists have merely copied what he wrote.*

Of Milo's sons the elder, Geffrey, married a daughter of William de Rughdon,† but beyond this there appears to be no mention of him, except that he was succeeded by

1274. a son, Laurence de St. Maur, who, in 1274, obtained from King Edward I a grant for a market, to be held at his Manor of Rode, in Somerset, upon the Thursday in every week, and also to hold a fair

---

* At the same time it must be remembered that Roger de St. Maur is stated as being the founder of two families, only one of which can be traced, and that not in a very satisfactory manner. It is possible, but hardly probable, that the St. Maurs of Penhow came from the other, but even then the connection would only be rendered more distant.

† Dugdale.

there every year upon the eve, day, and morrow of St.
Margaret, the Virgin.* In 1282 we find him
1282. acknowledging the service of half a knight's fee
for his own inheritance in Wilts, and one-third of
a knight's fee for the inheritance of Sibilla, his wife, in the
county of Northumberland.† In August of the same
year he led an expedition against the Welsh. In
1295. 1295 he was exempted from the general summons
of persons holding land by military tenure, for
1297. the King's expedition to Gascony (June 14).†
In July, 1297, he was summoned to perform
military service beyond the seas.† This summons can
only have arrived after his death which had taken place
the previous winter. He left one son, Nicholas.*

Nicholas de St. Maur did his homage, and had livery of
his father's lands. He also had been summoned in July,
1297, for military service abroad, and appears to have
attended the summons, and gone furnished with horses
and arms.† In 1298 he was summoned to per-
1298. form military service against the Scots, by a letter
dated May 25, and in June, 1300, he was again
1300. summoned for a similar purpose.† In 1306 he
again served there in the retinue of Henry of
Lancaster, the younger son of Edward Crouchback, Earl
of Lancaster. In 1313 he obtained a pardon, as
1313. an adherent of the Earl of Lancaster, for having
participated in the death of Gaveston, and in the
same year was summoned to Parliament as representative
of Gloucester.† In the following years, 1314,
1314–17. 1316, 1317, he was summoned to perform
military service against the Scots.† In 1316 he
was certified as Lord or joint Lord of the following
hundreds and townships :—North-Molton in Devon,
Hampton-Maysi in Gloucester, Yonkill and Weston in
Hereford, Woolverton and La Road in Somerset, Eton-

* Dugdale.
† Parliamentary writs and writs of military summons, Public
Record Office.

Maysi, Poulton, and Witham in Wilts.* His first wife had been Eve de Meysi, who had brought him considerable property, but had not lived long. (Note 1.) His second wife was Helen, the eldest of the three daughters and coheirs of Alan la Zouche of Ashby, in Leicester. By this marriage he gained considerable importance as well as more property. (Note 2.) He died in 1317, leaving a son, Thomas. His wife, Helen, survived him, and married Alan de Cherleton.†

1317. Thomas de St. Maur was only 9 years of age at the time of his father's death. He became, in consequence, a ward at the disposal of the Sovereign, Edward II, who almost immediately granted letters patent to Hugh le Despencer, the elder, giving him the wardship of the Manors of Hampton-Maysi, in Gloucester, and Eton-Maysi, in Wilts, which the late Nicholas had held, as part payment of certain debts which were owed him by the King.‡ (Note 3.) This wardship was to be held during the minority of Thomas, who does not, however, appear to have lived many years after coming of age. Little further can be found about him, except that he founded the Priory of Dulton, in Wilts, annexing it, as a cell, to the Priory of Semplingham, in Lincoln.† The successor to the estates was Sir Nicholas de St. Maur, Knight, who served in the wars in France in the retinue of Maurice de Berkeley in 1348, and again in the 1348. retinue of Thomas de Holland in 1360. He was summoned to Parliament from 1352 to 1352-61. 1361.† He married Muriel, the daughter and heiress of James, the son and heir of Richard, Lord Lovel, by whom he had two sons, Nicholas and Richard, the former of whom died young.†

Richard de St. Maur inherited all his father's estates,

* Parliamentary writs and writs of military summons, Public Record Office.
† Dugdale, also Complete Peerage (Jacob).
‡ Public Record Office, Pat. Roll, 10 Edward II, part 2, mem. 6, 28.

which appear to have been considerable. (Note 4.) In
1387 he served in the wars in France, in the
1387. retinue of Richard, Earl of Arundel, Admiral of
England. He was also summoned to Parliament
1381. from 1381 to 1401.* He married Ela, the daughter
and coheir of Sir John St. Loe, Knight, and died
May 15, 1401, leaving three sons, Richard, John, and
Nicholas, of whom both the latter died without issue.*
By her testament, dated 1409, Ela bequeathed her body
to be buried in the new chapel of Staverdale Priory, next
to her husband's grave. She left her son Nicholas twenty
pounds, her son John a set of beads of coral, garnished
with gold, and made him her heir male, whilst Alice, her
grand-daughter, was made her heir female.*

Richard de St. Maur served in Ireland under Thomas,
Duke of Surrey, the Lieutenant of that realm, in
1399. 1399, and afterwards in France, in 1402. He
was summoned to Parliament from 1402 to 1407,
and died the following year, leaving no male issue. His
wife, Mary, received at his death a considerable
1408. dowry, and his daughter, Alice, inherited the remainder of his property. This daughter was born
either just before or just after his death in the house of
Thomas Cressy, citizen and mercer of London, in the
parish of St. Laurence, in Cripplegate Ward, and was
baptised in the church of St. Laurence. She married Sir
William le Zouche, Knight, of Totnes, who performed
fealty, and had livery of her lands.*

Thus the elder of the two families started by Milo de
St. Maur came to an end in an only daughter. We will
therefore now go back to his second son, William, for
from him apparently are descended the St. Maurs or
Seymours of the present day. Sir William de St. Maur,
Knight, was expressly called " of Penhow,"† which was
one of the border castles in Monmouth erected against the

---

* Dugdale and Rev. A. Jacob.
† Notes on Penhow Castle.

Welsh, and which, as has been already noticed, had formed part of the possessions of the family for some time. These possessions Sir William evidently determined to increase, for, in 1235-6, he entered into an agree-

1235. ment with Gilbert Marshall, Earl of Pembroke, to wrest the Manor of Woundy or Undy (as it was called later) from a Welshman, Morgan ap Howell, Lord of Caerleon,* an attempt which appears to have been successfully carried out, the manor being subsequently divided between the Earl and Sir William.   An old Latin record, which is transcribed in Vincent's manuscript baronage in the College of Arms, No. 20, says : " Gilbertus Marescallus, comes Pembrochiæ tenetur præbere domino Willo de S. Mauro consilium in quantum poterit, secundum leges Angliæ, ad perquirendum manerium de Woundy, de Morgano filio Hueli, tali conditione quod si præd ; Willus dictus menerium perquirere poterit, dictus Gilbertus habebit medietatem dicti manerii, et aliam medietatem faciat extendi dicto Willo, per probos et legales homines ad hoc ex utraque parte electos ita quod pro qualibet summa 20 L. redditus dictus Gilbertus dabit Willo de S. Mauro decem libras.   Et quod idem Willus de S. Mauro teneat medietatem dicti manerii in manu sua, donec inde plenam solutionem, sicut præscriptum est, receperit.   Et si forte contigerit, quod idem Willus de consilio dicti Gilberti defecrit, dictus Willus de S. Mauro remaneat solutus et quietus de obligatione, quam dictus Gilbertus fecit super dictum manerium de Woundy."

Sir William de St. Maur thus became possessed of the Manor of Undy in addition to that of Penhow.† The latter place he made his residence, and soon transformed it into a larger and more important castle, surrounded by a large park, both of which he named St. Maur.‡ He also dedicated the church there to St. Maur, the patron

---

* Notes on Penhow Castle.

  † Dict. Nat. Biog., and J. R. Planché, Journ. Archæolog. Assocn., 13, 327-8.

  ‡ Complete Peerage (Jacob).

saint of the family,* who seems to have been of some importance in ancient days, for even now churches are to be found abroad that were dedicated to him. Camden, in his chronicles of events in Ireland, 1361, also mentions him : " On the feast of St. Maur the Abbot, there happened a violent wind, that shook or blew down the pinnacles, chimneys, and such other buildings as over-topped the rest ; trees without number and several steeples ; particularly the steeple of the Friar's Preacher's." (Note 5.)

Sir William's signature appears as witness to two charters of Gilbert Marshall, and to three of Walter Marshall, two being undated, and the third bear-1245. ing the date 1245.† He married the 3rd daughter of William Marshall, Earl of Pembroke, but nothing more is to be found about him except that his son, Roger, is mentioned as succeeding him.

Sir Roger de St. Maur inherited his father's possessions at Undy and Penhow. He is mentioned as Lord 1269. of the Manor of the former in 1269. He died before 1300, and was succeeded by his eldest son, Roger.‡ (Note 6.)

It is at this period that we first find mention made of the arms of the St. Maur family which, from a seal appendant to a grant of messuage to Thomas Elliot, of the chapel of Undy, surrounded by this inscription : " Sigill, Rogerii de Seimour," appear to have consisted of two angel's wings, joined, tips downward. In an MS. of Percy Enderby, which was in the possession of S. R. Bosanquet, Esq., in 1867, he records that in the " South windows at Penhow there were in the centre the arms of Seymour, Gules, 2 wings conjoined, or." In his History of Modern Wiltshire, vol. i, p. 115, Sir Richard Colt Hoare says : " Percy Enderby, in his book entitled

---

* Complete Peerage (Jacob).
† Notes on Penhow Castle.
‡ Augustine Vincent's Manuscript Baronage, 1613.

PENHOW CASTLE AND CHURCH, FORMERLY CALLED ST. MAUR, IN MONMOUTH.

From an Old Print.

Cambria Triumphans, informs us, that the arms, now
borne by Seymour (viz. : a pair of wings) were, in his
time, visible in the church at Penhow ; both cut in stone
and in painted glass ; and I have been informed by a
friend of mine, who lately visited Penhow at my request,
that he perceived the wings on two old windows, belonging to a tenant at that place, and which being rather
singular as to their application and situation, I think
worthy of remark."*

  Of Roger de St. Maur but little is known, except
1314. that he lived in the year 1314, and married Joan,
   daughter of ——— Damarel, of Devonshire,† by
whom he had two sons, Sir John St. Maur and Sir Roger

  St. Maur, the former of whom died about 1358,
1358. leaving a son, Roger, born in 1340, who in turn
   left an only daughter who married into the family
of Bowlays, near Penhow, and apparently brought her
inheritance of Penhow Castle into that family.‡

  Sir Roger St. Maur, or Seymour as we may now call
him, became Lord of the Manor of Woundy in succession
to his father. He does not, however, appear to have
spent much of his time there, preferring to reside at
Evinswinden, in Wilts.§ He married Cecilia, daughter
of John de Beauchamp, Baron of Hache, in Somerset.§

  Camden says : " From William de St. Maur, knight,
who first settled at Woundy, descended Roger de St.
Maur, knight, who married one of the heiresses of the
illustrious John Beauchamp (this John Beauchamp of
Hache married Cecilia, daughter of Beauchamp, Earl of
Warwick, as may be seen in Sir William Dugdale's Antiquities of Warwickshire), the noble Baron de Hache,
who was descended from Sybill, one of the coheiresses of
that most puissant William Marshall (so called from his

 * A drawing of one of these windows may be seen in Sir R.
Colt Hoare's History of Modern Wiltshire.
 † Vincent's MS. Baronage ; also Complete Peerage (Jacob).
 ‡ Dict. Nat. Biog.
 § Vincent's MS. Baronage ; also Complete Peerage (Jacob).

office), Earl of Pembroke ; and from William Ferrers,
Earl of Derby ; Hugh de Vivon ; and William Malet,
men of eminent worth in their times.   The nobility of all
which, as also of several others, have (as may be made
evident), concentred in the Right Honourable Edward de
St. Maur or Seymour, now Earl of Hertford, a singular
encourager of virtue and learning ; for which qualification he is deservedly famous."

In his description of the county of Somerset, Camden
again says: "The Beauchamps, otherwise de Bellocampo,
have flourished in great honour from the time of Henry II,
especially since Cecilia de Fortibus, descended from the
Earls of Ferrariis, and from the famous Marshall of
England, William, Earl of Pembroke, was married into
this family.   But in the reign of Edward III, the estate
was divided by sisters, between Roger de Sancto Mauro
and John Meriel, both of them sprung from ancient and
honourable ancestors.   This is the cause why Henry VIII,
after he had married Jane Seymour, Edward VI's mother,
made Edward Seymour, her brother, Viscount Beauchamp."

This marriage not only greatly advanced the importance
of the Seymour family, but brought them a considerable
increase in wealth for, as we have seen, the Lady Cecilia
            was one of two sisters, the last of the Beauchamp
1363.   family, and, in 1363, the entire possessions of that
            family were divided between them.* (Note 7.)
She died in 1393, having survived her husband, by
whom she had five sons, the eldest of whom, William,
being the only one about whom any information is to be
gathered.

This Sir William Seymour, knight, resided for the
most part at Undy. (Note 8.)   He is mentioned, in
1362, as attending the Prince of Wales to his government of Gascony, after first obtaining the King's letter
of protection, dated from Bamberg on February 8 of that

* Camden.

year.   He married Margaret, daughter of Simon de Brockburn, and died in 1390, leaving a son, Roger, born in 1366.* (Note 9.)

1393. Within three years of the death of his father, Roger Seymour inherited all the possessions of his grandmother, Cecilia, in addition to the property already received from his father.   He was at this time 27 years of age.*   He married Maud, daughter and coheir to
    Sir William Esturmy, knight, of Wolfhall in 1420. Wilts,† and died in 1420, leaving a son, John,
    born in 1402.   Camden says : "The Esturmies had been bailiffs and guardians of the forest of Savernake, by right of inheritance, from the time of Henry III. The Earl of Hertford, descended from this Roger, had in his possession their hunter's horn of a mighty bigness and tipped with silver.   The Esturmies are famous for being the founders and patrons of the hospital of the Holy Trinity at Easton, near Marlborough, in Wilts."

John Seymour inherited all his father's possessions, which had been so greatly encreased by his marriage, at the age of ' 18.   Being also heir to his cousin, Sir Peter
    de la Mere, knight, he became of still greater
1431. importance.   In 1431 he served as Sheriff of the
    county of Southampton, and in the following year of Wiltshire.   Soon after this he was made a knight, and appears to have become one of the most important of the gentlemen of Wilts ; for, in the list of names of the
    gentlemen of that county returned by the Com-
1434. missioners in 1434, his name appears first, after
    those of the elder knights and William Westbury, Justiciarus.   He also served as Sheriff of Gloucester and
    Somerset, and again of Southampton in 1437.
1437. In 1451 he served in Parliament as one of the
    knights for the county of Wilts, this Parliament

* Vincent's MS. Baronage;   Complete   Peerage   (Jacob);
Edmundson's Peerage ; Camden.
    † History of Modern Wiltshire.

being one held at Reading.* His wife was Isabel, daughter of Mark Williams, of Bristol, by whom he had a son, John.†

Isabel Seymour, who had been married in 1424, survived her husband for many years, dying April 14, 1463. 1485.‡ Two years after her husband's death, in 1463, she took the vow of perpetual chastity in the collegiate church of Westbury, *inter missar solempnia*, in the presence of Bishop Carpenter, who gave her his benediction and put upon her the vidual vesture, June 3, 1465.§ She was possessed in fee of divers messuages, cottages, and gardens, in the town and suburbs of Bristol ; and held in dower, or by joint feoffment with her late husband Sir John Seymour, various lands in the counties of Southampton, Wilts, Hereford, and Somerset. Her heir was found to be her grandson, John Seymour of Wolfhall, in Wilts, who at the time of her death was 34 years of age. His father and mother had both predeceased his grandmother.‖

John Seymour, described as of Wolfhall (the Ulfela of the Saxons), in Wilts, served as Sheriff for that county in 1458. He married Elisabeth, daughter of Sir Robert Coker of Laurence Lydiard, in Somerset, and died in 1463, a month or two before his father, leaving two sons, John and Humphrey, the latter of whom settled at Evinswinden,¶ and married the daughter and coheiress of Thomas Winslow of Burton, Oxon. The Seymours of Oxford and Gloucester were directly descended from him. Elisabeth Seymour died 1472.**

The elder brother, John Seymour of Wolfhall, was born in 1450. He was, therefore, barely 14 years of age

* Vincent's MS. Baronage ; Camden ; Complete Peerage (Jacob), &c.
† Close Roll, 23 Henry VI (endorsement).
‡ Genealogist.
§ Bishop Carpenter's Register at Worcester, vol. i, fol. 192.
‖ Genealogist, vol. xii, N.S., p. 74.
¶ The old name for Swindon.
** Vincent's MS. Baronage ; Complete Peerage (Jacob), &c.

when his father and grandfather died. He was twice married, first to Elizabeth, daughter of Sir George Darell, of Littlecote in Wilts, by Margaret, daughter of John, Lord Stourton; secondly to a daughter of Robert Hardon, by whom he had one son, Roger, who in 1491. turn left four daughters, his coheirs. The death of John Seymour occurred in 1491.* By his first wife, Elizabeth, he left numerous issue :

Sir John Seymour, of whom we will speak next.

George Seymour, who was Sheriff of Wilts in 1499.

Robert Seymour.

Sir William Seymour, who was made a Knight of the Bath at the marriage of Arthur, Prince of Wales, November, 1501.†

Margaret Seymour, who married Sir William Wadham, knight.

Jane Seymour, who married Sir John Huddlestone, of Warleston, in Cumberland.

Elizabeth Seymour, who married John Crofts, Esq.

Catherine Seymour, who died unmarried.

* Genealogist.
† Hume, 3, 411.

C

SIR JOHN SEYMOUR.

Sir John Seymour inherited most of the family possessions.   He was born about the year 1474*, and
1492. succeeded his father in 1492.†   In 1497 he
attended the King at the battle of Blackheath, in
Kent, against the Cornish rebels under the command of
Lord Audley.   On this occasion he was only
1497. acting as a volunteer, but he displayed such marks
of a great military genius, that the King's attention
was drawn to him, and he received the honour of knighthood in the field.‡   In 1508 he was made Sheriff
1508. of Wiltshire.†   Five years later he made a campaign in France and Flanders, and was present
1513. at the sieges of Terounne and Tournay.†   At the
latter place he succeeded in performing such signal
services that the King, who was present, conferred upon
him the honour of Knight Banneret.   He was also present
at the action of Guinegaste, otherwise called the Battle of
the Spurs, on account of the precipitate retreat of the
French.

After his return to England he served at different times
as Sheriff of Dorset, Somerset, and Wilts, and appears to
have been held in great favour at Court, for he was appointed one of the knights of the body to the King.   In
1517 he obtained for himself and his eldest living
1517. son, Edward, the constablewic of Bristol Castle,
with power to enjoy the same in as ample a manner

---

* The Dictionary of National Biography mentions 1476 as
the probable year of his death, but the accompanying portrait was
taken in the 62nd year of his age, so that as he died in 1536 he
cannot have been born later than 1474.

† Dict. Nat. Biog. ; Collins' Peerage, 1, 149.

‡ Collins' Peerage.

SIR JOHN SEYMOUR.

From a picture at Stover, the property of H. St. Maur, Esqr.

as Giles, Lord d'Aubeny, had done.* In 1520 he was
nominated one of those who attended the grand
1520. interviews, held between Guisnes and Ardres,
between King Henry VIII and James, King of
France. On this occasion he had in his retinue one chaplain, 11 servants, and 8 led horses.†

In 1522, by command of the King, he joined the Royal
retinue at Canterbury, where Henry was to meet
1522. Charles V upon the latter's arrival in England.
Shortly after this he was appointed one of the
Commissioners to the county of Wilts to inquire into the
possessions of Cardinal Wolsey. In 1532 he
1532. attended the King to Boulogne upon his second
interview with the King of France,‡ and acted on
this occasion in the capacity of groom of the bedchamber.

There is not much further information to be gathered
as to events of Sir John Seymour's life. We find, indeed,
that he was named in a Commission of the Peace for
Wiltshire in the 24th year of Henry VIII, and among
the grants for the same county in March, 1531, and
February, 1532,§ but there is little else. After having
made his mark as a soldier in his younger days, he appears to have been satisfied with the favour and confidence shown him by the King and to have devoted a
considerable portion of his time to attendance on the
King's person; indeed, in 1535 he had the honour of
receiving a visit from the King at his country seat of
Wolfhall (September 10), where he entertained the Royal
party for several days.‖

His character must have been such as to render him
both liked and respected by all parties at the Court, or he
could never have avoided being mixed up in some of the

* Brewer, State Papers, July 15, No. 3474; September 20,
No. 4446.
† Complete Peerage (Jacob) and Guthrie's Peerage.
‡ Dict. Nat. Biog.; Collins' Peerage, I, 149.
§ Gairdner, Letters and Papers, Henry VIII, vol. v.
‖ Dict. Nat. Biog.

many intrigues of the time ; yet it appears that he had
one enemy for certain, for, in a letter of his to Cromwell,
we read: "As everybody has furnished you with venison,
I send you a winter tegge of my own killing. I trust
you will remember me against my enemy, Essex,* who
works me all the ill in his little power."†

It is possible that history might have had more to tell
us about Sir John Seymour if it were not that his career,
busy as his life had been, sinks into insignificance beside
those of his children, whose names were so soon to fill all
England. He is in fact best known to us as being the
father of a Queen, of a Protector of the Realm, and grandfather of a King.

He married Margery, daughter of Sir Henry Wentworth, of Nettlested, in Suffolk, a Knight of the Bath
and ancestor of the Earls of Cleveland. Her grandfather,
Sir Philip Wentworth, had married Mary, daughter of
John, seventh Lord Clifford, whose mother, Elisabeth, was
daughter of Henry Percy (Hotspur) and great great grand-
daughter of Edward III.‡ He died December 21,
1536. 1536, and was buried in the chapel at Easton
Priory, whence his remains were removed in 1590
by his grandson Edward, Earl of Hertford, to the church
at Great Bedwyn, in Wilts, where most of the Seymours
have been interred. Here a great monument was erected
to him, with a long inscription, which consisted chiefly of
an account of his many children. The accompanying
pictures show this monument before, and after, it was
defaced in order to allow two fresh windows to be opened
in the church. (Note 10.)

Sir John had six sons and four daughters, viz. :—

Sir John Seymour, knight, who died July 15, 1520,
  unmarried.§

* Probably Sir William Essex.
† Gairdner, Letters and Papers, Henry VIII, vol. v, 1531-2.
‡ Notes and Queries, 1 ser. viii, 51-2 ; Harl. MS. 6177.
§ Dict. Nat. Biog.

TABLET TO JOHN SEYMOUR IN GREAT BEDWYN CHURCH, WILTS.

TOMB OF SIR JOHN SEYMOUR, KNᵗ
IN GREAT BEDWYN CHURCH.
The arms restored from Aubrey's sketch, circa A.D. 1658; and the shields arranged
in the order set down in his MS.

SIR JOHN SEYMOUR'S TOMB IN GREAT BEDWYN CHURCH.
Before the alteration.   From an old print.

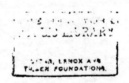

SIR JOHN SEYMOUR'S TOMB IN GREAT BEDWYN CHURCH.
Shewing the alterations recently made.

Sir Edward Seymour, who succeeded him and afterwards became Duke of Somerset. We will speak of him later.

Sir Henry Seymour, knight, who married Barbara, daughter of Morgan Wolfe, Esq., by whom he had three sons, of whom there is no issue remaining. He took no part in politics, but was made a Knight of the Bath, February 27, 1547, together with his elder brother, then Earl of Hertford, and many others, on the occasion of the Coronation of Edward VI. In 1551, the King, in whose service he was, rewarded him for his zeal by giving him some large grants of land, and in the following year enriched him still further. On his mother's death, in 1550, he found himself her sole executor. He died in 1578, leaving (in addition to the sons already mentioned) seven daughters, from one of whom, Jane, are descended the Barons Rodney.*

Sir Thomas Seymour, afterwards Baron Seymour of Sudley and High Admiral of England. We will speak of him later.

John Seymour and Anthony Seymour, both died young, leaving no issue.*

Jane Seymour, who became wife of Henry VIII and Queen of England, and of whom we will speak next.

Elizabeth Seymour, who married three times : first, Sir Henry Oughtred ; then Gregory, Lord Cromwell ; and finally John Pawlet, second Marquis of Winchester.*

Margery Seymour, who died in childhood.*

Dorothy Seymour, who married Sir Clement Smith, knight, of Little Baddaw, in Essex ; the father of Sir John Smith, knight, Ambassador to Spain.†

* Dict. Nat. Biog.
† Inscription in Great Bedwyn Church, printed in Aubrey, p. 375-6.

[The Norman People ; La Chenaye des Bois ; Public Records ;
Wiltshire Archæological Magazine ; British Museum MSS. ;
Cotton MS. ; Harleian MS. ; Dictionary National Biogra-
phy ; Gairdner's Letters and Papers ; Notes and Queries ;
Brewer, State Papers ; A Complete Peerage, Rev. A. Jacob ;
Vincent's MS. Baronage ; The Genealogist ; Camden ;
Bishop Carpenter's Register ; Edmondson's Peerage ; Col-
lins' Peerage ; Dugdale's Baronage ; History Modern
Wiltshire, Sir R. Colt Hoare ; J. R. Planché, Journal
Archæological Association ; Notes on Penhow Castle, by
O. Morgan and J. Wakeman, 1867 ; &c.]

JANE SEYMOUR, WIFE OF HENRY VIII, AND QUEEN OF ENGLAND.

From an old print.

JANE SEYMOUR.

1509. Jane Seymour was born about 1509, apparently in her father's house of Wolfhall. Some tapestry and bedroom furniture which she worked there as a girl came later into the possession of Charles I, who presented it to William Seymour, Marquis of Hertford, in 1647. During the struggle between Charles and the Parliament, Seymour had to compound with the latter in order to retain these relics, the sum to be paid amounting to sixty pounds. It is uncertain if any of these things are still in existence.*

Jane Seymour has been stated by Miss Strickland to be the subject of a portrait in the Louvre gallery, which was said to represent one of the French Queen's maids of honour, although no name is stated in the inscription. The portrait appears probably to have been that of Anne of Cleves, but it had not been identified at the time Miss Strickland wrote.†

All that we know for certain of Jane's early life is that she was attached to Catherine of Aragon's household, as lady in waiting, not long before Catherine ceased to be Queen, and was subsequently placed in the same position with Anne Boleyn.‡ She was described by Chapuys, the Emperor's ambassador in England, in 1536, as "of middle stature and no great beauty," but though he did not praise her for her beauty, he did for her intelligence.‡

1535. On September 10, 1535, she appears to have been at Wolfhall on the occasion of the King's visit to

* Dict. Nat. Biog.; Wilts Archæolog. Mag., xv, 205.
† Dict. Nat. Biog.
‡ Dict. Nat. Biog.; Letters and Papers of Henry VIII, xi, 32.

her father and to have assisted in entertaining him.*   Up
to this time she had passed unnoticed amongst the other
ladies of the Court; but, during the few days of his visit,
the King was able to discover the many brilliant qualities
of her mind, and the charm of her manner.   Pleased by
her conversation he, from that time, took more notice of
her and frequently sought her company for a short period,
during the various Court functions ; a preference which
speedily excited the jealousy and ill-feeling of the Queen,
Anne Boleyn, and of many of the Court beauties.

In February of the following year it has been
1536. stated that the King gave her some costly presents,
and it is most probable that he may have offered
them to her.   There is nothing, however, to show that
she accepted his gifts ; indeed, from her conduct soon
after, it is more than probable that she may have declined
them.   An old story says that she possessed a locket containing a portrait of the King, which flew open on one
occasion when the Queen, in a fit of temper, struck at her
with such a force as to tear the locket from her neck,†
but this appears to be the only present ever actually
mentioned and was one certainly that she could scarcely,
with civility, have refused.

The story of the presents probably originated from the
gossip of the other ladies of the Court who, in their
jealousy, were not likely to adhere too strictly to
the truth.   Chapuys, however, gives credence to it in
a gossiping letter which he wrote to the Emperor on
February 21, 1536.   " Upon the whole, the general
opinion is that the concubine's (Anne Boleyn's) miscarriage
was entirely owing to defective constitution and her utter
inability to bear male children ; whilst others imagine
that the fear of the King treating her as he treated his
late Queen,—which is not unlikely, considering his
behaviour towards a damsel of the Court, named Miss

* Dict. Nat. Biog.
† Fuller's Worthies.

Seymour, to whom he has latterly made very valuable presents."*

In March, however, the King actually did send her a purse full of sovereigns, together with a letter, said to contain dishonourable proposals. I think it will be generally agreed that her behaviour on this occasion refutes any story of her having accepted gifts previously. Chapuys, writing to the Emperor on April 1, says : " Just at this moment I receive a message from the Marchioness (of Dorset) confirming the information I once had from Master Geliot (Eliot ?), namely, that some days ago, the King being here in London, and the young Miss Seymour, to whom he is paying court, at Greenwich, he sent her a purse full of sovereigns, together with a letter ; and that the young damsel, to whom he is paying court, after respectfully kissing the letter, returned it to the messenger without opening it, and then, falling on her knees, begged the royal messenger to entreat the King, in her name, to consider that she was a well-born damsel, the daughter of good and honourable parents, without blame or reproach of any kind ; there was no treasure in this world that she valued as much as her honour, and on no account would she lose it, even if she were to die a thousand deaths. That if the King wished to make her a present of money, she requested him to reserve it for such a time as God would be pleased to send her some advantageous marriage."†

Thus did a young girl reply to the advances of a King, and that King Henry VIII ! Need more be said before we cast aside, with all the contempt they deserve, these tales and insinuations, brought forward by idle scandalmongers in the past to destroy a maiden's honour ?

To the surprise of many, this answer of Jane Seymour's appears to have pleased the King, and to have made him like and respect her more than before. Chapuys, in his letter to the Emperor, proceeds to say :

* Spanish State Papers, 1536.
† Spanish State Papers, 43, 1536.

"The Marchioness also sent me word that in consequence of this refusal, the King's love for the said damsel had marvellously encreased, and that he had said to her that not only did he praise and commend her virtuous behaviour on the occasion, but that in order to prove the sincerity of his love, and the honesty of his views towards her, he had resolved not to converse with her in future except in the presence of one of her relatives, and that for this reason the King had taken away, from Master Cromwell's apartments in the palace, a room to which he can, when he likes, have access through certain galleries without being seen, of which room the young lady's elder brother and his wife have already taken posession."* The brother referred to is Sir Edward Seymour, afterwards Duke of Somerset and Protector of the Realm, a man whose honour no one has ever dared to call in question.

Seeing the way the King's affections were tending, many courtiers, not of Anne Boleyn's party, made haste to press their advice and wishes upon young Jane Seymour. She was advised, even beseeched, by those who hated the Queen, " to tell the King frankly, and without reserve, how much his subjects abominate the marriage contracted with the concubine (Anne Boleyn), and that not one considers it legitimate, and that this declaration ought to be made in the presence of witnesses of the titled nobility of this kingdom, who are to attest the truth of her statement should the King request them on their oath and fealty to do so."† Chapuys himself, in his letter, appears to have been very anxious to lend a helping hand in endeavouring to persuade Jane to assist in the schemes of the Catholics, and, by her influence with the King, to bring about Anne Boleyn's fall, and thus aim a blow at the Reformation, towards which Anne was inclined.†

Jane Seymour, however, does not appear to have acted upon the suggestions made to her ; in fact, during her

* Spanish State Papers, 43, 1536.
† Chapuys to the Emperor. Spanish State Papers, 43, 1536.
‡ Chapuys to the Emperor. Spanish State Papers, 1536.

short period of power she made a point of never interfering in political or religious matters, knowing that it was none of her business to meddle in the affairs of the country. The fate of Anne Boleyn depended upon the King's humour or caprice. No word of Jane's could have hastened or delayed her fall, which was inevitable. Anne Boleyn did not suffer because the King had wearied of her, but because of her own inconstancy, which rendered her unfit to continue the wife of any man, or to remain a Queen of any nation.

Soon after the commencement of Anne Boleyn's trial, or rather of the preliminary proceedings, Jane Seymour moved to a house belonging to Sir Nicholas Carew, about seven miles from London. Before the 15th of May, the day of Anne's trial, she was moved to a house on the Thames, within a mile of Whitehall, and it was here that she learnt of Anne's condemnation from Sir Francis Bryan. The King, himself, called upon her that afternoon.*

On the day of Anne Boleyn's execution, Archbishop Cranmer issued a dispensation for the marriage of Henry VIII and Jane Seymour without publication of banns, and in spite of the relationship " in the third and third degrees of affinity " between the parties.†

The next morning Jane Seymour was privately taken down to Hampton Court Palace, where she was formally betrothed to the King.‡ It has generally been stated that their marriage took place the same day in the church near Wolfhall, and that the wedding banquet took place in a large barn near that house. This story is, however, uncorroborated by any contemporary correspondence.§ Eight

* Dict. Nat. Biog.

† In Notes and Queries, vol. vii, p. 42, there is a detailed pedigree tracing the descent of Jane Seymour, through Margaret Wentworth, her mother, by an intermarriage with a Wentworth, and a grand-daughter of Hotspur, Lord Percy, from the blood royal of England.

‡ Friedmann, Anne Boleyn, ii, 354.

§ Letters and Papers, x, 411 ; Wilts Archæolog. Mag., xv, 140, *seq.*, containing a drawing of the barn.

days certainly elapsed between the betrothal and the marriage, and Jane Seymour appears to have spent that time under the paternal roof.* On May 29, or the day previous, she arrived in London and the marriage was celebrated, in private, on the 30th, in "the Queen's closet at York place."†

It was now just upon Whitsuntide and, in the ensuing festivities, Jane was openly introduced to the Court as Queen of England.‡ On June 29, St. Peter's Eve, "the King paid the citizens the compliment of bringing his fair Queen to Mercer's Hall, and she stood in one of the windows to view the annual ceremony of setting the city watch."§ (Note 11.)

* Dict. Nat. Biog.

† Letters and Papers, x, 413–14. Froude, in explanation of what to modern eyes appears to have been the most indecent haste, says : "The Privy Council and the Peers, on the same grounds which had before led them to favour the divorce from Catherine, petitioned the King to save the country from the perils which menaced it, and to take a fresh wife without an hour's delay. Henry's experience of matrimony had been so discouraging, that they feared he might be reluctant to venture upon it again. Nevertheless, for his country's sake, they trusted that he would not refuse." . . . . "The indecent haste (in performing the marriage) is usually considered a proof entirely conclusive of the cause of Anne Boleyn's ruin. To myself, the haste is evidence of something very different. Henry, who waited seven years for Anne Boleyn, was not without some control over his passions ; and if appetite had been the moving influence with him, he would scarcely, with the eyes of all the world fixed upon his conduct, have passed so gross an insult upon the nation of which he was the Sovereign. The precipitancy with which he acted is to me a proof that he looked on matrimony as an indifferent official act which his duty required at the moment ; and if this be thought a novel interpretation of his motives, I have merely to say that I find it in the statute book.

"Similarly on the death of Jane Seymour, the Council urged immediate re-marriage on the King, considering a single prince an insufficient security for the future." See a letter of Cromwell's to the English Ambassador at Paris on the day of Jane Seymour's death in the State Papers, a portion of which is quoted by Froude.

‡ Dict. Nat. Biog.

§ Lives of the Queens of England, Miss Strickland. Froude's Hist. England.

KING HENRY VIII.

From an Old Engraving.

The new Queen was well received both by the people and the Court, the members of the latter congratulating the King " upon his union to so fair and gentle a lady."[*] It may not be out of place to remark here that Chapuy's unfavourable description of her appearance was not generally shared. It is true that she could not lay claim to great beauty, but her features appear to have been pretty and pleasing and, had it not been for an excessive paleness, she might have been called beautiful.   Sir John Russell (afterwards Earl of Bedford), " having been at Tottenham, a parish church, with the royal pair " gave it as his opinion " that the King was the goodliest person that was there, and that the richer Queen Jane was dressed the fairer she appeared ; on the contrary, the better Anne Boleyn was apparalled the worse she looked ; but that Queen Jane was the fairest of all Henry's wives, though both Anne Boleyn, and Queen Catherine in her younger days, were women not easily parallelled."[†]   Jane's chief charm, however, consisted in the kindness and goodness of her disposition, which qualities were specially evinced in her treatment of the Princesses Mary and Elizabeth, to whom she exhibited marks of an almost maternal tenderness,[†] and in the invariable kindness which she showed to the Princess Mary, between the King and whom she successfully effected a reconciliation.[‡]

Mary of Hungary wrote in praise of her to Ferdinand, King of the Romans, and described her as " a good imperialist," while Cromwell wrote to Gardiner of the King's marriage—" he (the King) has chosen, as all his nobles and council upon their knees moved him to do, the most virtuous lady and veriest gentlewoman that liveth."[§]   The following letter, from Chapuys to the Emperor, written on June 6, may be of interest : " . . .

[*] Dict. Nat. Biog.
[†] Lives of the Queens of England, Miss Strickland. Froude's Hist. England.
[‡] Wood, Letters of Illustrious Ladies, ii, 262.
[§] Cromwell to Gardiner. Gairdner's Letters and Papers, Henry VIII, let. 29, p. 17.

Mass over, I accompanied the King to the apartments
of the Queen, whom with the King's pleasure I kissed,
congratulating her on her marriage, and wishing her
prosperity. I told her besides that although the device
of the lady who had preceded her on the throne was
'the happiest of women,' I had no doubt she herself
would fully realise that motto. I was (said I) sure that
your Majesty would be equally rejoiced, as the King
himself had been, at meeting with such a virtuous and
amiable Queen, the more so that her brother* had once
been in your Majesty's service. It was almost impossible
to believe (I added) the joy and pleasure which Englishmen of all ranks had felt at the marriage, owing especially
to the rumour that had circulated abroad that she was
continually trying to persuade the King, her father, to
restore the Princess to his favour, as she formerly was.
Among the many felicities which I enumerated, I said to
the Queen, certainly the chief one was the Princess, in
whom, without having had the pain and trouble of bringing her into the world, she had such a daughter that she
would receive more pleasure and consolation from her
than from any other she might have. I ended by begging
her to take care of the Princess's affairs; which she
kindly promised to do, saying that she would work in
earnest to deserve the honourable name which I had
given her of pacificator, that is, 'preserver and guardian
of the peace.'

"After this address of mine the King, who in the
meantime had been talking with the ladies of the Court,
approached us and began making excuses for the Queen,
saying that I was the first Ambassador to whom she had
spoken; she was not used to that sort of reception; but
he (the King) imagined that she would do her utmost to
obtain the title of 'pacificator' which I had greeted her
with, as besides being herself of kind and amiable disposition and much inclined to peace, she would make the
greatest efforts to prevent his taking part in a foreign

* Sir Edward Seymour.

war, were it for no other thing than the fear of having to separate herself from him."*

A curious example of the haste with which everything had been done by Henry VIII is that Miles Coverdale, who had just been completing the publication of his Bible, which he had dedicated to the King and Anne Boleyn, found himself suddenly compelled to print the initials of Jane's name across that of Anne.†

The Whitsuntide festivities over, matters appear to have gone on smoothly and satisfactorily for a time. On June 8, Queen Jane was made a present of Paris Garden, in July she accompanied the King on a journey through Kent to Canterbury, whence they journeyed to Dover to see the pier which had not long been commenced, and in August she went on a hunting expedition with her husband.‡

Parliament, meanwhile, had, in July, settled that the succession to the Crown should be vested in Jane's children, to the exclusion of the Princesses, Mary and Elizabeth, and that the Coronation should take place at Michaelmas.† A report, however, soon spread that the Queen was not likely to bear children and the ceremony of the Coronation was delayed, and although her name was introduced into the bidding prayer by Cranmer, it was generally rumoured that she would never be crowned at all unless she became a mother.§ Chapuys wrote to Granville : ". . . The Coronation of this Queen has been delayed till after Michaelmas. Suspicious persons think it is to see if she shall be with child ; and if not, and there is danger of her being barren, occasion may be found to take another. I am told on good authority that this King will not have the prize of those who do not

* Spanish State Papers, vol. 5.
† Dict. Nat. Biog.
‡ Dict. Nat. Biog. Lives of the Queens of England, Miss Strickland.
§ Gairdner's Letters and Papers, Henry VIII; Dict. Nat. Biog.

repent in marriage ; for within eight days after publication of his marriage, having twice met two beautiful
young ladies, he said and showed himself somewhat sorry
that he had not seen them before he was married
. . . ."* Again, writing to Charles I, Chapuys says :
". . . . The Queen's Coronation which was to have
taken place at the end of the month is put off till next
summer and some doubt it will not take place at all.
There is no appearance that she will have children."*
The alarm that this was now occasioning the King caused
him again to think of the Princess Mary, to whom he
had been reconciled through the efforts of Jane, as his
successor, and we find Chapuys writing—". . . On
the King's return from hunting she (the Princess) will go
to the Court to be named heiress of the Crown in default
of issue by the present Queen, and none is expected on
account of the complexion and disposition of the King
. . . ."†

The great friendship of the Queen towards the Princess
Mary had been, ever since the marriage, causing some
alarm to the followers of the Reformed Church, who had
hoped to obtain her assistance to their cause, the more so
as her brother, now Viscount Beauchamp, was believed to
favour their views. The Queen, however, showed no
preference for either religious party, doubtless thinking
that, whatever her own views might be, she had no
business or occasion to meddle in church affairs. This
caused her to be viewed with some disfavour by the
Reformers but to be held in greater esteem by the
Catholics, at that time the more powerful party. Luther,
in a letter to Nic Hausmann, says : ". . . Alesms
writes from England that the new Queen, Jane, is to be
crowned at Michaelmas. He says that she is an enemy
of the Gospel, and the state of the kingdom is so altered
that Antonius (Barnes) lies hid and keeps quiet, yet he is

* Gairdner's Letters and Papers, Henry VIII, lett. 8, p. 10, and
No. 528, p. 215.
† Gairdner's Letters and Papers, Henry VIII, 493, p. 200.

not free from danger."* Cardinal Pole, on the other hand, wrote in great praise of her, describing her as "full of goodness."† The Catholics, indeed, might well have deemed themselves the favoured party, for the only occasion on which Jane ever attempted to sway Henry's mind, was during the Pilgrimage of Grace and in favour of the restoration of the dissolved Abbeys. In a letter to Cardinal du Bellay, we read, "At the beginning of the insurrection the Queen threw herself on her knees before the King and begged him to restore the Abbeys, but he told her prudently enough to get up, . . . and not to meddle in his affairs, referring to the late Queen . . ."‡

In the December following Jane returned to London with the King, and on the 22nd of that month they rode in great state through the City.§ The winter of 1536–7 was one of extraordinary severity, and in the January we find a record of her crossing the frozen Thames, on horseback, to Greenwich Palace, accompanied by the King and the whole Court.‖

1537.

In March, to the great joy of the King and of the whole country, it was announced that the Queen was with child.¶ Being of a delicate constitution it now became necessary for her to lead a more quiet and retired life, and the coronation was, therefore, once more postponed. Prayers were ordered to be said at mass for her safe delivery, and she was removed to Hampton Court where, in September, she took to her chamber.**

"The splendid Gothic banqueting hall," says Miss Strickland, "was finished at this juncture, for Queen Jane's initials are entwined with those of her husband among the decorations. . . . At the entrance of the

* Gairdner, 475, p. 188.
† Strype's Memorials, i, ii, 304.
‡ Gairdner, 860, p. 345.
§ Dict. Nat. Biog.
‖ Lives of the Queens of England, Miss Strickland.
¶ Gairdner's Letters and Papers, vol. xii.
** Notes and Queries, 3rd ser., i, 186.

chapel, on each side of the doorway, is a species of a coloured stone picture, containing Henry's arms and initials on the right, and Queen Jane's arms with the interchanged initials J. H. and H. J., with love-knots intertwined. The motto, arms, and supporters of Jane Seymour as Queen are among the archives of Herald's College. Over the shields is inscribed 'BOUND TO OBEY AND SERVE,' in English. Her supporters were, on the right side, a unicorn, with a collar of roses around his neck, alternately a red and a white one. It seems the unicorn was adopted for her as the emblem of chastity. On the left side was a horse ducally collared. Her family shield of the Seymour arms is entire, not impaled with the royal arms, emblazoned in an escutcheon of the usual broad form ; the crown of England is over the shield, and beneath it is written ' REGINA JANE.' "*

On Friday, the 12th of October, the Queen gave birth to a son,† and on the same day wrote to Cromwell to announce to him and to the Privy Council the birth of an heir to the throne "conceived in lawful matrimony." This letter was signed " Jane the Quene."‡

Her health, however, was not by any means satisfactory, although at first there appeared no cause for anxiety. With rest and care she would doubtless have recovered, but, unfortunately, it appears to have been a rule that a Queen of England should attend her infant's christening, which in this case took place very soon after the child's birth. The baptism took place in the evening, by torch-light, and the ceremony lasted till midnight. The Queen was carried from her room to the chapel on a sort of pallet or sofa, on which she reclined propped up by cushions and wrapped in a crimson velvet mantle, and during the whole of the proceedings King Henry remained

* Lives of the Queens of England, Miss Strickland.
† " The report that the Cæsarian operation was performed in her case was an invention of the Jesuit, Nicholas Sanders."—Dict. Nat. Biog.
‡ Gairdner's Letters and Papers ; Cotton MS.

KING EDWARD VI.

From a portrait at Stover, in the possession of H. St. Maur, Esqr.

seated at her side.* An account of the ceremony is to be found in Gairdner's Letters and Papers. (911.) The Princess Elizabeth carried the chrysome and, on account of her tender age, was in turn borne in the arms of Viscount Beauchamp, the Queen's brother.†

The exertion of this long ceremony, however, was too great for Jane's strength. "What with the procession setting out from the chamber, and the braying of the trumpets at its entrance when it returned (the herald especially notes the goodly noise they made there) ; and, in conclusion, the exciting ceremonial of bestowing her maternal benediction on her newly baptized babe, the poor Queen had been kept in a complete hurry of spirits for many hours."‡ It appears, in addition, that she had caught a cold, as the result of which and perhaps also of improper diet, she fell seriously ill and soon after expired, Wednesday, October 24, twelve days after the birth of her son, Edward, afterwards King Edward VI.§

Her death appears to have caused the King greater sorrow than any other event of his reign and, whatever his behaviour may at times have been, there seems no doubt that he had become deeply attached to her. On no other occasion was he ever known to have exhibited signs of such genuine grief, and he who hated black to such an extent that no one had ever dared to wear it about the Court, went into mourning himself for several months, an attention which he paid to the memory of none of his other wives.‖ That the people in general also shared his grief may be seen by an old ballad (Bell, Ancient Poems of the Peasantry of England), which was very popular at the time.

Froude says of her character, "Although she makes no figure in history, though she took no part in State

* Lives of the Queens of England, Miss Strickland.
† Letters and Papers, 911.
‡ Lives of the Queens of England, Miss Strickland.
§ Strype's Memorials ; Fuller's Church History, Brewer.
‖ Lives of the Queens of England, Miss Strickland ; Dict. Nat. Biog.

questions, and we know little of her sympathies or opinions, her name is mentioned by both Protestant and Catholic with unreserved respect. . . . Her uprightness of character and sweetness of disposition had earned her husband's esteem, and with his esteem an affection deeper than he had perhaps anticipated. . . . She was also deeply regretted by the whole Court whom she had attached by the uncommon sweetness of her disposition. . . . "

Queen Jane's body was embalmed and lay in state at Hampton Court till the 12th of November, when it was removed with great pomp to Windsor and buried in the choir of St. George's Chapel,* where the following epitaph was inscribed above her tomb :

> " Phœnix Jana jacet, nato Phœnice, dolendum
> Sæcula Phœnices nulla tulisse duas." (Note 12.)

According to the King's commands and to his last will and testament, his remains were, at his death, to be laid by her side. He further ordered that " Both their statues were to be placed on the tomb : the effigy of Jane was to recline, not as in death, but as one sweetly sleeping ; children were to sit at the corners of the tomb, having baskets of roses, white and red, made of fine Oriental stones—jasper, cornelian, and agate, ' which they shall show to take in their hands, and cast them down on and over the tomb, and down on the pavement ; and the roses they cast over the tomb shall be enamelled and gilt, and the roses they cast on the steps and pavement shall be formed of the said fine Oriental stones.' "† This beautiful idea, however, was never carried out. The materials for it were indeed gradually collected and placed in the chapel, but they were stolen or destroyed during the Civil War.‡

Later on, when seeking for a place in which to lay the body of Charles I, the searchers came upon the coffins of

* Dict. Nat. Biog.; Letters and Papers, Henry VIII, vol. xii.
† Lives of the Queens of England, Miss Strickland.
‡ Dict. Nat. Biog.

Henry and Jane, beside whom they laid the headless corpse of the murdered King ; and again, when George IV was seeking in the vaults for the plain lead coffin containing Charles, Queen Jane's coffin was found close to that of Henry VIII, whose enormous skeleton an accident had exposed to view. King George (all praise to his kindly feeling !) refused to allow Jane's coffin to be interfered with, and finally caused the vault to be closed up.*

For a long time after Queen Jane's death, the bed and apartment in which she died and in which Edward VI was born, were shown to the public, and they are mentioned by Hentzner, who saw them in the latter part of Elizabeth's reign. In more recent years, however, every fragment of the furniture of the Queen's apartments has been removed, and the very apartments altered, even to the beautiful entrance from the great staircase, which has been walled up. Tradition, however, still asserts that, in spite of these changes, " ever as the anniversary of Edward VI birth-night returns, the spectre of Jane Seymour is seen to ascend those stairs, clad in flowing white garments, with a lighted lamp in her hand."†

Only two documents with Jane's signature appended remain to us. One announcing the birth of her son has already been noticed here, the other is merely a warrant addressed to a park-keeper in 1536 for the delivery of two bucks.‡

Catalogues of her jewels, lands, and the debts owing to her at her death are among the British Museum MSS. (Royal) and at the Record Office.§ All her property reverted to the King.

There are several portraits of Queen Jane, but few of them are satisfactory to my mind. There is a certain stiff-

* Lives of the Queens of England, Miss Strickland.
† Lives of the Queens of England, Miss Strickland.
‡ Cotton MS.; Vesp., F. 3, 16.
§ Dict. Nat. Biog.

ness about the pictures of that period, especially in the women's portraits, which always gives me the impression that the likenesses are not likely to be good. A half-length picture, believed to be by Holbein, is at Stover, a sketch by Holbein is at Windsor, replicas of a finished portrait by the same artist are at Woburn Abbey and at Vienna. The Woburn picture was engraved in a medallion by Hollar and also by Bond for Lodge's " Portraits " ; the Vienna picture was engraved by G. Büchel. Copies of the painting belong to Lord Sackville, the Society of Antiquaries, the Marquis of Hertford, Sir Rainald Knightley, and the Duke of Northumberland. A miniature by Hilliard is at Windsor. There was also a portrait group, by Holbein, of Henry VIII, his father, mother, and Jane, which was destroyed by the fire at Whitehall in 1698, a small copy of which is at Hampton Court.*

[Lives of the Queens of England, Miss Strickland ; Dict. Nat. Biog. ; Gairdner's Letters and Papers, Henry VIII ; Notes and Queries ; Spanish State Papers ; Friedmann's Anne Boleyn ; Froude's History ; Wood's Letters of Illustrious Ladies ; Strype's Memorials ; Cotton MS. ; Fuller's Church History, by Brewer ; Bell, Ancient Poems ; British Museum Royal MSS. ; Wilts Archæolog. Mag., &c.]

---

* Dict. Nat. Biog.

SIR THOMAS SEYMOUR, BARON SEYMOUR OF SUDELEY.

From an old print.

SIR THOMAS SEYMOUR, BARON SEYMOUR OF SUDELEY, AND HIGH ADMIRAL OF ENGLAND.

Thomas Seymour was the fourth son of Sir John Seymour of Wolfhall, by Margery, daughter of Sir Henry Wentworth (who was descended from John 1508. of Gaunt), and he was born about the year 1508.

He must not be confused with a Sir Thomas Seymour who was Sheriff of London 1516, Lord Mayor of London 1526 and 1530, Mayor of Staple at Westminster, and who was frequently employed in commercial negotiations by Henry VIII. This Sir Thomas died December 11, 1532.*

Of Thomas Seymour's childhood and early years, there is but little information to be found. He appears to have entered the profession of arms in his youth, and to have become so proficient as greatly to excel in the jousts and tournaments which, under the encouragement of the King, were so much in vogue at the time.

It is at the age of 22 that he first comes into 1530. public notice. He was then in the service of Sir Francis Bryan, who regularly employed him on his 1536. frequent embassies.† The marriage of his sister, Jane, to King Henry VIII in 1536, and of another sister, Elizabeth, to Gregory, son of Cromwell, however, placed him before long in a much better position. On October 1 following he was granted in survivorship the Stewardship of Chirk and other castles and manors on the borders of Wales, and not long after was

---

* Dict. Nat. Biog.; Letters and Papers, vol. iv; Greyfriars Chronicle; Ellis, Shoreditch, p. 54.
† Letters and Papers, Henry VIII, v, 323-325.

made a Gentleman of the Privy Chamber. The following year he was granted the castle and manor of
1537. Holt in Cheshire and, on October 18, he received
the honour of knighthood, on the occasion of
the christening of his nephew, afterwards Edward VI.*

In 1538 he was attached to an embassy to the French
Court under Sir Anthony Brown, and during this
1538. year and the next received some large grants of
land, including Coggeshall Abbey and Monastery in
Essex, Romsey Abbey in Hampshire, and Coleshull in
Berkshire.† (Note 13.)

In July a marriage was proposed by the old Duke of
Norfolk between his daughter, the beautiful Mary,
1538. widow of the Duke of Richmond, and Sir Thomas
Seymour. On the 14th of this month, Rafe
Sadleyr wrote to Cromwell : " The day the King removed
from Westminster to Hampton Court, the Duke of
Norfolk made a suit to him touching the jointure of his
daughter, the Duchess of Richmond, and spoke about her
marriage, mentioning two persons, one being Sir Thomas
Seymour. The King has spoken to Sir Thomas about it,
and he, considering that Cromwell's son has married his
sister, preferred him to have ' the mayning of the matter.'
The King desires him to speak to the Duke at some time
convenient, and soon, as the Duchess goes into the
country to-morrow or next day." The proposed alliance,
however, came to nothing, owing chiefly to the difficulties
raised by the Earl of Surrey, Norfolk's son, who had
become a bitter enemy of the Seymour family ever since
his failure in France, where his command had been taken
from him and given to the Earl of Hertford.‡

In 1539 Sir Thomas was one of the escort sent over to
Calais to meet Anne of Cleves and bring her to
1539. England.§ (Note 14.) After her marriage with

* Wriothesley's Chronicle, i, 69.
† Cf. Addit. M.S. 15,553, f. 72 ; Dict. Nat. Biog.
‡ Tytler's Henry VIII.
§ Chron. of Calais, p. 168–173.

sive alliance with France,* and on the 6th was deputed to take the seal from the Lord Chancellor Wriothesley. There was some talk at this time of making him Governor of the King's person, but the project was quickly abandoned.†

Lord Seymour, one would have thought, might have been well contented in attaining both rank, influence, and wealth in so short a time. Although sprung from an ancient and honourable family, he had been but a younger son of a simple knight, and now, having scarce reached the prime of life, he found himself among the most influential men in the kingdom, a Peer of the Realm, High Admiral of England, uncle to the King, and brother of the Protector. All this, however, was not enough. His limitless and unprincipled ambition could not brook any other subject in the Realm holding a higher office ; he must be Protector at any cost. Like his brother, he was brave, accomplished, handsome, and of stately bearing. Unlike his brother, his ambition was purely selfish, his religion was naught, his moral life full of sin, his treatment of his dependants unscrupulous and unjust. Latimer in one of his sermons described him " as a man furthest from the fear of God that he ever knew or heard of in England," and of whom " he had heard so much wickedness that he ever wondered what would be the end of him."‡

Considering his ambition, his want of principle, and of moral or religious feeling, it can readily be understood that he would stop at nothing to attain his purpose—that of supplanting his brother. Determined to advance himself to this end, he commenced immediately after Henry's death to pay his addresses to the Princess Elizabeth, then 15 years of age.§ Here, however, he met with a decided refusal, for she sent him the following letter in reply to

* De Selve, Corresp. Pol., pp. 109-114.
† Greyfriars Chronicle, p. 54; Lit. Remains, Edward VI, p. 114.
‡ Froude's Hist.
§ Wood's Letters, Royal and Illustrious Ladies, iii, 191-2.

one of his proposing marriage :* " My Lord Admiral, the letter you have written to me is the most obliging, and at the same time the most eloquent in the world. And as I do not feel myself competent to reply to so many courteous expressions, I shall content myself with unfolding to you, in few words, my real sentiments. I confess to you that your letter, all elegant as it is, has very much surprised me ; for besides that neither my age nor my inclination allows me to think of marriage, I never could have believed that any one would have spoken to me of nuptials at a time when I ought to think of nothing but sorrow for the death of my father. And to him I owe so much, that I must have two years at least to mourn for his loss. And how can I make up my mind to become a wife before I shall have enjoyed for some years my virgin state, and arrived at years of discretion ?

" Permit me, then, my Lord Admiral, to tell you frankly that, as there is no one in the world who more esteems your merit than myself, or who sees you with more pleasure as a disinterested person, so would I preserve to myself the priviledge of recognizing you as such, without entering into that strict bond of matrimony, which often causes one to forget the possession of true merit. Let your highness be well persuaded that, though I decline the happiness of becoming your wife, I shall never cease to interest myself in all that can crown your merit with glory, and shall ever feel the greatest pleasure in being your servant, and good friend, Elizabeth. February 27, 1547."

In spite of this Seymour does not appear to have

---

* Wood's Letters ; Leti, Vita de Elizabetta, vol. 1, p. 171.

Leti, in writing his life of Elizabeth, had evidently access to many valuable original letters, some of which have now perished ; but as those which remain prove, on comparison, to have been faithfully, though freely, translated by him, there is no reason whatever to doubt the authenticity of the remainder, though the originals may be lost. The letter inserted in the text confirms the report of our historians as to Seymour's proposal immediately after Henry's death.

CATHERINE PARR, WIDOW OF HENRY VIII, AND WIFE OF LORD SEYMOUR, OF SUDELEY.

From an Old Print.

relinquished hope at once, but endeavoured, through a gentleman of the household named Fowler, whom he bribed, to obtain the King's approval and influence.[*] Young Edward, however, was too wise to meddle in such an affair, whereupon Seymour transferred his attentions to the Princess Mary and to Anne of Cleves, both of whom immediately rejected his suit.[†]

There now remained but one more chance of his contracting a royal alliance. This was with Catherine Parr, the late King's widow, who had already been married three times, first to Sir Edward Burgh, secondly to John Nevill, Lord Latimer, and lastly to Henry VIII. Between this lady and Seymour there had already been some incipient love passages while she was the widow of Lord Latimer, and Seymour now renewed the intercourse with such success that within two months or so of the late King's death she became privately his wife.[‡] (Note 15.)

Having accomplished his purpose, Seymour was now confronted with the difficulty of how best to announce the marriage. To his brother he was determined not to go for assistance; the King and Princess Mary, if won over, he thought would be sufficient. Edward's letter was managed through Fowler, but Mary, to whom Seymour applied in person, refused her assistance, saying that the request appeared to her " too strange to meddle with."[§] Whilst this was going on the truth was discovered, and the Council and Protector were " much offended."[‖]

The marriage being an accomplished fact, and there being no remedy for it, the matter was passed over; and to cover any unpleasant feeling, on the breaking out of the Scotch war, the Admiral (Seymour) was desired to take command of the fleet. He preferred, however, to remain at home and carry on his schemes during his

---

[*] Froude's Hist.
[†] De Selve, Corresp. Pol., pp. 154-5.
[‡] Dict. Nat. Biog. ; Froude's Hist.
[§] Froude's Hist.
[‖] Lit. Remains, Edward VI, p. 215.

brother's absence with the army, and so deputed the Lord
Clinton to command the fleet, reserving to himself the
management of the Admiralty.*

His first step was, if possible, to get himself appointed
Governor of the King's person, and, with this object in
view, he began carefully to examine precedents in the
hope of showing that, in cases of a King's minority, it
was usual for one uncle to have the custody of the King's
person while the other was Protector of the Realm.† In
addition to this, he encouraged young Edward to come to
his house as frequently as possible, ostensibly to visit his
stepmother, gave him large presents of money for his
privy purse, bribed his attendants, and formed a league
with some of the dissatisfied nobility, notably the Marquis
of Dorset and the young Earl of Rutland, with the
object of securing votes in Parliament and gaining such
interest in the country as would enable him to raise an
army if required. He also succeeded in obtaining, without the Protector's knowledge or sanction, a new and
more ample patent for his office of High Admiral, with
an addition of 200 marks to the salary.‡

On April 5, before the outbreak of the Scottish war, he
visited the western ports and made, soon after, an expedition against a pirate named " Thomessin," who had seized
on the Scilly Isles and used them as a base whence he
could easily prey upon the traders of all nations.§ Instead
of attacking and capturing this pirate, however, Seymour
came to a friendly understanding with him to share the
spoil and the control of the islands.‖ He then made an
attempt on Lundy Isle, which he occupied, and so arranged
matters as to win over the pirates and privateers to his
own ends, in spite of the remonstrances of the French
Ambassador and the commands of the Protector.¶

* Froude's Hist. ; Dict. Nat. Biog.
† Dict. Nat. Biog.   ‡ Froude's Hist., &c.
§ De Selve, Corresp. Pol., pp. 130, 189.   ‖ Dict. Nat. Biog.
¶ Oppenheim, Administration of the Navy, 1897, pp. 101,
104 ; Chron. Henry VIII, ed. Hume, 1889, p. 161.

In July he received a large grant of manors and estates situated chiefly in Gloucestershire, North Wilts, and Wales, which were ostensibly given to him as an accomplishment of the intended gifts of the late King. Soon after this, in order to secure more fully the aid of the Marquis of Dorset, he lent him several large sums of money, without taking any security, and persuaded him to send his young daughter, the beautiful and accomplished Lady Jane Grey, at that time but 10 years old, to reside in his house, promising that he would not fail to bring about a marriage between her and the young King as soon as he should obtain control of the latter's person.* (Note 16.)

Seymour was now becoming more confident of the ultimate success of his plans. His efforts, however, were by no means relaxed, for he seized every opportunity of slandering the absent Protector, assuring the King that the Scottish invasion "had been madly undertaken, and was money wasted in vain," and urging him to take the government into his own hands. He also tried to persuade Edward to write a letter on his behalf to the Parliament, which met on November 4, but the young King was too shrewd to meddle in such a matter.† To add to the anger he felt at this refusal, a dispute arose over some jewels, which the Protector retained as Crown property, but which he claimed as having been given to his wife by Henry VIII.‡ The little caution and control he had hitherto exhibited now deserted him. He declared openly that, if his demands as to the Governorship of the King's person were refused, he would make it "the blackest Parliament that ever was in England," he would "take his fist to the ear of the proudest that should oppose him," and declared "that he could live better without the Protector than the Protector without him."§

---

* Froude's Hist. ; Haynes.
† Froude's Hist. ; Dict. Nat. Biog.
‡ Froude's Hist.
§ Froude's Hist. ; Haynes.

E

His wild language and his general insolent bearing could not long escape the notice of the Council, who now required him to appear before them and explain his actions. He took no notice of their summons, however, and dared anyone to imprison him. In vain did the Protector send his friends to reason with him, pointing out the injury he was doing to the country, already in an unsettled state owing to the youth of the King and the religious disputes, and begging him to submit to the orders of the Council, who, in all probability, would have sent him to the Tower at once if Somerset had not smoothed matters down to some extent and quieted the Admiral for a time by giving him further grants of land.*

1548. Thus matters stood in the spring of 1548, and nothing much occurred till the summer, when it was decided by the Council to send two expeditions into Scotland, one by land and one by sea, the command of the latter being entrusted to Lord Seymour, who having collected the fleet, started about July or August, taking with him about 1,200 land forces. With these he made two descents on the coast of Scotland, one at St. Ninians, in Fife, and the other at Montrose, but was defeated on each occasion, and, having lost more than half his force, returned to England the latter end of August.†

On September 5, his wife, Queen Catherine, died in childbed.‡ Hers had not, it appears, been a happy marriage. Being Queen-Dowager, the Princess Elizabeth had, not unnaturally, been entrusted to her care, and resided with her in Seymour's house. Thrown thus constantly into her company, it was not long before the Admiral had begun to renew his advances to the Princess, whom he soon commenced to treat with such indelicate familiarity that the Queen grew jealous, and caused her to be removed.§

* Froude's Hist.
† Dict. Nat. Biog.; Froude's Hist.
‡ She was buried in the chapel at Sudeley with much pomp, the Lady Jane Grey going as chief mourner.
§ Haynes; Froude's Hist.; see Raumer and Wright's Collections.

Lord Seymour's intrigues had all along been carried on with unabated vigour. He had endeavoured to ingratiate himself with the landowners who were offended by Somerset's measures. He had endeavoured to secure adherents, with the assistance of Dorset and Northampton, among those gentlemen and yeomen who had nothing to gain by the maintenance of the existing Government. He had acquired all the stewardships and manors he could in order to increase his influence in the country. He had begun to store arms and ammunition in Holt Castle, and had arranged with Sharington, the fraudulent treasurer of the Mint at Bristol, for money sufficient to raise ten thousand men, an army he openly boasted about.* With the pirates and privateers he had always continued on friendly terms, in spite of the many complaints made against them, which came before him at the Admiralty, and to which he paid no attention. When some notorious pirate was captured he was invariably, before long, set at liberty. The cargoes of such piratical craft as were taken were never restored to the merchants who owned them, and the Admiral's followers were frequently to be seen wearing ornaments known to have been plundered.†

Such was the state of affairs at the time of Queen Catherine's death, almost immediately after which he began again to attempt to win the hand of Elizabeth, whose servants he bribed in order to open a direct correspondence, which she appears to have encouraged considerably. So certain did he soon become of his ultimate success, owing to her encouragement, that he began to make the minutest inquiries into her fortune and the management of her estates, and even to offer his counsel as to various exchanges of property.‡ (Note 17.)

However much the Council and the Protector, however, might be inclined to overlook Seymour's other misdeeds, they had no intention of allowing him to marry Elizabeth

* Dict. Nat. Biog. ; Haynes ; Froude.
† Froude's Hist.
‡ Haynes.

and thus obtain a power which would enable him to throw
the country into confusion, if not into a civil war. Russell
and others repeatedly warned him against any attempt at
marrying the Princess or carrying on his schemes for
obtaining more power, but it was of no avail. Seymour
thought himself sufficiently strong to defy all. He
counted on the adherence of Dorset and Northampton,
on his munitions of war at Holt Castle, and on the money
to raise an army which Sharington was to supply. He
began to talk openly to the Earl of Rutland of ending the
Protectorate, and even approached Wriothesley on the
subject. In the latter he found himself at once mistaken.
" My lord," said Wriothesley, " beware how you attempt
any violence. It were better that you had never been
born, yea, that you had been burnt quick alive, than that
you should attempt it." *

As much of the conspiracy as Wriothesley had heard,
he communicated at once to the Council, and shortly after
the Earl of Rutland brought an accusation against Seymour, apparently concerning the words he had spoken to
him. Several Council meetings were held and, as a result,
the Protector summoned Seymour to an interview. The
latter refused to attend, upon which the Council sent Sir
Thomas Smith and Sir John Baker to arrest him
1549. at Seymour Place, January 17,† and to convey him
to the Tower.

Some time previous to this the Lady Jane Grey, whom
her father had handed over to Seymour, and who became
one of his household, being apparently his ward,‡ had
been sent back to her father's house by order of the
Council. During her residence in his house, Seymour
appears to have treated her with every courtesy and kindness, and to have intended to marry her to the King.
Though but a child of eleven, the following letter from

* Froude's Hist.
† Dict. Nat. Biog. ; State Papers.
‡ Wood's Letters of Royal and Illustrious Ladies ; Sir Harris
Nicholas, Memoirs of Lady Jane Grey, p. 14.

her to Seymour is not without interest, as showing not only the esteem she had for him, but as an example of her own draughtsmanship. The penmanship of the original is remarkably beautiful. A fac-simile may be seen in Wood's Letters of Royal and Illustrious Ladies :

"My duty to your lordship in most humble wise remembered, with no less thanks for the gentle letters which I received from you.

"Thinking myself so much bound to your lordship for your great goodness towards me from time to time, that I cannot by any means be able to recompense the least part thereof, I proposed to write a few rude lines unto your lordship, rather as a token to show how much worthier I think your lordship's goodness, than to give worthy thanks for the same, and these my letters shall be to testify unto you that, like as you have become towards me a loving and kind father, so I shall be always most ready to obey your Godly monitions and good instructions, as becometh one upon whom you have heaped so many benefits. And thus, fearing lest I should trouble your lordship too much, I most humbly take my leave of your good lordship. Your humble servant, during my life, Jane Grey." This letter is endorsed, "My Lady Jane, 1st October, 1548."

The Admiral being safely lodged in the Tower, his adherents were speedily taken and imprisoned also ; Sir John Harington, Sir William Sharington, Sir Thomas Parry, John Fowler, and Mrs. Ashley, the Princess Elizabeth's governess, being placed in the Tower on the 18th, the day following the Admiral's arrest.* Many of his friends and accomplices, however, as usual in such cases, made haste to save themselves at his expense. An inquiry had already been commenced respecting the conduct of Sharington, and Seymour had endeavoured to shield him by taking into his custody all the compromising books and papers he could get, and by strongly asserting his innocence. He had even declared that certain large sums were owed to him by Sharington, whereas, in reality, the debt was the

* Dict. Nat. Biog.

other way about, in the hope of enabling · his friend to account for some of the deficit.* Now, however, Sharington threw himself on the mercy of the Council and confessed all his frauds at the Bristol Mint, amounting to about £40,000.

The Earl of Dorset confessed the Admiral's agreement with him to marry Jane Grey to the King. The cannon foundries were discovered, and over thirty pieces of cannon and quantities of powder and shot were seized, as well as all the arms in Holt Castle. The secret dealings with the pirates were laid bare, and all the other features of the conspiracy,* which might have been successful had it been better managed.

An inquiry had also been begun to ascertain how far the Admiral had gone in his attempts to win the Princess Elizabeth, and Sir Thomas Tyrwhit had been sent down to Hatfield, at the beginning of February, to interview the Princess. The following letter was sent by her to the Protector on February 6. It follows the long letter, dated January 28, which was printed in Haynes' Burleigh papers, and more recently in Miss Strickland's Queens of England (vol. 4, p. 40), and precedes the formal confession which she made on the following day : " My lord, I have received your gentle letter and also your message by Master Tyrwhit, for the which two things especially (although for many other things) I cannot give your lordship sufficient thanks, and whereas your grace doth will me to credit Master Tyrwhit, I have done so, and will do so as long as he willeth me (as he doth not) to nothing but to that which is for mine honour and honesty. And even as I said to him and did write to your lordship, so I do write now again, that when there doth any more things happen in my mind which I have forgotten, I assure your grace I will declare them most willingly, for I would not (as I trust you have not) so evil an opinion that I would conceal anything that I knew ; for it were to no purpose, and surely forgetfulness may well cause me to hide things,

* Froude's Hist.

but undoubtedly else I will declare all that I know. From Hatfield, the 6th of February, your assured friend to my little power, Elizabeth." *

The Princess's confession amounted to very little, certainly to far less than she could have said had she been inclined. Her governess, Catharine Ashley, and Parry the coifferer, however, on their examination, confessed to the most astonishing particulars as to the improper freedoms which Seymour had used towards the Princess,† —making disclosures that, in honour of Elizabeth's great name, we will not repeat here. Suffice it to say that her governess and most of the persons about her were immediately dismissed for gross neglect of duty in permitting such things to pass unnoticed.‡

On the 20th of February, the Lord Privy Seal, Southampton, and Secretary Petre were sent to examine the Admiral and his confederates in the Tower.§ They reported to the Council that he was accused of forming, with Sharington and others, a conspiracy against the Government, and of committing many misdemeanours in his office of High Admiral; that he was charged with protecting pirates and sharing in their plunder, and finally with refusing justice to those who complained to him of these outrages. (Appendix A.) As a result of these examinations,‖ thirty-three articles of accusation were drawn up against him,¶ and on the 23rd, the whole Council, with the exception of the Protector, Archbishop Cranmer, and Baker, waited upon him in the Tower and exhorted him to make some reply to these charges.** Seymour, however, refused to make any reply or defence and demanded an open trial.†† This the Council would not

* Wood's Letters of Royal and Illustrious Ladies.
† Haynes; Froude's Hist.
‡ Froude's Hist.
§ Dict. Nat. Biog.; Froude.
‖ These are printed in Haynes, pp. 65–107.
¶ These are printed in Acts, P.C., 1547–50, pp. 248–256.
** Dict. Nat. Biog.; Froude.
†† Dict. Nat. Biog.; Froude.

grant, owing probably to the fear that the Princess Elizabeth's character might be damaged if the disclosures necessary in an open trial were to become public property.

Many of the charges against him had, in the meantime, been fully proved, not only by witnesses but also by his own letters.* The Council, therefore, reported the result of their interview with Seymour, to the King, and to the Protector on the following day. (Note 18.) A deputation from both Houses of Parliament was then sent to him, consisting of the Lord Chancellor, the Earls of Shrewsbury, Warwick, and Southampton ; Sir John Baker, Sir Thomas Cheney, and Sir Anthony Denny. These, however, failed to gain any satisfactory reply, for, though the Admiral went so far as to admit the truth of the first three charges, he steadfastly refused to make any reply to the others.†

After considering the matter and the evidence before them, the Council unanimously declared that his offences amounted to high treason, and, on the 25th, framed a Bill of attainder which was introduced into the House of Lords,‡ and read a first time on the spot, and a second and third on the two days following, without a dissenting voice.§ In the Commons, however, Seymour still had some adherents, and there the question was debated for some time in a crowded house of fully 400 members.‖ In the end the Bill passed its third reading in the Lower House, March 4, only ten or twelve members voting against it.¶

The Bill was now sent to the Crown with a request that

* Froude's Hist.
† Froude's Hist.; Dict. Nat. Biog.
‡ Printed in Statutes of the Realm, IV, i, 61–5.
§ Dict. Nat. Biog.
‖ Dict. Nat. Biog.; Froude's Hist.
¶ Lords' Journals, i, 345, *et seq.* In the Dict. Nat. Biog. Mr. Pollard says : "An Act of 1547 had swept away all treasons created since the statute of 1352, and the Council's decision has been generally regarded as illegal ; but Seymour's dealings with pirates and measures for securing adherents might plausibly be construed as 'levying war upon the King,' and his connivance at Sharington's frauds as 'counterfeiting the King's money,' while his general conduct was undoubtedly a menace to the peace of the realm."

"justice might have place," and the Council waited on the King for a warrant appointing the date and place of execution ; but "forasmuch as the Council did perceive that the case was so heavy and lamentable to the Lord Protector, if the King's Highness was so pleased, they said that they would proceed without further troubling or molesting either His Highness or the Lord Protector."

Somerset, it seems, on the authority of Elizabeth, would still have interfered to save his brother, and it was found necessary to prevent an interview between them if the sentence was to be carried out.* From the first he had endeavoured to overcome the Admiral's jealousy by kindness, and he maintained the same tenderness to the end. Seymour's last action, however, showed that his hatred had not diminished.

The warrant was signed on the 17th of March, and the execution appointed to take place on the 20th, on Tower Hill. Ever since the sentence had been pronounced, Seymour seems to have exhibited the greatest rage and resentment against the Council and against his own friends, but more than all against his brother. If we are to believe Latimer, he spent his last days writing letters to Elizabeth and Mary, urging them to conspire against the Protector, and, lest these letters should be seized, he concealed them in the sole of his shoe. When before the block his last words were an injunction to his servant not to fail in delivering them.† For the rest, he went boldly to his death, and met it without flinching, though it took more than one blow of the axe to sever his head from his body.‡

* "I heard my Lord of Somerset say, that if his brother had been suffered to speak with him, he had never suffered, but great persuasion was made to him."—Elizabeth to Mary, quoted in Froude.

† The words were overheard. The servant was examined, and the letters were found. They had been written with great ingenuity. "He made his ink so craftily and with such workmanship as the like had not been seen. He made his pen of the aglet of a point that he plucked from his hose."—Latimer's Sermons, quoted in Froude's Hist.   ‡ Froude's Hist.

"Lingard, Maclean, and others have maintained that Seymour's abilities were superior to those of his brother, but the evidence is not conclusive. He was undoubtedly a capable soldier, of great personal powers and handsome features, and he won the affections of many of those with whom he was brought into contact. But these qualities were marred by unscrupulous ambition, an overbearing disposition, and, according to Latimer, moral profligacy.* He was accurately described by Elizabeth as 'a man of much wit and very little judgment.' " †

Lord Seymour's body was apparently taken to the Tower and there buried, though some have said it was removed to Great Bedwyn, in Wilts. He left no children, his only daughter having died in infancy.‡

There is a portrait of him, by Holbein, at Longleat ; a miniature, by the same artist, is at Sudeley, in the possession of Mrs. Dent, who has reproduced it in her "Annals of Winchcombe and Sudeley." Anonymous portraits are at Sudeley, in the Wallace Collection, and in the possession of Sir G. D. Clerk, Bart.§ (Note 19.)

[Sir John Maclean's Life of Sir T. Seymour (privately printed in 1869, and not in the British Museum Library) is written mainly from contemporary MSS., addit. MSS. 5751 (ff. 295, 307), 5753 (ff. 20, 48, 137), 6705 (f. 62), 19398 (f. 52) ; Froude's Hist. ; Letters and Papers, Henry VIII ; Greyfriars Chronicle ; Ellis, Shoreditch ; Wriothesley's Chronicle ; State Papers, Henry VIII ; Chronicles of Calais ; Lords' Journals ; Oppenheim, Administration of the Navy ; Correspondence Politique ; Literary Remains, Edward VI ; Wood's Letters of Royal and Illustrious Ladies ; Bapst., Deux Gentilshommes Poètes, pp. 338–9 ; Cotton MS. ; Latimer's Sermons ; Dictionary National Biography ; Tytler's Henry VIII, &c.]

---

* Cranmer also described him as one of the most profligate and desperate persons that ever lived.
† Quoted from Dict. Nat. Biog.
‡ Edmundson's Peerage.
§ Dict. Nat. Biog. (cf. Cat. Victorian Exhib., Nos. 185, 209, 443, 1077 ; Cat. First Loan Exhib., No. 181).

EDWARD SEYMOUR, EARL OF HERTFORD AND FIRST DUKE OF SOMERSET.
From a picture at Bulstrode, by kind permission of the Lady Gwendolen Ramsden.

SIR EDWARD SEYMOUR, DUKE OF SOMERSET, EARL OF HERTFORD, VISCOUNT BEAUCHAMP, AND BARON SEYMOUR.

Edward Seymour was born about 1506,* and is first mentioned as acting in the capacity of Page of Honour to Mary Tudor on her marriage with the King of France in 1514.† His youth was passed first at Oxford and then at Cambridge,‡ at which places he not only obtained such education as was then thought sufficient, but was also able to devote much of his time to such exercises of arms as were then in vogue, and in which he became as proficient as the best men of his day.

On the 15th of July, 1517, he was associated with his father in a grant to be constables and doorwards of Bristol Castle, and to enjoy the same with as ample powers as had belonged to Giles, Lord Daubeney.§ This appears not to have been the first time that he received notice from the King, for, in the previous year, his name is mentioned amongst those of the Gentlemen of the Privy Chamber.‖

In 1522 he appears to have been deputed, with his father, to attend upon Charles V during his visit to England,¶ and, in the following year, he accom-

1506.

1514.

1517.

1522.

* According to an inscription on an anonymous portrait at Sudeley (Cat. Tudor Exhib., No. 196).
† Dict. Nat. Biog.
‡ Wood, Athenæ Oxon., i, 210; Cooper, Athenæ Cant., i, 107.
§ Brewer, State Papers, Nos. 3474, 4446.
‖ Brewer, State Papers, No. 2735.
¶ Chapuys, Letters and Papers, Henry VIII, x, 1069.

panied the Duke of Suffolk in an expedition into France.*

Cardinal Wolsey, who was then the King's first
1523. minister, was so much interested in this campaign, owing partly to his hatred of the French,
that he went over to Calais that he might superintend the
management of the expedition in person.   The English
army numbered about 14,000 men, but these were soon
joined by the Imperialists, under the Count de Bure, to
the number of 11,000 foot and 6,000 horse.   The Cardinal's idea appears to have been to march straight into
the heart of France, and he made the mistake, owing to
his anxiety to rush forward and strike one decisive blow,
of leaving in his rear many fortified places such as
Terouenne, Hedin, and Montreuille.   They took Corbic,
then crossed the Somme, took Roye and Montdidier—
the latter having a garrison of 1,200 men—and several
other places, and struck terror into the French by appearing within 7 leagues of Paris.   This success had been
very rapid, but now the want of caution, shown by the
Cardinal in his orders, began to tell.   The Imperialists
had received no pay, and refused to continue ; the English
were unable to replace the artillery and transport horses
they had lost in their hurried march ; the winter was fast
approaching ; and the French were collecting two armies,
one in their front, and the other in their rear.   There was
nothing for it but to return to Calais, which was done in
good order and with great skill, and to withdraw the
garrisons that had been placed in the towns they had
captured.   The expedition thus proved fruitless.

In this campaign Seymour appears to have rendered
considerable service.   He was present at the
1524. capture of Bray, Roye, and Montdidier, and
received the honour of knighthood on November 1 at the hands of the Duke of Suffolk.†

On his return home he was placed on the Commission

* Dict. Nat. Biog.; Martin's Hist. Eng., 311 ; Lloyd's Statesmen and Favourites, 145.
† Dict. Nat. Biog.

for the Peace in Wiltshire,* January 12, and soon after was appointed Master of the Horse to the Duke of Richmond.† He appears now to have become a
1525. personal favourite of the King's, who made him an esquire of his household.‡ This liking seems to have been due, in the first place, to Henry's passion for tilts and tournaments, in which Seymour made a considerable show. On one occasion we find him chosen as one of the challengers in a tournament which took place at Greenwich during some Christmas festivities.

In July, 1527, when Cardinal Wolsey was sent over to make negotiations for peace with the French
1527. King,§ Sir Edward Seymour accompanied him, and was present at the interview at Amiens, where the Cardinal's appearance rivalled that of King Francis, though the latter was attended by the King of Navarre and the chief nobility of France.

In 1528, Sir Edward received some grants of lands belonging to various monasteries which were dis-
1528. solved as a consequence of Wolsey's visitation, and, in March of the following year, he was granted the stewardship of the manors of Henstridge, in Somerset, and Charlton, in Wilts. (Note 20.) In 1530 he received, jointly with his brother-in-law, Sir Anthony Ugh-
1530. tred, the manors of Kexby, Leppington, and Barthorpe, in Yorkshire, all formerly the property of Wolsey.‖ In September he was appointed esquire to the body to the King, who continued to show great favour towards him, occasionally lending him money, and more frequently borrowing it.¶ (Henry VIII appears seldom to have remembered his debts, though he was less forgetful of those due to him.)

---

* Brewer, State Papers, Henry VIII, No. 1049 (12).
† Brewer, State Papers, Henry VIII, Nos. 1512, 4536.
‡ Dict. Nat. Biog.
§ Chron. of Calais, p. 37.
‖ Dict. Nat. Biog.
¶ Letters and Papers, Henry VIII, vols. 4, 5, and 6.

In 1532, Seymour, together with his father, accompanied
the King to Boulogne to meet Francis I.* During
1532. this year a dispute, apparently originating from a
transaction of the previous year,† arose between
him, on the one side, and Lord Lisle and John Dudley,
afterwards Duke of Northumberland, on the other, about
some lands in Somerset. (Note 21.) This quarrel lasted
many years, and was the subject of a great deal of correspondence, which is now in the Record Office.‡ On the
last day of this year we find Seymour presenting the
King with a sword having a gilded hilt, with the word
" Kalenders " upon it, as a New Year's gift.§

For the next three years he appears to have divided his
time between his attendance at Court and his private
affairs, and to have kept out of the events that occurred at
that time, taking no part in the downfall of Wolsey or
the marriage and death of Anne Boleyn. His position
required him, however, to be frequently at Court, and he
attended Anne's coronation, at which he officiated as
carver for the Archbishop, who sat at the Queen's
1535. board.‖ In March, 1535, he received a grant of
various lands in Hampshire, formerly belonging to
the Convent of the Holy Trinity, Christchurch, London,
and in October he received a visit from the King at his
seat of Elvetham, in Hants.¶

The King was now beginning to make advances to the
Lady Jane Seymour, who, as we have seen in her
1536. life, rejected his proposals and gifts, a refusal which
rendered her still more attractive to the King,
unaccustomed as he was to find virtue and honour
amongst the ladies of his Court. He therefore, as we
have already noticed, promised on his honour not to see

* Dict. Nat. Biog.
† Gairdner's State Papers.
‡ Wood's Letters of Illustrious Ladies, iii, 41 ; Gairdner's
Letters and Papers, vols. 7-11.
§ Gairdner's State Papers (686).
‖ Gairdner's State Papers (562).
¶ Dict. Nat. Biog.

or converse with her except in the presence of at least one of her relatives. Sir Edward Seymour was, in consequence, made a Gentleman of the Privy Chamber, and given apartments in Greenwich Palace, which he now occupied with his wife (Anne), where the King might at times come and converse with Jane in their presence.*

On the 5th of June, a week after the marriage of Jane Seymour to Henry VIII, Sir Edward was created Viscount Beauchamp, of Hache, in Somerset, and two days later he received a grant of the manors of Ambresbury, Easton Priory, Chippenham, and Maiden Bradley, all situated in Wiltshire. (Note 22.) A month later he was made Chancellor and Chamberlain of North Wales, and Captain and Governor of the Isle of Jersey,† an appointment which had just been vacated by Sir Thomas Vaux, Lord Harrowden. January 30 of the following year he was granted the manor of Muchelney, in Somerset.‡

1537. In addition to these lands, and to those previously granted him, he now had the paternal estate, which he had inherited from his father, who had died in the winter of 1536. (Note 23.)

On May the 22nd he was made a Privy Councillor, and was appointed one of the Commission for the trial of Lord Darcy and Lord Hussey, who had taken a leading part in the "Pilgrimage of Grace."§ On the 15th of October he was present at his nephew's, Edward VI's, christening, at which function he was deputed to carry the Princess Elizabeth.‖ Amongst the honours conferred on that occasion, he received the Earldom of Hertford.¶ (Note 24.)

His influence and power were now becoming great, and he might soon have reached one of the highest places

* Letters and Papers, Henry VIII, x, 601.
† Gairdner's State Papers.
‡ Dict. Nat. Biog.; Tanner's Notitia, p. 601, says Maiden Bradley was granted at the same time.
§ State Papers, Henry VIII.
‖ Wriothesley's Chronicle, i, 68.
¶ Gairdner's Letters and Papers, 939.

that a subject could occupy but that a severe blow was in
store for him, affecting not only his private affections, but,
in addition, causing him to lose much of his importance
at the Court. This was the death of his sister, Queen
Jane. There is a curious document in Gairdner's State
Papers (732) which describes him, amongst other nobles,
and which seems of sufficient interest to find place here.
"The names of all the nobility in England, their ages,
and their activeness.* The Duke of Norfolk, 72 years,
the chief and best captain. The Duke of Suffolk, of the
same age, a good man and captain, sickly, and half lame.
The Marquis of Exeter, 36, lusty and strong of power,
specially beloved, deseased of the gout, and nearer unto
the crown of any man within England. The Marquess
of Dorset, 26, young, lusty, and poor, of great possessions, but which (?) are not in his hands, many friends of
great power, with little or no experience, well learned, and
a great wit. The Earl of Oxford, of 66 years, a man of
great power and little experience. The Earl of Arundel,
60, a man of great power, little wit, and less experience ;
his son young and lusty, of good wit, and like to do well.
The Earl of Shrewsbury, of great power, young and
lusty, of little wit, and no experience. The Earl of
Derby, the greatest of power and land, young, and a child
in wisdom, and half a fool. The Earl of Cumberland, a
man of 50 years, of good power, without discretion or
conduct. The Earl of Westmoreland, of like age, of a
great power, without wit or knowledge. The Earl of
Rutland, of like age, of great power, with small wit, and
little discretion. The Earl of Essex, an old man, of little
wit and less experience, without power. The Earl of
Sussex, of 50 years, of small power and little discretion,
and many words. The Earl of Wiltshire, of 60, of

* This is printed by Brady, not as an entire document but as
part of a document " found lately among some loose papers in the
Archivio di Stato at Rome." The date must be after July, 1538,
when the *young* Earl of Shrewsbury, Francis, succeeded his father,
and before the following November, when the Marquis of Exeter
was arrested.

small power, wise, and little experience, Queen Anne's father. The Earl of Hampton and Admiral of England, made by the King ; wise, active, and of good experience, one of the best captains in England. The Earl of Bath, old and foolish. The Earl of Worcester, young and foolish, and of great power in Wales. The Earl of Hertford, young and wise, of small power, and brother unto the last Queen deceased. The Earl of Huntingdon, of 60 years, of great power, little discretion, and less experience."

Though now " of small power," the Earl of Hertford continued to be employed in various ways. At 1538. the close of this year, probably December, he was appointed one of a Commission for the trial of the Marquis of Exeter, Lord Montagu, and others.* In the May previous he is mentioned among those present at the execution of Friar Forest.† In March, 1539, he 1539. was sent over to France to inspect the fortifications and secure the defences of Calais and Guisnes, returning in April, on the 16th of which month he was given a grant of Chester Place, outside Temple Bar.‡ In the following August he received a visit from the King at Wolfhall, which lasted four days. Particulars of this visit may be seen in the Wilts Archæological Magazine (xv, App. No. iv). In order to make room for the King's numerous suite, Hertford was compelled to utilise the famous old barn there, which he had at first fitted up as a ball room, as a lodging for himself and his family.§ At meals, of which there were two a day, covers were laid for 200, but this large number was not entirely composed of the King's suite ; the more important of the neighbouring gentry, who were invited, thinking it necessary to the

* Dict. Nat. Biog.
† Wriothesley's Chron.
‡ Wriothesley's Chron.
§ This barn, of stone, wood, and thatch, was 172 feet long and 26 feet wide, inside measurement. There is a drawing of it in the Wilts. Archæolog. Mag., vol. xv.

F

upkeep of their dignity to bring as many attendants with them as possible.   The expenses of this entertainment did not fall altogether upon Lord Hertford, for the King's purveyors provided a great part of the banquets, and the gentry of the neighbourhood assisted with presents of game, fish, fowls, &c.

Towards the end of August he received a grant of the Charterhouse at Sheen,* and, in the December following, was sent by the King to meet Anne of Cleves at Calais, and escort her to London.   According to a letter of his to Cromwell this new marriage of the King's gave him the greatest satisfaction.†

In the early part of May, his private fortunes were considerably advanced, for he succeeded to the 1540. Sturmy Estate, being cousin and heir to Sir William Sturmy, or Esturmy.‡   As these estates joined his own, they were of great value to him.   The estate at Maiden Bradley had come to him partly by a grant from the King and partly from his second marriage with Anne, daughter of Sir Edward Stanhope.   These estates, as well as those he had received before, were now entailed upon the children of his second wife by special Act of Parliament.§   The two sons he had had by his first wife Catherine, daughter of Sir William Fillol, were thus completely cut out from the succession, not only of the property but of the titles as well.   (Note 25.)   According to many of the chroniclers of the time, Hertford seems to have been greatly influenced in the matter by his second wife.   From the first he is said to have been divorced,‖ but there appears to be some doubt about it.   In any case she appears to have been dead before Hertford married Anne Stanhope, and certainly some time before the Act

* Wriothesley's Chron., i, 105.
† Letters and Papers, xiv, i, 1275.
‡ Gairdner, State Papers, grants in July, 1541, 947 (38).
§ Act of 1540.—Gairdner, State Papers.
‖ According to a manuscript note in Vincent's Baronage in the College of Arms, which has been generally copied.

for disinheriting her sons was passed.* Concerning this special entail, Heylyn writes :† " There goes a story that the Earle having been formerly employed in France, did there acquaint himself with a learned man, supposed to have great skill in magick ; of whom he obtained, by great rewards and importunities, to let him see, by the help of some magical perspective, in what estate all his relations stood at home. In which impertinant curiosity, he was so far satisfied, as to behold a gentleman of his acquaintance in a more familiar posture with his wife, than was agreeable to the honour of either party. To which diabolical illusion, he is said to have given so much credit, that he did not only estrange himself from her society at his coming home, but furnished his next wife with an excellent opportunity for pressing him to the disinheriting of his former children." Can it be that the above unlikely tale was the foundation for the later story of Catherine's unfaithfulness which has obtained general credence ? It almost seems so.

Hertford's power was now again increasing, and even Cromwell's fall during this year made no 1541. alteration or diminution in the favour with which Henry regarded him. He had been made a Privy Councillor, and, during the preceding year, had been very diligent in the discharge of such business as came before the Council,‡ in recognition of which activity, probably, he was made a Knight of the Garter§ (January 9). Shortly after this he was employed, together with Sir Edward Carne, in a mission to France to settle the boundaries of the English and French territories near Calais, but no satisfactory arrangement could be made with the French commissioners.‖ In February he was deputed to report

* Pollard, England under Protector Somerset, p. 319.
† Heylyn's Edward VI.
‡ Pollard, England under Protector Somerset.
§ Gairdner, State Papers, 440.
‖ Gairdner, State Papers, 510, 523-30; Corr. de Marillac, pp. 257-266.

upon the state of the defences at Calais,* and to remove Sir John Wallop, the governor of that town, and place Sir Edward Rangeley in his stead. Soon after his return home, he received a great mark of the King's favour and trust, for to him was entrusted the principal management of affairs in London, in conjunction with Cranmer and Lord Audley, during Henry's progress in the north, which lasted from July to November ;† immediately after which he was employed in a matter of the utmost delicacy, being, together with Cranmer, the recipient of the charges of adultery made against Catherine Howard.‡

In September, 1542, Hertford served in a cam-
1542.   paign on the borders of Scotland, under the Duke of Norfolk, and was appointed Warden of the Scot-
tish marches with very large powers, enabling him to levy and arm the tenants, farmers, and inhabitants of the northern counties, to confer titles and determine causes, &c. He soon found, however, that he was unable to carry out all that he desired to do for the safety of the borders, owing to the supineness of the Council of the North, and that he was making enemies for himself through his habit of writing full and true accounts of what was going on to the King, a proceeding which, though pleasing to Henry, did not meet with approval in other quarters. Indeed his friend Paget had to write and caution him on this subject on more than one occasion. (Note 26.) Fortunately, perhaps, for him, he was recalled in November, at his own request.§

He now resumed his attendance at Court, and soon received another mark of the King's favour, for, in December, he was made Lord High Admiral. This post, however, he did not retain long, for on his appoint-ment as Great Chamberlain, the January following, he

* Gairdner, State Papers ; Proc. Privy Council, vii, 130.
† State Papers, i, 660–690.
‡ Hume, Chron. Henry VIII, p. 82.
§ Gairdner, State Papers ; Hamilton Papers (from the Longleat MSS.).

1543. resigned in favour of Lord Lisle.* Later in the year he again had the honour of entertaining the King for a few days at Wolfhall.†

On the 5th of March, in the following year, he was appointed Lieutenant-General in the North, with
1544. orders to prepare an army for the invasion of Scotland, for the purpose of punishing the Scots, who had broken the existing treaty, and made an alliance with France.‡ Accompanied by Sir Ralph Sadler, he repaired to Newcastle to await the arrival of the army and fleet, and to arrange about supplies, which, being scarce in the north, had to be brought from London and other ports. Proclamations had meanwhile been issued naming Henry guardian of the young Scottish Queen and Protector of the Realm,§ and many of the Scotch Protestants had offered to join Hertford and to assassinate Cardinal Beaton, who was looked upon as the author of the war. Hertford, however, refused their assistance.

Owing to contrary winds, the expedition was delayed for some time at Newcastle, but on the 1st of May the Earl set out with 200 sail of transports and arrived in the Firth of Forth on the 3rd. He at once began operations by burning St. Menance and removing the shipping he found there. On the 4th, he landed ten thousand men at Grantham Cragg, took Blackness Castle, and advanced upon Leith. Here he was confronted by about 6,000 Scottish horse, with some artillery, who, however, retired upon Edinburgh after firing a few shots. The garrison of Leith made so slight a resistance that the town was captured with the loss of but two or three men.‖

Hertford was now reinforced by the arrival of 4,000 light horse under Lord Evers. Leith was made into the headquarters of the expedition, the fleet was brought

* State Papers, Henry VIII.
† Dict. Nat. Biog.
‡ Dict. Nat. Biog.
§ Proclamations, Addit. MS., 32654, 49, 58.
‖ Hertford's Letters, Addit. MS.

into the harbour, the heavy artillery and stores were landed, and in a few days the Earl commenced his march on Edinburgh. On the way he was met by the Provost of Edinburgh, who had come to offer a capitulation of that town, on the condition that the inhabitants should be allowed to depart with all their goods and that the town itself should not be burnt. Hertford, however, would listen to no terms, insisting on an unconditional surrender.*

Meanwhile the garrison of Edinburgh had received a reinforcement of about 2,000 horsemen, under the Earl of Bothwell and Lord Hume, and resolved to defend the town. Their resistance, however, was not of long duration, for on the following day the Canongate was blown in by Sir Christopher Morris and the city captured. In the attack the Scots lost about 200 slain, and the remainder took refuge in the castle, the strength of which preserved it from assault.†

The Earl, whose orders from the King and Council were to do all the damage he could,‡ set fire to the town after it had been pillaged for two days, and completely burnt it, the Abbey and Palace of Holyrood being destroyed with the rest. At the same time the country for six miles round was laid bare by Lord Evers' light horsemen.

The army now retired to Leith, and the fleet was sent out to find and destroy all the shipping it could find in the Firth. In addition it destroyed many towns and villages on the banks, as well as the fortress on Inchgavey.

This done, the Earl placed all his heavy artillery on board the fleet, which was also loaded with spoil, removed the shipping from the harbour, destroyed the pier, and burnt the town. On May 15th he was already on the

* Correspondence of Lord Hertford, Addit. MS., 32654 ; Froude, &c.
† Correspondence of Lord Hertford, Addit. MS., 32654 ; Froude, &c.
‡ Hamilton Papers.

march in the neighbourhood of Dunbar, where a Scottish force was drawn up to oppose him. No action, however, took place, and the town was set on fire in the night. On the 18th the army was back at Berwick.*

The celerity and success of this expedition, which had only lasted eighteen days, were highly approved of by the King and Council, the more so as a considerable portion of the Earl's army was required at once to take part in an expedition into France. Lord Hertford himself returned in June, and the King, who intended to command the French expedition in person, chose him as Lieutenant of the Realm, under the Queen Regent, during his own absence.†

The Earl did not, however, have to contend with the difficulties of this appointment for long, for on the 13th of August, being summoned by the King, he joined the army at Hardelot Castle, where he was employed as one of the Ambassadors to settle terms of peace with the French representatives. These negotiations proving fruitless, Henry continued the siege of Boulogne, which he had already invested. This town soon surrendered to him.‡

"If the accounts given by the French writers of those times be true, Henry owed his success to treachery. Thus far at least is certain. De Vervins§ was afterwards brought to trial for his conduct on the occasion. He was charged with having agreed with the Earl of Hertford to capitulate for the sum of 150,000 rose nobles, and with having procured the assassination of Phillipe de Corse, whose honest bravery had thwarted his treacherous designs. The charges were considered as having been fully proved, and De Vervins was beheaded."‖

Charles V had meanwhile been privately carrying on

* Froude's Hist. ; Lord Hertford's Correspondence, &c.
† Rymer, xv, 39 ; State Papers, Henry VIII, i, 765.
‡ Mémoires du Mareschal Vieilleville, 1822, i, 152.
§ The Governor of that town.
‖ Nott. Surrey's Works, 69.

negotiations with the French, with the result that, within five days of the capture of Boulogne, a peace was concluded between him and the French King. Being thus left to carry on the war alone, Henry sent a deputation, of which Hertford was the head, to attend a conference of the three Powers at Calais (October 18). No result following this conference, Hertford and Gardiner were despatched to Brussels, where, after considerable difficulties and delays, they obtained three interviews with the Emperor, from which, however, they obtained no satisfactory terms for an alliance.* They were therefore recalled (November 21st), and preparations were made to renew the war, Hertford being given the command of the army.†

The following January, having examined and reported on the defences of Guisnes, the Earl joined his army at Boulogne, and successfully defeated a determined attack made by the French on that place. They had encamped before it to the number of 14,000 men, while Hertford's force numbered barely half the number. Undeterred, however, by the odds against him, the latter had sallied out in the morning, before dawn, with about 4,000 foot and 700 horse, and surprised the French with the suddenness and determination of his attack. They fled, panic-stricken, leaving their guns, stores, and ammunition to the victors.‡

1545.

Matters had not, meanwhile, gone so well for the English in the north, where they had suffered a severe defeat at the hands of the Scots. It was thought advisable, therefore, to recall Hertford, whose signal victory had saved Boulogne for the time, and send him to the north as Lieutenant-General in place of the Earl of Shrewsbury.§ This was accordingly done in May, but it was not till August that the expedition was ready to start,

* State Papers, 63, 119–36, 147.
† State Papers, Addit. MS., 25114, ff. 312, 315.
‡ Life and Reign Henry VIII, Herbert, p. 250.
§ Rymer, xv, 72.

as Hertford found himself obliged to spend the whole summer making preparations, owing to the state in which his predecessor had left the army. Early in September he began his march, by Kelso and Jedburgh, meeting with but little opposition, and destroying everything in his path. According to a list which is still extant, he destroyed five market towns, two hundred and forty-three villages, and many castles and monasteries. This expedition did not occupy long, for he returned to Newcastle on the 27th.* (Appendix B.)

In October, Hertford returned to London to attend Parliament and the Council, on whose business he 1546. was engaged throughout the winter, and remained there till March, when he was sent to supersede the Earl of Surrey in the command of Boulogne, the latter having failed to hold his own against the French.† In April he was appointed Lieutenant-General within the English pale in France and, having successfully re-opened the communications between Calais and Boulogne, which had been broken through Surrey's incompetence, was ordered to treat for a peace, which was concluded on April 7, but of which the terms were none too satisfactory for the English. In September, after a visit home, he again returned to Boulogne to destroy the fortifications there, according to the terms of the treaty.‡ In October he seems to have been at Windsor, and, from that time to Henry's death, he appears to have been much at Court and to have been most assiduous in his attendances at the Council board, where his diligence and energy won for him the respect and affection of the other Councillors.§

Owing to his rapid advancement, Hertford was now one of the most powerful nobles in England, and was generally looked upon as the head of the Protestant

* Hamilton Papers, vol. 1 ; State Papers.
† State Papers, xi, 60.
‡ State Papers, i, 877, 879 ; De Selve, Corr. Pol.
§ Pollard, England under Protector Somerset.

faction, which was making great strides in the country, and towards which it was believed the King was inclining. This placed him in direct opposition to the Duke of Norfolk, the greatest and most powerful noble in the land. The Duke, however, being old and inclined towards peace and quiet, had already once endeavoured to bring about an alliance between the two families through a marriage between his daughter, the Duchess of Richmond, and Sir Thomas Seymour, Hertford's brother, but had been foiled in his project by his own son, the Earl of Surrey. He now again endeavoured to bring about the match, but with a similar result, and, not long after, the dramatic fall of his house left the Seymours without any powerful rival.* It has generally been asserted that Hertford took a prominent part in the downfall of the Howards, but though he officiated at Surrey's trial, he took no part in bringing it about, nor did he do anything afterwards to injure Norfolk. In his capital book, England under Protector Somerset, Mr. Pollard says : " Between Surrey and Hertford, indeed, there was no love lost. Hertford had taken part in the condemnation of Surrey three years before for his midnight frolic in the City,† but it was Surrey who, detesting Hertford as an upstart, had scorned the proposed marriages between his and Hertford's children. He had dedicated poems and made other advances to Hertford's wife, which she had haughtily declined, and he had been enraged beyond bounds by his recall from the French command in Hertford's favour. But his fall was due to other causes. By quartering with his own the royal

* Wriothesley's Chron., i, 177 ; Howard, Earl of Surrey, 1473–1554; Bapst., 358 ; Henry Howard, Earl of Surrey, 1517(?)–1547.

† On 1st April, 1543, Surrey was charged before the Privy Council with breaking windows in the City and shooting stones at peaceable citizens, and was sent to the Fleet. His companion in this prank was Sir William Pickering, afterwards Ambassador to France, and a suitor for Elizabeth's hand (Acts of the Privy Council, i, 104 ; Bapst., Deux Gentilshommes Poètes à la Cour d'Henri 8, p. 269).

arms,* by claiming the protectorate for his father, he had roused Henry's jealous fear for his son's secure succession, and it was Henry himself who drew up the charges against him. In this task he was aided by Lord Chancellor Wriothesley ; but both Wriothesley and Sir Richard Southwell—Surrey's original accuser—were staunch adherents of Surrey's own religion, and bitter enemies of Hertford."†

The King's life was now fast drawing to a close and Hertford was kept in constant attendance upon 1547. him. On January 28, 1547, Henry breathed his last at York House, now Whitehall, which he had confiscated from the Bishop of York.‡ He had spent the previous day in earnest conversation with Hertford and Sir William Paget, pointing out to them the condition of the country, urging them to follow out his scheme of uniting the Scotch and English Crowns by a marriage between Mary and young Edward, and earnestly commending the latter to the care of Charles V and Francis I. The Earl and Paget were with him to the last, receiving his injunctions and commands, and to them was entrusted Henry's last will.§

Some of the conditions contained in the latter, however, Hertford thought it advisable to set aside, and, immediately on Henry's death, he held a long conversation with Paget, pointing out his own views to him and promising, should he receive his assistance, to be guided at all times by his advice. (Note 27.) Paget falling in with his ideas, it was agreed between them that Henry's death should be kept secret till the young Prince could be brought to London, and that only so much of Henry's commands and of the contents of the will, as were

---

* There was also the hideous charge that Surrey had urged his sister, the Duchess of Richmond, to assume the same relation to Henry VIII as Madame D'Étampes held to Francis I.
† Pollard, England under Protector Somerset.
‡ Greyfriars Chron.
§ Froude's Hist., &c.

absolutely necessary, should be made public at first.*
(Note 28.)

Within an hour of the King's death, Hertford hurried
off to fetch the Prince, who was at the time with Elizabeth at Hatfield, and returned with him to London on
the 31st, on which day the King's death was officially
announced.† The Council being in session, the terms of
Henry's will were immediately discussed, by which it
appeared that the royal authority was to be delegated
upon sixteen executors, of whom the Earl of Hertford
was one, with twelve Councillors to assist them.   Paget
then proposed that, as their number was too great for the
proper carrying out of their regal powers, one man should
be selected to bear the outward symbols of royalty, and
proposed that the Earl of Hertford should be chosen as
Protector.‡   After some discussion this proposal was
agreed to, in spite of the vehement opposition of
Wriothesley, the Council, however, expressly stipulating
that the Protector should only act "with the advice and
consent of the rest of the executors."§   At the same time
an enquiry was held into the intentions of the late King,
by which it appeared that he had intended to confer
honours upon various noblemen, a thing that was now
done.   Hertford was made High Steward of England
(February 2), Treasurer of the Exchequer and Earl
Marshal of England (February 10), created Baron Seymour of Hache (February 15), and Duke of Somerset
(February 16).‖   In the patent conferring the Barony it
expressly said, as one of the reasons for conferring it,
that the name of Seymour should not fall into oblivion,
sunk in the titles he was to bear ; for to that name the
King expressed a great attachment, on account of its

* Froude's Hist.; Dict. Nat. Biog.; Tytler, England under
Edward VI and Mary.
   † Lit. Remains, Edward VI.
   ‡ Dict. Nat. Biog. ; Froude's Hist.
   § Acts of the Privy Council, 11, 4–7.
   ‖ Dict. Nat. Biog.

EDWARD VI. KING OF ENGLAND.

From an old print.

having been borne by "his most beloved mother, Jane, late Queen of England." These new titles were limited on the children of his wife Anne, in strict conformity with the Act of 1540.

Somerset was now almost all powerful, but one great obstacle yet remained in his path. This was Wriothesley, who had been the chief opposer of his elevation to the dignity of Protector, and who was likely to prove a serious obstacle to the execution of his designs. Wriothesley, however, now made a fatal mistake. He took upon himself a power that was not his, and used the Great Seal without a warrant, for which serious offence he was immediately called before the Council. Instead of attending their summons he returned a threatening answer, which resulted in his being removed from the Chancellorship and from the Council.* (March 6.) On the 11th Somerset received a patent as Governor of the King and Protector of the Realm, by which he was empowered to name any fresh Councillors and to consult with such only as he should think proper.† By this patent his power was very much increased, for he was no longer so dependent on the Council. (Note 29.)

It is probable that in the history of England no statesman has ever had so difficult a task as that which now fell to Somerset's lot ; for never had the condition of affairs at home and abroad been more dangerous. The people at home were disunited both in politics and in religion, the poor were ground down with poverty and oppression, and the exchequer was not only empty but the coinage had been debased to the lowest point it has ever reached, except under the administration of Warwick. Although a nominal peace had just been concluded with France, the two nations remained practically at war, while the relations with Scotland were as hostile as they had been throughout Henry's reign. The fortifications round the English pale in France and round the English coast were in the worst

* Acts of the Privy Council, 11, 48-59.
† Froude's Hist. ; Acts of the Privy Council, 11, 63, 67.

condition, and the navy had received no pay for months. The Pope was summoning all the powers of Rome to assist in firmly re-establishing the Catholic power in the kingdom, and even Charles V was not to be depended upon should he be able to conclude the war he was then engaged on.*

Somerset at once took matters in hand and, by means of vigorous action and energy, soon succeeded in fortifying Newhaven, Blackness, the forts at Boulogne, Portsmouth, and other places. About £35,000 (of our money) was at once sent to pay the arrears of the navy and workmen. Another large sum was sent to Calais to relieve its most urgent necessities. Commissioners were appointed to examine the state of other defensive places. Musters were held once a month, and the export duty on corn to Newhaven, Calais, and Boulogne was removed. The royal household expenses, which had been £28,000 during the previous six months, were reduced to £14,000, out of which even the coronation expenses were paid.† The alloy in the coinage was reduced as far as possible at once, the improvement being met partly by making the coins smaller as well as purer ; but, even with this altera-tion, Somerset was unwilling that the young King's reign should commence with such debased money, and so coined the first issue in dies of the former reign, intending to make a further improvement the following year.‡

All this, however, was not done without great difficulty and some opposition. The corruption in high places which had begun under Henry VIII still continued and could not at once be checked. Somerset's position was by no means secure. The Council, with the King's con-sent, could remove him at any time, and many of them were already jealous. Indeed his very patent as Pro-

* Pollard, England under Protector Somerset.

† This economy continued during Somerset's power, but under Warwick's rule these expenses were increased to £56,000.— Pollard, England under Protector Somerset.

‡ See Pollard, England under Protector Somerset.

tector was only signed by seven of them, and the statute still remained by which the King could, later on, repeal all the Acts which had been passed during his minority. " This," says Mr. Pollard, " cast a shadow of doubt over the measures of Edward VI, and gave colour to the contention that the Protector and his Council had no authority to disturb Henry's settlement in Church and State, on which Gardiner and Bonner based their opposition to the Government. It was thus, invested with a crippled authority and assured of doubtful support, that the Protector entered on a task which would have taxed the power of Henry VIII, and set to work to effect a revolution not merely in the established beliefs of the people, but in the spirit of administration and in the laws upon which it was based."

The dismissal of Wriothesley and the changes that were made in the Council only slightly modified the difficulties in Somerset's way, but he was a man who was very tenacious of his opinions—opinions formed long before—which made him a believer in constitutional freedom. This, in spite of all opposition, he now endeavoured to carry out.*

One of his first actions was to set about reforming the abuses of the Church, but, though some of his reforms were most sweeping, he endeavoured always to act with prudence and moderation and to recognize the right of individuals to follow any religion they pleased. (Note 30.) This principle of a universal toleration he practically effected. Not a single soul suffered death or torture on account of his religious views during Somerset's protectorate. In Henry's reign the fires at Smithfield had been ever busy. In Mary's and Elizabeth's they continued equally so. But during this interregnum Somerset would not allow one single soul to suffer, although there is no doubt that, in certain cases, great pressure was brought to bear on him.†

* Pollard, 1901, England under Protector Somerset.
† Pollard, 1901, England under Protector Somerset.

His first act in ecclesiastical matters was to compel (February 6) all Bishops to exercise their office " durante beneplacito," and this was followed later on (November) by an Act ordering that their appointment should be by letters patent, which practically reduced them to the position of mere State officials, and so deprived them of their former power. A visitation was then made having for its object the assertion of the. royal supremacy, the enforcement of the new law that services were to be held in English instead of Latin, and the removal of all such images as were likely to lead to idolatrous worship. This was strenuously opposed by the Bishops, Gardiner and Bonner, whose opposition reached such a pitch that it was found necessary to imprison them, if only for the sake of the public peace. (Note 31.) This occurred in June. The month following a book of homilies was published, and in November the administration of the Communion in both kinds was authorized by Parliament, who, at the same time, granted all colleges, chantries, and free chapels to the King.*

The Protector had, on the 26th July, received a grant of 8,000 marks a year for the time he should hold office, in order that he might be better able to maintain his position with suitable dignity, and, on August 10, he received a grant authorizing him to bear an augmentation to his coat of arms. It consisted of a part of the royal arms, and comprehended whatever Queen Jane had been allowed to bear, except the crown and the distinctive marks of royalty. (Note 32.) This grant was couched in the most complimentary terms, and extended, through the Protector, to the entire Seymour family for ever.

Somerset's hands were now very full, not only with Church matters, but also with negotiations with Scotland. "He held in his hands," says Mr. Pollard, "all the threads of government ; except when away on his Scottish campaign or on tours of inspection he never missed a meeting of the Council, and he seems to have been

* Dict. Nat. Biog.

present at every sitting of Parliament. The management of foreign affairs he retained in his own hands, assisted only by two secretaries, who were almost exclusively Secretaries for Foreign Affairs. All diplomatic correspondence was submitted to him, and he dictated or directed the tenor of all communications to foreign States." The Ambassadors were always received by him, often alone. He superintended all measures for the defence of the kingdom, and for carrying on such wars as the country was engaged in, and in addition to all this he gradually pushed on his great schemes for the progress of religion and social reform.* As regards the Church matters, his moderate schemes and gradual innovations were not by any means satisfactory to the ultra Protestants, who now began to pull down crucifixes and images in the churches and to behave with great license. In vain Gardiner appealed to the Protector, who, not wishing to check the progress of the Reformation solely on account of the behaviour of a few fanatics, made a point against him by replying that it was not worse to destroy an image than to burn a Bible. In a letter he wrote to him he said : " Let a worthless worm-eaten image be so disposed, and men exclaimed as if a saint were cast into the fire."†

The Scottish affairs were, however, at this period, of much greater importance. The Protector's policy was, for those times, a good one. The amalgamation of the two kingdoms of England and Scotland was the great object. This he desired to do by a marriage between Edward and Mary, which would be the first step towards joining the two kingdoms into one empire, under one King, who should be, he said, King of Great Britain. In this idea Somerset was, indeed, far ahead of his time, as may also be seen by his prayers, in which he addresses God as " Defender of all nations," as against the usual form, " Defender of our nation." He began by claiming

---

* Pollard, England under Protector Somerset.
† Froude's Hist.

G

the fulfilment of the marriage treaty, which had been ratified by the Scots Parliament in 1543, and insisted upon the advantages both countries would receive thereby. The Scotch people for the most part were in favour of the union, but the Queen Regent of Scotland was a Guise, and Henry II of France was her adopted brother. Her opposition was in the end fatal, joined, as it was, with that of the priests. Somerset endeavoured to remain at peace with France, and at the same time endeavoured to embroil her with the Emperor Charles V. Could this be done, he would have leisure to carry out his plans on Scotland secure from foreign invasion. The quarrel between France and the Emperor, however, only came about in time to save England from invasion under Warwick's rule some three or four years later.*

At the commencement of his protectorate, indeed, Somerset had entered into a treaty of peace with Francis I; but this King dying, his successor, Henry II, refused to ratify it, and declared his intention of regaining Boulogne, and of assisting the Scots, whose young Queen he intended to marry to the Dauphin. Ships, men, money, and supplies were poured into Scotland by the French King. In vain did Somerset endeavour to come to terms, even hinting that Boulogne might be restored before its proper time. The Council were too impatient, and the Scottish expedition then just starting, hurried on by their order, broke off all negotiations. Somerset was chosen to lead the army, and was soon at Newcastle with 18,000 men and 60 ships.†

Towards the end of August the army marched to Berwick, the fleet, under Lord Clinton, keeping pace with it along the coast. Leaving that town, Somerset crossed the Tweed (September 4), and skirting Dumbarton, which he thought not worthy of attack, arrived before Musselburgh on the 8th. Here he found himself confronted by a Scotch army, far exceeding his own in

---

* Pollard, England under Protector Somerset.
† Pollard, England under Protector Somerset.

numbers, and holding an almost impregnable position, on rising ground, flanked by the sea on one side and a marsh on the other, and in front protected by the River Esk. Perceiving the strength of the position, Somerset shifted his ground nearer the sea, in order to receive more assistance from the fleet, whereupon the Scots, perhaps thinking that he meant to try and re-embark his army, left the rising ground and crossed the Esk shortly before dawn (September 10). The battle commenced immediately, the Scottish left, composed for the most part of 4,000 Irish archers and some light horse, charging the English right, in doing which they came under the fire of the fleet, and were thrown into such confusion that they soon broke and fled. On the other flank, however, the Scots were for a time more successful, for Lord Grey, apparently against orders, left his ground and charged their pikemen with his horse. The Scotch infantry stood firm, and having thrown themselves in vain against their long pikes, Grey's horse turned and fled, hotly pursued by the Scots. At this juncture, however, Warwick advanced his men-at-arms and Italian musketeers, whom he had kept in good order in spite of the flying horse which came charging upon them, and met the Scots, whose ranks were now disordered through the eagerness of the pursuit. A fierce struggle ensued, but it was not of long duration. The Protector, with Sir Ralph Sadler and Sir Ralph Vane, had succeeded in rallying the cavalry, and brought them on to a second charge. The Scots, taken in flank, were seized by a panic, and broke and fled in all directions, throwing away their arms, and even such clothes as impeded them. The rout soon became a massacre, in which it has been said that over 10,000 of the Scots were slain and 1,500 taken prisoners, whilst the English loss was barely 200.*

* Accounts of this battle are so numerous that it has seemed unnecessary to give more than the shortest account here. For further details see De Selve, p. 203; Froude; Pollard; Knox's Works; Bannatyne Club, vol. 1; Teulet, Papiers d'états sur

Somerset's projects were not, however, much advanced by this victory, brilliant and decisive as it was. He advanced as far as Leith and burnt it; but Mary had meanwhile been removed to Stirling, and he was unable to go further, his army having been only provisioned for a month.* Garrisons, however, were left at Inch Colin, Broughty Crag, and Roxburgh, at which place he erected fortifications, working at them with his own hands for two hours a day, in order to hasten and encourage his men.*

The campaign he had just completed was very much thought of, both on account of the speed and success with which it had been carried out, and of the very small losses that had been incurred, and in their joy the City of London proposed to receive him with a triumphal procession. This honour he declined; but in spite of his wishes, on his approaching London on October 8, the Lord Mayor and Aldermen went out to meet him, and he was marched through the City in triumph, followed by the 80 pieces of cannon he had captured.† On the day following, the Council ordained that in future his designation should be, in royal phrase—" Edward, by the grace of God, Duke of Somerset, Protector of the Realm"; and an order was issued by the King that " our uncle shall sit alone, and be placed at all times, as well in our presence at our court of Parliament, as in our absence, next on the right hand of our seat royal in our Parliament chamber." ‡ It was also proposed that a further grant of lands, to the value of £500 a year, should be given him, but this gift Somerset refused for that time, owing to the distressed state of the revenue, which he considered could ill afford such rewards.

At the meeting of Parliament, on November 4,

l'histoire Écossaise; Patten, Expedition into Scotland, 1548; Complaynt of Scotland; Early Eng. Text Society; Hamilton Papers.
* Ibid.
† Wriothesley's Chronicle, i, 186.
‡ Dict. Nat. Biog.; Froude's Hist., &c.

Somerset's wishes for the moderation of some of Henry's severe laws were discussed and embodied into statutes. All the laws of treason made since 1352 were repealed, as well as the Six Articles Bill, the Acts against the Lollards, and the sharper clauses of the Act of Supremacy.* As regards the law of treason, which had been unjustly severe hitherto, not content with modifying it to make it a reasonable statute, Somerset added a last clause, one of the most important of the Tudor reign, as affecting the liberty of the subject. It stipulated that no one could be " indicted, arraigned, condemned, or convicted for any offence of treason, Petit treason, misprision of treason . . . ." unless he " be accused by *two sufficient and lawful witnesses*, or shall *willingly, without violence*, confess the same." At the same time the former Act of Parliament placing restrictions on the printing of the Old and New Testaments or any other books teaching or expounding the Scripture was repealed. This affected not only Protestant but also Catholic works and thus practically established a universal tolerance and was the foundation of the liberty of the Press.†

"The importance of these enactments," says Mr. Pollard, " has seemed to justify a full description, for they effected a more abrupt constitutional, as distinguished from a religious, change in the spirit of the laws than occurred at any other period in English history except during the great Rebellion and the Revolution. To sweep away almost the entire system of treason laws and heresy laws—an inveterate growth of two centuries—was nothing less than a revolution ; but the temper which it illustrated is equally apparent in the treatment which Parliament itself received at the Protector's hands. His administration was marked by a fuller recognition of the powers of Parliament than had been accorded to it since the early days of the Lancastrian kings, and the history of Parliament during that brief period is notable for freedom

* Dict. Nat. Biog.
† Pollard, England under Protector Somerset.

of debate, immunity of its members from molestation on
account of their words or actions, and total absence of
attempts on the part of Government to influence either
elections to, or proceedings in, Parliament. The prevailing freedom of debate is amply exemplified in the
journals of the two Houses, and it is, perhaps, not entirely
without significance that the journals of the Lower House
commence with the first session of the Parliament summoned by Somerset. . . ." Many Bills that came up
were voted against by influential persons in such a
manner at times as to become an act of direct hostility to
the Government, but in no case did Somerset show any
resentment or remove such opponents from the authority
which they had received at his hands. Nor, when a Bill,
however distasteful to himself, had once been passed by
Parliament did he ever arrange for the refusal of the royal
assent ; he even went so far as to recognize the right of
Parliament to be consulted in the management of foreign
affairs, and insisted that treaties on the King's part should
be ratified by Parliament.*

During the same session, Somerset made an attempt to
suppress vagrancy, which was increasing at a great rate
and almost threatened to disturb the peace and quiet of
country districts. An Act was passed by which any able-
bodied vagrant, who was roaming about the country without honest means of self-support or without seeking
employment, was to be brought before the two nearest
magistrates who, on being satisfied of the said person's
idle living, might cause him to be branded on the breast
with the letter "V" and hand him over to some honest
neighbour who should cause him to work for two years
without wages, but should feed, clothe, and house him
during that period. Should the vagrant refuse to work,
or run away, he might be branded on the cheek or forehead with the letter "S" and adjudged a slave for life.
Only as a last resource might he be tried and sentenced
as a felon. The details of the Bill mentioned that

* Pollard, England under Protector Somerset.

SOUTH VIEW OF BERRY POMEROY CASTLE.

From an old print.

children of beggars were to be taken from them and brought up in some honest calling. If no householder could be found to take charge of a slave, he was to be adjudged to his town or parish to work in chains on the highways or bridges. Collections were to be made in the parish churches every Sunday for the relief of the deserving poor. The slaves of private persons were to wear rings of iron on their necks, arms, or legs. As their crime was the refusal to maintain themselves, so if they could earn or obtain any kind of property, they were entitled to their freedom. About this time the Protector established a colony of foreign weavers on his estate at Glastonbury, which afforded employment for many Protestant refugees as well as for the unemployed of this country, and which answered so well that, after Somerset's death, the Council continued it under their own management.[*]

The Protector did not, however, have everything his own way during this session of Parliament, for an Act was passed, during its last days, making his protectorate dependant upon the King's pleasure, instead of on the duration of his minority. This Act never passed the Great Seal and was probably instigated by some of his enemies, and no doubt chiefly by his brother, Sir Thomas Seymour, who was almost openly working for his overthrow.[†]

During this year Somerset purchased the castle and property of Berry Pomeroy, in Devonshire, which has remained in the family ever since. The castle, however, has been in ruins for many years. (Note 33.)

In the early part of this year the Council issued a proclamation against ceremonies and, at Easter, 1548. published a new Communion office.[‡] An order for the removal of images from every church soon

[*] Knox's Works, iv, 42, 564; Froude's Hist.; Pollard, England under Protector Somerset; Acts, P.C., iii, 415, 490; Strype's Eccle. Mem., II, i, 378; Dict. Nat. Biog., &c.
[†] Archæologia, xxx.
[‡] Dict. Nat. Biog.

followed, and the people were allowed and encouraged to neglect confession. In the autumn the visitation of the universities of Oxford and Cambridge commenced. (Somerset had been elected Chancellor of the latter the previous year.)

The haste with which these orders were issued does not seem to have been approved of by the Protector. His signature is indeed affixed to the proclamations but, as Protector, it was necessary that he should sign all such documents as were approved by the Council, whether he agreed with their contents or not. Indeed, his moderation was causing some annoyance to the more zealous reformers who, as usual, would have wished to condemn to the stake everyone who differed in the slightest degree from their own religious views, and Calvin wrote him several letters to urge him on to greater severity against what he termed "the unbelievers."[*]

During the summer Somerset received a grant of lands from the King, and also inherited the large possessions in Dorsetshire belonging to Sir William Fillol, his first wife's father. (Note 34.)

Foreign affairs were, meanwhile, causing the Protector great uneasiness, both in regard to Scotland and to France. Although there was no actual war with the latter, frequent hostilities kept taking place around Boulogne, where the disputes over the fortifications were constantly recurring.[†] The French King also had determined to thwart Somerset's plans of marrying Mary of Scotland to Edward, and kept sending money and supplies to the Scots, in doing which he was encouraged and assisted by the Pope.

The Protector, however, did not recommence the war without having in the meanwhile done all he could to come to terms with the French King, without whose assistance the Scots could not have sustained another campaign. Captured ships and prisoners were exchanged

[*] Froude's Hist., Letter, Calvin to Protector.
[†] Dict. Nat. Biog. ; De Selve, Corresp. Pol.

with the French, and the cession of Boulogne was once more discussed. But Henry required all the other possessions in France as well. Negotiations again fell through, and Somerset made preparations for a war which seemed inevitable, but which did not actually commence till the following year.[*]

As to Scotland, Somerset found himself forced to adopt different measures. He had, after his last campaign, doubtless imagined that the Scots would recognize the futility of attempting a prolonged resistance, and he had brought back with him to London the Earls of Huntley and Bothwell, and some other prisoners, whom he had treated with great consideration, in the hope that, on their return, they would show their people the advantages of the union of the Crowns. The Lowlands were almost entirely in the hands of the English ; Dundee, Dalkeith, Dunbar, Haddington, and many other places had been captured and garrisoned. Offers had been made for the surrender of St. Andrews, Perth, and Edinburgh. In all these places, and indeed wherever the English had established themselves, efforts were made to introduce the Protestant religion, in the hope that, could the two countries be once united in religion, the last hindrance would be removed to their becoming one nation. At the same time the Protector had often issued writings to the Scotch people, putting before them all the advantages of a union.[†] Mr. Pollard says : " No record has been discovered of the full details of the plan of union which Somerset had in his mind, but the indications that have survived suggest that it embodied not a few of the conditions upon which union was eventually accomplished, and upon which alone it was possible." The King was to be Emperor of Great Britain, Scotland was to retain her autonomy, free trade was to be established between the two kingdoms, and all laws prohibiting "interchange of marriage" were to be abolished.

[*] Pollard, England under Protector Somerset.
[†] Pollard, England under Protector Somerset.

Somerset's plans, however, though well conceived, failed for two reasons. One was the condition of affairs at home, where the Council's acts were causing the people to rise ; the other was the opposition of the French King, who kept supplying the Scotch nobility with money, frequently sent them arms and supplies, and was endeavouring to bring about a marriage between the Scottish Queen and the Dauphin. This last was too great a danger to be overlooked, and in the end forced Somerset to adopt fresh measures. Hitherto he had dealt with the Scots as with another nation, carefully relegating to the background Henry VIII's claim of suzerainty, which would only annoy the Scotch to no purpose. Now he must either find and put forward a claimant to the Scottish throne, or take his stand upon this claim of suzerainty. He naturally chose the latter, and informed the French Ambassador that if the French marriage took place he would send assistance to the rebels in Guienne, which, he added, with significance, had once been an English province.*

In the spring (February), Somerset had sent a proclamation or exhortation to Scotland, pointing out the great advantages that must result to both nations by an amicable union of the Crowns, and attributing the cause of war to Arran and his party.† He had also gained over many of the Scottish nobility to his views by means of heavy bribes, and he was able to count on the assistance of the Protestants. In spite of his efforts, however, a marriage was arranged between the young Queen Mary and the Dauphin of France, and a French army was sent to Scotland from Brest to bring back the young Queen.

On hearing of this, Somerset at once (April) despatched Lord Grey de Wilton and Sir Thomas Palmer with an army to anticipate the arrival of the French force, and to prevent Mary being taken out of the country. They crossed the borders on the 18th, and took Haddington,

---

* Pollard, England under Protector Somerset.
† This exhortation is printed by R. Wolfe, 1548.

in which they left a strong garrison of 2,500 men, ravaged and wasted all the country round Edinburgh, and returned to Berwick without accomplishing the object of their mission, for the French fleet had meanwhile sailed safely away, bearing with them the Queen, who was shortly after married to the Dauphin.*

Somerset's Scottish policy, and his dreams of a peaceful union of the two nations, were thus shattered, and to add to his trouble the Scots now regained their courage, and marched southward, taking Home Castle, and besieging Haddington, to the relief of which it was necessary to send supplies and reinforcements at once (August). But what was perhaps a more bitter blow than the failure of his scheme, was the behaviour of his own brother, whose plots and intrigues were threatening to plunge the country into a civil war.

Lord Seymour, whose ambition was greater than his ability, had always envied the high position of his brother, and endeavoured in every way to bring about his fall and usurp his place. An unscrupulous and hard man, his want of success hitherto had gradually changed his envy into a bitter hatred, which was somewhat aggravated by the jealousies and disputes of their two wives. Somerset, on the other hand, being of a gentler and more forgiving disposition, had always shown his brother the greatest kindness. The marriage of the Admiral to the Queen Dowager, so soon after Henry's death, had not unnaturally annoyed him, but he had quickly forgiven it, and had, on the occasion of the birth of his brother's daughter, written him a most affectionate letter (August 31). On frequent occasions, when some more than usually reckless deed or saying of the Admiral's had come to light, he had written him kindly letters pointing out 'the folly of his plots and intrigues, and begging him, for the good of the country, to desist from them. It was all of no avail. The Admiral persisted in his designs, which eventually reached such a pitch that it became impossible to overlook

* Dict. Nat. Biog., &c.

them any longer.   Somerset made one last effort,
1549. and sent for him (January, 1549) in order to
reason with him, but he refused to come.   He
was then arrested by order of the Council, sent to the
Tower, tried, and executed.   When the Bill of Attainder
was passed, Somerset showed the greatest reluctance in
assenting to it, and, according to Queen Elizabeth, he
would still have interfered to save him, but the Council
prevented him from even having an interview with the
condemned man.   The Admiral's death, however, involved
Somerset in a good deal of odium, and was a severe blow
to his power.*

In the same session of Parliament which had condemned his brother, a Bill was now passed (January),
called the Act of Uniformity.   At the same time another
was passed, permitting the marriage of priests and regu-
lating tithes.†   It does not seem that Somerset had very
much to do with the bringing in of these Bills.   Foreign
affairs and internal troubles required all his attention, and
for his own part he would doubtless have preferred to
leave such fresh innovations to a more suitable period.
To add to the internal troubles of the country, a Bill had
been passed in the Lords some time before, much against
the Protector's wishes, allowing everyone to enclose his
lands as he pleased.   The Commons, indeed, had rejected it, but nevertheless the nobility and gentry continued to enclose lands and to turn arable fields into
pasture.   This caused great hardship amongst the people,
numbers of whom had been thrown out of work by
the dissolution of the monasteries, for the monks had up
to that time been the chief cultivators of the soil, and
employed large numbers of labourers.‡   Somerset brought

* Tytler ; Froude ; Hayward, Edward VI ; Dict. Nat. Biog. ;
Lords' Journals, &c.
† Dict. Nat. Biog.
‡ A discourse of the Common Weal of this Realm of England,
Lamond, 1893 ; Froude's Hist. ; Pollard, England under Pro-
tector Somerset.

the matter to the notice of the Council, but met with so much opposition that he resolved to take matters into his own hands. He accordingly issued a proclamation against all new enclosures, and appointed Commissioners to hear and determine causes. The gentry, however, paid no heed to the proclamation, and continued to enclose lands.*

Upon finding this, Somerset appointed another Commission to go into the country and enquire into the condition of all estates, towns, villages, and hamlets, with power to imprison such as might offer opposition, and to send to himself the names of those who had broken the law. At the same time he established a Court of Requests in his own house, where men might come for justice, and avoid the long delays experienced in the ordinary law courts.*

The Commissioners were hailed by the people with great joy, for it seemed as if their wrongs would now soon receive redress, but they were destined to disappointment. A report was duly sent in by the Commissioners to the Protector, who drafted it into a petition to be presented to Parliament in the form of an Enclosure Bill. This was summarily rejected by the House of Lords. A second Bill was then prepared, which eventually passed the Lords, but was rejected by the Commons, and a third Bill suffered a similar fate. Speaking of this Bill, Mr. Pollard says : † " There was thus nothing novel or revolutionary in either the aims or the methods of the Protector. They were indeed essentially conservative, and their object was to stay the agrarian revolution that was going on in favour of the rich at the expense of the community at large. The Protector sought merely to enforce statutes passed in the two preceding reigns ; his policy was the traditional policy of the Yorkist and Tudor rulers,

* A discourse of the Common Weal of this Realm of England, Lamond, 1893 ; Froude's Hist. ; Pollard, England under Protector Somerset.

† Pollard, England under Protector Somerset.

and the Commission he appointed was closely modelled
on that sent out by Wolsey in 1517."

The people, seeing the failure of the Protector's efforts
on their behalf, now became more discontented than ever,
and the counties of Oxford and Buckingham broke into
an open revolt which, however, was soon subdued by
Lord Grey. In June the people of Norfolk rose as well
as the counties of Devon and Cornwall ; the former on
account of the enclosures, the latter more on account of the
religious changes lately forced upon them by the Council.
The Norfolk rebellion was finally crushed by Warwick,
but not until August, and only after great difficulty.
That in Devon was suppressed by Lord Russell.*

Whilst these events had been taking place at home,
matters abroad had assumed an equally alarming aspect.
The Scotch had eventually captured Haddington and
every other English garrison with the exception of
Lander. The Protector desired to make a fresh invasion
and re-conquer the various fortresses, but the want of
money rendered such a plan impossible. In spite of all
his efforts the coinage had become more debased, and the
debts to the Antwerp money dealers had increased. The
exchequer was empty, and no more loans could be contracted. The position in France was equally bad.
Blackness, Ballemberg, and Newhaven had all been
captured, and the French were pressing hard on Boulogne,
although, as yet, no war had formally been declared.†

This had, of course, not all occurred in one moment.
The relations between the two countries had been strained
for some time, and the Protector had been warned that
an attack on Boulogne was likely to take place in the
summer. To make matters worse, his brother's conspiracy had encouraged the French to believe that there
was such secret dissatisfaction in England that an invasion

---

* Pollard, England under Protector Somerset ; Froude's Hist. ;
Dict. Nat. Biog., &c.

† De Selve, 410 ; Pollard, England under Protector Somerset ;
Wriothesley's Chronicle, 11, 20.

had every chance of success, and agents were sent by them to England and Ireland to encourage a civil war. The large pirate fleet, which owed its existence to the Admiral's encouragement, was made welcome in the French ports, whence it could with security prey upon the English traders, and commerce was in consequence almost at a standstill.*

In August of the previous year, a ray of hope had appeared, for the country people round Bordeaux had risen in revolt against the taxation by which they were oppressed, and had applied for assistance from England, but, before anything could be done to help them, the rebellion had been suppressed by Henry II, who had thus once more become free to continue his antagonism to Somerset's policy in the north, in which he was greatly assisted by the Pope, who sent him large supplies of money with which to prosecute the campaign in Scotland, and to attack the English possessions in France.†

What could be done at this juncture it appears that Somerset did, or endeavoured to do, by doing his utmost to bring about a peace at home by entering into negotiations for an offensive and defensive alliance with the Emperor Charles,† but all his efforts were fruitless. Hampered as he was by the Council, many of whom were against him, and by his other enemies, and perhaps more than all by an empty exchequer, his power was fast declining. The anxiety caused by the difficulties that beset him, coupled with the continual weariness occasioned by the enormous amount of work he insisted on personally carrying out,† began seriously to affect his health. His temper, usually so mild and equable, became now so hasty and violent that at times none dared speak to him but Paget, whose advice was no longer well received. Even the court which he had established in his own house for redressing the wrongs of the poor no longer gave him or the people satisfaction, for the men who

* Froude's Hist.
† Pollard, England under Protector Somerset.

managed it made it as unjust and corrupt as any of the
law courts of the day.* (Note 35.)

In the summer of 1549, matters stood thus : The
exchequer was empty and no loans could be raised, yet
the Council determined on an invasion of both Scotland
and France. The people at home were dissatisfied and
almost in revolt, yet the Council had announced a new
Commission of Enclosures, a Heresy Commission, had
prohibited mass from being held, and published a new
Prayer-Book. Somerset appears to have disapproved of all
these plans. Finding an alliance with the Emperor hopeless and knowing that England could not carry on two
wars single-handed and without money, he was inclined
to treat for peace with France, which would lead to a
cessation of hostilities in Scotland, by anticipating by a
few years the restoration of Boulogne which, in any case,
was to be given back to the French in 1554, according to
the treaty made by Henry VIII. As to the religious
innovations, he approved the Prayer-Book as a whole, but
was too moderate and tolerant to entirely support the
prohibition of the mass and the Heresy Commission. The
first Prayer-Book of this reign had, together with the first
Act of Uniformity, been drawn up under his own immediate influence, and was written in such a manner as to
retain many portions of the former Catholic matters of
faith. It was intended as a book of prayer which might
be suited to all parties, and indeed has been described by
a High Churchman in this generation as preferable to the
book of Common Prayer in use at this day. It left the
real presence to be assumed, enjoined abstinence from
flesh during Lent, and permitted prayers for the dead and
auricular confession.† In the second Prayer-Book, however, all these things were specially forbidden, and the
change it made in religion was too great and sudden to
win the Protector's approval. In fact, in pursuance of
his policy of moderation and of hearing both sides,

* Froude's Hist.
† Pollard, England under Protector Somerset.

Somerset had for some time permitted Cardinal Pole to write to him from abroad and had even entered into a controversy with him over the merits of their respective creeds. Plenty of instances of this correspondence are to be seen in the State Papers, notably a letter written by the Duke, June 4, 1549, in answer to one of the Cardinal's, dated May 6, in which he expressed the hope that at last the Cardinal perceived the abuses of the Church of Rome and that he would now take advantage of the King's clemency and return home. At the same time he enclosed a copy of the book of Common Prayer.*

But it was the Enclosure Commission that had raised the greatest discontent at home, and Somerset had a violent dispute with the Council over it. The people, driven to fury, had taken the law into their own hands, had levelled hedges, filled ditches, torn down the walls and palings of parks, and driven away or killed the deer. The sternest measures had been necessary to subdue the many risings and the misery in the country had consequently increased. The Protector spoke his mind openly. He told the Council " that he liked well the doings of the people " ; " the covetousness of the gentlemen gave occasion to them to rise ; it were better they should die than perish for lack of living." Before matters came to a crisis he had endeavoured to allay the disturbances by issuing a proclamation, on his sole authority, that all illegal enclosures should be levelled by a certain date and granting a free pardon to almost all those who had taken part in the riots. This, however, had done no good. The Lords and gentry had immediately armed their retainers and attacked the people, and for some time many counties were in a state of civil war. It was only after much bloodshed that peace was finally restored.†

This desperate crisis through which the country was

* State Papers ; Froude's Hist.
† Pollard, England under Protector Somerset ; Froude's Hist. ; A discourse of the Common Weal of this Realm of England, ed. Lamond, 1893 ; John Hales, &c.

H

passing must be laid to the blame of the gentry, through
their greed, and to those of the Council who, out of
jealousy, had all along endeavoured to frustrate Somerset's
policy at home and abroad, and had been the promoters
of all the new laws which caused irritation amongst the
people, at the same time opposing such reforms as
Somerset attempted to alleviate the country's distress.
Mr. Pollard says of this juncture, "The Government
of England was shaken to its base, its hold on Scotland
and on France was relaxed, and at home it was confronted
with the prospect of a prolonged and bitter social war.
In the midst of the convulsion, the Council bethought
itself of saving its face and its pockets by attributing the
condition of England not to the original malady but to
the remedies that Somerset had prescribed.   It prepared
to remove not the disease but the physician."[*]

For a long time the Earl of Warwick had been in-
triguing against the Protector, and he had formed a
powerful party amongst the Council and the nobility, not
the least of whom was Wriothesley, now Earl of Southampton, who had never forgiven his own dismissal from
office.   The Catholics also were ready to join in any
attempt that would bring about the overthrow of a
Protestant ruler, while many of the Protestants themselves were discontented at the tolerance that Somerset
had shown.   The present state of matters at home and
abroad seemed too good an opportunity to be lost.   The
blame of every failure was cast on Somerset by Warwick
and his party, and no chance was lost of damaging his
government in the eyes of the people.   His plans being
sufficiently advanced, Warwick waited on Somerset, in
September, with two hundred captains who had assisted
in suppressing the late risings and demanded extra pay
for their services.   This being refused, he succeeded in
enlisting their support for his own ends.[†]

Secret meetings of the disaffected Councillors were now

* Pollard, England under Protector Somerset.
† Chron. Henry VIII, 185-6; Dict. Nat. Biog.

held to debate upon Somerset's overthrow, and the King's attendants were bribed in order that they might the more easily get possession of his person. Hearing of this, the Protector removed most of the King's attendants and replaced them by his own. The Court was at the time at Hampton Court Palace, and Somerset had with him, Cranmer, Paget, Cecil, Petre, Sir Thomas Smith, and Sir John Thynne, who had all been his supporters throughout. Finding the conspiracy becoming serious, Somerset caused handbills to be distributed in the neighbouring towns and villages calling on the peasantry to arm themselves. "Good people, in the name of God and King Edward, let us rise in all our power to defend him and the Lord Protector against certain lords and gentlemen and chief masters, who would depose the Lord Protector, and so endanger the King's royal person, because we, the poor commons, being injured by the extortions of gentlemen, had our pardon this year by the mercy of the King and the goodness of the Lord Protector, for whom let us fight, for he loveth all just and true gentlemen which do no extortion, and also the poor Commonwealth of England." A commission was issued under the King's seal requiring all liege subjects to rise and repair with harness and weapons to Hampton Court , to defend the Crown. The Corporation of London was commanded to arm and despatch 1,000 men, and, in a private letter, Somerset ordered the Lieutenant of the Tower to admit no member of the Council within its gates. (Note 36.) At the same time he sent his son, Sir Edward Seymour, with a letter to Russell and Herbert, who were returning from the suppression of the Western rebellion, entreating them to bring their army to the defence of the King's person.* (Note 37.)

On the same day, October 6, he sent Petre to London to interview the separating Councillors and threaten them with arrest if they proceeded in their rebellious designs.

* Dict. Nat. Biog.; Froude's Hist.; England under Protector Somerset; Acts, P.C., 11, 330-6; Chron. Henry VIII, p. 186

Petre found them sitting at Ely House, Holborn, where they had been drawing up an indictment against the Protector. On receipt of the message they sent letters to the chief nobility in England, describing the Protector's evil deeds and demanding their assistance. They also demanded and obtained the assistance of the Mayor and Aldermen of London and of the Lieutenant of the Tower. By the 8th they had assembled fifteen thousand men, and had received promises of assistance from Russell and Herbert, who halted their army and sent to Bristol for cannon.* Petre, doubtless looking upon the Protector's cause as lost, remained with the Council.

Meanwhile, in response to the Protector's proclamation, about ten thousand men had assembled at Hampton Court,† but, on hearing further news of the Council's proceedings, Somerset left that place with the King and repaired to Windsor, October 7, whence he wrote to the Council marvelling at their detaining Petre and vouchsafing him no answer, and saying that if any violence was intended to the King's person he would resist till death, but that if no harm was meant towards His Majesty, he was prepared for his own part to listen to any reasonable conditions they might have to offer in order to avoid the shedding of Christian blood. (Note 38.) "For we do esteem the King's wealth and tranquillity of the realm, more than all other things ; yea more than our life."

After some more correspondence on either side, from which it appears that Somerset was quite willing to resign his office provided the King's authority was not lessened thereby, a meeting took place at Windsor between the King and the separating Councillors, October 12, which

* Chron. Henry VIII, p. 189 ; Froude's Hist. Pollard, England under Protector Somerset :—"Herbert and Russell both had a private grievance against the Protector. The former had seen his park ploughed up as an illegal enclosure, and the latter had been reprimanded for exceeding his instructions in his severity towards the rebels."

† Chron. Henry VIII, p. 186.

ended in the withdrawal of the proclamation of treason
which had been issued against the Protector.   The following day, however, a long list of charges was brought
against him, after hearing which, the King caused him to
be arrested and confined in the Beauchamp Tower.*

On the next day, October 14, he was removed to
London, where some of his adherents had already been
imprisoned, notably Sir Thomas Smith, Sir Michael
Stanhope, and Sir John Thynne.†   On his way he rode
through Holborn between the Earls of Southampton and
Huntingdon, and was followed by 300 gentlemen on
horseback, and the citizen householders stood with halberts on the sides of the streets through which he passed.
At Sopher Lane, he was received by the Lord Mayor,
the Sheriffs, the Recorder, and many knights of special
note, who, with a great train of officers and attendants,
bearing halberts, escorted him to the Tower.   At the
same time a letter was sent by the Council to the Lieutenant of the Tower, ordering him to allow no one to
speak to Somerset or the other prisoners, and not even to
allow any of their servants to go abroad.‡

The articles laid to Somerset's charge referred to
various alleged malversations of office, his usurpation of
power and dignity, his neglect of the King's interests both
at home and abroad, and several other matters, the whole
of which accusations were couched in the most extravagant
and violent terms.

Mr. Pollard says, " The more violent of these charges,
the talk about ' devilish and evil purposes,' the ' subversion
of law and justice ' and traitorous behaviour, may be dismissed as mere stage thunder intended to frighten the
people into acquiescence in the revolution.   It is incon-
ceivable that there should be any truth in them when it
is remembered that those who made them restored
Somerset, six months later, to his place at the Council

* Froude's Hist., &c.
† Dict. Nat. Biog.
‡ Froude's Hist.

board. It is obvious that the only charges in which
the Councillors themselves believed were those of improper and arbitrary use of his power as Protector, and
of the ill success of his Government. Some of these
were partially, if not wholly, true ; that Somerset was
overbearing towards his colleagues is unquestionable, and
we may well believe that he gave offices to his personal
adherents. Such deeds were not peculiar to him or to
his age. That his government had been attended by
ill success is obvious, but it is not so obvious that the
fault was his. The real cause of failure was the social
trouble which finally broke out in rebellion, but this
event was precisely what the Protector laboured so persistently to prevent. He knew that no state could be
really strong in which the mass of the people were or
felt themselves oppressed, and his proclamations, enclosure commissions, and Bills in Parliament were all
designed to remove this feeling and to strengthen
England against her enemies. The commission which
the Councillors alleged as the cause of the social disturbances came after they had begun, and to prevent
their development. Their real cause was one which
the Council found it necessary to ignore, and that
was the persistent opposition of the Lords and gentlemen
which spoilt the Protector's remedies and precipitated
social war. Even so, the knowledge that Somerset was
on their side probably prevented numbers of the Commons from joining in revolt who might otherwise have
done so." This peril at home, Mr. Pollard points out,
aggravated perils abroad. Levies meant for France or
Scotland were employed in Norfolk and Devon, and the
wonder is that the reverses suffered were not greater.
Somerset was accused of leaving Boulogne defenceless,
yet its state cannot have been so bad, as it resisted a large
French army all the winter. The war itself in France
might not have occurred had Somerset been allowed by
the Council to offer the terms he desired. In Scotland
all Somerset's conquests remained in English hands, and

he kept receiving assurances of further support from many of the Scots. "Had Somerset remained in power, the English position might perhaps have been retrieved. His accusers, however, did little in practice to justify their accusations ; within a few months of their accession to power almost every fortress in Scotland which the Protector left them had been recaptured by the Scots, and a disgraceful peace was made which gave up every point for which the Tudors had struggled."*

What caused the Council to turn against the Protector was their fear of further efforts on his part to redress the wrongs of the people. They feared his meeting Parliament in November when Bills for the redress of grievances were to be proposed. They hated his love of liberty, his toleration, his abolition of the treason laws, in fact everything that was best and noblest in his government, and were determined to end his power at any cost.†

After his fall came Warwick's administration. The change was immediate and terrible.· Religious persecution commenced at once with the greatest fury, and the fires at Smithfield burned continuously ; new laws in religion were made almost daily ; a peace was concluded with France as disgraceful as that with Scotland ; Boulogne was given over in six weeks for less than half the sum formerly agreed on, and the arrears of the French pension were altogether omitted. Ships of war were laid by to rot and no new ones built ; the building of fortifications was stopped and many were even demolished. Garrisons of soldiers were reduced and many disbanded. The courts of law became so corrupt that none dared seek them. The coinage, which Somerset had been so careful to improve, was at once debased to the lowest point it has ever reached. The chantry lands were granted to private persons, and all Church plate that could be found was seized. Enclosures recommenced all over the kingdom. The poor were ground down to despair.

* Pollard, England under Protector Somerset.
† Pollard, England under Protector Somerset.

Parliament was packed with Warwick's followers, and even the Council was changed to admit a greater number of his partisans. In fact, the condition of the nation both at home and abroad was suddenly put back by something like a hundred years.*

The enemies of the Reformation had gloried in the fall of one of their most powerful opponents, and Bonner and Gardiner wrote to the Earl of Warwick, congratulating him upon his having freed the Church from its dangers, and priding themselves on the share the Church had taken in the matter. They expected that the Reformation would now be stamped out in England, but in this they were grievously disappointed, for Warwick followed the advice of the most zealous among the reformers and even persecuted others, so it was no wonder that later on the Bishop of Arras complained to Sir Philip Hobby that the Catholics were receiving no reward for having assisted so strongly in the Duke's fall.†

The latter bore his reverses with more equanimity than he had borne his prosperity and, during his imprisonment, set himself to study works of moral philosophy and divinity. A book upon patience having made a strong impression on his mind, he wrote a preface to it. This book is called "The Spiritual and Precious Pearl," and his preface is well reasoned and shows a great respect for moral philosophy and a firm belief in the Christian religion. Upon his liberation he caused an edition of it to be published which contained the preface he had written.‡

The Protector was unable to deny some of the charges brought against him and, being assured that he would be gently and leniently dealt with if he would acknowledge to the truth of the whole, he made a full confession of

* Pollard, England under Protector Somerset.
† Froude's Hist.
‡ Brit. Mus. Cat. and Hazlitt Collections.

everything laid to his charge on December 23, at the
same time attributing his guilt to his ignorance and folly,
and not to any malicious design.*

On the 2nd of January, a Bill was brought into
Parliament against him, accompanied by his con-
1550. fession. This last was thought so strange a thing,
as he was known to be innocent of several of the
charges, that many of the Peers could not believe it to be
genuine. The House, therefore, deputed the Earls
Bath and Westmorland, the Bishops of Hereford, Lich-
field, Worcester, and Westminster, with the Lords
Cobham and Morley, to see the Duke and learn whether
he had voluntarily signed the confession. The following
day they reported to the House that he acknowledged
his handwriting and confessed his faults and errors.
These articles which he confessed were vastly different
to the charges originally drawn up but finally abandoned.
They had been so modified as to amount to a mere vote
of censure. This explains Somerset's readiness to confess
them in order to end the matter, for the very things he
was now charged with doing he had been expressly authorised to do by his patent as Protector.†

The Bill previously mentioned proceeded to implore
the King's mercy and to beseech him to commute the
punishment to imprisonment during the royal pleasure.
It then settled upon the Duke and Duchess a list of manors
and estates that appears quite astonishing and excites
wonder as to how he could have amassed so much
property. (Note·39.) The Duke was freed from the
payment of tenths, reserved by the letters patent by
which many of these estates had been granted. But other
fines and reliefs were still confirmed to the King. Then,
in lieu of the fines and ransom (which the King was
pleased to take on this occasion) the Bill gave him a set
of manors and estates which adds to the wonder excited
by the former list. (Note 40.) It also gave (by a sweeping

* Froude's Hist.
† Pollard, England under Protector Somerset ; Froude's Hist.

clause) all his other lands to the King ; except those which by this act, were settled upon him and his Duchess. This arrangement was to take place from the 6th of the preceding October. All the Duke's personalty was forfeited to the King from the same time, but His Majesty was to pay, out of the court of augmentations, a set of annuities from which the Duke and Duchess were, of course, to be held discharged. The custody of the forest of Savernake was settled upon the Duke and his heirs, and he was to hold the same by the service of a fourth part of a knight's fee, &c.*

At this time there was a dispute between the Duke and Lord Audley, apparently about some property, and the House deputed several members to negotiate between them. These reported that the law was decidedly in favour of the Duke. The House, however, sent to entreat him to have some consideration for the Lord Audley, and he agreed to grant him 40 marks a year and give him any security he pleased.*

The Bill for imposing a fine upon the Duke was all this time progressing through the House. The amercement was £2,000 a year in land, the forfeiture to the King of all his goods, and the loss of his places.†

On being informed of these proceedings, he wrote to the Lords of the Council professing his obligation to them for bringing his case to a fine, and professing the innocence of his intentions, the frankness of his confession, his want of knowledge and judgment, and his reliance on the King's mercy.‡

Those who desired his destruction dared not proceed further at present. He was therefore liberated on the 6th,§ upon his giving a bond of £10,000 for his good behaviour, and on condition that he should stay at the King's palace at Sheen or at his own house at Sion, and

* Papers of 11th Duke of Somerset.
† Dict. Nat. Biog., &c.
‡ Froude's Hist.
§ Wriothesley's Chron., 11, 33 ; Acts, P.C., 11, 383.

should not go more than four miles from them or come
to the King's Council unless he was summoned. (Note
41.) He was also to promise that, if the King should
come within four miles of either of these houses, he
should at once withdraw himself.* On the night of his
liberation he dined with Sir John Yorks, one of the
Sheriffs of London, where the Lords assembled to meet
him.†

On the 16th of February, the Duke received a full
pardon, and, before many weeks had passed, was invited
to the Court at Greenwich, where he was well received by
the King and Council, and dined with His Majesty.
On April 10 he was sworn a Privy Councillor, and
resumed his attendance on the 24th, taking precedence of
all the other members. He was constant in his attendances for the next eighteen months.‡

About this time the Duke appears to have rendered
some service to the Duchess of Suffolk, who, on May 9,
wrote to Cecil, saying that she much desired a match
between Somerset's daughter and her son, but that she
wished to let the parties have their free choice.

To effect a reconciliation between Somerset and
Warwick, a marriage was now proposed between Lord
Ambrose Dudley, the Earl's eldest son, and Lady Anne
Seymour, the Duke's eldest daughter. This was duly
solemnized on June 3, the King being present, and on
the 4th a great part of Somerset's estates were restored to
him.§ (Note 42.) On the 5th he received permission,
during his lifetime, to retain 200 persons, resident within
the King's dominions, and to give them his livery,
badges, and cognizance, over and above all such servants
as attended him in his household or were under him in
any office of stewardship, &c. As the law at that time
forbade anyone's keeping more persons about them than

* Froude's Hist.
† Pollard, England under Protector Somerset.
‡ Dict. Nat. Biog., &c.
§ Dict. Nat. Biog.

were absolutely necessary, this may be taken as a mark of great favour.*

The Duke had regained some of his influence in ecclesiastical matters, and was now sent, with others, to interview Gardiner, who had been in the Tower for a long time without any proceedings being taken against him. Gardiner, however, refused to say anything unless he was first of all set at liberty. This Somerset endeavoured to obtain, but without success. Neither was he more successful in his efforts to obtain the pardon of the two Arundels, who had been concerned in the Cornish insurrection ; indeed, his efforts, though probably inspired solely by a desire for justice, alarmed Warwick's party, who feared his attempting to regain the Protectorate, and therefore determined to thwart him in every way, especially in the matter of Gardiner's release.†

Just about this time, October 18, an excellent opportunity arose for Warwick and his friends to show their ill-feeling and openly insult the Duke. On this day, Lady Seymour, his mother, died.‡ As the King's grandmother, it seemed natural that a State funeral should be accorded her, and this placed Somerset in a difficult position, for, if he ordered a public funeral it might arouse jealousy and would certainly imply that the Court should go into mourning, whereas if he ordered a private funeral he might be accused of disrespect to the King. He accordingly consulted the Council, from whom he received the following reply, which appears an extraordinary one when we see that on August 4 Lord Southampton had been buried in state, and that, on March 7 ensuing, the Lord Chamberlain was interred with similar honours. The Lords " weighed with themselves that the wearing of dole and such outward demonstration of mourning not only did not any-ways profit the dead, but rather served to induce the living to have a diffidence of the better life to

* Froude's Hist.
† Froude's Hist.
‡ Dict. Nat. Biog.

come to the departed in God by changing of this transitory life ; yea, and divers other ways did move and cause scruple of coldness in faith unto the weak ; besides, that many of the wiser sort, weighing the impertinent charges bestowed upon black cloth and other instruments of those funeral pomps, might worthily find fault with the expense thereupon bestowed—considering, therefore, how at this present the observation of the times of outward mourning and wearing of the dole was far shortened and omitted, even among mean persons, from that it was wonted to be ; considering, further, how private men should reserve their private sorrows to their own houses, and not diminish the presence of their Prince with doleful token," the Council, in the name of the King, "did specially dispense with the said Duke for the wearing of dole either upon himself or upon any of his family, or the continuing of other personal observances such as heretofore were had in solemn use, as serving rather to pomp than to any edifying."*

The House of Commons still favoured the Duke, and, in the early part of the year, had consulted about restoring him to the office of Protector.† This plan was stopped by their prorogation, but, in December, he received a very great mark of favour from the King, for, upon the distribution of a band of horsemen among the nobles, as many as 100 were appointed to him.

Warwick was, meanwhile, still quietly working for his final overthrow. He endeavoured to ruin him in 1551. the royal favour by means of certain emissaries who beset the King continually with tales and insinuations against him, and used every means of causing him such mortification as he hoped might drive him into some act or expression which would prejudice him in the eyes of the rest of the Council. For some time his attempts were unsuccessful, for Somerset used the greatest caution, and continued to enjoy the royal favour

* Froude's Hist.
† Dict. Nat. Biog.

and to be invested with greater powers by the Council who, May 10, made him Lord Lieutenant of the counties of Bucks and Berks, and sent him to preserve order in the counties of Oxfordshire, Wilts, Hants, and Sussex, which were threatening an insurrection.*   About this time, Somerset is said, but apparently without foundation, to have made interest with the Lord Strange to persuade the King to marry his daughter Jane, and also to act as a spy to advertise him when any of the Council should speak privately with His Majesty, and, if possible, acquaint him with what was said.   In spite of all his efforts, however, his enemy's schemes soon began to take effect.   The King became more attentive to the calumnies that were told him, and the Duke himself began to lose the patience he had till then shown, and to show his provocation at the daily affronts to which he was exposed by Northumberland's party.   This state of things was aggravated by an unfortunate occurrence.   Richard Rich, Lord Chancellor, though outwardly concurring with the Council, was beginning secretly to favour the Protector's restoration to power and sent him several letters acquainting him with the doings and intentions of Warwick and his party.   One of these letters, unfortunately, he entrusted to a new and ignorant servant with instructions to deliver it safely.   The letter was simply addressed " To the Duke," and the servant therefore delivered it to the first Duke he came across, who happened to be the Duke of Norfolk, a bitter enemy of Somerset's.†

All through the summer of 1551, Warwick and the Council had been making new changes and inno-
1551. vations in the religious services, which, though applauded by the more zealous reformers, had placed the country in a state of ferment.   Princess Mary was their greatest difficulty, but the Council, thinking themselves secure, determined, on August 9, to put down

* Dict. Nat. Biog.; Froude's Hist.; Pollard, England under Protector Somerset.
† Burnet, 2, 182.

her resistance. "They considered how long and patiently the King had laboured in vain to bring her to conformity —and how much her obstinacy and the toleration of it endangered the peace of the realm." They decided, therefore, that her chaplains should in future be compelled to use the English service, established by law, in her chapel ; while Edward was to write and reprove her for her stubbornness.* Somerset was the only one to openly take her part.† His name is, indeed, attached to the various resolutions of the Council, but as, when in power, he had permitted her "to keep her sacrificing knaves about her," so now he endeavoured to prevent their withdrawal ; he even went further, and strongly urged a general toleration, a desire which was later added as a crime to the list of charges against him. It is indeed probable, as Froude says, that he was getting somewhat weary of Protestantism, seeing what Protestantism had become, and preferred to superintend his architects and masons to attending chapel and hearing violent sermons.‡

Warwick's administration meanwhile had been causing such widespread discontent that Somerset's followers began to regain courage and to make plans for his restoration. As early as the last days of the session, February, 1550, the idea had been discussed amongst many members of the Lower House, but the dissolution had prevented anything further being done in the matter.§ It had not, however, escaped Warwick's notice, and, fearing the result of a discussion in Parliament, he had resolved to do without one as long as he could, or at any rate until he had made certain of Somerset's destruction.‖

The latter of course was not ignorant of the schemes that were being formed against him, and seems to have thought of seizing and imprisoning his three greatest

* Froude.
† Dict. Nat. Biog.
‡ Froude, Letter, Burgoyne to Calvin.
§ Tytler, 11, 15 ; Pollard, England under Protector Somerset.
‖ Pollard, England under Protector Somerset.

enemies, Warwick, Northampton, and Pembroke. Whether he would have done so or not, there is no proof to show, and nothing was done in the matter. Somerset himself was ill during the whole of September and unable to attend the meetings of the Council, and during his absence his enemies had time to formulate their designs. On the 4th of October he was summoned to attend them, apparently only for the purpose of seeing Warwick created Duke of Northumberland, and many of his adherents advanced likewise.*

Three days later Sir Thomas Palmer, "a brilliant but unprincipled soldier," revealed a plot, which he alleged had been made by Somerset in April, to raise the people in the north and to murder Warwick.† To this confession he added, during the next few days, that Somerset meant to have secured the Tower, raised the city of London, killed the horses of the gendarmes, secured the Great Seal with the aid of the apprentices, and invited Warwick, Northampton, and others to a banquet at Lord Paget's house, where they were all to be slain.‡ (Note 43.)

Such was Palmer's story. How false a one may be seen by the fact that Warwick himself confessed before his own death that Somerset had through his means been falsely accused ;§ and that Palmer, before his death, also declared that the evidence to which he had sworn had been invented by Warwick, and had been maintained by himself at Warwick's request.‖ (Note 44.)

On the 11th, the Council ordered an enquiry into Somerset's debts to the Crown. This, coupled with Warwick's advancement, raised his suspicions that some scheme was being carried out against him, but he made no move, and continued his attendances at Court and at

* Dict. Nat. Biog.
† Dict. Nat. Biog.; Froude.
‡ Froude; Wriothesley's Chronicle, 11, 56–57.
§ Simon Renard to Charles V, MS., Record Office.
‖ Simon Renard to Charles V, MS., Record Office.

the Council Board as if nothing had happened. On the 16th he was suddenly arrested and sent to the Tower in the evening, and during the next few days the Duchess of Somerset, the Earl of Arundel, Lord Grey, Sir John Thynne, Sir Miles Partridge, Sir Michael Stanhope, Sir Thomas Arundel, Sir Thomas Holcraft, John Seymour, David Seymour, and many others were imprisoned.* In all so large a number of people were arrested, against whom there was no charge, that it appears as though an attempt was being made to persuade the people that some huge conspiracy had been discovered.

Somerset's popularity had been so great that Warwick thought it necessary to take the greatest precautions in order to avoid a rising of the people. London was over-awed by a great parade of gendarmerie, and the city elders were ordered to " be greatly circumspect to see good and substantial watches and warding" kept, and were told that this was necessary because Somerset had plotted " to destroy the city of London and the substantial men of the same."† In order further to distract the minds of the people, several measures of reform were promised but never carried out, and fearing the meeting of Parliament, which was to take place in November, Warwick contrived to have it prorogued to the end of January.‡

This gave him three more months in which to bring his schemes to a head. November was spent in a series of private examinations of the prisoners in the Tower, but no evidence of such importance as to suit Warwick's plans could be secured. Palmer, by himself, was not a man whose confessions would obtain much credence, and Crane, the other principal witness, had nothing of importance to confess,§ yet if Warwick was to succeed, evidence must be forthcoming. An order was therefore sent to Sir

---

* Pollard, England under Protector Somerset, p. 289.
† Pollard, England under Protector Somerset, p. 289.
‡ Council Warrant Book, Royal MSS., 18, c. 24, f. 142 b.
§ Pollard, England under Protector Somerset ; Journal in Lit. Remains, Edward VI.

I

Arthur Darcie to permit the newly appointed Commissioners to have access to the prisoners "when and as
often as they shall think convenient ; and farther to be
assisting to the said Commissioners for the putting the
prisoners, or any of them, to such tortures as they shall
think expedient."*

Even these extreme measures failed to produce sufficiently incriminating evidence, and what was procured
seems to have been added to by Warwick himself, through
whose hands the written depositions passed. "Only the
deposition of Crane survives,† and that with the Earl of
Arundel's confession, or rather Northumberland's version
of it, constitutes the sole material on which to base an
estimate of the truth of the charges against Somerset. He
himself confessed nothing, and one day during the last
week in November,‡ Northumberland wrote to Sir Philip
Hoby and the Lieutenant of the Tower complaining of
Somerset's silence, and ordering them to strip from him
the Garter and Collar of the Order, even at the cost of
personal violence."§

The special commission for taking the indictments had
been issued on November 16. The Crown had then no
more difficulty in procuring indictments than it has now.
True bills were returned as a matter of course. Two were
now returned by the Middlesex grand jury ; one charging
Somerset with having, on April 20, 1551, assembled with
Sir Michael Stanhope, Sir Miles Partridge, Sir J. Holcroft,
and others, at Somerset House, for the purpose of imprisoning Warwick and seizing the Great Seal and Tower
of London and depriving the King of his authority ; and
further with inciting the citizens of London to rebellion
against the King with drums and trumpets and shouts of

* Acts, P.C., 111, 407.
† State Papers (Domestic), Edward VI, xiii, No. 65.
‡ Harleian MSS., 523, f. 26.
§ Pollard, England under Protector Somerset, p. 291. These
details are taken from England under Protector Somerset, by
Pollard, who took them from the Baga de Secretis, in the Record
Office.

Liberty. The other charging him with having, on May 20, conspired with others to take and imprison Northumberland, Northampton, and Pembroke. A similar indictment was returned by the city jury which, however, found that the treason had been committed at Holborn, while the jury of Kent placed the scene at Greenwich on April 21. It will be seen by these indictments that no mention is made of any plot of assassinating Northumberland and others. It seems clear, therefore, that such a charge is unfounded, else it would certainly have been mentioned. No reference to it either is made in the questions addressed to Somerset in his examination,* and neither Paget (at whose house report says the assassination was to have taken place) nor Arundel, both of them mentioned as accomplices and both enemies of Northumberland, were ever brought to trial on the matter, nor were they even questioned. The story doubtless arose from the entry in Edward VI's journal, a very unreliable authority, containing practically only what Northumberland chose to tell him. The only charges against Somerset were those in the indictment. These, as we have seen, consisted of two : assembling with others to take and imprison Northumberland, Northampton, and Pembroke, and raising the citizens of London to rebellion with drums and trumpets and shouts of Liberty. By law it was treason for twelve or more people to assemble together for the purpose of killing or imprisoning a Privy Councillor, but only if such persons refused to disperse when ordered to do so by the Sheriff.† It is doubtful if Somerset and his friends ever met in such a number or with such a purpose, and they had certainly never been called on to disperse. The charge of treason on this count could therefore not be sustained, and was abandoned at the trial. As regards the second charge in the indictment, it was felony by law to call unlawful assemblies by bell, trumpet, or other instruments, or to incite them to action by outcry or deed, but no proof was forthcoming

* Tytler, 11, 48-51.
† Statutes of the Realm, Rec. ed., 111, 104-108.

that Somerset had done so. Instead there exists plenty proof to the contrary in chronicles and diaries kept by citizens at the time as well as in the State Papers, for nowhere is there any mention made of such a proceeding on Somerset's part.*

The last possible charge, according to Mr. Pollard, was that the incitement was only by open word. Such an offence required evidence. Somerset denied the charge, as did also his friends Vane, Stanhope, and Partridge, even when they were about to die. To support it there were only Palmer and Crane, men not to be relied on and who afterwards confessed to the falseness of their accusations. The very Act upon which these accusations were brought was one which had been passed after Somerset's first fall, an Act totally contrary to the one made during his protectorate, and which was only temporary, as it was to expire at the end of the following Parliament. The Council as a whole do not appear to have ever been consulted on the charges, and the things with which he was charged were directed solely against Warwick and his friends, the very men who ordered his arrest, made their own accusations, produced their own witnesses, whom they examined themselves, who acted as counsel and judges at the trial, and who finally decided upon the sentence and execution.*

At five o'clock in the darkness of a winter morning (December 1), Somerset was taken in a barge from the Tower to Westminster Hall to stand his trial. Still in fear of a popular demonstration, an order had been issued by the Council the day before that every householder should keep to his house, and a large force was held in readiness to suppress any outbreak. But the order was unheeded. At break of day "Palace Yard and the court before the hall were thronged with a vast multitude, all passionately devoted to Somerset, all execrating his rival."†

The Court was now formed, Lord Winchester sitting

* For detailed account, see Pollard, England under Protector Somerset.
† Froude's Hist.

as High Steward. It had been carefully chosen, only 26 out of 47 temporal peers having been summoned. Men supposed to have a leaning towards Somerset were carefully excluded. Amongst them were Lord Chancellor Rich, the highest judge in the land, the Earls of Oxford and Shrewsbury, and the Lords Clinton and Willoughby; Paget, Arundel, and Lord Grey de Wilton had been confined to the Tower. Of those present the first were Suffolk, Northumberland (Warwick), Northampton, and Pembroke, all of them bitter enemies of Somerset.*

At nine o'clock the prisoner was led to the bar and the trial commenced. No witnesses were produced, their depositions being read, with the exception of Lord Strange, and he only said that Somerset had asked him for assistance in bringing about a marriage between the King and his daughter Jane, and also to give him secret information of the doings of the Council—matters of small importance, and which Somerset denied on oath. When the evidence of Crane and Palmer was read, the Duke desired that the former might be produced to confront him, the latter, he said, was a worthless villain. Indeed there was much that could have been brought against the characters of both these witnesses. When he objected to them he was told that the worse they were the fitter they were to be his instruments. "Fit instruments, indeed, but rather for others than for me," retorted Somerset. The reading of the evidence over, the Lords consulted together. The Duke of Norfolk and others held there was no proof of treason, and Warwick agreed readily, knowing that a lighter verdict would be sufficient for his purpose. On the charge of felony there was some argument, and several Peers spoke out saying it was not right that Northumberland, Northampton, and Pembroke should assist at the trial of a prisoner charged with conspiring against themselves only. But Northumberland would not retire, he

* Pollard, England under Protector Somerset, p. 300.—Taken from the Lord High Stewards of England in the Harleian MSS. 2194.

replied that a peer of the realm might not be challenged and, the majority present being his partisans, a verdict of felony was passed and Somerset was condemned to death.* (Note 45, Appendix C.)

The anxious crowd waiting at the doors had, however, only heard of the acquittal on the first charge and, as the Serjeant-at-Arms led the way with the axe turned from the prisoner, they imagined he was altogether acquitted and, mad with joy, sent up a shout "again, and again, and again, which pealed up to Charing Cross, and was heard in Long Acre." The crowds lining the route back to the Tower cried "God save him!" "God bless our good Duke!" and wherever the news reached church bells were rung merrily and bonfires were lit. Deep was the rage when the truth became known.†

During the period of imprisonment that followed, Somerset again occupied himself with reading and writing. In a little calendar which he possessed, and which is still in existence, he wrote the following heads of his reflections the day before his death. They are inscribed on the fly-leaf as follows: "Fere of the Lorde is the begynning of wisdome." "Put thy trust in the Lord with all thine hart." "Be not wise in thyne owne conceyt but fere the Lord." "From the Towar the day before my dethe 1551 (–2) E. Somerset." This same calendar was afterwards used by his daughter-in-law, Catharine Grey, during her imprisonment in the Tower and inside the cover, she wrote her name, "Catherine Seamoure, Catherine Hartford."‡

Nearly two months elapsed after Somerset's trial without any attempt being made to carry out the sentence. Although the Council had been packed with Warwick's adherents and the King's mind poisoned with the misrepresentations made by his enemies against Somerset,

* Pollard, England under Protector Somerset.
† Wriothesley's Chron., 11, 63; Acts, P.C., 111, 462; Stowe, p. 607.
‡ This calendar is in the Stow MS., 1066, in the British Museum.

yet there was still some doubt as to whether King and Council would agree to his execution. The general public did not for one moment believe that it would be carried out, and Warwick found it necessary to spread about false stories of pardons offered and refused, and to pretend that there had been a gigantic conspiracy.* Parliament had been summoned to meet on January 23, and it was known that neither House would suffer the Duke's execution to take place. Warwick knew that he could not prorogue them again, and that if he was to destroy his enemy, the deed must be done before their meeting.

His craftiness was equal to the occasion. "On the 18th of January," says Mr. Pollard, "Edward drew up in his own hand 'certain points of weighty matters to be immediately concluded on by my Council.'" Among them was the following note : "The matter for the Duke of Somerset's confederates to be considered as appertaineth to our surety and quietness of our realme, that by their punishment example may be showed to others." In other words, the Council was ordered to take measures for bringing to trial Somerset's confederates, who were in prison but had not yet been tried. The Council met to discuss the matter on the following day, but before Edward's memorandum was submitted to its consideration, it had by means of interlineations and erasures, been made to read as follows : "The matter for the Duke of Somerset *and* his confederates to be considered . . . , that by their punishment *and execution according to the lawes*, example, etc. . . . ."† The order for the trial of Somerset's confederates had become an order for the execution of the Duke. He was not directly referred to in the King's original note ; in the amended version laid before the Council, his was the only execution contemplated, for arrangements could scarcely be made for his confederates' execution before they had been tried."‡

* Pollard, England under Protector Somerset.
† This document is in the Cotton MSS., Vesp., F. 13, f. 171.
‡ Pollard, England under Protector Somerset.

The ruse succeeded. The forgery passed undetected and the Council were easily persuaded to appoint January 22, *the day before the meeting of Parliament,* as the date on which Somerset was to die.

The execution was appointed to take place on Tower Hill at eight o'clock in the morning,* and the same elaborate precautions against a tumult or attempt at rescue, as had been taken at the trial, were ordered for the execution. The citizens were to keep to their houses, a thousand men were brought up from the country and paraded on Tower Hill, where with the gendarmerie they formed a dense ring round the scaffold. The people, however, again paid no attention to the orders and by daybreak the great square and every approach to it were crowded with spectators.†

Shortly before eight o'clock, Somerset, dressed in his richest and most magnificent apparel, and looking as handsome and as composed as ever, arrived, surrounded by the various officers of state, the King's guards, and an escort of a thousand men from the Tower.‡ On reaching the scaffold he knelt down and said a short prayer, after which he made the following speech to the assembled people in the same distinct and even voice with which he always spoke :

" Masters and good fellows. I am come hither to die ; but a true and faithful man as any was unto the King's Majesty and to his realm. But I am condemned by a law whereunto I am subject, as we all, and therefore to show obedience I am content to die. Wherewith I am well content, being a thing most heartily welcome to me ; for the which I do thank God, taking it for a singular benefit as ever might have come to me otherwise. For, as I am a man, I have deserved at God's hand many deaths ; and it has pleased His goodness, whereas He might have taken me suddenly, that I should neither have known

* Original Letters (Parker Soc.), 11, 731-2.
† Froude's Hist.
‡ Froude's Hist.

EDWARD SEYMOUR, EARL AND MARQUIS OF HERTFORD, AND FIRST
DUKE OF SOMERSET
From an old print.

Him or myself, thus now to visit me and call me with this present death as you do see, where I have had time to remember and acknowledge Him, and to know also myself, for the which I do thank Him most heartily. And, my friends, more I have to say to you concerning religion : I have been always, being in authority, a furtherer of it to the glory of God to the uttermost of my power ; whereof I am nothing sorry, but rather have cause and do rejoice most gladly that I have so done, for the greatest benefit of God that ever I had, or any man might have in this world, beseeching you all to take it so, and to follow it on still ; for, if not, there will follow and come a worse and great plague."*

" Suddenly came a wondrous fear upon the people after those words of him spoken, by a great sound which appeared unto many above in the element as it had been the sound of gunpowder set on fire in a close house bursting out, and by another sound upon the ground as it had been the sight of a great number of great horses running on the people to overrun them ; so great was the sound of this, that the people fell down one upon the other, many with bylles (?), and others ran some this way, some that way, crying aloud, ' Jesus save us, Jesus save us.' Many of the people crying ' This way they come, that way they come, away ! away ! ' And I looked when one or other should strike me on the head, so was I stunned. The people being thus amassed, espy Sir Anthony Brown upon a little nag riding towards the scaffold, and therewith burst out crying in a voice, ' Pardon ! pardon ! pardon ! ' hurling up their caps and cloaks with these words, ' God save the King, God save the King ! ' The good Duke all this while stayed,† and with his cap in his hand waited for the people to come together, saying these words to their words of pardon, ' There is no such thing,

* Ellis, Original Letters, 2nd series, 11, 215–6 ; Pollard, England under Protector Somerset.
† It is said that Somerset might easily have escaped in the confusion.—See Harleian MSS., 353, f. 121.

good people, there is no such thing, it is the ordinance of God thus for to die wherewith we must be content ; and I pray you now let us pray together for the King's Majesty, to whose grace I have been always a faithful, true, and most loving subject, desirous always of his most prosperous success in all his affairs ; and ever glad of the furtherance and helping forward of the Commonwealth of this Realm.' At which words the people answered, ' Yea ! yea ! yea ! ' and some said with a loud voice, ' That is found now too true.' To whose grace I beseech God to send and grant to reign most prosperously to the pleasure of God."*

Having finished his speech, Somerset unbuckled his sword and presented it to the Lieutenant of the Tower. His rings he handed to the executioner, and after a few words with the Dean of Christchurch, laid his head quietly and composedly on the block.† Three times he was heard to murmur, "Lord Jesus save me."‡ Then the executioner's arm fell and all was over.

The people, disappointed in their hopes of a pardon, and touched by the manner in which he had met his end, now broke through the soldiery and, mounting the scaffold, dipped their handkerchiefs in his blood, so that they might have some token to preserve of the memory of a man who had always been their friend and who had espoused their cause on so many occasions.§ (Note 46.)

"So," says Mr. Pollard, "died Somerset, without a word of reproach against his enemies, without a regret for the life he was losing, and with a confidence born of a clear conscience, that whatsoever he had done he had done for the glory of God and the welfare of his country. Exactly 19 months later Northumberland stood on the same scaffold. In abject degradation he declared that

* For the sake of legibility it has been necessary to alter the spelling of the above, otherwise it has not been changed.
† Froude.
‡ Dict. Nat. Biog.; Pollard; Froude.
§ Harleian MSS., 353, ff. 139 onwards; Stow; Holinshed; Wriothesley's Chron., 11, 88–9; Chron. Queen Jane (Camden Society); Ellis, Orig. Letters, 2nd series, 11, 216.

he had lived the life of a hypocrite, that his faith had really been that of the Bishops he deprived and the priests he persecuted, and piteously he begged for life, ' Yea, even the life of a dog.'[*] In politics a simple faith may be but a poor substitute for the arts of Macchiavelli, and Somerset may have been no match for the craft and subtlety of his rival, but when the hour came he could at least die with decency and spirit."

Somerset's body was interred in the Tower, on the north side of the choir of St. Peter's, between the two deceased Queens, Anne Boleyn and Catherine Howard. Nineteen months later the body of Northumberland was laid headless by his side.

It may seem strange that the King should have appeared so callous and indifferent to the fate of an uncle who had always shown him the greatest kindness, and to whom he had certainly been attached up to this period ; but it must be remembered that Edward was but a boy and that, in Bishop Burnet's words, " There was all possible care taken to divert and entertain the King's mind with pleasing sights, as will appear by his journal ; which it seems had the effect that was desired ; for he was not much concerned in his uncle's preservation." The journal indeed, during this period, contains nothing but references to various sports and amusements, till January 22, when we find this brief entry. " The Duke of Somerset had his head cut off upon Tower Hill, between 8 and 9 o'clock in the morning."[†] (Note 47.)

Most historians writing of that time, have given us their opinion of his character ; and it would have seemed needless to add one more word concerning it, were it not that historians, to my mind, have persistently treated his faults and his virtues as if he had been a politician of the present century, instead of considering them in conjunction with the peculiar laws, manners, and customs of a remote

* See Northumberland's speech on the scaffold, Brit. Mus. Royal MSS., 12A, 26.
† Journal in Lit. Remains, Edward VI.

period. It is easy for us now to criticise and judge
according to our present notions and ideas; easy to
imagine to ourselves what should have been done or what
we ourselves would have endeavoured to do. But would
we have done it? Let us imagine ourselves in his place;
by birth but sons of a knight; brought up with but scanty
education, amidst wars with Scotland, wars with France,
insurrections at home, and the plots and strife of two great
religious parties; spending our youth amidst the hardships and dangers of foreign campaigns, and the even
greater dangers of a Court full of jealousies and underhand
intrigues. Let us imagine ourselves then suddenly called
on to fill the highest place that it is possible for a subject
to occupy, amidst the jealousy of the rest of the nobility
and the implacable hatred of our own brother. Should
we have managed better? I venture to think not.

The Protector was proud and haughty, but not too
overbearing; ambitious of power, but only that he might
do good to the people; wealthy, yet generous; intent on
reforming the abuses of the Church, but moderate in his
reforms and ready to tolerate the views of others. Faults
he certainly had, the greatest of which perhaps for a man
in his position was being good-natured and forgiving; a
fatal error and one which cannot generally be charged against
the great men of any time. He did not use his enormous
power to crush his foes when he might have done so, and in
consequence they took advantage of this weakness to crush
him. However much his Government may have failed, it
must be owned that he was throughout actuated by the best
of motives. Liberty! Liberty! was his political motto;
and in pursuit of this high aim he dared single-handed to
enter into a struggle with the Council, the Parliament, the
nobility, and the gentry. Shall we blame him for this
Quixotic courage, which few statesmen have dared to
show, or shall we not rather admire him for it? Liberty!
the country was not yet ripe for it then. Liberty! it is
ours now; and what are we that we should blame a man
for being in advance of his time, or blame the measures

and actions of one of the pioneers of that freedom for which we have cause to thank God every day of our lives ?

Perhaps nowhere can a better idea of his life and character be gathered than in Mr. Pollard's essay,* which I venture to quote : "With all his faults of method and character, Somerset had instincts of genuine states-manship, which raised him above the personal ambitions and unprincipled time-serving of his colleagues. His means were inadequate, his time was short, and the men with whom he worked had no eye for the loftiness of his aims, and no sympathy with the motives that impelled him. Yet his achievements were of no mean order. He was born before his time, a seer of visions and dreamer of dreams ; but his visions were visions of the future, and his dreams were dreams that came true. Immediate failure was but the prelude to ultimate success. His repeal of the heresy laws, his removal of the restrictions on the Printing Press, his refusal to persecute for religious opinion, anticipated some of the reforms which are justly ranked amongst the greatest of the privileges enjoyed by Britons. The policy of sympathy towards the poor which the Protector by means of a transient authority sought to enforce, is now compelled by the surer method of a liberal franchise. England and Scotland have become the Great Britain of which Somerset dreamt, a realm having 'the sea for a wall, mutual love for a garrison, and no need in peace to be ashamed, or in war to be afraid, of any worldly power.' The religious revolution, so far as he carried it, has been permanently established. The treason laws which he abolished are now a by-word, and that love of liberty which proved a stumbling-block to his contem-poraries is become the corner-stone of the British con-stitution. So long as civil and religious freedom remain ideals of English-speaking peoples, the Protector Somerset will be entitled to grateful remembrance as one who brought his country at least one step nearer toleration, and added at least one stone to the temple of liberty."

* Pollard, England under Protector Somerset.

The Duke of Somerset had been married twice ; first to Catharine, daughter of Sir William Fillol, knight, of Fillol Hall, in Essex ; secondly to Anne, daughter of Sir Edward Stanhope, knight, of Suffolk. By the former he had two sons—

> Sir John Seymour, of whom we will speak presently.
> Sir Edward Seymour, of whom we will speak presently.

By the latter he had three sons and six daughters—

> Sir Edward Seymour, who by Act of Parliament (1540) was to receive the honours and estates of his father, and of whom we will speak later.
> Sir Henry Seymour, of whom we will speak later.
> Edward Seymour, who died unmarried in 1574.
> Anne Seymour, who was twice married ; first to Ambrose Dudley, son of the Earl of Warwick, and 2ndly to Sir Edward Unton, knight, of Farringdon, in Berks.
> Margaret Seymour, who died unmarried. She was at one time engaged to the Lord Strange but ceased all communication with him after his behaviour at her father's trial.*
> Jane Seymour, who it was said was intended by the Duke to have married Edward VI. (Note 48.) She afterwards became Lady-in-Waiting to Queen Elizabeth, and died unmarried at the age of 20.
> Mary Seymour, who married Andrew Rogers, of Brainston, in Dorset.
> Catherine Seymour, who died unmarried.
> Elizabeth Seymour, who married Sir Richard Knightley, of Falvesley, in Northants, and died in 1602.

These daughters were all brought up with great care, their father being a man of considerable learning himself ;

* Biog. Dict. of Celebrated Women. 788.

ANNE, DUCHESS OF SOMERSET, DAUGHTER OF SIR E. STANHOPE,

From an old engraving.

for he was a good French scholar, an excellent Latin one, had a fair knowledge of German, and was able to hold his own in theological discussions with the best men of his day. They were taught Latin and French and were reckoned extremely clever for their writings, which made a considerable mark at the time. On the death of Margaret of Valois, the sisters, Anne, Margaret, and Jane, wrote 104 Latin distiches in her honour.* These were so highly thought of that they were soon translated into French, Italian, and even into Greek. Some scholars of the time enlarged upon the subject and upon the writers. Sonnets, epigrams, and odes poured in, in various languages, and the poetesses have been handed down to posterity attended by a train of poets. (Note 49.)

At the time of their father's imprisonment they were residing at Sion House, and, on their mother's arrest, were subjected to a severe examination, together with the whole household, in reference to the jewels of the Duchess, of which apparently they had been robbed by some of their domestics.† At their father's death, their mother and brothers being in the Tower, four of them were left without a home, and were sent by the Council to reside with their aunt, Lady Cromwell, who does not appear to have appreciated the charge. (Note 50.)

The Duchess of Somerset appears to have been kept a prisoner in the Tower‡ till after the accession of Mary, who released her, amongst others, on August 3, 1553.

The Parliament then restored to her certain properties, and gave her all such household stock as remained at Killingworth, lately the property of the Duke of Northumberland, so that she had the gratification, not only of seeing the destruction of her enemy, but of sharing in his spoils.§ She subsequently married Francis Newdigate,

---

* These verses have been published in Latin and English.
† Fragmenta Regalia, Addit. MS. 5498, f. 26, date Nov. 16 1551.
‡ Dict. Nat. Biog.
§ Burghley State Papers, 1, 193.

her late husband's steward,* and died in 1587. She was
buried in the chapel of St. Nicholas in Westminster Abbey,
where a fine monument was erected to her memory in the
form of a temple made of various coloured marbles.

She was a proud and haughty woman and is generally,
though I think erroneously,† supposed to have aided, by
her jealousy of Queen Catherine Parr, in bringing about
the ill-feeling shown by Lord Seymour, of Sudeley,
against the Duke of Somerset, his brother. One thing
she undoubtedly did, and that was to use all her influence
in bringing about the Act of 1540, by which her children
were to succeed to all the family estates and honours to
the total exclusion of the sons of Somerset's first wife.

There are two portraits of her, both anonymous, one
belonging to the Duke of Northumberland and the other
to the Earl of Stanhope. Of the Duke of Somerset
there are several portraits, one by Holbein, belonging to
the Duke of Northumberland, which has been engraved by
White, Honbraken, and others ; and several anonymous,
two of which are at Sudeley.

[England under Protector Somerset, by A. F. Pollard ; Dic-
tionary National Biography ; Froude's History ; Sadlier's
State Papers ; Haynes's Burghley Papers ; Ellis's Original
Letters ; Adit. MSS. British Museum (Hamilton Papers) ;
Hist. MSS. Commission ; Papers of 11th Duke of Somerset ;
Calendar's Domestic, Venetian, Foreign, and Spanish State
Papers ; Harleian MSS. ; Cottonian MSS. ; Brewer and
Gairdner's Letters and Papers, Henry VIII ; Wiltshire
Archæolog. Mag. ; Acts of the Privy Council, Nicholas and
Dasent ; Lisle Papers in the Record Office ; Greyfriars
Chronicle ; Literary Remains, Edward VI ; Wriothesley's
Chronicle ; Rymer's Foedera ; De Selve, Corresp. Pol. ;
Machyn's Diary ; Wood, Athenæ Oxon. ; Cooper, Athenæ
Cant. ; Wood's Letters of Royal and Illustrious Ladies ;
Burnet's Hist. of the Reformation ; Corr. de Marillac ; Pro-
ceedings, Privy Council ; Memoires du Maréchal de Vielle-
ville ; Nott, Surrey's Works ; Herbert, Life and Reign

---

* Dict. Nat. Biog.
† Burnet's Hist. of the Reformation.

MONUMENT IN WESTMINSTER ABBEY, ERECTED TO ANNE, DUCHESS OF
SOMERSET, THE DAUGHTER OF SIR E. STANHOPE.

Henry VIII; Teulet, Papiers d'État relatifs a l'histoire d'Écosse; Patten, Expedition into Scotland; Bannatyne Club, vol. 1; Knox's Works; Strype's Eccles. Mem. Archæologia, 30; Lords' Journals; Tytler, Life of Henry VIII; Hayward, Edward VI; Lamond, A Discourse of the Commonwealth of this Realm of England; Hales; Stow's Chronicle; Lodge's Portraits; Narrative of the Reformation; Friedman's Anne Boleyn; Camden Society Publications; Letters of Cardinal Pole; Zürich Letters; Genealogist, new ser., vol. xii; Mem. du Bellay; Somerset's Works in British Museum Library; Camden's Annals; Speed's History; Grafton's Chronicle; Baker's Chronicle; Church Quarterly Review, Oct. 1892; Cobbett's State Trials; Gent.'s Mag.; Hall's Chronicle; Fabyan's Chronicle; Leland's Commentaries; Fuller's Church Hist.; Holinshed's Chronicle; Lloyd's State Worthies; Nott's Works of Henry Howard, Earl of Surrey; Fox's Acts and Book of Martyrs; Maitland's Essays on the Reformation; Eng. Hist. Review, Oct. 1886, July 1895; Hoare's Modern Wiltshire; Lingard's Hist.; Dixon's Hist. Church of Eng.; Spelman's Hist. of Sacrilege; Worthies of England; Athenæ Brit., Myles Davies, vol. 11; Collinson's Somersetshire; Gasquet and Bishop, Edward VI and the Common Prayer, &c.]

As the reader will perceive, we now have two branches of the Seymour family to deal with : that of the Duke of Somerset's progeny by his first wife, Catherine, and that by his second wife, Anne. On that of the latter, as we have seen, the family honours and estates were settled by an Act of Parliament, in 1540. It would be confusing and almost impossible to continue the history of these two branches at the same time. We will, therefore, confine the annals for the present to the descendants of Anne. The issue of these, as will be seen later, eventually fails, and the title then reverts to the elder branch according to the Act. When that occurs, we will retrace our steps to the sons of Catherine and follow their progeny down to the present time.

K

HENRY, LORD SEYMOUR.

Henry Seymour was the second surviving son of the
Duke of Somerset, by his second wife, and was
1540. born in the year 1540.* His youth saved him
from imprisonment at the time of his father's trial,
and during Mary's reign he lived, like the rest of his
family, in retirement.

After his father's death, when an inquiry was made by
Parliament into the Duke of Somerset's estates, he
1552. was granted some portions of the property which
he apparently either sold or exchanged, for, on
1559. June 18, 1559, he was able to complete the purchase of a large estate in Gloucestershire, called
Gastling or Frampton Cotterell, in the parish of Frampton, owned by John Bush, of Boulton, Wilts, and lately
occupied by Lady Cecilia Berkeley.†

Henry Seymour was apparently inclined to lead a
military life, but for some time he was unable to rise into
any notice, not it appears from want of ability, but from
his family being out of favour. Queen Elizabeth indeed
advanced him at the same time that she restored his
brother to the Earldom of Hertford, but the
1560. latter's marriage to Lady Catherine Grey (1560)
roused Elizabeth's anger, and for a time spoilt his
1564. chances of preferment. Whilst the Earl of Hertford was in the Tower, Henry Seymour did what
he could to obtain his pardon, and was a constant
messenger on his brother's behalf to Elizabeth's various
favourites.‡ This caused the Queen to look with greater

* Dict. Nat. Biog.
    † Letters and papers, Seymour family, coll. by 11th Duke of
Somerset.
    ‡ State Papers, Domestic, Elizabeth.

1566. displeasure upon him, and we find a letter from the Earl of Hertford to Cecil (June 24, 1566) complaining of the continuance of the Queen's heavy displeasure and that his brother, Henry, was bearing part of the penalty.*

Lord Seymour's qualities as a soldier were, however, too great to be entirely overlooked and although, the country being at peace, he had no opportunity of distinguishing himself, he was employed in various matters of importance in the country and was made one of the Commissioners of Musters, in which capacity he 1569. returned a certificate, October 10, 1569, of all the able men, horses, armour, and weapons of the county of Southampton.†

In December, 1574, he received a lease of the 1574. Manor of Banwell, which was granted to him by the Bishop of Bath, at the Queen's request.‡

The next few years passed without anything occurring worthy of mention, but a time was soon to come when Lord Seymour might have an opportunity of distinguishing himself. The great Spanish Armada 1587. was being prepared for the invasion of England, and the Prince of Parma's army was being collected ready to be carried over the Channel. The news of these great preparations duly reached Elizabeth, but, like our Government of the present day, she made but scanty preparations, preferring to trust to useless diplomacy, and thereby aggravating the danger. The Armada was indeed defeated in the end, but, as in a more recent crisis, its defeat was due more to the courage and enterprise of private individuals than to any preparation on the part of the Government of the country.

Lord Henry Seymour and Captain Winter were sent 1588. in January with the few Queen's ships that could be spared them to watch the coast off Kent and

* State Papers, Domestic, Elizabeth.
† State Papers, Domestic.
‡ State Papers, Domestic, vol. xiv, p. 17.

K 2

Sussex, and prevent the landing of the Prince of Parma's army, whilst Drake was to watch for the Armada's approach, and then join Admiral Howard's squadron.* The ships, however, appear not to have been ready, for on February 18, Howard wrote to Walsingham to say that Seymour had an extreme cold and was very ill, " but yet he will not forbear to do all services and to be stirring abroad," and, as the ships were only then receiving their victuals he had taken Seymour and Gray to Rochester, where they soon regained their health. " I thank God," writes Howard, " they are much amended. I think if I had not made them come to Rochester they would not have been able to have gone to the seas with me; but I found by my dear Lord Harry that how sick soever he were, he would not tarry behind me."†

At the end of February, Lord Henry sailed with Howard's squadron in the " Elizabeth Bonaventure." A mishap, however, soon befell him, for the fleet being driven by stress of weather into Flushing, his ship ran aground. The accident is described in Howard's letters to Burghley : " The ' Elizabeth Bonaventure' in coming in, by the fault of her pilot, came aground on the sand where there had been a hulk cast away but a month before, having in her one of the best pilots in the town. I must commend my Lord Henry Seymour wonderfully for his honourable mind ; for although many of the ship went out to save themselves for fear, he would by no means stir out of her, but said he would abide her fortune, and so encouraged them all. I and Sir Wm. Winter came presently aboard of her, where we found my Lord Harry sparing no labour for her help."‡ In another he says, " through the personal exertions of Lord Henry

* Bernardino de Mendoza to the King. Spanish State Papers, Paris Archives, written January 16, 1588.
† Howard to Walsingham, February 14, in Laughton's Defeat of the Armada.
‡ Howard to Burghley, March 9, in Laughton's Defeat of the Armada.

Seymour (she) got off safe, without making a spoonful of water ; unless a ship had been made of iron it were thought to be impossible, she being twenty-seven years old and in constant service."*

In April, Seymour was deputed to guard the narrow seas with his fleet. He had now moved into a ship called the "Rainbow," of 500 tons, which was manned by 250 sailors, 30 gunners, and 70 soldiers. His squadron was composed of 16 of the Queen's ships, but so many gentlemen and private persons furnished others at their own expense, that before long he had close upon 50 vessels under his command. Of these 23 were coasters, the largest of which was 160 tons, their total tonnage amounted to 2,248 tons, and they carried between them 1,210 men.† (Note 51.) In May, having parted from the Lord Admiral, Seymour wrote to Burghley saying that he was now at Blackness, and requesting an order for the re-victualling of his fleet, which was already short of provisions.‡ A few days afterwards he sent to Walsingham a list of the ships and hoys provided by various coast towns, with full details about each, and a request that an order for provisions for six weeks at least might be sent to him.§ No attention appears to have been paid to his request, although an order was all that he required, as he states in his letter to Burghley that a Mr. Domall, of Blackness, had offered to supply any order for victuals, ammunition, or anything else required.‖

On the 17th of June, he wrote again to Walsingham to report that the Spanish fleet was at Ushant, a piece of information he had probably received from Drake, and stating that he was fully certain that the Prince of Parma's

---

* Howard to Burghley, in State Papers, Domestic, Elizabeth.
† Burghley State Papers, Murdin.
‡ Seymour to Burghley, May 22. State Papers, Domestic, Elizabeth.
§ Seymour to Walsingham, May 28. State Papers, Domestic, Elizabeth.
‖ Seymour to Burghley, May 22. State Papers, Domestic, Elizabeth.

enterprise would not go forward and that the Isle of Wight would probably be his mark. He also recommended the immediate recall of the Commissioners who had been sent to treat with the Prince of Parma.*

During this time Lord Seymour had been cruising about the narrow seas, keeping a strict watch, and only returning to the English coast when driven by stress of weather. On the 23rd of June, he sent a letter to Walsingham again urgently asking for a supply for his ships, enough for at least six weeks.† He had as yet received none from the Government, and would have been unable to keep his fleet at sea but for the generosity and public spirit shown by the brothers Musgrave, Captains of Yarmouth and Lyme, who had already supplied one month's victuals at their own cost and now promised to supply enough for another month.† He further told Walsingham that, in his opinion, the Prince of Parma was not likely to attempt anything that year for want of shipping, although he had 30,000 trained soldiers in readiness.†

On July 12 he wrote complaining of the weather, which had been more like winter than summer, with continual gales, one of which had just driven him back to the English coast, and enclosing a note of the coast ships that were discharged or absent from want of victuals. He also added that he thought it vain for the Spaniards to heap on braveries for the conquering of little England, which had always been renowned, and was now most famous, by its great discovered strength.‡ On the 18th he sent another letter containing some information, and earnestly requesting a supply of money, his men having remained unpaid for 16 weeks, and it being all he could do to keep them from mutiny.‡

* Seymour to Walsingham, May 28. State Papers, Domestic, Elizabeth.
† Same to same, June 23, June 26. State Papers, Domestic, Elizabeth.
‡ Same to same, July 12. State Papers, Domestic, Elizabeth.

The Armada was now approaching, and he received a letter from Sir Francis Drake announcing its arrival, and directing him to be ready to lend his assistance. (Note 52.) He had at last got some supply of provisions and powder, and his fleet was fully manned. Many gentlemen of standing now joined him and things wore a brighter aspect, especially since news arrived of the success of the English in their first action against the Armada.[*]

Seymour immediately set sail and joined the Admiral with all his fleet, and took part in the engagement that proceeded all the way up the Channel. He formed one of the Council that determined to drive the Spaniards from the harbour, into which they had fled, by means of fire-ships and, after the success of that scheme, he took a prominent part in the engagement that ensued, attacking, with the help of Sir William Winter in the "Vanguard," one of the largest Spanish galleons, which they drove into the body of the fleet in such a crippled state that it sank during the night; after which they each attacked one of the largest and best equipped of the Spanish fleet, doing them such damage that their crews ran them ashore on the coast of Flanders in a sinking state. Here the Spaniards were soon overpowered by the Zealanders and taken prisoners into Flushing.[†]

Lord Henry was unable to take any further part in the pursuit, as he was now ordered back to guard the English coast and prevent the Prince of Parma from embarking his army. This order seems to have grieved and annoyed him, for in his letter of August 1 to the Queen describing the battle, &c., he signs himself " Her Majesty's most bounden and faithful Fisherman,[‡] H. Seymour," and his next letter to Walsingham shows his annoyance. (Note 53.)

[*] Seymour to Walsingham, July 25. State Papers, Domestic, Elizabeth.

[†] State Papers, Domestic, Elizabeth.

[‡] The fleet on the coast was probably composed mostly of fishing boats and private craft, the larger ships being required elsewhere. See Laughton, foot-note to Seymour's letter to the Queen.

If we are to judge by Lord Seymour's letters (inserted in the Notes) there were several factions and jealousies amongst the fleet, and the other leaders did not intend that he should gain any portion of the honour and glory of a great victory.* Let no blame, however, be imputed to those great and gallant seamen whose names are for ever famous. Men are but men, and jealousy has always, and will always, exist amongst the greatest and most successful commanders on sea and land. Seymour had not been bred to the sea like the others, although when the time came he showed an ability that surprised them. He was of a great family, and well received and known at Court. If he were permitted to do great deeds, his name and fame would be extolled, and less notice would be paid to the deserts of the great men with him—men who had spent their lives braving the dangers of the ocean and fighting in foreign seas. They doubtless looked upon Seymour as of a different class to themselves, and they were right. He was not one of them. Equal they might be in courage, daring, and ability, but there equality must cease. Birth, rank, and influence made a gap between them that was not easily filled up.

One, however, the Lord Admiral Howard, had no other reason to influence his conduct unless it were jealousy, pure and simple. So Seymour apparently thought, but let us hope that in this he was mistaken. Howard's courage and abilities place him so high that none can wish to cast ever so slight an aspersion on his character.

Seymour obeyed his orders promptly, and remained in the station he was appointed to till all fear of an invasion was over, although he freely expressed his intention of not continuing in any command once his duty to his country no longer called upon him for service.†

When the fleet he commanded was disbanded, Seymour returned to Court, where he received the thanks of

* Seymour's Letters to Walsingham during August. State Papers, Domestic, Elizabeth.
† Seymour to Walsingham. State Papers, Domestic, Elizabeth.

1589. the Queen for the services he had rendered, and was appointed to the Governorship of the island of Guernsey. (January.)*

He does not appear to have taken part in any further affairs of the period, and we find no mention of 1600. him afterwards, except that in 1600 he made a claim for the continuance of a pension of £300 which the Queen allowed him, and which had fallen into arrear.

He married Joan, daughter of Thomas, Earl of Northumberland, but left no issue.† The date of his death is uncertain.

From the little information there is to be gathered about his life it is difficult, if not impossible, to attempt to gauge his character with any accuracy. He was seriously handicapped at the outset of his career by the attainder against his family, and later by the rage of the Queen at his brother's marriage. Afterwards he found himself in the important and responsible position of guarding England's shores against a projected invasion of 30,000 men, and he showed great resource, daring, and courage in his engagement with the enemy and the handling of his fleet. He appears to have been a capable and courageous leader, and to have carried out to the satisfaction of all, such duties as were entrusted to him. This is all we know. Had his opportunities been greater he might have made himself a lasting name or he might have failed entirely. We cannot tell, but such record as remains tells us that he did his duty well in the position that he occupied, and no man can be expected to do more.

[Dict. Nat. Biog.; Letters and Papers relating to Seymour family, collected by 11th Duke of Somerset; State Papers, Domestic, Elizabeth; Letters, Bernardino de Mendoza to the King of Spain, Spanish State Papers; Papers relating to the Defeat of the Spanish Armada, ed. Laughton; Burghley State Papers, ed. Murdin.]

---

* Bernardino de Mendoza to the King, March 4, 1589. Spanish State Papers.
† Dict. Nat. Biog.

EDWARD SEYMOUR, EARL OF HERTFORD.

Edward Seymour was the eldest surviving son of the Duke of Somerset, by his second wife, Anne, and upon him therefore were the honours and estates of his father settled by the Act of 1540. He was born on the 25th of May, 1539, and baptized soon after, having for his godfathers the Dukes of Norfolk and Suffolk.*

1539.

He was educated together with the young prince until the latter's accession to the throne, and received the honour of knighthood at his coronation, February 20, 1547. On April 7th, 1550, he was sent to France as one of the English hostages, and was absent three weeks.† On this occasion he was equipped entirely at the King's expense.

1547.

1550.

On the death of his father he became de jure Duke of Somerset, for the attainder against the Duke did not affect his dignities or estates. He was never, however, permitted to enjoy them, for his father's enemies almost immediately brought an Act into Parliament‡ "for the limitation of the late Duke of Somerset's lands," in which a clause was inserted declaring that not only all lands and estates belonging to the late Duke were to be forfeited, but all his dignities and titles as well, that is, as far as they affected his issue by his second wife.§ Hitherto Edward Seymour had always been styled Earl of Hertford, but he now became Sir E. Seymour, and found himself almost dependent for his support upon his father's former agent, Sir John Thynne.

1552.

* Gairdner, Letters and Papers, xiv, i, 1026, 1033.
† Dict. Nat. Biog.
‡ 5 Edward VI.
§ Cobbett, State Trials, i, 526–7.

The Seymour family, however, made strenuous efforts, through their friends in Parliament, to recover some of the family property, with the result that a court or committee was appointed, with the Marquis of Winchester at its head, to apportion such lands to the Duke's children as had been the patrimony of their respective mothers, and to arrange for due compensation in the case of any such lands as had been sold. (Note 54.) As the outcome of this inquiry, Sir Edward Seymour received a considerable number of manors and estates in the eastern portion of the county of Wilts, and was given full compensation for Somerset Place, which had been confiscated with the rest. The restitution of these properties was carried out by means of letters patent, and the King undertook the payment of the late Duke's debts.*

It will be remembered that the Duke of Somerset during his Protectorate had shown the Princess Mary very great kindness, especially in the matter of pursuing her religion unmolested. The Princess was not one to entirely forget such kindness, and, on her accession to the throne, she not only left the Seymours in peace in the exercise of their Protestant faith, but released the Duchess of Somerset from her imprisonment in the Tower, and granted her some lands. She also permitted an Act to be passed restoring Sir Edward Seymour in blood,† and apparently thought of creating him Earl of Hertford, but from this she was dissuaded by her ministers.‡

The accession of a Protestant Sovereign, however, promised to improve matters still further. Elizabeth also had cause to remember many kindnesses received at the hands of the Protector, and to show her gratitude for these, within two months of her inheriting the throne, she

* Papers relating to Seymour family, collected by 11th Duke of Somerset.

† But with an express proviso that he should not succeed in consequence of this restitution to any of the lands forfeited by the attainder of the Duke.

‡ Dict. Nat. Biog.

created Seymour, Baron Beauchamp and Earl of
1559.　Hertford, January 13, 1559.*　In support of this
title he was granted £20 a year out of the customs
of Southampton.

The Earl of Hertford was now in a position when great
things might have been expected of him, for he was in
great favour with his Sovereign, and many roads of
preferment were open to him.　His affections, however,
were at that time greater than his ambition, and he soon
incurred the everlasting enmity of the Queen by secretly
marrying† the Lady Catherine Grey, whose claim
1560.　to the throne was such as to form a latent menace
to the peace and security of Elizabeth's reign.

The Lady Catherine was one of the Suffolk family, whose
pretentions to the Crown rested on the fact that Frances,
Duchess of Suffolk, was the daughter of Princess Mary,
younger sister to Henry VIII.　The Duchess's elder
daughter, Lady Jane Grey, had been proclaimed Queen
of England on the death of Edward VI, and had been
sent to the scaffold by Queen Mary.　The younger
daughter, Lady Catherine, only remained ;‡ but, in view
of what had already occurred, it was not unnatural that
Elizabeth should regard her every action with suspicion
and dread, especially as, according to Henry VIII's will,
Lady Catherine stood next to Elizabeth in the succession
to the Crown, now that Lady Jane was dead.

The Lady Catherine was born in 1540,§ and receiving
the same careful education as her sister, became equally
learned and accomplished.　On the 21st of May, 1553,
she was betrothed to Henry Herbert,‖ afterwards second
Earl of Pembroke, whose father took an active part in

* Dict. Nat. Biog.
† In November or December, Dict. Nat. Biog.
‡ It appears there was a third, a younger sister, Lady Mary
Keys.
§ Notes and Queries, 8th series, vii and viii, February to August,
1895 ; Cal. State Papers, Dom. Add., 1580, 1625, p. 404.
‖ Notes and Queries, 8th series, vii and viii, February to August,
1895 ; Cal. State Papers, Dom. Add., 1580, 1625, p. 404.

the schemes of the Duke of Northumberland. No marriage was ever consummated,* however, and after the execution of Lady Jane Grey and her father, the Duke of Suffolk, the Earl of Pembroke became afraid for his own future if he should be found to have married the heir to the Crown, and so procured a divorce or annulment of his marriage contract.†

During the remainder of Mary's reign Lady Catherine lived under the care of the Duchess of Somerset, and it was during these years that an attachment sprung up between Catherine and young Seymour, which was apparently viewed with approval by her mother, the Duchess of Suffolk.‡ Nothing, however, could be done while Mary was in power, but on Elizabeth's accession their hopes of success grew greater, for both found themselves looked upon with more favour, Catherine being given a place about the Court and Seymour being created Earl of Hertford.

They now set about endeavouring to gain Elizabeth's consent to their union through the intercession of the Duchess of Suffolk, but, unfortunately for them, the latter died (December, 1559), before she had been able to do anything in the matter.§ Several small matters that occurred at the time soon began to show them that Elizabeth's consent was not likely to be obtained, and, despairing of success if they appealed to her, they resolved to be married in private and to await a more suitable time for making public their union. Hertford's young sister, Jane Seymour, was taken into their confidence ; and 1560. one day at the latter end of 1560, when the Queen was hunting at Eltham, and the two young ladies had been excused from accompanying her, the latter seized the opportunity, and, having escaped unnoticed

* Notes and Queries, 8th series, vii and viii, February to August, 1895 ; Cal. State Papers, Dom. Add., 1580, 1625, p. 404.
† Craik's Romance of the Peerage ; Dict. Nat. Biog.
‡ Harleian MS., 6286.
§ Craik's Romance of the Peerage ; Dict. Nat. Biog.

from Whitehall, proceeded to Hertford's house in Cannon Row.* It was quickly arranged between them that the marriage should take place at once, and Lady Jane went out to procure a clergyman, who had doubtless been told to hold himself in readiness, and who appears to have been a Protestant lately returned from Germany. The marriage was duly solemnized in the Earl's room, and such was their haste and inexperience that it never occurred to them to get suitable witnesses. The priest and Lady Jane were the only persons present at the union of the heir to the throne to the head of one of the great houses of England.†

Lady Catherine returned immediately afterwards to Whitehall, and resumed her occupations about the
1561. Court, and in June Hertford went to Paris with Mr. Thomas Cecil, afterwards Marquis of Exeter, chiefly with the object of studying the French language. This trip does not appear to have been attended with success. Cecil gave way to the dissipations of Paris and made no progress. His tutor, Thomas Windebank, not liking to report this to Thomas Cecil's father, laid all the blame on Hertford, and a good deal of correspondence ensued between the Duchess of Somerset and Sir William Cecil over the accusations unjustly laid to Hertford's charge.‡

Lady Catherine's condition, meanwhile, was causing some remark about the Court, seeing which she confided her marriage to Mistress Saintlow (afterwards the famous Countess of Shrewsbury) and sought her advice. The news soon spread, and in August it became a matter of common knowledge. Elizabeth at once sent her to the Tower, and, in a letter, ordered the Lieutenant of that place to examine her most strictly as to her marriage; " and let her certainly understand that she shall have no manner of favour except she will show the truth, not only

* Harleian MS., 6286.
† Harleian MS., 249; Cooper's Life and Letters of Arabella Stuart.
‡ Cal. State Papers, Domestic.

what ladies or gentlewomen of this Court were thereto privy, but also what lords and gentlemen ; for it doth now appear that sundry personages have dealt therein, and, when it shall appear more manifestly, it shall increase our indignation against her if she will forbear to utter it." Saintlow was also to be taken to the Tower, and to be frightened into some confession by being told that Catherine had confessed all.* No confession, however, resulted from these examinations.†

Elizabeth evidently thought that she had come upon some deeply-laid plot, and, although entirely mistaken in this, she never got over her suspicions. She had, indeed, already had some cause to be afraid, for, not long before, a scheme had been formed by Philip of Spain for carrying off Lady Catherine and then raising her claim to the English throne under pretence of the alleged bastardy of Elizabeth.‡

As soon as Hertford heard that his marriage had been discovered, he at once returned to England, arriving at the end of August, and on September 5 was sent to the Tower. Two days afterwards he was visited by the Lord Treasurer and other official persons, and examined on a list of charges that had been formally drawn up, and on the 12th the Lady Catherine was similarly examined.§ They both declared themselves married.§

On the 24th, Lady Catherine gave birth to a son, Edward, Lord Beauchamp. A commission was immediately appointed, headed by Parker, Archbishop of Canterbury, to make full enquiries and "judge" of her "infamous conversation" and "pretended marriage," and to make more sure of their verdict, Elizabeth so hastened this commission that only a few hours were allowed in which to procure witnesses for the defence.§

* Craik's Romance of the Peerage ; Parker Corr., p. 149 ; Aiken's Court of Elisabeth, 351–2.
† Sir E. Warner to the Queen ; State Papers, Domestic.
‡ Wright, Elisabeth, i, 7, 8 ; Cal. Hatfield MSS., i, 279.
§ Cal. State Papers, Domestic, 1561.

Both Lady Catherine and the Earl adhered steadfastly to the fact that they were married, and in their separate examinations agreed in every detail of the ceremony. Their description of the clergyman and of the positions occupied by the four persons present and many other minute details tallied exactly. Lady Catherine also produced the ring used on the occasion, which consisted of five gold links, on each of which was engraved a line of verse composed by the Earl, and which could hardly have served for any other purpose than that of a wedding-ring.* Unfortunately for them the Lady Jane Seymour, who had assisted at the marriage, had died a few months previously, there was no documentary evidence to support their statements, and the clergyman who had performed the ceremony could not be found. It appears that the latter was afraid to come forward at the time, and the short notice allowed in which to collect witnesses did not permit of any extensive search being made for him.

The commission proceeded to announce its decision on the 12th May, 1562. It was to the effect that 1562. there had been no marriage, and that the child must be declared illegitimate.† According to an Act passed in 1536, it had been made treason for a person of the royal blood to marry without the Sovereign's consent, and had Elizabeth chosen she could have proceeded to much greater severities under that Act than she could by merely declaring the marriage illegal. The latter course, however, suited her best for, in following it, she hoped not only to bring discredit on Lady Catherine but to remove a future danger in the shape of her son by casting a doubt upon his birth, whereas had she proceeded under the Act she must have acknowledged the marriage and, though it might have enabled her to remove the mother, the son might have become a more dangerous

* Craik's Romance of the Peerage.
† Harleian MS., 6286, contains a detailed account of the commission's proceedings.

rival. In addition the popularity of the Earl and Countess of Hertford was too great for Elizabeth to venture upon any extreme measures against them.

Popular feeling ran so high indeed in favour of the prisoners, and the decision of the Commissioners was so generally regarded as unjust,* that Elizabeth did not for the moment dare to award any punishment otherwise than to continue their imprisonment in the Tower, to the Lieutenant of which she gave strict orders that they were to be kept separate. These orders, however, were not strictly enforced, and the Earl had many opportunities of seeing and conversing with his wife, with the result 1563. that on the 11th of February, 1563, a second son was born, who was christened Thomas.†

The news of this event added greatly to the Queen's anger and, in consequence, Hertford was brought up before the Star Chamber and accused of three capital crimes, namely, " of breaking prison, of debauching a lady of the blood royal, and of abusing her a second time." He was fined £5,000 for each offence, £15,000 in all, and the Lieutenant of the Tower was dismissed for having permitted the intercourse. The Earl, however, was never called upon to pay this enormous sum, which it is doubtful if he would have been able to do, for the Queen soon remitted £10,000 of it in consideration of an immediate payment of £1,000, and later on remitted the remainder for a further payment of £1,187.‡ (Note 55.)

There appears at this time to have been some project amongst a portion of the Protestant leaders of settling the Crown on Lady Catherine and her children, for we read in Quadra's letter to the King of Spain, March 18,§ " It is true that Cecill is playing his game to give the Crown to the Earl of Hertford as Lethington understands, but the

* Aikin's Court of Elizabeth, 353.
† Craik's Romance of the Peerage ; Dict. Nat. Biog.
‡ Wilts. Archæolog. Mag., xv, 153. The fine was not finally remitted till 1571. See Note.
§ Spanish State Papers.

L

adherents to such a course will be weak in comparison to the Catholic party who favour the Queen of Scotland, as some of the heretics side with Huntingdon and some have no fixed plan, but will follow the strongest." In another letter, in speaking of a meeting to discuss the succession, he says, "I think they (the Catholic leaders) saw that when the principal of them were all here together, the city being so much in favour of the Earl of Hertford on the ground of religion, the Crown might be given suddenly to Lady Catherine, his wife, and the rest of them all taken prisoners and put safe under lock and key. They have, therefore, gone to their homes without doing anything in this business of the succession except to notify another Parliament in October."* The Lady Catherine and Hertford appear, however, to have had nothing to do with these plots, and not to have desired to make any claim upon the Crown.

Their imprisonment continued during the summer months, but the plague breaking out in London, Elizabeth commanded that they should be removed from the Tower, the Lady Catherine being consigned to the custody of Sir John Grey at his house of Pirgo, in Essex, and Lord Hertford being given over to the custody of his mother and Francis Newdigate, her second husband.† Strict orders were given that no intercourse should be permitted between them, but that they were still to be treated as prisoners.

It is possible that Elizabeth, if we may judge by her letters, was inclined now to abate her severity, and possibly in the end to grant a pardon, should the Earl and Countess conform to her desires during this new phase of their imprisonment. But if any thoughts of showing greater leniency ever entered her head, they were speedily dispelled to make way for her old anger and hatred. John Hales, a learned man, chose this inopportune moment to publish his assertion of Lady Catherine's

* Quadra to the King, April 24.—Spanish State Papers.
† State Papers, Domestic.

claim to the royal succession* and Elizabeth's fears and jealousies were at once aroused. (Note 56.) Hertford was sent for and re-committed to the Tower, 1564. May 26, 1564, and a stricter supervision was kept over Lady Catherine.

Sir John Grey dying on November 21, the Lady Catherine was removed to the custody of Sir William Petre,† who had just retired from the post of Secretary of State and lived for the most part at Ingatestone, in Essex. There she remained until May, 1566, when the Queen ordered her removal to the custody of Sir John Wentworth, of Gosfield Hall, in Essex. This gentleman appears to have been by no means pleased with the responsibility of the charge committed to his care and to have repeatedly, but ineffectually, petitioned the Queen to relieve him of the burden. He died in September, 1567, upon which Lady Catherine was confided to the care of Sir Owen Hopton, of Cockfield Hall, Yoxford, in Suffolk.‡

During all this time Lady Catherine and her friends had made strenuous endeavours to obtain the Queen's pardon, but without success. Hertford also had gained the sympathy of many of the most influential people about the Court, but nothing could now shake Elizabeth's determination to keep them in custody. Her fears for the stability of her own power were too great, and were further increased by the sympathy and affection with which her prisoners were regarded by the people. The continued worry and misery of imprisonment had told severely upon Lady Catherine's health. She had written more than once craving the Queen's pardon for the only offence she could or would acknowledge, that of having married without her Majesty's consent. Sir John Grey,

---

* Harleian MS., 537. This pamphlet of Hales's caused a considerable commotion, known as the "Tempestas Halesiana."

† Notes and Queries; Lansdowne MS., 102, Art. 57.

‡ Notes and Queries, 8th ser., vii and viii, February to August, 1895, by W. L. Rutton.

whilst she was with him, had written drawing a sad picture of her sufferings. "The thought and care she taketh for the want of Her Highness's favour pines her away. Before God I speak it, if it comes not the sooner, she will not long live thus. She eateth not above six morsels to the meal. If I say unto her 'Good Madam, eat somewhat to comfort yourself,' she falls a weeping, and goeth up to her chamber ; if I ask her what the cause is, she answers me, 'Alas, uncle, what a life is this to me, thus to live in the Queen's displeasure ! But for my Lord and my children, I would to God I were buried."* On the 12th of December, Sir John again wrote representing her pitiable state. The last few days she had not left her chamber nor yet her bed ; he never went to her but found her in tears ; and earnestly begged Cecil "for the mutual love which ought to exist between Christian men, and for the love wherewith God hath loved us" to endeavour to procure some favour from Elizabeth.† Lady Catherine also wrote about the same time : "What the long want of the Queen's Majesty's accustomed favour towards me hath bred in this miserable and wretched body of mine, God only knoweth, as I daily more and more, to the torment and wasting thereof, do otherwise feel than I am well able to express ; which if it should any long time thus continue, I rather wish of God shortly to be buried in the faith and fear of him than in this continual agony to live."‡ These appeals, it might be thought, would have softened the heart of most women, but Elizabeth seems to have been singularly wanting in those attributes of sympathy and kindness with which her sex, for the most part, are endowed.

Lady Catherine remained a prisoner in the custody of Sir Owen Hopton at Cockfield Hall, Yoxford, in Suffolk, until her death, which occurred January 27, 1568.§ She does not appear to have suffered from any

* Ellis's Original Letters, CL, xiv.
† Ellis's Original Letters, CL, xvi.
‡ Ellis's Original Letters, CL, xvii.
§ Dict. Nat. Biog.

malady, but to have gradually pined away from sheer unhappiness at being totally separated from those she loved. An affecting account of her last hours is given in one of the Harleian MSS.* It appears that she realized that her end was near and spent the previous night in prayer with those about her. In the early morning, between six and seven o'clock, she requested to see Sir Owen Hopton, and spoke to him as follows : "I beseech you, promise me one thing, that you yourself with your own mouth will make this request unto the Queen's Majesty, which shall be the last suit and request that ever I shall make unto Her Highness, even from the mouth of a dead woman ; that she would forgive her displeasure towards me, as my hope is she hath done. I needs must confess I had greatly offended her in that I made my choice without her knowledge, otherwise I take God to witness I had never the heart to think any evil against Her Majesty. And that she should be good unto my children, and not to impute my fault unto them, whom I give wholly unto Her Majesty ; for in my life they have had few friends, and fewer shall they have when I am dead, except Her Majesty be gracious unto them. And I desire Her Highness to be good unto my Lord, and, for I know this my death will be heavy news unto him, that Her Grace will be so good as to send liberty to glad his sorrowful heart withall." She then called for her box of trinkets and, taking from it a ring with a pointed diamond in it, she handed it to him, saying, "Here, Sir Owen, deliver this unto my Lord ; this is the ring that I received of him when I gave myself unto him and gave him my faith." "And there is my weddingring," she continued, taking another ring out of the box. (Note 57.) (It was the same ring, consisting of five gold links engraved with the Earl's verses, that she had exhibited to the Commission of Enquiry.) "Deliver this also unto my Lord, and pray him, even as I have been to

* XXXIX, f. 380, printed in Ellis's Original Letters, 2nd ser. vol. II.

him, as I take God to witness I have been, a true and
faithful wife, that he would be a loving and a natural
father unto my children ; unto whom I give the same
blessing that God gave unto Abraham, Isaac, and Jacob."
She then handed him a third ring, saying, "This shall be
the last token unto my Lord that ever I shall send him ;
it is the picture of myself." This ring bore a death's
head on it, surrounded with the words, "While I live,
yours." Her strength was now exhausted and, after a
little time, finding the end at hand she exclaimed, "So
here he is come. Welcome, death," and passed peace-
fully away with a joyful countenance.

"Thus," says Mr. Craik, in his Romance of the Peerage,
"died, without one of her blood near her, cast out, as it
were, and abandoned to strangers and servants, the great
grand-daughter of Henry VII, within 60 years from the
time when that great King wore the crown. Old men
might still remember when her mother's mother was first
the betrothed of the future Emperor of Germany and
then the Queen of France ; and it was but as it were
yesterday that her elder sister, whose heir and representative she was, had been proclaimed Queen of England.
She had not lived 30 years, and for half of that space her
existence had been little else than a succession of miseries.
From the time when she was a girl of 14 the few
months of her stolen and perilous intimacy with Hertford
—extending at most over little more than the two years
1559 and 1560—were the only interval of anything like
happiness that she had known. It were hard to say
whether the seven years that preceded that gleam of
troubled and treacherous sunshine, or the seven that
followed it, had been the darker. The slaughter of a sister
and a father, the ruin of her family, and all her own peculiar
wrongs at that period, floods of tears as we are told they
wrung from her eyes, probably did not crush the life of
her heart as much as did the hard usage she afterwards
experienced. That would bring most of the wearing-out-
sickness of hope deferred. All that is known of her,

too, would lead us to believe that she was of a gentle and affectionate nature, and ill-constituted for being so roughly tried—except, indeed, that the meek, considerate, and patient spirit, which we have seen manifesting itself so touchingly in the closing scene of her life, would also beautify and bless the whole course of it.　With so kind a heart she could not but win the attachment of every living thing that came near her.　It used to be one of the traditions about her among the people of Yoxford, that after her death a little dog which she had would taste no food, but went and lay down and died upon her grave."

The Lady Catherine was buried at Yoxford with all the pomp and ceremony befitting her rank, but later on her remains were removed to Salisbury, either by her husband or grandson.*

It has often been alleged that Hertford had entered into this marriage to advance himself, but such could not have been the case, and the allegation is practically disproved by the love and affection exhibited in his letters.　When they first met, Lady Catherine had just been divorced by Pembroke, who dared not face the danger of a union with a lady so nearly allied to the throne but whose claim appeared hopeless, her elder sister and father had been beheaded by Mary, her family was ruined, and she herself was in disgrace.　A marriage with her could bring no advancement and was certain to meet with severe punishment if not with death.　Yet Hertford was prepared to face anything if he could only win her for his wife, and when their marriage was discovered, instead of remaining abroad in security and trying to raise a party to assert her claim to the Crown, he returned at once to share her imprisonment and never countenanced or took part in any plot against Elizabeth, though success would have gained him his freedom.　The more the facts of his marriage are studied, the more does it appear that he never had any ulterior view, and that he looked upon the Lady Catherine as a true and lovable woman and not

* Notes and Queries.

as a possible Queen. Had this not been the case, he
surely would have taken the precaution to procure substantial witnesses to his marriage, so that no doubt might
afterwards be cast upon its validity. His very careless-
ness in this matter is a proof that he had no designs upon
the throne, and that love, and love only, was the cause
of the marriage ; and that love lay so deep in his heart
and memory that, though he was afterwards twice married,
he gave strict injunctions that, at his death, his remains
should be laid by Catherine's side, an order that was
duly carried out. (Note 58.) In life the lovers were
separated, but in death they repose together in the ancient
and beautiful cathedral of Salisbury.*

Although Lady Catherine was now dead, Elizabeth
continued to keep the Earl of Hertford in the Tower,
but towards the latter end of the year he was re-
1571. moved and remained, until 1571, in a somewhat
easier confinement in various country houses.†

When eventually his release came, it found him somewhat broken in health and spirits. The long confinement
and the anxiety he had endured on his wife's account, had
told heavily upon him. His best years had been spent in
prison, and his energy for a time was sapped. Being still
out of favour he, not unnaturally, elected to remain quiet
for a time, though he never ceased to endeavour to have
the validity of his marriage and the legitimacy of his sons
made clear to the world. This doubtless caused him to
seek Elizabeth's favour more than he would otherwise
have done. Elizabeth was selfish, cruel, vindictive, a
woman probably without a heart or soul, but she had
courage, and was now firmly seated on the throne, and it
was possible that in one of her more generous moods she
might, as eventually she did, do justice to his children.
It was doubtless better to rely upon one of these spasmodic
flashes of generosity than to hope for anything from the
cold, calculating spirit of James, whose cowardice was too

* Life and Letters of Lady Arabella Stuart.
† Wilts. Archæolog. Mag., xv, 153.

great to allow of any generosity or justice towards a possible rival, as Hertford's son might become.

On the 30th of August, Hertford was created M.A. of Cambridge and, on February 2, 1572, was ad-
1572. mitted a member of Gray's Inn.* About the same time he was appointed one of the judges for the trial of the young Duke of Norfolk, who was accused of treasonable practices, into which he had apparently been drawn by his attachment to Mary, Queen of
1578. Scots. In 1578 he was placed on the Commission for the Peace in the county of Wilts, and the year
1579. after was appointed one of the Commissioners for musters in the same county.* For a considerable time he had been endeavouring to recover certain lands that he claimed should have come to him from the distribution of his father's estates, and succeeded in obtaining a confirmation of certain grants, though not without meeting with considerable opposition. What he claimed and received was not nearly so much as he considered he was entitled to, but, as he himself said, he wished only to place what he had got on a secure footing, and to avoid further disturbance. At the foot of one of the papers relating to his petitions for a confirmation of title, he wrote, "Note.—This that I seek is but a feather of mine own goose : whereas if I were ambitiously disposed . . . I should have claimed restitution of the whole once meant me by Queen Mary, contrary to me in Religion."† (Note 59.) The income accruing from the lands originally restored to him by Parliament had been kept during his minority and afterwards during his imprisonment, so that he had at his disposal, after his release, a considerable sum of ready money.

In October, 1586, he was sent in company with Lord Admiral Howard in command of a strong escort
1586. to remove the Queen of Scotland from the castle where she was to another within a few miles of

* Dict. Nat. Biog.
† Wilts. Archæolog. Mag., xv, App., No. vii.

Windsor.* Early in the following year he was
1587. one of the Commissioners sent by Elizabeth to
Flanders,† and at the alarm occasioned by the approach of
the Spanish Armada, he was one of those noblemen who
raised bands of horsemen to join the large army of 81,000
men, under the Earl of Leicester and Lord Hunsdon,
        which was paraded before the Queen. In 1590,
1590. he erected a great monument at Great Bedwyn to
        his grandfather, Sir John Seymour, and the fol-
lowing year he built Easton church, but appears to have
been somewhat niggardly in his expenditure over it, for it
has been described as a mean edifice.

About this year, during one of the Queen's pro-
        gresses through the country, we are told that
1591. she was sumptuously entertained by the Earl
        of Hertford at Elvetham in Hampshire. "In
spite of the former treatment he had received at her
hands, he appears to have been anxious to win some
favour from her, probably for the sake of his children.
Elvetham, which was little more than a hunting-seat, was
far from possessing sufficient accommodation for the
Court; but the Earl, who was probably one of the
richest noblemen in England, supplied its deficiencies by
very extensive erections of timber, fitted up and furnished
with the greatest elegance. He also caused a large pond
to be dug containing three islands, artificially constructed
in the likeness of a fort, a ship, and a mount, for the
exhibition of fireworks and other splendid pageantries.
The water was made to swarm with swimming and wading
sea gods, who blew trumpets instead of shells, and recited
verses in praise of her Majesty: finally, a tremendous
battle was enacted between the Tritons of the pond and
certain sylvan deities of the park, which was long and
valiantly disputed, with darts on one side and large squirts

* Bernardino de Mendoza to the King of Spain, October 20.
—Spanish State Papers.
† Bernardino de Mendoza to the King, February 12.—Spanish
State Papers.

on the other, and suddenly terminated, to the delight of all beholders, by the seizure and submersion of old Sylvanus himself."* (Appendix D.)

Elizabeth quitted Elvetham so highly gratified by the attentions of the Earl, that she made him a voluntary promise of her especial favour and protection ; she was, however, unable to overcome her former anger against him, and soon forgot her promise.

In October, 1595, it was found, by an examination of the papers of a Dr. Aubrey, that the Earl had taken 1595. various opinions upon the validity of his marriage, and had caused a record of it to be secretly put into the Court of Arches.† At the very time of this discovery Hertford renewed his petition to have the declaration of the invalidity of his marriage set aside.‡ Elizabeth's wrath was again aroused, and she committed him at once to the Tower, and gave orders that his son, who till now had always been called Lord Beauchamp, should henceforth be styled Mr. Seymour. Several lawyers and others were also imprisoned over this matter.†

The Earl had been married a second time to Frances, daughter of William, Lord Howard of Effingham, and sister to the Lord Admiral. This lady came at once to endeavour to obtain his liberty, but without success ; for though the Queen, to whom she was related, affected to be well disposed towards her, and regularly sent her small presents of game and dishes from her own table, 1596. yet she refused to see her.† (Note 60.) On the 3rd of January following, however, the Earl was released.

During the remainder of Elizabeth's reign, Hertford's attendances in the House of Lords, either by person or by proxy, seem to have been very frequent, and he was on some occasions appointed one of the Commissioners for

* Aikin's Court of Elizabeth, 11, p. 283.
† Aikin's Court of Elizabeth, 11, p. 366.
‡ Cal. State Papers, Domestic, 1595, p. 121 ; Addenda, 1580–1625, pp. 406–8.

proroguing Parliament, but, being so much out of favour
at Court, he took little part in any important
1602. political affairs.   On the 29th of May, 1602, he
was made Lord Lieutenant of Somerset and Wilts,
and Custos Rotulorum of the latter shire in 1603.   His
jurisdiction as Lord Lieutenant included the cities of
Bristol, Bath, Wells, and Salisbury, and empowered him
to raise and muster the trained bands, to lead them against
enemies or rebels, to execute martial law when necessary,
to suppress insurrections and unlawful assemblies, and
appoint all officials and officers under him.*

The Queen was now approaching her end, and as yet
no definite arrangement had been made as to who was to
be her successor, nor could she be prevailed upon to state
her wishes and make her choice.

When the Queen was dying, Beaumont writes : " In
this state " (she was very weak and her speech had left
her) " I do not think she can make a will or declare her
successor.   The Lords of the Council have already begun
to call together the Earls and Barons of the kingdom who
are in the city, and have sent for the greater number of
those absent, among whom the Earl of Hertford has refused to come.   On the night of the 23rd of March, the
Lord Admiral, the Lord Keeper, and the Secretary, Cecil,
approached the bedside of the Queen, and asked her to
name her successor.   She seemed still speechless, and,
perhaps to test the state of her intellect, they asked if the
King of France should succeed her.   She returned no
answer ; and when they proposed the King of Scotland,
she still remained mute.   A third time they spoke, and
proposed the Lord Beauchamp, eldest son of Catherine
Grey (and the Earl of Hertford).   That name pierced
even ' the dull, cold ear ' of approaching death.   Elizabeth
for an instant recovered speech, and with inextinguishable
hate she spent her last efforts against the son of her dead
rival.   She said hastily, ' I will have no rascal's son in my
seat' ; and spoke no more in this world."

* Commission to the Earl of Hertford.—State Papers, Domestic.

Soon after the accession of James I, he was sent[*] as Ambassador Extraordinary to Bruxelles about the 1605. treaties of commerce, made by France and England with Spain and the Archduke. "It was evidently well understood by this nobleman, that his wealth alone had obtained for him what was styled the honour of this appointment, and that he would be expected to serve the King chiefly at his own cost. For this reason probably, as well as on account of his advanced age, he at first peremptorily refused to go ; and it was not till after the receipt of a ' very express letter from the King, to enjoin him to obedience, all excuses set apart,' that he yielded to take upon him so heavy a burden. But no sooner had Hertford pledged himself to the undertaking, than he declared with spirit, that he would now be 'as free as another' in his preparations."— "Nothing seems to have been omitted by him which his own credit, or the dignity of his country, could be thought to require."[†] He sailed from Dover on April 9th, with Sir Thomas Edmondes (designed to be the resident Ambassador), two barons, sixteen knights, and a great number of gentlemen, and above 300 persons in rich liveries. During the passage, a Dutch man-of-war sailed by and refused to strike her flag, whereupon the English captain (Sir W. Monson) prepared to attack him. The Ambassador would not, however, give him leave, and thus the first indignity of that nature received by the English from the Dutch, whose sovereignty was not yet so much as acknowledged by any potentate in Europe, was allowed to pass unnoticed.[‡]

Arriving at Dunkirk, he was honourably received there by Diego Orles, the governor of that town. The Baron of Brabanson, captain of the Archduke's archers, attended him ; and all the ordnance in the town, as well as on the ships, was fired. At Nimport, where the Master of the

[*] April 19, 1605.
[†] Aikin's Memoirs of James I, p. 224.
[‡] Howard, Talbot, and Cecil, Papers, vol. 3, p. 249.

Ordnance was sent to entertain him, he received a similar reception from Pedro d'Alega, governor of the town and Great Bailiff of France. The Archduke and the Infanta also made a great parade, being accompanied by knights of the Golden Fleece and Spaniards and Italians of great name.* Having seen the Archduke ratify the treaty on May 1, he left Bruxelles for home eight days afterwards, viâ Ghent and Flushing, leaving gifts, valued at £3,000, to the Archduke's attendants. In this expedition he spent £10,000 out of his own pocket in addition to the King's allowance, an enormous sum for those days.† (Note 61.)

Soon after this there appear to have been some differences between Hertford and Lord Mounteagle, and the Earl of Salisbury was, with others, appointed to arbitrate in the matter. Their decision appears to have greatly annoyed the Earl, who went so far as to say that he had expected better usage, in respect not only of his cause but of his expense and services during his embassy. To this Lord Salisbury replied that, considering how things stood between his Majesty and the Earl's house, the King had done him a special favour by employing him in such a capacity. This led to an angry argument, in which Hertford practically called Salisbury a liar. The latter, within an hour, sent him a direct challenge by his servant, Mr. Knightley, which was at once accepted. All arrangements were made and St. James fixed upon as the place of meeting. The King, however, had heard something about the quarrel and sent some of his followers to prevent the meeting, which they succeeded in doing.‡

The Earl was now getting old but he was still fated to undergo more trouble. His grandson privately 1609. and without permission followed his own former example and married a lady of the blood royal.

* Grimstone's Hist. Netherlands, 1345; Mem. Peers of England, 295; Rapin, 2, 170; Hist. M. de Thou, 14, 347.
† Aikin's Memoirs of James I.
‡ Aikin's Memoirs of James I, p. 226; Donne's Letters, p. 214.

This apparently occasioned him great alarm and grief, for he feared an unfortunate ending to his family from this second contact against the wishes and the power of his Sovereign. We read : " When the aged Hertford was forced to appear before the Council, on the occasion of his grandson's misdemeanour in having married one of the royal race, how strange must have been his feelings, and all the old wounds of his youth must have been re-opened. It is no wonder that, as he read the paper ordering him to appear, and recounting the circumstances of the flight of the lovers, his hand should tremble in such a manner that the scroll he held was half consumed by the taper he read it by."* (Note 61A.) As he was found, however, to have had nothing to do with the marriage or the subsequent escape he was soon released.

During the previous year he had been re-appointed
1612. Lord Lieutenant of the Counties of Somerset and Wilts, and in June, 1612, he was made high
1619. steward of the revenues to the Queen, an appointment which he held until March, 1619.†

In 1620 he made his will, limiting his estates on his third wife, then on the heirs male by her, remainder
1620. to his eldest son, Lord Beauchamp, and his heirs ; remainder to Thomas Seymour, his second surviving son. He thus followed what may almost be called the family rule of cutting off his eldest son to begin with.‡

During the last few years he had become very old and decrepit, but he continued his attendance at Court and about the King, whom he always accompanied on his visits to the House of Lords, where his age and weakness
made him almost an object for pity. His last
1621. appearance there was in January,§ 1621, very shortly before his death which occurred on the

---

* Miss Costello, Memoirs of Eminent Englishwomen.
† Dict. Nat. Biog.
‡ Papers relating to Seymour family, 11th Duke of Somerset.
§ D'Ewes, Autobiography, p. 170.

6th of April, at Netley, in Hampshire. He was buried
in Salisbury Cathedral in the same tomb to which he had
removed the body of his first wife, Lady Catherine Grey.
(Note 62.)

Whatever Lord Hertford's faults may have been, and
doubtless he had as many as other people, one cannot
help feeling considerable astonishment and admiration at
his continued loyalty—a loyalty which at all times seems
to have been part and parcel of the character of his
family. We see him first just old enough to see his
father's life unjustly ended on the scaffold and to find his
own name taken from him as well as all his possessions,
again unjustly. We then see him compelled to use
secrecy and stealth in marrying the lady of his choice
and condemned to see her suffer an imprisonment of
seven years, full of tears and misery, and only ended by
her death ; to find himself a prisoner for an even longer
period ; to be fined .enormous sums ; to have his
children's rights of birth denied before all the world,
thus bringing shame and dishonour on his lady and himself ; and all this again unjustly. Such treatment might
well have turned the heart of any man against a Sovereign,
from whom he received nothing but cruelty, and against
a country where such injustice was permitted to take
place. Yet he never took part in any of the plots and
factions of the time ; he never attempted to form a
party to bring forward the claims of his wife or children
to the throne, even though many powerful nobles showed
their readiness to assist him ; he never thought of sub-
verting Elizabeth's power or hindering the succession
of James. Throughout all his troubles, even when in
the darkest depths of such despair as may be engendered
by continued cruelty, unjust imprisonment, and the sight
of the misery endured by those he loved, his thoughts
and actions remained loyal, steadfast, and true to his
Sovereign and to his country.

By his first wife, Lady Catherine Grey, he had two
sons—

MONUMENT IN WESTMINSER ABBEY, ERECTED TO FRANCES,
COUNTESS OF HERTFORD.

1. Edward Seymour, Lord Beauchamp, of whom we will speak later.
2. Thomas Seymour, who was born in the Tower. Various notarial instruments were drawn up declaring his legitimacy, namely, in November, 1580, October 30, 1589, October 21, 1590, October, 1592, October 23, 1588. In 1596 he was unwittingly brought into a plot against Elizabeth.* He had accompanied Sir John Smythe to what he imagined was a review of troops, but when the force was drawn up in a hollow square of three sides, Sir John addressed the men asking them if they would follow him or rather a better man than himself, namely, a nobleman of the blood royal, brother to the Earl of Beauchamp. He further spoke of traitors about the Court and that he desired to bring about a reformation and redress the wrongs of the people. Seymour was very angry with him and blamed him openly for making such a speech, and then rode off the field and sought the Lord Treasurer to whom he related the occurrence.† Seymour married Isabel, daughter of Edward Onley, of Catesby in Northants and died on August 8, 1600, leaving no issue. He was buried in St. Margaret's, Westminster.‡ Isabel survived him, dying in 1619.

The Earl's second wife was Frances, daughter of William, Lord Howard of Effingham, whom he married before 1582.§ (Note 63.) She died on the 14th of May, 1598, without issue,‖ and was buried in St. Benedict's chapel in Westminster Abbey. On the very spot where formerly stood the altar of the Saint, Lord Hertford erected to her memory a fine monument of various kinds

---

* State Papers, Domestic.
† State Papers, Domestic, Elizabeth, Add.
‡ Walcott, St. Margaret's, p. 29.
§ Wilts. Archæolog. Mag., xv, 200–1.
‖ Chamberlain Letters, p. 10.

M

of marble.   She was represented recumbent, in her robes ;
her head resting on an embroidered cushion, and her feet
on a lion's back.   The upper part of the structure consisted partly of arches and obelisks, and was ornamented
with ensigns and devices.

His third wife, whom he married in December, 1600,
was Frances, daughter of Thomas, Viscount Howard of
Bindon, and widow of Henry Pranell, citizen of London.*
(Note 64.)   This marriage was performed clandestinely,
without banns or licence, and not in the parish church.
The clergyman, Thomas Montford, was punished for
performing it by being suspended for three years.†   This
Frances was a woman of great birth and beauty, but
otherwise without any great qualities, except that of good
nature, even this gift being to some extent marred by her
vanity and folly.   Her first marriage to Pranell did not
last long, and his death left her a young, rich, and beautiful widow.

She was now courted by many gentlemen, amongst
whom Sir George Rodney seems to have been the most
favoured, but finally she consented to marry the Earl of
Hertford.   Rodney, thereupon, after viewing their bridal
procession from a room in an inn at Amesbury, in Wilts,
wrote her a set of verses in his own blood, and, after
having despatched them, fell upon his sword and put an
end to his existence.‡   (Appendix E.)

Her pride in her family and descent was very great,
and she was fond of boasting of it, but upon such occasions the Earl of Hertford, who seems to have been
greatly attached to her, used to cover her with confusion
by playfully saying, "Frank, Frank, how long is it since
you were married to Pranell?"

At Hertford's death she became possessed of £5,000 a
year, which she had persuaded him to leave her, and, after
a time, married the Duke of Richmond, who appears to

* Dict. Nat. Biog.
† Strype, Whitgift, ii, 333, 453.
‡ Printed in Lodge's British Portraits.

FRANCES, DAUGHTER OF THOMAS, VISCOUNT HOWARD OF BINDON, AND THIRD
WIFE OF THE EARL OF HERTFORD.

From an Old Print.

have made himself ridiculous for a long time previously by following her about in all sorts of foolish disguises. The Duke, however, did not live long, upon which she began to have thoughts of raising herself to a still higher position by marrying King James, but the old monarch was too wary to be caught, and she continued to remain a widow.*

"This ridiculous notion she permitted to take full possession of her mind; and, in order to keep up a suitable dignity, she declared that she would never condescend to sit at the board with a subject. She thus saved her dinners and preserved her grandeur; being in the habit of exhibiting to her guests a table loaded with covered dishes, which appeared to contain the choicest viands, and, after their departure, mortified, she trusted, at not being permitted to share her meal, she sat down to a very simple repast for one.

"The same childish love of display was also shown in her assumption of extreme sanctity; for she caused it to be generally bruited abroad that religious conferences were continually held at her house, and that she listened to sermons from the most eminent divines, all of which was known to be but 'empty air,' like her Barmecide dinners, and only occasioned much mirth at her expense."† When she witnessed the christening of the Queen of Bohemia's child, she produced a huge inventory of plate as her gift. This passed from hand to hand, and her generosity was greatly admired. The Queen, however, never got the plate, though she may have kept the inventory. (Note 65.)

She died without issue on October 3, 1639, and on the 28th was buried in Westminster Abbey.‡

---

* Miss Costello, Memoirs of Eminent Englishwomen, vol. 1, 403, *et seq.*
† Miss Costello, Memoirs of Eminent Englishwomen, vol. 1, 403, *et seq.*
‡ Dict. Nat. Biog.

[Gairdner's Letters and Papers, xiv, 1, 1026, 1033; Dict. Nat. Biog.; Cobbett's State Trials; Papers relating to Seymour family, coll. by 11th Duke of Somerset; Calender, State Papers, Elizabeth, Domestic, and Addenda; Notes and Queries, 8th ser., vii and viii; Craik's Romance of the Peerage; Harleian MSS.; Parker Correspondence; Aikin's Court of Elizabeth; Aikin's Memoirs of James I; Wright, Elizabeth; Calendar, Hatfield MSS.; Wilts. Archæolog. Mag., xv; Spanish State Papers; Lansdowne MS.; Ellis's Original Letters, 2nd series; Life and Letters of Lady Arabella Stuart, Mrs. Smyth; Howard, Talbot, and Cecil, Papers; Rapin's History; De Thou; Donne's Letters, p. 214; Grimstone's History of the Netherlands; Memoirs, Peers of England; Sir Simon D'Ewes, Autobiography; Walcott, St. Margaret's, p. 29; Chamberlain Letters, p. 10; Strype, Whitgift; Lodge's British Portraits; Memoirs of Eminent Englishwomen, Miss Costello, vol. 1, p. 403 *et seq.*; Litt. Remains, Edward VI; Description of Salisbury Cathedral; Doyle's Official Baronage; Lords' Journals; Camden's Elizabeth; Hallam's Constitutional History; Froude's History; Dugdale; Bailey's Succession to the English Crown; Bedford, Hereditary Right; Luder's Right of Succession to the Crown in the Reign of Elizabeth; G. E. C. Peerage; Collins's Peerage; Machyn's Diary.]

EDWARD SEYMOUR, LORD BEAUCHAMP.

Edward Seymour was born in the Tower on the 24th of September, 1561, and was educated at Magdalen College, Oxford, where he matriculated on December 22nd, 1576.*

1561.

As we have already seen his father's marriage had been declared illegal, and he was looked upon by Elizabeth as a natural son. In spite of this, he appears always to have been called Lord Beauchamp, and his father and friends made strenuous efforts to have the declaration of illegitimacy rescinded, but without any practical result during Elizabeth's reign.†

Lord Beauchamp was of considerable importance at the time from the fact of his being of royal birth, and of thereby having a claim upon the succession to the throne, only two others, Lady Arabella Stuart and James VI of Scotland, being in a position to become his rivals. James was the more powerful of these, having some adherents in England, and being able to bring some force, if necessary, to assert his claim ; but Lord Beauchamp had many friends in England, some of them being amongst the most powerful of the nobles, and he might possibly have plunged the country into a civil war, after Elizabeth's death, had he elected to bring forward his claim. Indeed, the strength of Lord Beauchamp's party, including as it did Cecil, Raleigh, Lord Howard of Effingham, and many others, probably prevented Elizabeth from using severer mea-

* Dict. Nat. Biog.
† State Papers, Domestic, Elizabeth.

sures against him and against his father during her life-time.*

In June, 1582, he married his cousin Honora, daughter of Sir William Rogers of Brianston, in Dorset.†

1582. This marriage was accomplished without the know-ledge or sanction of the Earl, his father, who was so enraged that he forcibly separated the young couple and confined Beauchamp in one of his country houses. The latter soon managed to make his escape, but was retaken on his road to London, and placed under a stricter guard.

Lord Beauchamp was now in an unfortunate position, for he could only look to an angry father to whom he had given a double offence, to a haughty grandmother whose family pride made her still less inclined to forgive, and to a Queen in whose eyes his very existence was a crime. Not having obtained her permission for his marriage, he suspected that his detention was partly owing to her orders, and though she declared that he was no prisoner of hers, and was detained without her warrant, there is no doubt that Elizabeth was greatly annoyed, and that she had something to do with his imprisonment.

Seeing no prospect of an early release, Lord Beauchamp addressed a petition‡ to Lord Burleigh, the same minister who was so great a friend to the old Duchess of Somerset, and begged that the Queen and Council would grant him the benefit of the laws of the realm. No immediate result followed his petition, but not long after he became reconciled to his father and obtained his release.

In 1596 he was called before the Council and sub-jected to a severe examination for having, together

1596. with his brother, accompanied Sir John Smith to Essex on an occasion when the latter made a treasonable speech to the troops at a review in that county.§ It appeared, however, that he had accom-

* State Papers, Domestic, Elizabeth.
† State Papers, Domestic, Elizabeth.
‡ Calender State Papers, Domestic.
§ Calender State Papers, Domestic.

panied him in complete ignorance of his treasonable intentions and no further proceedings were taken against him.

At the time of Elizabeth's death, Lord Beauchamp's name was mentioned to her during her dying moments in connection with the succession, and had the effect of rousing her to a last access of rage in which she exclaimed, "I will have no rascal's son in my seat." In spite of Elizabeth's wishes, however, many noblemen 1603. waited on the Earl of Hertford and offered him their services in bringing forward Lord Beauchamp's claim to the throne,* but neither father nor son were inclined to urge a claim which must have dragged the country into a civil war. They both tendered their allegiance to James although, by Act of Parlia-1604. ment, Beauchamp remained the rightful heir to the throne for one year after James' accession, when the latter's title was settled by statute.†

During all these years Lord Beauchamp's legitimacy had never been satisfactorily proclaimed, although many appeals had been made against the unjust sentence of the Commission which had declared his father's marriage illegal.‡ In consequence of this the elder branch of the Seymour family had made several claims to the succession of the Protector's honours and estates which were entailed on them, by the Act of 1540, in default of any issue of the Earl of Hertford.§ No success, 1606. however, attended their efforts, and, in 1606, the marriage of Lady Catherine Grey and the Earl of Hertford was finally established " when the priest who had joined them being produced, and all other circumstances agreeing, a jury at common law found it a good

* Calender State Papers, Domestic.
† Dict. Nat. Biog.
‡ Papers relating to those appeals may be seen in the Cotton MS., vol. c, 16, fols. 412, 458, 516, 522, and in Sir Julius Cæsar's notes in Lansdowne MS., 732.
§ Papers, Seymour family, coll. by 11th Duke of Somerset.

marriage."* Even this, however, does not seem to have
placed Lord Beauchamp's rights on a secure basis,
1608. and he found it necessary, May 14, 1608, to
obtain a patent that he and his heirs male,
immediately on the death of his father, should be Barons
of Parliament, and have place and voice there, as well as
for the title of Earl of Hertford. It is curious to notice
that even in these letters patent the name of his father is
not even mentioned.†

Lord Beauchamp died before his father (in July, 1612),
and was buried at Great Bedwin, whence his
1612. remains were afterwards removed to Salisbury
Cathedral. On his gravestone was erected a brass
plate with the following inscription : "Bellocampus eram,
Graia Genetrice, Semerus, tres habui natos, est quibus
unus soror." This allusion to his mother might well
puzzle anyone who did not know that she had been
Lady Catherine Grey. Lord Beauchamp left three sons
and three daughters—

Sir Edward Seymour, who was created a Knight of
the Bath at the creation of Charles, Prince of
Wales. He matriculated from Magdalen College,
Oxford, April 16, 1605, and graduated B.A.
December 9, 1607. June 1, 1609, he married
Anne, third daughter of Robert Sackville, 2nd
Earl of Dorset. This lady brought him a portion
of £6,000, whilst he received a settlement of
£800 a year from his father. He had a son and
two daughters who all died in infancy, and he
himself pre-deceased his father and grandfather
and was buried September 15, 1618. His widow
afterwards married Sir Edward Lewis, knight,
and had one son, Edward, who died in infancy.
Sir William Seymour, of whom we shall speak later.
Sir Francis Seymour, knight, of whom we shall
speak later.

* Ellis, 2nd series.
† State Papers, Domestic, James I.

Anne and Mary Seymour, who both died in infancy.
Honora Seymour, who married Sir Ferdinand Sutton,
Knight of the Bath, and, at that time, heir apparent
to Edward, Lord Dudley. She had one girl,
Frances, who was afterwards made Baroness
Dudley, and married Lord Ward.

[Papers of Seymour family, coll. by 11th Duke of Somerset;
Dictionary National Biography; Calendar State Papers,
Domestic, Elizabeth; Calendar State Papers, Domestic,
James I; Cotton MS.; Lansdowne MS.; Ellis, 2nd series;
Cornhill Magazine, March, 1897; Collins's Peerage; G. E. C.
Peerage.]

FRANCIS SEYMOUR, BARON SEYMOUR OF TROWBRIDGE.

Francis Seymour was born about the year 1590* and
was apparently, together with his elder brother,
1590.   brought up under the care of his grandfather, the
Earl of Hertford.   Upon the escape of his brother
1611.   and Lady Arabella in June, 1611, he was confined
to his lodging, by order of the King, under suspicion of having aided in their escape.   Nothing could, however, be proved against him and he strongly urged his utter
ignorance of the whole affair, upon which he was liberated
after a detention of a few weeks.†

On October 23, 1613, he received the honour of
knighthood at the hands of James I, at Royston,
1613.   and in May, 1620, he went into the Low Countries
for the purpose of fighting a duel with a Mr.
John Savage, of Worcestershire, with whom he had
entered into a quarrel at Bath.‡ The result of this
meeting, if indeed it ever actually took place, is not
recorded.

On December 26 of this year, Sir Francis was returned
to Parliament as member for Wiltshire, and from
1620.   that time devoted himself to a political career, in
which he soon rose to power and distinction.   In
1624.   1624, when the King was anxious to withdraw
from war with Spain, but desired to send an army
into the Palatinate and applied to the House for the

* Dict. Nat. Biog.
† Calendar State Papers, Domestic, James I.
‡ Sir F. Popham to the Earl of Pembroke.—State Papers,
Domestic, James I.

FRANCIS, LORD SEYMOUR OF TROWBRIDGE.

From an old engraving.

necessary supplies, Seymour rose and made a very telling speech in which he strongly advocated war with Spain, but opposed the sending of any force into the Palatinate on account of the enormous cost and the heaviness of the King's debts. His words voiced the general opinion of the House, and not a member rose to oppose him.*

In June of this year he was commissioned with the other Sheriffs of Wiltshire to examine into and collect the debts due to the King for recusancy by certain persons in that county.†

On the 10th of May he was again returned member for Wiltshire and, in June, he moved a request 1625. to the King for the proper execution of the laws against Catholics, saying that their duty to God must not be forgotten, and that it was right that the laws already existing against priests and Jesuits should be duly enforced. This proposal led to an animated discussion in which member after member rose to express their approval of Seymour's action, and finally it was referred to a committee by whom, however, the tone of the petition was considerably modified before it was presented to the Lords for their approval.‡

The King had summoned this Parliament with the intention of obtaining large supplies from it in order to carry out his plans—plans which had already been strongly objected to by the Commons during the preceding session, and for the carrying out of which they were determined not to grant any large subsidy. It was perhaps to create a delay before the question of supply arose that Seymour had so earnestly pressed the petition for enforcing the law against Catholics, over which it was certain that the King and the Commons would have a long dispute. Gardiner says of this moment, " It would still be some time before the petition on religion reached the throne. What Charles expected the Commons to do as soon as they had relegated

* British Policy, Seeley ; Gardiner, v, 342, 345.
† State Papers, Domestic, James I.
‡ Gardiner.

their religious grievances to the House of Lords, it is
impossible to say. Supply stood next in order to be
treated of ; but though 12 days of the session had passed
away, giving him time to reflect on the attitude of the
Commons, he had taken no steps to explain to them the
real meaning of the vague demands which he had made in
his opening speech.

" If he expected that, when once the petition on religion
was cleared out of the way, the Commons would lay at
his feet the vast treasures which he needed, but the amount
of which he had not ventured to specify, he was soon
bitterly undeceived. Scarcely had the petition left the
House, when Sir Francis Seymour rose and proposed the
grant of one subsidy and one-fifteenth, or about £100,000.
Seldom has a motion more simple in appearance been
more momentous in its consequences. The vote proposed was as nearly as possible one-tenth of the sum
which Charles required to fulfil his engagements. It
therefore implied, under the most courteous form possible,
a distinct resolution of the House to give no adequate
support to the war in which the King was engaged.

Seymour gave no reasons for his abrupt intervention.
As far as he is personally concerned, it is not difficult to
find an explanation for his conduct. He had been one of
the most eager in the last Parliament to engage England
in a war with Spain, one of the most decided in protesting
against any attempt to involve Parliament in extensive
military operations on the Continent. He was therefore
only consistent with himself in refusing the supply necessary to carry out a policy of which he disapproved." After
some discussion, the House raised the proposed supply to
£140,000.

Finding that Seymour was becoming a powerful leader
in the House, owing to the courage he exhibited in
openly expressing his opinion, the Duke of Buckingham
deemed it wise to try and win him over, and began to
make overtures to him to that effect. These advances
were at once rejected, upon which the Duke endeavoured

to regain some measure of popularity for himself by showing more readiness to put aside his engagements with France and to oppose the Catholics in England. One of his old allies, however, now stood in the way of his projects. This was Williams, the Lord Keeper. Buckingham determined on his removal from office, and, through a friend, approached Seymour on the matter, declaring that if the Commons "would set upon the Lord Keeper, they should be backed by the greatest men in the kingdom." Seymour saw the plot, and answered quickly and sharply, "I find nothing in the Lord Keeper but the malice of those great men."

On August 5, he made a spirited and determined attack on the King's foreign policy, during which he made accusations of peculation in high places, and denounced the sale of offices at Court. As on former occasions, his speech carried the House with it, and the supplies required were again refused. Gardiner says, " If there was a man in the House who would be consistent with himself in attacking the foreign policy of the Crown, it was Sir Francis Seymour, the proposer of the restricted supply which had been granted at Westminster. In itself the fact that the Government had entered into engagements with foreign Powers so extensive that it did not venture directly to ask the Commons for the means of fulfilling them, was calculated to give rise to the gravest suspicions, and Seymour, the old opponent of the system of Continental war, was not likely to treat such suspicions lightly. This meeting of Parliament, he argued, had been the work of those who sought to put dissensions between the King and his people. It was absurd to suppose that it needed a Parliament to procure £40,000 for the fleet. As for the rest that had been said, he had no confidence in the advisers of the Crown. He did not believe that peace had been made in France, and he hoped that English ships would not be used as abettors of the French King's violence against his Huguenot subjects. Then turning to the past, Seymour said, ' We have given three subsidies and three-fifteenths to the Queen of Bohemia, for which she is nothing the better. Nothing hath been done. We know not our enemy. We have set upon and consumed our own people.' What he wished was that they might now ' do somewhat for the country,' and they would then give his Majesty a seasonable and bountiful supply." This speech showed in every sentence Seymour's distrust of Buckingham's capacity and intentions, and, in answering him, it was necessary for Mr. May, on behalf of the Government, to enter into a long defence of its foreign policy.

On August 10, Sir Francis made a very powerful and personal speech again denouncing peculation in high places and the sale of preferments at Court, and, on the 17th, when there was a debate as to the reason why the English ships were lying idle when they should have been keeping the coasts clear of pirates, during which the House began to get excited and angry, Seymour rose and openly stated what was probably in the minds of all, but what no one had summoned up sufficient courage to express. " Let us lay the fault where it is," he said, " the Duke of Buckingham is trusted, and it must needs be either in him or his agents." This was the first occasion on which anyone had dared attack the powerful favourite by name, and it made a great impression.*

The King was now finding that it would be difficult, if not impossible, for him to carry out his own or his favourite's plans so long as such steady patriots as Coke, Seymour, and Phelps were there to influence the House.

Upon their being re-elected to the Parliament 1626. summoned in February of the following year, he devised a scheme for procuring their absence. A sheriff, he found, was supposed to attend exclusively to his duties in his own county, and could not, therefore, sit in Parliament. Coke, Phelps, and Seymour were made sheriffs, the latter being appointed to Wilts.

In July the King dismissed several Justices of the

* Gardiner.

Peace whom he knew were certain to oppose the forced loan which he was about to try and raise from the people without the consent of Parliament. Amongst these Justices was Seymour. But Seymour's turn came. In the following March he was elected Member for Parliament both for Wiltshire and Marlborough,* and when the old question of supply arose, he stood up and said, "If his Majesty shall be persuaded to take what he will, what need we to give ?"

1627.

Sir Francis, however, was now beginning to realise that the Commons might go to greater lengths in their opposition to the King than their constitutional powers admitted of, and so began to incline towards Wentworth's more moderate policy. On the 29th of April, when the Bill on the liberty of the subject came before the House, he made a powerful speech in favour of modifying it. Later on he gave his support to Wentworth's Habeas Corpus Act, and joined him in advocating that a joint committee of the two Houses should be appointed to consider the Petition of Right. Their proposal was opposed by Eliot, and, though it met with favour in the House of Lords, it was rejected by the Commons.

February 14, 1630, Sir Francis, who had been living in the country since the dissolution of the last Parliament, wrote to Secretary Coke to complain of the way in which the Saltpetre men were exceeding their commission. He said that they cared not in whose houses they dug, claiming that their commission gave them the right to dig in any house and even room, at any time, and that their behaviour was occasioning great grievance to the people. Of his own knowledge he could show that they had dug up many malting rooms, and the entrances and halls of private houses, and forced men to carry their saltpetre in their own carts during seed time and harvest at one groat a mile, besides breaking down houses in cases of opposition.† This complaint seems to

1630.

* Dict. Nat. Biog.
† State Papers, Domestic, Charles I.

have been the means of causing some abatement of the evil.

On May 2, 1634, Sir Francis was charged before the Council Board by Anthony Wither, Commissioner 1634. for the reformation of clothing, with having affirmed that the Commission for clothing was against the dignity of a Justice of the Peace, that it was an innovation and would lead to the decrease of the cloth industry, and with having, when sitting with the other Justices at the Assizes at Salisbury, suggested that the Commissioner should refer to the Justices of that county, and, upon his refusal to do so, with having said that the Commissioner would not submit the Commission to the censure of the Justices and clothiers, as if, he had added, the Justices of the Peace did not best know what were fittest for the good of the country.*

Upon this Sir Francis and the other Justices laid an information against Anthony Wither, stating that he had asked certain clothiers of Salisbury to sign a certificate to the effect that they made cloth of the finer sorts of yarn, spun from Wiltshire wool by farmers' wives and others, whereas in reality the yarn brought to their market was of a coarser sort, made by market spinners, and " was made so false through divers ways of conceit, that it was impossible to make true cloth thereof." An inquiry was instituted in which it appeared that Wither had spoken of Sir Francis as the " most malicious man against his commission," and had brought forward his accusations out of spite. In the end Wither was committed by the Council, when he acknowledged that his committal was just and expressed his hearty sorrow to Sir Francis for his behaviour.†

During the summer of this year Seymour was in frequent correspondence with Lord Strafford, whom he complimented upon the great fame he had obtained by

* State Papers, Domestic, Charles I.
† State Papers, Domestic, Charles I.

his administration in Ireland, in one of his letters dated June 20.*

In May, 1639, he was amongst those who refused to pay ship money, a tax illegally levied by the King, but nothing seems to have resulted from this refusal. About this time he completed building the castle of Marlborough, in which his descendants resided for a considerable time, but which eventually became an inn.†

In March, 1640, he was elected without opposition as member for Wilts,‡ in what has been termed the Short Parliament, and, on the dissolution, was re-elected for the same shire in what became the famous Long Parliament. Having taken his seat he again began to show the greatest interest and activity in political affairs, taking a prominent part against Ecclesiastical grievances in April, and, in November, heading a strong attack against the actions of the Government. (Appendix F.) His opinions, however, were gradually undergoing a change. The more fierce and unreasonable the popular party, to which he had belonged, became, the more his inclinations were beginning to turn against them. The impeachment of Strafford was perhaps what caused him finally to disassociate himself from the popular party and throw his weight and influence upon the side of the King.

It was probably also this attachment to the Earl of Strafford that caused the King to create him Baron Seymour of Trowbridge, Wiltshire, on the 19th of February, 1641. The patent of this creation dwells upon Seymour's wisdom and respectability, the ancient splendour of his family, and his loyal affection towards the rights and fortunes of the Crown.*

1639.

1640.

1641.

---

* Letters and Papers, Seymour family, coll. by 11th Duke of Somerset.

† Letters and Papers, Seymour family, coll. by 11th Duke of Somerset; Evelyn's Diary, ed. Bray, 1, 289.

‡ State Papers, Domestic, Charles I.

N

Having taken his seat in the House of Lords he exerted himself on Strafford's behalf and voted against his attainder, although his competence to vote was challenged by the opposite party on the ground that he was not a member of that House when the charges against Strafford were first brought before it.

When matters came to a crisis between Charles and the Parliament, Seymour was one of those who signed the declaration which stated that the King had no intention of making war, and, when hostilities were begun by the Parliament, he repaired to the King at York, and 1642. joined in the voluntary subscription for raising horses for the King's service, offering for his part to provide and maintain 20 for three months.*

At the beginning of autumn Seymour accompanied the Marquis of Hertford, who had been appointed Lieutenant-General of the West, and assisted him in raising and collecting the Royalist forces, in doing which he journeyed as far as Glamorganshire, where he was able to raise a few troops. During the following months he followed the fortunes of the Marquis of Hertford, and took part in most of the engagements that took place between the Marquis's force and the Parliamentary army.

In December of the next year he joined with many other peers in writing to the Council in Scotland 1643. to protest against a proposed invasion of England to which the Scots had been invited by the Parliament, but, though employed for some time about the King, he soon rejoined Hertford's army in the west.

In 1645, he appears as Chancellor of the Duchy of Lancaster, and was appointed† one of the Com-1645. missioners for the preservation and well ordering of the city and university of Oxford, as well as for the counties of Oxford, Berks, and Bucks, and the garrisons therein, during the King's absence; and not long after he was named as one of the nobles to whom

* State Papers, Domestic, Charles I.
† State Papers, Domestic, Charles I, May 8.

the King entrusted the Militia.* In February he was selected as one of the Commissioners appointed to treat with the Parliament at Uxbridge and, on the completion of the proceedings there, he returned to Oxford, where he remained till the surrender of that place on the 22nd of June.

From the first he had been pronounced a delinquent by the Parliament, but soon after his capture he was permitted to compound for retaining his estates by a payment of £3,725, and does not appear to have suffered any imprisonment or molestation, although he continued to be looked upon with considerable suspicion by the Parliament. He apparently continued to assist the King to the best of his ability, both financially and by actively joining in various projects for his restoration, a fact that did not escape notice, for Halton and Hely frequently wrote to Cromwell giving an account of his doings, but as nothing serious could ever be proved against him he escaped all punishment.†

On the Restoration he was re-appointed Chancellor of the Duchy of Lancaster by Charles II, and once 1660. more began to show a keen interest in political affairs, seldom being absent from his place when any debate of importance was being carried on in the House of Lords.

He did not, however, live long to enjoy his renewed 1664. political activity, for he died in 1664, July 12. His remains were buried in the chancel at Great Bedwyn.‡

Of Sir Francis Seymour's life and character we cannot form an opinion, unless we attempt to judge them from the scanty records that remain to us. Except during his Parliamentary career, there is but little mention of him, except in documents of small interest referring to his

* State Papers, Domestic, Charles I.
† Papers relating to Seymour family, coll. by 11th Duke of Somerset ; Thurloe's State Papers, 4, 610.
‡ Aubrey, Top. Coll., Wilts., p. 378.

office of Chancellor of the Duchy of Lancaster. Clarendon seems to have had a high opinion of him, and it may not be amiss to quote what he says, in reference to him, in his history : "He was a man of interest and reputation ; he had always been very popular in the country, where he had lived out of the grace of Court ; and his parts and judgement were best in those things which concerned the good husbandry and the common administration of justice to the people. In the beginning of the Parliament, he served as Knight of the Shire for Wilts, where he resided ; and behaving himself with less violence in the House of Commons, than many of his old friends did, and having a greater friendship for the Earl of Strafford, he was, by his interposition, called to the House of Peers, where he carried himself very well in all things relating to the Crown ; and when the King went to York, he left the Parliament and followed his Majesty, remaining firm in his fidelity."

Sir Francis was twice married ; first to Frances, daughter and heiress of Sir William Prynne, knight, of Alington in Wilts ; secondly to Catharine, daughter of Sir Robert Lee, knight, of Billesley, in Warwickshire. By the former he had two children :

> Sir Charles Seymour, who succeeded his father in the Barony, and of whom we must speak next.
> Frances Seymour, who married Sir William Ducie, of Tedworth, in Gloucestershire, who was afterwards created Viscount Downe in the Kingdom of Ireland.

By his will, dated September 5, 1662, Lord Seymour bequeathed to his wife the sum of £600 a year and left her his house in St. Martin's Lane with the plate and furniture contained therein as well as £500 in cash. After leaving many small legacies, chiefly to old servants, he left the whole of his estates, charged with these payments, to his son Charles, who was made his sole executor.

FRANCES, LADY SEYMOUR OF TROWBRIDGE,
DAUGHTER OF SIR W. PRYNNE.

From an old print.

CATHERINE, DAUGHTER OF SIR ROBERT LEE, SECOND WIFE OF
SIR FRANCIS SEYMOUR, BARON SEYMOUR OF TROWBRIDGE.

From an old engraving.

[Dict. Nat. Biog.; Calendar State Papers, James I; Gairdner's History; British Policy, Seeley; State Papers, Domestic, Charles I; Evelyn's Diary, ed. Bray, 1, 289; Letters and Papers, Seymour family, coll. by 11th Duke of Somerset; Aubrey's Top. Coll., Wilts., 378; Notes and Queries, 2nd series, vols. vi and vii; Clarendon State Papers, ed. Macray; Clarendon's History of the Rebellion; Strafford Papers, i, 264; Foster's Eliot; Journals, House of Lords; Journals, House of Commons; Official Returns of Members of Parliament; Nalson's Collection, 1, 779; Dugdale's Baronage; Thurloe's State Papers, 4, 610, 324.]

SIR CHARLES SEYMOUR, BARON SEYMOUR OF TROWBRIDGE.

He succeeded his father July, 1664, but only survived him for a year, dying on August 25th, 1665. He was buried at Trowbridge. He had been twice married ; first to Mary, daughter of Thomas Smith, of Foley, in Wilts. ; secondly, to Elizabeth, daughter of William, Lord Alington, of Horsheath, in Cambridgeshire. By the former he had one son and two daughters :

Edward Seymour, who died young.
Catharine Seymour, who died unmarried.
Frances Seymour, who married Sir George Hungerford, knight, of Cadingham, in Wilts.

By the latter he had five sons and two daughters :

Edward Seymour, who died young.
William Seymour, who died young.
William Seymour, who died young.
Sir Francis Seymour, who afterwards became Duke of Somerset, and of whom we shall speak later.
Sir Charles Seymour, who afterwards became Duke of Somerset, and of whom we shall speak later.
Elizabeth Seymour, who died young.
Honora Seymour, who married Sir Charles Gerard, of Harrow-on-the-Hill, and who died 1731.

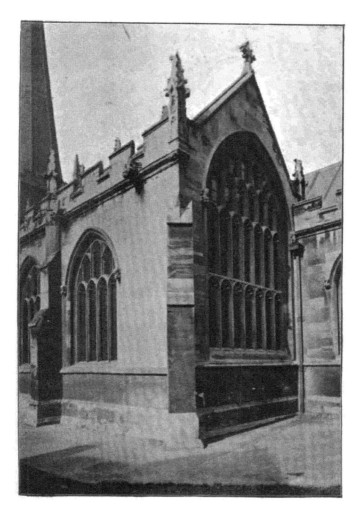

SEYMOUR CHAPEL, TROWBRIDGE CHURCH, WILTS.

TROWBRIDGE CHURCH, WILTS.

Left hand window showing the Seymour Chapel.

SIR WILLIAM SEYMOUR, MARQUIS OF HERTFORD, AND 2ND DUKE OF SOMERSET.

William Seymour was born in 1588, and was educated at Magdalen College, Oxford, where he exhibited considerable talent and a great aptitude for learning. He matriculated from there on April 16, 1605, and received the degree of B.A. December 9, 1607.* With all the talents he possessed it seemed probable that a great career might be in store for him, but, like his father and grandfather, he spoilt his chances by contracting an early and clandestine marriage.

1588.

The Lady Arabella Stuart was first cousin to James I, and stood next to him in the succession to the English Crown. Many indeed considered her claim as preferable to his in that she had been born and bred in England, whereas James was to all intents and purposes a foreigner. The English nobles who favoured the idea of an English monarch were, however, divided in their opinions as to whether to support Arabella or Lord Beauchamp and, as neither of these seemed inclined to assert their claim, no opposition was in the end made to James's accession.

Lady Arabella had been brought up by her mother, but, after her father's death, they found themselves in very reduced circumstances, for all their estates in Scotland were seized by James, and those in England by Elizabeth. A claim was brought forward asserting Arabella's right to the estates and to the earldom of her father,† but no notice of it was taken by either Elizabeth or James, so the mother and daughter remained practically destitute.

* Dict. Nat. Biog.
† Harl. MS., 289, fol. 196.

On the death of her mother Lady Arabella was given over to the care of the old Countess of Shrewsbury, who introduced her to the Court and began to set about to find some great, if not royal, alliance for her. On Lady Arabella's first presentation she had the honour of twice holding a conversation with the Queen, and afterwards dined in the presence, being throughout made much of by those about the Court, and receiving many compliments on the talents she exhibited. She appears indeed to have been well educated and accomplished, for she knew French and Italian well, was a good musician, an excellent dancer, and a good and skilful writer.*

Her attendances at Court became frequent, and Elizabeth received her with some favour. Indeed, it seems likely that the Queen may at one time have thought of naming her as her successor, for one day she said to the French Ambassador, speaking of Lady Arabella, " Look at her well. She will one day be attired just as I am, and will be a great lady ; but I shall have gone before her."†

Whatever the Queen may have really meant by this speech, there is no doubt that the Countess of Shrewsbury was fully determined upon her granddaughter occupying a great position, and she began by arranging a marriage between her and Robert, Lord Denbigh, son of the Earl of Leicester.‡ Unfortunately for the success of her scheme, this nobleman died the same year. Many more matches were proposed for her during Elizabeth's reign. James wanted to wed her to the newly made Duke of Lennox ; § the Pope suggested the brother of the Duke of Parma ; § Elizabeth herself was accused by James of trying to persuade the King of France to get rid of his wife and marry Arabella ; ‖ and the latter herself seemed

* Miss Costello, Lives of Eminent Englishwomen ; MS. at Hardwick Hall.
† Craik's Romance of the Peerage.
‡ Labanoff, v, 436.
§ Miss Costello, Lives of Eminent Englishwomen ; State Papers, Scotch, ser. xix, fol. 108, MS.
‖ State Papers, Scotch, lix, fol. 6, MS.

WILLIAM SEYMOUR, EARL AND MARQUIS OF HERTFORD, AND
SECOND DUKE OF SOMERSET.

From an Old Engraving.

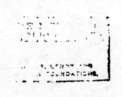

to fancy a union with a son of the Earl of Northumberland.* (Note 66.)

Nothing, however, came of these schemes, and, towards the end of Elizabeth's reign, a new idea entered 1602. Lady Arabella's head, which was to marry William Seymour, an attachment having sprung up between them, though Seymour was but a boy of fifteen, and she was his senior by a good many years. This love affair, innocent as it might seem to most, did not escape Elizabeth's watchful eye, and Lady Arabella was arrested and confined for a time.

On the accession of James a plot was discovered, in which Cobham and Raleigh were seriously implicated, as well as many Catholics, for seizing the 1603. Lady Arabella and conveying her to Spain, so that one of James's rivals would be secure and might at any time be brought forward to contest his sovereignty. (Note 67.) In the trial which followed, and at which Arabella was present, it appeared that a letter from the conspirators had once been sent her, but that she had laughed at their proposals and acquainted the King with the matter.† The latter was fully persuaded of her innocence, and treated her afterwards with considerable favour, giving her an allowance of £800 a year, and sending constant supplies of provisions for her retainers.‡ (Note 68.)

Being now so well received by the King, Lady Arabella thought fit to fall in with all his desires, and outwardly gave up her desire to marry Seymour, whom the King playfully termed "the forbidden fruit." This had the effect of bringing her into still greater favour, so that, before long, she became one of the principal channels through which solicitations were made to the King, and was able to procure many good places for her relatives and friends, while she received considerable sums of money for

* D'Israeli, Curiosities of Literature, 2nd ser.
† Lodge ; Jardine, i, 434.
‡ Miss Costello, Lives of Eminent Englishwomen ; Lodge.

advancing the suits of others.   In this manner she found herself able to keep up a great show and live at a most extravagant rate, which reached such a pitch that, in one of Chamberlain's letters describing a Court masque, we read that in the matter of jewellery she far surpassed a lady of the Court who was said to be furnished with jewels to the amount of over £100,000.* (Note 68A.)

This extravagance, as may be supposed, led her frequently into serious monetary difficulties, to free herself from which she resorted to extraordinary measures.   In 1608 and 1609 she frequently entreated the King for a grant of various English and Irish monopolies, and, on one occasion, she went so far as to commence a suit for the recovery of some lands that should have belonged to her, on the strange plea of the bastardy of the late Queen.† (Note 69.)

In December of this same year she was suddenly
1609.   accused of having entered into a treaty of marriage with some person whose name is not mentioned but who, in all probability, appears to have been William Seymour.   In consequence of the suspicions entertained about her she was placed in confinement, together with her servants, and even had to appear, in answer to the charge, before the House of Lords, where she denied any intention of marrying without the King's consent, and pleaded her poverty as an excuse for her discontent.   This plea of hers being believed by the King, she was at once set free and restored to favour, and, in order to remove the apparent cause of her discontent, James presented her with plate to the value of £200, as a New Year's gift, in addition to a thousand marks, to pay her debts, and at the same time increased her allowance to £1,600 a year.‡ (Note 70.)

In spite of Arabella's denial, there appears no doubt

* Chamberlain's Letter to Carleton.
† Chamberlain, Report of Suit commenced in the Exchequer Court.
‡ Winwood, iii, 117.

that she had continued her attachment towards William Seymour, and, as she was frequently at Woodstock, the latter had every opportunity of visiting her there whilst he was at Oxford. These meetings had apparently gone on for some considerable time with the result that, on February 2, 1610, the two plighted their troth to each other.

The betrothal, although intended to be kept a secret for the time being, by some means leaked out, and both Arabella and Seymour were brought before the Council when they both declared that they never intended marrying without the King's consent. They were therefore liberated.* (Note 70A.)

Seymour, indeed, does not appear to have at any time been anxious to bring about the marriage which he no doubt realised would be a most unsuitable one, not merely from the danger both would incur in contracting it, but from the disparity of age that lay between them. He had allowed himself to be led on, weakly enough, until he had actually become betrothed, and, once that was done, his honour would not allow him to draw back from the engagement unless he received the free consent of the lady to whom he was affianced. He determined, however, to make one effort for his freedom and sent a message to the lady, in which he pointed out the extreme danger in which both of them would stand if they proceeded with their intended marriage, owing to the King's displeasure, the fact that neither of them had ever intended to disobey his commands, the difference in their positions, she being a lady of royal blood fit to mate with any of the highest degree, whilst he himself was but the second son of an earl, without hope or expectations, and who had already presumed too high, and promising that he would never give her any cause of trouble if it pleased her to desist from her intended resolution towards him.† (Note 71.)

This message does not appear to have had the intended result, for the Lady Arabella took no notice of it, and

---

* Craik's Romance of the Peerage.
† Wilts. Archæolog. Mag., xv, p. 157.

held him to his engagement. She was now again in favour with the King who imagined that her folly was over, and who, to show his good will, granted her, on the 22nd March, the Irish monopoly for which she had previously petitioned. James's confidence was, however, misplaced, for Arabella continued to arrange meetings with Seymour, and persuaded him to marry her privately at Greenwich on the 22nd of June. (Note 72.)

The secrecy of the marriage was no better kept than that of the betrothal, and, as soon as the news reached the ears of the King, both parties were arrested, the Lady Arabella being confined in the custody of Sir Thomas Parry at Lambeth, and Seymour being sent to the Tower, on July 8th, to which he was welcomed by Melvin, the poetical minister, with the following distich :—

> " Communis tecum mihi causa est carceris ; Ara-
> Bella, tibi causa est, Araque sacra mihi."*

Their confinement was not, however, severe, and Seymour was able to pay occasional visits to Lambeth. This light imprisonment continued during that year, throughout which Lady Arabella made many appeals for pardon to the King and Council, but without success.† (Note 73.) The King was evidently afraid of granting a release to his prisoners, and he further feared their managing to escape him. At the same time, in view of the sympathy that their punishment might raise amongst the people, he did not think it wise to place them under severer restraint. There was a middle course, however, which seemed to ensure the security of their persons, and that was to remove them so far apart that communication between them would be difficult, even by letter, so that they would be prevented from concerting any plan of escape. Adopting this course. James ordered that Lady Arabella should be transferred to the keeping of the Bishop

* Lodge ; Letter of Dudley Carleton ; Nichols, 2.
† State Papers, Domestic, James I.

1611. of Durham, on March 13, 1611, and be removed by him to his remote diocese.* (Note 74.)

The worthy bishop duly started to carry out his instructions, but he had got no further than Highgate, when his charge was apparently taken so ill that he dared not proceed farther. She was therefore placed in the house of a Mr. Conyers, and a physician was called in to attend her. The day following, March 14, she wrote to the Council stating that she was so weak that it would occasion her death if she were removed further, and asking for a delay in which to recover her strength, which she stated would come the sooner if she was not continually molested.† On the 16th the Bishop wrote to the Council in the same strain, and said that she refused to start at once upon the journey. A delay of a month was granted upon these representations, but in the meantime Arabella had been taken as far as Barnet, where she was now permitted to remain in the custody of Sir James Crofts.‡

The old Countess of Shrewsbury now came to her assistance, and arranged a plan by which she might escape and join her husband. In order to gain the time necessary for the various preparations for escape, Lady Arabella, though fast recovering her strength and activity, continued to appear ailing, and, without much difficulty, persuaded the Council to grant her another month's respite.§

During this time, with the aid of Lady Shrewsbury, all measures were duly concerted with Seymour, who was still in the Tower, and, on the 4th of June, Lady Arabella, having carefully disguised herself " by drawing a pair of great French-fashioned hose over her petticoats, putting on a man's doublet, a man-like perruque, with long locks over her hair, a black hat, black cloak, russet boots with red tops, and a rapier at her side," walked boldly out of

* State Papers, Domestic, James I.
† Lady Arabella to the Council; State Papers, Domestic, James I.
‡ State Papers, Domestic, James I.
§ State Papers, Domestic.

the house, attended by one retainer only. After walking about a mile and a half she reached a small inn where Crompton, a confidential servant, was waiting with horses. Getting astride on one of these she rode some thirteen miles down the Thames to where two boats were awaiting her, one containing her gentlewoman and maid, the other her luggage and her husband's. Having entered her boat she caused the men to cross over to the Woolwich side, and then rowed down to Gravesend, on reaching which the watermen were exhausted, but were with some difficulty induced to row out to a French barque that was lying in readiness.*

Lady Arabella had started between three and four in the afternoon, and did not get on board the barque till the following morning. Seymour had not yet arrived, and she determined to wait for him, but those who were with her, fearing that he might not have been able to effect his escape, and knowing that severe penalties awaited them if captured, paid no heed to her desires, and at once put out to sea.*

Meanwhile Seymour, attired in a wig and beard or black hair and in a tawny cloth suit, had escaped from the Tower with the aid of a cart that had brought him some billets of wood. After walking some distance he found the boat that was waiting for him and got safely to Lee, only to meet with the disappointment of finding the French barque already gone. He succeeded, however, in persuading a Newcastle collier that was passing to take him to Calais for £40,† but, owing to contrary winds, he was compelled to land at Ostend, whence he proceeded to Bruges to await tidings of Arabella.

It was not till the afternoon following their escape that the Government learnt of Arabella's flight, a piece of news that threw the King and Council into great perturbation. Their first thought was to send an express messenger to

* John More to Sir Ralph Winwood.—Printed in Eminent Englishwomen, Miss Costello.
† John More to Sir Ralph Winwood.

the Lieutenant of the Tower, enjoining him to set a strict guard over Seymour. "That," replied the Lieutenant, "he would thoroughly do, that he would." On proceeding to Seymour's apartment, however, great was his consternation to find his prisoner gone.*

Hasty orders were now sent to a pinnace lying in the Downs to make all speed and scour the French coast in search of the fugitives, and a proclamation was issued forbidding any person from assisting or harbouring them. Communications were also sent to the foreign Powers describing their offence, and requesting that they should be seized and returned.†

The Lady Arabella had meanwhile caused her followers to anchor off the French coast so as to await Seymour's appearance, and it was not long before the King's pinnace came upon them. On seeing it they at once hoisted sail, and fled towards Calais. Their barque, however, was no match for the pinnace, and before long they were overhauled and compelled to strike, though they did not give in until thirteen large shot had been poured into their vessel.‡

The Lady Arabella seems to have borne up against her capture with considerable fortitude, and openly expressed her joy at her husband's escape. On her return she was placed in the Tower, and an enquiry was held into all the circumstances of her escape, by which it appeared that Lady Shrewsbury had been the prime mover in the matter, and had given Arabella £850 to assist her escape.‡ Lady Shrewsbury was therefore committed to the Tower, as well as Seymour's servant, one Batten, who had provided him with his disguise. A search was also instituted for young Rodney, who was found to have provided the boats, but he had escaped, having accompanied Seymour to Ostend.§

* Craik's Romance of the Peerage.
† State Papers, Domestic, James I.
‡ John More to Sir Ralph Winwood.
§ State Papers, Domestic, James I.

On the 30th of June a warrant was issued for defraying the cost of the pursuit and capture of Lady Arabella out of such money as she was possessed of at the time of her escape, and all her jewels were taken from her, ostensibly for the purpose of paying her debts.[*]

The unfortunate lady was kept a close prisoner in the Tower for the remainder of her life. What with her grief at her confinement and the serious attacks of illness to which she became subject, her mind gradually became deranged,[†] but it was not till the sixth year of her imprisonment that death came to her release. She died in the Tower, September 25, 1615, leaving no issue, and was privately buried, by night, in Westminster Abbey. (Note 75.)

Though neither good-looking nor graceful she was gifted with considerable cleverness, and her many letters which remain show a great vivacity and a purity and elegance of style uncommon at that age. (Appendix G.) Her better qualities, however, seem to have been considerably marred by a somewhat flighty disposition, and by her love of a lavish display which led her into all sorts of extravagances. As an instance of the former, it may be sufficient to note that in April, 1613, an order was issued for her closer confinement, as well as Lord Grey's (who was also in the Tower), because it appeared that she had received love messages which the latter sent her by one of her maids, and, as an instance of her vanity, we find that, in Feb. 1613, though a prisoner in the Tower, she bought four gowns in one morning, one of which cost £1,500.[‡]

William Seymour, in the meantime, had remained abroad, living chiefly under the protection of the 1611. Archduke, who refused to deliver him up,[§] though constantly urged to do so by James. The latter,

---

[*] State Papers, Domestic, James I.
[†] Winwood, iii, 454.
[‡] State Papers, Domestic, James I.
[§] The Lord Treasurer to the Minister, Winwood, ii.

LADY ARABELLA STUART, COUNTESS OF HERTFORD.

From an old print.

however, took the greatest precautions to have him carefully watched and all his doings immediately reported. The Minister at Brussels was ordered " to carry always a watchful eye to observe what entertainment he doth find there ; how he is respected ; to whom he most applies himself, who especially resort unto him, and what course he purposeth to take, either for his stay or his remove."*

Seymour's grandfather, the old Earl of Hertford, had strongly disapproved of all his doings, and endeavoured to have his friend, young Rodney, removed from him, as many of Seymour's actions were attributed to Rodney's influence. He also appears greatly to have feared that Seymour's ideas on religion were undergoing a change, and that he might be won over by the Catholic party, and so sent John Pilling, Seymour's old tutor, to Paris (to which place Seymour had removed in September), to remonstrate with him and dissuade him from any errors in religion. At the same time (November) the Earl agreed to make him an allowance of £200 a year.†

The King, finding that it was not likely that Seymour would be delivered up to him, now changed his 1612. course and sent him an order forbidding him to set foot in England or in any of the English possessions, an order to which Seymour promised a faithful compliance, adding that he was glad of an opportunity to show his obedience, which he would maintain however difficult it might be to him, and thanking the King for the mildness of his proceedings, and begging an increase of his favour.‡ In spite of his promise Seymour appears during the following year to have visited Dunkirk, a fact which duly reached the ears of his grandfather, who wrote to him very strongly on the subject of his disobedience. (Note 76.) The Earl, indeed, though he continually expressed bitter disappointment at the reports which reached him of his grandson's doings, seems to have

* The Lord Treasurer to the Minister, Winwood, ii.
† State Papers, Domestic, James I.
‡ Seymour to the Council, State Papers, Domestic, James I.

treated him with considerable kindness, increasing his allowance to £400 a year, and paying his debts upon several occasions.

Upon the death of Lady Arabella, William Seymour renewed his petitions for pardon and for permission 1615. to return home. There being no longer any reason for keeping him in exile, the Council con- 1616. veyed to him the King's permission to return on January 5, 1616.* On the 10th of February Seymour arrived in London, and on the following day was received by the King, who granted him his pardon and restored him to favour.*

On the 3rd of November Seymour was created a Knight of the Bath at the same time as the young Prince 1618. of Wales, and in April, 1618, he married Frances, eldest daughter of Robert Devereux, second Earl of Essex.* In August of this same year he took the courtesy title of Lord Beauchamp on the death of his eldest brother, by which he became heir to the House of Hertford.*

In December, 1620, he was returned member of Parlia- ment for Marlborough, but he only retained this 1620. seat for a few weeks, for, February 14, 1621, he was called to the House of Lords as Baron Beau- champ. In April following, by the death of his grand- father, he became Earl of Hertford, and was summoned to the House of Lords "to take his place accord- 1621. ing to the new creation of that earldom and not otherwise." It will be remembered that his father had never been able to obtain more than a grant that he and his issue should become Barons of Parliament and Earls of Hertford upon the death of the old Earl, who was not mentioned as his father in the grant, and that he was therefore to obtain a new title instead of succeeding in the natural course of events. The marriage of Lady Catherine Grey and the Earl of Hertford was therefore not yet recognised by law as valid, although it was no

* State Papers, Domestic, James I.

longer disputed that there had been a marriage. Had the law, as laid down by the Commissioners in the time of Elizabeth, been strictly adhered to, the Earl of Hertford's lawful issue must have been considered extinct, in which case, according to the entail settled by the Act of 1540, the title should have gone to Sir Edward Seymour, of Berry Pomeroy, the head of the elder branch of the family, instead of to William Seymour. The means adopted, however, exactly suited the policy of James, for, by them, William Seymour received his grandfather's estates, and was granted the same honours as his grandfather had held, but his claim to royal descent through Lady Catherine was not acknowledged, and thus the chances of his becoming a possible rival for the throne were greatly minimized.

Being more devoted to study and to his books than to a life of political activity, the new Lord Hertford lived more or less in retirement at one of his country houses, and seldom attended the meetings of Parliament. He was not always, however, able to avoid employment, and in February, 1626, he was made a member of the Committee of Privileges, and presented the reports on the petitions of the Earls of Bristol and Arundel, and, in July, 1628, he was made Assistant Commissioner for the disafforesting of Roche and Selwood forests.*

Although out of favour at Court, his influence in the country had become very great, and, as Charles and his people drifted farther apart and the prospect of serious disturbances grew more imminent, the King thought it would be good policy to bring him into employment. On the 23rd of March, 1639, he was appointed Lord Lieutenant of Somerset, his jurisdiction including the cities of Bath, Bristol, and Wells.* A few weeks previously he had been, together with many other nobles, requested to join the King at York, and had expressed his readiness to go there with such retinue as

---

* State Papers, Domestic, Charles I.

the short notice might allow him to collect.   His commission as Lord Lieutenant, however, now kept him busy in
the West, and he was unable to join the King, to whom,
however, he sent the sum of £1,000, with assurances of
further assistance should such be required.*

The following year he was sworn a member of the Privy
Council and created a Marquis† (June 3).   Two
1640. days later he was introduced into the House of
Lords by the Marquis of Winton and the Earl of
Essex, and preceded by the Lord Chamberlain, the Earl
Marshall and Garter, all in their robes. Having delivered his
patent of creation, he was conducted to a seat next below the
Marquis of Winton. The King's reasons for granting this
advancement are given in the patent of creation, in which
Hertford's virtues are first mentioned and particularly
named, then the loyalty of his family is remarked, and lastly
his high birth and connection with royalty itself are mentioned.   In support of this new honour the Marquis was
to receive £30 a year out of the customs of the port
of London, and he was to be released from the fees
which the Hanaper office were wont to exact on such
occasions.

Hertford was very friendly with the Earl of Essex, his
brother-in-law, and other nobles who were out of favour
at Court, chiefly owing to their desires for having a proper
and settled government.   In this he fully concurred with
them, and, during August and September, he joined with
Bedford and Essex in petitioning the King to return to a
constitutional method of government.‡ Hertford's sympathies were indeed entirely on the side of the people and
Parliament, and all his friends were of the same party. The
unconstitutional methods of the King met with his open
disapproval, and he frequently opposed Charles's demands
in the Upper House.

In October, he was appointed one of the Commissioners

* State Papers, Domestic, Charles I.
† Dict. Nat. Biog. ; Clarendon's Hist.
‡ State Papers, Domestic, Charles I.

sent to treat with the Scots at Ripon,* after the latter had sent a petition to the King. The negotiations, however, brought no satisfactory result. November 19, he was deputed by Charles, with the consent of the Lords, to visit the Earl of Strafford in the Tower,† and he seems to have done his best to dissuade his friends from proceeding to extreme measures against that unfortunate nobleman. Not long after he was appointed, together with the Earl of Bristol, to confer with the Commons over some accusations which the latter had presented against Sir George Ratcliffe.†

The struggle between the King and the Parliament had by now assumed such dimensions as to threaten a civil war, and it became necessary for every man of any importance to throw in his lot upon one side or the other. Much as Hertford disapproved of the King's methods, the fact did not escape him that the Parliament was overstepping the limits it should have observed, and was no longer making use of constitutional methods in its opposition to the King. The Parliament hitherto had contented itself with opposing the King in furthering the rights of the people, but they now began to assume an authority that belonged to the King only as head of the Church and State. Always a strenuous upholder of constitutional authority, Hertford had hoped that the reforms needed would be brought about by constitutional and peaceful methods, but he now saw that the supreme head of the State was likely to be in danger. This fact alone was sufficient to decide his course of action. His sovereign was threatened. As a loyal subject he at once hastened to protect him.‡

At this critical period the Earl of Newcastle resigned his position as Governor to the young Prince of
1641. Wales, and the choice of a new one was likely to add to the King's difficulties. Newcastle, however, sug-

* Clarendon's Hist., 1, 189.
† Journals of the House of Lords.
‡ Clarendon's Hist. of the Rebellion.

gested the Marquis of Hertford for the post, as being perhaps the only man whose appointment would be sure to
please both the Parliament and the people. Charles favoured
the suggestion, and on the 17th May, Hertford was appointed Governor to the Prince of Wales.*   In speaking
of his appointment in his History of the Rebellion, Clarendon says :—" The Marquis of Hertford was a man of
great honour, interest, and estate, and of an universal
esteem over the whole kingdom ; and though he had
received many and continued disobligations from the
Court, from the time of this King's coming to the throne,
as well as during the reign of James, in both which
seasons more than ordinary care had been taken to dis-
countenance and lessen his interest ; yet he had carried
himself with notable steadiness from the beginning of
the Parliament in the support and defence of the King's
power and dignity, notwithstanding all his allies, and
those with whom he had the greatest familiarity and
friendship, were of the opposite party ; and never concurred with them against the Earl of Strafford, whom he
was known not to love, nor in any other extravaganzy.

"And then he was not to be shaken in his affection to
the government of the Church ; though it was enough
known that he was in no degree biassed to any great inclination to the person of any churchman.   And with all
this, that party carried themselves towards him with profound respect, not presuming to venture their own credit
in endeavouring to lessen his.   It is very true he wanted
some of those qualities which might have been wished to
be in a person to be trusted in the education of a great
and hopeful Prince, and in forming of his mind and
manners in so tender an age.   He was of an age not fit
for much activity and fatigue, and loved and was even
wedded so much to his ease, that he loved his book above
all exercises, and cared not to discourse and argue on those
points, which he understood very well, only for the
trouble of contending (and had even contracted such a

---

* Clarendon's Hist. of the Rebellion.

laziness of mind that he had no delight in an open and liberal conversation) ; and could never impose upon himself the pain that was necessary to be undergone in such a perpetual attendance ; but then those lesser duties might be otherwise provided for, and he could well support the dignity of a Governor and exact that diligence from others which he could not exercise himself ; and his honour was so unblemished that none durst murmur against the designation. And therefore His Majesty thought him very worthy of the high trust, against which there was no other exception, but that he was not ambitious of it, nor in truth willing to receive and undergo the charge, so contrary to his natural constitution. But in his pure zeal and affection for the Crown, and the conscience, that in this conjunction his submission might advance the King's service, and that the refusing of it might prove disadvantageous to His Majesty, he very cheerfully undertook the province, to the general satisfaction and public joy of the whole kingdom, and to the no little honour and credit of the Court, that so important and beloved a person would attach himself to it under such a relation, when so many, who had scarce ever eaten any bread but the King's, detached themselves from their dependence, that they might without him and against him, preserve and improve those fortunes, which they had procured and gotten under him and by his bounty."

Hertford's acceptance of this post seems to have been done more to satisfy the people than with the intention of really carrying out the duties of the post, for, though he always remained with the Prince, he does not appear to have ever interfered in the management of his education, being doubtless satisfied of the ability of the Prince's tutors.

Shortly after his appointment, the Parliament were seized with the fear that the Prince might be 1641. removed out of the kingdom, and demanded him to give them an undertaking that he would be constant in his attendance on the Prince, and that he

would not let him be conveyed out of the kingdom.[*]
This demand was made while Hertford was in the House,
but, ignoring the insolence of its tone, the Marquis
replied in a courteous and dignified speech, in which he
said that much as he felt himself bound to obey their
injunctions on ordinary occasions, this demand was one
which he most decidedly refused to agree to.[†]

Shortly after this episode, the King accompanied the
Queen to Dover to see her safely embarked upon a
voyage to France. The wind, however, being unfavour-
able, they were obliged to wait there for several days,
upon which the King instructed Hertford to remove the
Prince to Richmond so that there might be no reason for
anyone suspecting that the latter might be transported to
France. As soon as the Queen had safely embarked,
Charles sent an express messenger to Richmond to ask the
Marquis to bring the Prince to meet him at Greenwich.
It so happened that just at this time Hertford was seriously
indisposed, and not fit for a journey.[‡]

In the meantime Parliament had been thrown into a
great state of alarm, for a young Welshman, named
Griffiths, a member of the House, possessing more
assurance than ability, and who was annoyed over some
refusal he had met with, informed them that he had
discovered a design for removing the Prince to France,
and that, unless they acted at once, he would be beyond
their reach.[§] Upon this the Parliament sent an express
message to Hertford ordering him at his peril not to let
the Prince leave Richmond unless he himself accompanied
him. This message, arriving at the same time as the
King's, placed Hertford in a difficult position. Determined, however, to obey the King without, if possible,
angering the Parliament, he left his bed, ill as he was, and
accompanied the Prince to Greenwich in person.[‖]

[*] State Papers, Domestic, Charles I.
[†] May 3, 1642, Dict. Nat. Biog.
[‡] Life of Clarendon, 1, 81.
[§] Clarendon's Hist. of the Rebellion, 1, 436.
[‖] Clarendon's Hist., 1, 437 ; Life of Clarendon, 1, 81.

In January of this year Hertford was put on a special
Commission to inquire into the state of the royal
1642. revenues and expenses. This Commission does
not appear, however, to have had time to do much,
for, in April, the King removed to York, and Hertford
had to follow him with the Prince. They arrived at that
town on the 20th, and were welcomed by an escort of
between eight and nine hundred horse.*

On the 13th June, seeing that a call to arms was now
inevitable, Hertford subscribed to the engagement for the
defence of the Monarchy and Protestant religion, and on
the 22nd made a voluntary contribution of sufficient
money to pay for sixty horses for the King's service for
three months.† Many others joined in this, and a long
list of subscribers was drawn up. The cost of a horse
was reckoned at 2s. 6d. per day.

On the 2nd of August he was appointed Commissioner
of array and Lieutenant-General in the West, with power
to levy such bodies of horse and foot as he should find
necessary for His Majesty's service. His authority was
to extend from Oxford to Land's End and from Southampton to Radnor and Cardigan.‡ Hertford, as well as all
those appointed to act under him, had great influence in
the western counties, and therefore had great hopes of
success. This he shows plainly in a letter he wrote at the
time to the Queen of Holland to inform her of the
manner in which he had been commanded by the King to
dispose of the Duke of York, and in which he craves
pardon for the freedom and exultation with which he
writes upon this occasion.§

The Marquis set out at once, on receipt of his commis-
sion, accompanied by the Earl of Bath, Lord Paulet, Lord
Francis Seymour, Henry Seymour, Sir Ralph Hopton, Sir
John Berkeley, and many others of importance in the

---

* State Papers, Domestic, Charles I.
† State Papers, Domestic, Charles I.
‡ Dict. Nat. Biog.
§ Antiquarian Repertory, 2, 290.

West, and went to Bath, where the Assizes were then
being held, and where he hoped to meet all the more
important of the Somersetshire gentry. Finding these for
the greater part well affected towards the King, he held a
consultation with all the chief men to decide upon the
best means of raising a large force and upon the most
suitable place for establishing their headquarters. The
Marquis himself fancied Bristol as being the most suitable
town, and many agreed with him ; the majority, however,
were strongly in favour of Wells, and Hertford was
eventually persuaded to make that town his headquarters.*
This point decided, he removed there at once, and set
about allaying the apprehensions of the people by doing
everything in a peaceable manner and according to the
laws of the realm, at the same time employing the
gentry who had followed him in raising troops about the
country.

The Parliament, meanwhile, were well informed of all
these doings, and had already despatched a large force to
the West partly to divide more effectually the North and
South, but more especially to seize Hertford, Paulet,
Seymour, Hopton, and others, whom they had already
declared to be delinquents.† They also sent envoys to
the West to go about and persuade the people that the
Marquis's sole object was to put the Commission of Array
in force, by which each yeoman and farmer would lose a
great portion of his property.† By this means many of
the people were won over to the side of the Parliament,
and a considerable number joined the Parliamentary force
for the purpose of surrounding and surprising the Marquis at Wells.

The latter's whole force did not amount to more than
500 men, composed of troops of horse raised by Mr. John
Digby, Sir Francis Hawley, Sir Ralph Hopton (who had
some dragoons raised at his own expense), about 100 infantry, and the retinues of Lord Paulet and 28 of the

* Clarendon's Hist., 2, 2–5.
† State Papers, Domestic, Charles I.

leading gentry who had joined him, when the Parliamentary General, Sir E. Hungerford, appeared before Wells with 12,000 men, horse and foot, and some cannon.*

Having erected barricades, the Marquis remained unmolested in the city for two days, when, finding that some of his trained men were beginning to desert, he thought it best to endeavour to retire. He therefore marched boldly out of the city at noon and marched to Somerton, and thence towards Sherborne in the face of the enemy, who were so surprised at this boldness that, in spite of their overwhelming superiority of numbers, they made no attempt to attack him.

On arriving at Sherborne he was joined by Sir John Berkeley, Col. Ashburnham, and other good officers, but desertions had been so numerous at Wells that, even with this addition, his force now numbered little over 400. A few days after his arrival, the Earl of Bedford, General of Horse to the Parliament, appeared before Sherborne with 7,000 foot, eight full troops of horse, and four pieces of cannon.† Undeterred by the odds against him, Hertford held the town and castle for five days (during which he challenged the Earl of Bedford to a duel, an honour which the latter declined),† and so disheartened the enemy by the vigour and gallantry of his defence that, at the end of that time, the Earl sent to ask if he would allow him "to fairly and peaceably draw off his forces and march away." This request the Marquis haughtily refused, saying "that, as they came thither upon their own counsels, so they should get off as best they could." The enemy thereupon retired, leaving him for some weeks undisturbed at Sherborne.

At the end of this time, hearing of the loss of Portsmouth, and that some troops he was expecting had been sent for by the King, as well as that the people of the county were all declaring for the Parliament, he saw that

---

* Clarendon's Hist., 2, 6.
† Clarendon's Hist., 2, 329.

it would be impossible for him to further the King's cause where he was, and so determined at all costs to join His Majesty. With this object he marched to Minehead, where he expected to get shipping to transport his small force into Wales. On his arrival, however, he found that the people were against him, and that all their boats but two had been carefully sent away. The Earl of Bedford having followed him, and being now within four miles, the Marquis crossed into Glamorganshire with Lord Paulet, Lord Seymour, and a small force of foot and the smaller cannon, leaving Sir Ralph Hopton, Sir John Berkeley, Mr. Digby, and other officers with the horse (amounting to about 120) to march into Cornwall in the hopes of raising some troops in that county.*

During his march through Wales the Marquis succeeded in raising some troops, and reached the King at the head of 2,000 foot and one regiment of horse about the time a Treaty was begun between the King and Parliament.*

By this time a force had been raised in Cornwall which, however, required assistance as it was hard pressed. An army was therefore sent to its aid, and whilst on the march to Devon, an express was sent from the King at Oxford to the leaders of the Cornish army, "That Prince Maurice and the Marquis of Hertford, with a very good body of horse, would join them, and were already hastening through Somerset ; also that Sir William Waller was being sent by the Parliament into the West with a new army." It being now necessary that the King's forces should be joined, the Cornish army marched eastward, leaving sufficient garrisons to hold Plymouth and Exeter in check and so relieve the Cornish people, and waited at Tiverton for fresh orders from the Marquis.†

About the middle of June, Hertford, with Prince Maurice, who was his Lieutenant-General and so second in command, arrived at Chard with about 1,700 horse, a 1,000 newly levied foot, and seven or eight field pieces.

* Clarendon's Hist.
† Clarendon's Hist., 2, 127, 132.

Here they were joined by the Cornish army, which consisted of 3,000 excellent foot, 500 horse, 300 dragoons, and four or five field pieces. With this army the Marquis first marched on Taunton, the garrison of which fled to Bridgewater, only to leave again the next day. In three days he was master of Taunton, Bridgewater, and Dunstar Castle, all being surrendered to him without bloodshed.* He remained at Taunton for seven or eight days to settle garrisons in these places. During this time they lost much of the goodwill of the people, for, though the Cornish army behaved with great steadiness, having been disciplined to it by Sir Ralph Hopton for a considerable time, the men brought by the Marquis and Prince Maurice behaved as if they had been in an enemy's country. This soon produced a coolness between the Marquis and the Prince, the former insisting on a more stringent discipline, whilst the latter was strongly averse to it.*

They now found that, by dint of forced marches, Sir William Waller, with the Parliamentary army, was within two days' march, and, as he had Bristol at his back whilst the Marquis had only the open country to draw supplies from, it was determined to engage him before he got stronger, and then continue their march to Oxford, whither they were now ordered.†

The Marquis was at Somerton and Sir William Waller at Bath, when a skirmish occurred in which the enemy routed a small body of the King's dragoons. This led the Marquis to draw up his army and advance ; whereupon the enemy retired to Wells, which, however, they almost immediately evacuated and retired to the summit of Mendip Hill. The march having been long and the day being late, the Marquis remained at Wells with the infantry and baggage. Prince Maurice, however, determined to reconnoitre further, and, with the Earl of Carnarvon, Sir Ralph Hopton, Sir John Berkeley, and two regiments of horse, advanced to the top of the hill,

* Clarendon's Hist., 2, 275-281.
† Clarendon's Hist.

the enemy meanwhile retiring in good order, guarded by a large force of horse which kept facing about to keep Prince Maurice in check.*

The latter, thinking they were but running away, followed as far as a village called Chewton, where, a favourable opportunity occurring, the Earl of Carnarvon, with great gallantry, charged and routed the whole body of horse, pursuing them for above two miles, when he suddenly came upon a large force of cavalry, sent by Sir William Waller to assist his rearguard. With considerable difficulty he managed to retire in good order till he met the Prince, when, finding that they could not well retire further in face of so strong a force, they resolved on the bold but hazardous plan of charging. This was done with such force and determination that the enemy were completely routed.*

The Marquis remained eight days at Wells, whilst Sir William Waller awaited further reinforcements at Bath.*

Matters being in a bad state in Devon, Hertford found himself obliged to send Sir John Berkeley with a regiment of horse into that county, but, in order not to weaken himself too much, he ordered him to send back Sir James Hamilton's regiment of horse which had been left in Devon, and which, by its license, was doing much harm to the King's party in the minds of the people.*

Hertford now advanced to Frome and on to Bradford, four miles from Bath. Each day produced sharp skirmishes, but Sir William Waller, having the better position, would not be drawn into a general engagement. Upon this Hertford advanced to Marsfield, five miles beyond Bath on the way to Oxford, hoping by this means to draw him out, for Waller's instructions were to prevent him from reaching that town. This move was successful, for Waller now drew his whole army out to Lansdowne, where, however, he took up such a favourable position that, if he was attacked, it must be at a disadvantage. The battle that ensued, on July 5th, has been called the battle of

* Clarendon's Hist.

Lansdowne, and will be best described in Clarendon's own words :—

"Sir William Waller, as soon as it was light, possessed himself of that hill, and after he had, upon the brow of the hill over the highway, raised breastworks with faggots and earth, and planted cannon there, he sent a strong body of horse towards Marsfield, which quickly alarmed the other army, and was shortly driven back to their body. As great a mind as the King's forces had to cope with the enemy, when they were drawn into battalia, and found the enemy fixed on the top of the hill, they resolved not to attack them upon so great disadvantage ; and so retired again towards their old quarters, which Sir William Waller perceiving, sent his whole body of horse and dragoons down the hill to charge the rear and flank of the King's forces ; which they did thoroughly, the regiment of Cuirassiers so amazing the horse they charged, that they totally routed them ; and, standing firm and unshaken themselves, gave so great a terror to the King's horse, who had never before turned from an enemy, that no example of their officers, who did their parts with invincible courage, could make them charge with the same confidence, and in the same manner they had usually done. However, in the end, Sir Nicholas Slanning with 300 musqueteers, had fallen upon and beaten their reserve of dragoons, Prince Maurice and the Earl of Carnarvon, rallying their horse, and winging them with the Cornish musqueteers, charged the enemy's horse again, and totally routed them ; and in the same manner received two bodies more, and routed and chased them to the hill ; where they stood in a place almost inaccessible. On the brow of the hill there were breastworks, on which were pretty bodies of small shot and some cannon. On either flank grew a pretty thick wood towards the declining of the hill, in which strong parties of musqueteers were placed ; at the rear, was a very fair plain, where the reserves of horse and foot stood ranged ; yet the Cornish foot were so far from being appalled at this disadvantage, that they desired to fall on, and cried out 'that they might have leave to fetch off those cannon.' In the end, order was given to attempt the hill with horse and foot. Two strong parties of musqueteers were sent into the woods, which flanked the enemy ; and the horse and other musqueteers up the roadway, which were charged by the enemy's horse and routed ; then Sir Bevil Greenvil advanced with a party of horse, on his right hand, that ground being the best for them ; and his musqueteers on the left ; himself leading up his pikes in the middle ; and in the face of their cannon, and small shot from the breastworks, gained the brow of the hill, having sustained two full charges of the enemy's horse ; but in the third charge, his horse failing, and giving ground, he received, after other wounds, a blow on the head with a poll-axe, with which he fell, and many of his officers about him ; yet the musqueteers fired so fast upon the enemy's horse that they quitted their ground, and the two wings, who were sent to clear the woods, having done their work, and gained those parts of the hill, at the same time beat off their enemy's foot, and became possessed of the breastworks ; and so made way for their whole body of horse, foot, and cannon to ascend the hill ; which they quickly did, and planted themselves on the ground they had won ; the enemy retiring about demi culverin shot behind a stone wall upon the same level, and standing in reasonable good order. Either party were sufficiently tired and battered to be contented to stand still. The King's horse were so shaken, that of 2,000 which were upon the field in the morning, there were not above 600 at the top of the hill. The enemy were exceedingly scattered, too, and had no mind to venture on plain ground with those who had beaten them from the hill ; so that, exchanging only some shot from their ordnance, they looked upon one another till the night interposed. About 12 o'clock, it being very dark, the enemy made a show of moving towards the ground they had lost ; but giving a smart volley of small shot, and finding themselves answered with the like, they made no more noise ; which the Prince observing, he sent a common soldier to hearken as near the place, where they were, as he could ; who brought word 'that the enemy had left lighted matches in the wall behind which they had lain, and were drawn off the field' ; which was true ; so that, as soon as it was day, the King's army found themselves possessed entirely of the field, and the dead, and all other signs of victory. Sir William Waller being marched to Bath, in so much disorder and apprehension, that he left great store of arms and ten barrels of powder behind him, which was a very seasonable supply to the other side who had spent in that day's service no less than fourscore barrels, and had not a safe proportion left."

After this victory the Marquis at once sent to Oxford to inform the King, and to ask for a regiment or two of horse and some ammunition. The Earl of Crawford was at once sent to him with his regiment of 500 horse and a supply of powder.*

Having rested a few days at Marsfield, Hertford started to march to Oxford and join the King's army, thinking that a better plan than staying to attend to Waller, who was still at Bath, where he was waiting for fresh troops from Bristol. The latter, however, hearing that Sir Ralph Hopton and many distinguished officers in the Marquis's army were badly wounded, and believing that the army was short of ammunition, and probably discouraged by their severe losses, quickly gathered fresh men from Bristol, Wilts, Gloucester, and Somerset, and followed the Marquis towards Chippenham.*

Early the next morning Hertford, hearing of the enemy's approach, drew back his army through Chippenham, and drew it up in order of battle on ground that gave his infantry every advantage, well knowing that his horse, being weary, would not be of any great assistance. Waller, however, who trusted his horse as much as he distrusted his new levies of foot, declined the engagement. Hertford, having waited all night, marched the following day towards Devizes, having arranged a very strong rear-

* Clarendon's Hist.

guard to repel any attacks of the enemy. This the rear-guard did so well that Waller, despairing of overtaking him, sent a messenger to him with a letter, offering him a pitched battle in a place of his own choosing, out of the way. Perceiving this to be only a ruse to delay the march, Hertford took the messenger with him for some miles before returning any answer. During the whole of this day the enemy pressed hard on his rear, but without effect, and the army reached Devizes in safety.*

The Parliamentary army had been daily increasing in strength, and Hertford now saw that, owing to the openness of the country and its suitability for cavalry attacks, it would be impossible to get his infantry safely to Oxford. He decided, therefore, to break through with Prince Maurice and the cavalry and bring relief from Oxford, which was but thirty miles distant. This was successfully done the same night, the force reaching Oxford in the early morning.*

Sir William Waller, meanwhile, had surrounded Devizes and attacked it on every side, but without success. Hearing, however, of the Earl of Crawford's advance to join the army with horse and ammunition, he sent a strong party in that direction which surprised and completely routed him. Encouraged by this success he sent a messenger into the town to summons the leaders to surrender ; this they would not do, but agreed to treat with him on condition that hostilities should cease during the negotiations. By this means they trusted to gain time for aid to reach them.*

The Marquis, meanwhile, had not been idle, and, having obtained from the King all the horse, to the number of 1,500, and two cannon, that could be spared, under the command of Lord Wilmot, started off in the evening of the same day he had arrived (Monday), and, at noon on Wednesday, arrived within two miles of the town.†

The enemy had been told of their approach, and, de-

* Clarendon's Hist.
† Clarendon's Hist., 2, 287–293.

termined to prevent the junction of the two forces, drew away from the town and took up a position on Roundway Down, over which they were bound to pass.*

The army in the town, thinking this a stratagem and not having heard of the approach of help, as all the messengers had been intercepted, were somewhat late in coming out to take their share in the battle; a delay which enabled Waller to advance quickly against the Marquis and Lord Wilmot, who were forced to await his charge on the best ground they could get. In his haste and contempt of the small force opposed to him, Waller now made a fatal mistake, for, leaving his foot, he advanced with his horse only. His cuirassiers went first, but, after a sharp conflict, were routed, and, in their flight, charged on to their own supports. At the same time Lord Wilmot charged, attacking one division after another with such success that, in half an hour, the whole body of Waller's horse was totally routed and dispersed.*

The foot still stood firm, but their cannon was soon taken and turned against them by Lord Wilmot, and the Cornish foot, having now arrived from the town, charged them in rear and completely routed them. Sir W. Waller with difficulty escaped, and reached Bristol with only a few followers.*

The King now resolved to make an attempt upon Bristol, and on July 24th two armies sat down before it, one commanded by the Marquis and Prince Maurice, the other by Prince Rupert. On the following day a council was held as to the best manner of taking the town, the Marquis and his officers being of opinion that, as there was no army near to relieve it and the works being very strong, a regular siege would be the surest manner, the more so as there was believed to be a very strong party in the city who were favourable to the King, and whose influence might make itself felt after a few days of a close siege.†

* Clarendon's Hist., 2, 287–293.
† Clarendon's Hist.

P 2

Prince Rupert was in favour of an immediate assault, and eventually carried his point.   It was therefore decided to assault the town the next morning, which was done with such courage and impetuosity that it was soon taken, though not without great loss.   It appears probable that the town would not have been captured had there not been treachery or cowardice on the part of the defendants, who threw down their arms as soon as Colonel Washington with a few men had reached the top of the rampart ; the towns-people, however, inflicted great loss on Prince Rupert's men by firing from their windows as they passed through the streets.*

Soon after the capture of Bristol an unfortunate rupture took place between the Marquis and Prince Rupert. It appears that the latter, as well as Prince Maurice, were annoyed that a Prince should be second in command to the Marquis, who had not been brought up as a soldier. The latter, on the other hand, though he permitted Prince Maurice to have almost the entire military control, did not approve of his assuming more than became his station as Lieutenant-General, and frequently crossing acts of his in the management and governing of the country, about which he knew more than the Prince.   When Bristol was taken, the Marquis took to himself the command-in-chief, both because he was head of the army and Lord-Lieutenant of that city, which came particularly into the commission he had received from the King ; he was, therefore, not unnaturally annoyed when Prince Rupert entered into a treaty with the inhabitants and completed it, without taking his advice or noticing him in any way ; and accordingly, not to be outdone, he gave the government of the city to Sir Ralph Hopton without consulting the Princes.   On hearing this Prince Rupert sent a messenger to the King asking if he might not himself take the government of the city ; and His Majesty, not knowing that a Governor had already been appointed, answered in the affirmative.*

* Clarendon's Hist.

Almost immediately after, Hertford's report arrived, and then the King saw what had occurred and what a difficult position he himself was now in ; and, as none of his advisers could show him what to do, he resolved to go to Bristol in person. On his arrival there, he succeeded, by flattering both and putting the matter as a great personal favour to himself, in inducing each party to give way in some measure, and finally made an arrangement agreeable to the pride of both, namely, that Prince Rupert should, nominally, be Governor, and that Sir Ralph Hopton should be Lieutenant-Governor and have the real management of the city.*

An army was now sent to Dorchester, but the King kept the Marquis with him to attend on his own person ; "for though he well saw he should undergo some inconveniences by withdrawing the Marquis from that employment, the opinion of the soundness of his religion and integrity of his justice, rendering him by much the most popular man in those parts, and was exceedingly tender of giving the least umbrage and distaste to his lordship, upon whose honour and friendship he relied entirely, and would as soon have trusted his crown upon his fidelity as upon any man's in his three kingdoms, yet he discerned plainly that the Prince and Marquis would never agree together," &c.*

The King then declared to him, " that he would make him a Gentleman of his Bedchamber, and Groom 1644. of his Stole (January), and that he would always have his company and advice about him " ; and seems to have thought so highly of him that he trusted him with his counsels perhaps more than anyone else. Many of the King's wisest followers, however, thought that a greater success would have attended the army had Hertford again been in command, and if the Prince had gone with His Majesty's force and only interfered in purely military matters.*

Some time after this a fresh difference arose between

* Clarendon's Hist.

Prince Maurice and the Marquis. It appears that the Earl of Carnarvon had captured Dorchester and Weymouth, the latter being then a very important place. The Marquis, who was still nominally in command of the army, had promised the government of this place, when it should be captured, to Sir Anthony Ashley Cooper, a most suitable man for the appointment, and had raised some officers and men so as to form a garrison for its defence, without in any way lessening the army.

Prince Maurice, however, wanted to place some follower of his in this command, and in the end the matter had to be brought before the King, who, after due consideration, gave it as his opinion that the Marquis was in the right, and therefore appointed his nominee.*

During the remainder of the war Hertford remained in constant attendance on the King, and took no further active part in any of the military operations.

It will be remembered that Hertford had been brought up at Oxford, in which college he took a great interest, which was not lessened even during the stirring times that had followed. In his younger days he had become M.A. and B.A., and June, 1643, he had been elected Chancellor of the University, a post which he held 1645. till 1647. He was now, May 8, 1645, appointed one of the Commissioners for the preservation and well ordering of the city and University of Oxford, as well as for the counties of Oxford, Berks, and Bucks, and the garrisons within them during the King's absence.† He was also one of the nobles to whom the King entrusted the militia.

On the 28th of January of this year he was appointed one of the sixteen Commissioners sent to treat with the representatives of Parliament at Uxbridge, and after the completion of the treaty made at that place, he returned to 1646. his duties at Oxford, remaining there till the surrender of that city, June 24, 1646. Under the

* Clarendon's Hist.
† State Papers, Domestic.

articles of this surrender he was able to compound for the retention of his estates.*

During the subsequent confinement of the King, Hertford remained in constant attendance on 1648. him. In September, 1648, he was made one of the Gentlemen of the Bedchamber, and during the same month was one of the Commissioners for the treaty of Newport. When Charles was to be tried, Hertford joined with the Duke of Richmond, the Earl of Southampton, and the Earl of Lindsay in offering themselves as a sacrifice for the safety of the King's person, urging that as Privy Councillors they had been the advisers of the measures now imputed to the King as criminal, that the exclusive responsibility for his acts rested upon them, and that therefore they should meet with the punishment instead of the King.†

After the execution of King Charles, these same noblemen requested leave from the Parliament to bury his body in a suitable place and attend it themselves to the place of interment. The first part of this request was readily granted, but a restriction was placed upon the latter part, namely, that they should not meet the body till it was outside London. A further request they made, that the Bishop of London should be permitted to perform the funeral service, was refused. "They attended the funeral to Windsor; but, not being able to find, in the chapel, the place where the English princes used to be interred, they caused a grave to be made near a spot where they were told there was a vault in which Henry VIII and Queen Jane Seymour were buried. Here they privately buried the King. They had indeed no power to prepare or do anything, having obtained leave only to be present. They were not allowed to have more than three servants each to accompany them into the castle. They found the church so wild a place that they did not know it again; for the soldiers of the

* Dict. Nat. Biog.
† Clarendon's Hist.; Dict. Nat. Biog.

garrison had broken down all the wainscot, rails, and partitions, defaced all the monuments, and turned the whole into a barn or stable."* (Note 77.)

Having thus performed the last sad rites for the Sovereign he had so faithfully followed, Hertford found himself now compelled to undergo his own troubles. These, however, were not as great as they might have been, for he had earned the respect and esteem of Cromwell and the Parliament by his continued upright and honest behaviour. On July 22, 1650, the Council wrote to him saying that, though he was to remain in confinement according to the Act passed against him and others as delinquents, he might make a choice of any of his houses in Wiltshire or at Yelverton in which to live.† He accordingly chose Netley, in Hampshire. On November 22 he was made to enter into recognisances with the Council of State, binding him in the sum of £20,000, or two sureties of £10,000, to remain at Netley and be of good behaviour, and appear whenever called upon to do so within ten days of the summons. Shortly afterwards he received a permit to come to London at the request of the Solicitor-General, which visit over he had 1651. again to return to Netley.† On March 17, 1651, the Council wrote to him to say that they considered it might be prejudicial to the peace of the Commonwealth and the security of those parts if he remained there longer, and accordingly ordered him to remove himself and his family to his house at Amesbury on or before the 1st of April. They further said that they understood that many dangerous and disaffected persons resorted to his house, and that several of his servants were described as such, and they insisted that these practices should be put a stop to.†

In November a dispute arose between the Marquis and Lord Hereford which almost led to a duel, but the Council, hearing of it in time, caused them both to

* Clarendon's Hist., 1, 370.
† State Papers, Domestic.

appear before them and bound them over to keep the peace.* The cause of the dispute appears to have been that they had throughout been on opposite sides, and the Marquis looked upon Hereford as a traitor, and, further, would not acknowledge his title, which the late King had declared he had no right to. Mr. Selden supported the King in this opinion, and from an inquiry made after the Restoration it appeared that Hereford had no claim upon the title of Viscount which he had taken.*

Before many months had passed, the restrictions placed upon Hertford's liberty were removed, and he was permitted to compound with Parliament for the removal of the Act of delinquency passed against him, by paying the sum of £8,345. At the same time he was removed from the Chancellorship of Oxford.*

During the remainder of the usurpation he continued to live in a quiet manner in the country, but at the same time never lost an opportunity of assisting the King's cause. During the latter's exile, he regularly sent him £5,000 a year. The Marquis of Hertford and Lord Southampton were the principal persons on whom Charles II relied for the furthering of his cause in England. They kept him well informed as to every event that occurred, and warned him of any new 1654. danger that appeared to threaten him.† On one occasion in 1654, when the news they received gave them reason to fear that Cardinal Richelieu was inclined to give up Charles to Cromwell, they contrived to despatch Henry Seymour at once with the news to the King, and accompanied it with the sum of £3,000, so that the latter would be enabled to leave France if necessary.†

Cromwell himself had a high opinion of Hertford's abilities, and, knowing the esteem in which the latter was held throughout the country, made several attempts to win him over to his side. On one such occasion he sent

* State Papers, Domestic.
† Clarendon's Hist. of the Rebellion, 3, 522.

to invite him to dinner, an invitation which was duly accepted, amounting, as it practically did, to a command. On Hertford's arrival he found himself treated with the greatest respect and, after dinner, in the drawing-room, the Protector informed him that he had desired his company in order that he might speak with him and receive his advice. "For," he said, "I am not able to bear the weight of business that is upon me, I am weary of it, and you, my lord, are a wise man, of great experience, and well versed in the business of government, pray advise me what I shall do." Hertford replied that, seeing he had always been a faithful servant of the King's and one of his Privy Council, it was not consistent with his principles that he should give him advice, nor was it fair the Protector should ask it. Cromwell, however, continued to press him, whereupon, in the end, the Marquis said : "Sir, I will declare to your highness my thoughts, by which you may continue to be great, and establish your name and family for ever. Our young master is abroad, that is, my master, and the master of us all ; restore him to his crown, and by doing this, you may have what you please." Cromwell, in no way angered by this speech, said that he feared he had gone so far that the young gentleman could not forgive, upon which the Marquis replied, "that, if his highness pleased, he would undertake with his master for what he had said." Cromwell, however, said, "that in his circumstances he could not trust"; and thus they parted, the Protector being left with a still greater respect for the steadfastness and loyalty of Hertford's character.*

When the Restoration came, Hertford was one of the nobles who met the King at Dover, May 26. The following day, at Canterbury, he was made a Privy Councillor and invested with the Garter (he had previously been made a member of that order in Jersey, January 12, 1659).

1660.

* Lives of the Friends and Contemporaries of Lord Chancellor Clarendon, by Lady Theresa Lewis, vol. iii, 122–3.

On the 18th August the Marquis appeared before the House of Lords and informed them that it appeared that a patent had been granted to the Marquis of Worcester to the prejudice of other peers. It was a patent to be Duke of Somerset. The matter was at once referred to a Committee, and Worcester then confessed that such a patent had been made and left in his hands by the King, but that the conditions upon which it was granted had never been performed, and he was therefore prepared to deliver it up to His Majesty.* (In justice to Charles it must be said that he had granted this patent long before, and apparently in ignorance of Hertford's claim to the title.)

Worcester having abandoned his claim, an Act was now passed, September 13, restoring the Marquis of Hertford to the Dukedom of Somerset, with all the privileges formerly granted to that title, as if the Act of attainder against his great-grandfather, passed in the reign of Edward VI, April 12, 1552, had never been made. When the King gave his assent to it he added, " that as this was an Act of an extraordinary nature, so it was done for an extraordinary person, who had merited as much of his royal father and himself as any subject could do, and therefore hoped no man would envy it."

Thus, after a long and eventful life, did Sir William Seymour at last succeed in recovering the family honours. He did not, however, live long to enjoy them, for he died on the 24th of October in the same year, and was buried at Great Bedwyn, November 1.

This Duke of Somerset's life deserves more notice than has generally been accorded to it. He was a man of great and varied abilities, and was endowed with great strength of mind and character. His tastes were more those of the student and philosopher than those of a man of action, yet when the time came he proved himself a courageous and capable soldier and general, and exhibited the talents of a great statesman in ruling over the counties which he was appointed to govern during the Civil War. He had

* Journals of the House of Lords, 11, 133, 138, 153.

been in his youth first imprisoned and then exiled by James, and later had suffered the effects of Charles's ill favour, yet when the latter was in danger he had hastened to his side, and had willingly undergone the hardships and dangers of war on his behalf, though he found himself obliged to battle against his own friends. Such was the esteem which his conduct earned for him from both parties that, after he had left the army in the field on account of Prince Rupert's behaviour and had become Charles's constant companion and friend, he was employed as prime agent in all public and private negotiations with the rebels, who looked upon him with such reverence that they held his person sacred, though he frequently put himself in their power, and allowed him the utmost freedom in conversing or corresponding with any members of their party. Nor were his personal services all that he gave his master, for he spent his private means on his behalf. Not only did he contribute large sums towards the payment and equipment of the troops, many of which were raised at his sole expense, but he supplied the King with many large sums of ready money, on one occasion as much as £60,000, and during the fifteen years of Charles II's exile he regularly gave him £5,000 a year. So great was his loyalty to the Crown, as head of the English Constitution, that he was ready to spend his life and fortune in the service of a King from whom, during his prosperity, he had never received a kindly word or the slightest mark of favour. If any man deserves the epithets of faithful, just, loyal, and true, surely it is this Duke of Somerset.

By his first wife, Arabella, he had no issue ; but by his second, Frances, daughter of Robert Devereux, Earl of Essex, he had five sons and four daughters—

William Seymour, who died young, unmarried.
Robert Seymour, who died young, unmarried.
Henry Seymour, Lord Beauchamp, who was born in
    1630. He followed his father throughout the

FRANCES, DAUGHTER OF ROBERT, EARL OF ESSEX, MARCHIONESS OF HERTFORD
AND DUCHESS OF SOMERSET.

From a Picture at Petworth, by kind permission of the late Lord Leconfield.

MONUMENT ERECTED IN GREAT BEDWYN CHURCH TO FRANCES,
DAUGHTER OF ROBERT, EARL OF ESSEX, AND WIFE OF WILLIAM,
EARL AND MARQUIS OF HERTFORD AND SECOND DUKE OF SOMERSET.

Civil War, towards the close of which his health became seriously injured. He was employed frequently in visiting the West of England, communicating with the King's friends, and sending in reports as to the state and feeling of the country. In 1651 he was taken by the Parliament and sent to the Tower to be kept a close prisoner for ten days for treason (April 9). His imprisonment, however, was of much longer duration, for, April 16, he was examined by order of the Council of State, who at his request allowed him to see his physician in the presence of the Lieutenant of the Tower; April 17, he was permitted to engage a servant, provided the latter was vouched for by the Lieutenant of the Tower, and his further examination was put off for a week; April 24, he petitioned to be allowed to take exercise about the Tower, a request that was granted on the 28th. At the same time Lady Beauchamp with her maid were allowed to join him for ten days on condition they did not leave the Tower and spoke to no one except in the presence of the Lieutenant. On May 6, Lady Beauchamp was permitted to remain with her husband, on the same conditions, until further notice. September 9, Lord Beauchamp was bailed out on a bond of £10,000, with two sureties of £5,000 each. September 17, he was granted permission to go into the country.* During this time his health had broken down completely and, hoping a greater change might bring about a recovery, he went over to France soon after his release, and died there in 1654. He had married Mary, daughter of Arthur, Lord Capel of Hadham, by whom he had one son and three daughters, viz. :—

William Seymour, born 1651, who became third

* State Papers, Domestic.

Duke of Somerset, and of whom we must speak later.

Frances and Mary Seymour, who died young.

Elizabeth Seymour, who, by a warrant from Charles II, June 28, 1672, assumed the title of Lady and the rank of a Duke's daughter, which, by her father's decease during the lifetime of her grandfather, she had been debarred from. August 31, 1676, she married Thomas, Lord Bruce, afterwards Earl of Aylesbury, and, as heir to her brother, brought Tottenham Park, Savernake Forest, and other possessions into that family.*

John Seymour, who became fourth Duke of Somerset, and of whom we shall speak later.

Edward Seymour, who died young.

Frances Seymour, who was married three times; first to Richard, Viscount Molyneux; secondly to Thomas, Earl of Southampton; thirdly to Conyers, Lord Darcy, afterwards Earl of Holderness. She died without issue.

Arabella Seymour, who died unmarried.

Mary Seymour, who married Heneage Finch, second Earl of Winchelsea.

Jane Seymour, who married Charles Boyle, Lord Clifford of Lanesborough, son and heir of Richard Boyle, first Earl of Burlington and second Earl of Cork.

The Duke of Somerset had made his will, August 15, 1657. In it he took great care of his daughters, Frances, Mary, and Jane, and of his granddaughter Elizabeth. Amongst other properties, he bequeathed amongst them the manors of Savage, Darell, and Esturmy. His other estates were left in such a manner that in course of time they all devolved upon his granddaughter and passed into

* Papers relating to Seymour family, coll. by 11th Duke of Somerset (case of Lord Aylesbury and the Duke of Somerset).

the Aylesbury family. This lady benefited still further upon the death of her grandmother, Frances, Duchess of Somerset, in May, 1673. Amongst other things she received, were the portrait of William, the second Duke, the portrait of William, the third Duke, the double picture of Frances, Duchess, and her brother, when children, and the Seymour pedigree at Tottenham.* The latter was a great scroll, six feet wide and twenty-four feet long, beautifully illustrated with miniatures, arms, seals, deeds, and grants.

[Letters and Papers of Seymour family, coll. by 11th Duke of Somerset; Life and Letters of Lady Arabella Stuart, Cooper; Life of Lady Arabella Stuart, by E. J. Bradley (Mrs. Murray Smith); Lives of Eminent Englishwomen, Miss Costello; Harl. MS.; Dict. Nat. Biog.; Wilts. Archæolog. Mag., xv; State Papers, Domestic, James I; Dugdale's Baronage; Clarendon's Hist. of the Rebellion; Life of Clarendon; State Papers, Domestic, Charles I; Journals of the House of Lords; Collins's Peerage; Gardiner's Histories of England and of the Great Civil War; Antiquarian Repertory, 2, 290; Winwood's Memoirs; D'Israeli's Curiosities of Literature; Rymer's Foedera; Complete Peerage; Rushworth's Historical Collection; Birch's Memoirs of the Reign of Elizabeth, 11, 506; Lodge's Portraits of Illustrious Personages, ed. Bohn; Whitelocke's Memoirs; Nichols's Progresses of James I; Edinburgh Review, July, 1896; Forster's Alumni, Oxon.; Nicholas Papers (Camden Society), 11, 66; Courthorpe's Historical Peerage; Metcalfe's Book of Knights; Hutching's Dorset; Memoirs of James I, Aikin, &c.]

---

* Papers relating to Seymour family, coll. by 11th Duke of Somerset (case of Lord Aylesbury and the Duke of Somerset).

WILLIAM SEYMOUR, 3RD DUKE OF SOMERSET.

He was born in 1651, and succeeded his grandfather in the title in 1660. He died, unmarried, at the age of 20, at Worcester House, in the Strand, September 12, 1671, and was interred at Great Bedwin, where he lies without any monument to mark his last resting-place.* (Appendix H.) His great estates, Tottenham Park, Savernake Forest, &c., devolved upon his sister Elizabeth, whilst the title went to his uncle, John Seymour.

* Genealogical Hist., 539.

WILLIAM SEYMOUR, THIRD DUKE OF SOMERSET.

From an Old Engraving.

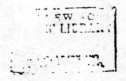

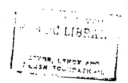

JOHN SEYMOUR, FOURTH DUKE OF SOMERSET.

From a Picture in the Council Chamber at Salisbury.

JOHN SEYMOUR, 4TH DUKE OF SOMERSET.

He succeeded his nephew in the title in 1671, but did not live to enjoy it long, for he died four years afterwards, April 29, 1675, at Amesbury, in Wilts, whence his body was conveyed to Salisbury and buried in the Cathedral there on June 10.

By his death without issue the title of Marquis became extinct, as that had been limited to the descendants of William Seymour, created Marquis of Hertford in 1641.

He had married Sarah, daughter of Sir Edward Alston, knight, President of the College of Physicians. This lady was the widow of George Grimston, son of Sir Harbottle Grimston, Master of the Rolls.

The Duchess not only survived him but his successor as well, living till October, 1692. She led a retired life, but became well known and distinguished by her extensive charity. She showed a great attachment to the Seymour family for, by her will dated May 17, 1686, she left two manors and other lands of great value, limited in the strictest manner, to Charles Seymour, 6th Duke of Somerset, and his heirs. (Note 78.)

She also left to her trustees, Lord Delamere, Sir Samuel Grimston, and Sir William Gregory, the sum of £1,700 with which to erect an almshouse at Froxfield for 30 poor widows, ten of whom were to be ministers' widows living in Wilts, Berks, or Somerset ; ten to be chosen out of the Duchess's manors in Wilts ; five to be widows from London or Westminster ; the remaining five to be other widows from Wilts, Berks, or Somerset. A further sum of £200 was to be spent in providing durable furniture. As an endowment she left the manors of Frox-

Q

field, Hewish, and Shaw, with all their lands, and some houses at Milton and Fifield. When the income should exceed £400 a year, the surplus was to go towards providing accommodation for 30 more widows. Later on, in a codicil, she added the manor and farm of Cherrington to the endowment, and gave £500 more for building and £100 more for furnishing. The advowson of Hewish she left as a provision for the chaplain.*

* Will of Sarah, Duchess of Somerset.

SARAH, DUCHESS OF SOMERSET, DAUGHTER OF SIR EDWIN ALSTON.

From an Old Print.

MONUMENT IN SALISBURY CATHEDRAL TO JOHN SEYMOUR,
FOURTH DUKE OF SOMERSET.

MONUMENT IN WESTMINSTER ABBEY, ERECTED TO SARAH,
DUCHESS OF SOMERSET, DAUGHTER OF SIR E. ALSTON.

FRANCIS SEYMOUR, 5TH DUKE OF SOMERSET.

He was, as we have seen, the 4th son of Charles, Lord Seymour of Trowbridge, who was grandson to Francis Seymour, third grandson of Edward, Earl of Hertford, and brother to William the second Duke.

He was born May 25, 1655, and on June 10 was baptized at Preshute. At the age of ten he succeeded his father as Baron Seymour, and at twenty he succeeded to the title of Duke of Somerset and Earl, but not Marquis, of Hertford ; the latter honour, as we have seen, having become extinct.

He only held the title for three years, dying in 1678, under the following circumstances : During a trip abroad he was persuaded by some French friends to accompany them to the church of the Augustines at Lerice where, though they were all men of rank, they are reported to have grossly insulted some ladies of the noble family of Botti. This so exasperated the husband of one of them, Horatio Botti, that he set out in search of the aggressors and, chancing to see the Duke standing at the door of his inn, he immediately shot him.*

Mr. Hildebrand Alington (afterward Lord Alington), who was travelling with him, at once demanded satisfaction of the State of Genoa, in which this occurrence had taken place. To pacify him, the Genoese did their utmost to apprehend Horatio Botti, and issued a large reward for his capture. Botti, however, had escaped. After some time, as a sort of atonement to the King of

---

* Collinson's Somersetshire.

England for the death of so illustrious a subject, an effigy of Botti was publicly hung.

In justice to the Duke, it may be said that all agreed that he was entirely innocent of taking any active part in the affair, but some measure of blame must still rest on him for not doing his utmost to restrain his companions.

His body was brought back to England and was buried at Preshute on October 15, 1678.

CHARLES SEYMOUR, 6TH DUKE OF SOMERSET.

Charles Seymour, "the proud Duke of Somerset" as he has generally been called, on account of his stately manner of living and his extreme haughtiness, was 1662. born on the 12th of August, 1662,* and was baptized at Preshute.

At the age of 15 he was sent to Trinity College, Cambridge,† where he remained for some years to 1678. complete his education, although within a year of his entering that place he found himself compelled to take up the responsibilities of his position as Duke of Somerset upon the sudden and tragic death of his elder brother.

The estates accompanying the title were very few and of small value, owing to the expenses of his predecessors. His ancestor, William, the 2nd Duke, had, as we have seen, greatly encumbered his property during the Civil War in order to raise money for the King's service and through his liberality to Charles II during the usurpation, nor had he lived long enough after the Restoration to reap any pecuniary reward for his loyalty. Of the estates that remained he had also, as we have seen, left the greater part to his daughters and grandchildren.

Charles was, in consequence, far from well off for his position, and it became necessary that he should contract some alliance which would place him in more 1682. favourable circumstances. This he was soon able to do for, on May 30, 1682, he married the Lady

---

* Memoirs of the Kit Cat Club.
† Dict. Nat. Biog. ; Lodge's Portraits.

Elizabeth, sole daughter and heiress of Josceline Percy, last Earl of Northumberland.* This lady was without doubt the greatest match in the kingdom, and amongst other properties which she brought to her husband was Sion House which, it will be remembered, had been built by the 1st Duke of Somerset, but had been confiscated on his downfall and given to his rival. So great was the eagerness with which Charles entered into this alliance that he agreed in the marriage articles that himself and his heirs should relinquish the name of Seymour and adopt that of Percy instead.† The Lady Elizabeth, however, was far too sensible a woman to make him adhere to this disagreeable obligation, which had been chiefly insisted on by her ambitious grandmother, and released him from it as soon as she came of age and was able legally to do so.

The Lady Elizabeth Percy was born on the 26th of January, 1667, and in 1671 had, as the only surviving child of the last Earl of Northumberland, inherited the whole of the estates of the house of Percy, which included the Baronies of Percy, Lucy, Poynings, Fitz-Payne, Bryan, and Latimer. She had been carefully brought up by her grandmother, who was determined to arrange her marriage as she thought best without in any way consulting her granddaughter's predilections. Thus it came about that, in 1679, Charles II's proposal of the Duke of Richmond as her husband was refused, and Lady Elizabeth was formally and legally contracted to a sickly boy, Henry, Earl of Ogle, the heir apparent to the Dukedom of Newcastle.‡ This youth was made to take the name of Percy, and was immediately after the ceremony of the betrothal, sent abroad to travel until such time as he and his bride should have arrived at an age when the marriage might be consummated. Scarcely a year had passed, however, when this boy died, upon which Lady Elizabeth's grandmother

* Kit Cat Club.
† Craik's Romance of the Peerage.
‡ Collins, ii, 469.

CHARLES SEYMOUR, SIXTH DUKE OF SOMERSET.

From a picture at Bulstrode, by kind permission of the Lady Gwendolen Ramsden.

at once set about finding another match for her, her choice this time falling upon Mr. Thynne of Longleat, in Wilts, one of the richest commoners in England, who, on account of his wealth, was nicknamed "Tom of Ten Thousand,"* and was the man that Dryden introduced as "wise Issachar, his wealthy western friend," in his description of the Duke of Monmouth, in his Absalom and Achitophel.

The Lady Elizabeth was now nearly 15, but, though she consented under her grandmother's pressure to go through the form of marriage, nothing could induce her to consummate the act,* and immediately after the ceremony she fled to Lady Temple at The Hague, where it was soon after arranged she was to remain unmolested for a year.   Soon after her arrival she appears to have again met the young Count Konigsmark, who had previously paid her a great deal of attention in England and had been looked upon as a suitor for her hand.   Whether she in any way encouraged his addresses or not does not appear ; but the Count certainly seems to have imagined that were she free he would have but little further difficulty.   There seemed but one important obstacle in his way—her husband.   This obstacle was soon removed.   Mr. Thynne was set upon one Sunday evening, February 12, 1682, when he was passing along Pall Mall, and murdered by three foreigners, who after their capture confessed that they had been hired to do the deed by Count Konigsmark.   (Note 79.)

Upon the news arriving that for the second time she had become a widow, the Lady Elizabeth returned at once to England,† and her grandmother once more set about searching for a suitable match.   This time her choice fell upon Charles, Duke of Somerset, and, all parties being willing on this occasion, the marriage took place three months after the death of Mr. Thynne.

* Craik's Romance of the Peerage, 329, iv.
† The Domestic Intelligencer, 1682, Feb. 15, 23, March 23.

By this alliance the Duke of Somerset became a very wealthy man, for, in addition to the property already mentioned, he became possessed of Petworth House, Alnwick Castle, and Northampton House, which he re-named Northumberland House. The latter was situated in the Strand district, and was only pulled down in recent years to make way for Northumberland Avenue.

His importance had now considerably increased, and he began to be looked upon with favour at Court. 1683. The year after his marriage he was made a Gentle-man of the Bedchamber, and the following spring 1684. (April 8) was made a Knight of the Garter.* On 1685. the death of Charles (February 6), whose funeral he attended as second mourner, he was one of the Privy Councillors who signed the proclamation of James II, who, shortly after his accession, made him a Lord of the Bedchamber.† On the 2nd of August he was given the command of a regiment of Dragoons, then called the Queen's, but which later became the 3rd Hussars, which was employed in suppressing the insurrection of the Duke of Monmouth, and for the same purpose he raised the militia of Somersetshire.‡

Charles was now apparently in great favour, and might have become conspicuous at the Court of James II, 1687. but that he preferred his principles to his chances of advancement. In July of this year the King de-termined to give an official and public reception at Windsor to the Papal Nuncio, Ferdinand Adda, Archbishop of Amasia, and the duty of introducing the Pope's delegate fell to the Duke of Somerset as First Lord of the Bedchamber. This duty, it appears, involved breaking the law of the land as it then stood, and Somerset resolutely refused to be a party to such a proceeding.§ In vain his friends pleaded with him, pointing out how the loss of the royal

---

* Lodge.
† Kit Cat Club.
‡ Lodge.
§ Burnet's Hist. of his Own Time.

ELIZABETH PERCY, DUCHESS OF SOMERSET.

From an old print.

favour would ruin his career. Somerset stood firm. The King himself expostulated with him, saying, "I thought, my Lord, that I was doing you a great honour in appointing you to escort the minister of the first of all crowned heads." The Duke replied, "Sir, I am advised that I cannot obey your Majesty without breaking the law." "I will make you fear me as well as the law," said the King, now in a towering rage; "do you not know that I am above the law"? "Your Majesty," answered the Duke, "may be above the law, but I am not, and while I obey the law I fear nothing." At the time of this episode the Duke was but 25 years of age, and his firmness and spirit were greatly liked by the people, in whose estimation he was thenceforth raised on high. The King, however, never forgave him, and he was immediately deprived of his place at Court and of the command of his regiment, and during the next few months he was removed from the Lord Lieutenancy of the East Riding of Yorkshire.

The staunch feelings of the Duke in regard to religion had made him view James's leanings towards the 1688. Catholics with considerable suspicion, and when matters came to a crisis and the Prince of Orange was invited to come over and give his assistance to the Protestant Church, Somerset was one of the first noblemen to join him.* Like many others, however, he does not seem to have ever intended that the Crown should be given to William of Orange, but only that James's government should be put an end to, and that, if the latter would not conform to the laws of the country and to the oath he had sworn at his coronation, that it should be given to the Princess, so that the succession should still descend in the right course. As a result of this feeling, he was always looked upon coldly by William, although, once the matter had been settled, he took the oath of allegiance and expressed his readiness to conform to the new government; indeed, so far did he show his willingness to enter into the new order of things, that he carried the

* Kit Cat Club.

Queen's sword at the coronation, and not long after entertained William at his house at Marlborough, on the latter's journey to and from Ireland.

In 1689 he was elected Chancellor of the University of
1689.   Cambridge,* and, in the following year, succeeded
        Lord Halifax as Speaker of the House of Lords.
1690. Although disliked by William he gained the favour
        of the Princess Anne, with whom the Duchess
became on friendly and intimate terms, and on one occa-
        sion was able to render her a slight service ; for,
1692. when the Princess was ejected from the cockpit in
        April, 1692, he received her at Sion House and
made her welcome, in spite of the order forbidding anyone to countenance her.†

In 1701, Somerset became President of the Council,
        and was further appointed one of the Lords of the
1701. Regency during the King's absence on his last
1702. visit to Holland.   The year following he was
        made Master of the Horse, an appointment which
he held for some years, and, on Queen Anne's accession,
        he became a Privy Councillor.   In 1703, when
1703. the Archduke of Austria was proclaimed King of
        Spain at Vienna, and was journeying to his new
kingdom viâ Holland and the Channel, Somerset was
detailed by the Queen to receive him at Portsmouth and
escort him to Windsor.   A magnificent reception was
1706. prepared on this occasion, and the Duke took a
        very prominent part in it.   In 1706 he was made
one of the Commissioners for the union with Scotland.

By attaching himself to no party, the Duke had no serious political foes for some time, and continued to enjoy his places and the Queen's favour.   Although he does not appear to have fully approved of Marlborough's
        Government, he supported him during the Mini-
1708. sterial crisis of February, 1708.‡   Matters, how-

* Kit Cat Club.
† London Gazette, 2758.
‡ Lodge.

ever, not turning out to his satisfaction he threw in his lot with the Tories, by whom, however, his assistance does not appear to have been appreciated or desired, if we are to judge by the manner in which St. John and others tried to oust him from his place in the Council.

In 1712 (January) he was suddenly deprived of the Mastership of the Horse and of his place at the Council Board, on its being reported to the Queen that, in his zeal for the Protestant succession in the House of Brunswick, he had entered into a secret correspondence with the Elector of Hanover. There appears to have been no harm or disloyalty in this correspondence, but the Queen was particularly touchy on such matters, and never quite forgave him for what she looked upon as needless interference in her business.

1712.

Although out of favour himself, his Duchess did not lose any of her influence over the Queen, and retained her position at Court as Groom of the Stole and first Lady of the Bedchamber, in which appointments she had succeeded the Duchess of Marlborough, and no efforts of her enemies were able to remove her. The Duchess continued to use her influence, which was chiefly directed towards persuading the Queen of her duty of securing the Protestant succession. Her efforts in this direction having soon been noticed, the floodgates of party virulence were at once opened upon her, though without effect. Swift, in his "Windsor prophecy," poured forth the grossest and most vulgar abuse upon her, and went so far as to accuse her of having murdered her first husband. The whole poem was so grossly violent and the accusation so untrue that his friends persuaded him to withdraw the publication, but his repentance came too late. Copies had already been issued in some quantity, and he had to bear the fruits of his indiscretion. The Queen and the Duchess were greatly annoyed and, in revenge, carefully excluded him from any higher Church preferment, upon which, knowing whom he had to thank

for the loss of an expected Bishopric, Swift continued to
pour forth his abuse in his poems* :   (Note 80.)

> " Now angry Somerset her vengeance vows
> On Swift's reproaches for her murder'd spouse :
> From her red locks her mouth with venom fills,
> And thence into the royal ear distils."

When Queen Anne's recovery was despaired of,
Somerset succeeded in disconcerting the schemes
1714. of some of the other Councillors, with regard to
the succession, by suddenly appearing at the
Council Board (where he had not appeared for three
years) at Kensington, to which he had not been summoned, and, with the support of Shrewsbury, Somers,
and Argyll, taking the steps necessary to ensure the
peaceful succession of George I.   "But for the Duke
of Somerset (acting with Shrewsbury and Argyll) the
Council which met upon Queen Anne's death might, and
probably would, have recalled the Stuarts ; but no man
not at once Duke and Seymour, if unconnected with the
Cabinet, would have pushed uninvited into a Cabinet
Council, and compelled the members to make instant
choice between their safety and their predilections.   This
act of impudent patriotism saved the Protestant succession, and those who grudge the pride of the Seymours
may remember with advantage the incident in which it
was most conspicuously shown."†

Upon the death of Queen Anne, August 1, the Duke's
name was placed second in a list of 19 Peers whom
George I had, by a previous deed, added to the seven
great officers of state, as Guardians of the Realm until his
arrival.   The Duke concurred in every step necessary for
the tranquillity of the country, and was employed with
Shrewsbury and Cowper in receiving the Seals from Lord
Bolingbroke and closing up the doors of his office.‡

* Forster's Life of Swift ; also Sheridan.
† The Great Governing Families of England, by Sanford and
Townsend.
‡ Kit Cat Club.

When King George landed at Greenwich, September 18, the Duke was nominated one of the new Privy Council and, September 27, was restored to his place as Master of the Horse. He now found himself once more in considerable favour with his Sovereign and in a position where it was possible for him to acquire great influence and power ; but, for the third time, his principles and pride caused him to quarrel with his King and to retire from the Court. Two years after the accession of George, Sir William Wyndham, Somerset's son-in-law, was accused of having entered into a treasonable correspondence with the Pretender, and a warrant was issued for his arrest. Hearing of this in time, Wyndham went into hiding, and Somerset applied on his behalf, to the King, asking that Sir William should not be confined but be admitted to bail, should he voluntarily surrender himself. As there seemed no immediate prospect of effecting the arrest, the King willingly pledged his word to that effect, but no sooner had Sir William delivered himself up, than he was at once confined to the Tower, and all applications for bail were refused. Highly incensed at this dishonourable breaking of the King's pledge, Somerset expressed his indignation in no measured terms, for which he would have been dismissed from the Mastership of the Horse, had he not anticipated the King's intention by resigning his appointment in the most offensive manner he could think of. On October 25 he paraded his servants outside Northumberland House, dressed in the family livery in place of the royal one, and, sending for a common dust-cart, caused all the badges of his office to be thrown into it. Then, marshalling his men around the cart, he proceeded in great order to the courtyard of St. James's Palace, where, his retinue having formed up on either side of the cart, he gave the command " to shoot the rubbish," upon which all the royal liveries and his badges of office were turned out into the mud, a fitting place he considered for the property of a monarch who could not keep his pledged word. This done, he marched slowly back to Northumberland House in the same order.*

After this, the Duke would never again accept any office at Court, even though, in June, 1747, George II nominated him one of the Privy Council.* Henceforth he resided quietly in his own home, chiefly at Petworth, and devoted himself to the management of his estates.

His first wife, Elizabeth Percy, had died in 1723, and the titles of Northumberland and Percy were practically extinct. It will be remembered that Somerset had, on his marriage, agreed to take the name of Percy, but had afterwards been released from this obligation. He desired, however, to retain the Northumberland honours in his family, as having married the last of the Percyes, but only on condition that they should remain secondary to the name of Seymour. The following letters, from the originals at Stover, show his feelings on the subject, and are not without interest. They are all addressed to Serjeant (Sir Thomas, afterwards Lord Chief Justice) Pengelly :—†

Petworth,
January 8, 1723.

Sir,

On this unfortunate occasion of the death of my poor wife, she being possessed of several Baronies in right of her family and also in King Charles I reign in right of a then writ of summons to call her grandfather to the House of Lords, in his father's lifetime, and he being then placed next to the Lord Audley but as the third Baron, there arose a dispute he claiming place as the first Baron in England. The House, February 5, 1628, referred it to the Committee for privileges, as appears by the Journal, but the sudden dissolution of that Parliament prevented the Committee making their report, and by consequence, the resolution of the House upon it ; and there being twelve years before another Parliament met, her great grandfather died, so that her grandfather became Earl of Northumberland. That and the troubles which began early in

---

* Kit Cat Club.
† This gentleman assisted the Duke greatly in his legal affairs. Many of the Duke's letters to him are in the possession of the author at Stover, Devon.

that Parliament 1640 prevented the determination of the Precedency, and these Baronys not having had any opportunity until this melancholy occasion to attest its rightful demand I sent Cockell last week to Syon and to London to search for materials to support the right of my children, and also to speak to Mr. Anstis upon it, and then to lay all these things before you, to receive your orders in what farther he is to do in case we are deficient in any one thing, which I think we cannot well be, if he hath done according to my directions, when you have seen and considered all we can produce to support the Precedency. I shall desire to have your opinion whether as the case now is, that these five Baronys have been so long dormant I ought not to insist to have them all inserted in this first writ of summons to call Lord Hertford up to the House of Lords. I have no mind that he shall demand his writ until all these matters are looked into and very well considered by you, whose judgment is very much valued and will have its weight with, your most humble servant, &c.

Petworth,
January 17, 1723.

Sir,

I do return thanks for the very great care expressed in yours of the 12th, relating to the Baronys now in my son Hertford, and as I have all the reason in the world to depend on your judgment and advice in this and in everything else I do accept of it: and I have sent Cockell back with the state of the case you were pleased to deliver him, when he hath waited on you then he is to communicate your directions to Mr. Anstis, the proper way for my son to demand his writ for the barony of Percy only, and to take the same place on the Baron's bench next to Lord Audley as his great grandfather Northumberland did before him; after this Cockell is to go to Lord Hertford to acquaint him and all my other children with it. I believe great care ought to be taken in entrusting the world with any farther intentions at present until I am something better able to enter into business.

I am, etc.

Petworth,
May 14, 1723.

Sir,

The conversation you mention to have had with my son Hertford, as to the title of Northumberland will deserve a farther consideration. Mr. Anstis will be a very proper person to be discoursed with upon it, for I shall hardly be brought to consent that the Duke of Somerset's eldest son shall bear the title of another family; therefore, I shall propose to know what objection may be against a patent to create him Marquis of Hertford and Earl of Northumberland, but this earldom to be in the patent to him and to the heirs male of his body lawfully begotten. In failure of such, then to his sisters successively, and to their heirs of their bodies: or whether I can have it, having a superior title, to me and to the heirs of my body lawfully begotten, either of these ways the most feasible to secure the title of Northumberland in my family, etc.

———————

Petworth,
May 25, 1723.

SIR,

I am sorry to give you so much trouble in the affair you are pleased to mention in your letter of the 23rd on the title of Earl of Northumberland. My son having already spoke to the King upon it and His Majesty's answer hath most certainly secured that title going into another family for one year or two at least; and as you write that Mr. Anstis hath cleared my questions concerning the creating my son, Marquis of Hertford; in my lifetime; I am confirmed in resolution never to give my consent to have my son take a patent on any other terms, than to be created Marquis of Hertford to him, and to the heirs male of his body lawfully begotten, and Earl of Northumberland to him and to the heirs male of his body lawfully begotten. In failure thereof, the earldom to descend to his two sisters successively and to their heirs of their bodies, and go on of course to their children. As my own paternal estate and that of their mothers will descend to them, it is not an unreasonable request when all things are rightly considered, with the services I have done the King before and since his accession to the crown, and the steadiness which my son hath at all times shown for His Majesty's service, and my birth and estate, etc., that I may plead a much better pretence, than many others who have had titles, and others asking every day. E. of Coningsby's earldom is to his daughters and other precedents may easily be found. Therefore since you have had a good deal of trouble in this affair, I desire to add one more, to communicate this letter to my son that he may ask the King for these two titles on these conditions. Neither are the titles to be separated, nor the succession to the earldom to be varied one tittle. According to His Majesty he may then proceed to get or not to get a warrant signed, for if there is any hesitation in the King, let the whole fall until a more favourable opportunity do happen; for I am utterly against his asking any of the ministers, to assist him in his request, for it is not a matter of that consequence.

I am, etc.

CHARLES SEYMOUR, SIXTH DUKE OF SOMERSET.

From an Old Print.

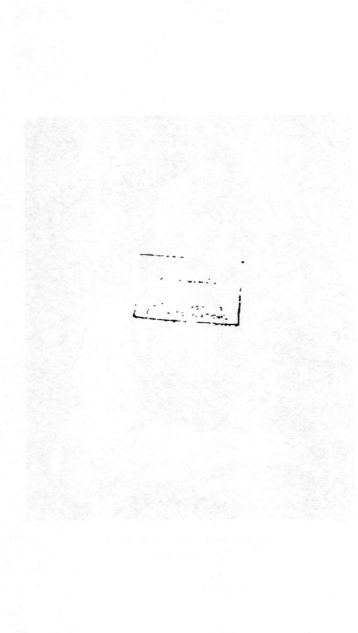

The Duke was fond of show, and, whenever possible, invariably attended all great public ceremonies. At the funeral of Charles II he was one of the supporters to Prince George of Denmark, the chief mourner. He carried the orb at the coronation of James II, and the Queen's crown at the coronation of William and Mary. At King William's funeral he was one of the supporters of the pall, whilst the Duchess walked as chief mourner. He carried the orb at the coronation of Queen Anne, at that of George I, and also at that of George II.*

Some years previous to his death, the Duke retired from all public affairs to his seat at Petworth, in 1748. Sussex, where he died December 2, 1748, and was buried in Salisbury Cathedral.* In July, 1750, a very fine marble statue, representing him in the early period of his life, was executed by Rysbrack at the expense of two of his daughters, the Marchioness of Granby and Lady Guernsey.* It was raised on a square pedestal and habited after the manner of Vandyck, with ensigns of the Garter, in the Senate House of the University of Cambridge ; he is represented leaning on his left arm and holding a roll in his hand. (Note 81.)

" The Duke was of middle stature and well formed ; his complexion was dark and his countenance expressive. He had a good flow of words generally at his command ; but, owing to an impediment in his speech, appeared to considerable disadvantage in the company of strangers. His judgment was, for the most part, correct, and his acquaintance with the sister arts, music and poetry, by no means superficial."* His principal feeling seems to have been an unbounded pride, founded upon his high birth and expectations, which often influenced his conduct to the prejudice of all the better qualities of his heart. His rank entitled him to take precedence on most occasions, when he developed as much loftiness of demeanour as if he had been invested with regal honours. Like a Turkish

* Kit Cat Club.

R

The Duke was fond of show, and, whenever possible, invariably attended all great public ceremonies. At the funeral of Charles II he was one of the supporters to Prince George of Denmark, the chief mourner. He carried the orb at the coronation of James II, and the Queen's crown at the coronation of William and Mary. At King William's funeral he was one of the supporters of the pall, whilst the Duchess walked as chief mourner. He carried the orb at the coronation of Queen Anne, at that of George I, and also at that of George II.*

Some years previous to his death, the Duke retired from all public affairs to his seat at Petworth, in 1748. Sussex, where he died December 2, 1748, and was buried in Salisbury Cathedral.* In July, 1750, a very fine marble statue, representing him in the early period of his life, was executed by Rysbrack at the expense of two of his daughters, the Marchioness of Granby and Lady Guernsey.* It was raised on a square pedestal and habited after the manner of Vandyck, with ensigns of the Garter, in the Senate House of the University of Cambridge; he is represented leaning on his left arm and holding a roll in his hand. (Note 81.)

"The Duke was of middle stature and well formed; his complexion was dark and his countenance expressive. He had a good flow of words generally at his command; but, owing to an impediment in his speech, appeared to considerable disadvantage in the company of strangers. His judgment was, for the most part, correct, and his acquaintance with the sister arts, music and poetry, by no means superficial."* His principal feeling seems to have been an unbounded pride, founded upon his high birth and expectations, which often influenced his conduct to the prejudice of all the better qualities of his heart. His rank entitled him to take precedence on most occasions, when he developed as much loftiness of demeanour as if he had been invested with regal honours. Like a Turkish

* Kit Cat Club.

R

Bashaw, he made his servants acquainted with his wishes by signs. The country roads through which he travelled were often cleared by avant couriers before his approach, so that he might pass without obstruction or observation. " Get out of the way," cried one of his servants one day to a man leading a pig by the roadside. " Why ? " said the fellow. " Because my Lord Duke is coming, and he does not like to be looked at," rejoined the servant. " But I will see him, and my pig shall see him too," exclaimed the enraged yokel, and he held the pig up by the ears till the Duke and his retinue had passed by.*

Some remarkable anecdotes illustrating his intolerable pride are told on various authorities. His second Duchess once tapped him familiarly on the shoulder with her fan, when he turned round, in great displeasure, and observed, " My first wife was a Percy, yet she never took such a liberty."* His children were taught to obey his injunctions with the most profound respect. The two younger daughters were accustomed to stand and watch him alternately whilst he slept in the afternoons. On one occasion, it being very hot and feeling very tired, the Lady Charlotte sat down. The Duke by chance suddenly woke, and expressing his surprise and displeasure at her disobedience, declared he would remember it in his will. He left Lady Charlotte £20,000 less than her sister.*

On another occasion he sent for a celebrated painter, James Seymour, to take the portraits of some of his race-horses, and at dinner one day drank to him, saying, " Cousin Seymour, your health." The artist replied, " My Lord, I really do believe that I have the honour of being of your Grace's family." Highly offended, the Duke rose from the table and told his steward to pay the painter and dismiss him. Another artist was then sent for, but finding himself incapable of completing the pictures in the same style, he had the honesty to acknowledge his incapacity to the Duke, and humbly advised him to

* Kit Cat Club.

CHARLOTTE, DAUGHTER OF DANIEL, EARL OF WINCHELSEA,
DUCHESS OF SOMERSET.

From a portrait at Petworth, by kind permission of the late Lord Leconfield.

recall Seymour. This the Duke eventually did, but the artist replied, " My Lord, I will now prove myself one of your Grace's family, for I won't come."*

Sir James Delaval once laid a wager of £1,000 that he would make the Duke give him precedence. The latter was so touchy on such matters that it was considered impossible. Delaval, however, finding out the precise time at which the Duke must enter a narrow lane on his way to town, stationed himself there in a coach emblazoned with the arms of Howard, and a number of servants in like livery, who called out when the Duke approached, " Way, way, for the Duke of Norfolk." Somerset, though he always expected his due, was also very particular in regard to that of others, and knowing it would be a breach of etiquette for him to take precedence of the Duke of Norfolk, naturally caused his men to draw aside, leaving the way clear to Delaval. This stupid joke, which passed for wit at that time, was much talked about.*

The Duke was a member of the Kit Cat Club and one of its chief supporters. (Note 82.) His first wife was, as we have already seen, a daughter of the last Percy, Earl of Northumberland. She is said to have been one of the best bred, as well as the best born lady in England. Her wealth was immense. Burnet tells us : " She maintained her dignity at Court with great respect to the Queen and sincerity to all others. She was by much the greatest favourite when the Queen died, and it would have continued, for she thought herself justified in her favour to her when she was ashamed of it elsewhere. Not long before the Queen died, she told me she designed to leave some of her jewels to the Queen of Sicily (who was the only relation I ever heard her speak of with much tenderness), and the rest to the Duchess of Somerset, as the fittest person to wear them after her."†

The Duke's children by her were—

* Kit Cat Club.
† Burnet's Hist. of his Own Time.

Algernon Seymour, seventh Duke of Somerset, of
    whom we must speak later.

Lord Percy Seymour, born June 3, 1686, who
    served in Parliament for the borough of Cocker-
    mouth, in Cumberland, and died unmarried, July 4,
    1721.

Lord Charles Seymour, born in 1688, who died un-
    married January 4, 1711.

Lady Elizabeth Seymour, who married Henry
    O'Brien, Earl of Thomond, in Ireland, and died
    without issue.

Lady Catharine Seymour, who, in 1708, married Sir
    William Wyndham, Bart., of Somersetshire, and
    by him was mother to the Earl of Egremont.
    She died 1713.

Lady Frances Seymour, who died unmarried, May 10,
    1720.

Lady Anne Seymour, who married Peregrine Osborne,
    Marquis of Carmarthen, and afterwards Duke of
    Leeds.   She died November 27, 1722.

The Duke's second wife was Charlotte, daughter of
Daniel, Earl of Winchelsea, whom he married February 4,
1725, nearly three years after the death of his first wife,
who died November 23, 1722.   She bore him the following children :—

Lady Frances Seymour, born July 8, 1728, who
    married John Manners, commonly called Marquis
    of Granby, eldest son of the Duke of Rutland, on
    September 3, 1750.   She died January 25, 1760.

Lady Charlotte Seymour, born September 21, 1736,
    who married Heneage, afterwards Earl of Aylesford,
    October 6, 1750.

[Particulars of Charles, Duke of Somerset's life, are to be found
    in the following works :—Memoirs of the Kit Cat Club;
    Dict. Nat. Biog.; Boyer's Reign of Queen Anne; Wyon's
    History of Queen Anne; Craik's Romance of the Peerage;

PERCY SEYMOUR, LORD BEAUCHAMP.

From a picture at Stover, the property of H. St. Maur, Esqr.

Reresby's Diary; Evelyn's Diary; Burnet's Hist. of his Own Time; Collins's Peerage; G. E. C. Peerage; Macaulay's Hist.; Lodge's Portraits of Illustrious Persons; Lingard's Hist. of England; Jesses' Court of England; The London Gazette, 2758; Luttrel's Brief Historical Narration; Aungier's Syon Monastery; Forster's Life of Swift; Swift's Works, ed. Scott; The Great Governing Families of England, by Sanford and Townsend; De Fonblanque's House of Percy; Dryden's Works; Burke's Romance of the Peerage; Wentworth's Journal; Walpole's Correspondence; London, Past and Present, by Wheatley and Cunningham, &c.]

ALGERNON SEYMOUR, 7TH DUKE OF SOMERSET.

Algernon Seymour was born November 11, 1684,[*]
1684. and was apparently educated at Trinity College,
Cambridge.   Before arriving at full age he was
returned to Parliament as member for Marl-
1705. borough, June 14, 1705.   This was the last
English Parliament before the union with Scotland
in 1707, and became, in that year, the first Parliament of
Great Britain.[†]

January 25, 1706, he was appointed Lord Lieutenant
and Custos Rotulorum of the county of Sussex.
1706. The comparative peace and quiet of a parliamentary life did not, however, suit his taste, and he
longed for a sphere of greater personal activity.   This
inclination led him to make a trial of the military
1708. profession and, in May, 1708, he joined Marlborough's army at Brussels as a volunteer, and
served in that capacity throughout the campaign in
Flanders, during which he was present at the taking of
Lille and the battle of Oudenarde, and distinguished
himself so far as to be chosen as bearer of Marlborough's
despatches, announcing his victory to the Queen, by
whom he was received with great distinction.[†]   We read
in the Gazette of that time : " St. James's, November 26.
This afternoon the Right Honble. the Earl of Hertford
arrived here express from his Grace the Duke of Marlborough, to Her Majesty, with an account that his Grace
had passed the Scheld, and relieved the town of Brussels,

* Dict. Nat. Biog.
† Collins's Peerage.

ALGERNON SEYMOUR, SEVENTH DUKE OF SOMERSET.

From a Picture at Petworth, by kind permission of the late Lord Leconfield.

FRANCES, DAUGHTER OF HENRY THYNNE, COUNTESS OF HERTFORD,
AND AFTERWARDS DUCHESS OF SOMERSET.

From a portrait at Stover, in the possession of H. St. Maur, Esqr.

which was besieged by the late Elector of Bavaria. His lordship was received by the Queen with great distinction."

The experiences he had undergone confirmed Hertford in his taste for the military profession and, early 1709. in the following year, he accepted a commission as Colonel of the 15th Foot, and again joined Marlborough's army. During the next few months he served with diligence in that army, and took part in the capture of Tournay, the battle of Malplaquet, and the fall of Mons, which closed that campaign. The next year he served again under Marlborough, and afterwards took part in every campaign down to the peace of Utrecht in 1713.*

The peace once ratified he returned to England, and shortly after married Frances, eldest daughter and coheir of Henry Thynne, only son and heir of Thomas, first Viscount Weymouth. This marriage did not, however, tempt him to forsake the profession in which he had already distinguished himself. His former services were rewarded with the Governorship of Tynemouth 1715. Castle and Clifford Fort and, in 1715, he received a further mark of favour in being appointed Captain and Colonel of the 2nd troop of Horse Guards, and, on the accession of George I, he was made Lord of the Bedchamber to the Prince of Wales.*

The country being at peace and the duties of his command not affording a sufficient scope for his energy, he now again entered the arena of politics and served, during the next few years, as member for Marlborough and for the county of Northumberland.

On the death of his mother in 1722, when his father, as we have already seen, put forward a claim to the 1722. honours of the House of Percy, he prematurely and therefore wrongly assumed the title of Baron Percy,† but relinquished it as soon as his mistake was made clear to him. His mother being the last of the

* Collins's Peerage.
† G. E. C. Peerage.

Percys, it had been expected that he would succeed to
her Baronies of Percy, Lucy, Poynings, Fitz-Payne, Bryan,
and Latimer, and his father was at some pains to get him
called to the House of Lords as Marquis of Hertford,
Earl of Northumberland, and Baron Percy, but, owing to
the many difficulties placed in his way, the matter
remained in abeyance for the time.

In 1726 he was appointed Lord Lieutenant of Wiltshire; the year following he was made Brigadier-
General and, in 1735, Major-General of the Horse.
1737. On September 26, 1737, he was appointed
Governor of Minorca.*

During most of his life he seems to have suffered from
frequent attacks of gout, which grew worse as he got
older and which, during the whole of the next year, kept
him confined to his residence at St. Leonard's Hill.†
Lady Hertford in many of her letters mentions the
solitary life she led there, but without complaining of it,
for being a clever woman she found plenty resources in
reading and working and relaxation in riding, of which
she appears to have been very fond.

In 1739, Lord Hertford was made Lieutenant-General
of the Horse and, during this year, resided chiefly
at the family seat at Marlborough, the beautiful
gardens of which Lady Hertford speaks of with delight in
her letters to Lady Pomfret.‡

On May 6, 1740, Lord Hertford was appointed
Colonel of the royal regiment of Horse Guards
and, March 13, 1742, was made Governor of the
1742. Island of Guernsey.* He does not appear, however, to have taken up his residence there, for,
during this year, he rented a place called Richking's Park,
situated a little north of Colnbrook, from Lord Bathurst.
Lady Hertford was so pleased with the beautiful scenery

* Collins's Peerage.
† Correspondence of the Seymours, MS. (St. Leonard's Hill
was about two miles from Windsor.)
‡ Corresp. of the Seymours, MS.

ALGERNON SEYMOUR, SEVENTH DUKE OF SOMERSET.

From a portrait at Stover, in the possession of H. St. Maur, Esqr.

on this estate that she persuaded her husband to purchase it.   In her letters to her friend Lady Pomfret, she describes the house as standing in a small park of about a mile and a-half round, laid out in the French style, interspersed with pretty woods and lawns.   In the park was a small but deep lake supplied by a pretty stream, and in one of the woods was a cave, from the back of which gushed a spring which fell into a basin, from which again it overflowed and poured along a channel cut in the pavement.   The entrance was overhung with periwinkle, and the top shaded with beeches, huge elms, and birch. Dispersed over the park were covered benches, seats under shady trees, and little arbours interwoven with lilacs, woodbines, syringa, and laurel.*

In December, 1748, Lord Hertford succeeded his father as Duke of Somerset, and, on the 24th of March following, he was made General of the Horse.   It was now proposed that he should be granted the honours of the House of Percy which he had been unable to obtain upon his mother's death, but he does not appear to have been so anxious now as formerly for, in 1744, he had suffered a bitter blow by the loss of his only son, a lad of great promise, and there remained but daughters to succeed him.   On their behalf, however, he made an application to the Crown with the result that, on October 2, he procured a new patent of creation as Baron and Earl of the kingdom of Great Britain, by the name, style, and title of Baron Warkworth of Warkworth Castle, in Northumberland, and Earl of Northumberland ; to hold the same to him, and the heirs male of his body, and in default of such issue to Sir Hugh Smithson, bart., of Stanwick, in York, his son-in-law, and to his heirs by the Lady Elizabeth, his daughter ; and, in default of such issue, the dignities of Baroness Warkworth and Countess of Northumberland to that lady, and the Barony and Earldom to her heirs male.†   At the

1748.

1749.

---

* Corresp. of the Seymours, MS.
† See original patent.

same time, October 3, he received a grant, by letters
patent, of the dignities of Earl of Egremont and Baron
Cockermouth of Cockermouth Castle, in Cumberland,
with remainder to Sir Charles Wyndham, the eldest son
of his sister, Lady Catharine Seymour ; and in default to
Percy Wyndham O'Brien, of Shotgrove, in Essex (afterwards Earl of Thomond), and to the heirs male of his
body.*

The Duke of Somerset was a man of many and great
accomplishments and might have made a much greater
figure in history, but that he was of a weak constitution,
which had become seriously impaired by the hardships of
the campaigns he had gone through in his younger days,
as a result of which he was for some time almost an
invalid.   Though his preference had run towards a
military career, in which he had made his mark, he did
not confine himself to that alone.   He was an active and
steady member of Parliament, and took considerable
interest in the work and discoveries of men of science.
About the year 1749 he was chosen as President of the
Society of Antiquaries.†

He only survived his father two years, dying on
February 17, 1750. By his wife, Frances Thynne,
1750. who survived him, he had two children—

> George Seymour, Lord Beauchamp, born Septem-
> ber 11, 1725, who died of small-pox at Bologna, in
> Italy, on his 19th birthday, 1744.   His godfathers
> had been George I and Henry, Earl of Thomond,
> and Queen Caroline (then Princess of Wales) had
> been his godmother.   The following account is
> given of his character : " This young nobleman
> was so amiable in his person, and of so sweet a
> disposition, as endeared him to all that had the
> honour to know him ; and, in the little time he
> lived, showed an excellent turn of thought, far

* See original patent.
† Butler's Collections.

GEORGE, LORD BEAUCHAMP.

From a picture at Stover, the property of H. St. Maur, Esqr.

FRANCES THYNNE, DUCHESS OF SOMERSET.

From an old print.

above his years, and a behaviour, in all respects, that could not fail of rendering him an ornament to his country, and a shining example to posterity."[*]

Elizabeth Seymour, who married Sir Hugh Smithson, bart., who became Earl of Northumberland in July, 1740. She was given Sion House by her father, and enlarged and beautified it considerably.

The Duke and Duchess, together with Lord Beauchamp, were buried at Westminster Abbey, in St. Nicholas Chapel.[†]

The Duchess was a great friend of Mrs. Elizabeth Rowe, whom she persuaded, in 1736, to add two books to the History of Joseph, which she had been prevailed upon to publish. After the loss of both her husband and son, she had recourse to the solace of religion. (Note 83.) Her drawing-room was converted into a chapel, and she expressed herself resigned to the Divine will. The Duke had left her the house near Colnbrook, of which she was so fond, and which had been re-named Percy Lodge.[‡] Here she passed her time in the greatest tranquillity, surrounded only by her oldest servants and seeing but a few selected friends, her chapel and library almost sharing her day. She was greatly attached to the children of her daughter, especially of the boy, on account of his strong resemblance to his uncle.[§]

She corresponded constantly with Lady Luxborough, and occasionally with Mr. Shenstone. The latter, with Mr. Graves, of Claverton, and Mr. Whistler, of Whitchurch, formed a little triumvirate which considered most matters of taste as their special province; in this they were joined by the Duchess, who was looked up to as an arbitress in such matters.[†]

[*] Collins's Peerage.
[†] Register of Westminster Abbey.
[‡] Hall's Collec. of Letters, 1, 186.
[§] Corresp. of the Seymours, MS.
[‖] Shenstone's Works, 3, 262; Select Letters, 1, 186.

In some of the stanzas of the "Rural Elegiacs," addressed by Shenstone to the Duchess, her taste and virtue are highly extolled, as indeed they were by others amongst the most eminent writers of the day. It seems that she desired to see the poem, and Lady Luxborough undertook to convey it to her, with a flattering letter from the poet. From some unaccountable delay, the Duchess did not receive it till long afterwards. She then wrote to Mr. Shenstone, acknowledging that she was much flattered, indeed, she said, a great deal too much; but she expressed a wish to decline being named in the printed copy. Mr. Shenstone seems, however, to have misunderstood her letter and to have supposed that she wished the ode altogether suppressed. This the Duchess, in a letter to Lady Luxborough, strongly deprecated, saying that her only wish had been to decline celebrity for herself.*

[Dict. Nat. Biog.; Corresp. of the Seymours, MS. at Stover; Hall's Select Letters; Shenstone's Works; Collins's Peerage; G. E. C[ockayne's] Peerage; Butler's Collections; Marlborough Despatches, ed. Murray; Craik's Romance of the Peerage, &c.]

* Corresp. of the Seymours; Hall's Select Letters, 1, 179, 184.

For want of male issue the Dukedom of Somerset and Barony of Seymour now devolved upon Sir Edward Seymour, bart., the seventh in lineal descent from Edward, first Duke of Somerset, by his first wife, Catharine Fillol. We must, therefore, retrace our steps and, commencing with the Protector Somerset's sons by his first wife, trace the progeny of the elder branch down to the present time, when they have at last regained, by inheritance according to the Act of 1540, the honours that should have been theirs in the first instance.

SIR JOHN SEYMOUR.

John Seymour was the Duke of Somerset's eldest son by his first marriage, and appears to have been looked upon with some dislike by his father, for he was specially cut out, by the Act of 1540, from any prospect of inheriting either his father's honours or estates, which were strictly limited upon the younger branch and, failing them, upon his younger brother. He was thus absolutely disinherited.

During the period of his father's first imprisonment he was returned member of Parliament for Reading, but he never sat in that Parliament, for Warwick and the Council were too nervous to bear the thought of a Seymour being in the House of Commons at a period so critical to their designs, and so sent a peremptory order to the Sheriff for the election of some one else.*

Up to that time he had led a very retired life, taking no part in either the military, political, or Court affairs of the period. We find him, however, on one occasion deputed to escort the Princess Elizabeth to Hatfield and see her safely lodged there, no very enviable task, especially as his uncle, the Admiral, then at the zenith of his power, charged him with some very coarse messages to the Princess, which he does not appear to have delivered.†

At the time of his father's second arrest, Sir John Seymour was amongst those who were imprisoned in the Tower (October 16, 1551), where his name, " IHON SEYMOUR," till recently remained inscribed in large

* Pollard, England under Protector Somerset, p. 276.
† Haynes, State Papers, Edward VI.

letters on the wall of the Beauchamp or Cobham tower in the Tower of London.*

After his father's death he petitioned Parliament for his restoration to the lands that had belonged to his mother. (Note 84.) The Parliament, however, confirmed the Act of 1540, but (as the late Duke appeared to have sold much of the property that had come to him by his two wives) it ordered that full compensation should be made to their respective children out of the lands that still remained. This Act proceeded to settle all the Duke's property, most of which was to go to the King, and to deprive the children of all their titles, honours, dignities, and pre-eminences. It also confirmed the attainders against the Duke and those who had suffered with him.†

The Marquis of Winchester, who was Master of the Wards and Liveries, was appointed to apportion the lands that were left amongst the Duke's children. He began by ascertaining the names and• values of such estates (formerly the patrimony of Catharine Fillol) as had previously been sold. As a compensation for these he awarded (by a formal limitation) the manor of Maiden Bradley to Sir John Seymour, excepting all the lands in Yarnfield and in Baycliff, and, as this manor was deemed to be of more value than the properties in lieu of which it was given, the estimated difference was annually appointed to be paid to the Duke's children, by his second marriage, to whom it was secured and entailed with great care and nicety.‡

Sir John Seymour was thus reinstated to a part of his father's former possessions. He did not, however, live to enjoy them, and appears to have remained a prisoner in the Tower and to have been ill for some considerable time before his death, which occurred December 19,

---

* Bailey's Tower of London, p. 166.

† Act 5th, 26 Edward VI, for limitation of the Duke of Somerset's estates, 23-53.

‡ Limitation of the Manor of Maiden Bradley to Sir John Seymour.—Papers, 11th Duke of Somerset.

1552.* So little is known of his life that we have no direct information respecting his character, but the very absence of notoriety, together with the readiness which the King and Parliament, as well as his own relatives, showed in restoring him to wealth and dignity, shows that his former treatment must have been unjust and his father's dislike ill-founded.   His will, which consists of but eleven lines, written with his own hand and during his illness, evinces benevolence, gratitude, and a great regard for his younger brother, notwithstanding that the latter had always been preferred before him, a fact that would have led to the greatest bitterness between most brothers.†

His first two bequests were to two women as a reward for their patience in nursing him, then followed some small legacies to his servants or followers, after which he left the leases of Bridgenorth, Chorley, and Hovington to one Richard Whiting.   Finally he made his brother, Sir Edward Seymour the elder, his full executor and residuary legatee.†

He was buried the 19th of December at the hospital of Savoy,* apparently with some pomp.

[Pollard, England under Protector Somerset, p. 276; Bailey's Tower of London, p. 166; Machyn's Diary; Haynes, State Papers, Edward VI; Sir John Hayward's Life and Reign of King Edward VI, in Kennet, vol. ii, p. 321 ; Papers of Seymour family, coll. by 11th Duke of Somerset.]

---

* Machyn's Diary, pp. 10, 27, 326.
† Papers, 11th Duke of Somerset.

SIR EDWARD SEYMOUR.

Edward Seymour was born about the year 1529.[*] He
was the second son of the Protector Somerset, by
1529. his first wife, and appears to have been looked
upon with greater favour than his elder brother
John for, though he was cut off from the succession by
his father, in the Act of 1540, yet it was arranged by that
Act that the honours of the Duke might revert to him in
case of the failure of the younger branch.

At the age of 18, his education having been completed,
he accompanied his father during the latter's last
1547. expedition into Scotland, and greatly distinguished
himself at the battle of Musselburgh, where he
took part in the mistaken charge of Lord Grey's horse,
after the repulse of which, though badly wounded, he
was of the greatest assistance in rallying the scattered
cavalry and leading them back to a second and more
successful attack.   As a reward for his services during the
campaign, he received the honour of knighthood at the
hands of the Protector.[†]

During the next few years he seems to have been in
almost constant attendance on his father and, when the
latter was at Hampton Court with the King and was
endeavouring to raise a force to protect the King's
1550. person from the Council, he was chosen as bearer
of the letters sent to the Lords Russell and
Herbert, who were returning from the west with an army,
to entreat their assistance.[*]   Soon after he was sent to
the Tower with his father, but was released with the

[*] Dict. Nat. Biog.
[†] Jekyl's Cat. of Knights, MS. ; Froude.

latter after some weeks' confinement. The next
1551. year, however, saw them both in the Tower again.
This time they were not so fortunate as before.
1552. The Duke only left his prison for the scaffold, in
January, and Sir Edward appears to have remained a prisoner till the summer.

The following year he succeeded to the Maiden Bradley
and other estates left him by his brother, whose
1553. full executor he was made by a will dated December 7, 6th Edward VI, the probate of which bears
date April 26, 1553.* What he received from his brother
did not, however, constitute all his possessions, for he
had previously been granted the reversion of a large
house and estate in Somersetshire, the latter comprising
a deer park and considerable other lands, which had
formerly belonged to his father, and had since been
granted to Humphrey Colles, Esq., by the King, for a
term of 21 years. On February 20 of this year, Sir
Edward granted a further term of 15 years to this same
gentleman.†

The Act of Attainder which had been passed was
chiefly directed against the Duke and his heirs by his
second wife, so that it did not strictly affect Sir Edward.
But to set at rest all doubt upon the subject an Act was
now passed, March 27, for his restitution in blood and
for settling upon him the manor of Maiden Bradley and
the surrounding property left him by his brother. This
Act did not, however, restore to him any other possessions of his father's but, on the contrary, expressly reserved
the whole of them to the King.‡

Sir Edward appears to have been looked upon with
considerable favour by the King, for, in the early part of
the summer, the latter granted to him the manor of

---

* Collins's Peerage.
† A lease to Humphrey Colles.—Papers, 11th Duke of Somerset;
Blackstone, 2, 38.
‡ Act for the restitution in blood of Sir E. Seymour.—Journ.
House of Commons, 1, 26; Journ. House of Lords, 1, 440.

S

Banwell, in Somerset, and entered into an arrangement which secured to him some other large properties. This transaction was very complicated and was not finally completed till the year 1558. It appears that on April 16, 1553, Sir John Thynne sold to Sir Edward Seymour the manor of Sevenhampton (also called Sevyngton), his mills and lands in Kingswood, his lands in Mere, his lands in Henbury Saltmarsh, in Gloucester, his lands at Cirencester, his lands at Berkeley known as Okeley Park, and various other estates. On June 1, Sir Edward gave all this property to the King in exchange for the castle of Berry Pomeroy, the manors of Berry and Bridgetown Pomeroy, the advowson of the vicarage of Berry, the manor of Middleton (or Milton), and part of the possessions of the late Priory at Taunton. (Note 85.) This was confirmed by letters patent on June 10. Almost immediately afterwards Sir Edward disposed of a great portion of these properties in various ways.* On September 6 of the same year he received a grant from the King, at Ely, of the lordships and manors of Walton, Shedder, and Stowey, the park of Stowey, and the hundred of Water-stock, with their appurtenances, in the county of Somerset, to him and his heirs for ever. These properties had been amongst those confiscated at his father's attainder.†

The great changes that were made in the management of religious affairs, on the accession of Queen Mary, compelled the Seymours to retire into private life, and, during the whole of this reign, Sir Edward devoted himself to his private affairs. (Note 86.) Although the manner in which many belonging to his religion were now persecuted must have been very painful to him, he does not seem to have taken part in any of the rebellions that were planned at that time, although a certain amount of suspicion appears to have rested upon him, for, on the

---

* Papers, 11th Duke of Somerset ; Risdon's Survey of Devon, 177.

† Strype's Memorials, 11, 502.

occasion of Queen Elizabeth's coronation, we find his name mentioned, amongst others, of those who received a full pardon for what they had done.*

The accession of Elizabeth does not appear to have been of any benefit to him beyond assuring him peace in 1558. the exercise of the Protestant religion ; indeed, the only transaction of any kind he appears to have had with the Queen was in 1560, when she borrowed £100 from him, which was to be repaid before Xmas. 1563. In return she gave him a promissory note which has not yet been redeemed.

In 1562, he married Jane, daughter of John Walsh, Esq., Serjeant-at-Law, and afterwards one of the Justices 1562. of the Common Pleas, who gave him the lease of the rectory of Berry Pomeroy. This had formerly belonged to the Monastery of Merton, so celebrated for its statutes, but had been let for a term of 41 years in the reign of Henry VIII, and, after passing through several hands, had eventually come into the hands of Walsh.†

On May 26, 1565, Sir Edward obtained exemplifications of the two Acts which had been passed 1565. for the restitution in blood of himself and his half-brother of the same name, now Earl of Hertford. By virtue of these Acts that nobleman might eventually have become the heir-at-law to Sir Edward, so they were to him the most interesting documents.‡

In 1583, Sir Edward was appointed Sheriff for the county of Devon,§ and appears to have held several 1583. other offices in that county, such as Deputy Lieutenant and Justice of the Peace. He appears to have been diligent in the execution of his duties in the county and to have been accurate and diligent in making the returns required from time to time by the Council. From those that remain we find that, although

* Rymer's Foedera, 15, 544, 558.
† Papers coll. by 11th Duke of Somerset.
‡ Exemplification of Acts.
§ Collins's Peerage.

cut off from any of his father's honours, and by law but a simple knight, he was almost invariably styled Lord Edward Seymour, even in State documents.* This seems to show that his position evoked considerable sympathy, which was shown in thus addressing him by a higher title than he was legally entitled to.

During the year 1584, we find an interesting return made by him and Sir John Gilberte, of all the 1584. demi-lances and light horse in four of the hundreds of Devon (September 30), and an Instrument of Association for Devon, signed and sealed by him, together with Sir John Gilberte, Sir Francis Drake, and many others.† (October.)

On the approach of the Spanish Armada, Sir Edward was placed in command of a body of troops in 1588. Devon, but when the alarm of an invasion was over these were disbanded. On August 26, 1589. 1589, we find a curious letter from Gilberte and Cary, to the Council, in which they acknowledge the receipt of their order for safely bestowing the prisoners from a Spanish ship, brought in to Dartmouth, and for making an inventory of the ordnance, munition, &c., contained therein. They add that they had found 85 pipes of wine on board, but in such bad condition that they could make but 67 full pipes of the best of it, and with that the wines were indifferent and sour. They had ventured, they said, presuming on the Council's approval, to bestow one of these pipes on Lord Edward Seymour, as a slight return for his having been kind enough to cumber his house at Berry Pomeroy with all their Spanish prisoners until the ship was cleared, and that, but for him, they would not have known where to bestow them.† We may hope that either their verdict on the wine was wrong or that Sir Edward was not troubled with too delicate a palate, so that he may have appreciated this handsome reward.

* State Papers, Domestic, Elizabeth.
† Laughton.

From this time on Sir Edward continued to reside at Berry Pomeroy, and to spend both his time and his energy in improving both that and the Maiden Bradley estate. He lived to a good old age, dying 1593. on May 6, 1593.* (Note 87.) He was buried at Berry Pomeroy.

From the period in which he lived, an age of the greatest activity and enterprise, and distinguished as he was by extraordinary talents, he might have been expected to have become one of the most conspicuous of his family. But its peculiar circumstances were discouraging, and, though in early days he had acquired some military fame, the storm that ruined so many of his connections strongly inculcated a lesson which he was too prudent to forget. Accordingly, after the fall of his father, he retired altogether into private life, became immersed in business, and devoted himself to the aggrandisement of his family, which he purposed chiefly to effect by the increase of his property, over which he spared neither trouble nor money. In this pursuit he was greatly assisted by his father-in-law, Mr. Walsh, but his success must also be attributed to his own extraordinary diligence and sagacity.

By his wife, Jane, he only had issue of one son—

Edward Seymour, of whom we will speak next.

[Papers of Seymour family, coll. by 11th Duke of Somerset; Dict. Nat. Biog.; Froude's Hist.; Rymer's Foedera; Blackstone; Risdon's Survey of Devon; Acts of Edward VI; State Papers, Domestic, Elizabeth; Journals, House of Lords; Journals, House of Commons; Collins's Peerage; Laughton; Strype's Memorials; Jekyl's MS. Catalogue of Knights, &c.]

---

* Collins's Peerage.

SIR EDWARD SEYMOUR, 1st BARONET.

Edward Seymour was born in 1562–3, and when but two or three years of age was betrothed by his father 1563. to Elizabeth, the daughter of Sir Arthur Champernowne, a near neighbour and an intimate friend 1566. of his.* This family of Champernowne resided at what was then a magnificent old place, called Dartington Hall, situated but a few miles from Berry Pomeroy, and were of great antiquity as well as celebrated both in English and French history for their former chivalrous achievements.†

The actual marriage between these children took place ten years afterwards.* Although this may appear 1576. now to have been a ridiculously early age, there was, in those days, a strong reason for marrying children very young ; for, in the case of the father's decease, it was the custom for the lord or guardian to have the right of marrying his ward to whomsoever he chose, which frequently resulted in the ward being sold to the highest bidder, and many guardians cared little to whom they sold a child so long as the transaction was profitable to themselves. Once a child had been married, however, it no longer ran this risk, and thus parents arranged marriages for their children, even when in the cradle, so as to insure their safety in case of their own death.‡

On June 19, 1583, though but just 20 years of age, Edward Seymour was appointed as Deputy Vice-1583. Admiral for the county of Devon by Mr. Hill, the then Vice-Admiral, who had been appointed to that

* Seymour Papers, 11th Duke of Somerset ; Collins's Peerage.
† Intro. to Risdon's Survey of Devon, 18 ; Life of Sir W. Raleigh, 1, 11.
‡ Blackstone's Commentaries, 2, 71 ; Aikin's Memoirs of Elizabeth, 2, 28.

post by the Earl of Lincoln, High Admiral of England.*
About the same time he was also made Sheriff of Devon,†
and February 9, 1586, we find a letter from him to the
Council, from which it appears that he had then been
made Vice-Admiral of Cornwall.‡

On the death of his father, in 1593, he succeeded to all
1593.　his estates which, through the latter's care and
good management, had become considerable.
(Note 88.) He now began to engage himself
very much in the affairs of the county, in doing which he
was careful to act always under the directions of Lord
Bath, the Lord Lieutenant of Devon, and a great friend
of the Seymour family. On August 27 of this year,
Mr. Seymour and Mr. Carey received copies of the Privy
Council's letters from Lord Bath, in which it was ordered
that they were henceforth to be specially employed in
Her Majesty's service on the coast of Devon. They
were to confer together, at the earliest opportunity, as to
the best means of appointing and disposing the bands
and companies of trained and untrained men in their command, and to make a return specifying the results of the
distribution of their forces, which was, however, left
almost entirely to their own discretion.§

On October 28 of the following year, Mr. Seymour
1594.　received a special licence, under the Great Seal,
enabling him to enter upon all his father's lands.
(Note 88A.)

In 1595 he was again nominated Sheriff of Devon,‖
1595.　and was joined with Mr. George Carey in a commission to take up, for the use of the royal
household, certain provisions in the county of
Devon. They were ordered to take these things at an

* Mr. Hill's commission and indenture between him and Mr.
Seymour.
† List of Sheriffs in Risdon's Survey of Devon.
‡ State Papers, Domestic, Elizabeth.
§ Letters from Lord Bath to Mr. Seymour.—Family Corre-
spondence.
‖ Collections for Devon, 101.

appraised value in preference to all others, an exercise of the prerogative of purveyance, which existed at that time and indeed long afterwards. (Note 89.)

During this year another attempt at invasion was made by the Spaniards and one of their fleets burnt off Penzance.[*] The Lord Lieutenant being absent, the Council sent their instructions for the defence of the coast direct to the Deputy Lieutenants and, in another letter, gave directions that Mr. George Carey, of Cockington, near Torquay, should have the command of all the bands near his house, for the defence of Torbay, and that Sir John Gilberte should command such as were near his dwelling at Greenland. Upon the latter's excusing himself, however, on the plea of indisposition, the command was given to Mr. Seymour on August 18. As a result of this, Seymour received a commission as Colonel from the Lord Lieutenant on September 5.[†]

Colonel Seymour's regiment consisted of 1,600 able men, but of these only 916 appear to have been furnished with arms of any kind. (Note 90.) The office of a Colonel was then, however, very different to what it is now, as it carried with it a command over a certain district. Colonel Seymour's jurisdiction extended over eight hundreds of the south division of the county and reached from Dartmouth to Plymouth.[‡]

In October, Colonel Seymour received permission from the Council, together with Gilberte and Carey, to requisition all arms that they could find in the possession of ecclesiastical persons. As the clergy, for the most part, had always good stores of weapons secreted in their houses, Seymour and the others were, by this means, soon able to arm the greater part of their men.[§]

---

[*] Lives of the Admirals, 1, 457.
[†] Letters from the Lords of the Council to the Deputy Lieutenants.—Seymour Papers, coll. by 11th Duke of Somerset.
[‡] Letters from the Council, Lord Bath, and others.—Seymour Papers.
[§] Privy Council to Lord Bath.—Seymour Papers.

In June, 1596, a disagreement arose between Colonel
1596. Seymour and Mr. Arthur Champernowne, whom
he had appointed as Captain in his regiment on
October 27, of the previous year, on account of
the latter's having written direct to the Council, complaining that his band of 200 men was not complete,
several of them having been taken away to be trained,
and asking their permission to replenish it by taking
men from other places in the district commanded by
Seymour, whose permission he had never sought, and to
whom he had not reported his deficiency of men. At the
same time, when ordered to muster and train his band
and parade them by fifties before Sir Ferdinando Gorges,
commanding at Plymouth, he had purposely mustered
several companies of untrained recruits, belonging to
Colonel Seymour's force, who were naturally reported
upon by Sir Ferdinando as ill-appointed and undisciplined.
The Colonel, as may be imagined, was highly displeased
at this attempt to make him appear negligent in his
command, but, after some words had passed, the matter
blew over for a time.*

On the 31st of October, Seymour was appointed a
Deputy Lieutenant for the county of Devon by the Privy
Council, on the recommendation of Lord Bath.†

During the whole of this year he was busily engaged,
first in levying troops for service in Ireland, which
1598. were not, however, required in the end; and,
secondly, in carrying out the orders and disposi-
tions of the Council for the safety of the county of Devon
in case of another Spanish invasion, which they had
reason to expect.‡ (Appendix I.) Throughout this he was
constantly hindered by Champernowne, who appears to
have been jealous of the superior command entrusted to
Seymour, and to have done all he could to persuade the

---

* Letters of Col. Seymour, Sir F. Gorges, and Lord Bath.—
Seymour Papers.
† Letter from Lord Bath to the Lord Keeper.—Seymour Papers.
‡ Letters from the Council to Lord Bath.—Seymour Papers.

Council to give him an equal power or else to let him supplant his superior officer. Champernowne, it appears, could never be got to carry out diligently and punctually the orders he received, and, in consequence, became most unpopular with the other officers as well as with the men. In the end his behaviour became so bad that he was severely reprimanded by the Lord Lieutenant, who threatened to deprive him of his command, and appears not long after to have been obliged to actually carry out his threat.* (Appendix J.)

The fears of a Spanish invasion were now subsiding, and the Council deemed it no longer necessary 1599. to keep up the expense of a large armed force.

The regiments that had been specially raised for the emergency were therefore gradually disbanded, amongst them being Colonel Seymour's. The latter continued, however, to reside at Berry Pomeroy and to busy himself with the affairs of the county.

On the accession of King James in this year, Colonel Seymour received a pardon from that monarch 1603. (November 1), but for what offence, if any, we are unable to discover. That it did not put him out of favour is shown by his receiving a licence, on November 22, to hold a cattle market at Bridgetown on every Thursday, and to have an annual fair there on the 28th of April in each year.† He was also chosen to serve in Parliament as knight of the shire for the county of Devon,‡ and appointed sheriff for the same, in which capacity he was very nearly getting into trouble through the misconduct of one, Lawrence, who he had appointed as his deputy.§

1611. King James was now proposing to raise money by the creation of Baronets, each of whom was to

* Letters of Col. Seymour, Lord Bath, A. Champernowne, and the Council.—Seymour Papers.
† Blackstone's Commentaries, 3, p. 32.
‡ Collins's Peerage.
§ Collections for Devon, 101 ; Seymour Correspondence, MS.

pay a large sum for the honour, but in an indirect manner. Every gentleman who had maintained a certain number of foot soldiers for service in Ireland, or was prepared to put down a sum of money as an equivalent, was to receive the honour. Amongst others it was conferred on Seymour. According to the patent of creation he was supposed to have maintained 30 men, at his own expense, for the service in Ireland. Whether he really did so or not, is not clear, but there is no doubt that shortly after he had to pay the sum of £1,095, presumably as a composition in lieu of service; that sum being reckoned the equivalent to the maintenance of 30 men for three years.[*] The whole transaction is somewhat obscure, unless we are to think that he was not aware that he was afterwards to purchase the honour he received, for he makes no mention of money, but, writing to Salisbury, from Lupton, on the 12th of June, thanks that nobleman for deeming him worthy to be recommended for advancement into the order of Baronets, and requests that he may have a grant of the wardship of his son-in-law, Mr. Parker; and, writing again on the 21st, thanks his lordship for being created a baronet and for the grant of the wardship of Mr. Parker, which had now come to him through the death of the latter's grandfather.[†] The patent of creation is dated the 29th, and it seems possible that the wording of it may have been the first intimation he received that he was expected to pay for his new dignity.

Sir Edward Seymour was always on a very friendly footing with Lord Burleigh and Sir Robert Cecil, and doubtless owed much of his employment during Elizabeth's reign to the good offices of these ministers, as well as to the assistance of Lord Bath. He appears to have been a very careful and diligent officer and justice, and was at one time particularly complimented by the Lord Lieutenant upon his accounts and his care of such public

[*] Papers, 11th Duke of Somerset.
[†] State Papers, Domestic, James I.

papers as came into his hands, and the copies he took of those he wrote, tend to confirm this account of him.[*] From the time of his death to the commencement of the Civil War, we scarcely find a letter or paper of any consequence, relating to public affairs, in the possession of the family. They seemed to have turned their attention chiefly to their private affairs.

Sir Edward died April 11, 1613, and was buried, with great solemnity, in the church at Berry Pomeroy 1613. on May 27, when a funeral sermon, full of his praises, was preached by Barnaby Potter, afterwards Bishop of Carlisle. This oration was printed at Oxford during the same year, and an abstract of it appeared later, in 1741, in " Memorials and Characters, together with the lives of divers eminent and worthy persons."[†]   (Fol. 485.) *Elizabeth*

By his wife ~~Jane~~ *Elizabeth*, daughter of Sir Arthur Champernowne, he left five sons and four daughters :—

Sir Edward Seymour, who succeeded him, and of whom we must speak later.

John Seymour, who married a sister of Sir Richard Slanning.   (Appendix K.)

William and Walter Seymour, who died unmarried.

Richard Seymour, who married a daughter of . . . . ~~k~~ Ashley, and had one son, ~~who died unmarried~~.

Bridget Seymour, who married John Bruen, Esq., of Admerston, in Wilts.

Mary Seymour, who married Sir George Farewell, knight, of Hill Bishop, in Somerset.

Elizabeth Seymour, who married George Cary, Esq., of Cockington, Devon.

Amy Seymour, who married Edmund Parker, Esq., of Borrington, in Devon, from whom are descended the Lords Borrington, afterwards created Earls of Morley.

[*] Letters from Lord Bath.—Seymour Papers.
[†] Collins's Peerage.

SIR EDWARD SEYMOUR'S MONUMENT AT BERRY POMEROY CHURCH.

[Seymour Correspondence and Papers, coll. by 11th Duke of Somerset; State Papers, Domestic, Elizabeth; State Papers, Domestic, James I; Risdon's Survey of Devon; Life of Sir Walter Raleigh; Aikin's Memoirs of Elizabeth; Blackstone's Commentaries; Collections for Devon; Lives of the Admirals; Collins's Peerage; G. E. C[ockayne's] Peerage; Edmundson's Peerage; Prince's Worthies of Devon.]

SIR EDWARD SEYMOUR, 2ND BARONET.

Edward Seymour was born about the year 1585, but
no mention is anywhere made of his early years, so
1585.   we can only presume that they were passed at
some college or else in attendance on his father ;
but, although no particulars are to be found as to his
education and his earlier years, he appears to have shown
marks of promise, for we find that, on James's accession
to the throne of England, he received the honour
1603.   of knighthood at the hands of that King, at
Greenwich, on May 22, although he was but
18 years of age.*

In April, 1613, he succeeded to all the possessions of
his father, and, in December of the same year, he
1613.   was appointed Governor of Dartmouth, which was
then a very important place.†   He does not
appear, however, to have taken any leading part in the
public affairs of the time, preferring a peaceful and quiet
country life to the arduousness and danger of a more
distinguished public career.

He did not, however, avoid such public duties as he
was able to attend to in the county of Devon,
1617.   where he resided at the family seat of Berry
Pomeroy.   On March 5, 1617, he was appointed
a Deputy Lieutenant of the county of Devon by Lord
Bath,‡ and, in February, 1620, he was given the
1620.   command of a regiment raised in South Devon,
with power to appoint or nominate his own officers.
We find a Mr. Tremayne and a Mr. Glanville appointed

* Collins's Peerage.
† Seymour Papers.
‡ Lord Bath's commission to Sir E. Seymour.—Seymour Papers.

captains by his order about this time. He kept a portion of this regiment at Tavistock, while the remainder he quartered at Totnes, close to his own home.*

In this year he appears to have been employed in some way as an officer of the Admiralty, with certain powers on the Devonshire coast, for we find a petition, apparently presented in May, by Robert Dure to the Council, on behalf of certain merchants of St. Malo, in France, which states that a ship of theirs had been taken and brought into Plymouth by a Rochelle pinnace, and that the officers of the Admiralty refused to take it in charge, but aided and abetted their captors in embezzling and selling the goods therein, maltreating the master and mariners, and had finally sold the vessel for a very small sum. The petition requested that Sir Edward Seymour, James Bagg, and Thomas Harding, the Admiralty officers, should be called before the Council to answer for their conduct.† Whether this accusation was untrue, or whether these officers were acting under orders from the Admiralty, does not appear, but certain it is that no notice was taken of the complaint.

1622.

On the accession of Charles I, Sir Edward served in Parliament as member for Hillington, and afterwards, on two other occasions, as member for Totnes.‡

1625.

About this time he appears to have entered into some speculations on his own account, keeping one or more ships, perhaps for trading, but more likely for privateering, for, on April 28, 1626, we find a letter from the Mayor of Dartmouth to the Council which states that a warlike ship, belonging to Sir Edward Seymour, had come into Dartmouth with an Irish barque, going from Newhaven to Dundalk, and that, in searching the prize, a priest from Douay was discovered.†

1626.

In May of the same year we find Sir John Eliot com-

* Seymour Papers.
† State Papers, Domestic, James I.
‡ Collins's Peerage, Parliamentary summons.

plaining to the Council that, as Vice-Admiral of the
county, he was entitled to a-half of the value of all ships
captured within his district, but that, a ship called the
" Joshua " having been taken, the reward, amounting to
£1,000, had been given to Sir Edward Seymour by the
Duke of Buckingham.* It seems probable that it was
one of Sir Edward's own ships that had made the capture,
for he seems to have begun to enter more boldly into the
privateering business, and, according to a letter from Sir
John Drake to Nicholas, dated December 4, he seems to
have made a valuable capture of a richly laden French ship
                which he brought into Plymouth about that time.*
1627. In an Order of Council, made June 29, 1627,
                mention is even made of one of his ships, the
" Reformation of Dartmouth," which is stated to have
been a man-of-war.

The following year he endeavoured to obtain the
appointment of Vice-Admiral of Devon, and wrote to
Nicholas upon the subject, saying that both Sir James
Bagg and Sir John Drake were weary of the work, but
that he himself would be most thankful for the appointment, "a thankful debtor " he calls it, and that if the
tenths might be got with it, he would add a brace or
leash of hundred pounds.* In spite of this offer he did
not then get the coveted appointment, but continued to
act in his capacity as an officer of the Admiralty, part of
the duties of which, as we see by a letter from the King
                to him and his fellow-officers, was to appraise ships
1631. and cargoes found derelict upon the high seas or
                brought in as prizes into port.†

During all this time Sir Edward continued to be diligent in the exercise of his duties as a justice and deputy
lieutenant, but the Admiralty business appears to have
                been the most congenial to his mind and to have
1633. received the greater part of his attention. On
                July 31, 1633, he received an order from the Lords

* State Papers, Domestic, Charles I.
† Letter from the King, June 23.—State Papers, Domestic.

of the Admiralty, from Whitehall, to "romage" and search His Majesty's "pink," the Great Seahorse, which had set out for the South, but had returned to Plymouth, and which was in command of Captain Quaile, and to examine the commander and the ship's company as to what gold, jewels, pinks, ships, or merchandize, had been taken by them, and report the same.* It is curious to note that this is the first document among the State papers in which the Seymour name is spelt in the old way. The letter is addressed to Lord Edward St. Maur.

About this time Sir Edward received the appointment of Vice-Admiral for the county of Devon, which 1636. he had always been so desirous of receiving, and appears to have exercised the duties of that position with great diligence.* His private affairs had all along engaged a great portion of his attention, and he had so prospered in his management that he was able to enlarge and beautify his castle of Berry Pomeroy, where he constantly resided, and upon which he is stated to have spent upwards of £20,000,† an expenditure which can readily be conceived if we read the description of that place as it then was, or even by an examination of the ruins as they appear to-day. (Note 91.)

The disputes between the King and the Parliament were now growing more and more dangerous, and it became plain that a civil war could not long be delayed. Like the rest of the Seymours, Sir Edward threw in his lot with his Sovereign, though his advancing age and ill-health made it impossible for him to become of any real service in the field. He made an attempt, how-1642. ever, to join the King's forces for, when, in 1642, the people of Devon were summoned to assemble at Modbury by the High Sheriff, in the King's name, he insisted upon accompanying his son to that place with a few men the latter had hastily raised. His effort did not

* State Papers, Domestic, Charles I.
† Risdon, p. 203; Prince, Danmonii Orientales Illustres, p. 492.

T

meet with the success it deserved for, on the march thither, the party was set upon and captured by a body of Parliamentary horse, and Sir Edward was sent a prisoner to London.*

His imprisonment was not, however, of long duration, for, after the lapse of a few weeks, he was exchanged and, upon his release, retired to Berry Pomeroy. There he found that his goods had been seized by a party of horse, in spite of the resistance made by his bailiff and retainers, and sold for the sum of £89 12s. 6d.†

Realising that his age and health would not permit him to take any active part in the military proceedings in the West, he continued to reside at Berry Pomeroy, leaving his son to take his place in the field. This did not, however, secure him from further molestation at 1647. the hands of the Parliament who, July 18, 1647, sequestered the whole of his Devonshire estates (the Wiltshire ones he had made over to his son some years before), urging as an excuse for this proceeding his old offence of having started for Modbury, in obedience to the King's summons.† The sequestration does not appear to have been properly carried out, although his rents were received by the Parliament, for he continued to reside at 1659. Berry Pomeroy, where he died, October 5, 1659, "very much lamented, having, by an obliging temper, attracted the love of his country; and, by a prudent management, gained the character of a person of honour, conduct, and experience." He was buried at Berry Pomeroy.‡

By his wife Dorothy, daughter of Sir Henry Killegrew, knight, of Laroch (or Lathbury) in Cornwall, he had six sons and five daughters—

Sir Edward Seymour, bart., of whom we will speak later.

Henry Seymour, of whom we will speak next.

* Letters from the Commissioners for Sequestration.
† Seymour Papers, 11th Duke of Somerset.
‡ Collins's Peerage.

BERRY POMEROY CASTLE.

From an Old Print.

Sir Joseph Seymour, who married Bridget, daughter of — Anderson.

Thomas Seymour, who married Anne, daughter of Sir Richard Anderson, knight, of Penley, in Herts. In 1667 he was made Clerk of the Hanaper for life.*

Robert and John Seymour, both of whom died young. (Note 92.)

Elizabeth Seymour, who was twice married ; first to Sir William Courtenay, of Powderham Castle, in Devon ; secondly, to Sir Amos Meridith, bart., of Timberley Hall, in Cheshire.

Mary Seymour, who married Sir Jonathan Trelawney, bart., by whom she was mother to Sir J. Trelawney, bart., Bishop of Winchester.

Margaret Seymour, who married Francis Trelawney, brother to the above Sir Jonathan.

Anne Seymour, who married Dr. Stourton.

Catharine Seymour, who married Sir Thomas Hall, of Bradford, in Wilts.

[Letters and Papers of Seymour family, coll. by 11th Duke of Somerset ; Collins's Peerage ; G. E. C[ockayne's] Peerage ; Beatham's Genealogical Tables ; State Papers, Domestic, James I ; State Papers, Domestic, Charles I ; Risdon's Survey of Devon ; Prince's Danmonii Orientales Illustres ; Parliamentary Summons, &c.]

* Beatham's Genealogical Tables.

HENRY SEYMOUR.

Henry Seymour was born in the year 1612, and at an
early age was made a page of honour to Charles I.
1612. When but sixteen years old we find him serving
as captain in Sir Benjamin Tichborne's regiment,
1628. and, from a letter of Secretary Conway's, dated
August 18, he appears then to have been willing to
leave his company,* probably having some better or more
congenial appointment in view.   It appears, indeed, that
he must have returned to Court not long after, for,
1638. on March 23, 1636, he is expressly mentioned as
His Majesty's servant in a grant giving him the
office of Comptroller of the Customs, after the death of
John Holloway and Martin Hardrett, as assuring him the
same fees as these gentlemen had enjoyed.*

On the breaking out of the Civil War he was still in
attendance on the King, but being anxious to take an
active part in his master's cause, he was permitted to
accompany the Marquis of Hertford to his command in
the West and repaired with him to Wells, after-
1643. wards taking part in the retreat of the small Royalist
army to Sherborne Castle, where he was chosen as
the bearer of the Marquis's challenge to the Earl of Bedford.†   For some time after he continued to follow the
fortunes of Hertford's army but, as matters became more
hopeless, he left that force to attach himself to Prince
Charles, to whom he had been appointed Groom of the
Bedchamber.

* State Papers, Domestic, Charles I.
† Clarendon's Hist. of the Rebellion, vii, 185.

HENRY SEYMOUR.

From a picture at Knoyle, by kind permission of Mrs. Alfred Seymour.

In August, 1648, he was the bearer of a message from
Prince Charles to the Earl of Warwick, concerning
1648. the surrender of the fleet,* and in the beginning
of September he was captured and confined in the
prison of Peterhouse by the Parliament.† He did not,
however, remain there long, for he managed to effect his
escape† about the 15th of the same month, and
1649. returned to the Prince who, in the following year,
again sent him to England, charged with the last
message he was able to send the King, his father, before
the latter's execution.‡

In September of the same year he left Jersey, where he
was in attendance on Charles, and went to Ireland upon
some business of the King's.§ He returned in
1650. time, however, to accompany Charles to Scotland in
1650, but, on his arrival there, he was voted away
from the King because he made no scruple of speaking
against that part of the newly formulated declaration which
he considered to touch the honour of the late King.
He was examined upon several occasions by a committee
upon this matter, but insisted that he could not do otherwise after having been the bearer of a certain message from
the late King to the present one, just before his murder.‖
The first act of the Scots on Charles's entering their
country had been to vote away all his English followers,
with the exception of the Duke of Buckingham and Henry
Seymour, so it is evident that the only reason for his
afterwards being voted away by the Scots was that he
would not agree in full to their declaration.‖ After the
Scotch defeat at Dunbar, Henry Seymour was left at
Aberdeen.¶

As soon as he was able to get a ship, Seymour left

* Clarendon, xi, 69.
† State Papers, Domestic.
‡ Ludlaw's Memoirs, ed. Firth, 11, 286.
§ Gardiner's Commonwealth, 160, 207.
‖ State Papers, Domestic.
¶ Cal. Clarendon Papers, 11, 69, 77, 87.

Scotland and went to join Charles in Paris, where
1651. he resumed his attendance as Groom of the Bedchamber.* During the next few years he was
frequently employed in making secret journeys to England
to interview the King's friends, and on most of these occasions returned with sums of money subscribed by the
Royalists in England. He appears more than once to
have been the means whereby the Marquis of Hertford
sent over the £5,000 a year which he regularly gave
Charles and, on one occasion, brought £3,000 from that
nobleman to Paris, so that the King might have the means
of escape should the French, as seemed likely, decide to
give him up. His last journey was in January,
1654. 1654, when he collected £1,920 in England, with
which he returned to Paris. Almost immediately
afterwards he obtained a pass from Cromwell, on representing that he would be solely engaged in his private
affairs,† and returned to England, where he was soon after
arrested and committed to the Tower, June 17, on the
charge of high treason.‡

In April, 1656, he was released on bail in order that he
might recover his health, which had suffered from
1656. the confinement of his prison but, upon some
rumour of Royalist activity in the country, he was
summoned in September and again lodged in the Tower
on October 1, whence he addressed a petition,
1657. February 3, begging that he might again be
admitted to bail as he had committed no offence
and found his health was being ruined by restraint.‡
No immediate result followed this petition, but the following May he was released, upon his agreeing to certain
conditions, which appear to have been rather severe, even
for that time.§

Upon the Restoration he continued in his appointment

* Clarendon.
† Dict. Nat. Biog. ; Cal. Clarendon Papers.
‡ State Papers, Domestic.
§ Cal. Clarendon Papers, iii, 303.

of Groom of the Bedchamber, and was again made
1660. Comptroller of the Customs. Soon after he was
appointed Clerk of the Hanaper and returned to
Parliament as member for Eastloe, which he continued to
represent for the next 21 years.* On December 6, he
petitioned for a lease of Crown lands, partly for his
advancement in marriage and partly as a recompense for
his loss of land owing to his long service. This loss he
estimated at £500 a year. This petition was
1661. apparently favourably received, for, November 30
of the following year, he obtained a lease in reversion of certain lands and tenements belonging to the
Duchy of Cornwall, for his own life and that of Edward
Seymour, his nephew, and also received a pension of £500
a year on November 18.†

In February, 1663, he received a lease of Castle Hay
Park, in Staffordshire, and at various times re-
1663. ceived other smaller grants and leases. His
former services were indeed very highly rewarded
by the King, for the Duchy leases alone were computed
to be worth £40,000 during the time he had them.‡

During the first few years of the Restoration he ap-
1666. pears to have resided at Westminster, but, in 1666,
he removed to Langley, in Bucks, which he rented,
and which, three years afterwards, he purchased from the
trustees of Sir William Parsons. Here he erected
1669. and endowed some almshouses, after obtaining a
grant of the manor from the Crown.

Having reached the age of 57 he now retired from
public life and spent his few remaining years
1686. quietly at Langley, where he died on the 9th
March, 1686.

He had been twice married ; first to Elizabeth, daughter
of Sir Joseph Killegrew, and widow of William Basset,
of Claverton, which lady died in 1671 ; and secondly to

---

* Returns of Members of Parliament.|
† State Papers, Domestic, Charles II.
‡ Marvell.

Ursula, the widow of George Stawell, Esq., of Cotherston, in Kent, and daughter of Sir Robert Austen, of Bexley, in Kent. By his second wife he had one son—

> Sir Henry Seymour, of Langley, Bucks, who was born October 20, 1674, and who, at the age of seven (1681) was created a baronet by Charles II, in consideration of his father's approved loyalty and great services, and whilst he was still living. The limitation of the patent was to his heirs male, with remainder to his father and his heirs male. Sir Henry was returned as member of Parliament for Eastloe, in 1699, and served in six other Parliaments until the time of his death in 1714. He was buried at Langley. As he had died unmarried, his estate at Langley devolved upon Sir Edward Seymour, bart., grandfather to the 9th Duke of Somerset, who sold it to Lord Masham, who in turn sold it to the Duke of Marlborough.

[Letters and Papers relating to Seymour family, coll. by 11th Duke of Somerset; Dict. Nat. Biog.; State Papers, Domestic, Charles I; State Papers, Domestic; State Papers, Domestic, Charles II; Ludlow's Memoirs; Clarendon's Hist. of the Rebellion; Calendar Clarendon Papers; Hoskins's Charles II in the Channel Islands; Gardiner's Commonwealth; Andrew Marvell's Seasonable Arguments; Burke's Extinct Baronetage; Collins's Peerage; Ormonde Letters, &c.]

SIR EDWARD SEYMOUR, 3RD BARONET.

Edward Seymour was born in 1610, and as soon as he
had attained a reasonable age was returned to
1610. Parliament as knight of the shire for the county
of Devon, serving in the last two Parliaments of
1640. Charles I, the latter of which was summoned in
1640.*

Some time previous to this he had been given over the
Maiden Bradley and other Wiltshire property by his
father, who contented himself with the Devonshire estates ;
and December 3, 1639, we find him petitioning the King
to grant him and his heirs permission to hold a market on
every Friday at the town of Maiden Bradley, in lieu of
the market anciently held there on the Monday, and also
to hold a yearly fair there on St. Mark's Day, of which he
should receive the tolls and privileges. (Note 93.) He
further petitioned for a grant to confirm to him and his
heirs certain liberties, franchises, and privileges within the
manor and parish of Maiden Bradley, which had been held
hitherto by grants from former sovereigns and by several
charters under the Great Seal.†

In July, 1642, he received a commission as Colonel
from the King, and, on November 9, was em-
1642. powered to raise a regiment of 1,200 men. The
form of the commission is peculiar. The first
object proposed is to repel and subdue the traitorous
attempts of the Earl of Essex, the Lord Brooke, and
others. Then follows the preservation of peace, the
support of the laws, and of the Protestant religion.
Seymour was authorised to appoint officers to this regi-

* Parliamentary Summons.
† State Papers, Domestic, Charles I.

ment, in the absence of the Marquis of Hertford, commanding in the West, but otherwise was to be under that nobleman's orders. The soldiers were to be paid by the King.*

Soon after this, Sir Edmund Fortescue, High Sheriff of Devon, summoned the people to Modbury in the King's name, and Edward Seymour started for that place with his father. They were, however, taken prisoners on the way by some Parliament horse and sent to London. The father, as we have previously seen, was soon exchanged, and Edward Seymour also recovered his liberty after some weeks, either by escape or exchange. It is not certain which.

On April 16, 1643, Colonel Seymour received a second commission, this time from the Marquis of Hertford, authorising him to raise 1,500 foot, including officers, the appointment of the latter being again left to his discretion. This commission differed materially from the former one, for the objects now mentioned were the defence of the King's person, that of the two Houses of Parliament, the Protestant religion, the laws of the land, the liberty and property of the subject, and the privileges of Parliament.†

Having raised his regiment, Colonel Seymour appears to have operated in the north of Cornwall and South Devon for some months. The Parliamentary forces, somewhat further north, were at that time commanded by Lord Stamford, an old and intimate friend of Seymour's, and, though engaged on opposite sides, their correspondence always remained of an affectionate nature. On July 27, Stamford wrote asking for a partial exchange of prisoners, so that it appears that their operations were frequently directed against each other's forces.‡

1643.

* Col. Seymour's Commission; Clarendon's Hist., 2, 397, 1, 715; Betham.
† Col. Seymour's Com. from Lord Hertford.—Papers, 11th Duke of Somerset.
‡ Corresp. of the Seymours.—Papers, 11th Duke of Somerset.

On the 10th of September, Colonel Seymour received an order from Prince Maurice, now commanding in the West, to summon the town and castle of Dartmouth, and, Seymour's force not proving strong enough to storm the place, the Prince soon afterwards brought a portion of his army to its assistance and, after considerable difficulty, succeeded in capturing it. Colonel Seymour was then placed in command of the garrison as Governor of Dartmouth, his commission for which appointment had been signed by Hertford on August 12.[*] It contained the fullest powers, and authorised him to receive the contributions and imposts levied on behalf of the King.

Dartmouth appears, at this time, to have had a considerable trade, for, at the time of its capture, the harbour contained no less than 44 ships, of from 40 to 300 tons, and 32 barques.[†] In addition to these Seymour found a great quantity of ammunition in the town, together with over 50 cannon, 57 muskets, and 35 barrels of powder.[‡] A quantity more was seized on board a ship called the "Seraphine," which had been detained in harbour.

Upon his appointment to the command of the garrison, Colonel Seymour took up his residence at Dartmouth, and started to make regulations suitable to the times. Having received an order from the King for the legal adjudication of such prizes as might be brought in, he established a little Court of Admiralty to deal with such cases, and appointed Dr. Joseph Martin as judge. All ships found at sea without a proper warrant from the King's officers were adjudged lawful prizes, and all commanders of vessels were made, on entering Dartmouth, to deliver up all their arms and ammunition to the Governor (according to an old custom observed at that port), petitioning him for their restoration when they went to sea again.[§]

[*] Col. Seymour's Com.—Papers, 11th Duke of Somerset.
[†] A list of ships in Dartmouth Harbour.—Papers, 11th Duke of Somerset.
[‡] Clarendon's Hist., 2, 311.
[§] Corresp. and Seymour Papers of 11th Duke of Somerset.

During the ensuing winter Seymour repaired to the King at Oxford, returning through Exeter, and then journeyed into Cornwall, returning through Tavistock. The object of these journeys is not mentioned in any of his letters.

On January 10 he was authorised to erect a powder mill at Totnes, which was soon completed.* He 1644. had already a great magazine at Dartmouth, which the new powder mill was to keep supplied, but the demands upon his store were great, for he had to supply the Cornish army, as well as the forces and strongholds in his own neighbourhood, and, on August 3, he received a further order from the King to supply Sir John Berkeley, the Governor of Exeter, with all the powder and match he might require. He seems to have been a very able and diligent manager of these stores, and to have kept all receipts and delivery notes for the various kinds of arms and ammunition he supplied with the greatest care.† (Appendix L.)

In April the King's forces were besieging Plymouth and Sir Richard Grenville, who was in command, sent to Colonel Seymour asking for all the assistance the latter could spare from Dartmouth. Seymour sent him 300 men and such stores of arms and ammunition as he could, though not nearly as much as he would have desired to send or as were required. So numerous of late had been the applications from all quarters that even the large stores at Dartmouth had been unable to supply them all, and, as the stores in other places grew less, so did the demands upon Seymour become greater.‡

On March 21st, by an order from Bedford House, Seymour was authorised to appoint watches at the beacon fires, and to distribute horsemen and musketeers at convenient places along the coast between Teignmouth and

* Warrant for erecting powder mill.—Papers, 11th Duke of Somerset.
† MS. Warrant.—Papers, 11th Duke of Somerset.
‡ Corresp. of the Seymours, coll. by 11th Duke of Somerset.

Plymouth. He was also to call the inhabitants together and enlist them, if necessary, to raise fortifications, appoint officers, and provide arms and ammunition. Such was the general order, the details and carrying out of which was left entirely to his own discretion. Sir Edmund Fortescue and Colonel Henry Cary were associated with him in this matter, but each of them was to act independently of the others in his own particular district.*

On May the 7th Seymour was ordered to send his regiment to join Prince Maurice, and he elected to take the command himself, leaving his brother-in-law, Sir Amos Ameridath, as his deputy in command at Dartmouth. He joined Prince Maurice before Lyme, but appears to have returned to Dartmouth at the end of the month or the beginning of the next.*

Towards the latter end of June the King's party in the West found themselves hard pressed. Sir Amos Ameridath, who had returned to his command, wrote to Seymour in the most pressing manner for some more culverins for his fort, as he was apprehending an attack from the Earl of Essex, then at Crediton ; Prince Maurice, who was at Heavitree, about 2 miles from Exeter, wrote to inform him that Weymouth had been captured, and that he might shortly expect an attack on Dartmouth ; and Sir John Berkeley, Sir Peter Ball, and others, wrote in some alarm giving him the latest intelligence of the movements of the contending armies, by which it appeared the King had come to Chard, and exhorting him to see to the careful victualling of his garrison, and above all to secure all persons who refused the protestation. On this last point Seymour appears to have been very careful, perhaps more so than Sir John Berkeley and his friends really desired.*

The siege of Plymouth still continued, and again, July 19, Sir Richard Grenville wrote asking for reinforcements. Before these could be raised, however, the aspect of affairs was completely changed by the receipt of the news of the disaster at Marston Moor, which caused the

* Corresp. of the Seymours, coll. by 11th Duke of Somerset.

greatest alarm to the King's party in the West. Sir Francis
Fulford at once came to Seymour for protection (July 22);
Colonel Arundel wanted to bring his regiment to Dartmouth ; and Sir John Berkeley wrote for all the match
and oakum that could possibly be spared, for the defence
of Exeter, where he should have kept a supply.*

Colonel Seymour, however, was now himself in difficulties. Hitherto he had done his best to assist others
by meeting their demands, even at the risk of seriously
reducing the strength of his own garrison, to strengthen
which he had applied, some time before, to the King,
through Sir Edmund Fortescue, who was with him. That
knight had done his best to persuade Charles to send
some reinforcement to the West, and had used all the
interest he could command amongst friends at Court for
the same purpose, but hitherto without effect. He now
(August 23) wrote again to Seymour telling him not to
despair, as he felt confident he would soon succeed in
obtaining the necessary supplies.* Such a letter at this
time can but have been intended as friendly encouragement, for, had it been possible for him to obtain any supplies, they would have now been too late to be of any
great service.

Colonel Seymour remained at Dartmouth for some
time after this, and we find him mentioned in his capacity
as Governor of that place on October 26.* He appears,
however, to have been in Exeter, engaged on some other
duty, at the time of the surrender of Dartmouth.

As Colonel Seymour had all along stood forward as the
most conspicuous and active member of the elder branch
of the Seymours, it is not to be wondered that he should
be specially selected for punishment by the Parliament,
now that victory was theirs. His Maiden Bradley estate
and other properties in Wiltshire were now seized and
sequestered (October 27), and the rents owing at Michaelmas and still unpaid were also taken. These amounted
to £166 10s. 0d. The estate itself was let by Parlia-

* Corresp. of the Seymours, coll. by 11th Duke of Somerset.

1645. ment to one William Raddish, on March 24, 1645, at a yearly rental of £160. At the same time the Berry Pomeroy estate, which had been made over to him by his father, was also sequestered, but, no tenant being put in possession, his father continued to reside there. The rents and profits of this estate do not appear to have been actually taken by the officers of the Parliament, but remained in the hands of the tenants, so that the Seymours were left without any income from either property.*

This state of things, however, did not last long, for the Parliament proposed, on June 27, to compound with all delinquents, that is, with all those who had served their King, and appointed July 3 as the day on which the compositions were to take effect. A committee was appointed to settle these compositions, and, until the day of its meeting, the present tenants were not to be disturbed. With this committee Colonel Seymour was able to compound for his estate at Maiden Bradley for the sum of £1,200 ; but, as the place had already been let by the Parliament, he was unable to take possession until the new tenant could be got rid of.†

This, however, was but a minor consideration, as matters turned out, for the Parliament had by no means done with him yet. They now asserted that, as he had been absent on the King's business, in Exeter, at the time of the surrender of Dartmouth, although he was still Governor of that town, he was not entitled to any benefit under the articles of that surrender. He was in consequence kept a prisoner in Exeter for some years, being only occasionally let out on bail for short periods. This treatment he, not unnaturally, considered unjust, and he frequently petitioned that some end might be put to it.

1651. Writing from the Marshalsea, in Exeter, where he was confined, in 1651, he says :—"Truly I

* Papers, Seymour family, coll. by 11th Duke of Somerset.
† Order of the Committee for Compounding and petition of E. Seymour.—Papers of 11th Duke of Somerset.

consider it very hard that having an absolute discharge at Goldsmith Hall," and having been "punctual
in observing all acts and ordinances——I should be
hurried away to prison and no bail taken." (He had
been hurriedly sent for and again confined during one of
the short periods of liberty allowed him.)

Troubles and misfortunes, however, do not appear to
have crushed his sense of humour, for, in a letter begging
his correspondent to again lay his case before the Council
of State, he says that, if his request for liberty be denied,
he had found a way to be even with them :——"For, if not
granted, I intend to send up my wife——and I pray advise
the Council of State from me, in relation to their own
quiet, let them grant my request rather than be punished
with her importunity." In justice to this lady, the subject of his joke, it may not be amiss to state here that
there remain on record many of her acts of loyalty,
courage, kindness, and generosity, the latter qualities
being frequently exerted as well upon her foes as upon
her friends.

Even this threat of Seymour's did not procure his
liberty, for we find him still a prisoner at Exeter in June,
on the 13th of which he was permitted to go, in company
with an officer, for 8 or 10 days, to transact some business concerning Mr. Wallop, about which that gentleman
seemed particularly anxious.*

During the following autumn he appears to have been
eventually released and to have retired to his country
seat, where he led a life of the greatest tranquillity so long
as he was permitted to do so. He continued, however,
to be regarded with the greatest suspicion, and there
seems no doubt that Cromwell himself believed him to
have entered into several of the conspiracies of the time
for the King's restoration.† Whether his conduct was
such as to give occasion for any such feeling, or not,
there is nothing to show, but we find that on Novem-

---

* State Papers, Domestic.
† Thurloe's State Papers, 4, 610.

1655. ber 27, 1655, he was obliged to enter into an engagement to surrender himself, whenever required, into the custody of General Desborough, or that of Sir John Copplestone, and not to act against the Protector or the present Government, nor go out of the county of Devon, except into Exeter, without the leave of the Protector, or that of one of the officers above mentioned.*

On November 21, Colonel Seymour granted a lease of Totnes Castle for 999 years to Mr. W. Bogan, of Gitcombe, for the consideration of £300 ; and, shortly after, with the consent of his father, he sold it outright to the same gentleman, together with all its appurtenances, the reserved rent payable by the Corporation, and all his property in the town of Totnes, for a further sum of £400.†

This property was probably sold in order to assist the King, for we find that Seymour was one of His Majesty's most active partisans at this time, and that about this period he contrived to send him a considerable sum of money. This does not appear to have been the only occasion on which he rendered such pecuniary 1658. assistance, for, in the year 1658, he appears to have repaired in person to the King's Court abroad, bringing with him a welcome gift of £1,000.‡

In the autumn of the following year he succeeded to the baronetcy through his father's death, and, in 1659. 1660, upon the restoration of Charles II, he was the first to sign "the declaration of the Gentrie of the King's party in the county of Devon." (Note 94.) Almost immediately afterwards he was made Deputy Lieutenant for Devon, and appointed to the command of the same regiment in Devon that he had before

* Col. Seymour's engagement to surrender himself.—Papers, 11th Duke of Somerset.
† Original Deed of Sale at Stover.—Papers, 11th Duke of Somerset.
‡ Papers, 11th Duke of Somerset.

U

1664. commanded.* Soon after he was made Vice-Admiral for the same county, and was returned to Parliament as member for Totnes, which he continued to represent during this reign and the next.

It has always been supposed that the castle of Berry Pomeroy, on the embellishing of which his father had spent so large a sum of money, was plundered and burnt down during the Civil War ; but, from a settlement which he made in this year, it appears that the castle was still standing uninjured. There was, in addition, a mansion house in the park of Berry Pomeroy, and a capital house, farm, barton, &c., probably the same that still remain near the church.*

1676. On August 31, 1676, Sir Edward was appointed Colonel General of all the trained bands of horse and foot, raised and to be raised in Devon, and Captain and Governor of the castles and block-houses in the town and port of Dartmouth.† About the same time, in company with some other gentlemen, he was officially thanked by Lord Bath, in the name of the King, for the diligence he had shown in suppressing all seditions and discontents in the county.‡ (Note 95.)

1688. In 1688 he was chosen member for the city of Exeter, an honour that, for a wonder, appears to have cost him very little, and was soon after called upon to advise an association of persons desirous of welcoming the Prince of Orange.

He died December 7th of the same year, at the age of 78, and was buried at Berry Pomeroy.§ As we have seen, he had shown himself a most active officer and zealous partisan of Charles, for, on the outbreak of the Civil War, his father having become too old for service, he was the Colonel and Governor of Dartmouth who so dis-

* Papers, 11th Duke of Somerset.
† Sir E. Seymour's Commission.—Papers, 11th Duke of Somerset.
‡ Corresp. of the Seymours.
§ Collins's Peerage.

ANNE SEYMOUR, DAUGHTER OF SIR WILLIAM PORTMAN.
From a portrait at Knoyle, by kind permission of Mrs. Alfred Seymour.

tinguished himself.* The little notice taken of him by
Clarendon is hardly to be accounted for, unless we are to
suppose that the enmity which subsisted between that
nobleman and the son could influence the pen of the
historian in recording the merits of the father. Sir
Edward Seymour, indeed, as well as all the family, of
either branch, had been a strenuous supporter of the
House of Stuart, so long as loyalty could, by any arguments, be reconciled to the constitution. When these
became irreconcilable, the whole family turned against
that House and welcomed the Prince of Orange. What
we have been able to find concerning Sir Edward himself
is but very little compared to what there might have been
to tell, had his actions only been chronicled; but every
writer who mentions him speaks in unqualified praise of
his behaviour during the whole of the stormy times in
which he lived. He appears to have been looked upon
as a soldier of great courage and ability, and, when in
Parliament, as a statesman of the steadiest principles,
esteemed by all for his honour and integrity. The chief
occasion upon which he took a leading part in the House
of Commons was in his attack upon Lord Danby.

He had married Anne, daughter of Sir William Portman, of Orchard Portman, in Somerset, and by her had
five sons and one daughter—

> Sir Edward Seymour, who succeeded him and of
> whom we must speak later.
> John Seymour, who was made a colonel in the
> English service, and who married a daughter of
> Sir Richard Kennedy, knight.
> Hugh Seymour, who became a captain of distinc-
> tion in the English Navy, and was killed in an
> engagement with the Dutch, when commanding
> the "Foresight." (Note 96.)
> William Seymour, who died unmarried.
> Henry Seymour, who, by the will of his mother's

* Betham's Genealogical Tables.

brother, Sir W. Portman, inherited the large estate of the Portmans at Orchard Portman, and, pursuant to the same will, added, by Act of Parliament, the name of Portman to his own. He was twice married ; first to Penelope, daughter of Sir William Hazlewood, knight, of Maidwell, in Northants ; and secondly to Millicent, daughter of William Fitch, Esq., of High Hall, in Dorset. After his death, without issue, Millicent Seymour Portman married G. Founes, Esq., of Dorset.

Elizabeth Seymour, who married Sir Joseph Tredenham, knight, of Tregony, in Cornwall.

Lady Edward Seymour survived her husband and died in 1694. Her will, made in December, 1692, is curious from the amount of legacies it contained. Nineteen of these, the only ones consisting of money, amounted only to £345. The remainder were silver dishes, spoons, looking-glasses given her by the King of Spain, a sword given to her husband by Charles II, and many other such articles, which she desired might remain in the Seymour family for ever. "One of them," writes the 11th Duke of Somerset, "probably on account of its small value, has remained longer than she had reason to expect, and that is a buff coat, which she says was her husband's. It is still one of the antiquities of Berry Pomeroy."

[Family Papers and Correspondence of the Seymours, coll. by the 11th Duke of Somerset ; Collins's Peerage ; Betham's Genealogical Tables ; Thurloe's State Papers ; State Papers, Domestic, Charles I ; State Papers, Domestic ; State Papers, Domestic, Charles II ; Clarendon's Hist., &c.]

SIR EDWARD SEYMOUR, SPEAKER OF THE HOUSE OF COMMONS.

From a portrait at Stover in the possession of H. St. Maur, Esqr.

SIR EDWARD SEYMOUR, 4TH BARONET.

Edward Seymour, called by Guthrie "the great Sir Edward," was born in 1633,* and grew up into 1633. a remarkably tall and handsome man. Few private gentlemen in England ever had so large or so continued a share in public transactions as he had, for, from the time of the Restoration (when he was 27 years of age) to the time of his death, he was a member of the English Parliament, always representing the city of Exeter, except on three occasions, when he was returned for Hindon, Devon, and Totnes. It has been generally agreed that he had a great command of speech, and that his eloquence was of a style particularly adapted to an English House of Commons. In consequence he became of the highest importance to the Court upon any emergency, and, being possessed of plenty of spirit, he was always either the first man in the Ministry or the leader of the Opposition.

Edward Seymour commenced his Parliamentary career in 1661, and, being in some favour at Court, owing 1661. probably to his father's long and devoted services to the King, soon after received the post of Commissioner of Prizes in the Navy.*

In this year, when both the King and the Parliament were ready, the one to give up and the other to 1667. impeach the Earl of Clarendon, Seymour distinguished himself by being the first man to charge that nobleman openly in the Commons with many great and serious crimes. His speech brought about an animated debate in the House, as a result of which the

* Dict. Nat. Biog.

Commons decided to impeach the Earl for treason and other offences and misdemeanours, upon 17 articles which they drew up against him, only one of which, however, really amounted to the graver charge.

The impeachment decided upon, Seymour was chosen to deliver it to the House of Lords, which he did in a few dignified and well-chosen words. The issue of this, as may be seen in history, was the Earl's abrupt departure from the kingdom, after which an act of banishment was passed against him.

The leading part taken by Seymour in this matter was doubtless the cause of the hatred with which Lord Clarendon regarded him, and which resulted in that nobleman's making as little mention as he could of the Seymours of Devonshire in his History of the Rebellion.

In October, 1668, Seymour was appointed a Deputy Lieutenant for Wiltshire,* and soon after was
1668. granted the post of Treasurer of the Navy, which carried with it a salary of £3,000 a year. In
1672. May, 1672, he was again appointed a Commissioner of the Navy, for which he received another £500 a year,* and in June he was made Clerk of the Hanaper in Chancery for life.

On the 18th of February in this year, he was unanimously elected Speaker of the House of Commons,
1673. in the place of Sir Job Charleton, who had been compelled to resign through ill-health. This selection shows the great esteem with which he was regarded in that House, for the Speaker's chair had always, up to this time, been filled by a member of the legal profession, and he was, therefore, the first gentleman, not bred to the law, whose abilities were considered such as to fit him for so important a position.

The following month he was sworn a member of the Privy Council, an elevation which was viewed with considerable disapproval by some of the more independent

* State Papers, Domestic, Charles II.

members of the House, one of whom, Sir Thomas Little-
ton, started a debate on the subject (October 27), in
which he said to the Speaker, "you are too big for that
chair and for us, and you that are one of the governors of
the world, to be our servant, is incongruous." The discussion grew somewhat warm, but in the end it turned
completely in Seymour's favour, upon which the latter
rose from the chair, which he had refused to vacate during
the debate, and, in a neat speech, "complimented the
House to the effect that he held no employment a greater
honour to him than that which he had in their
service."*

On the 4th of November another warm debate arose,
in which it was moved that the French alliance and the
evil councillors about the King were a danger to the
nation, and the more ardent members of the House were
for Seymour's putting the motions to the vote immediately.
Seymour, however, was not to be made to precipitate
matters in any such manner, and, understanding from the
looks and gestures around him that there was some idea of
holding him forcibly in the chair until the motion was
passed, he, as Reresby puts it, "very nimbly" skipped out
of it, leaving the House to rise in great confusion.

Edward Seymour appears to have been one of the
proudest of all his family, in fact, his pride at times
amounted almost to arrogance, but at the same time it
was a pride of the right kind, and enabled him to carry out
the duties of his position in a manner that a less spirited
man would have shrunk from. Though generally represented as the most haughty and arrogant Speaker that
ever presided over the debates of the House of Commons,
it has been generally admitted that this very quality was
necessary to his position, and proved most advantageous
in preserving the dignity of the House, both inside and
out, and in keeping order between the unruly factions
that divided it. His courage, dignity, and haughty bearing inspired his fellow-members with respect and even

* Parl. Hist., iv, 593.

fear, so much so that "one day when the House was sitting in Committee, in consequence of a violent discussion, blows were struck, and some members had even drawn their swords, Mr. Seymour resumed the chair as of right, although contrary to all the usages of Parliament, and instantly reduced the House to obedience."*

Many other instances of his haughty bearing are related, a few of which will suffice to show the intensity of his pride and his determination to uphold the dignity of the House. On one occasion, when a message was brought that the King was sitting on his throne and desired his immediate attendance to hear the prorogation of Parliament, he refused to leave the chair until the Bill of Supply had been returned from the House of Lords, according to precedent, and, when warned that His Majesty was both impatient and angry, declared that "he would be torn by wild horses sooner than quit the chair."* On another occasion, when driving through Charing Cross, his carriage broke down, upon which he ordered the beadles to stop the next gentleman's that passed, and, upon the gentleman's expressing annoyance and surprise at being turned out of his own coach, replied in the most dignified manner that it was fitter that another should walk the streets than the Speaker of the House of Commons. Another time he gained much applause in the House by ordering the Mace to take Serjeant Pemberton into custody for not paying him sufficient respect. "He saw me," said Seymour, "and paid me no respect, though I was near him or very slightly."*

That his assumption of extreme authority frequently enabled him to influence the decision of the House appears to be without a doubt. Burnett, though as an enemy of his there may be reasons for regarding his statements as somewhat exaggerated, tells us that "he knew the House and every man in it so well, that by looking about he could tell the fate of any question. So, if any thing was put, when the Court party was not well gathered together,

* Manning's Lives of the Speakers.

he would have held the House from doing anything, by a wilful mistaking or misstating the question. By all that he gave time to those who were appointed for that mercenary work, to go about and gather in all their party. And he would discern when they had got the majority. And then he would very fairly state the question, when he saw he was sure to carry it."*

In March of this year, when the new Parliament assembled, Seymour was again unanimously chosen 1679. Speaker. He had, however, now quarrelled with Danby, and the King and the Court party feared that their objects would not be obtained with so powerful and determined a Speaker in the chair, and so determined to prevent his election. Seymour himself, at first, had declined the proffered honour, urging that " the long sittings of the late Parliament had so impaired his health, that he doubted he should not be well able to undergo the service of the House, as would be expected from him." He was, however, earnestly urged to accept the position, and finally accepted.*

The King and the Earl of Danby were determined not to approve this choice, and, consequently, when Seymour presented himself and announced that he had been elected Speaker, the Chancellor, according to his instructions, told him that His Majesty intended to reserve him for other services and therefore required the Commons to elect some one else. Although this refusal had been worded with great tact and in the most complimentary terms, the Commons saw through the manœuvre at once and became greatly irritated. A discussion immediately took place, when Sir John Ernly stood up and said " That he had an order from His Majesty to recommend Sir Thomas Meers to them to be their Speaker, as a person well known in the method of practice of Parliaments, and a person that he thought would be very acceptable and serviceable to them." This announcement was received with angry shouts of " No! No!" and amidst the

* Burnett's Hist. of his Own Times.

general tumult that followed, Mr. Sacheverel said that "It was never known that a person should be excepted against, and no reason at all given," and that "it was done purposely, to gratify some particular person." Mr. Williams argued that "For above 100 years, it had not been known that a Speaker presented was ever excepted against ; and the thing itself of presenting him to the King, as he humbly conceived, was but a bare compliment." Sir Thomas Clarges pointed out "That there were Parliaments long before there were Speakers chosen ; and afterwards, for the ease of the House amongst themselves, they pitched upon a Speaker. All our lives and liberties are preserved by this House, therefore we are to preserve the liberties of it." Mr. Garraway urged, "If Mr. Seymour be rejected, and no reason given, pray who must choose a Speaker, the King or we ? It is plain not we." Many other members rose, all protesting against the King's action, and, after a stormy debate, the House adjourned.*

The following day the Commons sent up a humble petition to His Majesty, pointing out that the matter seemed to them to be of so great importance that they desired that a few days might be given them in which to consider the matter, it being impossible for them to come to an immediate resolution on the subject. This was on a Saturday, and the King consented to allow them till the following Tuesday, upon which day they drew up another representation, full of expressions of loyalty but firmly insisting that it was their undoubted right to elect their own Speaker and that, according to this usage, " Mr. Seymour was unanimously chosen, upon the consideration of his great ability and sufficiency for that place, of which we had large experience in the last Parliament," and hoping that His Majesty would be pleased to rest satisfied with their choice. Charles immediately replied that they were but wasting their time, and desired them to return and carry out his bidding at once.

* Grey's Debates, 6, 402.

The abruptness and incivility of this order did not tend to conciliate the House who again sent up a representation insisting upon their rights, but, at the same time, couched in conciliatory though firm language. Charles, finding himself now in difficulty, adopted his usual course when in such circumstances and prorogued Parliament, after the Commons had sat for six days without a Speaker. The following week they were again summoned, when the House, not wishing to delay the business of the nation by continuing a struggle with so obstinate a Sovereign, elected to compromise matters for the time and so chose William Gregory, Serjeant-at-Law, to be their Speaker.*

Seymour thus became once more a private member and before long incurred a certain amount of unpopularity, by joining with Halifax in strongly opposing the Bill for the exclusion of the Duke of York (afterwards James II) from the succession to the Crown. In a long and obstinate debate upon the subject, after complaining that his life had been greatly endangered by the malevolence of the Duke's enemies, Seymour said, " Sir, I confess I am very much against the bringing in this Bill, for I think it a very unfortunate thing, that whereas His Majesty hath prohibited but one thing only, that we should so soon fall upon it. I do not see there is any cause we should fear Popery so much, as to make us run into such an extreme. Have we not had great experience of the Duke's love for his nation ? Hath he not squared his actions by the exactest rules of justice and moderation ? Is there not a possibility of being with the Church, and not of the Court of Rome ? Hath he not bred up his children in the Protestant religion, and showed a great respect for all persons of that profession ? Would it not be a dangerous thing for him (I mean in point of interest) to offer at any such alteration of the religion established by us as is needlessly, nay, unjustly apprehended ? Can any man imagine that it can be attempted,

* Hist. MSS. Comm., 12 Rep. vii, 157.

without great hazard of destroying both himself and his family ? and can so indiscreet an attempt be expected from a Prince so abounding in wisdom and prudence ? But though we should resolve to have no moderation in our proceedings against Papists, yet I hope we shall have some for ourselves. It cannot be supposed, that such a law will bind all here in England, any in Scotland, and is it not disputed, whether it will be binding in Ireland ? so that, in all probability, it will not only divide us among ourselves, but the three kingdoms one from another, and occasion a miserable civil war ; for it cannot be imagined that the Duke will submit to it : and to disinherit him for his religion, is not only to act according to the Popish principles, but to give cause for war with all the Catholic princes in Europe : and that must occasion a standing army, from which there will be more danger of Popery and arbitrary government, than from a Popish successor or a Popish King." In spite of his efforts, however, the Bill of Exclusion passed the Commons but was eventually rejected by the Lords, to the great joy of the King.

Notwithstanding Seymour had, previous to the bringing in of this Bill, rendered himself generally popular by being the chief promoter of the Habeas Corpus Act, with which his name must ever remain associated, yet the majority of the Commons, who had espoused the Bill of Exclusion, upon its failure in the Upper House, addressed a request to His Majesty that he should remove Lord Halifax and Edward Seymour from his Council and presence for ever ; the former for having been the chief instrument of rejecting the Bill amongst the Lords, and the latter for having been active in the same cause in the Commons. Failing in this they determined to impeach Seymour upon four articles, relative to corruption and maladministration in his office as Treasurer of the Navy.* This accusation, however, they found it impossible to sustain and so the matter subsided, no articles against him being ever exhibited in due form.

* Macpherson's Original Papers, 1, 106.

Although Seymour had taken an active part in upholding the Duke of York's right to the succession, he appears
to have frequently endeavoured to persuade him to change
his religion so that no obstacle should remain to debar
him from the people's confidence ; and, when he found
his persuasions of no avail, he originated a proposal to
ensure the security of the Protestant religion
1681. during the reign of the future Catholic King.
This was that the Prince of Orange should be
appointed Regent to James, upon the latter's accession.
The Prince of Orange had already been over to England
once and he now paid a second visit during the summer
of this year. During his stay he was invited to dine at
the Lord Mayor's in the City, an invitation which he
readily accepted, doubtless remembering the former entertainment he had had there. The relations between the
City and the Court were at this time, however, very
strained, and his acceptance of the former's hospitality
was likely to cause great annoyance to the King. Halifax, Hyde, and Seymour, therefore, endeavoured to
dissuade the Prince from going, but without any effect,
upon which Seymour posted off to Windsor and persuaded the King to send a letter demanding the Prince's
immediate attendance, a command which prevented the
latter from being present at the dinner and so saved a
probable further quarrel between the City and the Court.*
The following year Seymour was still associated with
Halifax whom he supported in his endeavours to
1682. obtain Monmouth's pardon and restoration to
favour, but he soon began to draw near to Roches-
1683. ter, with whose party he generally acted from the
summer of 1683, when the Privy Seal had been
given to Halifax, to the disappointment, as some said,
of Seymour.
As he had been an enemy to the Exclusion Bill, so,
1685. upon King James's accession, he was a strenuous
asserter of his right, and, although he disapproved

* Macpherson's Original Papers, 1, 125-6.

of some of the King's measures, yet he deemed nothing
but a manifest attack upon the religion or liberties of
the land a sufficient plea for an alteration in his conduct.
Accordingly he was assiduous against the Duke of Monmouth and his adherents when they threatened an
insurrection.

In his speech at the opening of Parliament, King
James asked to have his revenue settled and continued,
as it was in the lifetime of his brother. This request was
unanimously granted, one speech only being made against
it, by Seymour, in which, however, he did not directly
oppose the grant but stated that the elections had been
carried on so much under Court influence, that it was the
duty of the House to ascertain, first of all, who were the
legal members, before proceeding to business of importance
which might affect the laws and religion of the nation.[*]

Macaulay, who seems generally inclined to be unjust to
Seymour, thus describes the scene :—" When in the
Commons, after the King's speech, it was proposed that
the House should go into Committee for the purpose of
settling a revenue on the King, Seymour at once stood up
to speak. How he stood, looking like what he was, the
chief of a dissolute and high-spirited gentry, with the
artificial ringlets clustering in fashionable profusion round
his shoulders, and a mingled expression of voluptuous-
ness and disdain in his eye and on his lip, the likenesses of
him which still remain enable us to imagine. It was
not, the haughty cavalier said, his wish that the Parliament
should withhold from the Crown the means of carrying on
the government. But was there indeed a Parliament?
Were there not on the benches many men who had, as all
the world knew, no right to sit there, many men whose
elections were tainted by corruption, many men forced by
intimidation on reluctant voters, and many men returned
by corporations which had no legal existence? Had not
constitutional bodies been remodelled, in defiance of royal
charters and of immemorial prescription? Had not

* Fox's Hist. of the Reign of James II, 147.

returning officers been everywhere the unscrupulous agents of the Court ? Seeing that the very principle of representation had been thus systematically attacked, he knew not how to call the throng of gentlemen which he saw around him by the honourable name of a House of Commons. Yet never was there a time when it more concerned the public weal that the character of Parliament should stand high. Great dangers impended over the ecclesiastical and civil constitution of the realm. It was a matter of vulgar notoriety, it was a matter which required no proof, that the Test Act, the rampart of religion, and the Habeas Corpus Act, the rampart of liberty, were marked out for destruction. 'Before we proceed to legislate on questions so momentous, let us at least ascertain whether we really are a legislature. Let our first proceedings be to enquire into the manner in which the elections have been conducted. And let us look to it that the enquiry be impartial. For, if the nation shall find that no redress is to be obtained by peaceful methods, we may perhaps ere long suffer the justice which we refuse to do.' He concluded by moving that, before any supply was granted, the House would take into consideration petitions against returns, and that no member, whose right to sit was disputed, should be allowed to vote."

Amidst a solemn silence, Seymour sat down. Not a cheer greeted the close of his fine oration, not a member had the courage to second it. What he had said was but too true ; the elections had been carried on by the Court party in the most unprincipled and scandalous manner, and it was but right that the strongest protest should be entered against such proceedings. Many of the House sympathised with the speech, which voiced their own thoughts, but the nominees of the Court were many and powerful, and they dared not even applaud a speech with which they agreed, and which none of them would have dared to make, for fear of the Court's disfavour.*

* Burnett, 1, 639 ; Evelyn's Diary, 1685 ; Barillon.

" Haughty," " dissolute," " voluptuous," Seymour may
have been. It matters not. He was the only man who
dared, unsupported, to uphold the honour of the House,
with which was involved the safety of the country and of
the Protestant religion.

During the same session, the King demanded, amongst
other things, a standing army. This led to a heated
discussion in the House. The courtiers argued, with
some force, upon the great superiority of a standing
army to a half-trained militia, asking in a mocking
manner whether the defence of the country was to be
entrusted to the Beefeaters, and how the Devonshire
Militia, which had fled from Monmouth's scythemen,
would be likely to face the troops of France.* The
House, however, was not to be taken in by any arguments. The danger of a standing army in the hands of
James was too great. "The general feeling," says
Macaulay, "was expressed by the first of the Tory
county gentlemen of England, Edward Seymour. He
admitted that the militia was not in a satisfactory state,
but maintained that it might be remodelled. The
remodelling might require money ; but, for his part,
he would rather give a million to keep up a force from
which he had nothing to fear, than half a million to keep
up a force of which he must ever be afraid. Let the
trained bands be disciplined ; let the navy be strength-
ened ; and the country would be secure. A standing
army was at best a mere drain on the public resources.
The soldier was withdrawn from all useful labour. He
produced nothing : he consumed the fruits of the
industry of other men ; and he domineered over those
by whom he was supported. That the nation was now
threatened, not only with a standing army, but with a
Popish standing army, with a standing army officered by
men who might be very amiable and honourable, but
who were on principle enemies to the constitution of the
realm." The debate continued for some time, and, in

* Macaulay's Hist. of England.

the end, a supply was granted to the Crown, but a Bill was also passed for making the militia more efficient.

As Seymour had almost prophesied in his speech, it soon became apparent that King James was aiming at nothing less than the subversion of the Established Church. Hitherto Seymour's principles of honour, justice, and integrity, which had marked out his plan of politics, had led him to support the King as the hereditary and rightful head of the constitution, but now that the King was preparing to subvert that constitution, the same principles caused Seymour to turn against him. When he saw that nothing further could be done to influence the King in the right direction, he joined with others to invite the Prince of Orange to stand between the people and the reinstation of Popery.

On the 15th of November, 1688, in company with all the firm churchmen of the adjacent parts, he 1688. met the Prince of Orange at Exeter, nine days after the latter's arrival. For a long time Seymour had been the head of the "Western Alliance," a body composed of the chief gentry in the west of England, and had thus obtained great influence in those parts. This now enabled him to take the lead, with the consent of the Prince, in causing Articles of Association to be drawn up which each had to sign upon joining the party. By this means he made more sure of the fidelity of those who came in, for, once their signature was appended, it was not so easy for them to leave, as they might be inclined to do should their project be threatened by failure.*

Seymour was generally looked upon as the most important of those who had first come to join the Prince. "In birth, in political influence, and in Parliamentary abilities, he was beyond comparison the foremost among the Tory gentlemen of England." It is not surprising therefore that William should, on his arrival, have commenced to make much of him. His first

* Burnett's Hist.; Rapin, 2, 777.

x

attempt at flattery, however, was not very successful. "I think, Sir Edward,"[*] he said, meaning to be very civil, "that you are of the family of the Duke of Somerset." "Pardon me, Sir," replied Seymour, who never forgot that he was the head of the elder branch, "the Duke of Somerset is of my family."[†]

Sir Edward's prompt action in forming the Association gained him the confidence of William, who made him Governor of Exeter, and left him in charge of the surrounding district when he himself advanced towards London.[‡] It appears plain, however, from Sir Edward's subsequent behaviour, that in taking part with the Prince of Orange he had no other intention than that of forcing James to adhere to his coronation oath. He had no idea of actually dethroning that monarch to put William in his place.[§]

Even after James's flight he appears still to have been prepared to assist in reinstating him, provided 1689. the security of the constitution and of the Protestant religion were assured. This caused him to join Rochester in strongly declaring, in the Parliament assembled at Westminster, January 22, against the vote of the throne's being declared vacant, and the motion for filling it with the Prince and Princess of Orange.[||] This, in all probability, was the reason why he was not chosen as Speaker of that Parliament, although probably more fitted for that position than any other member. As soon, however, as the majority of voices had settled the point, he expressed himself as willing to adhere to the new order of things.

In February he urged the House to form themselves into a grand committee to discuss the affairs of the nation and secure the liberties of the people, before the throne

* It was just about this time that he succeeded his father.
† Macaulay's Hist. of England.
‡ Harleian Miscellany, 1, 439–440.
§ Clarendon, State Letters.
|| Rapin, 3, 42.

should actually be filled. He also protested against limiting the duration of Parliaments to three years. On the 2nd of March, the new Sovereign having been duly installed, he took the oath of allegiance to the new king to the great joy of all the Court at receiving so great an accession of strength.* He declared also in the House that, though he had not taken part in the setting up of the new government, he was prepared now to give it his cordial support in all that might be necessary for the pacification of Ireland.†

Soon afterwards Sir Edward again came forward in defence of his old ally, Halifax, in the House of Commons. On this occasion John Hampden had made a very bitter speech, attacking Lord Halifax and ascribing all the disasters of the year to him and the others who had, in the days of the Exclusion Bill, attempted to negotiate between William and James, and demanding the exclusion from the King's councils and presence of the three noblemen who had been sent to him at Hungerford. Upon this Seymour rose and declared that, much as he disapproved of the manner in which the administration had lately been conducted, he was unable to concur in the vote which Hampden had proposed. "Look where you will," he said, " to Ireland, to Scotland, to the navy, to the army, you will find abundant proofs of mismanagement. If the war is still to be conducted by the same hands, we can expect nothing but a recurrence of the same disasters. But I am not prepared to proscribe men for the best thing that ever they did in their lives, to proscribe men for attempting to avert a revolution by timely mediation."‡

In November we find him proposing and the Commons resolving that an address should be presented to His Majesty " that he will please to issue out a proclamation for the apprehending Colonel Ludlow, who stands

* Journals of the House of Commons ; Letter from Ronguillo.
† Grey's Debates, June 22, 1689.
‡ Macaulay's Hist., iii, 515 ; Boyer's Life of William.

attainted of high treason, by Act of Parliament, for the murder of King Charles I ; and that he will please to propose a reward to such as shall apprehend him."[*] Whether he was obliged to make this proposition, or not, in the course of his duty as leader of his party, we cannot now determine ; but it seems unfortunate that he should have appeared as prime mover in the matter, for the fact of his having previously received a considerable portion of Colonel Ludlow's forfeited estates in Wilts, has since given rise to the accusation that he was determined to drive their former owner out of the country.[†]

Early in March, 1692, Sir Edward was made a Privy Councillor and appointed a Lord of the Treasury. 1692. (Note 97.) This greatly annoyed many of his Tory followers, who had looked upon him as their leader in a war against placemen and Dutchmen, nor did it give him any satisfaction, as his pride was sorely wounded by finding that, at the Board of Treasury, he would have to sit below Richard Hampden. This at first he flatly refused to do, but was eventually mollified by being given a seat in the Cabinet, and by a special recommendation to the Queen. "I bring you," said King William, "a gentleman who will, in my absence, be a valuable friend."[‡]

During this year many earnest debates took place in the Commons as to the events of the war on land and sea, and frequent complaints were made as to the preference given to aliens over Englishmen in the various commands. Seymour's love for foreigners had never been great ; in fact, hitherto, he had not troubled to conceal his aversion to them. On this occasion, however, he did not hesitate to take their part. "I have no love," he said, "for foreigners as foreigners : but we have no choice. Men are not born generals : nay, a man may be a very valu-

* Journals, House of Commons; Guthrie; Rapin.
† Ludlow, Memoirs, 1894, ii, 511.
‡ Macaulay's Hist., iv, 185.

able captain or major, and not be equal to the conduct of an army. Nothing but experience will form great commanders. Very few of our countrymen have that experience ; and therefore we must for the present employ strangers."[*]

In March, 1694, Sir Edward lost his place through the formation of a Whig ministry, and was never 1694. more employed during that reign, for the remainder of which he continued to be the leader of the Tories and the most formidable opponent of the Whigs. During the debates in Parliament he did not confine his censures to the ministers only, but seized every opportunity of reflecting on the King ; but with such caution, and in such ambiguous terms, as to evade the possibility of impeachment. For instance, he did not in plain words call him a usurper, but he openly disputed his title of "rightful and lawful king."

During the same year both the people and the Parliament were thrown into a great state of excitement by a rumour that arose, that the two great corporations, the City of London and the East India Company, had bribed and corrupted many of the great men in the Commons. Soon afterwards the names of Trevor, Seymour, and Leeds were freely mentioned as amongst those who had received the largest sums. These three being perhaps the most important and influential persons amongst the Tories, their opponents now saw a great chance of dealing a crushing blow at that party, and prepared to take full advantage of it. Wharton was especially busy in the matter, stirring up his friends to demand an official inquiry into the matter, but, before their plans were perfected, the subject was brought before the House in an unexpected manner.[†]

It appears that one day, while a Bill of little interest was being discussed, the postman arrived, and members hurried to the Bar to receive their letters, during the

* Macaulay's Hist., iv, 302.
† Macaulay's Hist., iv, 548.

distribution of which the noise of their conversation almost drowned the voices of the members who were speaking. Seymour, who was always very punctilious that the rules of the House should be rigidly adhered to, called upon the Speaker to reprimand such members as were responsible for the disturbance; upon which an angry discussion arose in which one of the offenders, stung by Seymour's remarks, made a pointed allusion to the rumours that were current. "It is," he said, "undoubtedly improper to talk while a Bill is under discussion; but it is much worse to take money for getting a Bill passed. If we are extreme to mark a slight breach of form, how ought we to deal with that corruption which is eating away the very substance of our institutions?" This speech brought about a most stormy debate, which was frequently interrupted by loud cries of "The Tower!" and which ended in Wharton carrying his point of having an immediate and searching inquiry.[*]

Trevor was found to have taken money right and left and was compelled to leave the House. No proof, however, could be discovered against Seymour,[†] but he continued to be suspected, and by almost every historian is suspected still, for the tongue of slander once let loose never fails to leave some stain upon its victim. There appears no doubt that heavy bribes were offered to Seymour, but, according to the depositions of Sir Basil Firebrass and others, he had steadfastly refused to accept them.

During the elections that followed soon afterwards, the Whigs were nearly everywhere triumphant, so much so that they were emboldened to put forward candidates for even the strongest Tory seats. Seymour's seat at Exeter had, hitherto, been held unassailable, but his popularity had suffered through the allegations brought against his

[*] L'Hermitage, March, 1695; Journals of the House of Commons.

[†] Journals, House of Commons, March 12; Vernon to Lexington; Burnett, ii, 145.

honour, and two strong candidates were brought forward against him. The contest, one of the longest and fiercest in history, not only attracted the attention of the whole kingdom, but was deemed of such importance that even foreign governments watched it with interest. The poll remained open for five weeks, during the whole of which time the freemen of Exeter were feasted at the expense of the rival candidates. Eating, drinking, and brawling took up so much of the electors' time that it was not till the last day that the votes had come in, in sufficient quantities to show who was the victor. In the end Seymour was defeated after one of the most exciting, and probably the most expensive contests of the age.*

The borough of Totnes, however, still remained open for him, so that his defeat did not cost him his seat in Parliament, where he continued to be as active 1697. as ever. In 1697, he advanced the sum of £10,000 to the Treasury,† and, at the opening of Parliament, urged the House to postpone the question of supply until the King's speech had been thoroughly discussed. Later on in the same year he made a long speech in defence of Sir John Fenwick, which failed to effect his purpose, but which was remarkable from the number of quotations it contained from ancient history. Much of this oration was in Latin.‡

During the elections of the following year he was returned member for Exeter by a large majority, 1698. although he took but little trouble in the contest, and, in fact, was absent most of the time.§ During the session of this year he advocated reducing the Civil List to the former amount of £600,000.‖

1699. In 1699, Sir Edward's son was killed in a duel by Captain Kirke, and the loss seems to have affected

* Macaulay's Hist., iv, 617 ; L'Hermitage Despatches.
† Dict. Nat. Biog.
‡ Oldmixon, iii, 153, 159.
§ Macaulay's Hist., v, 129.
‖ Dict. Nat. Biog.

him so seriously that, for a time, he could think of nothing but revenge. So deep did this feeling become that he even forgot his usual punctilious observance of forms, and so far forgot himself as to appear in Westminster Hall whilst it was being deliberated whether Kirke should be brought to immediate trial or released on bail, and deliver an harangue against standing armies. "Here," he said, "is a man who lives on money taken out of our pockets. The plea set up for taxing us in order to support him is that his sword protects us, and enables us to live in peace and security. And is he to be suffered to use that sword to destroy us?"* This oration does not appear to have affected the case, for Kirke was eventually found guilty of manslaughter only; but, however much we must blame Seymour for his unwarrantable interference in a Court of Justice, some palliation is to be found in the severe loss he had just sustained, which aggravated, to an extent that almost became a mania for the time, his hatred of a standing army.

During this same year he led the many attacks that were made in the Commons upon Somers and 1700. the Dutch favourites, and in the following spring was the chief promoter and manager of the Resumption Bill.

On the prorogation of this Parliament, in April, he went to Kensington to take leave of the King. At this time he appears to have been confident of a political reaction which would place his party in power, for, when William told him that he would think no more of the past, hoping that they might be better friends in future, Seymour abruptly answered, "I doubt it not."†

In the new Parliament which met in this year, Seymour showed himself willing to give the King every 1701. assistance towards commencing a fresh campaign. This new attitude of his is to be attributed to

* Macaulay's Hist., v, 242.
† Bonnet's Despatch, ap. Ranke, v, 214.

the recognition of the Pretender by the King of France, which made an invasion of England once more appear within the bounds of possibility.

On the accession of Queen Anne, who at that time showed a great partiality for the Tory party, Sir 1702. Edward became a great favourite and his influence increased considerably. On the meeting of the first Parliament in this reign he drew the attention of the House to the fact that the new East India Company had bought several seats at the elections and demanded an inquiry, as a result of which his charges were fully proved, and not only were several seats declared void but some few members were even imprisoned.*

On the 14th of April, he was appointed Comptroller of the Household. On the 17th he was admitted into the Privy Council, and, in May, he was made Ranger of Windsor Forest. The Queen's intention to distinguish him from the rest of the party, in a peculiar manner, was visible in nothing more than in the offer of a peerage, with which Her Majesty complimented him soon after. This offer he declined, in his own person, as he saw a great probability of the Dukedom of Somerset reverting to his descendants by his first marriage; but he accepted it in the person of his eldest surviving son by his second marriage.

During the dependance of the Bill against occasional conformity, which was the first measure that effectually disunited the Tories in this reign, Sir Edward was a warm friend of that Bill; but he concurred in all measures for securing the Protestant succession. He also begged permission to bring in Bills for resuming all the grants made in the late reign and for applying them to the public use. These Bills miscarried through the influence of the Whigs, who were daily gaining ground. After this he became the champion of the Tories and made it a point to harass the ministers and clog their measures; so much so, that the Queen's resentment was

* Burnett's Hist. of his Own Times, iv, 463.

1704.   at last aroused and he was in consequence dismissed from office in April, 1704.

During his attendance upon Parliament afterwards, he still continued the steady patriot (Note 98) ; but it was not long before he retired to his seat at 1708. Maiden Bradley, where he died on February 17, 1708. (Note 99.) It is said that his death was accelerated by a fright he received from an old woman who gained admittance to his house and assaulted him in his study, during the absence of the household at some neighbouring fair.*

"Of the character of Sir Edward Seymour," says Mr. Manning in his Lives of the Speakers, "we have several versions, all pretty well comparing in general points. Mr. Noble, in his continuation of Grainger, describes him as 'a man of morose disposition, but of great good sense, invincible obstinacy, and incorruptible integrity, feared more than loved, and respected more than esteemed.' The wags were pleased when they could annoy this impersonation of pride and haughtiness. One gave him a petition, of no moment, to present to the House ; Seymour took it from his pocket with his accustomed gravity, and putting on his spectacles, began to read :—'The humble petition of Oliver Cromwell— the devil!' The laugh was so loud and long, that the old man, throwing down the paper, hastened from the House, confused, and in wrath at the insult to his dignity." His pride indeed rivalled, if it did not excel, that of Charles, Duke of Somerset, who lived during the same time, and it frequently led him into unnecessary if not foolish actions. Thus we are told that when summoned to the Privy Council by Charles, he walked to the head of the room, and, leaning over that King, "whispered too audibly, that he should not prevaricate with himself." And, that "hardened in his pride by age, he treated William III with the airs of an equal, if not a superior, and when dismissed from his place of

* Rapin's Hist., 1751, iv, 65.

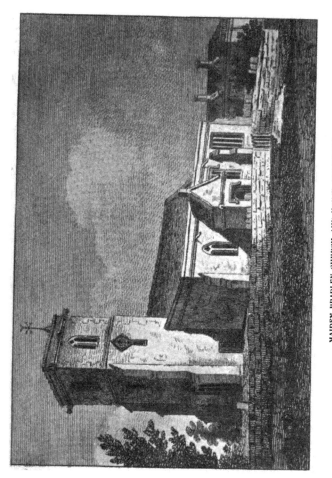

MAIDEN BRADLEY CHURCH AND HOUSE, WILTSHIRE.

From an old print.

MONUMENT ERECTED TO SIR EDWARD SEYMOUR IN MAIDEN BRADLEY CHURCH.

Comptroller of the Household by Anne, sent word that he would return his staff by the common carrier."[*]

But it is not by his exhibitions of an overwhelming pride that we must judge him. "Every Englishman," continues Mr. Manning, "though he laughs at his peculiarities, must love his virtues, and venerate him as the man to whom we are principally indebted for the Habeas Corpus Act. Temperate in the use of wealth, he was frugal, yet liberal in his expenditure, nor did he enrich himself and his family as he might have done. Proud of his ancestry, and haughty as he was, yet he would not accept a Barony from Queen Anne ; but he permitted the eldest son of his second marriage to take the title of Conway, whose descendants now possess one of the old Seymour titles, the Marquisate of Hertford. In private life he was worthy if not amiable ; true to his two wives, and to his children careful, if not kind ; to his tenants and attendants, a good, though not a bountiful, landlord and master."

One serious allegation has continually been made, and will doubtless continue to be made, against his honour. This was the accusation of his having received large bribes from the East India Company. Such an imputation, however, will scarcely be credited by any fair-minded person in view of the facts, as far as these can now be examined. A full inquiry was, at the time, held upon the matter and he was acquitted of the charge by a House of Commons, of whom perhaps the greater part may be said to have been against him, and the depositions of the witnesses examined showed that he had rejected all such offers of money. Had he accepted large sums, he must have had something to show for them, yet we are told that he was frugal in his expenditure and that, at his death, his fortune was found to be much of the same value as when he inherited it. "Sir Edward Seymour," we read in Collins's Peerage, "though he inherited a large paternal estate, though he married two wives, with considerable

* Hist. of the House of Commons, Townsend.

portions each, though he had enjoyed lucrative appointments almost from his very youth, and though he lived without profuseness but with as much economy as splendour; yet the personal estate, which he left at his death, and the real ones which he had purchased, did not amount near to what a person of the strictest probity might have, without blemish, added to his patrimonial fortune."

It seems indeed probable that Seymour may have been a loser in the end by his transactions with the government, for in 1696, he gave considerable assistance to the Treasury out of his own private means and does not appear to have ever been repaid. We read, "The finances of the country were never so low and hopeless as in 1696. The ordinary resources of revenue were exhausted. The public servants did not know where to look for their next quarter's salary. The King was bent upon a compulsory clause for bringing in of plate; and the Exchequer was as thankful as any private bankrupt for the smallest contribution. Sir Edward Seymour lent it—£10,000 in money, and offered to furnish £10,000 in cattle to the victuallers."* Is it likely that a man who would thus sacrifice his private fortune in the assistance of his country, would stoop to accept bribes offered him by wealthy corporations for furthering their Bills? Let the reader judge for himself.

Sir Edward Seymour was twice married; first to Margaret, daughter of Sir William Wale, knight, of London; secondly to Letitia, daughter of Francis Popham, Esquire, of Littlecote, in Wilts. By the former he had two sons—

> Sir Edward Seymour, who succeeded him, and of whom we shall speak later.
> William Seymour, who entered the army at an early age. January 1, 1692, he received a commission

* Edinburgh Review, Oct. 1841; Letters Illus. of the Reign of William III, by J. Vernon.

MARGARET, DAUGHTER OF SIR WILLIAM WALE, AND WIFE OF SIR EDWARD
SEYMOUR, OF BERRY POMEROY.

From a Picture at Knoyle, by kind permission of Mrs. Alfred Seymour.

GENERAL WILLIAM SEYMOUR.

From a portrait at Stover, in the possession of H. St. Maur, Esqr.

as Major and Captain of a company in the 2nd Regiment of Foot Guards, " the Coldstreamers," and was permitted to take rank as the youngest Lieutenant-Colonel of Foot.* During the same year he was captured by a French privateer. On his release he obtained the command of Cutts's Regiment, which he commanded with great distinction at the siege of Namur, and at Landen, where he was wounded, July, 1693.† July 18, 1698, he was appointed to the command of a regiment of Marines.‡ In 1702, he served as Brigadier under the Duke of Ormond, in the expedition to Cadiz. In 1706, he was appointed Major-General of Marines‡ and Lieutenant-General of the forces. (Note 100.) He died, unmarried, February 9, 1728.

By the latter he had six sons and one daughter—

Popham Conway Seymour, who was killed by Captain Kirke in a duel, June, 1699. The duel is supposed to have originated by one of them calling the other a coxcomb for wearing red-heeled shoes. Macaulay, however, gives a different account :—" Conway Seymour had lately come of age. He was in possession of an independent fortune of £7,000 a year, which he lavished in costly fopperies. The town had nicknamed him 'Beau Seymour.' He was displaying his curls and his embroidery in St. James's Park on a midsummer evening, after indulging too freely in wine, when a young officer of the Blues, named Kirke, who was as tipsy as himself, passed near him. 'There goes Beau Seymour,' said Kirke. Seymour flew into a rage. Angry words were

* State Papers, William and Mary.
† Dict. Nat. Biog. ; D'Auvergne, Campaigns in Flanders, 1693, p. 90.
‡ Treasury Papers.

exchanged between the foolish boys. They
immediately went beyond the precincts of the
Court, drew, and exchanged some passes. Seymour
was wounded in the neck. The wound was not
very serious ; but, when his cure was only half
completed, he revelled in fruit, ice, and burgundy,
till he threw himself into a violent fever. Though
a coxcomb and a voluptuary, he seems to have had
some fine qualities. On the last day of his life he
saw Kirke. Kirke implored forgiveness ; and the
dying man declared he forgave as he hoped to be
forgiven." By his death the Conway estates
devolved upon his brother Francis.

Francis Seymour, who was created Baron Conway,
March 17, 1702. In 1750, he was created Earl
of Hertford, and afterwards Marquis of Hertford
and Earl of Yarmouth. (Appendix M.) He
died in 1794. From him are descended the subsequent Marquises of Hertford.

Charles Seymour.

Henry Seymour, who entered the army as a Captain
but died young.

Alexander Seymour, who died young.

John Seymour, who became a Colonel in the army,
and was appointed Governor of Maryland.*

Anne Seymour, who married William Berkeley,
Esquire, of Pill, in Somerset, and was mother to
Henry William Berkeley, Esquire, who, by Act
of Parliament, assumed the name of Portman,
and was member of Parliament for Somerset, in
1741.

[Boyer's Annals of Anne; Collins's Peerage; G. E. C. Peerage;
Macaulay's History of England; State Papers, William and
Mary; Treasury Papers; Bulstrode Papers, Nov. 1667;
Wyon's History of Queen Anne; Dict. Nat. Biog. ; Letters

---

* Treasury Papers.

Illustrative of the Reign of William III, by Vernon;
Eachard's History of England; D'Auvergne, Campaigns in
Flanders, 1693; Luttrell's Brief Historical Narration; Rapin's
History; Ranke's History; Townsend's History of the
House of Commons; Evelyn's Diary; Reresby's Diary;
Hist. MSS. Commission, 7th and 12th Rep.; Manning's
Lives of the Speakers; Coxe's Life of Marlborough; Christie's
Life of Shaftesbury; Ludlow's Memoirs; Dalton's English
Army Lists; Grey's Debates; Burnett's History of his Own
Times; Cook's History of Parties; Harleian Miscellany;
Clarendon, State Letters; Fox's History, James II; Mac-
pherson's Original Papers; Parliamentary History; State
Papers, Charles II, &c.]

•

SIR EDWARD SEYMOUR, 5TH BARONET.

Although eldest son of so great a man as Sir Edward
Seymour, the 4th Baronet, Edward does not appear to
have possessed an ambition equal to that of his father.   His
brothers, as we have seen, almost all entered the military
profession, and those of them who attained manhood made
some name for themselves.   Edward Seymour, however,
was cast in a different mould, and appears to have preferred a peaceable retreat at Maiden Bradley to the invidi-
ous situation of those who moved in a more exalted
sphere.   He took little or no part in the public transactions of the time, and, in consequence, there is but little
that is recorded about him.

On the death of his father he made his appearance in
the House of Commons, being returned by the
1708. borough of Totnes, and in 1710 and 1713 he
served as member for Great Bedwyn.*   A Parlia-
1713. mentary career, however, seems to have had but
little attraction for him.   He took no part in any
debates and appears to have seldom attended the sittings
of the House.   After the Parliament of 1713, he did not
seek re-election but retired to Maiden Bradley, where he
spent the remainder of his years in the ordinary pursuits
of a country gentleman.   He died at that residence,
December 29, 1740, at the age of 80 or thereabouts.†

He had married Letitia, sole daughter of Sir Francis
Popham, of Littlecote, Knight of the Bath, and niece to
his father's second wife.   She died in 1738.   By her he
had numerous issue—

* British Parl. Regist., 49.
† Collins's Peerage.

ELIZABETH, DAUGHTER OF ALEX. POPHAM, DOWAGER VISCOUNTESS
HINCHINBROKE, AND WIFE OF FRANCIS SEYMOUR OF SHERBOURNE.

From a portrait at Knoyle, by kind permission of Mrs. Alfred Seymour.

Edward Seymour, who became 8th Duke of Somerset, and of whom we will speak later.

Francis Seymour, of Sherbourne, Dorset, who married Elizabeth, the dowager Lady Hinchinbroke, mother to John, Earl of Sandwich, and daughter of Alexander Popham, Esquire, of Littlecote, by whom he had issue two sons: Henry, who married Caroline, only daughter of William, Earl Cowper, July 24, 1753, and Francis, who died an infant. He had also one daughter, Mary, who married John Bailey, of Sutton, in Somerset, November 30, 1758. He was elected member for Bedwin, in 1727, and for Marlborough, in 1734. He died in December, 1761.

Alexander Seymour, who died unmarried, April, 1731.

William Seymour, of Knoyle, in Wilts, who married Elizabeth, daughter and heir of — Hippye, of Frome, in Somerset.

Letitia Seymour, who married John Gapper, Esquire, of Wincaunton, in Somerset.

Margaret Seymour, who married Richard Jones, Esquire, of Ramsbury, in Wilts.

Elizabeth Seymour, who married Henry Hungerford, Esquire, of Fiefield, in Wilts.

Anne Seymour, who married William Scroggs, Esquire, of Chute Lodge, in Wilts.

Helena Seymour, who died unmarried.

Mary Seymour, who married the Rev. Mr. Hammond.

Jane Seymour, who married William Colman, Esquire, of Gornhey, Devon.

Catherine Seymour, who married John Philip Fuhr, of Bristol, a Hamburgh merchant.

EDWARD SEYMOUR, 8TH DUKE OF SOMERSET.

Edward Seymour was born in December, 1694.
There appears to be no record of his earlier
1694. life, nor does he appear to have taken any active
part in the politics and government of the time.

When 22 years of age he married Mary, daughter of
Daniel Webb, Esq., of Monkton Farley, in
1716. Wilts, the niece and heiress of William Somner,
Esq., of Seend, near the Devizes.

In 1741 he served in Parliament as one of the representatives for Salisbury, but appears to have
1741. retired after the death of his wife, not very long
after.

After her decease, Lord Aylesbury and other friends endeavoured to persuade Seymour's father that a marriage
should be proposed between Edward Seymour and the
Duke of Somerset's eldest daughter, apparently in the
hope that the match would be the means of keeping a
portion of the Seymour estates in the Seymour family,
the Duke having no son living and the estates being at
his absolute disposal. (Note 101.) It was thought that
the Duke would favour such an alliance, seeing that by
Lord Beauchamp's death, without issue, the title must
devolve upon Edward Seymour. Nothing, however,
came of this idea ; nor is it to be wondered at when we
remember that, however much the Duke might have
favoured such a scheme, he could not well suggest it,
and Sir Edward Seymour's pride would never have
permitted him to take the initiative, as it was impossible
for him to forget that he was the head of the Seymours,

EDWARD SEYMOUR, EIGHTH DUKE OF SOMERSET.

From a Picture at Knoyle, by kind permission of Mrs. Alfred Seymour.

whilst the Duke was but the younger branch of the family.*

Edward Seymour was on his road to town when the news of the decease of the Duke arrived. He 1749. was playing chess, when the innkeeper entered to congratulate him on his accession to the title. To this, however, Sir Edward paid no attention, and completed his game without a single word or sign. The next day, on his way to town, he met Lord Holland, on horseback, who rode up to the carriage, and, speaking through the window, strongly urged him to claim the title at once. This Seymour proceeded to do; but it was not without some difficulty that he established his claim to the Dukedom, for, though the matter appeared clear enough in the eyes of the law, there were many, in high places, who would gladly have seen the Seymour family removed from the House of Lords and their power and prestige lowered in the eyes of the world. For this purpose one or more claimants were produced and a good deal of underhand intrigue carried on. (Appendix N.) The claimants, however, being unable to uphold their false position, eventually retired from 1750. the field, and the enemies of the family found it beyond their power to delay or prevent justice being done. Seymour's right to the succession was proved by Sir Dudley Rider, Attorney-General, and a report was made to His Majesty, whereupon, November 25, 1750, he was summoned to the House of Peers.†

The following year he acted as chief mourner at the funeral of Frederick, Prince of Wales, April 13, 1751. 1751. In 1752, February 11, he obtained a grant of the offices of Warden and Chief Justice 1752. in Eyre of all His Majesty's forests, parks, chases, and warrens beyond Trent; and was

---

* Corresp. of the Seymours, coll. by 11th Duke of Somerset.
† Corresp. of the Seymours, coll. by 11th Duke of Somerset; Collins's Peerage.

also constituted Lord Lieutenant of the county of Wilts.*

1757.   He died at Maiden Bradley on the 12th of December, 1757, leaving the following issue :—

Edward Seymour, 9th Duke of Somerset, of whom we will speak later.

Webb Seymour, 10th Duke of Somerset, of whom we will speak later.

William Seymour, born February 12, 1719. He studied the law as a member of the Inner Temple, and was called to the Bar in 1744.

Francis Seymour, born August 25, 1726. He became Vicar of Wantage in Berks, Canon of Windsor, Dean of Wells, and Chaplain-in-Ordinary to His Majesty. On the 24th October, 1749, he married Catharine, daughter of the Rev. — Payne, of Holme-Lacy, in Hereford, and sister to the Countess Dowager of Northampton. By her he had issue, viz., Mary Seymour, born at Salisbury, October 5, 1751 ; Edward Seymour, born at Milford, near Sarum, February 14, 1754; Francis-Compton Seymour, born at Easterton, near Market-Lavington, January 28, 1755; Catharine Seymour, born at Cliff-Hall, near Market-Lavington, November 1, 1756 ; Fanny Seymour, born at Bath, April 11, 1761.

Mary Seymour, born May 15, 1729. On October 20, 1759, she married Vincent Biscoe, Esquire, of Austin-Friers. She died of small-pox at Seend, July 21, 1762, leaving issue a daughter, Mary, born August 30, 1760 ; and a son, Joseph Seymour Biscoe, born September 5, 1761.

* Collins's Peerage.

EDWARD SEYMOUR, NINTH DUKE OF SOMERSET.

From a portrait at Stover in the possession of H. St. Maur, Esqr.

EDWARD SEYMOUR, 9TH DUKE OF SOMERSET.

Edward Seymour was born January 2, 1717, and succeeded his father to the title December 12, 1717. 1757. About this time he formed an attachment to the Lady Dungarven which appeared to be 1757. reciprocated. There was, however, a considerable delay in the arrangements for the match, owing to many difficulties and arguments with her trustee as to the settlements; but these appeared to have eventually been practically overcome, for the settlement deeds were drawn up and had been seen and approved by both parties. Suddenly, however, the lady changed her mind and admitted a new attachment and a determination to marry the Lord Bruce.*

Whether this disappointment seriously affected the Duke or not we cannot tell, but certain it is that he took no further active part in politics, but settled down to lead a quiet and retired life at Maiden Bradley, seldom leaving the seclusion of this country seat for any purpose.

For several years before his death, which took 1792. place January 2, 1792, he shut himself up even more closely and developed such a curious and extraordinary dread of the small-pox that it amounted almost to a mania. (Note 102.) He never would touch a letter, but made a servant open it and hold it up against a glass window, through which he read it.*

He carried the orb at the coronation of George II, who made him a Privy Councillor, and attended his funeral, in 1760, as principal supporter to the Duke of

* Corresp. of the Seymours, coll. by 11th Duke of Somerset.

Cumberland, the chief mourner. In 1783 he was fortunate enough to receive a pension of £1,200 a year from the King.* (Note 103.)

It will be remembered that, at the commencement of the book, mention was made of a branch of the St. Maur family which was still in existence in France in 1800, and is believed to exist there still. In 1783 the head of this branch wrote to the Duke of Somerset, desiring to find out particulars and proofs which might show him to be a member of the Seymour, or rather St. Maur, family. (Appendix O.) The Duke was able, after some researches, to satisfy him to some extent on this point.

Owing to the seclusion and retirement of his life in the country, where he kept but few servants and did no entertaining, his fortune, which at first had been but small, gradually increased, and, with the aid of a careful and skilful management such as he exercised, became more fitted to his position. He died unmarried.

* Corresp. of the Seymours, coll. by 11th Duke of Somerset.

MARY, DUCHESS OF SOMERSET, DAUGHTER OF T. BONNEL, ESQ.

From a Portrait at Bulstrode, by kind permission of the Lady Gwendolen Ramsden.

WEBB SEYMOUR, 10TH DUKE OF SOMERSET.

Webb Seymour was born November 22, 1718, and when quite young inherited his grandfather's seat at Monkton Farley.

In 1751 he was made a Justice of the Peace for the county of Wilts, and in 1754 was admitted to the freedom of the city of Taunton.

In 1765, December 11, he married Mary Anne, daughter and heiress of John Bonnel, Esquire, of Stanton Court, Oxfordshire, who died July 22, 1802, having borne him four sons, only two of whom, however, survived; the others, it is said, having died more on account of the excess of care which she lavished upon them than from any inherent weakness.

He succeeded to the title of Duke of Somerset in 1792, but only held it for a year, dying in 1793. His sons were :—

Edward Seymour, who died young.
Webb Seymour, who died young.
Edward Adolphus Seymour, who became the 11th Duke of Somerset, and of whom we will speak later.
Webb John Seymour, of whom we will speak next.

LORD WEBB SEYMOUR.

Lord Webb Seymour was born in the spring of 1777. He commenced his education at the school of Ramsbury, in Wiltshire, whence he went to Christchurch, 1794. Oxford, where he began to reside in 1794.* "It was not long after this time that his character developed itself into a steadiness of purpose and an unshaken determination to cultivate his mind according to a preconceived scheme of improvement, rare in a young man of his rank, and much more so at that time than in the present age."* He adopted a plan, which even the studious and reading men of the University seldom thought it necessary to pursue. He resolutely declined all invitations, and during the whole of his residence at college was never seen at a wine party. "Such a course," says Mr. Hallam, "whatever in this more studious age may be thought, brought down at that time on his head the imputation of great singularity; but his remarkable urbanity of manners, and the entire absence of affectation, preserved to him the respect and regard of those from whose society he thus seemed to withdraw. The reason which Lord Webb gave for thus sacrificing all convivial intercourse was characteristic of his modesty. He felt, he said, that his parts were slow; that he acquired knowledge with less facility than many of his contemporaries; and that he could not hope to compass the objects which he had in view, if he gave up the evening hours, as was then customary, to the pleasures of conversation.

"Lord Webb Seymour was neither a very good scholar, in the common sense of the word, nor by any means the

* Biog. Not. of Lord Webb Seymour, by H. Hallam, in Life and Correspondence of F. Horner, 1853.

LORD WEBB SEYMOUR.

From a bust at Bulstrode, by kind permission of the Lady Gwendolen Ramsden.

contrary. He knew well, on every subject, what he knew at all, and his character rendered him averse to spread his reading over a large surface. He read slowly and carefully, possibly too much so; but on this account he forgot little, he was by this means uninformed on many subjects of general literature. But his peculiar quality was the love of truth, and, as is perhaps the case with all true lovers, he loved that mistress the more in proportion as she was slow in favouring his suit. It was said of him that he would rather get at anything by the longest process; and, in fact, not having a quick intuition, and well knowing that those who decide instantly are not apt to understand what they decide, he felt a reluctance to acquiesce in what the world calls a common-sense view of any philosophical question."

At first Lord Webb attached himself to the study of anatomy and chemistry and fitted up a laboratory in his rooms for the study of the latter science, but his ambition soon went further. After acquiring a considerable knowledge of physical history and philosophy, he became engrossed in metaphysical theories.*

In these pursuits, which he shared with a few friends, Lord Webb passed his time at college till the end 1797. of 1797, when he was seized with the desire of spending a few years at the University at Edinburgh, being attracted by its high reputation for moral and physical philosophy.*

"It was not long after his settling at Edinburgh that he became intimate with Mr. Horner, as well as 1800. with other individuals of a remarkable constellation who illustrated that city; especially Dr. Thomas Brown and Mr. Playfair. Under the auspices of the latter he carried on his enquiries in geology; a science then hardly more than nascent, and to which Lord Webb's attention had been drawn during his residence at Oxford. He travelled in company with Mr. Playfair on several occasions over a great part of Scotland, and some-

* Biog. Not. of Lord Webb Seymour, by H. Hallam.

times in England. Mr. Playfair became also the instructor of Lord Webb in mathematics, to which he addicted himself for some years with great assiduity, and not without injury to his health."*

During the next few years he became a most intimate friend of Mr. Horner. "Both ardent in their cultivation of natural philosophy, and deep in metaphysical enquiry, they read Bacon together, and compared their notes on every branch of study. The slowness of Lord Webb's mind, no doubt, gave greater depth and accuracy to Mr. Horner's researches, while Mr. Horner's greater activity stimulated and quickened that of Lord Webb."†

His Lordship stood aloof from public affairs, not from a want of interest but from a natural reserve coupled with ill-health and a feeble constitution which showed him but too plainly that it was not for him to enter the arena of political and party strife.† He did not, however, forget for a moment the duty he owed to his country when the latter was in danger, and, when an invasion of 1803. England was threatened by Bonaparte, he immediately left his studies, his associates, and the quiet life he loved, and for which only was he by nature fitted, to join a battalion of volunteers in Devonshire, which before long he was selected to command.‡

During his residence in that county he lived at Torquay, and spent such time as could be spared from his military duties in studying the geology of the country. At the end of two years, however, the scare of invasion being over and the country being once more secure, he gave up his appointment and returned to Edinburgh.‡

A change, however, had come over him. Hitherto he had been a very active man and a great walker, following 1805. his studies of geology in the field and thinking nothing of distances to be traversed. Now his "digestive organs began to fail, and to require a continual

* Biog. Not. of Lord Webb Seymour, by H. Hallam.
† Quarterly Review, 1843, 135.
‡ Biog. Not. of Lord Webb Seymour, by H. Hallam.

attention, which he was not ill-disposed to afford; but which came, as often happens, to engross much of his thoughts, and to shut him out from many pleasures, both intellectual and social, which he was formed to enjoy. With no manifest disease, a gradual languor stole over his mind and body, frequently relieved by transient rallying, but on the whole silently increasing for the rest of his life. Edinburgh continued to be his principal quarter; but the loss of some friends, and the removal of others to England, conspired with the decay of his health, to break off, except at intervals, or at least to relax the vigour of those philosophical speculations which he had pursued in the society of a Horner and a Brown. He came not more than two or three times to England afterwards; for the last, in the winter of 1816, when he remained in London for several months."*

It must not, however, be thought that this bodily failing turned Lord Seymour away from his studies. He found himself indeed compelled to give up his mathematical studies and now devoted himself to the fine arts, though with more regard to the philosophy of the emotions of taste than to purely technical knowledge. His study of geology also was not abated, though he was now debarred from pursuing this study in the field.*

In 1810 he purchased a small property call Glenarbach,
        beautifully situated on the banks of the Clyde.
1810. As he himself said he began to find it necessary
        from his bad state of health to spend a certain
portion of the year in a retirement which would allow him an uninterrupted pursuit of his own peculiar objects of scientific research, and where the pure air and quiet might aid to strengthen his weak constitution. After
        living there some time, however, he found him-
1814. self no better, and in 1814 he was back again
        in Edinburgh.†

* Biog. Not. of Lord Webb Seymour, by H. Hallam.
† Lord Seymour to Hallam, in Life and Corresp. of F. Horner, App. A.

He was now beginning to be unequal to much continuous exertion, but his love of acquiring knowledge was as great as ever, though as time went on his reading became more miscellaneous and less laborious. 1819. This quiet and studious life continued till 1819, when he gradually succumbed to pulmonary consumption and died on April 19.*

"Nothing," says Mr. Hallam,† "except a few pages on geology, ever appeared from the pen of Lord Webb.‡ But he had been much accustomed to commit his reflections to paper ; and whatever he wrote was clear, precise, and full of thought. He left a considerable quantity of notes designed for a work on the philosophy of the human mind, which, before the entire failure of his health, he had not ceased to contemplate in distant prospect; though, from the slowness of his composition, arising partly from the great labour which he gave, it was not likely, perhaps, under the most favouring circumstances, that he would have given his reflections a methodical form. It was at one time the wish of some of his friends, and especially of his nearest relation, that these fragments of his long-cherished speculations should be given to the world. But it is believed that they were found, on examination, to be in so unconnected a state, as to cause this intention to be abandoned.

"It would be doing the utmost injustice to the memory of this most lamented person, were I only to dwell on his intellectual character, or even on those qualities which have been already mentioned—his love of truth and desire of improvement. Not only was Lord Webb Seymour a man of the most untainted honour and scrupulous integrity, but of the greatest benevolence and the warmest

* Biog. Not. of Lord Webb Seymour, by H. Hallam.
† Life and Corresp. of F. Horner, by H. Hallam, ed. by L. Horner.
‡ He wrote a paper on geology, which may be seen in the Transactions of the Royal Society of Edinburgh, vol. vii, 303. Also the description of a clinometer. Both these papers were highly thought of.

attachment to his friends. This was displayed in a constant solicitude for their success, their fame, their improvement ; and in a sincerity which made no concessions to their vanity, while its delicate and gentle expression endeared him still more to those who were worthy to be his friends. Neither his constitution, nor his habits of reflection, admitted of strong emotions : he scarcely knew anger, or any of the violent passions ; and, perhaps, in considering the mild stoicism of his character, the self-command, which never degenerated into selfishness, we are not mistaken in fancying some resemblance between him and Marcus Aurelius. He would at least, in other times, have surely chosen the philosophy of the Porch ; but with all the beneficence and kindliness which only the best disciples of that school seem to have evinced."

There are many letters of Lord Webb's left to us—letters from which much may be learnt and that well repay the time spent in perusing them. Many of these are yet in private hands, but a good many, addressed to Mr. Horner and Mr. Hallam, have been published.* Space forbids their insertion here, and the following must merely serve as a sample, of which it has been said : "Which, if ever there be a manual compiled from the wisdom of our most experienced observers, and the high principle of our best writers, for the guidance of men in public life, will find its proper place." And again :—"What a lesson may public men of all parties take from these dignified admonitions of this kind, upright man ! "†

Edinburgh,
27th March, 1816.

MY DEAR HORNER,

For a long while past I have been anxious to write to you upon a subject on which I cannot enter without some embarrassment. Our views and sentiments upon politics have been growing wider

---

* Many may be read in the Life and Corresp. of F. Horner, by H. Hallam, ed. by L. Horner.
† Quarterly Review, 1843, 135-139.

and wider apart for the last two years, and though such differences
between friends must be expected in the course of life, and mutually
indulged, yet any material error in politics threatens to detract so
much from your high character, and so much from the good which
your talents and virtuous intentions may produce to the country,
that I cannot refrain from telling you I think you are in the
wrong, and how I think you have come to be so. That you
think me equally in the wrong, follows of course ; and you are of
course amply prepared with a defence against any argument I
should offer against the opinions you have entertained respecting
the characters, measures, and events of the grand story we have
witnessed. Such discussion could only have the effect of calling
up your habitual trains of thought, and those warm feelings which
they have produced, and which in turn have done so much to produce them. I shall therefore address you in another way, and
venture to place my authority in the balance against yours; with
all respect for your more extensive and accurate knowledge upon
political matters, your closer intercourse with men and things, and
your daily and hourly reflections upon them ; yet trusting on my
side to the calmness of the station from which I am allowed to
look on, to my freedom from the keenness of party warfare, and to
the constant exercise of a judgment which my friends allow to be
tolerably candid on other subjects, and for which, on the present,
I can see no source of bias, except what might have disposed me
to lean too much towards your side—I will tell you plainly my
opinion of the state of your mind, and leave it to any weight that
I may have with you to bring that opinion under your serious consideration in some quiet hour.

It seems to me, then, that, from your habitual antipathy and
active zeal against the members of our present government, and
your warm attachment to friends with whom every private, as well
as public, feeling has made it almost A RELIGION to agree, your
favour and aversion have been extended to every person and event,
according to their connection with, or opposition to, the one party
or the other. Thence has arisen the indulgent tenderness towards
Buonaparte and his adherents,—a tenderness which always increased, not so much, I believe, with the decline of their fortunes,
as with the swelling triumph of their enemies : thence the ready
suspicion of meanness, treachery, and selfishness in the Allies—
the angry censure of every step that did not accord with the most
high-minded notions of political morality, and the insensibility to
a generosity and rectitude in the great outlines of their conduct,
to which the history of the world affords few parallels : thence the
asperity against the Bourbon family, whose weakness and bigotry
were for ever dwelt upon, while the difficulties of their situation
were forgotten, and what was humane and liberal in their policy
overlooked: thence the apprehensions of a revival of a superstitious

reverence for royalty—while it was not considered that the restoration of the old dynasty was connected with the deliverance of Europe from the threatening evils of a military despotism of the most profligate character—and that with respect to France, the weakness of the executive power favoured the growth of civil liberty at home, while it promised security to her neighbours. The prevalence of such partial views in your mind may in some degree be ascribed to certain noble sentiments which the circumstances of the times made you cherish in early youth, an admiration for talent and energy of character, and the wish to see those only who possess them at the head of affairs, a hatred for the corruptions of superannuated governments and bright hopes for mankind from their overthrow, an abhorrence of the crafty domineering of priests, and a scorn of the ignorance, the incapacity, and the low vices, so often occurring in the families of princes, when the line has long been seated quietly on the throne. But the main source of bias is the constant society of your party friends in London. I can conceive no situation more seducing to the mind than to be going on among a set of men—most of whom are united in the harmony of friendship and social enjoyment—all extolling the talents and principles of each other—all ardent for the same objects, though each impelled by a various mixture of private and public motives—all anxious to detect, to communicate, and to enlarge upon whatever is to the disadvantage of their adversaries, and to keep out of sight whatever presents itself in their favour—all vieing with each other, not only in every public debate, but at every dinner, and in every morning walk, to magnify the partial views to which each by himself is naturally led. Most men, when long actuated by any keen interest in their private affairs, are liable to bias; how much more must this be the case when a number of minds are re-acting upon each other in the strenuous prosecution of a common cause, when there is the mutual support of each other's authority, no reference to opinion beyond the limits of the party, and the proud notion that the good of the country depends mainly on the practical adoption of their own principles? Look around, among all you have ever known, and name me a man whose judgment you would have said beforehand could remain firm and right under such warping influence. And how seldom in history do we find an active associate of any sect or party retaining a tolerable degree of candour. Such reflections should make you occasionally suspect yourself—as well as those of your party friends on whose understandings and integrity you place the strongest reliance. It was a striking lesson to remark last year and the year before the unprejudiced judgment and language of the Whigs, who were at a distance from the struggle between the parties, when compared with the sentiments of those who were engaged in it: and on the former side of this contrast I am happy to place Jeffrey, J. Murray, Dugald Stewart, Mr. Wilson, Mr. J. Clark, Lord Minto, and Hallam. Perhaps your consciousness of a high spirit of independence makes you too little on your guard against the influence of those around you. There are many cases in which I could trust to the candour of your judgment ; but not so when certain strong feelings are connected with the point in question. Above all, I could not trust you where your affections are involved ; for that warmth of heart and steadiness of attachment, which are such charms in your character, must then interfere, and I have observed them to do so.

I wish that your party friends were more aware of the light in which their temper and conduct appear to many people, who, with no strong feeling either for or against ministers, are anxious for the best interests of their country and mankind. Men thus disposed, and with various degrees of intelligence, are, I imagine, pretty numerously scattered throughout the island ; and these are the men whose approbation they must be ambitious of, if their motives are pure, and whose support, if they are prudent, they must be eager to gain. During the last two years they would have often found the sentiments of such people at variance with their own. They would have found them sometimes lamenting, and sometimes indignant, to see men who profess themselves patriots and philanthropists steadily turning away from every joyful event and every bright prospect—to dwell upon the few intermingled occasions of regret, or censure, or despondency—and uttering naught but groans over the fate of Norway, or Spain, or Saxony, or Genoa—while our own country and half the civilised world felt as if breathing when first risen from a bed of imminent death. I wish your friends could have heard in secret the opinions of the impartial upon the justice and expediency of the war last year ; I wish they could now hear the expressions I have heard— of dread at the idea of any man being in office whose indulgent favour of Napoleon might render it, in however small a degree, more likely that he should escape from his confinement and again throw the world into confusion.

Opposition in Parliament is generally conducted upon one very false principle, namely, that the measures of ministers must in every case be so far wrong as to deserve upon the whole very severe reprobation. I will not suppose this principle to be speculatively recognised ; but it seems at least to be practically adopted. Now it is plain that where a set of men have the good of the country mainly at heart, and have tolerable capacities for business, though their talents be neither profound nor brilliant, and though their principles lean rather more than is right in favour of the Crown, yet their measures must in all probability be often as good as circumstances will admit of, and sometimes entitled to praise for unusual prudence or magnanimity. On such occasions justice is, for the most part, denied them altogether by the opposition side of the House ; or, if praise is bestowed at all, it is bestowed in feeble terms, and with reservations much insisted on; but what is denied them in Parliament is granted by an impartial public without doors, with proportionate disgust at the bitter and unremitting censures of factious enmity. Upon this point I must add, that I heard it said (by a friend too) that you hurt yourself in the opinion of the public by some want of candour towards the latter part of the last session.

Do not conceive that I am insensible to the benefits which the country derives from a vigorous opposition. But I am confident that these benefits might be greatly increased, and every interest of the opposition party much advanced, if the temper, which party is sure to generate, were better controlled by those at least whose talents place them at its head ; and if their views, freed from the bias of that temper, accorded more with the sentiments of an enlightened and almost neutral part of the nation. Opposition, even when carried on with the spirit of Sir Francis Burdett, is a check to abuses and a safeguard to our liberty; there are few, however, with intelligence superior to that of the mob, who would favour his political objects. Mr. Whitbread's conduct in opposition was of a higher character: a friend of the people, and a firm foe to corruption, he was entitled to a great respect; yet there were occasions when I could not have wished to see Mr. Whitbread in office, from the fear of his acting upon those mistaken notions, and with that vehement and perverse spirit which appeared in his attacks upon Government, and which sometimes made him even go beyond the sentiments of his own political friends. There are higher stations in opposition than that of Mr. Whitbread—higher, from a display of more temperate and candid judgment. I would fain see you occupying the highest in this as well as in other respects; and I would fain know that the dignified propriety of language and demeanour which you have so successfully cultivated in the House was founded upon just and moderate views of events, and men, and manners.

Believe me, my dear Horner,
Yours ever, very affectionately,
WEBB SEYMOUR.

[Edinburgh Review, July to October, 1843, p. 279 onwards ; Edinburgh Review, November to February, 1818 ; Quarterly Review, vol. 72, 1843, p. 135 onwards ; Life and Correspondence of F. Horner, by H. Hallam, ed. by L. Horner, containing a short biographical notice of Ld. Webb Seymour, by Hallam, App. A., and a great number of his letters.]

Z

EDWARD ADOLPHUS, 11TH DUKE OF SOMERSET.

1775. Edward Adolphus Seymour was born at Monckton Farley, in Wilts, on the 24th February, 1775. He was educated first at Eton and then at Christchurch, Oxford, where he matriculated on
1792. January 31, 1792.*

1793. The following year he succeeded to the Dukedom through the death of his father, December 15, and having still a minority of three years he became somewhat richer than his immediate predecessors, who were certainly by no means well off for their position. He continued his education at Oxford, however, where from the first he devoted himself to science and mathematics, for both of which studies he displayed great aptitude. He received his degree
1794. of M.A. on July, 1794, and continuing to remain a member of the college received the honorary degree of D.C.L. July 3, 1810.†

1795. In 1795, he took a long tour through the most interesting parts of England, Wales, and Scotland, an account of which was published by Mitchell, in 1845. During this tour he seems to have occupied himself chiefly with the study of geology. In
1797. 1797 he was elected a Fellow of the Royal Society, and in 1816 was made a Fellow of the Society of Antiquaries. For some years he was president of the Royal Institution, in which he took great interest

---

* Dict. Nat. Biog.
† Annual Register, 1856; Gent's. Mag., 1855; Forster's Alumni, Oxon., 1715-1886.

EDWARD ADOLPHUS SEYMOUR, ELEVENTH DUKE OF SOMERSET.

From a portrait at Stover in the possession of H. St. Maur, Esqr.

1801. and, from 1801 to 1838, president of the Royal Literary Fund, and vice-president of University College, London.*

In 1814, he assisted Mr. Lancaster in his scheme for the universal diffusion of education amongst the 1814. poor, by becoming patron of an institution, established near Maiden Bradley, for training village schoolmasters ; an attempt which unfortunately failed, and produced a loss of £1,200.†

In 1820 he became a Fellow of the Linnean Society. From 1826 to 1831 he was vice-president of 1820. the Zoological Society, and from 1834–7 president of the Linnean Society. He was also a member of the Royal Asiatic Society.‡

He carried the orb at the coronation of William IV, in 1831, and again at the coronation of Queen 1831. Victoria, in 1838. In 1837 he was made a Knight of the Garter by William IV. He died at 1855. Somerset House, Park Lane, August 15, 1855, and was buried in the cemetery at Kensal Green.§

The Duke was a very handsome man, with a kind and genial expression, and was a generous and frank patron of men of science and letters, some of whom owed a good deal of their eventual success to his encouragement and assistance at the commencement of their careers. His own attainments were considerable, and, though he did not publish many of the results of his mathematical and scientific researches, a great part of his time was spent in the study of these sciences.‖ Two small treatises, however, which he contributed to the press attracted no little attention at the time. These were " The Elementary Pro-

---

* Annual Register, 1856 ; Dict. Nat. Biog.
† Edinburgh Review.
‡ Dict. Nat. Biog., &c.
§ Dict. Nat. Biog.
‖ The quantities of MSS. in the author's possession at Stover attest the diligence with which he worked.

perties of the Ellipse deduced from the Properties of the Circle," published in 1842, and " Alternate Circles and their Connection with the Ellipse," published in 1850.

He was extremely well versed in historical and antiquarian knowledge, and P. F. Tytler, the historian, attached great value to his judgment in these matters.* He was, moreover, an excellent landlord, taking keen interest in the management of his estates, and popular amongst his tenantry. Unlike most landed proprietors he supported the repeal of the Corn Laws, and showed his confidence in that measure by making large purchases of land during the depression which followed it.†

He was twice married, first on June 24, 1800, to Charlotte, 2nd daughter of the 9th Duke of Hamilton and Brandon, who died June 10, 1827. Secondly, in 1836, to Margaret, eldest daughter of Sir Michael Shaw Stewart, Bart., of Blackhall, Renfrew, who survived him for some time, dying at Somerset House, July 18, 1880.

By his first wife he had the following children :—

> Edward Adolphus Seymour, born 1804, who became 12th Duke of Somerset, and of whom we shall speak next.
> Archibald Henry Algernon Seymour, born 1810, who became 13th Duke of Somerset.
> George Spencer Adolphus Seymour, born 1812, who died without issue.
> Algernon Percy Banks Seymour, born 1813, who became 14th Duke of Somerset.
> Charlotte Jane Seymour, who married Archibald Blount, Esq., of Orchill, Bucks.
> Jane Anne Wilhelmina Seymour, born 1806.
> Anna Maria Jane Seymour, born 1807.
> Henrietta Jane Seymour, born 1809.

* The Duke made considerable researches into his family history, and at one time meant to have written a book, Annals of the Seymours. All his MSS. and notes for this are in the author's possession, at Stover.

† Dict. Nat. Biog.

MARGARET, DAUGHTER OF SIR MICHAEL SHAW STEWART, AND SECOND WIFE
OF THE ELEVENTH DUKE OF SOMERSET.

From a drawing at Stover, in the possession of H. St. Maur, Esqr

[Annual Register, 1856; Dict. Nat. Biog.; Gent's. Mag., 1855, 11, 425; Tour of the Duke of Somerset through parts of England, Wales, and Scotland, in 1795, published 1845; The Duke of Somerset's Own MSS., &c., at Stover; Times, August 16, 1855; Forster's Alumni, Oxon., 1715-1886; Forster's Peerage; G. E. C[ockayne]'s Peerage.]

EDWARD ADOLPHUS, 12TH DUKE OF SOMERSET.

Of Lord Seymour's early childhood there is little to record.   He appears to have been a great favourite with his grandfather, the Duke of Hamilton, and with 1804.   his uncle, Lord Webb Seymour ; his education was carefully attended to, even fencing being included before the age of nine.   He is said up to this time to have shown a somewhat indolent disposition, which, however, soon gave way to activity upon his being sent to Eton.*

After some years at this College, he went to Christchurch,† whence, his college career being duly finished, he was sent abroad to travel.   Amongst other places he visited Russia, but of his doings and adventures we have no record, as no letters or papers relating to these five years are to be found.‡

In June, 1830, he married Jane Georgina, the youngest daughter of Mr. Thomas Sheridan,† and 1830.   sister to the Hon. Mrs. Norton and Lady Dufferin, the ceremony taking place in the evening, at the house of Sir James Graham, in Grosvenor Place.

A few weeks after his marriage he was elected member of Parliament for the town of Okehampton,† and began seriously to enter the arena of politics.   This necessitating his passing a considerable portion of his time in town, he settled down at 18, Spring Gardens.

The following year, 1831, Parliament was dissolved, upon which he stood, and was elected as a Whig 1831.   for theborough of Totnes.

* Letters and Memoirs, by Lady G. Ramsden.
† Dict. Nat. Biog.
‡ Letters and Memoirs.

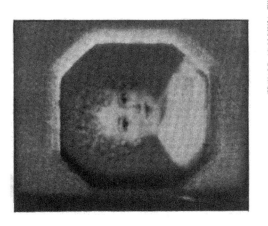

EDWARD ADOLPHUS, TWELFTH DUKE OF SOMERSET

From miniatures at Bulstrode, by kind permission of the Lady Gwendolen Ramsden.

JANE GEORGINA, DUCHESS OF SOMERSET, DAUGHTER
OF THOMAS SHERIDAN.

From a miniature by kind permission of Lady Gwendolen Ramsden.

In the autumn of 1834 Lord and Lady Seymour took a tour on the Continent, visiting, amongst other 1834. places, Frankfort, Wiesbaden, and Paris. Their trip was, however, curtailed owing to the dissolution of Parliament, which necessitated Lord Seymour's again standing for the borough of Totnes. Within three months of his election there was a change of 1835. Government, and he was appointed Lord of the Treasury under Lord Melbourne. This necessitating re-election, he was again returned for Totnes.*

During this same year (1835) he fought a duel with Sir Colquhoun Grant ; this being perhaps the last duel fought in this country. It was brought about in the following manner. Sir Colquhoun Grant challenged him with having been privy to the elopement of his only daughter with Lady Seymour's brother, R. B. Sheridan. Seymour refused either to acknowledge or deny the charge, preferring to be suspected of complicity in the matter rather than that any similar accusation should be brought against his wife. As a matter of fact, he knew nothing whatever about the elopement, not even that it had taken place. Shots were exchanged, Seymour firing in the air. His ignorance of the transaction was then explained, and the matter ended.†

During this year and the next there is practically nothing to record, "but he has left an interesting record of his own mental development during that period in the following 'Reflections,' many of which were obviously suggested to him by his experience of public life, and show the spirit in which he himself entered on it."

"The Relation of Thought to Oratory. *

"Why is it that those men who are most given to reflection and to the exertion of their thoughts are often least capable of expressing them ?

* Letters and Memoirs.
† Dict. Nat. Biog.

" The first and most palpable reason which occurs to me is, that their thoughts are probably more intricate and continued, not so loose and undetached as those of the generality of men. The ideas of great thinkers may be often, as Johnson says somewhere, inductile and unmalleable, so that they cannot easily be brought into a shape fitted for expression. The solution is not, however, sufficiently explanatory, and I am inclined to believe that several other causes contribute to this result. There seems, indeed, to be an unfortunate discrepancy between the two powers of thinking and speaking, which tend very much to prevent their being united in the same individual. This will, I trust, appear plain if we consider what a man does when he wishes to think correctly. He first, probably, looks upon his subject as much as possible separate from the words in which it is conveyed to him ; for such, I remember, is the advice of Locke, and, as it will strike every one, is the safest way to avoid prejudice and misconception. He thinks as far as he is able without the intervention of words, but he takes more especial care to avoid those strings of words which, from some temporary application, frequent usage, or sometimes merely from the harmony of sound, have been long continued and accustomed to go together. Such words he either omits, or, if he has need of them, he detaches them from their association, he weighs cautiously their insulated, their intrinsic worth, and never for a moment allows his mind to think of them in any other sense than that which he has prescribed. After this labour has been performed, and when he has sufficiently balanced in his mind the difficulties and probabilities on each side of the question, he draws his inferences and obtains his result. But this result comes forth from his mind, as metal from a crucible, in a pure and unadulterated state, not only with no adventitious questions attached to it, but without any epithets or any other of the usual concomitants of opinions. In this state, however valuable it may be to himself as an immutable truth, or as a predominant probability, it is not in a state to be communicated to others : it is a piece of pure gold, but it must be well coined and stamped before it will be generally received.   He is obliged, therefore, to discard his usual habits and mental exertion, and to turn his attention to words—to seek out, in short, appropriate phrases, epithets, and metaphors, to mix his truth with the alloy of language that it may pass current in the world. The superficial thinker, or rather, perhaps I should say, the unphilosophical thinker, takes his question, on the contrary, with all the language in which he finds it enveloped, considers it all at once, and, if he arrives at the same conclusion, it must be rather by the acuteness of his mind than the adequacy of his means.   But, then, he possesses his conclusion and all the arguments on which it is founded ready for immediate expression ; he has used his words in the loose sense of common language, and in that sense they will be readily received ; he needs no definition of terms, no restriction of meaning ; he did not chemically analyse the coin which was given him for examination, but, after looking a little at its superscription and trying its jingle on the floor, he has it ready to pay whereon he may desire.   Such appears to me to be one of the disadvantages under which a calm, unprejudiced reasoner labours when he is opposed by the ready eloquence of a superficial thinker.   I believe that in speaking of Parliamentary debates I might even go further, and say, what at first hearing appears paradoxical, that a prejudiced mind is the most readily adapted for eloquence and oratorical display.   Whenever a question is mooted, the prejudiced man comes to the discussion with a number of sentiments already enlisted on his side. 'Prejudice,' as Burke says in speaking its eulogy, ' is of ready application in the emergency ; it previously engages the mind in a steady course, and does not leave the man hesitating in the moment of decision, sceptical, puzzled, and unresolved.   Prejudice renders a man's virtue his habit, and not a series of unconnected acts.   Through just prejudice his duty becomes a part of his nature.'

Burke seems here to have fallen into the very error I was just mentioning, of using inappropriate epithets. How can prejudice be ever called just? ' Prejudice' means (see Johnson) 'judgment founded beforehand without examination.' Now, however correct that judgment may chance to be, it is no more just than it would be to pass sentence on a culprit before trial."

" Ridicule as a Test of Truth.

" Ridicule, as it appears to me, is not a fair test of truth—' Ridiculune acri fortius ac metius plermuque secat res '; this, if at least it be a truth, must be applied with some modification. The reductio ad absurdum is an allowable mode of arguing in mathematics, but must not be used in religion, in morality, or politics. In religion, certainly, it must not be used as a weapon against matters of faith, for it appears to me that Protestant divines are inconsistent who would allow us to ridicule the doctrine of transubstantiation, but forbid us to reason in the same manner about the Trinity, and many articles of our creed. We should never laugh at errors in religion ; the subject is too grave, too important, too vital ; yet there is much scriptural authority for laughing at the errors of men. I always feel shocked at that passage in ' Paradise Lost,' where Milton describes the building of Babel, and the consequent punishment of the confusion of tongues ; and then he adds that the angels mocked at the miseries of men, and that there was ' laughter loud in heaven.' Surely this degrades the angels ; we should not laugh if we saw children in foolish ignorance risking their lives and happiness ; yet Milton had some apparent authority for this in the expressions of Scripture. When man had tasted the forbidden fruit, God said : ' Behold, man has become as one of us.' Now this speech was, as St. Chrysostom and others explain it, a bitter irony to Adam, who, instead of becoming like a god, was degraded and fallen from the state of man. Does not David also say that at the punishment of the wicked the just shall look and laugh over them, and Job says the innocent man shall mock them ? Jeremiah says that the deeds of sinners are vain and laughable. Is it not even said of the Deity that he shall laugh over the death of the wicked ? Such passages in Scripture are dreadful and incomprehensible. Laughter over an unrepentant sinner appears unworthy of a Christian. It is cruelty usurping the place of pity. It is curious to observe how much use is made of ridicule in all polemical disputes. Even in the earliest times, and down to the present day, different sects ridicule each other. The coarse ribaldry of Luther, and the vulgar wit with which the church replied to him, seems as if it had been imagined the Reformation could be settled by personal aspersions and recriminations. We find Milton making jokes against Episcopacy, and Pascal wittily mocking the doctrines of the Jesuits. In matters of religion ridicule is a dangerous weapon ; it frequently injures those who use it, for it is like bringing an elephant into battle ; and sometimes the witty writer, like Diomed under the walls of Troy, wounds a deity while he aims at his antagonist."

"The Defence of Atheism.

" A man who writes in support of Atheism, and passes his time in trying to prove that there will be no future life, employs himself in a very melancholy occupation. The monks of La Trappe spent their leisure hours in digging their graves, but he occupies his life in proving that the grave will be eternal."

"Truth and Intellectual Acuteness.

"Hume says in one of his essays that men may be divided into profound and shallow thinkers ; the first miss the truth by going beyond it, the last do not penetrate far enough to reach it. Pascal says the same : ' Si on n'y songe pas assez, ou si on y songe trop on s'entête et l'on ne peut trouver la verité.' This seems to be true in almost every department of knowledge ; even in religion, although we are often told to think of it continually, yet we observe that those who do make it the constant subject of their thoughts imbibe notions which must be false, because if they were generally adopted they would be most pernicious. By this I mean that I consider any religious opinion to be necessarily false which militates against the existence of society, and of this kind are the opinions which enthusiasts or profound thinkers in religion usually adopt. The saying of Hobbes is frequently quoted : ' I am not so ignorant as others, because I have not read so much,' and we might sometimes with equal truth say : ' I am not fallen into so many errors as others, because I have not thought so much.' This is, in fact, what is meant when persons remark ' that suggestion is too ingenious to be true ' ; that is, ' you have missed the truth by going beyond it.' Much injury, as Bacon observed, has arisen to science by the love of generalising ; that is, reasoning too hastily from particulars to universals, or founding a theory upon a single fact, which is a vice peculiar to profound thinkers. Carneades, the sophist, used to say : ' If he is a very clever man, I shall the more easily succeed in deceiving him,' and there was much truth in this observation, for a clever man is more easily deceived by ingenious arguments than a stupid man, who seldom sees their force. Give Berkeley's essay to a shallow thinker, and he will soon put it aside as an extravagant absurdity ; but no clever man ever read it without being much puzzled and left in doubt whether or not matter really exists. These remarks might be applied to the national character of many countries. We all know how the Athenians were constantly led astray by an ingenious argument, and thus we find that the speeches of their favourite orators consist almost entirely of argument ; and, indeed, it must surprise every one who reads these orations to see how seldom (considering that they were addressed to a promiscuous audience) they appeal to

JANE GEORGINA DUCHESS OF SOMERSET, DAUGHTER OF THOMAS SHERIDAN, ESQ.
IN THE DRESS WORN AT THE EGLINTON TOURNAMENT.

From a painting in the possession of Lady Ulrica Thynne. By kind permission.

the passions. But this love of shrewd arguments and ingenious reasonings did not make them more difficult to be deceived ; a clever man would always deceive them. Now, the English, on the contrary, are not easily deceived ; they do not listen patiently to an ingenious argument. If the reasoning is very clever, they suspect it to be fallacious. They say of a clever child, ' He is too clever to live long,' and of a clever theory, ' It is too clever to last.' ' It is so brilliant that it must be false,' is a natural remark when one sees a fine head-dress of diamonds, and the same observation is frequently applied to a brilliant speech. The sound sense of the English, it is said, protects them against these deceptions ; if the people were more clever they would be more easily deceived. They are so sensible because they are so stupid ; this sounds like a paradox, but there is some truth in it. Now the Germans are more subtle and ingenious reasoners, and the consequence is that they are frequently puzzled about their own identity—a misfortune which can only happen to a profound thinker—' Si on y songe trop on s'entête.' "

The Parliament was dissolved this year owing to the death of William IV. Lord Seymour was again 1837. elected for Totnes, and continued Lord of the Treasury until 1839, when he resigned on being appointed Secretary to the Board of Control.*

During this year the famous Eglinton tournament took place, and Lady Seymour was chosen to preside over it as Queen of Beauty. So many accounts have been given of this revival of ancient days, that it is needless to enlarge upon it here.†

In June of this year Lord Seymour was appointed Under Secretary of State for the Home Depart-1838. ment ; this, however, barely lasted two months, Parliament being dissolved in August, when Lord

---

* Dict. Nat. Biog. ; Annual Register, 1885.
† Eglinton ; Dict. Nat. Biog.

Melbourne was succeeded by Sir Robert Peel. Lord Seymour was elected for Totnes without opposition, and, shortly after, accompanied by Lady Seymour, went to Italy, where they remained till the following spring.*

The following year he took a short trip to Norway during the time Parliament was not sitting, and, 1840. in the autumn of 1844, went for a yachting 1844. cruise with Mr. Cavendish Bentinck in the "Dream," returning in March of the following 1845. year, Lady Seymour and her children, meanwhile, remaining in Paris.*

In April, 1849, he was appointed Chief Commissioner of Woods and Forests, under Lord John Russell, 1849. and Chief Commissioner of Works and Privy Councillor in 1851.

In June, Parliament was dissolved, and he again successfully presented himself to his constituents at 1851. Totnes for re-election.*

Soon after the borough of Totnes was disfranchised, and Lord Seymour ceased to be a member of the House of Commons. During the time that he sat there he carried a Bill through the House, which received the Royal assent, for establishing a Board for the Superintendence of Railways. He voted for the repeal of the Corn Laws, and served on the Committee of the House to inquire into the state of the army during the Crimean War.†

Having lost his seat he took the opportunity of taking a holiday, and paid a second visit to Norway. His father, however, dying in August, he was obliged to return at once to take up his duties as Duke of Somerset in the House of Lords.‡

In this year he became First Lord of the Admiralty under Lord Palmerston, a post which he filled for 1859. seven years, until Lord Palmerston was succeeded

---

* Letters and Memoirs.
† Dict. Nat. Biog.; Annual Register, 1885.
‡ Letters and Memoirs; Dict. Nat. Biog.

by Lord Derby.* "The Duke's tenure of office was now ended, nor did he ever again seek to re-enter public life. Three years later he was invited by Mr. Gladstone to join the Ministry, but he declined. His doing so was the occasion of a just and temperate tribute to his character on the part of a paper in which such serious writing was uncommon. 'The refusal of the Duke of Somerset,' said Vanity Fair, 'to become a member of Mr. Gladstone's Administration endowed us no doubt with Mr Childers as First Lord of the Admiralty, and probably left the Cabinet much more amenable to the uncontrolled will of the Premier than would otherwise have been the case; but with all these advantages to set against it, the want of so strong a pillar of the Liberal Party in the Ministry must be accounted a loss even greater to the country than to the party itself; for the Duke is a strong Liberal, not only in matters of State, but, what is more important, in Church matters, and his Liberalism not being of the sort which is assumed for personal purposes, may be trusted even upon occasions when ordinary Liberals often go wrong from fear of personal consequences. The high rank and position of the Duke have, indeed, had upon his political conduct an influence for good, which is by no means the common rule, for he has put them to their proper and nobler uses as strongholds whence he may look justly and fearlessly upon men and things. In our system of government by party, it is perhaps necessary that jobbery should flourish as it does, yet the Duke of Somerset has never condescended to its use, either for himself or for his party; but it is only because he is too strong to be coerced like other leaders that he has been able to maintain and to carry out his strong sense of impartial justice. For this reason it is that he is said to be a proud man; and so he is, but his is a pride a little of which were better found in some others of our statesmen than much of the humility now accepted as meritorious. Indeed, the Duke apparently

* Letters and Memoirs.

dislikes humility, for, himself proud and sincere, yet liberal and just, he refused to serve under the most humble of Premiers.' "

During the next three years Mr. Gladstone and Mr. Childers went in for a Government of the greatest economy, which resulted in the greatest inefficiency of the army and navy, and might very possibly have terminated in a disaster to the country. We read of this period in the Quarterly Review :—" The cautious and strong sense of the Duke of Somerset has pronounced sentence on the Administration which he generally supports, and which he has vainly endeavoured to save from folly. In a caustic and terse epigram, which will never be forgotten, he has stigmatised for ever the military and naval policy of the present Administration :—' An army that can't march, and ships that won't swim,' as the result of three years of boastful economical government."

" The Duke's refusal, however," we see in his Memoirs,* " whatever may have been his political feelings at the moment, was mainly due to reasons of a very different nature. Six months previously he had lost his second son, Lord Edward St. Maur, and he was now overwhelmed with a sorrow from which he never wholly recovered. His subsequent life was one of a comparative retirement, and the fact that it was so is attributable to this cause. He was not, however, a man to allow himself to be unnerved by suffering. He sought alleviation in activity of a new kind.

" The Duke mentions in one of his later letters, that he learnt by experience that sorrow was best borne by forcing the mind to busy itself with some arduous and absorbing work. In the sorrow which had now fallen on him, and which was subsequently deepened by the loss of his eldest son a few years afterwards, he threw himself into the study of a class of questions and problems which had always roused his interest, but which, up to now, he had not examined systematically, namely, the results of scien-

* Letters and Memoirs, 12th Duke of Somerset.

EDWARD PERCY ST. MAUR.

From a miniature at Stover, the property of H. St. Maur, Esqr.

tific scholarship, and of science generally, as affecting historical Christianity. To this study he devoted himself for five years, making himself familiar with the writings of the most authentic scholars and critics—in especial, those of Germany ; and he finally, in 1871, produced a small volume, in which their conclusions are summed up. This volume is curiously characteristic of the writer. It is full of shrewd and dry humour, which sometimes suggests Gibbon. It is remarkable for the practical turn everywhere given in it to speculation. It is admirable for lucidity of arrangement and terseness of expression, and

1872. is for this reason full of intrinsic interest. The title of the volume is ' Christian Theology and Modern Scepticism.' " It was published in 1872.

The Duke still continued to be regular in his attendance at the House of Lords, and to take intense interest in all measures for the good of the country and the people.

1876. In 1876 we find him very busy over a Commission on Slavery, and also spending some of his time over his duties at the British Museum.*

He did not often speak in the House, but, when he did, the House always sat in wrapt attention, knowing they would hear the opinion of a clever and impartial man. His speeches were short and to the point and, often, amusing from the dry wit he exhibited. On one occasion he was speaking against a motion of Lord Halifax, relating to the Ameer, and, referring to Yakoob Khan, his son, said that heirs-apparent were sometimes irregular in their conduct and troublesome. All eyes at once were turned upon the Prince, who was present, and the Duke of Cambridge, sitting next him, burst out laughing ; but when he added that, amongst other slight irregularities, this heir-apparent had committed a few murders, and had even murdered the Commander-in-Chief, the Royalties were convulsed with laughter, in which the whole House joined.*

" Though the Duke, as has already been said, after the

* Letters and Memoirs.

death of his second son, never again took a prominent part in politics, yet the changes which, under the influence of Mr. Gladstone, were at this period taking place in the character of the Liberal party, turned him once again into a keen political critic.   Many of his letters—full of wit and shrewdness—bear witness to this fact ; but 1880.   evidence of it, still fuller and more important, is to be found in his short work on ' Democracy,' which he published in 1880."*

The Irish Land Bill was now attracting great attention, and I may perhaps be pardoned for quoting an extract or two concerning it from his letters.   April 22, he writes : " The Irish Land Bill, while it robs the landowners of their property, will in its results perpetuate the pauperism of the small tenants.   It does not even obtain the approval of the Irish, whom it was designed to gratify.   I suppose, however, that it will be carried in some shape in order to save the Government from a disastrous failure."   On April 24, he writes : " —— seems very well ; he is astonished and disgusted at the Irish Land Bill. Gladstone told him, some months ago, that he sympathised with his paper on the question.   —— bought up the tenant right from some of his tenants, but under this Bill they will recover the right for which they have been paid.   Nevertheless, this Bill again enables landowners to purchase the tenant right.   Who will be fool enough to buy what will probably be taken from them in a year or two hence ? " August 6, he says : " Last night we ended the Committee on the Irish Land Bill, one of the most discreditable measures that I remember in all my public life.   I feel ashamed of the ministers and of the Liberal party for proposing such a Bill, yet it could not have been rejected without causing a violent convulsion and a re-enactment of a similar law."   On August 20, he writes : " I was glad to leave town after the most discreditable Session which I can remember.   Irish ideas have demoralised British statesmen."   The following year he writes : " The

* Letters and Memoirs.

years slip away, and we cannot expect to go on much longer; but I fear that I may outlive the English Constitution, which the ministry are undermining."

"Early in the year of 1884 the health of the Duchess began to show signs of failing. By the autumn it 1884. gave the family grave cause for alarm; and on December 14 she died. The Duke's affection for her is evidenced in every letter he wrote her, and in none more than in the two short notes—the one announcing her death to Mr. Sheridan, the other thanking Lord and Lady Dufferin for their condolence—which are given in this chapter, and in their brevity and superficial address have a pathos which could hardly be found in any less restrained method of expression." *

40, Park Lane,
Dec. 15, 1884.

My dear Brinsley,

Georgy came up to town on Friday, and seemed well—said the drive had done her good. The young Duchess of Montrose called, and they talked and laughed together. On Saturday she felt sleepy, and did not get up, but the doctor felt her pulse, and said she would be better next morning. But in the night she had shivering fits; Gwen sent for the doctor, and he said she was better, but on Sunday morning she passed away in a quiet doze. She had suffered so much during the last eight months, and had nearly lost her sight, that it is for her a comfort, but to us a great loss, for she was always cheery and lively, even in the midst of her suffering.

Yours affectionately,
Somerset.

40, Park Lane,
Jan. 19, 1885.

My dear Dufferin,

I thank you and Lady Dufferin for your kind sympathy. It is a dreadful blank, after above fifty years of a most cheerful and affectionate companion, but I will not dwell further. My daughters, in the midst of their own sorrow, have done all they could to console me. At my time of life I cannot look forward to

---

* Letters and Memoirs.

any long period ; and, indeed, the sad condition of public affairs, both at home and abroad, reconciles me to depart.

I am glad to hear good accounts of you and of your journey and reception at Bombay. I take a great interest in your government, and hope that your health may enable you to deal with all the difficulties which at present surround you.

Yours affectionately,
SOMERSET.

" The Duke's foreboding that he should not long survive his wife proved to be correct. He survived her for but twelve months. Meanwhile, however, he seems to have had recourse to the same practical philosophy which he had before called to his aid, to assist him in bearing the loss of his favourite son. He gave his mind constant and active employment, and forced himself to take an interest both in public events and the lives of those around him."*

In the autumn of this year, following his usual custom, he went from Bulstrode to Stover, his house in 1885. Devon, taking his grand-daughter, as usual, with him. "His days were spent in his customary employments, and his evenings in reading or in playing at chess with his grand-daughter. He often drove out to visit various neighbours, particularly Sir Samuel Baker, who lived almost next door to him, and on one occasion he opened a cottage hospital in a village not far distant. He seemed, indeed, to be in his usual health, except for a pain in his foot, which gave him considerable uneasiness. Supposing this to be gout, he abandoned, for the first time in his life, the practice of walking when he went out to shoot, and took to riding on a pony. One day the pony started, and the Duke fell. The fact of his having lost his seat, owing to so slight a cause, is a proof that he was even then far less strong than he was thought to be ; but he seemed at the moment to be none the worse for the accident. From this time, however, he began to complain more frequently of a general sense of weakness, and also of the pain in his foot ; and the doctors regarded the

* Letters and Memoirs.

symptoms as very grave, and as indicating weakness of the heart." *

" The accounts which we received," one of his daughters writes, " caused great anxiety to my two sisters and to myself, and brought us to Stover, where we remained with our father during the few remaining weeks of his life. The increasing weakness had now confined him to his bed for the greater part of the day ; and it was only in the afternoon that he was moved on to the sofa. At times the pain which he suffered was very severe. We could see this by the expression of his face, though he never gave utterance to the least murmur or complaint.

"But his interest in all that was going on continued as keen as ever. The General Election was then in progress, and he liked us to read the reports of the newspapers from day to day ; and as the election appeared more and more to be going on as he thought best, he often exclaimed, ' Oh, I'm glad, I'm glad ! '

" At all times, and up to his last hour, he was most sympathetic, and took the greatest interest in whatever concerned his daughters and his grandchildren. To his daughters—for fear, no doubt, of making them unhappy—he never spoke as if he was dying ; but to his young grand-daughter,† one day, when she had spoken hopefully of his recovery, he said, ' Oh, yes, they try their best, and do all they can ; but I know very well it is only the beginning of the end.' And the end came very soon and very suddenly. One day my sister had been reading and talking to him during the morning at intervals, and then he had rested. In the afternoon he was assisted on to the sofa, and, as usual, wheeled into the next room—no worse, apparently, except, perhaps, more exhausted than usual after the moving.

" He gave his eldest daughter‡ some trifling commission to do for him downstairs, and turning to his grand-

* Letters and Memoirs.
† Mrs. F. C. Bentinck.
‡ Lady Hermione Graham.

daughter, who was sitting near, he asked her to read to him, for the second time, her brother's letter* she had received that morning. It was a schoolboy's letter, and he was much amused, and leant back on the cushions laughing. She thought he seemed 'strangely happy,' as she afterwards said ; and scarcely had she done reading it, and was talking to him about it, before she noticed he looked up suddenly 'with a surprised happy expression that was scarcely natural, as if he were seeing something far away and very beautiful ; and then his head sank as if he had fainted.' She rushed out into the passage and called her aunts, who came almost directly, but all was over. The doctor had told us to expect it. The action of the heart had failed."

The reader will remember the affection with which the Duke as a child was regarded by all who knew him. There was a happiness and a fitness in the death which thus found him full of an affection like that of which, in his earliest years, he had been the object.

The introduction to the "Letters and Memoirs of the 12th Duke of Somerset," says : "Personal records, where they are worth preserving and publishing, owe the fact of their being so to one or other of two reasons. The persons whose lives they refer to are exceptions, or else types. The 12th Duke of Somerset belongs to the latter class. Distinguished as he was alike by his talents, his attainments, and his character, his figure is calculated to interest the present generation, less on account of the degree to which he was greater than the majority of mankind, than of the striking example he offered in his own person of the qualities and the conduct which have distinguished an important body of his countrymen.

"In the schooldays of those who have not yet ceased to be young, what was called the governing class still governed England. It was a class composed principally of our old-established landed families. Its influence was felt everywhere, and was as great outside Parliament as

* R. H. St. Maur.

EDWARD ADOLPHUS, TWELTH DUKE OF SOMERSET.

From a bust at Bulstrode, by kind permission of the Lady Gwendolen Ramsden.

within it, and its members embodied, whether they were Peers or commoners, an unquestioned principle of hereditary political power. That principle, as we are all of us well aware, is not unquestioned any longer. On the contrary, the position and education which were considered, a short while since, as almost essential to fit men for public life, are now being represented as the things most likely to unfit them for it ; and the places once monopolised by Peers and country gentlemen we now see, to a growing extent, occupied by politicians and statesmen who are of an entirely different stamp—who are different in origin, in education, in temper, in ambition, and even, not unfrequently, in pronunciation of their mother tongue.

"Whether the new governing class will prove more satisfactory than the old is not a question we are concerned to discuss here. But the old is certainly well worth study—worth it even from the point of view of its enemies, as a factor in our national life which they believe to be disappearing ; whilst those who regard it in a less prejudiced spirit cannot fail to see in it one of the most remarkable bodies that have ever played a part in history, not only uniting in itself the most opposite social characteristics—the accomplishments of fashion and scholarship, with the tastes and hardihood of the country, and a vigorous enjoyment of leisure with an instinctive aptitude for business—but, above all, offering in its tone, temper, and conduct that singular mixture of the aristocratic and democratic elements which is peculiar altogether to the landed aristocracy of England.

"Of the sort of public man produced by this governing class, Edward, 12th Duke of Somerset, was an almost ideal representative. His public life lasted for five and thirty years, beginning with his entrance into Parliament in 1830, as M.P. for Okehampton, and ending in 1866, with the ending of his tenure of office as First Lord of the Admiralty. Many and important as were the posts which he occupied during this period, it is, if we consider him in the light of a public man only, as First Lord of the Admiralty that he principally claims attention ; in which position, for complete grasp of his subject, for shrewdness, and for administrative capacity, those qualified to judge declare that he has never been surpassed. . . . .

" Born to all the advantages which, in the earlier part of the century, distinguished descent and the highest rank would ensure, he was an example of their best and their most characteristic results. An accomplished scholar, an acute philosophical thinker, a keen sportsman, a laborious member of Parliament, a welcome figure in the gay and fashionable world, and husband to the most beautiful and wittiest woman of her generation ; he was a man whose life was as blameless as his position and his career were brilliant, and the charm of his character, regarded as a husband and father, was equalled only by his stainless integrity as a statesman. As a statesman, indeed, he might have risen to even higher eminence than he did, if it had not been for a great private affliction—the loss of his second son, Lord Edward St. Maur. This almost coincided in point of time with the Duke's retirement from the Admiralty, and so profound was the grief it caused him, that his spirits never recovered themselves, nor did he ever again have heart to re-enter public life."

The Duke of Somerset was Lord Lieutenant of the county of Devon, Governor of the Royal Naval College, Portsmouth, and a trustee of the British Museum.

By his wife Jane Georgina, daughter of the late Thomas Sheridan, Esq., he had the following issue :—

> Edward Adolphus Ferdinand, born July 17, 1835. In 1856 he went as an Attaché with Lord Granville to attend the Coronation of the Czar, Alexander II. The same year he went to Palestine, whence, after a short time, he hastened to the war then going on in Persia, joining Sir J. Outram's force and receiving great praise from that commander for the services he performed. The Indian Mutiny

EDWARD ADOLPHUS FERDINAND, EARL ST. MAUR.

From a portrait at Bulstrode, by kind permission of the Lady Gwendolen Ramsden.

breaking out shortly after, he at once joined the relief columns as a volunteer, marched to Cawnpore and the relief of Lucknow, and was mentioned more than once in despatches for his excessive gallantry. On his return home he joined the 4th Dragoon Guards ; but soldiering in times of peace had no attractions for him, and he resigned after a few months. The Volunteer movement next received his attention, and he took the greatest pains in raising a Company in Wilts, in spite of the discouragement he received on all sides. This he shortly followed by raising a Company of Mounted Infantry in Devon. On the breaking out of Garibaldi's war of independence in Italy, however, he left these occupations, being impelled to do so by the great chance now before him of assisting the cause of Freedom. He at first enrolled himself as a private, but the fact of his having already held a Commission soon caused him to be made a Captain and Military Secretary to Brigadier-Colonel Peard. Needless to say that, on account of his father's position as Lord of the Admiralty, he found it necessary to engage in this campaign under an assumed name, which, however, before long he had made respected and esteemed by exhibiting the same soldierly qualities which had already earned honourable mention for him in India. (Appendix P.) At the close of the war he visited several countries and employed himself in learning their languages, a thing for which he appears to have had a special gift. In July 1863, he was summoned to the House of Lords in his father's Barony of Seymour, and took his seat as Earl St. Maur. His health, however, was gradually giving way, and he found himself obliged to spend his winters abroad, for the most part at Tangiers. Coming home in September, 1869, he was suddenly taken ill at his father's house in Dover

Street, and died the day following, deeply mourned by those who knew him and understood him, and, as was remarked in a newspaper at the time, " He left few better or braver men behind him."

Edward Percy, born August 19, 1841. When 18 years of age he was sent to Vienna as an Attaché, where he remained about a year, afterwards spending some months in travelling about to various countries on the Continent. He was then sent in the same capacity to Madrid in 1861, but came home again after some months in order to pass an examination in the languages he had learnt. At the same time he published an article on Spanish " Church and Exchequer " in the Fortnightly Review, which received considerable praise. In 1862 he went to America at the time of the war between the North and South, and was a witness to several engagements, though he took no part in the operations of either side. After this he spent some time at home and in Italy, but in 1865 he started on a tour through parts of India—a tour from which he never returned. Whilst shooting at Yellapoor he was badly bitten by a bear, and had to undergo the amputation of his leg, an operation from which he was not strong enough to recover. He died a day or two afterwards, deeply mourned by all who knew him, for he was very popular. The very natives, though, as a rule, easily affected, displayed a most unusual and genuine grief, exclaiming, with tears in their eyes, " His heart was very large."   (Appendix Q.)

Jane Hermione, born January 1, 1832, who in 1852, October 26th, married Sir Frederic Ulric Graham, Bart., of Netherby, Cumberland.

Ulrica Frederica Jane, born January 12, 1833, who in 1858, June 1st, married Lord Henry Frederic Thynne, 2nd son of the 3rd Marquis of Bath.

Helen Gwendolen, born November 14, 1846, who,

EDWARD PERCY ST. MAUR.

From a portrait at Bulstrode, by kind permission of the Lady Gwendolen Ramsden.

JANE GEORGINA DUCHESS OF SOMERSET, DAUGHTER OF THOMAS SHERIDAN, ESQ.

From a bust at Bulstrode, by kind permission of the Lady Gwendolen Ramsden.

in 1865, August 10th, married Sir John William Ramsden, Bart., of Byram, Yorks.

[Letters, Remains, and Memorials of Edward Adolphus, 12th Duke of Somerset, K.G., ed. by W. H. Mallock and Lady G. Ramsden, 1893; Letters of Lord Ferdinand St. Maur and Lord Edward St. Maur, ed. Lady G. Ramsden; Annual Register, 1885; Spencer Walpole's Life of Earl Russell, ii, 423; Dict. Nat. Biog.; Times Newspaper; Vanity Fair.]

Jane Georgina, Duchess of Somerset, was the daughter of Thomas Sheridan, Esq., and grand-daughter of the famous Richard Brinsley Sheridan. Her two sisters were the beautiful and accomplished ladies the Hon. Mrs. Norton and Lady Dufferin, both of whom became so well known for their literary attainments.

She was married in 1830, at the age of 20, and some years afterwards (1839), when still Lady Seymour, was chosen as the Queen of Beauty at the memorable Eglinton Tournament, when she carried out the somewhat difficult duties of that position to the complete satisfaction of all.

But it was not her excessive beauty that caused her to be sought after and appreciated by all in the circles in which she moved. Great as it was, it was enhanced by the kindliest expression and the most winning smile. Her voice was sweet and melodious, her manner had the rarest charm, and her conversation sparkled with wit, which was not reserved only to shine in society, but remained the same when alone with her family—a simple and natural wit, owing its origin as much to the original way in which she viewed things and instantly spoke her thoughts, as to the quickness and cleverness of her brain. Devoted to country pursuits, full of interest in her garden and her farm, she gathered from the trivial events of the day materials for giving ever-renewed amusement to her family.

The queer sayings or oddities of speech emanating from the cowman, and the homely wisdom of the hen wife, passed through the sparkling medium of her memory, enlivened the quiet winter evenings with much innocent merriment.

While in society amongst her friends and acquaintances she would delight by her ready repartee, her apt Latin or other quotations, but she was careful that no spark of ill-nature should ever mar her speech. Brimming over as she was with natural fun and good-humour, she endeavoured always to amuse, to cheer, or to comfort, but never to wound the feelings of others for the mere sake of a witty remark or apt retort. Some yet living may recall a few of her amusing and clever sayings, but they must remain treasured in some remote corner of their memory. The very occasions which brought them forth have long been forgotten, and of what interest would the mere words be without the voice, the expression, the smile, and the charm of manner ? There can be no record made, nor should there, for she herself did not desire that she should be remembered for her wit or her beauty alone; her letters, amusing as they were, always ended with a request for their destruction, and no portrait worthy of the name did she ever have done as a record of herself.

Her character had another more enduring and nobler side. Admired as she was for those qualities which caused her to shine above others, it was her kindly and noble heart that secured the lasting affection, the love, of all. Only those whom she had comforted and cheered in trouble, in sickness, or in sorrow knew the depth of feeling, the strong affection, the loving devotion that lay hidden beneath the sunshine of her nature. When sorrow, at the loss of both her sons, had banished almost all the brightness and joy of her life, she did not give way entirely to a useless grief, but exerted herself to maintain a cheery presence to comfort her husband, and to live for those she loved around her. Even to the last, when oppressed with advanced age, ill-health, and frequent suffering, she maintained her spirit and courage. Flashes of the old brightness sparkled out again, so that even those about her could not realise the gravity of the situation ; but her mind was stronger than her body, and she died rather suddenly, December 14, 1884, after many months of illness. To the last all her thoughts and words were for the care and comfort of those she was leaving.

FINIS.

NOTES.

___

NOTE 1.

On the death of her father, she inherited the Manor of North Molton in Devon, and half the Manor of Gatesten in Herts. (Dugdale.)

NOTE 2.

He died seized of certain lands in Basingburne in Cambs, certain lands in Hampton-Meysi in Gloucester, the Manor of Polton juxta Crekelade, with the advowson of the church and manor of Eton-Meysi in Wilts, and the Manor of Northam in Devon. (Dugdale.)

NOTE 3.

He inherited the Manors of North Molton in Devon, Eton-Meysi and Wittenham in Wilts, Winfred-Egle in Dorset, Castle-Cary, Mershe, North-Bawe, South-Bawe, Rade, Corscombe, Prestelege, Blakeford, and Wincaulton in Somerset. (Dugdale.)

NOTE 4.

He inherited the Manors of Winfred-Egle in Dorset ; Witten-ham, Laugenham, Hulpringham, Westbury, North-Molton, in Devon ; Hampton-Meysi, Clifton, Bradeston, Stryntescombe, in Gloucester ; Castle-Cary, Mershe, Brockton, Rade (Rode ?), Stoke, Hallow, Presteley, Blakeford, a fourth of Immere, a third of Lokynton, the borough of Wincaulton, in Somerset ; and the moiety of the hundred of Westbury in Wilts. (Dugdale.)

NOTE 5.

There was also an Abbess, one of three sisters, in Ireland, who took or was given the name of St. Maur. She had no connection with the St. Maur family, but was probably given the name on account of her following so closely the principles laid down by St. Maur, the Abbot. Particulars of her life may be found in

"Lives of the Irish Saints." In Notes and Queries, I find the following curious passage: "Amongst the many strange derivations given of the name of Mona or Man (the island) I find one in an old unpublished MS. by an unknown author of the date about 1658, noticed by Feltham (Tour through the Isle of Man, p. 8). The name of the island is there said to have been derived from Maune, the name of the great apostle of the Maun, before he received that of Patricus from Pope Celestine. I have not any access to any life of St. Patrick in which the name of Maune occurs, but in the Penny Cyclopedia, under the head Patrick, I find it said, according to Nennius, St. Patrick's original name was *Maur*, and I find the same stated in Rose's Biographical Dictionary, but the article in the latter is evidently taken from the former." (Notes and Queries.)

Note 6.

An Assize in 1269 states that "Roger de St. Maur ought to have housebote and heybote at his house at Woundy, by the moiety of Magor Park, and upon his fee of Woundy, by the feoffment of Sir Barth. de Moor." (Dugdale.)

Note 7.

Cecilia Seymour's share consisted of the Manors of Hache, Shipton, Beauchamp, Murifielf, and a third of Shipton Malet, in Somerset; certain lands in Sturminster Marshall, in Dorset; the Manors of Boultberry and Harberton, in Devon; the Manor of Dourton, in Bucks; little Hawes, in Suffolk; and two-thirds of Snelling, in Kent. (A Complete Peerage and Camden.)

Note 8.

By a deed dated 1357, this William is styled: "Miles, filius et haeres Rogeri Seymour, Militis." This deed is dated from Woundy. (A Complete Peerage, taken from Dugdale.)

Note 9.

Simon de Brockburn of Brockburn, in Hereford, by Joan, sister and heir to Sir Peter de la Mere. (Vincent's MS.; Camden.)

Note 10.

"In the year 1829, the three shields on the upper part of the monument were still in existence; two of them were broken, but the fragments had been preserved by the care of the parish clerk, and were readily put together and secured in a bed of plaster of Paris. In the same year facsimiles of them were made in Bath stone by a clever sculptor at Oxford, and fixed in their respective places on the monument.

"The shield on the dexter side of the inscription, the only one that remained but little injured, is that of Sir John Seymour, viz., Gules, two wings conjoined and inverted Or, impaling Sable, a chevron between three leopard's faces Or for Wentworth.

"One-half of the shield over the inscription had been broken off; it bore the ensigns of Sir Henry Seymour, K.B., viz., Seymour, with a crescent Gules for difference, impaling Quarterly, 1. Argent, a fess between three martlets Gules, on a chief Sable, three wolf's heads erased Argent, for Wolfe of Gwerngotheyn; 2. Per Pale Sable and Azure, three fleurs-de-lis Or, for Wolfe Newton; 3. Or, three wolves passant Azure, for Nanfant; 4. Argent, on a chevron Gules, between three stag's heads caboshed Sable, three bugle horns Argent, stringed Or, for Le Sore of St. Fagans.

"On the sinister side of the inscription the arms are those of Seymour quartering the heiresses, with whom the family had previously intermarried, viz., Quarterly of six, 1. and 6. Seymour; 2. Vaire, for Beauchamp of Hache; 3. Argent, three demi-lions couped Gules, for Esturmy; 4. Per bend, Argent and Gules, three roses in bend counterchanged, for Macwilliams; 5. Argent, on a bend Gules, three leopard's faces Or, for Coker.

"The six shields on the face of the tomb, which were smaller than those above, having in the year above mentioned entirely disappeared, the spaces were filled up with newly sculptured bearings representing, 1. Seymour; 2. Beauchamp of Hache; 3. De Fortibus (through Beauchamp), viz., Argent, on a chief Gules, a label of five points Or; 4. Esturmy; 5. Mark Williams; 6. Coker.

"These are the arms now on the face of the tomb, but it has been recently ascertained from Aubrey's MS., so frequently quoted in this magazine by its indefatigable Editor, that of these six spaces five were originally filled with the bearings of Sir John Seymour's children.

"These were described by Aubrey, who visited the church in or about the year 1672.

"The sixth shield was wanting in Aubrey's time, and it is impossible to conjecture with any degree of probability, whose coat filled the vacant space, or whether it was ever filled at all. The arms of all Sir John's children, who grew up and lived to be married, are quoted by the Antiquary. Possibly the Earl of Hertford, who erected the monument, may have added his own arms, or the coat of Seymour impaling the sixth quarterings of Wentworth."—(Wiltshire Archæological and Natural History Magazine, 1860.)

NOTE 11.

List of the Manors granted by King Henry VIII to Queen Jane upon her marriage :—Cokeham, Bray, Hampstead, Marshall, Benham, Swallowfield, Newbury, Wakefield, Stratfield, Mortimer, in Berks : Langley Marreys, Wyrrerdesbury, Waddon, Cleydon, Burton, Wendover, in Bucks : Odcomb, Wilverton, in Cornwall : Gillingham, Pimperne, Eussect, Eundeville, Steeple, Crick, Wick, Weymouth, Portland, Helwell, Marshwood-vale, Cranbourn, in Dorset : Bradwell, Budley, Berdfield, in Essex : Bisleigh, in Glos'ter : Hoke, Mortimer, Worthymortimer, in Hants : Kings-lane, Litchdale, Berdesley, Brimerfield, Misserdere, Barton Chorle-ton, Doughton, Winston, in Hereford : Hechyn, Beckhampstead, Langley, in Herts : part of Beckhampstead and Langley, in Huntingdon : Southfrith, Erith, Shillingeld, Tong, Kingsdown, Swanscomb, in Kent : Duping, Stamford, Grantham, Kelby, in Lincoln : Bircham, in Norfolk : Fotheringay, Nassington, Yar-well, Upton, in Northants : Finmer, in Oxon. : Heygrove, Corry-mallet, in Somerset : Watting, Exbury, Hunden, Clarethall, Sud-bury, Leyham, Woodhall, Great Wallingham, Little Wallingham, in Suffolk : Banstead, Walton, Shyre, Purlright, in Surrey : Corsham, Marlborough, Berton, Devizes, Rowde, Merston Mersey, Sevenhampton, Highworth, Crickdale, Chelworth, Wotton, Tokeham, Winterbourn, Compton Basset, Somerford, Caynes, Chilton, Foliatt, in Wilts : Feckenham, Bromegrove, King's Norton, Odingley, Cliston, in Worcester.

List of the Castles granted by King Henry VIII to Queen Jane upon her marriage :—Odiham Castle, in Hants : Renchester Castle, in Kent : Fotheringay Castle, in Northants : Marlborough Castle and Devizes Castle, in Wilts.

List of the Chases and Forests granted by King Henry VIII to Queen Jane upon her marriage :—Wheddon Chase, in Bucks : Cranbourn Chase, Exmoor Forest, Bath Forest, Mendip Forest, in Dorset and Somerset : Melksham Forest, Penesham Forest, Blakamore Forest, Chippenham Forest, Bradon Forest, in Wilts.

(11th Duke of Somerset's MSS.)

NOTE 12.

This epitaph has been freely translated as follows :—

> " Soon as her Phœnix bud was blown
> Root-Phœnix Jane did wither ;
> Sad, that no age a brace has shown
> Of Phœnixes together."

NOTE 13.

Gairdner. Henry VIII. Vol. xiii, 1538, 221. Coggeshall Abbey, February 5.

2. Debts and bargains of the house of Coxalle (Coggeshall) to be discharged by Sir Thomas Seymour, viz. : To the King for unpaid first fruits, Seymour to re-deliver to the Abbot of Tower Hill all remaining obligations, £166. To the Countess of Kent for money borrowed, £189. To my lord of Essex for arrears of his fee, £4 10s. 0d. To Anth. Knyvett, Pygot of the Chapel, and Samfort, for arrears of their pensions. To Saunder for stuff for the house, to Highgate, for sheep remaining on the ground, and to Love, Cowper of Naylond, and Pecocke, etc. etc. . . . Seymour is to pay the Abbot £340 in compensation of charges sustained by him, for the house of Coxalle before and since the suppression, and for debts for which the Monastery of Tower Hill stands bound. The Abbot of Tower Hill shall also have a yearly pension of 100 marks for life, out of the lands of Coxalle, and Sir Thomas shall pay this annuity for the half year past, £33. 6s. 8d.

A second document to the same effect is in App. 12, vol. xiii.

646. (61) p. 246, to Sir Thos. Seymour.

Grant in fee of the late Monastery of Coggeshall alias Coxhall, Essex ; the principal or chief site and church, etc., of the same ; the rectories and advowsons of the churches, vicarages, and rectories of Childerditch and Coggeshall alias Coxhall and the advowson of a perpetual chantrey in the parish church of Coggeshall belonging to the said late monastery ; and all other manors, messuages, etc., in Coggeshall alias Coxhall, Magna and Parva Childerditch, Tillyngham, Thorndon, Wakeley, Brondewodde (Brendewode elsewhere), Springfield, Chelmesford, Borham, Tolshunt, Tregony, Tolshunt Major, Tuworth, Messing, Wakering, Fulnes, Fering, Kelden, Bradwell, Patteswike, Stysted, Revenhale, Colne Comitis, Halsted, Magna Ley, Magna Braxted, Canewdon, Burnham, Aldern, and Fulnes, Essex, Wyston, Suff, the parishes of All Hallows ad Fenum in the ward of Dowgate, and St. Boltulph without Algate London, and elsewhere in England and Wales which belonged to the said late monastery. Rent £25. 2s. 2½d.

The premises came to the King's hand by virtue of a fine, levied in the Octaves of St. Hilary, 29 Henry VIII, between the King and Henry More, Abbot and perpetual commendatory of the said Cistercian Monastery of St. Mary, Coggeshall, of the Manors of Coggeshall alias Coxhall, Chylderdiche, Tyllyngham, Kewton Hall, Lyons, Tolshunt Major, Chedingsell, Tutwyke, Bonseys alias Bouseys, Holfeld graunge and Bunhey gatehouse, and certain messuages in Coggeshall and other places before mentioned ; the Manor of Honyley graunge alias Wiston graunge, and certain messuages in Wiston, Suff ; and certain messuages etc. in the parishes of All Hallows ad Fenum in Dowgate Ward and St. Botolph without Algate ; and also by virtue of a charter of the said Abbot and convent of the said monastery, London dioc., dated Feb. 5. 29 Henry VIII, granting the said monastery and site to the King. Westm. palace, 18 March. 29 Henry VIII. Del 23 March.—P.S. Pat., p. 5, m. 44.

1155. John Forster to Sir Thomas Seymour. December 28. Sends the state of the house of Romsey according to his request. The house is out of debt. The plate and jewels are worth £300 or more. Six bells are worth £100 at least. The church is a great sumptuous thing, all of freestone and covered with lead, worth £300 or £400 more. (Here follow the rents of the Abbey of Romesey.) In answer to your letter by Mr. Flemynge whether the Abbess and nuns would be content to surrender their house, the truth is that in consequence of the motion made by your kinswoman and other friends, they will be content to do you any pleasure, but they would be loath to trust to the Commissioner's gentleness, as they hear that other houses have been straitly handled.—(Signed) Romesey. December 28.

Note 14.

Gairdner, Henry VIII. 1539. April 28. No. 867. Parliament.
Cap. 24. Assurance . . . of the commandry or lordship of Baddisley, Hants, to Sir Thomas Seymour, in tail male.
191. (38) Grant Elis. the Abbess and the convent of St. Mary and St. Ethelfreda, Romesey, Hants, to alienate . . . to Sir Thos. Seymour.
1192. (31) Sir Thos. Seymour. License to alienate (amongst other things) Weston Graunge to Robt. Cowper.
435. (18) Grants. Sir Thos. Seymour. A grant in fee for £1,299. 5s. 5d. of the Manor of Colleshull, etc.

The following occur in 1540 :—

611. (34) Sir T. Seymour. License to alienate . . . Chyderdyche Hall and Tyllyngham Hall . . . formerly belonging to the said Monastery of Coggeshall . . . to Sir Richard Riche, etc.
744. Attainted lands. IX. Lands late of Sir John Fortescue . . . to Sir John Semer, from Mich. 31 Henry VIII.
1500. Books of the Court of Augmentations. Leases of 32 Henry VIII. Sir Thos. Seymour. Glebe lands and tithes of Kyrkeby, Kendall Rectory, Westmorland. St. Mary's, York. December 10.

The following occur in 1541 :—

Grants. 947. June. (44) Sir Thos. Seymour. Grant in

fee, in exchange for the late Monastery of Coggeshall alias Coxhall, Essex, etc. . . . sold to the Crown. May 12. 33 Henry VIII, and for £2,693 2s. 11d., of the late Monastery of Edington, Wilts, etc.

(60) Sir Thos. Seymour. License to alienate the manors and hundred of Melkesham, Wilts, etc. etc. . . . all of which belonged to the late Monastery of Amesbury, Wilts, to Hen. Brounker. Westm. June 26.

(61) License to alienate rents, customs, and services, of that chief mansion of John Warneford in Sevenhampton . . . June 26.

(83) License to alienate Tonesleas, etc. June 30.

1056. (18) License to alienate . . . Petwyke, Berks . . . July.

1308. (26) License to alienate . . . Manor of Inglesham, Berks. July.

Note 15.

Later on his marriage was brought up as an accusation against him. "You married the late Queen so soon after the late King's death, that if she had conceived straight after, it would have been accounted a great doubt whether the child born should have been accounted the late King's or yours, whereby a marvellous danger might have ensued to the quiet of the realm."—"Articles against Seymour."

Note 16.

The Lord Marquis of Dorset's confession to the Council. No. 4, State Papers :—"The Lord Marquis Dorset sayeth, that he was fully determined that his daughter, the Lady Jane, should no more come to remain with the Lord Admiral. Howbeit my Lord Admiral himself came unto his house and was so earnest with him in persuasion, that he could not resist him. Among the which persuasions, one was, that he would marry her to the King's Majesty; saying further, that if he might get the King at liberty, he durst warrant the said Lord Marquis, that the King should marry his said daughter. And further, the said Lord Marquis sayeth, that Sir William Sharrington was as earnest, and travailled as fore with my lady his wife, that she should be content to let the said Lady Jane come to my Lord Admiral; and, as I think, used the persuasions that my Lord Admiral did: and so persuaded her at the last to agree so; and then he could not but consent. And that he the said Lord Marquis was so seduced and aveugled by the said Lord Admiral, that he promised him that, except the King's Majesty's person only, he would spend his life and blood in his the said Lord Admiral's part against all men. Wherefore as it were for an earnest penny of the favour that he would show unto him, when the said Lord Marquis had sent his daughter to the said Lord Admiral, he sent unto the said Lord Marquis immediately £500, parcel of £2,000 which he promised to lend unto him, and would have axed no bond of him at all for it, but only to have had the Lord Marquis's daughter for a gage. Also the said Lord Marquis further said, that the said Admiral, in communications with him in his gallery, at his house besides the temple, said, that he loved not the Lord Protector, and would not have any Protector, but said, he would have the King to have the honour of his own things ; for, said he, of his years he is wise and learned. Marry, he thought it meet the Lord Protector might be chief of the Council. And though he, the said Admiral, could not as then do that he would wish, to alter the thing, yet sayeth he Let me alone see me, I will bring it to pass within this three years.

" HENRY DORSETT."

NOTE 17.

A portion of Thomas Parry's confession. State Papers. "When I went unto my Lord Admiral, the third and fourth time after he had asked me, how her Grace did, and such things, he had large communication with me of her, and questioned with me of many things, and of the state of her Grace's house, and how many persons she kept ; and I told him 120 or 140, or thereabouts. And he asked me, what houses she had, and what lands ; and I told him where the lands lay as near as I could, in Northampton-shire, Berkshire, Lincoln, and others.

"Then he asked me, if it were good lands or no ; and I told him they were out in lease, for the most part all, and therefore the worse.

"And he asked me also, what state she had in the lands, for term of life, or how : and I said, I could not perfectly tell, but I thought it was such as was appointed by her father's will and testament, the King's Majesty that dead is. Then he asked me, whether she had out her letters patent or no? And I said no ; for there were divers things in them, that could not be assured yet to her ; and that a friend of her Grace's would help her to change a piece of land, which should be more commodious for her Grace. And he asked me who it was: and I said Morisyn, who would help her to have Ewelme for Apethorp. And then, as I remember, he said, ye may get your lands exchanged to better lands ; and let her then get out her letters patent ; and said, I would wish she had her lands westward or in Wales ; and said also, I will name or appoint one special piece in Gloucestershire, that was the Queen's, called the Bisley, in parcel of her exchange ; and I remember he told me then much of his three houses, Bewdley, Sudley, and Bromeham; and that he had been of late at them; and who lay at each of them; and what provisions he had for the same; and so compared the keeping of houses with the Lady Elizabeth, with less charge; and many such things," &c.

NOTE 18.

"When the Councillors waited on the King, the Lord Chancellor opened the matter and delivered his opinion for leaving it to the Parliament. Then every Councillor by himself spoke his mind to the same purpose. Last of all the Protector spoke—he protested that this was to him a most sorrowful business, and that he had used all the means in his power to keep it from coming to this extremity. But were it a son, or brother, he must prefer his Majesty's safety to them, for he weighed his allegiance more than his own blood; and that therefore he was not against the request that the other Lords had made, and said if he himself were guilty of such offences, he should not think he was worthy of life, and the rather because he was of all men the most bound to his Majesty, and therefore he could not refuse justice."—Cobbett's State Trials, vol. i, 493.

NOTE 19.

Lines attributed to Harrington, on the portrait of Lord Seymour of Sudley, afterwards in the possession of Henry Seymour, Esq.

None can deem right who faithful friends do rest,
Whilst they do rule and reign in great degree;
For then both fast and famed friends are prest
Whose faiths seem both of one effect to be.
But if that wealth unwind and fortune flee,
As never known, revolts the unfaithful guest;
But he, whose heart in life once faith links fast,
Will love and serve e'en after death is past.
Of person rare, strong limbs, and manly shape,
Of nature framed to serve on sea or land;
Of friendship firm in good state and ill hap,
In peace, head wise, in war skill great, bold hand:
On horse, on foot, in peril or in play,
None could excel, though many did assay.
A subject true to King, and servant great,
Friend to God's truth, enemy to Rome's deceit;
Sumptuous abroad, for honor of the land,
Temperate at home; yet kept great state with stay,
A noble house, and gave more mouths more meat,

Than some advanced on higher steps to stand.
Yet against nature, reason, and just laws,
His blood was spilt, guiltless, without just cause.

Printed in Nugæ Antiquæ, p. 330. The portrait and lines were given by Harrington to Elizabeth when she became Queen.

NOTE 20.

July 21, 1528. Duke of Richmond to Henry VIII. ". . . I have received two of your letters, dated Tittenhanger, the 10th, desiring the preferment of Sir Giles Strangwisshe and Sir Edward Seymer, master of my horse, to rooms vacant by the death of Sir Wm. Compton. I send a list of the offices and the fees appertaining. I presume you mean that one of the said gentlemen is to be preferred to the Stewardship of Canforde. . . ."—Brewer, State Papers, Henry VIII. No. 4536.

July 22, 1528. Magnus to Wolsey. ". . . The King has written to my lord of Richmond for two stewardships in the Duke's gift by the death of Sir Wm. Compton;—the one at Canforde and Corfe and my Lord's lands in Dorsetshire, fee 100s.; the other of my Lord's lands in Somersetshire, fee £6. 13. 4.—which he wishes given to Sir Giles Strangwisshe and Sir Edward Seymour. The King's letters mention only the first office, which cannot well be given to two persons. Sir Edward Seymour writes that both are intended for him. My lord, however, had already given the stewardship of Canforde and Corffe to Sir Will. Parre, his chamberlain, and of the Somersetshire lands to Geo. Cotton. . . ."—Brewer, State Papers, Henry VIII. No. 4547.

March, 1529. Grant. Sir Edward Seymour. To be steward of the Manors of Hengstrige and Charleton, Somersetshire, with power to appoint bailiffs and other officers, vice Sir Wm. Compton. Del Richemont, 5 March, 20 Henry VIII.—Brewer, State Papers, Henry VIII.

NOTE 21.

September 27, 1531. H. Earl of Northumberland (then John Dudley) to Cromwell. Has received his letter dated London the 24th inst. showing how Cromwell has moved the King in his behalf for the payment of his debt due to Sir Edw. Seymour at Michaelmas day, and how arrangement has been made with Sir Edward that he shall take no advantage at this time. Is much bound to the King for this. . . .—Gairdner's State Papers, Henry VIII. 435.

February 23, 1532. A bill of covenants comprised in a pair of indentures made February 6, 23 Henry VIII, between Lord Lisle and Sir Edward Seymour for the sale of Chadder Norton and other manors in Somerset. Seymour to pay a rent of £140, Lord Lisle will pay him £180 on March 1 at St. Paul's between 12 and 3 o'clock.—Gairdner's State Papers, Henry VIII. 817.

The following are of sufficient interest not to be out of place here :—

July, 1532. Indenture, dated July 24. Henry VIII, between Sir (Brian Luke), treasurer of the King's (chamber), Thomas Cromwell, master and treasurer of the King's (jewels), and Chr. Hales, attorney general, on the part of the King and Sir Edward Seymer, whereby the latter acknowledges the receipt of £1,000 from the King, by way of present, to be repaid in two instalments in July 1533 and 1534, or sooner, if demanded; for which Sir Arthur Darcy, Sir John Dudeley, Ric. Riche and Ric. Fermour, merchant of the staple of Calais, stand sureties.— Gairdner's State Papers, Henry VIII. 1205.

Privy purse expenses of King Henry VIII. Payments in November (1529).

. . . To Sir Edw. Seymore, on a reckoning between the King and him, £337 10s.

January, 1530. To Master Seymore, £376 17s. 5d.—Gairdner's State Papers, Henry VIII.

Lisle and Seymour. Complaint of Viscount Lisle against Sir Edw. Seymour for having got him to seal an indenture to his own prejudice, in the belief that it only concerned the purchase from Sir John Dudley of the reversion of the Manors of Norton Beauchamp, Lympisham Tornok, Saundeford, Abell, and Bridgewater, Somerset, to which it was necessary that he should give his assent.—Gairdner's State Papers, Henry VIII. 1551.

Note 22.

He was created Viscount Beauchamp in the following terms:— Ro. Pat. 1537. "The King, in consideration of the acceptable, good, and laudable service of his beloved and faithful servant, Sir Edward Saint Maure, knight, done, and to be done; as also of his circumspection, valour and loyalty, creates him Viscount Beauchamp, to him and the heirs male of his body hereafter to be begotten; and for his and their support of that honour grants them an annuity of twenty marks, arising out of the issues, revenues, profits, farms, and fines of the counties of Somerset and Dorset, payable by the Sheriff of the same, without any deduction. Witness the King at Tieling, June 5, in the twenty-eighth year of his reign."

Note 23.

The following letters and grants relating to property, &c., and all belonging to this year, may be of interest :—

Bishop Rowland Lee to Henry VIII. April 2, 1537. " . . . Of late I received a letter from my lord Privy Seal, whereby it appeareth your Majesty desires to have my house, etc. at the Stronde, for Lord Beauchamp, in exchange for one of his at Cewe (Kew) . . . When I attend on your Majesty at London, I have no other house there save that. And if I should take a house of that distance it should be tedious for me so far to seek my lodging. I beg your Majesty to suffer me to enjoy my said house . . . "—Gairdner. 806.

John Pakyngton to Cromwell. April 3. To this effect. My lord President is very sad and in heaviness because Cromwell has written to him that the King desires to exchange his house and tenantries in the Strond (Strand) with my lord Beauchamp for a house of his at the Cewe (Kew) for anempst Braynford (Brentford). He hopes Cromwell will remind the King of his faithful service here, so that if he has to give up his house he may be recompensed with other lands to the same value.—Gairdner. 821.

Bishop Rowland Lee to Cromwell. May 5. " . . . I have received, May 1, the King's letter and yours for exchange of my house in Stronde with lord Beauchamp. I am content to gratify my Prince, but marvel your lordship makes so little of my party that I should deliver my deed and know nothing of my recompense. I send it on your promise not to deliver it till I am recompensed, otherwise I have protested it shall never be my deed. Please give credence to my servant the bearer." From Wigmore, May 5.—Gairdner. 1139.

Viscount Beauchamp to Cromwell. To this effect. Wishes to know how he has fared since the writer's departure. Wishes Cromwell were with him, when he should have had the best sport with bow, hounds and hawks. Master Lister has brought such hounds as are loath to diminish his game and his hawks favour the partridges. Cromwell has one friend here, Mr. Edgar, who seldom forgets him. Mr. Penison is also here, who says the King promised his wife a jointure when he married. "I beg you therefore to put him in the book if the King distributes any of the forfeited lands in the North. I also beg your favour for my chaplain." Wolfhall. September 2.

There is a P.S. in his own hand, sending commendations to his brother-in-law (Henry) and sister, "and I pray God to send me by them shortly a nephew."

"Lands in the possession or reversion " of the Earl of Hertford. 1 Oct. 29 Henry VIII. First given him by the King £604 which with his inheritance amounts to £1,054. Annuity on his creation of Viscount Beauchamp £13 6s. 8d. Given him by the King at East Hampstead last summer £20. Annuity at his creation of Earl of Hertford £20. Total £1,107 6s. 8d., whereof fees of bailiffs, etc., amount to £91 15s. And there is yearly

paid to the Lady Sayntmor, his mother, for her jointure, £60, and
an annuity to Lord Lisle £120, and an annuity to one Quynten
£24.—Gairdner.   804.

(His creation as E. of Hertford was only on October 18, 1537,
so that either this date is retrospective, or he is called Earl by
anticipation.)

Note 24.

Grants (22) Sir Edward Sainct Maur, Viscount Beauchamp, a
patent granting him the title of Earl of Hertford with succession
in tail male of himself, and of —— (left blank) his present wife,
or any future wife, with £20 a year, in support of the title, out
of the customs and subsidies of the port of Southampton.   Del.
Hampton Court.   October 18, 29 Henry VIII.—Gairdner.
1008.

October 18.   Upon St. Luke's Day, the 6th day after the birth
of the aforesaid Prince Edward, Thursday, October 18, 1537,
29 Henry VIII, was Viscount Beauchamp, created Earl of
Hertford and Sir William Fitzwilliam, Lord Admiral, created
Earl of Southampton.

When the King had heard mass, the lords went into the
King's closet to put on their robes, and Fitzwilliam wore his
collar of the Garter.   Then Norfolk, Exeter, and Sussex, being
in their robes and collars, they went into the presence chamber,
where the King was standing under his cloth of estate, accompanied by his nobles.   There Lord Beauchamp was presented
first, being preceded by the officers of arms and Garter King-at-
Arms, bearing his patent of creation, which was then presented
by the Earl of Oxford, Lord Chamberlain, to the King, who
delivered it to Lord Thomas Cromwell "then secretary."   Sussex
bare his sword with the pummel upwards, and the Viscount was
led by Norfolk and Exeter.   Cromwell read the patent aloud,
and at the words "cincturam gladii," the King girt the sword
about his left shoulder.   Then the said Lord Secretary read out
the letters patent and delivered them to the King, who gave them
to the Earl of Hertford, who thanked the King.—Gairdner.   939.

Note 25.

"Sibi et heredibus masculis de corpore suo per dictum dominum
Annam procreat.   Et vide heredibus masculis de corpore suo per
aliquam mulierem post mortem dictæ dominæ Annæ, eidem
vicecomitis nubend legitime procreat" (to himself and the heirs
male of his body, and Anne, his then wife, that are either now
begotten of the said Anne, or may hereafter be legitimately
begotten of the said Anne, or any other wife he may hereafter

marry). And the other part entailed by the said letters patent: "Sibi et dominæ Annæ uxori ejus, et heredibus masculis de corpore ipsius vicecomitis per dictam dominam Annam legitime, aut aliam mulierem post mortem dictæ dominæ Annæ eidem vicecomiti nubend, remanere, inde heredibus femalis de corpore ipsius vicecomitis legitime procreat."

The Act of 1540 entailed the Maiden Bradley and Sturmy estates in the following extraordinary and unjust manner :—

The eldest son, John, was entirely overlooked and consequently disinherited. The Earl's estates were settled upon his children by his second wife and, in default of issue by that marriage, with the remainder to Edward Seymour, his second son by his first wife. In case of failure of Edward's issue the remainder was to Sir Thomas Seymour, the Earl's younger brother, and his heirs, remainder to the right heirs of Edward Seymour. Any future estate that should come to the Earl was by this Act settled in the same manner. This involved consequences that were not immediately foreseen, for by virtue of it, any estate subsequently conferred upon the Earl by grant from the Crown, was settled in a way which the King might not intend; and persons, who enfeoffed the Earl in their lands and tenements to their uses, were defrauded, as he became seised of the property to his own use. The following is a list of the manors and estates in Wilts, which belonged to the Earl on May 25, 1540. Names of manors :—

Woolton Eyvers, Burbage Sturmy, Sturmes Wyke, Studstecombe, Croston, Bedwin, Stapleford, Cowlifield Sturmy, Burbage Savage, Wolfhall, Tryhelden, Lydcombe, Homyngton, Ablington. Situation of estates :—Collingborne, Wilton, Marlborough, Westcombe, Bowden Swods, Collings Downes, Baylycliff, Box, Brodeton, Stapleford, Fitzwarren, Bedwyne, and Croston.

NOTE 26.

Sir William Paget to the Earl of Hertford. State Papers. "My duty to your good Lordship remembered. It may like the same to understand that the King's Majesty hath received your sundry letters, and taketh in good part your proceeding, and other advertisements contained in the same. Nevertheless (if it should please you to give me leave to write to you my poor advice, as I promised your lordship to do at your departing) I would wish that, if you fortune to find anything amiss there in those parts, you should rather amend them, if they be such as must and may be amended, with the advice of such others of the Council as be there with you than to signify hither that they be amiss, as you did lately, touching the laying of the Borderers to be of the garrison, whereby you say the King's Majesty was put to a

greater charge than needed ; and also the borders weakened by
the same : with which your advertisement some of your friends
here were offended, albeit the King's Majesty found no fault at it
and yet such reasons in the communing of that matter were
showed, as whereby it appeareth to me and the rest here, that if
inland men had been of the garrison, neither so many, nor yet so
notable exploits had been done within Scotland as hath been ; but
as the Italian saith, Basta, I trust your lordship will take this my
folly in good part, and think that men may better speak or do,
being present, than absent. Thus with my prayer that you and
the rest may have good success in the journey, I bid your good
lordship most heartily well to fare.

"From Westminster the day of April, 1543.
             "Your lordships unfained poor friend,
                                        "WILLIAM PAGET.

"Your lordship shall do well to salute now and then, with a
word or two in a letter, my Lord of Suffolk, and my Lord
Wriothesley, and such, as you shall think good, forgetting not
Mr. Denye."

NOTE 27.

Two years after, Paget wrote to the Protector : "What seeth
your Grace, marry, the King's subjects all out of discipline, out of
obedience, carrying neither for Protector nor King. What is the
matter ? Marry, sir, that which I said to your Grace in the
gallery. Liberty ! Liberty ! and your Grace's too much gentleness, your softness, your opinion to be good to the poor—the
opinion of such as saith to your Grace, 'Oh, sir, there was
never man that had the hearts of the poor as you have.' "

NOTE 28.

The Earl of Hertford to Sir William Paget. (Tytler's England
under Edward VI and Mary.)

"This morning, between one and two, I received your letter.
The first part thereof I like very well ; marry, that the Will should
be opened till a farther consultation, and that it might be well considered how much thereof were necessary to be published ; for
divers respects I think it not convenient to satisfy the world. In
the meantime I think it sufficient, when ye publish the King's
death, in the places and times as ye have appointed, to have the
Will presently with you, and to show that this is the Will, naming
unto them severally who be the executors that the King did specially
trust, and who be Councillors ; the contents at the breaking up
thereof, as before, shall be declared unto them on Wednesday in the

morning at the Parliament house; and in the meantime we to meet and agree therein, as there may be no controversy hereafter. For the rest of your appointments, for the keeping of the Tower, and the King's person, it shall be well done ye be not too hasty therein; and so I bid you heartily farewell. From Hartford, January 29, between three and four in the morning.

"Your assured loving friend,
"E. HERTFORD.

"I have sent you the key of the Will."

The Earl of Hertford and Sir Anthony Browne to the Council. (Tytler's England.)

"Your lordships shall understand that I, the Earl of Hertford, have received your letter concerning a pardon to be granted in such form as in the schedule ye have sent, and that ye desire to know our opinion therein.

"For answer thereunto, ye shall understand we be in some doubt whether our power be sufficient to answer unto the King's Majesty that now is, when it shall please him to call us to account for the same. And in case we have authority so to do it, in our opinion the time will serve much better at the Coronation than at present. For if it should be now granted, his Highness can show no such gratuity unto his subjects when the time is most proper for the same; and his father, who we doubt not to be in heaven, having no need thereof, shall take the praise and thanks from him that hath more need thereof than he.

"We do very well like your device for the matter; marry, we would wish it to be done where the time serveth most proper for the same.

"We intend the King's Majesty shall be a-horseback to-morrow by XI of the clock, so that by III we trust his Grace shall be at the Tower. So if ye have not already advertised my Lady Anne of Cleves of the King's death, it shall be well done ye send some express person for the same.

"And so, with our right hearty commendations we bid you farewell. From Enfield this Sunday night, at XI of the clock.

"Your good lordships assured loving friends,
"E. HERTFORD,
"ANTHONY BROWNE."

NOTE 29.

The Protector's prayer on commencing his administration.

"Thou Lord, by thy providence has caused me to rule. I am, by thy appointment, minister for thy King, shepherd for thy people.

By thee Kings do reign and from thee all power is derived ; govern me as I shall govern " ; etc. etc.

According to Gardiner, it was not the Protector who had caused the deposition of Wriothesley : " Your Grace," he said, " showed him so much favour that all the world commended your gentleness."—Froude's Hist.

NOTE 30.

Fuller, in his Church History, says of this : " Edward Semaure, the King's uncle, lately made Lord Protector and Duke of Somerset, ordered all in church and state. He, by the King's power, or if you please, the King in his protection, took speedy order for reformation of religion ; and being loth that the people of the land should live so long in error and ignorance, till a Parliament should be solemnly summoned (which for some reasons of state could not so quickly be called), in the meantime by his own regal power and authority, and the advice of his wise and honourable council chose commissioners, and sent them with instructions into several parts of the kingdom, for the rooting out of superstition." The substance of these injunctions to the number of thirty-six will be found in Fuller's Church History. Further on he again says : " Let us admire God's wisdom in our first reformers, who proceeded so moderately in a matter of so great consequence ; to reform all at once had been the ready way to reform nothing at all."

It is curious to find that one of the things in these injunctions to which Calvin took exception was the praying for the dead, which was one of the things he termed "tolerabiles ineptias" or tolerable fooleries.

NOTE 31.

The imprisonment and severe treatment of Gardiner were brought about by the Council, especially Cranmer. The Protector had little to do with it, being, indeed, absent in Scotland when Gardiner was summoned before the Council and imprisoned for neglecting their injunctions. When he returned he sent him his own physician, and did what he could to make his confinement more endurable. Their relations were always friendly and, even after his fall, Somerset did his utmost to obtain his release and to prevent his deprivation. This, indeed, was one of the causes that led to his death. In fact, Somerset, when in power, would never sanction the deprivation of any Bishop, even when Parliament required that of the Bishop of Worcester, and not one was deprived during his term of office.

(See England under Protector Somerset. Pollard.)

Note 32.

An augmentation of arms granted by King Edward VI to Edward, Duke of Somerset.

Or on a pile Gules between six Fleurs de Lis, Azure ; three Lions of the field passant Gardant, tongu'd and ungul'd Azure.

Note 33.

About this time the Duke had an opportunity, of which he was not slow to avail himself, of increasing his possessions. The Pomeroys had been established at the place which bears their name in Devonshire, ever since the Conquest, but from various causes had become greatly impoverished. Sir Thomas Pomeroy had mortgaged the greater part of his estates to Sir Wymond Carew for the sum of £2,300, and had granted him a long lease of the remainder without receiving any rent in return. The Duke of Somerset had before acquired some interest in the property, and he now redeemed the whole, and paid in addition £1,200 to Sir Thomas and Sir Wymond. The estates were very large, and comprehended the manors of Berry and Bridgetown Pomeroy, the adjoining parish of Sandridge, Harberton on the other side of Totnes, and Brixham by Torbay. Wyll and Eglyfford were also included in the schedule.

Berry castle was the principal seat. Around it were two parks of a large size, the wall of one of which still stands to mark a portion of its boundary. Without including these or the small interest which the Duke had before acquired, the annual value of the purchase was then computed to be at least £224. The vendor was pledged to its yielding that amount by a very peculiar arrangement ; for the Duke engaged to convey to Sir Thomas, before the next feast of Pentecost, lands in Devon of the clear yearly value of £148 ; but in case the Berry estate should fall short of the amount before mentioned, the Duke was to retain, out of the lands promised to Sir Thomas, as much as would cover the deficiency. In adjusting this amount, the value of the land was to be reckoned at ten years' purchase. The Duke also particularly and expressly stipulated to have all writings delivered up to him, which accounts for the Seymours afterwards possessing so many papers of the Pomeroys, some of which were of a date almost coeval with the conquest. The transactions in connection with this property took some time to settle. On the 7th July, 1548, the Duke agreed to make over to Sir Thomas Pomeroy an estate, for three lives, of the manors of Brixham, Sandridge, Wyll, Eglyfford, an estate in fee simple in the manors of Parkhurst and Lancraff, and to obtain for him the grant of the land of the late chantry of Plympton, in consideration of a fine of the castle and park of Berry Pomeroy, and of the manors of Berry Bridgetown and Harberton, to be levied by Sir Thomas and his lady. At the same time Sir Thomas Pomeroy signed a general release to free the Duke from the obligation contained in the former indenture, as well as from all recognizances into which he had previously entered.

The final deeds respecting the purchase of Berry Pomeroy were not ratified until the 29th of October, 1548. The amount finally mentioned is 3,000 acres of land, etc., and the fishery in the Dart.

(An account of the purchase of Berry Pomeroy by the 11th Duke of Somerset in his collection of Seymour family papers, letters, and notes.)

NOTE 34.

The grant of an additional revenue which the Protector had refused on his return from Scotland, was now again taken into consideration, and he now petitioned that in lieu of that which was intended for him, he might have a licence to purchase of the Bishop of Bath and Wells certain lands belonging to that see. This was granted and, as was the usual result of such licences, the church had to part with its property for much less than it was worth. In the end, however, it was found that the property did not yield as much as had originally been intended, and another grant from the Crown was therefore resolved upon. (Froude's Hist.)

By an Act in 1530, the large possessions in Dorsetshire, formerly belonging to Sir William Fillol, had been settled upon Sir Edward Seymour. Now that he was Duke of Somerset, he desired to increase his property in that part of England, and he now, July 20, received a grant of the manor of Wimborne, belonging to the Duchy of Lancaster. He already had great hereditary possessions in Wiltshire, to which the manors of Standen, North Standen, Okell, and Hungerford were now added. The grant also included the domain of Thetford, in Norfolk; certain lands in the forest of Chalfts, in Wilts and Hants; the manor of Cowfold, a part of the possessions of the late monastery at Malmesbury; the hundred of Rowburgh, Rushmore, and Hasils, in Dorset; a manor in Gloucester, and the manors of Reading and Whitley, part of the possessions of the late attainted monastery at Reading.

(11th Duke of Somerset's MSS.)

NOTE 35.

Sir John Thynne was said by Paget to have been amongst the worst of the Protector's friends. The following story is curious and of some interest. "William Wycherly examined saith—that about ten years past he used a rule called Circula Salamonis, at a place called Pembersham, in Sussex, to call up Baro, whom he taketh as oriental or septentrial spirit; where was also one Robert Bayly, the scryer of the crystal stone, Sir John Anderson, the magister operator, Sir John Hychely, and Thomas Gosling, in the which practice they had swords, rings, and holy water, when they were frustrated, for Baro did not appear nor other vision of spirit, but there was a terrible wind and tempest all the time of the circulation. And since that time he used no concentrate circule, but hath used the crystal to invocate the sprat called Scariot, which he called divers times into the crystal to have knowledge of things stolen; which sprat had given him knowledge an hundred time, and thereby men have been restored to their goods. And this practice by the crystal he hath at the command of my Lord Protector executed in the presence of Mr. Thynne, Mr. Whalley, Mr. George Blage, Mr. Chaloner, and Mr. Weldon; and by this means my Lord Protector's plate was found where deponent told his Grace it was hid. He saith that he can invocate the sprat into the crystal glass as soon as any man, but he cannot bind the sprat so soon from lying lies."—Froude's Hist.

Note 36.

Letter of the King to the Lord Mayor, Aldermen, and Citizens of London, in behalf of the Lord Protector.

Edward,
By the King.

Trusty and well-beloved, we greet you well. We charge and command you most earnestly to give order, with all speed, for the defence and preservation of that our city of London for us; and to levy out of hand, and to put in order, as many as conveniently you may, well weaponed and arrayed, keeping good watch at the gates; and to send us hither for the defence of our person, one thousand of that our city of trusty and faithful men, to attend upon us, and our most entirely beloved uncle, Edward, Duke of Somerset, governor of our person, and protector of our realm, dominions, and subjects, well harnessed, and with good and convenient weapons; so that they do make their repair hither unto us this night, if it be possible, or at least to-morrow before noon; and, in the mean time to do what appertaineth unto your duty, for ours and our said uncle's defence against all such as attempt any conspiracy or enterprise of violence against us or our said uncle, as you know best for our preservation and defence at this present.

Given under our signet, at our manor of Hampton-court the sixth of October, the third year of our reign.

You shall further give credit to our trusty and well-beloved Owen Cleydon, the bearer hereof, in all such things as he shall further declare unto you on behalf of us, and our said uncle the Lord Protector.

EDWARD.

SOMERSET.

(Haynes, State Papers.)

NOTE 37.

A letter of the Lord Protector to the Lord Russel, Lord Privy Seal, concerning troubles working against him.

After our right hearty commendations to your good lordship; here hath of late risen such a conspiracy against the King's Majesty and us, as never hath been seen, the which they cannot maintain but with such vain letters and false tales surmised as was never meant or intended of us. They pretend and say, that we have sold Boulogne to the French, and that we do withhold wages from the soldiers ; and other such tales and letters they do spread abroad (of the which if any one thing were true, we would not wish to live) : the matter now being brought to a marvellous extremity, such as we would never have thought it could have come unto, especially of these men, towards the King's Majesty and us, of whom we have deserved no such thing, but rather much favor and love. But the case being as it is, this is to require and pray you to hasten you hither to the defence of the King's Majesty, with such force and power as you may, to show the part of a true gentleman, and of a very friend : the which thing we trust God shall reward, and the King's Majesty in time to come, and we shall never be unmindful of it too.

We are sure you shall have other letters from them, but as you tender your duty to the King's Majesty, we require you to make no stay, but immediately repair, with such force as ye have, to his highness in his castle of Windsor, and cause the rest of such a force as ye may make to follow you. And so we bid you right heartily farewell.

From Hampton-court the 6th of October.

Your lordship's assured loving friend,

EDWARD SOMERSET.

NOTE 38.

A letter of the Lord Protector to certain Lords of the Council assembled at London. (Haynes, State Papers.)

My Lords, we commend us most heartily unto you : and whereas the king's majesty was informed that you were assembled in such sort as you do now also remain ; and was advised by us, and such other of his council as were then here about his person, to send master secretary Peter unto you, with such message as whereby might have ensued the surety of his majesty's person, with preservation of his realm and subjects, and the quiet both of us and yourselves, as master secretary can well declare to you : his majesty, and we of his council here, do not a little marvel that you stay still with you the said master secretary, and have not, as it were, vouchsafed to send answer to his majesty, either by him or yet any other. And for ourselves we do much marvel, and are right sorry, as both we and you have good cause to be, to see the manner of your doings bent with force of violence, to bring the king's majesty and us to these extremities. Which as we do intend, if you will take no other way but violence, to defend (as nature and our allegiance doth bind us) to extremity of death, and to put all to God's hand, who giveth victory as it pleaseth him ; so that if any reasonable conditions and offers would take place (as hitherto none have been signified unto us from you, nor do we understand what you do require or seek, or what you do mean), and that you do seek no hurt to the king's majesty's person ; as touching all other private matters, to avoid the effusion of Christian blood, and to preserve the king's majesty's person, his realm and subjects, you shall find us agreeable to any reasonable condition that you will require. For we do esteem the king's wealth and tranquility of the realm, more than all other worldly things ; yea more than our life. Thus, praying you to send us your determinate answer herein by master secretary Peter, or, if you will not let him go, by this bearer, we beseech God to give both you and us grace to determine this matter, as may be to God's honour, the preservation of the king, and the quiet of us all ; which may be, if the fault be not in you. And so we bid you most heartily farewell.

From the king's majesty's castle of Windsor, the 7th October, 1549.

Your lordships' loving friend,
E. SOMERSET.

NOTE 39.

List of manors and estates settled on the Duke and Duchess of Somerset by the Act for his fine and ransom, in the 3rd and 4th Edward VI.

In Wiltshire.

The manors of Sherston, Thornhill, Monketon next Chipnam, Echerfounte with the farm there, Alcanings with the farm there, Stapleford, Midgehall, Croston, Clatford, Huish, Froxfield, Amesbury, Brodtown, Easton Drewes, Cowlesfield in the parish of

Whiteparish, Trowbridge, Shalborn Dormer, Ramsbury, Maunton Preshute, Pewsey, Charleton, Knoll, Everleigh, Chelworth, Marlborough.

The estates of Monketon next Chipnam, Monketon next Broughton, Slaughtonford, Boxe, Wraxhall, Sopworth, Alington, Maiden Bradley, Collingburn, Brom farm, Corston parcel of Studley grange, Studley grange, Stuttiscombe, Wotton house, Fitzwarren, Titcombe, Oxenwood, Westcombe, Bedwin, Amesbury site, Amesbury Reve, Amesbury Farm, Easton Drewes, parcel of Biddenstoke, Burbage Savage, Sturmy, Wotton Rivers, Burbage Darell, Easton warrens, Collingbourn Dormer, West Grafton, East Grafton, Collingborn, Collingburn Kingston, Northwinterburn otherwise called Rabeston, Hippingscombe, Shalborn Escourt, Breydon otherwise called Temple Closes, Asserton, farm, Bedwin prebend, Langeden, Wike, Wolfhall, Mildenhall, the prebend of Acford, Rothefen prebends, Chrisbury late Cobhams, Alderbury hundred, Amesbury hundred, Kindwardston hundred, Silkley hundred, Hungerford (partly in Berks).

In Dorsetshire.

The manors of Kingston and Povington ; the estates of Estrington farm, Symesborough, the cell of Horton, the cell of Holme.

In Oxfordshire.

The manor of Brambury.

In Devonshire.

The manors of Ottery St. Mary, Topsham, Exminster, Tiverton, Fremington, Bulkeworthy, Beauforde, Uptomyne, Marsh, Plympton, Berry Pomeroy with the members of the hundred of Exmistre and Estyngton mouth, Shneford.

The estates of Tiverton Borough, Heaunton, Pemtherdon, Kydelcombe, Heaunton foreign, Raytakelrey Healpore, Tiverton hundred, Fremington hundred, Plympton hundred.

In Somersetshire.

The manors of Abbott, Ilminster, Hilcombe, Midleney, Haygrove, Bridgehampton, Southarpe, Turnock, Sandford, Periton, Windeyates, Cheddarm Westoker, Ilton, Pulton, Westpeminde, Balton's borough, Weston, Othery, Walton, East Brent, Stowey, Muddlesley, Mark, More, Wyke, Wollasington, Dunpole, Otecombe, Combe, Banwell, Chewe, Wokeye.

The estates of Spekington, Chellington, Westbarn farm, Pasture of Hickes park, pasture of Sheppard grove, Holt pasture, Lawrence, Lydeyarde, Beauchamp Shepton, Norton Beauchamp, Hache Beauchamp, Cheddar, Axbridge, Yerneshill, Westarnell, Downehead, Stowgurce, Wikefitzpaine, the farm of Bellerita,

Estbitroy, Westbitroy, Westoker hundred, Middle Sowye, North Penot, South Brent, South Brent Huish, Church lands, Stokeland Lovell, Honybere, Lyllestock, Wynford Rivers, Brampton Raff, Bishop's Cheddar, Blackford, Castle Cary, Yarnfield, the Pott and Marrey, Winterstoke hundred, Cheve hundred, Barton hundred, Brent and Wrington hundred, Whiteleigh hundred, Whelstone, Blackford hundred.

In Southamptonshire.

The manors of Evetham and Moksfount.

In Gloucestershire.

The manors of Standish, Trocester, Yeate, Weston Birte, Ablington, Standharst, Pulton, Marshfield.

The estates of Horton prebend, Frampton Cotterell, Northstanden, Standen, Okehill.

In Berkshire.

The manor of Whiteleigh and the estate of Eastbury.

In Lincolnshire.

The manor of Sleford.

In Warwickshire.

The manor of Belfall.

In Surrey.

The manor of Combernwell.

In Middlesex.

The manors of Stroud, Alcotes, Burston; and the estates of Sion, Covent garden, Liston, St. John's Wood, Isleworth.[1]

(11th Duke of Somerset's MS. relating to Seymour family.)

Note 40.

List of manors and estates given to the King in lieu of the fine and ransom which he was pleased to take of the Duke of Somerset.

In Somersetshire.

Wells, Wells foreign, Wells borough, Wellington, Wellington borough, Evercrick, Cranmer, the liberties of Wells, Woodmow, Dungate, Beniston park and hundred.

In Dorsetshire.

Canford, the town of Poole, Kingston large, Marshewodde, the isle of Purbeck, Knoll steeple, Chrich, Corfe castle, Chetred chase, Berdberry and Walford hundreds, Holt chase and park, Reading.

In Buckinghamshire.
Woodburn, Tinghurst.

In Huntingdonshire.
Bugden.

In Southamptonshire.
Hursboon, Ringwood, Christchurch constable, Christchurch hundred.

In Wiltshire.
Wotton Vetus, Vasterne park, Alborn, Ludgersall, Savernake forest, Chewte Finkeley, Dolles.

In Somersetshire.
Glastonbury, Norwood and Wirral, Mere, Berchers, Lympes-ham, Lymplesham, Estreate, Budeleigh, Streate, the liberties of the Hydes of Glastonbury, Widmore, North Petreton.

(11th Duke of Somerset's MS. relating to Seymour family.)

Note 41.

Somerset had built Sion house some time previously, and had made a fine botanical garden there. He was very fond of this, and was one of the first promoters of the science of botany in England. We are told that the property was formerly a convent, which was given him by Edward VI, and "that he began soon after to erect on its site the magnificent structure, whose shell, though variously altered, still remains (1803). The gardens were enclosed by high walls before the east and west fronts, and were laid out in a very grand manner, but being made at a time when extensive views were deemed inconsistent with the stately privacy affected by the great, they were so situated as to deprive the house of all prospect. To remedy that inconvenience, the Protector built a high triangular terrace in the angle between the walls of the two gardens; and this it was that his enemies afterwards did not scruple to call a fortification, and to insinuate that it was one proof, among others, of his having formed a design dangerous to the liberties of the king and people."

About the same time he built Somerset house on the site of that formerly occupied by Bishop Rowland Lee, who had been made to exchange it with Somerset for a house at Kew by order of Henry VIII. The building of it gave some offence to a certain section of the people, for it was built out of the stone, timber, and lead taken from the houses of the bishops of Worcester, Litchfield, and Llandaff; the parish church, St. Paul's cloister; two chapels; a charnel house; and the greater part of the church of St. John of Jerusalem, near Smithfield. It was one of the first attempts to restore ancient architecture in England. In later times James I, his Queen, Anne, and Catherine de Medici, held their court there, and the front to the river was rebuilt by Inigo Jones. The whole structure, with the water gate, was taken down in 1770 to be rebuilt into apartments for public offices.

"This Somerset house," says Fuller, in his Church History, "is so tenacious of his name, that it would not change a duchy for a kingdom, when solemnly proclaimed by King James, Denmark house, from the King of Denmark's lodging therein, and his sister Queen Anne her repairing thereof. Surely it argueth that this Duke was well beloved, because his name made such an indelible impression on this his house, whereof he was not full five years peaceably possessed."

Note 42.

The King gave him back the castle of Marlborough, all his lordships and manors of Burton, Ludgershall, Alborn, and Old Wotton; his parishes of Ludgershall, Great Vastern, Little Vastern, Alborn Chase, and Alborn Warren; the forests of Brudon and Savernake, in Wilts, and divers other manors and lands in the counties of Wilts, Hants, Dorset, Somerset, Middlesex, Berks, and Bucks.

(Seymour Papers, coll. by 11th Duke.)

Note 43.

Froude says, "It is to be remarked that in the subsequent proceedings, although the banquet was alluded to, the intended scene of it was not again mentioned. Neither Paget nor Arundel was tried, although, if any plot was really formed for the murder, Arundel was one of the principal persons concerned in it."

Note 44.

The Duke of Northumberland before his death earnestly entreated for an interview with Somerset's sons :—"Au quels il crya mercy de l'injustice qu'il avoit faict a leur Père, Protecteur de l'Angleterre, congnoissant avoir procuré sa mort a tort et faulsement. Palmer avant sa mort a confessé que l'escripture et l'accusation qu'il advouche et maintint contre le feu Protecteur estoit fausse, fabricquée par le dict duc (de Northumberland) et advoué par luy a la requeste du dict duc."—Simon Renard to Charles V.

(MS., Record Office.)

Note 45.

Lord Coke, commenting upon the trial, observes that, even admitting the tenth of the evidence, the verdict was not justified, because there had been no proclamation calling on the Duke and his confederates to disperse; and it was only by persisting, after such proclamation had been read, that his conduct came under the Treason Act. Northumberland probably anticipated the objection, and was contented with an ordinary verdict of felony under the common law (Froude's History). Edward, writing to his friend Barnaby Fitzpatrick, says, "after debating the matter from nine of the clock till three, the Lords went together, and there weighing that the matter seemed only to touch their lives, although afterwards more inconveniences might have followed, and that men might think they did it of malice, acquitted him of high treason, and condemned him of felony, which he seemed to have confessed."

(Litt. remains Edward VI.)

"But it is not however until the meeting of (the Council) Jan. 23, 1551-2, when we find an entry referring to the 'late Duke of Somerset,' that we learn how complete was Northumberland's triumph, as the Council is silent as to the trial and execution of his once all-powerful rival, though an entry on the preceding day authorises Sir Philip Hobby to supply the prisoner with money to be bestowed in alms before his execution." (Dasent's Preface to the Acts of the Privy Council in England. 1550-1552.)

Note 46.

During the next reign, when the Duke of Northumberland was being led through the city to his execution, a lady, who had retained one of these handkerchiefs, shook it in his face and cried out, "Behold the blood of that worthy man, that good uncle of that excellent King, which, shed by thy malicious practises, does now apparently revenge itself on thee."

Note 47.

The following curious story taken from the memorials of Archbishop Cranmer is perhaps worth reading. "The Arch. of Canterbury this year lost the Duke of Somerset, whom he much valued, and who had been a great assistant to him in the reformation of the church, and a true friend to it. His violent death exceedingly grieved the good Archbishop, both because he knew it would prove a great let to religion, and was brought about by evil men to the shedding of innocent blood, for the furthering the ends of ambition ; and begat in him fear and jealousies of the King's life. It is very remarkable what I meet with in one of my manuscripts (Harleian MSS., 425). There was a woman somewhat before the last apprehension of the Duke, wife of one Woocock, of Poole in Dorsetshire, that gave out, that there was a voice that followed her, which sounded these words always in her ears : ' He whom the King did best trust should deceive him, and work treason against him.' After she had a good while reported this, Sir William Berkeley, who married the Lord Treasurer Winchester's daughter, sent her up to London to the Council, with two of his servants. She was not long there, but, without acquainting the Duke of Somerset, whom it seemed most to concern (he being the person whom the King most trusted), was sent home again with her purse full of money and, after her coming home, she was more busy in that talk than before. So that she came to a market town called Wimborne, four miles from Poole, where she reported, that the voice continued following her as before. This looked, by the circumstances, like a practice of some Popish priests, accustomed to dealing in such frauds, to make the world the more inclinable to believe the guilt of the good Duke, which Somerset's enemies were now framing against him. And so some of the wiser sort thereabouts did seem to think ; for there were two merchants of Poole that heard her, and took note of her words, and came to the house of Hancock, minister of Poole, who was known to the Duke, counselling him to certify my lord of her. Which Hancock accordingly did, and came to Sion, where the Duke then was, and told him of the words. He added, ' whom the King doth best trust we do not know, but that all the King's loving subjects did think that his Grace was most worthy to be best trusted ; and that his Grace had been in trouble : and that all the King's loving subjects did pray for his Grace to the Almighty to preserve him, that he might never come in the like trouble again.'

" Then the Duke asked him whether he had a note of the words ; which when he had received from Hancock, he said to him, suspecting the plot, ' Ah ! sirrah, this is strange, that these things should come before the Councillors and I not hear of it. I am of the Council also.' He asked Hancock before whom of the Council this matter was brought ? Who replied, he knew not certain, but as he supposed. The Duke asked him, whom he supposed ? He answered, before the Lord Treasurer, because his son-in-law, Sir William Berkeley, sent her up. The Duke subjoined, ' It was like to be so.' This was three weeks before his last apprehension. . . . . Indeed it seemed to have been a plot of the Papists, and the Bishop of Winchester at the bottom of it."

NOTE 48.

"She was maid of honour to Queen Elizabeth, and in great favour with her royal mistress. She was buried in St. Benedict's chapel in Westminster Abbey with very great solemnity. Her corpse was brought from the Queen's armoury to the Abbey church, attended by all the choir of the said Abbey, and 200 of the court, and 60 mourners, etc. She had a great banner of arms borne : Mr. Clarencieux was the Herald attending ; and Scambler, Bishop of Peterborough, added to the solemnity a funeral sermon. On the east of the above mentioned chapel is a small but neat monument of black marble and alabaster, with small Corinthian pillars, embellished with gold, and adorned with coats of arms, etc., and an inscription to her memory." Camden also mentions a Latin inscription in verse, which was once to be found in the Abbey. This monument was erected by her brother.

"Ingenio præstans et vultu Jana decoro,
Nobilis arte fuit vocis, et arte manus,
Hanc Venus et Pallas certant utra debet habere,
Vult Venus esse suam, Pallas esse suam ;
Mors fera virginis figens in pectore telum,
Neutrius (inquit) erit, sed mihi præda jacet.
Corpore Jana jacet tellerum terra subibit,
Sed pius in cœli spiritus arce sedet."

These have been translated by Dr. Haddon thus :—

"For genius famed, for beauty loved,
    Jane bade the world admire ;
Her voice harmonious notes improved,
    Her hand the tuneful lyre.
Venus and Pallas claimed this maid,
    Each as her right alone,
But death superior power displayed,
    And seized her as his own.
Her virgin dust this mournful tomb,
    In kindred earth contains ;
Her soul, which fate can ne'er consume,
    In endless glory reigns."

(Printed in Life and Letters, Arabella Stuart. Cooper.)

NOTE 49.

Part of the Ode of Ronsard in praise of the three eldest daughters of the Duke of Somerset :

"Mais si ce harpeur fameux
    Oyoit le chant des Sirennes
    Qui sonne aux bords escumeux

Des Albionnes arènes ;
Son Luth payen il fendrait
Et disciple se rendrait,
Dessons leur chanson chrètienne
Dont la voix passe la sienne.

*   *   *

La science auparavant,
Si longtemps orientale,
Peu à peu marchant avant
S'apparoist occidentale ;
Et sans jamais se borner
N'a point cessé de tourner
Sant quelle soit parvenue
A l'autre rive inconnue.
La de son grave sourçy
Vint affoler le courage
De ces trois vierges içy
Les trois seules de notre age.
Et si bien les scent tenter
Qu'ores on les oit chanter
Maint vers jumeau, qui surmonte
Les notres, rouges de honte."

The following letter from Margaret and Jane to the King in 1548, translated from the original Latin (Howard Letters, p. 276), may be of interest as a specimen of their style of writing. "It cannot be expressed, O ! king most serene, with what hope and joy that literary gift which we have received from your highness has overflowed our spirit, and what a sharp spur we find it to be, in order to embrace those things and to cleave with all labour and sedulousness to those studies wherein we know your highness to take so much delight, and to be so deeply learned ; wherein we also, whom your serene highness wishes to see best instructed, hope to make some advancement. And these present tokens of your singular goodwill, which no power of words can do justice to, show plainly how many thanks are due from us, more than many others to your Majesty ; should we attempt any act or expression of thanks, your deserts, always proceeding more and more in perpetual vicissitude, would not only seem to press upon us but would certainly oppress us ; especially as we have nothing, nay, we ourselves are nothing, which we do not justly owe to your highness. Wherefore while forced to fly to your clemency, we yet doubt not that a prince of such heavenly kindness, who has loaded us with so many and so great benefits, will add also this one, that he will not think that those things are bestowed upon ungrateful persons which belong to a grateful spirit. Whereof these letters, which are wont to be substitutes for the absent, will be but a faint proof ;

while we pray for all happiness to your highness, with a long continuance thereof.

The most devoted servants to your Majesty,
MARGARET SEYMOUR.
JANE SEYMOUR.

(Wood's Letters of Royal and Illustrious Ladies.)

NOTE 50.

Elizabeth, Lady Cromwell, to Sir W. Cecil, A.D. 1552.

. . . . Your great gentleness, many ways shewed towards me, emboldeneth me to trouble you with these my letters, whereby it may please you to understand that, where it pleased the king's majesty and his most honourable Council to will me to take into tuition my four nieces, I thought it my duty, and the rather being moved by your friendly advice, declared unto me by your gentle letters, to satisfy the Council's honourable requests and not to refuse them; although if I should have declared unto my said honourable lords at that time what charge and other cares I, being now a lone woman, am troubled with, I doubt not but it would have pleased them, of their honours, to have accepted in good part my reasonable cause to have refused them. Wherefore, considering with myself the weighty burden and care which nature bindeth me to be mindful of, as well for the bestowing of my own children, as also for such poor family as my late lord and husband hath left me unprovided for, enforceth me to require your help and advice that hereafter, about Christmas next, or shortly after then, by your good means, my said honourable lords of the Council may understand that, when my said nieces have accomplished a full year with me, then my trust is that they shall be otherwise provided for and bestowed than with me; trusting that there be places enough where they may be, better than with me; and, as I do perceive by them many ways, much more to their own contentations and pleasings. And even as I was bold to write unto the king's Highness's most honourable Council, that I, being a lone woman, not nigh any of my kinsfolk, whereby I the rather am destitute of friendly advice and counsel, how to use myself in the rule of such company as now I am careful of, so now I am likewise bold to declare the same unto you, being not at any time either instructed by you or any other of my said honourable lords, how to use my said nieces; considering that I have, in some cases, thought good that my said nieces should not all wholly be their own guides, but rather willing them to follow mine advice, which they have not taken in such good part as my good meaning was, nor according to my expectation in them.

Trusting, herefore, so much in your worship, that you will so tender my aforesaid desire, as the same may so come to pass that my request herein may be satisfied in convenient time, and without any displeasure towards me for my good meaning. And thus I beseech the living God to send you continual health and much increase of honour. From Launde, the 25th Oct., 1552, yours always assured to her power.

ELIZABETH CROMWELL.

NOTE 51.

The names of all her Majesty's ships, and others that served under the Lord Admiral and the Lord Henry Seymore on the seas against the Spanish forces. Collected the 13th of December, 1588.

(Burghley State Papers, Murdin.)

Tonnage.	Ships.	Men.	Captains.
800	The Arke Rawleghe	400	The Lord Admiral.
600	The Elizabeth Bonaventure..	250	The Earl of Cumberland.
500	The Raynbowe	250	The Lord Henry Seymore.
500	The Golden Lyon	250	The Lord Thomas Howard.
1000	The White Bear	500	The Lord Edmund Sheaffield.
500	The Vanguard	250	Sir William Winter.
500	The Revenge	250	Sir Francis Drake.
900	The Elizabeth Jonas	500	Sir Robert Southwell.
800	The Victory	400	Sir John Hawkins.
400	The Antelope	160	Sir John Palmer.
1100	The Triumph	500	Sir John Furbusher.
400	The Dreadnought	200	Sir George Beeston.
600	The Mary Roase	250	Edward Fenton, Esq.
500	The Noneperely	250	Thomas Fenner, Gent.
600	The Hope	250	Robert Crosse, Gent.
	The Gally Bonavolia	250	William Bourough, Esq.
400	The Swiftshure	180	Edward Fenner, Gent.
300	The Swallowe	160	Richard Hawkins, Gent.
300	The Foresight	160	Christopher Baber, Gent.
250	The Aid	120	William Fenner, Gent.
200	The Bull	100	Jeremy Turner, Gent.
200	The Tyger	100	John Bostocke, Gent.
150	The Tremountain	70	Luke Warde, Gent.
120	The Scowte	70	Henry Ashley, Esq.
100	The Archates	60	Gregory Rigges, Gent.
70	The Charles	40	John Roberts, Gent.
60	The Moon	40	Alexander Clifford, Gent.
50	The Advice	35	John Herris, Gent.
50	The Spye	35	Ambrose Warde, Gent.
50	The Marlyne	35	Walter Goare, Gent.
40	The Sun	24	Richard Buckley.
30	The Synnet	20	John Shirrife.
	The Brigandine	36	Thomas Scott.
120	The George	30	Richard Hodges.
12,190	34	6,225	34

Coasters with the Lord Henry Seymore.

Tonnage.	Ships.	Men.	Captains.
160	The Daniel	70	Robert Johnson.
150	The Gallion Hutchens	70	Thomas Tucker.
150	The Bark Lane	70	Leonard Harvell.
60	The Fancy	30	Richard Fearne.
70	The Griffin	40	John Thompson.
50	The Little Hare	30	Matthew Railston.
75	The Handmaid	40	John Gattenbury.
150	The Marygold	70	Francis Johnson.
35	The Matthew	20	Richard Mitchel.
40	The Susan	20	John Musgrave.
140	The William of Ipswich	70	Barnaby Lowe.
125	The Katherine	60	Thomas Grymble.
120	The Primrose	60	John Cordwell.
60	The Anne Bonaventure	30	John Conny.
80	The William of Rye	40	William Coxon.
50	The Grace of God	20	William Fordred.
120	The Ellnatchen of Dover	70	John Lydgen.
110	The Robin	60	William Crippes.
38	The Hazard	20	Nicholas Tornor.
150	The Grace of Yarmouth	70	William Musgrave.
150	The May Flower	70	Alexander Musgrave.
100	The William of Bricklesey	50	Thomas Lambert.
60	The John Young	30	Reynold Veazey.
2,248	**23**	**1,210**	

NOTE 52.

Sir Francis Drake to the Lord Henry Seymour.   (Burghley State Papers, Murdin.)

Right Honourable and my very good Lord,

I am commanded by my good Lord, the Lord Admiral, to send you the carvel in haste with these letters, giving your Lordship to understand, that the army of Spain arrived upon our coast the 20th of the present, and the 21st we had them in chace ; and so coming up to them, there had passed some common shot between some of our fleet and some of them ; and as far as we can perceive, they are determined to sell their lives with blows. Whereupon his Lordship hath commanded me to write unto your Lordship and Sir William Winter, that those ships serving under your charge should be put into the best and strongest manner you can, and ready to assist his Lordship, for the better encountering of them in those parts where you now are. In the mean time, what his Lordship, and the rest following him may do, shall be surely performed. His Lordship hath commanded me to write hearty commendations to your Lordship and Sir William Winter. I do salute your Lordship, Sir William Winter, Sir Henry Palmer, and all the rest of those honourable gentlemen serving under you, with the like; beseeching God of his mercy to give her Majesty, our gracious sovereign, always victory against her enemies. Written aboard her Majesty's good ship the Revenge, off of Start, this 21st, late in the evening 1588.

Your Lordship's poor friend ready to be commanded,
FRANCIS DRAKE.

P.S.—This letter my honourable good Lord is sent in haste. The fleet of Spaniards are somewhat above a hundred sails, many great ships. But truly, I think not half of them men of war. Haste.

Your Lordship's assured,
FRANCIS DRAKE.

NOTE 53.

Seymour to Walsingham. Aug. 1. (Laughton papers relating to defeat of Spanish Armada.)

Sir, I have written to Her Majesty at large of our proceedings upon my Lord's honourable letters directed unto me for the re-inforcing my Lord Admiral's strength; so was I likewise desired and written by my Lord Admiral himself to hasten my forces to join the same to his, which I did perform. And where his Lordship was altogether desirous at the first to have me strengthen him, so having done the uttermost of my good will (to the venture of my life) in prosecuting the distressing of the Spaniards, which was thoroughly followed the 29th July, I find my lord jealous and loth to have me take part of the honour of the rest that is to win, using his authority to command me to look to our English coasts, that have been long threatened by the Duke of Parma.

So referring the rest unto Her Majesty's letters as (well as) to the messengers, the one Mr. Brown* and the other my Lieutenant, who both are witnesses of our actions, do take my leave. From aboard the Rainbow this 1st Aug. 1588, at anchor at Harwich at 3 in the afternoon.

Your assured friend to command,
H. SEYMOUR.

There is a postscript to this letter too long for insertion here, but which contains the following passage: "I pray God my Lord Admiral do not find the lack of the Rainbow and that company; for I protest before God, and have witness for the same, I vowed

---

* Brute Brown who was serving as a volunteer on board the Rainbow.

I would be as near or nearer with my little ship to encounter our enemies as any of the greatest ships in both armies, which I have performed to the distress of one of their greatest ships sunk, if I have my due. We are in a manner famished for lack of victuals, although the same hath been drawn at length (*i.e.*, drawn out as long as possible) yet by increase of soldiers the same is all wasted.

"I presume the Spaniards are much distressed for victuals, which I hope will be the cause to make them yield to Her Majesty's mercy.

"I do send my Lieutenant the rather to give you perfect notice of our lacks, as also I pray you to use Mr. Brown with some favour, who of good will came to see the service two days before I joined with the Lord Admiral."

Seymour to Walsingham. Aug. 12. (Laughton.)

. . . . This morning my Lord Admiral* sent unto me, desiring very earnestly to speak with me and Sir William Winter ; and the message was no sooner delivered but there was descried almost 30 sails afar off. I sent him word I had Her Majesty's present service in hand, whereby I could not attend him ; also I was directed by my Lords† to have a vigilant eye upon these coasts. But if my lord himself should come into the narrow seas, and that Sir Francis Drake should attend as Vice-Admiral, I pray you let me be called home, for by that I find by experience, by good observation, some seers of antiquity are not the same persons they are deemed. And even so do commit you to God. In haste, etc. . . . . .

Seymour to Walsingham. Aug. 18. (Laughton.)

. . . . Plain dealing is best among friends. I will not flatter you, but you have fought more with your pen than many have in our English navy fought with their enemies ; and but that your place and most necessary attendance about Her Majesty cannot be spared, your valour and deserts in such places opposite to the enemy had showed itself . . . .

. . . . For myself, as I have not spared my body, which I thank God is able to go through thick and thin, let not the same be spared to knit up all (harass) between Her Majesty and her service, so far forth as God will give us leave ; I will not say as the Duke of Parma, by Sir John Conway's letter which I sent you—"I am bound to revenge, and I will do it, asking God no leave." I will not trouble you any further, but if you have cause to employ me further, let all my wants be supplied and refer the rest to God. . . .

---

* Howard.
† Of the Council.

Sir, I should do the master of my ship wrong if I did not further his careful service, being a man of substance, most valiant, and most efficient besides concerning his charge. I would desire you to prefer him to Her Majesty's coat of ordinary, for I know ne'er a man in England that I would wish sooner to have care of the Prince's person, if they were driven to the seas, than him.

Spare me not while I am abroad, for when God shall return me, I will be 'kin to the bear, I will be haled to the stake, before I come abroad again.

* * * * *

Seymour to Walsingham. Aug. 19. (Laughton.)

Sir, I shall be glad to do Her Majesty all the service I can which in duty I am bound, as otherwise for my country. I find my Lord Admiral doth repair to these quarters, as I gather, to this end, to seek the Spaniards; whom when he shall find, I wish him no better advantage than he had upon our last conflict with them. But I hardly doubt the meeting of them this year, and for my own part desire to be spared at home for divers respects, which hereafter I may unfold. I know I am envied, being a man not suitable with them, and therefore my actions and services shall be in vain. Besides my summer ship, always ordained for the narrow seas, will never be able to go through with the northern, Irish, or Spanish seas, without great harm and spoil of our own people by sickness. I have hitherto (*invita Minerva*) maintained my honour and credit in all my services as best becometh me. I would be loth now to stand *ad arbitrium judicis*, and thereafter do pray you to respect your good, devoted friend, who hath many weighty irons of his own to look unto; and so do commit you to God. From aboard the Rainbow, the 19th Aug., 1588.

Your very loving assured friend,

H. SEYMOUR.

Postscript.—I shall be enforced to send away my cousin Knyvet and his company tomorrow to London, because of their short victuals and other lacks, which must be supplied if the service be any more commanded.

Seymour to Walsyngham. Aug. 23. (Laughton.)

. . . . As I have written unto you lately, my Lord Admiral now returned, I am subject to his orders and directions as long as he is in place; and as I perceive, his intention is to divide his company into two parts, whereof he wishes me to take the road of Margate or Gorend, and himself the Downs or Dover; which if

2 D

it be so, I desire to be called home, for I never loved to be penned or moored in roads. But so long as there is an expectation of the Spaniards to return I would not have the thought once to return before some better services be accomplished; which I hardly doubt will fall out to such advantage as we had at our last bickerings.

I find my lord and his company divided in manner to factions, which I would wish otherwise; neither doth it appertain unto me to meddle much therein, or otherwise to advertise, so long as his lordship is accountable for all.

I received direction from Sir Francis Drake and Sir John Hawkins for the discharge of some of our navy, by order, as it would seem, of better authority; which were discharged to the number of some needless vessels, and yet had made stay of Mr. Thomas Knyvet's company, according to your last direction; and withal by good hap, upon these last intelligences of the Spaniards, have made stay of the rest . . . etc. . .

NOTE 54.

Bishop Burnett says in his history: "There was a private bill put in about the Duke of Somerset's estate, which had been by Act of Parliament entailed on his son in the last reign. On the 3rd of March it was sent to the House of Commons, signed by the King; it was for the repeal of that Act. Whether the King was so alienated from his uncle, that this extraordinary thing was done by him for the utter ruin of this family, or not, I cannot determine; but I rather incline to think that it was done in hatred to the Duchess of Somerset and her issue. For the estate was entailed on them by Act of Parliament, in prejudice of the issue of the former marriage, of whom are descended the Seimours of Devonshire: who were disinherited and excluded from the Duke of Somerset's honours by his patents, and from his estate by Act of Parliament; partly upon some jealousies he had of his former wife, but chiefly by the power his second wife had over him."

Although this new Act deprived Sir Edward, the younger, of much of the property that would otherwise have come to him, it became of great benefit to Sir Edward, the elder, and his brother John, for a Commission was appointed, with Lord Winchester at its head, to apportion to each such lands as had belonged to their respective mothers and award due compensation for such as had been sold by the Protector, thus the elder branch of the family received some estates that according to the Act of 1540 would have gone to the younger. Sir Edward Seymour, the younger, received the following manors and estates by the award of the Master of Wards and Liveries. Manors—Collingborn Dormer,

Collingborn Sutton, Collingborn Kingston, Pewsey, Scalborne, Escorte, Marleborow (Marlborough) cum Burton, Eston Bradstock, West Grafton, East Grafton, Westcombe, Bedwyn. Estates—Savernake Forest, Burbage Darell, Shalborne, Westcote alias Dormer, Eston Warren, The Hundred of Sylkeley, Knoll, Bedwyn, site of Amesbury Priory, Borough of Amesbury, Littlecote pasture.

Note 55.

The fine of £15,000 was settled in the following manner :— £10,000 was almost immediately remitted by the Queen in consideration of £1,187 ready money. Of the remaining £3,813, the sum of £1,000 more was remitted through the good offices of Sir Thomas Smith, Secretary of State. A distraint was then laid upon the Earl's lands for the remainder, viz. £2,813, upon which he wrote the following statement to Sir F. Walsingham with the result that another £1,000 was remitted. Eventually the remainder was also remitted. A copy of the warrant of release is at Longleat.

The Statement.

" For Mr. Secretary Walsingham, who desired a note of the sum already paid in." (Written on the margin of the original.) " The sum set upon me in the Star Chamber was £15,000, my land never being distrained therefore, till a little before my coming in the Tower. At what time Her Majesty released £10,000 of the £15,000. After, when I was at the Tower, and made suit for the release of my poor tenants pityfully distrained for the remainder demanded, which was £5,000, Her Majesty said she would have one thousand paid afore she would release any part of the said £5,000. Whereupon was paid in £1,187. Shortly after, Her Majesty cut off £1,000 more. So as there remaineth to be paid £2,813 which my trust is Her Majesty will either wholly cut off, or at the least, the greatest part ; if it may please Her Majesty to remember the whole sum was first set but for terror, as also my humble return out of France upon the first call, my patient abiding Her Majesty's heavy displeasure in prison ten years lacking one month, my sundry great losses in the said space by my officers, and lastly, sithence Her Majesty's most happy favour restored, my diligent attendance and readiness these full six years, to do any service commanded which I shall be more able to perform when I may find some fruit of Her Majesty's favourable speeches and good opinion ; Her Majesty's gracious dealing in this behalf being more worth unto me than ten times the value of the remainder. Otherwise contrary to my own disposition I shall be enforced to leave

Her Majesty's comfortable presence by renewing my suit of travel, whereby in letting my land to most advantage, abating my maintenance, I may take order to pay my credit at home and at my return be able to serve Her Majesty where now for want, I cannot shew my affectionate mind if Her Majesty should any ways employ me." Endorsed "A remembrance of the Earl of Hertford for Mr. Secretary Walsingham." (Wilts Archæolog. Mag., xv, vii. Appendix.)

NOTE 56.

It seems that Hales had offended before, though he was soon liberated, but that he continued to urge the cause of Hertford and was again committed to the Tower. In Ellis, second series, we find, "From a letter of Sir William Cecil to Sir Thomas Smith, April 27th, 1564, it seems probable that the Lady Catharine and Lord Hertford's imprisonment, in a measure, owed their prolongation to the mistaken zeal of one John Hales, who had been Clerk of the Hanaper in the reign of Henry VIII. He says, here is fallen out a troublesome fond matter, John Hales has secretly made a book in the time of the last Parliament wherein he hath taken upon him to discuss no small matter, viz., the title to the crown after her Majesty. Having confuted and rejected the line of the Scottish Queen, and made the line of the Lady Frances mother to the Lady Catharine only next and lawful. He is committed to the Fleet for this boldness, specially because he hath communicated it to sundry persons. My lord John Grey is in trouble also for it. Besides this, John Hales hath procured sentences and counsels of lawyers from beyond seas to be written in maintenance of the Earl of Hertford's marriage. The dealing of his offendeth the Queen's Majesty very much. God give her Majesty by this chance a disposition to consider hereof that either by her marriage or by some common order, we poor subjects may know where to lean and to adventure our lives with contentation of our consciences."

In another, dated May 9th, 1564, Sir William Cecil says that he himself is not free from suspicion "because some of those committed upon the occasion had access to him in their suits."

"In this manner I am by commandment occupied, whereof I could be content to be delivered, but I will go upright, neither *ad dextram* nor *ad sinistram.*"

NOTE 57.

Verses by the Earl of Hertford engraved on the ring given by him to Lady Catherine Grey (Life and Letters of Arabella Stuart, Cooper, 169):—

" As circles five by art compact show but one ring in sight,
So trust united faithful minds with knot of secret might,
Whose force to break but greedy death no wight possesseth power,
As time and sequels well shall prove ; my ring can say no more."

NOTE 58.

The following letter of Lady Catherine's to her husband shows on what good terms they were. It is taken from a copy in the handwriting of the celebrated Duchess of Portland found among her papers at Longleat. A few sentences only, of a purely private nature, are withheld. The original letter is probably the one described as private and affectionate among the Duke of Northumberland's papers, Vol. III (Third Report of the Historical Commissioners, p. 47) :—

" No small joy, my dear lord, is it to me the comfortable understanding of your maintained health. I crave of God to let you sustain, as I doubt not but He will, you neither I having anything in this most lamentable time so much to comfort by pitiful absence each other with as the hearing, the seeking, and countenance thereof in us both. Though of late I have not been well, yet now, I thank God, pretty well, and long to be merry with you as you do to be with me. I say no more but be you merry as I was heavy when you the third time came to the door and it was locked. Do you think I forget old fore-past matters ? No surely I cannot, but bear in memory far many more than you think for. I have good so to do when I call to mind what a husband I have of you and my great hard fate to miss the viewing of so good a one. . . . . Thus most humbly thanking you, my sweet lord, for your husbandly sending both to see how I do, and also for your money, I most lovingly bid you farewell, not forgetting my especial thanks to you for your book, which is no small jewel to me. I can very well read it, for as soon as I had it, I read it over even with my heart as well as with my eyes ; by which token I once again I bid you once again *Vale et semper salles*, my good Ned.

" Your most loving and faithful wife during life,
"KATHERINE HARTFORD.

" I pray my lord be not jealous of a thing I shall desire you to do which is, to tell your Poet I think great unkindness in him for that I understand he should have come to me, but when he was wished he groaned . . . Well yet though he would not come to me, I would have been glad to have seen him ; but belike he maketh none account of me as his mistress which I cannot but take unkindly at his hands."—(See Wilts Archæolog. Mag., vol. xv.)

Some account of the Bible used in the Tower by the Earl of Hertford and Lady Catherine Grey. This was found at Longleat (see Wilts Archæolog. Mag., xv, 154):—

The little volume is described in the title page as *La Sainte Bible*, en Français à Lyon par Sebastine Honoré, 1558. At the top of the page is written the Seymour family motto, "Foy pour devoir," and at the foot, "E. Hertford," next to which is a signature "W. Wingfield." The Earl had also written a Greek sentence, signifying "In human affairs nothing is certain."

On the first fly-leaf at the end, in the Earl's handwriting, are the entries of the births of his two sons, born in the Tower:—

"Mon plus aisné fils Edouard Beauchamp fust né après le midi du jour, Mercredi 24 du Septembre, 1561, un peu après les deux heures, un quart d'heure ou demy heure."

"Mon second Thomas Seymour fust né Jeudy matin unzieme du Febury, 1563, environ quart d'heure après les dix heures. Dieu leur donne sa grande benediction paternelle. Amen."

Then follows a prayer in French in which allusion is made to the Queen's displeasure:—

"Dieu tout puissant père de toute consolation Que te mercie très humblement et très affectueusement de la grande misericorde et bonté infinie qu'il ta plu montrer en l'endroit de ma femme et moi en la delivrant hors des grands dangers d'enfantement et de maladie. Aussy en nous envoyant à tous deux les benedictions des œuvres de tes mains : te priant Seigneur Dieu, la consoler et fortifier en santé et patience : et aussy les petites creatures nos deux fils avec ta divine et chère protection et benediction. Par laquelle nous voyons bien que tu ne veut nous laisser l'âme désesperer de ta grande misericorde et bonté infinie ; mais comme père, nous voul . . . faire cognaistre ton affection paternelle. Il te plaist encore nous chatier de tes verges pour mieux nous faire te recognaistre et ta puissance absolue. Ainsy nous savons bien que c'est en ta seule puissance de rendre ton œuvre de grace . . . en la fin du tour accompli et parfait. Pour à quoi parvenir nous te prions tres-humblement que comme il t'a plus nous mettre en la mauvaise grace d'Elizabeth, notre Reine et maitresse, ainsi qu'il te plait luy mettre en l'esprit ta vertu de douceur et clemence, qui es accoutumé de pardonner les fautes à tous ceux qui de bon cœur les reconnaissont. Veuille donc regarder et pitier nous les dictes personnes ayant eu de long maux et estant encore battu de plusieurs tes verges . . . Seigneur, autant ou plus rigoureuse que jamais comme de l'affliction d'esprit de . . . et de plusieurs autres calamités. Console nous donc que selon que tu cognois que nous en avons besoin, et en nous faizant profiter tes chatiments à notre correction. Confirme nous en bonne patience, moderez ta rigueur selon ta sainte ordonnance, faiz que nous puissions jouir luy . . ."

Note 59.

The following paper contains the substance of several letters and documents concerning the Earl of Hertford's private affairs. Lord Wentworth and others had disputed his claims, and he sent the following statement (here compressed for want of space) to the Lord Treasurer in 1573 (see Wilts Archæolog. Mag., xv, p. 152):—

The Duke of Somerset, then Earl of Hertford, had lands of inheritance, in the year 1540, of the yearly value of	£2,400
The lands he acquired by purchase, grants, and increase of living from 1540 to Jan. 28, 1547 (the date of Henry VIII's death) were of the yearly value of ...	£2,000
His purchases and increase of lands from that date to the time of his own death in Jan. 1552, were of the yearly value of	£3,000
Making a total of	£7,400

The Earl claims that the whole of the above should have descended to him, and states that, when he was 14 years old and a ward of the King, all the lands that his father had acquired between 1537 and 1552, amounting to a yearly value of £5,000, were taken from him, thus leaving him only such lands as his father had possessed prior to 1537. He also states that it was arranged, by Lord Winchester's award, that he should be recompensed for certain lands sold by his father after 1547, but that he has received no such recompense, which was to have been made within a year, failing which it had been settled that he should receive lands of the value of the recompense awarded him, out of the confiscated property. At the time of the award Sir John Thynne and others of the chief officers of the Protector were in the Tower, and Lord Winchester had been unable to get full information as to the Protector's property. Acting on what information he could procure, however, he had awarded £753 14s. 3d. a year as recompense, but later on, finding that £81 a year more ought to have been awarded, he assigned the following manors to the Earl to make up that amount, viz.: North Perrott, Chillington, and Southarpe, in Somerset.

The Earl further states that he himself had remained contented with the arrangement hitherto, but on examining his rights when disputed by Lord Wentworth and others, he had discovered that he ought to have received still larger recompense, and that he ought not to have been paying certain rents, amounting to £400, which he had hitherto paid. He further states that his object is not to make fresh claims for what should have belonged to him, but only

to prevent further disturbance, and have his title confirmed to the
lands he already held.

He adds " That this statement was delivered by my Lord
Treasurer, by Mr. Attorney and Mr. Sollicitor, under their hands,
Termino Hillarii. Feb. 1573."

In a note at the foot of one of the papers is written in the Earl's
handwriting, " Note.—This that I seek is but a feather of myne
own goose : whereas if I were ambitiously disposed, or to ————
into the world as diverse would have done, I should have claimed
restitution of the whole once meant me by Queen Mary, contrary
to me in religion."

Note 60.

The following letter from Queen Elizabeth to " Good Francke,"
as she called Lady Hertford, may not be without some interest. It
was written Nov. 5, 1595, and is in the State Papers, Domestic,
Elizabeth :—

" Understanding your disposition to be troubled with sudden
impressions, even in matters of little moment, we do not forget
you in your Lord's misfortune, and therefore have thought it not
amiss, even by our own handwriting (your ladyship's brother being
absent whom otherwise we would have used), to assure you of the
continuance of our former grace, and to preserve your spirit from
those perturbations, which love to the person offending, and apprehension of the matter so far unexpected, might daily have bred in
you. It is not convenient to acquaint you with all the particular
circumstances of his offence, neither would it avail you, who have
been ignorant of all the causes ; but (to prevent any misapprehen-
sion that this crime is in its nature more pernicious and malicious
than an act of lewd and proud contempt against our own prohibition), we have vouchsafed to cause a ticket to be shown you by the
bearer, which may resolve you from further doubting what it is not,
and satisfy your mind for caring for that which care now remedies
not, being a matter both proved by record, and confessed by
repentance.

" It is far from our desire to pick out faults in such as he ; being
slow to rigour towards the meanest, we will use no more severity
than is requisite for other's caution in like cases, and than shall
stand with honour and necessity. Your ladyship will quickly
judge when you understand it, that his offence can have no colour
of imputation on you, and you will not be one jot the less esteemed
for any fault of his. You are therefore to trust to this assurance,
as the voice of that Prince to whose pure and constant mind you
are no stranger, and comfort yourself that you have served one who
still wishes your good, and cares for the contrary.

" For a farewell, you are to observe this rule, that seeing griefs and troubles make haste enough, unsent for, to surprise us, there can be no folly greater than by fearing that which is not, or by over-grieving for that which needs not, to overthrow the health of mind and body, which once being lost, the rest of our life is labour and sorrow, a work to God unacceptable, and discomfortable to all our friends."

It seems highly probable that Hertford in the end had to purchase his liberty, for we find in the State Papers, Domestic, Elizabeth, on April 22, 1600, a warrant for the instalment of a debt of £2,500, remainder of £50,000 due to Her Majesty by the Earl of Hertford ; £500 to be paid in six days after the date of the warrant, and £500 each Michaelmas and Easter following till the whole be paid.

Note 61.

The Earl of Hertford's command of ready money must have been very great for those times, for, in addition to what he spent on his embassy, he soon after undertook to discharge the King's debt of £15,180 due to diverse merchants. In return he was granted some lands of the late Duke of Suffolk's, in lieu of which, March 15, 1609, a warrant was issued to pay him an allowance. (State Papers, Domestic, James I.)

Note 61 A.

This, it would appear, is somewhat of an exaggeration. The following is Hertford's letter to Salisbury on receiving the letter brought by Francis Seymour :—

"My lord, this last night, at eleventh of the clock, ready to go to bed, I received this letter from my nephew, Francis Seymour, which I send your lordship here-inclosed ; a letter no less trouble-some to me than strange to think I should in those my last days be grandfather of a child that, instead of patience and tarrying the Lord's leisure (lessons that I learned and prayed for when I was in the same place whereout lewdly he is now escaped), would not tarry for the good hour of favour to come from a gracious and merciful King, as I did, and enjoyed in the end (though long first) from a most worthy and noble Queen, but hath plunged himself further into His Highness's just displeasure. To whose Majesty I do, by these lines, earnestly pray your lordship to signify most humbly from me how distasteful this his foolish and boyish action is unto me, and that, as at first upon his examination before your lordships, and his Majesty afterwards, nothing was more offensive unto me, misliking altogether the unfitness and inequality of the match, and the handling of it afterwards worse, so do I condemn this as worst of all in them both. Thus, my Lord, with an unquiet mind to think (as before) I should be grandfather to any child that hath so much forgotten his duty as he hath now done, and having slept never a wink this night (a bad medicine for one that is not fully recovered of a second great cold I took), I leave your Lordship with my loving commendations to the heavenly protection. From Letley, this Thursday morning, at four of the clock, the 6th of June, 1611. Your Lordship's most assured loving friend, HERTFORD.

"Postsc.—As I was reading my said nephew's letter my sise (?) took (as your Lordship may perceive) into the bottom of the letter; but the word missing that is burnt is *Tower to acquaint.*" (Harl. MS., 7003.)

Note 62.

In Salisbury Cathedral, after the inscription on the tomb " Sacred to the memory of Edward, Earl of Hertford," etc., may be read the following lines (Life and Letters of Arabella Stuart, Cooper):—

> Also to his dear and beloved wife,
> Catherine,
> daughter of Henry and Frances Grey, Duke and
> Duchess of Suffolk, and heiress of
> Charles Brandon, Duke of Suffolk, and Mary,
> sister of Henry VIII, and Queen of the French:
> by the will of her great uncle and
> Henry VII, her great grandfather.
> A matchless pair,
> who, after experiencing in many ways the
> hazards of a wavering fortune,
> at length repose here together in the same union
> in which they lived.
> She
> a rare model of virtue, piety, beauty, and fidelity,
> the best and most illustrious, not for her own
> age, but for all time,
> peacefully and piously breathed her last,
> on the 22nd of January.

(It will be noticed that the date is wrongly given; it should be the 27th.)

Note 63.

A letter from Frances Howard, the Earl's second wife, to him, describing a fall the Queen had from her horse. Printed in Wilts Archæolog. Mag., p. 158 :—

" Sweet Lorde, I thanke God moste humbly for your good helth and well doinge, and I most hartely desire Him to continue and increase the same, and I thanke you for so soon sending to me for I was a little melancholy for fere that you had not your helth, and I was sending my man Lennerd to you but you prevented me by your footman who met me as I was comynge home waytynge on the Quene abrode; but a lyttell before we were all grettly afraid for that her Majesties horse in stombling, fell withall, and she withall felle, but as she says, she lepped up frome hym, but her footman stode her in grate sted but thanks be to God she had no kynde of harme and presently after she wallked a fote halfe a myell. You may think what a fereful sight it was: her Majestie wolde have ridden on that horse agayne, but he would not suffer her to come on hys backe. She is very well, thankes be to God, and is determined to goe a prograce into Sussex, but when she will begin it is not known. There is no more speache of her goynge to Wansted and therefore you nede not stay the longer from hence but what she will goe she sayth it shall be to Nonsuche, and there you shall have a loggynge for so my Lord Lomley hymself told me and assured me for he is now att the Courte and there is no tyme appoynted when she will remove but you shall be sure of a loggynge at Nonsuche.

"Your most faithfull, lovying, and obediente wife during lyfe,
"FRANCES H————."

This letter was received June 11, 1582.

NOTE 64.

Lodge says, "She was born about the year 1578, and became, at an early age, under the influence of one of those extravagant predilections so frequent in youth, the wife of a person certainly of unsuitable rank. In this marriage originated much of the ridicule which has always been levelled at her character, and, as ridicule always deals in exaggeration, the condition of her first husband has been sunk by wilful misrepresentation to utter baseness. Whenever her name is mentioned his is sure to be coupled with it, and the description usually bestowed on him is 'one Prannel, a vintner's son,' for some have gone further, and asserted that his father was a mere ale-house keeper; but the truth is that his father, Henry Prannel, was an Alderman of London, and in a time too when none but the most respectable of the commercial order were elected to that degree. He had probably obtained his freedom of the city in the Vintners' Company, and hence this silly slander."

NOTE 65.

Lodge says: "Even in her dying moments she insisted on the observance of all the stately ceremonies to which she had accustomed herself, and was actually surrounded by the officers of her household, bearing white wands, and other ensigns of their respective stations, while a public record informs us that she condescended to accept from James, in partnership with another person, an exclusive patent for coining farthings."

NOTE 66.

A plot was formed amongst some of the Papists for obtaining possession of the Lady Arabella and taking her out of the country, after which they might marry her as best suited their designs. The following conversation between two Catholic agents was confessed by a Jesuit named James Yong. It is printed in Strype's Annals, iv, p. 102 :—

"When Roulston departed back again, he came to Stanley, who said, ' Thou art welcome, I hope. Thou shalt be employed in as good service for the Lady of which we have often talked.' At which time he said no more. Yet, being demanded after by one Dr. Stillington what the Lady was, ' Oh !' saith he, ' if we had her, the most of our fears were past, for any one that could hinder us in England. It is Arbella who keepeth with the Earl of Shrewsbury, whom most certainly they will proclaim Queen, if their mistress should now happen to die. And the rather they will do it, for that in a woman's government they may still rule after their own designments. But here is Symple and Rowlston, who, like cunning fellows, have promised to convey her by stealth out of England into Flanders, which, if it be done, I promise unto you she shall shortly after visit Spain.' "

This confession was confirmed soon after by Thomas Christopher, and another priest added the information that Sir William Stanley was to have a pension of three hundred crowns a month from the King of Spain if he succeeded in obtaining possession of Lady Arabella. (Strype.)

The idea, at this time, was to prevent her becoming a rival to Mary, Queen of Scots, in the succession to the English throne, but after that Queen's death she would be equally useful as a rival to James, should he not conform to the wishes of the Catholics. They therefore never ceased to endeavour to obtain possession of her until James was securely seated on the throne.

NOTE 67.

On the 17th of November Sir Walter Raleigh was, with others, accused of plotting to set Arabella on the throne. Count Aremberg was apparently to receive 600,000 crowns for bringing about the treason. Lord Cobham was to enlist the sympathies of

Archduke Albert, and, if he failed in that, to go on to the Spanish King and seek his assistance in planning an invasion of England. Arabella herself was to be persuaded to write three letters, one to the Archduke, another to the King of Spain, and a third to the Duke of Saxony, in which she was to promise three things in return for their assistance, viz., to establish a firm peace between England and Spain; to tolerate the Popish and Romish religion; to be ruled by her helpers and abettors in contracting her marriage.

Although Arabella's name was mentioned at the trial, she was not suspected of having taken any share in it, and was shown to have refused to write the required letters. She attended the trial, however, but as a mere spectator and, when her name was mentioned, Cecil rose and said:—"Here hath been a touch of the Lady Arabella Stuart, the King's near kinswoman. Let us not scandal the innocent by confusion of speech. She is as innocent of all these things as I or any man here. Only she received a letter from my Lord Cobham, to prepare her, which she laughed at, and immediately sent it to the King." Lord Nottingham then rose and said:—"The Lady doth here protest, upon her salvation, that she never dealt in any of these things, and so she willed me to tell the court."

The Attorney-General also declared Lady Arabella's complete innocence in the matter.

(Lodge. Life and Letters of Arabella Stuart, by E. Cooper.)

Note 68.

Lady Arabella Stuart to the Countess of Shrewsbury, Sept. 16, 1603. Sloan MS. 4164, fol. 178 :—

"Madame,—If you receive the letters I write, I am sure you see I fail not to write often how the world goeth here, both in particular with me and otherwise as my Intelligence stretcheth. Wherefore I rather interpret your postscript to be a caveat to me to write no more than how I do and my desire to understand of your health, that is, no more than is necessary than a new Commandment to do that which I already do. But lest, in pleasing you, I offend my uncle, I have adventured to write to him one superfluous letter more, and that I may include no serious matter in his, I send you all I have of that kind, which is that the King hath under his hand granted me the aforesaid mess of meat and £800 a year, and my lord Cecil will despatch it, I trust with all speed, for so his lordship promiseth. Your long expected messenger, by whom I should have understood your mind, is not yet come, and the Queen is going hence tomorrow; but the change of place will not cease my expectation till I understand from you, you have changed your mind in that matter, which if you do, I shall hope it is with a mind to come up shortly and let me know it yourself, according to a bruit we have here, which I would fain believe. You shall not fail to receive weekly letters, God willing, or some very great occasion hinder me.

"Mr. Elphinstone, who, you may see, is with me late as well as early, remembers his service to you. And so I humbly take my leave, praying the Almighty to send you all honour, happiness, contentment, etc.

"Your Ladyship's niece to command,
"ARABELLA STUART."

NOTE 68A.

At the creation of Henry Prince of Wales, a court masque was given by the Queen, at which Lady Arabella represented a nymph of the Trent. According to the description in Nichols's "King James," she wore the following extraordinary costume: "Her head tire was composed of shells and coral, and from a great murex shell in the form of a crest of an helm, hung a thin waving veil. The upper garments had the boddies of sky coloured taffataes, for lightness, all embroidered with maritime invention. Then she had a kind of half skirt of cloth of silver embroidered with gold, all of the ground work cut out for lightness, which hung down full, and cut in points. Underneath that came a base (of the same as was her body), beneath her knee. Her long skirt was wrought with lace, waved round about like a river, and on the banks sedge and seaweeds, all of gold. Her shoulders were all embroidered with the work of the short skirt of cloth of silver, and had cypress spangled, ruffed out, and fell in a ruff above the elbow. The under sleeves were all embroidered as the bodies. Her shoes were of satin, richly embroidered with the work of the short skirt."

NOTE 69.

On Dec. 8, 1604, there is the following entry in the Docquet book:—

"A Penson of 1000 li. paid for the La. Arbella for terme of her life without restraint from alienacon." (State Papers.)

A copy of that which the King's Majesty is to be moved to sign touching oats. July, 1608. (Lodge.)

"Our will and pleasure is, that there be given and granted unto our trusty and well-beloved cousin, the Lady Arbella Stuart, and unto her deputies or deputy, for and during the whole term of one and twenty years next after the date of our letters patent, sufficient power and authority, under our great seal of England, for us, and in our name and right, and to our use in all places, within our realm of England and Wales, to take yearly a bond or recognizance of five pounds of every inn-holder or hostler, wherein the said inn-holder or hostler shall be bound not to take any more than six-pence gain, over and above the common price in the market, for and in every bushel of oats which he or they shall sell in gross or by retail, unto any passengers or travellers. The said bushel also, or any other measure, to be according to the ancient measure or standard of England, commonly called Winchester measure.

And we will also, that our said well-beloved cousin, the Lady Arbella, or her deputy or deputies, shall take for every such bond or recognizance of every inn-holder or hostler the sum of 2/6, whereof one full fifth part, our will is that she or her deputy or deputies shall retain to her or their own use, in consideration of pains and charges. And our further pleasure is, that our said cousin shall have full power and authority to depute any person or persons, during the said term, for the execution of the foresaid power, so given and granted unto her.

> To our trusty and well beloved Sergeant at the Law,
> our Attorney General, and to any of them.

Two gentlemen made application for the grant at the said time, but as no record remains of its being obtained, the probability is that all three petitioners failed in their suit.

(Life and Letters of Lady Arabella Stuart, by E. Cooper.)

Note 70.

In the Docquet book for 1609, November 2, we find a letter from Sir Thomas Lake to the Lord Deputy of Ireland, requiring him "to cause a graunt under the great Seale of that Realme to be made to the Lady Arabella Stewart, her Deputies and Assignees, whereby they for 21 yeares shall have privelege to nominate such persons as shall sell wynes of any sorte, aqua vitæ, or usquebagh within that kingdom. Accordinge to a Mynute entered at Large in the private Signet booke, dated the 2nd. of November."

The Lady Arabella duly received this grant, but before long, either at the end of December or the beginning of January, she applied to have her debts paid in exchange for her renouncing this monopoly, as may be seen by the following letter :—

Lady Arabella Stuart to the Earl of Salisbury. (State Papers, James, Dom., L., fol. 69, MS.)

"Where your Lordship willed Ime to set down a note of those 3 things wherein I lately moved you. They are these :—The first, that I am willing to return back his Majesty's gracious grant to me of the wines in Ireland, so as your Lordship will take order for the paying of my debts when I shall upon my honour inform you truly what they are. The next, that his Majesty will be graciously pleased to augment my allowance in such sort as I may be able to live in such honour and countenance hereafter as may stand with his Majesty's honour and my own comfort. And lastly, that where his Majesty doth now allow me a diet, that he will be pleased, stead thereof, to let me have one thousand pounds yearly. Some other things I will presume to entreat your Lordship's like favour in that may stand me in stead ; but for that they are such as I trust your Lordship will think his Majesty will easily grant, I will now forbear to set them down.

> "Your Lordship's poor friend,
> "ARBELLA STUART."

This proposition of the Lady Arabella's was probably agreed to by the King for we find, from an entry among the Sloane papers, that, in January, 1610, James gave her a cupboard of plate of over £200 in value, a thousand marks to pay her debts, and a pension of £1,600 a year, which was probably in exchange for the Irish monopoly and for the dishes of meat with which she had till then been supplied.

NOTE 70A.

William Seymour to the Lords of the Council. (Harl. M.S. 7003, fol. 59.)

" May it please your good Lordships : — Since it is your pleasure (which to me shall always stand for a law) that I should truly relate under my hand those passages which have been between the noble Lady Arbella and myself, I do here in these rugged lines truly present the cause to your Lordship's favourable censure, that thereby his most excellent Majesty may by your Lordships be fully satisfied of my duty and faithful allegiance, which shall ever be a spur to me to expose my life and all my fortunes to the extremest dangers for his Highness's service, that I will never attempt anything which I shall have certain foreknowledge will be displeasing unto him. I do therefore humbly confess that when I conceived that noble Lady might with his Majesty's good favour and without offence make her choice of any subject within this Kingdom, which conceit was begotten in me upon a general report after her Ladyship's last being called before your Lordships, that it might be ; myself being but a younger brother, and sensible of mine own good, unknown to the world, of mean estate, not born to challenge anything by my birthright, and therefore my fortunes to be raised by mine own endeavour, and she a Lady of great honour and virtue, and as I thought of great means, I did plainly and honestly endeavour lawfully to gain her in marriage, which is God's ordinance common to all, assuring myself if I could effect the same with his Majesty's most gracious favour and liking (without which I resolved never to proceed) that thence would grow the first beginning of all my happiness ; and therefore I boldly intruded myself into her Ladyship's chamber in the Court on Candlemas day last (February 2), at what time I imparted my desire unto her ; which was entertained, but with this caution on either part, that both of us resolved not to proceed to any final conclusion without his Majesty's most gracious favour and liking first obtained ; and this was our first meeting. After that we had a second meeting at Mr. Baggs his house in Fleet Street ; and then a third at Mr. Boynton's, at both which we had the like conference and resolution as before ; and the next day save one after the last meeting, I was convented before your Lordships, when I did then deliver as much as now I have written : both then and now protesting, before God, upon my duty and allegiance to his most excellent Majesty, and as I desire to be retained in your Lordships' good opinions, there is neither promise of marriage, contract, or any other engagement whatsoever between her Ladyship and myself, nor ever was any marriage by me or her intended, unless his Majesty's gracious favour and approbation might have been first gained therein ; which we resolved to obtain before we would proceed to any final conclusion. Whereof I humbly beseech your Lordships to inform his Majesty, that by your good means, joined to the clearness of an unspotted conscience and a loyal heart to his Highness, I may be acquitted in his just judgment from all opinion of any disposition in me to attempt anything distasteful or displeasing to his Majesty, as one well knowing that the just disfavour of my sovereign will be my confusion : whereas his gracious favour and goodness towards me, may be the advancement of my poor fortunes. And thus my Lords, according to your commands, I have made a true relation of what was required, humbly referring the favourable construction thereof to your Lordships, having, for the farther hastening of the truth, and ever to bind me thereunto hereafter, subscribed my name the 20th of February, 1609.

"WILLIAM SEYMOUR."

NOTE 71.

Message from William Seymour to Lady Arabella. (Printed in Wilts Archæolog. Mag., p. 159.)

From the original rough draft :—" I am come from Mr. William Seymour with a message to your ladyship which was delivered unto me in ye presence of this gentleman, your servant, and therefore your ladyship may be assured I will neither add nor diminish, but will truly relate unto you what he hath directed me to do, which is this : he hath seriously considered of the proceedings between your ladyship and himself, and doth well perceive, if he should go on therein, it would not only prove prejudicial to your content-ment, but extremely dangerous to him, first in regard of the ine-quality of degrees between your ladyship and him, next, the King's Majestie's pleasure and commandment to the contrary, which neither your ladyship nor himself did ever intend to neglect : he doth therefore humbly desire your ladyship since the proceeding that is past doth not tie him or your ladyship to any necessity, but that you may freely commit each other to your best fortunes, that you would be pleased to desist from your intended resolution con-cerning him, who likewise resolveth not to trouble you any more in this kind, not doubting but your ladyship may have one more fitter for your degree (he having already presumed too high) and himself a meaner match with more security."

NOTE 72.

Memorandum of Lady Arabella's clandestine marriage on the fly-leaf of Mr. Hugh Crompton's account book, found at Longleat. (Printed in Wilts Archæolog. Mag., p. 161.)

"The 22nd of June, 1610, about 4 in the morninge my lady was married at Greenwiche to Mr. William Seymour.

"Witnesses to the marriage, Mrs. Byron, Mrs. Bradshawe, Mr. Rodney, Mr. Kyrton, Mr. Blange, the minister, Mr. Reeves, and myself (i.e., Mr. Hugh Crompton)," &c.

William Seymour's confession, signed by his own hand. (Bodleian Lib., Tanner MSS., 75, fol. 353.)

The examination of William Semar, Esq., before ye lordships of His Majesty's Privye Councell the 8th of July, 1610.

He confesseth that upon Fryday was fortnight he was marryed unto the Lady Arbella at Greenwich in the chamber of the sayd lady Arbella ther. That there was present one Blagew sonne of the Dean of Rochester who was the minister that marryed them, there were also present one Edward Rodné, Crompton—gent : usher to the lady Arbella, Edward Kyrton, and Edward Reve, Mrs. Biron and Mrs. Bradshawe, two servants to the Lady Arbella. The marryadge was on the Fryday morninge before sayd, between fouer and fyve of the clock, but without any Lycense as he con-fesseth.

He saith he came to Greenwich on the Thursday at night abowt twelffe of the clock, accompanied with the said Rodné and Kyrton and did sit upp in the Lady Arbella her chamber all the night untill they were marryed.

WILLIAM SEYMAURE.

NOTE 73.

The following letter from Arabella to the King, which is in the Harleian Collection, was written on her first being imprisoned :—

"May it please your most excellent Majestie, I doe most hartily lament my hard fortune, that I should offend your Majestie, especiallie in that whereby I have long desired to merit of your Majestie, as appeared before your Majestie was my Soveraigne ; and though your Majestie's neglect of me, my liking of this gentleman that is my husband and my fortune, drewe me to a contracte before I acquainted your Majestie, I humbly beseech your Majestie to consider how impossible itt was for me to imagine itt could be offensive unto your Majestie having fewe days before geven me your royall consent, to bestowe myselfe on anie subject of your Majestie's, which likewise your Majestie had done long since. Besides never havinge ben either prohibited any, or spoken to for any, in this land by your Majestie these 7 years that I have lived in your Majestie's house, I could not conceave that your Majestie regarded my marriage at all ; whereas if your Majestie had vouch-safed to tell me your mind and accept the free-will offering of my obedience, I would not have offended your Majestie, of whose gracious goodness I presume so much that, if it weare as con-venient in a worldly respect as mallice may make itt seame, to separate us whom God hath joyned, your Majestie would not doe evill that good might come thereof ; nor make me, that have the honor to be so neare your Majestie in blood, the first precedent that ever was, though our Princes maye have left some as little imitable for so good and gracious a Kinge as your Majestie as David's dealinge with Uriah. But I assure myself if itt please your Majestie in your own wisdome to consider throughlie of my cause, there will noe solide reason appeare to debarre me of justice, and your princlie favour, which I will endeavour to deserve whilst I breathe, and, never ceasinge to praye for your Majestie's felicitie in all thinges, remain, your Majestie's," etc., etc.

Both Prince Henry and the Queen appear to have interceded on several occasions in favour of the Lady Arabella, but without effect. The following letters from Arabella to the Queen may not be without interest :—

Lady Arabella Seymour to Queen Anne of Denmark.
(Lansdowne MS., 1236.)

"May it please your most excellent Majesty, since I am debarred the happiness of attending your Majesty or so much as to kiss your Royal hands, to pardon my presumption in presenting your Majesty in this rude form my most humble thanks for your Majesty's most gracious favour and mediation to his Majesty for me. Which your Majesty's goodness (my greatest comfort and hope in this affliction) I most humbly beseech your Majesty to continue. So praying to the Almighty to reward your Majesty with all honour and felicity both in your Royal self and yours, in all humility I cease. From Lambeth, the 22nd of July, 1610.
"Your Majesty's most humble and dutiful
subject and servant,
"ARBELLA SEYMOUR."

Lady Arabella Seymour to the Queen.   (Harl. MS., 7003.)

"May it please your most excellent Majesty to consider how long I have lived a spectacle of his Majesty's displeasure, to my unspeakable grief, and out of that gracious disposition which moveth your Royal mind to compassion of the distress, may it please your Majesty to move his Majesty in my behalf. I have presumed to present your Majesty herewith the copy of my humble petition to his Majesty against this time, when the rather I am sure his Majesty forgiveth greater offences as freely as he desires to be forgiven by him whose sacrament he is to receive. Though your Majesty's intercession at any time I know were sufficient. Thus hath my long experience of your Majesty's gracious favour to me and all good causes encouraged me to presume to address myself unto your Majesty, and encreased the obligation of my duty in praying continually unto the Almighty for your Majesty's felicity in all things. And in all humility I remain," etc.

Lady Arabella Seymour to the Queen.

"May it please your most excellent Majesty, I presume to send herewith a copy of my humble petition to the King's Majesty, whereby your Majesty may perceive (with less trouble than any other relation of mine) as much (in effect) as I can say of the condition of my present estate and hard fortune. Now to whom so fitly address myself with confidence of help and mediation as to your Royal person (the mirror of our sex?) and being for me, your Majesty's humble and devoted servant, and in a cause of this nature so full of pity and commiseration, I will wholly rely upon your Princely goodness, whom I humbly beseech to vouchsafe to enter into a gracious consideration of the true estate of my case and fortune, and then I nothing doubt but that in the true nobleness of your Royal mind your Majesty will be pleased to mediate for me in such sort as in your most Princely wisdom and favour the same shall be moved. And I shall always pray for the everlasting honour and felicity of your Majesty with all your Royal issue in all things, and will remain for ever, your Majesty's most humble and dutiful subject and servant,

"ARBELLA SEYMOUR."

NOTE 74.

When Lady Arabella heard that she was to be removed to the North under the care of the Bishop of Durham, she addressed the following letter to the Lord Chief Justice of England and the Lord Chief Justice of the Common Pleas. (Harl. MS., 7003, fol. 152):—

"My Lords,—Whereas I have been long restrained from my liberty, which is as much to be regarded as my life, and am appointed, as I understand, to be removed far from these courts of Justice, where I ought to be examined, tried, and then condemned or cleared, to remote parts, whose Courts I hold unfitter for the trial of my offence: this is to beseech your Lordships to inquire by an Habeas Corpus or other usual form of law what is my fault; and if, upon examination by your Lordships, I shall thereof be justly convicted, let me endure such punishment by your Lordships' sentence as is due to such an offender. And if your Lordships may not or will not of yourselves grant unto me the ordinary relief of a distressed subject, then I beseech you become humble intercessors to his Majesty that I may receive such benefit of justice as both his Majesty, by his oath, those of his blood not excepted, hath promised, and the laws of this Realm afford to all others. And though, unfortunate woman that I am, I should obtain neither, yet I beseech your Lordships retain me in your good opinion, and judge charitably till I be proved to have committed any offence, either against God or his Majesty, deserving so long restraint or separation from my lawful husband. So praying for your Lordships, I rest your afflicted poor suppliant,

"ARBELLA SEYMOUR."

NOTE 75.

The following letters to the King appear to have been written during the last year or two of Arabella's existence. They are to be found in the Harl. MS., 7003, fol. 87 and 146:—

"The unfortunate estate whereunto I am fallen by being deprived of your Majesty's presence, the greatest comfort to me upon earth, together with the opinion is conceived of your Majesty's displeasure towards me, hath brought as great affliction to my mind as can be imagined touching the offence for which I am now punished. I most humbly beseech your Majesty, in your most princely wisdom and judgment, to consider in what a miserable state I have been in if I had taken any other course than I did, for my own conscience witnessing before God that I was then the wife of him that now I am, I could never have matched with any other man, but to have lived all the days of my life as an harlot, which your Majesty would have abhorred in any, especially in one who hath the honour (how otherwise unfortunate soever) to have any drop of your Majesty's blood in him. But I will trouble your Majesty not longer, but in all humility attending your Majesty's good pleasure for that liberty (the want thereof depriveth me of all health and all other worldly comfort), I will never forget to pray for your Majesty's most happy prosperity for ever in all things, and so remain, your Majesty's most humble and faithful subject and servant,

                              "ARBELLA SEYMOUR."

"In all humility—in most humble wise—the most wretched and unfortunate creature that ever lived, prostrates itself at the feet of the most merciful King that ever was, desiring nothing but mercy and favour, not being more afflicted for anything than for the loss of that which hath been this long time the only comfort it had in the world, and which if it were to do again, I would not adventure the loss of for any other worldly comfort. Mercy it is I desire, and that for God's sake. Let either Freake or ——" (The rest of the MS. has been torn off.)

The following account is given of her end :—

"She had clung so long to hope ; she had indulged so many visions while Seymour was yet near her. But they were violently parted : his fate was unknown to her : her enemies had triumphed. Accusations, from which, although there was no foundation for them, she had no means of clearing herself, pressed frightfully upon her ; the past had been all uncertainty, the future was darkness, and the present utter despair. Her mind became confused with the magnitude of her affliction ; her body was wasted and worn with unwonted exertion ; her nerves destroyed by continued irritation. Like Tasso, in his dungeon, strange shapes and sights appalled her, and she saw some hideous phantom in every shadow that fell upon her prison floor. In vain she exerted all the powers that nature and education had given her ; in vain she tried to busy herself as before in her confinement; in vain she wrote petitions in the most moving language, poured out her sorrows in numbers—all was without effect. The blow had been struck, and fate was as remorseless as the king who refused her offerings and contemned her prayers.

"'Good, my lord,' she exclaims, in a letter to Viscount Fenton, 'consider the fault cannot be uncommitted; neither can any more be required of any earthly creature but confession and most humble submission.'

"There yet remain fragments of her papers found scattered in her prison; some written and crossed out, some begun and never ended; they are incoherent ravings or pathetic complaints. One letter is thus concluded: 'Help will come too late; and be assured that neither physician nor other, but whom I think good, shall come about me while I live, till I have his Majesty's favour, without which I desire not to live. And, *if you remember of old, I dare die*—so I be not guilty of my own death, and oppress others with my ruin too, *if there be no other way*, as God forbid, to whom I commit you.'—' I could not be so unchristian as to be the cause of my own death. *Consider what the world would conceive if I should be violently enforced to do it.*'

"And she thus writes in the agony of her spirit: 'In all humility the most wretched and unfortunate creature that ever lived prostrates itself at the feet of *the most merciful king that ever was*, desiring nothing but mercy and favour, not being more afflicted for anything than the loss of that which hath been this long time the only comfort it had in the world; and which, if it were to do again, I would not adventure the loss of for any other worldly comfort; mercy it is I desire, and that for God's sake.'

"That mercy came not, and was looked for in vain, till hope deferred made her heart sick even to death:

> " Where London's towre its turrets show
>   So stately by the Thames' side,
> Faire Arabella, child of woe,
>   For many a day had sat and sigh'd :
> And as she heard the waves arise,
>   And as she heard the bleake windes roare,
> As fast did heave her heartfelt sighes,
>   And still so fast her teares did poure."

(Memoirs of Eminent Englishwomen, Miss Costello.)

" Lady Arabella was buried in Westminster Abbey in the same vault with Mary Queen of Scots and Henry, Prince of Wales, but without any memorial of her resting-place. Camden says her

funeral was conducted in the night, and without pomp. An
epitaph was written for her by Richard Corbet, Bishop of Norwich.
The production is far from remarkable for poetical talent, and the
third and last lines are obscure :—

> "'How do I thank thee, death, and bless thy power,
> That I have pass'd the guard, and 'scaped the tower,
> And now my pardon is my epitaph,
> And a small coffin my poor carcass hath ;
> For at thy charge, both soul and body were,
> Enlarged at last, secured from hope and fear ;
> That amongst saints, this amongst kings is laid,
> And what my birth did claim, my death hath paid.'

" Ballard informs us that her coffin was at one time so shattered
and broken that her skull and body might be seen. Seymour
appears to have regarded his wife's memory with affection. It
may be taken as evidence of it, that he called one of his daughters,
by his second marriage with Frances, daughter of Robert
Devereux, Earl of Essex, by the name of Arabella Seymour."

(Memoirs of the Court of England.)

Note 76.

Letter from the Earl of Hertford to William Seymour when
abroad. Printed in Wilts Archæolog. Mag., p. 162. Oct.. 23,
1613 :—

"Your former great offences which I neede not expresse aded
to your course of life, ever since you escaped over the seas, not a
little agrevated by your late wilfull repaire to Duncerke, contrary
to his Majestie's pleasure, and my instructions sent you by your
tutor Pellinge, under pretence of fear of creditors in France, would
make any grandfather hate the memorie of suche a nephew. I
had thought his Majestie's gratious favour, that out of his princely
compacion on your weekness, drew from mee so greate an annall
allowance, my care of your education from your cradle, and your
dayly protestacion by letters that you would amend all your errors,
had been enough to have with-held you from Duncerk or any
other forbydden place, though it had ben with the losse of your
liberty, or at least drawen you for a time to Geneva, where your
Religion could not be corrupted, rather than to indevour payment
of your debts by a worse means then they were incurred. These
considerations make me fear, though you are not corupted in your
religion, from which God I hope will deliver my family, that you
are falen from his Grace and service without which you can never
prosper, nor any naturall care of myne take good effect. You writ
for payment of your debts and have prevayled with my worthy
friend the Lord Imbassador Ledger (Edmunds) to write for

increase of meanes, but do not consider how litle your ill government and profusse expense, doth incourage mee to contynew that
you have already. Is not £400 a yere from your aged grandfather
whose estate by debts and these like burdens stands more deeply
ingaged than his life-time is like to free, an exceeding greate allowance? which notwithstanding I have not long since paid to
Langrett your marchant in Paris, £100 for you whereof your
letter makes noe mention. To conclude, I advise you in the feare
of God, serve him, amende your course of life, be carefull not to do
any thinge that may offend your gracious Soveraigne, to whom I
wishe my selfe and all myne to be Saints, though to God we
cannot bee but sinners, live within your compasse, depend upon the
good advise and counsell of that worthey gent. the Lord Imbassador to whome you are muche bounde, his good indevours and
justification of your reformation may be greate means for you one
day to kisse that Royall hand, which may make you happie, and
bee a comfort to my old age. Whereas by your relaps you shall be
sure to rewin your selfe and what in you lyes tumble my graye
haires with sorrow to my grave. In this course upon farther triall,
I may be drawen to do for you what my meanes will give leave.
And ever so prayinge God to blesse you with his Holy Spirite, I
reste," etc.

Note 77.

Another account is somewhat similar :—"Their first step was
to proceed to St. George's Chapel, to select a proper resting-place
for his remains. That beautiful and interesting building was at
this period, internally a mass of ruins. The ancient inscriptions,
the architectural ornaments, the stalls and banners of the Knights
of the Garter, had been either torn down or defaced by the hands
of the Republicans and lay strewed in melancholy devastation on
the floor. It was found impossible to distinguish the tomb of a
monarch from the grave of a verger. At last, one of the noblemen
present, happening to strike the pavement with his staff, perceived
by the hollow sound that there was a vault beneath. The stones
and earth having been removed, they came to two coffins, which
proved to be those of King Henry the 8th and Queen Jane Seymour.
Though considerably more than a century had elapsed since their
interment, the velvet palls which covered their coffins were still
fresh. In this vault, over against the eleventh stall on the sovereign's side, it was decided to inter the body of King Charles."

(Memoirs of the Court of England.)

Note 78.

"—— Also out of the regard I have for the supporting the
honour of the Dukedom of Somerset, I do give and appoint the

manors of Powsey and Titcombe, Cum Oxenwood, with their
rights, members and appurtenances, in the county of Wilts, and
all messuages, farms, lands, tenements, and hereditaments, to the
said manors, or either of them, belonging, or reputed, or taken, to
be part, parcel, or member of them, or either of them. And all
that farm called Harding farm, with its rights, members, appurtenances, in the county of Wilts, unto Charles, Duke of Somerset,
for and during the term of his natural life," etc.

NOTE 79.

The lady's mother, thinking her too young, made an arrangement with Mr. Thynne that he should not live with his wife for a
year after the marriage. The lady then went abroad to pass the
time, and, during a visit in Holland, was seen by Count Konigsmark, who was much attracted by her.

The Count was one of the handsomest and best-bred men of
his time, his descent being from a noble German family who
formerly had been sovereign princes. He was, however, neither
rich nor honourable, and finding out through the lady's maid,
whom he bribed, that she was a great heiress, and, though married,
had not as yet consummated the marriage rights, he determined to
marry her. In order to do this, he thought that the quickest way
would be to get rid of her present husband, and therefore dispatched
G. Boroski, one of his servants, to England with orders to murder
Mr. Thynne. This servant, on his way, hired two foreign
ruffians, C. Vratz and J. Stern, and the three managed to waylay
Mr. Thynne one night as he was returning home through Pall
Mall and shot him in his chariot.

This murder created a great sensation and every effort was
made to bring the assassins to justice. The three men who committed the deed were caught and executed almost on the spot
where they had committed the murder, but the Count, though
brought to trial, managed to escape justice through a corrupt jury.
Lord Cavendish then challenged him to a mortal combat, but the
Count fled. He was, however, killed some years after whilst in
the execution of a most cowardly and wicked attempt on the
virtue of a most virtuous Princess in a foreign court.

NOTE 80.

Swift, in his Journal to Stella, has many passages referring to
the Duchess of Somerset. At first the references are moderate
and inoffensive, such as: "Your Duchess of Somerset, who now
has the key, is a most insinuating woman." Later, however, we
find him raging about "Your d——d Duchess of Somerset," and

writing, apparently in great fear of her influence against his party, "We must certainly fall if the Duchess of Somerset be not turned out ; and nobody believes the Queen will ever part with her." Soon after, in one of his poems, we find the lines :—

> " By an old murderess pursued,
>   A crazy prelate, and a royal prude,"

referring to the Duchess of Somerset, the Archbishop of Canterbury, and Queen Anne. The Windsor Prophecy, which was pretended to have been found in a grave at Windsor, and which was written in antique English, contains the following lines :—

> "And, dear England, if aught I understand,
>   Beware of CARROTS from NORTHUMBERLOND.
>   Carrots sown THYNN a deep root may get
>   If so they be in SOMER set :
>   Their CONYNGS MARK thou ; for I have been told
>   They assassin when young and poison when old.
>   Root out these carrots, O thou whose name
>   Is backwards and forwards always the same ;
>   And keep close to thee always that name
>   Which backwards and forwards is almost the same ;
>   And, England, would'st thou be happy still,
>   Bury the carrots under a Hill."

The references here made are to the Queen (Anna), Mrs. Masham (formerly Miss Hill), and to the Duchess of Somerset, whose hair was undoubtedly red.

NOTE 81.

The following is inscribed in the front of the pedestal :—

> Carolo
> Duci Somersetensi
> strenuo juris acedici defensori
> acerrimo libertatis publicae vindici
> Statuam
> Lectissimarum matronarum munus
> L.M. ponendum decrevit
> Academia Cantabriquiensis
> Quam praesidio munivit
> Auxit munificentia
> Per annos plus sexaginta
> Cancellarius.

The following is inscribed on the reverse :—

Hanc statuam
Suae in parentum pietatis
In academiam studii
Monumentum
Ornatissimae feminae
Francesca marchionis A. Granby conjux
Charlotta baronis de Guernsey
S.P. faciendam curaverunt
M.D.C.C.V I.

Note 82.

He instigated the idea that the portraits of the members of the Kit-Cat Club should be taken and made into a book. He himself was the first member to sit to Kneller for his portrait, which he presented to Jacob Touson. The mezzotint engravings from the originals by Faber, published in 1735, were dedicated to him in the following words :—" May it please your grace,—as this collection of prints owes its being to your liberality in setting the example to the other members of the Kit-Cat Club of honouring Mr. Touson with their pictures, and as your grace has ever been eminently distinguished by that noble principle for the support of which that Association was known to have been formed, the love of your country and the constitutional liberty thereof; but more especially as the arts and sciences have always found in your grace a most illustrious and indulgent patron—this work is humbly inscribed to your grace," etc. To the dedication are prefixed the armorial bearings of the Seymour family, and an enumeration of the various titles and situations of the Duke.

Note 83.

The two following letters from the Countess of Hertford, afterwards Duchess of Somerset, on the death of her son, George, Lord Beauchamp, are perhaps worthy of perusal as showing her great affection and her resignation to a superior power :—

" To the Rev. Dr. B——.

" Sir,—I am very sensibly obliged by the very kind compassion you express for me under my heavy affliction. The meditations you have favoured me with, afford the strongest motives for consolation that can be offered to a person under my unhappy circumstances. The dear lamented son I have lost, was the pride and joy

of my heart, but I hope I may be the more easily excused for
having looked on him in this light, since he was not so from the
outward advantages he possessed, but from the virtues and rectitude of his mind. The prospects which flattered me in regard to
him, were not drawn from his distinguished rank, or from the
beauty of his person, but from the hopes that his example would
have been serviceable to the cause of virtue, and would have
shown the younger part of the world, that it was possible to be
cheerful without being foolish or vicious, and to be religious
without severity or melancholy. His whole life was one uninterrupted course of duty and affection to his parents, and when he
found the hand of death upon him, his only regret was to think of
the agonies that must rend their hearts; for he was perfectly contented to leave the world, as his conscience did not reproach him
with any presumptuous sins, and he hoped his errors would be
forgiven. Thus he resigned his innocent soul into the hands of
his merciful Creator on the evening of the birthday which completed him nineteen. You will not be surprised, Sir, that the
death of such a son should occasion the deepest sorrow: yet at the
same time it leaves us the most comfortable assurance, that he is
far happier than our fondest wishes could have made him, which
must enable us to support the remainder of years which it shall
please God to allot for us here, without murmuring or discontent,
and quicken our endeavours to prepare ourselves to follow him in
that happy place, where our dear valuable child is gone before us.
I beg the continuance of your prayers, and am, Sir,

"Yours, etc., F. HERTFORD."

The second letter was written after an interval of ten years to a
lady friend:—

"I am sorry, good Mrs. ——, to find that your illness seems
rather to increase than diminish; yet the disposition of mind with
which you receive this painful dispensation, seems to convert your
sufferings into a blessing. While you resign to the will of God
in so patient a manner, this disease seems only the chastisement of
a wise and merciful being, who chasteneth not for his own
pleasure, but for our profit. Were I not convinced of this great
truth, I fear I must long since have sunk under the burden of
sorrow, which God saw fit to wean my heart from this vain
world, and show me how little all the grandeur and riches of it
avail not to happiness. He gave me a son, who promised all that
the fondest wishes of the fondest parents could hope; an honour
to his family, an ornament to his country; with a heart early
attached to all the duties of religion and society, with the advantage of strong and uninterrupted health, joined to a form, which,
when he came into Italy, made him more generally known by

the name of the English Angel than by that of his family. I
know this account may look like a mother's fondness ; perhaps it
was too much so once : but Alas ! it now only serves to shew the
uncertainty and frailty of all human dependance. This justly
beloved child was snatched from us before we could hear of his
illness. That fatal disease, the smallpox, seized him at Bologna,
and carried him off the evening of his birthday, on which he had
completed nineteen years. Two posts before, I had a letter from
him, written with all the life and innocent cheerfulness inherent
to his nature ; the next but one came from his afflicted Governor
(M. Dalton), to acquaint his unhappy father that he had lost the
most dutiful and best of sons, the pride and hope of his declining
age. He bore the stroke like a wise man and a christian ; but he
never forgot, nor ceased to sigh for it. A long series of pain and
infirmity, which was duly gaining ground upon him, shewed me
the sword, which appeared suspended over my head by an almost
cobweb thread, long before it dropped. As to my bodily pains, I
bless God, they are by no means insupportable at present. I
rather suffer a languid state of weakness, which wastes my flesh
and consumes my spirits by a gentle decay, than any frightful
suffering ; and am spending that remains of nature, which was
almost exhausted in continued care and anxiety for the sufferings
of a person dearer to me than one's self. My daughter, who is
very good to me, has sent me her youngest son, just turned of
four years, to amuse me in my solitude, because he is a great
favourite of mine, and shews a great deal of his uncle's disposition,
and some faint likeness of his person. It is high time to release
you from so long a letter, but there are some subjects on which
my tears nor pen know not how to stop, when they begin to flow.
I am, dear Madam,

     " Your sincerely affectionate friend, F. SOMERSET.

" July, 1762."

NOTE 84.

In consideration of the Manor of Sevenhampton and the lands
before mentioned, which Sir John Thynne had sold him, he made
over to that knight (June 2nd) his chief mansion house of the late
prebend or parsonage of Thauw and various lands and buildings belonging to it, in the county of Oxford, as well as tithes and oblations
there and in some adjoining places, and also the manor of Berry
Pomeroy with everything belonging to it, except what was called
its site, the castle, the two parks, and some lands of which the king
had the last year granted a lease of twenty years to one Robert
Robotham. He made over at the same time the moiety of his Manor
of Bridgetown and the half of all his lands there. The yearly value

of the estates are mentioned and are nearly equal. There was, however, a proviso that in case Sir Edward Seymour should, within five years, wish to have again the Manor of Berry Pomeroy and the half of the Manor of Bridgetown with the premises belonging to them, and would convey to Sir John Thynne a good and sufficient estate in the Manor of Maiden Bradley and the Manors of Chedder and Walton and his other lands in Somerset, or so much of them as might be equivalent to what he should desire to resume; that then Sir John Thynne should hold so much of the Devonshire estate to the use of Sir Edward Seymour. On the 15th of June, the Manor of Middleton (or Milton) was disposed of. Sir Edward sold it to Mr. Humphrey Coles.

(Seymour Papers, coll. by 11th Duke of Somerset.)

Note 85.

In 1553 Giles Kellaway was appointed steward of the lands in Devon; George Bold was bailiff at Maiden Bradley, and Jeffrey Upton receiver of the rents in Somerset. In 1556 Sir Edward took measures for securing to himself and his family the possession of his estates in Devon, or rather of those which had been purchased by the late Duke, and which were mostly held by Sir John Thynne. The conveyance of these estates to the Protector was now inspected and exemplified (April 22nd). This was apparently done at the request of Sir Edward Seymour. It would be needless to recapitulate this exemplification, but it embraced Walton Manor, Chedder, Winterstoke, Maiden Bradley, the Barton of Berry Pomeroy and half Bridgetown Pomeroy. In the following year Sir Edward was able to complete the arrangement with Sir John Thynne, by paying him £2,279, upon which Sir John released to him all the property that had belonged to Sir Thomas Pomeroy in Devon. On Nov. 2nd this transaction was followed by another to the same purpose, when Sir John renounced every claim he had in the manors of Berry and Bridgetown Pomeroy and in lands there and in Ipplepen. In Michaelmas term 1558, a fine was levied between Sir Edward and Sir John and his lady, of the Manor and estate of Berry Pomeroy, Ipplepen, Netherton, Langcombe, Afton, the advowson of the vicarage, the moiety of the manor of Bridgetown, and of the lands and houses which had been conveyed to Sir John in that place. In 1559 Sir Edward applied for an exemplification of those Acts of Parliament which related to the title by which he held his lands. The two most important ones were the 3rd and 4th of Edward VI, in 1550, and the 5th and 6th of the same King, passed in 1552. By permission of Queen Elizabeth, a full and separate exemplification of each of them was made out, April 5th. It is worthy of notice

that the last of them appears to recite incorrectly a former Act
passed in 1540.

(Seymour Papers, coll. by 11th Duke of Somerset.)

Note 86.

On Oct. 27th, 1563, there was executed an exemplification and
discharge of several charges that had been laid on the Manors of
Berry and Bridgetown Pomeroy, and in the following year another
was obtained of the fine that, in 1548, had been levied of the
Devon estates between Sir Thomas Pomeroy and the Duke of
Somerset. In 1565, some lands and a wood called Mockwood,
near Berry, Stanteswood, Short Mead, Underwood, and the
marshes near Totnes bridge, held by Jeffrey and William Bulky,
were conveyed to Sir Edward Seymour. Sir Edward continued,
by a series of small purchases, to extend his property round Berry
Castle. He bought, in 1566, Little Meadow or Mill Meadow,
the Mill leat belonging to small Brook Mill and Torr wood. In
1567 he freed the Bradley estate of a small yearly rent claimed by
the Stourton family. In 1570, desiring to procure stronger
security in the Devon estate, he obtained, from the Lord Treasurer
of England, a warrant for the deeds relating to its conveyance to
the late Duke. These were accordingly delivered by Christophus
Smith to Henry Dugdale of Clement's Inn, with a list which
shows that they consisted of ten different writings. He also
bought of John Rayche all his estate in the borough of Bridgetown or elsewhere in the parish of Berry. In 1571 he bought
from the Goodrudges several small properties in Bridgetown that
were mixed up with his own. In 1574 he purchased some more
property in Bridgetown that had belonged to the Martyns. In the
same year he purchased an estate close to Maiden Bradley from the
Lamberts ; it consisted of a messuage, Toft, garden and orchard,
160 acres of land supposed to be arable, 140 acres of meadow, 180
acres of pasture, and 100 acres of brake, all in Wiltshire ; twenty
acres of land, ten acres of meadow, twenty acres of pasture, and
forty acres of brake, in Somerset. He also bought two houses on
the south side of the street at Bridgetown. In May, 1577, he
bought some houses and lands in Denbury, amounting to sixty
acres, from the Earl of Bedford. He now, and for the next two
years, had a great deal of trouble in consequence of the transaction
which had taken place in 1553 with King Edward VI. For, as
Sir Edward had then made over to that King various estates, many
of them in Gloucestershire, had covenanted that he was seized in
fee simple of the premises, and, for performance of the covenant,
had become bound in a recognizance of two thousand pounds,
which had never been paid ; a precept was now directed to the

Sheriff of Somerset to ascertain what lands and of what annual value the said knight possessed within the Sheriffwick. An inquisition was, therefore, taken at Taunton (Aug. 27) by which Sir Edward appeared to be possessed of the Manor of Cheddar, net value £26 per annum, and of the Manor of Walton, of the net annual value of £20. Hereupon proclamation was made, according to custom, that if any one could show cause why the Queen should not take the above Manors in liquidation of the debt due to her, he should appear. As no one came forward, it was considered that the Queen should hold these Manors till the debt had been paid. As it was not paid by Feb. 12, 1578, separate briefs were issued to the Sheriffs of Wilts and Devon. The former now seized the Manor of Maiden Bradley till the debt should be discharged. The latter seized the Manor of Zeale Monachorum. All this does not appear to have disconcerted Sir Edward, who continued making his small purchases, and now bought more land at Denbury. The demands of the Government, however, became pressing, and he had to appear in Court, where he defended his case with skill. The judges, not being certain, then put off the trial till 1579, when Sir Edward again went to the Court, only to find the proceedings postponed for the second time. Whilst this was pending he purchased an estate called Rawes, Wooden Hame, and Woodey, not far from North Tawton. The case against him was now fixed for the 26th of Nov., and accordingly, on that day, he came in person into the court of Exchequer. It was found to be completely in his favour, and he was therefore restored to the lands that had been seized. On the 2nd of March, 1580, he bought some more houses and lands in Bridgetown, from Richard and John Savery. In 1581 he made a considerable purchase in the parish of Chumleigh, for which he gave £1,260 to Hugh and Robert Bury.

Sir Edward did not confine his purchases entirely to productive estate but was also anxious to obtain what was honorary. He now made a purchase that combined both, for he bought the castle and honour of Totnes, the Manors of Totnes, Cornworthy, Loddiswell, and Huish, with forty houses, ten cottages, five mills, two dove houses, forty gardens, forty orchards, a thousand acres of land, one hundred of meadow, two hundred of wood, two hundred of brake and heath, a rent of ten pounds and a right of free fishery in the Dart. These being held directly from the Crown, a license was required for the transfer, but the vendor Mr. Peter Edgcombe, got over this by a fine levied in the court of King's Bench. Sir Edward seems, at this time, to have thought of giving the name of Seymour instead of Pomeroy to the Berry estate, for, in some leases signed about this time, the name of Berry Seymour occurs. In 1583, he purchased the fourth part of the hundred of Haytor from Mr. Thomas Ford.

The Swan-head-ship of the county of Devon was another

honorary franchise which he was desirous of possessing. Swans, not marked or otherwise domesticated, were considered by the law in the nature of estrays and as such belonged to the King who had thus the right of granting to any subject all the birds of this species which might be found under such circumstances. The subject to whom they were granted was called the Great Swanherd and might transfer to others a part or the whole of his franchise. Lord Buckhurst now appointed Sir Edward Seymour his deputy in the Swan-head-ship for Devon. (Nov. 20.)

On Sept. 1st he bought two houses, two orchards, four acres of land, three acres of meadow, one acre of wood and three acres of marsh from John Blackler, these were situated in Bridgetown. In 1586 he obtained pardons of alienation for having purchased without a license some properties held immediately under the Crown. These were the hundred of Haytor, the castle of Totnes, and the Manors of Loddiswell and Huish.

In 1589 he bought another forty-seven acres in Denbury, with a right of using the water of Holly well. In 1592 he bought Langford Budville, in Somersetshire, and a house, garden, and two orchards in Bridgetown; also a house, orchard, and garden between Berry and Bridgetown.

(Seymour Papers, coll. by 11th Duke of Somerset.)

Note 87.

Mr. Seymour found himself possessed of the castle and honour of Berry, Berry Pomeroy and Bridgetown Pomeroy, with the advowson of the church of Berry, the castle and honour of Totnes, the Manors of Cornworthy, Loddiswell, Huish, Monnocken Zeale (alias Zeal Monacon), the manor of Losebear, a moiety of the hundred of Haytor, the site of the monastery of Torr, and divers other lands in Devon; the manor and lordship of Maiden Bradley and divers other lands in Wilts; and the house called the Lord Cheyne's house in London.

(Seymour Papers, coll. by 11th Duke of Somerset.— Collins's Peerage.)

An inquisition was taken (Sept. 20, 1593) of the landed possessions of the late Sir Edward Seymour. His estates appear by this to have been extensive but not compact. With respect to most of them, the acres are enumerated in round numbers, and of course, in an inaccurate manner. But with regard to some few, Rawes Woodenhame, Spickewyke, Wydecombe, and Ashburton, even this loose estimation is omitted. And indeed this omission is not much to be regretted; for where the quantities are stated, they appear to be exaggerated. Thus the estate in Berry Pomeroy, independent of other property in Devon, is made to contain 7,600 acres. Now the amount of Wilkin's general survey of it, is only 4,304 acres, 3 roods, and 23 perches. The Loventor estate was in the sixteenth century as it still is, the property of another family, and cannot, therefore, be considered as having served to swell the terrier of Sir Edward Seymour. And, without it, all the lands in the parish would not amount to the quantity that was stated to be his by the inquisition.

The names, not only of parishes and manors, but of smaller divisions of the estate were, in the sixteenth century, the same as they are at present, but the cultivation and mode of management were then very different. There appears to have been, at that time, on the Berry estate, not one mill nor a single orchard. The quantity of furze and heath was also much greater than it is at present.

This document shows too that, notwithstanding Sir Edward's knowledge of business, he had been dispossessed of an estate at Collaton, after having bought and paid for it.

The wording of this license is extraordinary from its comprehensiveness and particularity, and the precision with which it runs through the various modes and forms of that kind of property. It especially bars any molestation from the Judges of the Exchequer, the Sheriffs, and the Receivers of the Crown; as if Mr. Seymour had still been under some apprehension of being disturbed with regard to the estates obtained by exchange from King Edward the 6th. The grant contains, moreover, a complete remission of all dues that might be claimed by the Crown out of this property, excepting, however, any debt of obligation or recognition.

(Seymour Papers, coll. by 11th Duke of Somerset.)

Note 88.

A synopsis of the Lands that belonged to Sir Edward Seymour at the time of his death in 1593.

	Arable.	Meadows.	Pasture.	Wood.	Furze and heath.	Marsh.	Total acres.
Berry Pomeroy	3,000	1,000	2,000	600	1,000	—	7,600
Totnes, Cornworthy, &c.	1,000	100	300	200	200	—	1,800
Zeal Mouacon, &c.	500	200	500	40	500	—	1,740
Nycholas Nymett	40	10	30	10	40	—	130
West Nymett, &c.	300	600	100	600	300	40	1,940
Yealbourne and Paignton	40	3	20	1	10	—	74
Denbury and Tor Mowen } Cockington }	20 100	10 40	20 80	4 6	— 80	—	306
Maiden Bradley	2,000	200	200	300	50	—	—
Total	7,000	2,163	3,250	1,761	2,180	40	16,394

A Synopsis of Houses that belonged to Sir Edward Seymour at the time of his death in 1593.

	Messuages.	Tofts.	Cottages.	Mills.	Pigeon-houses.	Gardens.	Orchards.
Berry Pomeroy	200	100	100	—	—	200	—
Totnes, Cornworthy, &c.	40	—	10	5	2	40	40
Monacon Zeal and Losebear	20	—	—	—	—	20	20
Nycholas Nymett, &c.	1	—	—	—	—	2	1
Yealbourne and Paignton	1	—	—	—	—	1	1
Plymouth	1	—	—	—	—	1	—
Spickewyke	1	—	—	—	—	—	—
Ashburton	2	—	—	—	—	2	—
Denbury	1	—	3	—	1	4	—
Tor Mowen and Cockington	2	—	—	2	1	4	4
Maiden Bradley	100	100	—	1	1	—	4
West Nymett	6	—	6	—	—	6	4
Total	375	200	119	8	4	279	74

(Seymour Papers, coll. by 11th Duke of Somerset.)

Note 89.

How each Hundred in Devon payed towards the Composition for the provision of Her Majesty's household.

North Division.	£	s.	d.
Branton	6	6	0
Fremington	4	4	0
Sherewell	2	2	0
Witheridge	4	4	9
South Molton	4	4	0
North Tawton	4	5	2
Black Torrington	6	6	0
Hartland	2	0	0
Shebbere	4	0	0
Winkleighe	0	11	6
	£38	3	5

South Division.	£	s.	d.
Roxborough	2	17	8
Heytor	3	15	0
Cobridge	3	10	0
Stainborrow	3	10	0
Armington	2	10	0
Plympton	2	0	4
Lifton	3	0	0
Tavistocke	1	10	0
Exminster	3	0	0
West Budley	1	14	0
Crediton	2	0	0
Wonford	3	15	0
Teignbridge	2	3	0
	£35	5	0

East Division.	£	s.	d.
Axminster	5	8	6
East Budleigh	5	13	0
Colliton	3	12	0
Cliston	2	13	10
Ottery St. Mary	1	16	0
Hairidge	5	18	2
Henrioche	3	9	10
Halberton	2	7	3
Tiverton	3	10	10
Bampton	3	10	6
	£37	19	11

(Seymour Papers, coll. by 11th Duke of Somerset.)

NOTE 90.

The moiety of the South Division of Devon, October, 1595.

Colonel: Edward Seymour, Esq.
Captains: R. Champernowne, W. Grymes, W. Wrey, Ed. Giles.

Corslets with pikes	182
Calivers	365
Muskets	94
Bows	93
Bills	182

Men armed	916
Pioneers	160

Powder, match and bullets, of each 1,042; horses for carriages, 200; naggs for shot, 200; able men, 1,600.

(Seymour Papers, coll. by 11th Duke of Somerset.)

NOTE 91.

Prince's book, published in 1701, gives the following account of Berry Castle: "It was a castle, standing a mile distant towards the east from the parish church of BIRY aforesaid. What it was in its antique form, can hardly be calculated from what at present remains standing, which is only the front, facing the south in a direct line, of about 60 cloth-yards in length. The gate standeth towards the west end of the front, over which, carved in moorstone, yet remaineth Pomeroy's arms."—(viz., O. a lion ramp. G. within a bordure engrailed S.) "It had heretofore a double portcullis, whose entrance is about 12 foot in height, and 30 foot in length; which gate is turretted and embattled, as are the walls yet standing, home to the east thereof; where answereth, yet in being, a tower called St. Margaret's, from which several gentlemen in this county anciently held their lands. Within this is a large quadrangle, the north and east side whereof, the honourable family of Seymour, whose possession now it is, built; (a magnificent structure, at the charges, as Fame relates it, of £20,000;) but never brought it to perfection, for the west side of the quadrangle was never begun; what was finished may be thus described: before the door of the great hall was a noble walk, whose length was the breadth of the court, arched over with curiously carved free-stone, supported in the fore-part by several stately pillars of the same stone, of great dimensions, after the Corinthian order, standing on pedestals, having cornices or friezes finely wrought; behind which were placed in the wall several seats of free-stone also, cut into the form of an escallop shell, in which the company, when weary, might repose themselves.

"The apartments within were very splendid, especially the dining-room, which was adorned, besides paint, with statues and figures cut in alabaster, with admirable art and labour, but the chimney-piece curiously engraven, was of great cost and value. Many other of the rooms were well adorned with mouldings and fretwork; some of whose marble clavils were so delicately fine, that they would reflect an object true and lively from a great distance. In short the number of the apartments of the whole may be collected hence, if report be true, *That it was a good day's work for a servant to open and shut the casements belonging to them.* Notwithstanding which it is now demolished, and all this glory lieth in the dust buried in its own ruins; there being nothing standing but a few broken walls, which seem to mourn their own approaching funerals."

NOTE 92.

Robert Seymour apparently received the honour of Knighthood and was made Teller of the Exchequer, for we find a warrant, dated Nov. 17, 1623, to pay to William Twyne, clerk of the Kitchen, the sum of £1,842 surplusage of his account for expenses of the Commissioners sent to Southampton to attend to the reception of the Infanta, and to grant a discharge to Sir Robert Seymour, Teller of the Exchequer, for £200 by him previously advanced for the same service, without letters of Privy Seal. Sir Robert appears also to have acted as agent to the Earl of Bristol, for we find that nobleman writing, July 15, 1624, to say that he desired to spend some time in settling his own affairs, Sir Robert Seymour who managed them being dead.

(State Papers, Dom., James I.)

NOTE 93.

On July 9, 1644, Col. Seymour received, in addition, the whole of the Devonshire estates from his father, to whom he agreed to give an annuity in exchange, and also to make certain provisions for his younger brothers and sisters.

(Articles betw. Sir E. Seymour and Col. Seymour, papers of 11th Duke of Somerset.)

The settlement of the Maiden Bradley estate was executed chiefly on account of his marriage with a daughter of Sir William Portman. By the articles executed on that occasion, his father was to give him Maiden Bradley for his use and to settle it on his children. He also bound himself to settle the Devonshire estates in such a manner that they should come to him after his decease. (As we have seen he parted with them during his lifetime in

exchange for an annuity.) The Devonshire estates being mortgaged to the amount of £1,992. 0. 0. it was agreed that that amount was to be paid out of the Lady's portion of £3,000.
(Seymour Papers, coll. by 11th Duke of Somerset.)

Note 94.

The Declaration of the Gentrie of the King's Party in the County of Devon. (Printed by Roger Norton in 1660.)

We whose names are underwritten cannot but in all humility and gratitude acknowledge the infinite mercy of Almighty God to this Nation in giving such signal testimonies of his goodness towards it, by creating in men's hearts a confidence of the restoration of our native rights in Church and State so long suppressed by the ambitions and passions of factious and vulgar spirits, and that as we hope without the effusion of more blood or any farther devastation, He having wonderfully raised for our deliverance and to the perpetual honour of this Country, his excellency LORD GENERAL MONK, a person averse from those wicked designs and actions which others heretofore have practised on us, and to whose courage and conduct these nations are deeply engaged. And hearing there are a sort of malicious and uncharitable people, who by dispersing false rumours endeavour to have it believed that we and others of the KING'S PARTY are rather inclined to revenge and faction, than to the settlement of the peace of our Country; We therefore do think it our duty to declare to all the world, that we have it not so much as in our thoughts to contrive or do anything to the prejudice of the Public Settlement but (forgetting what is past) are resolved cheerfully and unanimously to submit and adhere to the determinations and Acts of Parliament, Praying to God to bless and prosper their Councels and Proceedings.

Baronets.	Esquires.	Esquires.
Edward Seymour.	Arthur Basset.	Edward Pyne.
Peter Prideaux.	Thomas Carew.	James Phodes.
Thomas Hele.	Francis Drewe.	Ames Pollarde.
Hugh Pollarde.	John Courtenay.	John Hancocke.
Courtenay Poole.	Henry Champernowne.	John Weare.
	Thomas Stuclye.	John Raymond.
Knights.	Robert Cary.	Robert Warren.
Francis Fullforde.	John Giffard.	Thomas Woode.
Henry Carew.	Edmund Tremaine.	Mark Cottle.
Richard Prideaux.	John Prouse.	Thomas Shapcote.
Peter Bulle.	George Yeo.	Robert Walker.
James Smyth.		

NOTE 95.

On account of his ill-health and advancing age, Sir Edward now resigned his command. Upon this he received the following letter from Lord Bath, which shows upon what good terms they were.

The Earl of Bath to Sir Edward Seymour. (Papers, 11th Duke.)

"Sir, I have received your two kind and most obliging letters for which I give you all imaginable thanks, but am infinitely sorry to hear of your indisposition of health and that it is now so inconvenient for you to continue your former command of the Militia of this county, out of whose hands it should never be taken during my Lieutenancy without your earnest and pressing desires, as now it is, and for your regiment I would never consent it should be under any other name than yours and for that reason because you will have it so at present, I am willing to transfer the same upon your most worthy grandson, to whom I have sent you enclosed a commission for him to be Colonel of your regiment, and another to make him a Deputy Lieutenant, with another deputation for yourself, assuring you that no man living doth or can more truly love and honour you and my ever honoured dear Lady at Berry, to whose service in particular I am eternally devoted, and beg pardon that I have not time at this present to write to her Ladyship, which I shall not fail to do very speedily, and in everything within my power gives perfect obedience to her commands. Thus with the presentment of my humble service to you both, wishing you all the health and prosperity in the world, and ever remain with all truth, Sir,

"Your most affectionate kinsman and most faithful servant,

"BATHE.

"April 9, 1686."

NOTE 96.

On March 14, 1664, Captain Hugh Seymour was ordered to Kinsale, in his ship the Pearl, by the following letter from the Duke of York :—

"The Duke of York to Captain H. Seymour.

"So soon as you have cleaned the ship under your command at Kinsale and received on board your victuals, you are with the first opportunity of wind and weather (in company of His Majesty's ships named in the margin, i.e., the Dartmouth, the Richmond, the Nightingale, and the Little Gift), to sail to the North West part of Ireland, and to ply out at sea about Black Rock, near Broadhaven, endeavouring to seize upon such Dutch ships as shall pass that way and to send them into Kinsale, if it may be, or else into the next convenient port, and cause them to be delivered unto such persons as shall be appointed there to receive prize goods ; and if no person be appointed in the said port for that purpose, then unto the Vice-Admirals of the county where such port shall be, or his deputy, to be by him secured until orders shall be given for their reception by some peculiarly appointed for that purpose. If any of the ships appointed to go with you shall not arrive at Kinsale before you are ready to sail, or being there shall not be in readiness to sail with you, you are in such case not to stay for them but to proceed to your station without them, leaving notice with the commanders, or (in case of their absence) with the Clerk of the Cheque at Kinsale, sealed up, where they may most probably meet with you ; and being met you are to act by joint advice and either separate yourselves or keep in a body, according as shall be judged best for the execution of these orders. Upon the arrival of Captain Rooth, in the Dartmouth, he is to command in chief, and you are to observe his orders, but until he arrive the commander of one of the fifth rate frigates (whose commission is of the oldest date) is to command. You are to continue plying in this station until the last day of April or 10th of May, as you shall find occasion ; which time being expired you are to sail to Orkney, there to clean the ship under your command and to expect further orders. You are to seize upon such ships as you meet with belonging to Hamburgh and send them in as aforesaid, taking care that the men on board them be civilly treated and neither the ship's furniture nor lading, as well what shall be between decks as in the hold, be embezzled ; the said ships not being intended to be brought in as prizes but only to be detained till further orders. And you are also to take notice that all ships belonging to Ameland and Embden are to be treated as Hollanders. Upon your seizing of the ships you are to take especial care that their tackle, apparell, furniture, and lading, be preserved from embezzlement, and you are to cause the masters and commanders of the said ships to produce all papers, writings, bills of lading, etc., concerning or relating to the said ships which you do cause to be sealed up in the presence and with the seal of the masters or commanders of the said ships and also with your seal, and you are speedily to send the same unto the Commissioners for prizes in the port whither you shall send the said ships or to such persons as they shall employ in the said port. You are to send sometimes in Sligo to enquire for orders. Given under my hand at St. James's this 14th of March, 1664.

"JAMES."

After this expedition Captain Seymour apparently went to the Mediterranean, for, on July 16, 1664, we find him returning home from Tangiers with a prize named the Golden Fountain which had been captured near Algiers. On March 13, of the following year, he was still in command of the Pearl and came into Portland Bay with her, accompanied by three prizes, laden with wine and brandy, which had formed part of the Holland fleet of 30 sail which was returning from Bordeaux. On October 1, of the same year, Lord Brounker and Sir J. Mennes wrote to the Navy Commissioners to inform them that they had heard that Capt. Seymour, late of the Pearl, had embezzled some goods taken from the Prince William prize at Erith, and asking that he might be examined. This accusation was apparently found to be without foundation. On Feb. 8, 1666, a warrant was granted to him and to John Seymour, in reversion, of the office of Searcher of the Customs in the port of London, and, on Feb. 12, we find him in command of the Foresight. In this ship he joined the fleet acting in the Channel against the Dutch, and appears to have distinguished himself on more than one occasion. In July, however, an important naval engagement took place in which he was killed. Sir John Clifford writing, on July 27, to Lord Arlington, says, in describing the battle that had taken place on the 25th and 26th, "Seymour, the brave commander of the Foresight, was killed."

That Hugh Seymour was highly thought of and was looked upon as a rising man in the Navy is shown by the following epitaphs, which would scarcely have been written for any man who was not well known and esteemed.

Epitaphium Hugonis Seimori, gloriosissimi centurionis in classe Regia, fortiter in Navali Proelio contra Baffavos 8 Calends Sextilias Anno Christi 1666 defuncti.

"Quisquis es antiquum mirare et nubile stemma
Quod Seimororum nomen et armia gerit.
Laus cuius per totum Anglorum clarvit urbem
Illius in tumba hac respice relliquias.
Nil marum O Frater, cum sint mortalia cuncta
At nostri Hugonis fama perennis erit."

(State Papers, Dom., Charles II. Also Papers coll. by 11th Duke of Somerset.)

Another Epitaph.

Épitaphe de Huges Seymour, fils d'Édouard Seymour, baronet, qui fut tué dans un combat naval contre les Hollandais en 1666.

"Nous delaissant ça bas au ciel tu te retires,
O Seymour regretté par tous tes vraies amis ;
Mais au ciel tu le pois delivre des envis
Que la-bas nous souffrons parmi tant de martyrs.

"Nous delaissant ton Dieu jamais tu ne delaisses,
Il ta laissé sortir de ce monde en sa paix,
Il ta même reçu dans son trés saint palais,
Pour y jouir tout saint de ces joyes célestes."

Note 97.

In April, 1692, Edward Seymour was one of those gentlemen who were asked by the exiled King, James, to come over and be witnesses to the birth of his second·child, which was about to take place.

His Majesty's letter to sundry Lords and others of the Privy Council. James R . . . . Whereas our royal predecessors used to call such of their Privy Council as could conveniently be had, to be witnesses to the birth of their children and whereas we have followed their example at the birth of our dearest son James, Prince of Wales, though even that precaution was not enough to hinder us from the malicious aspersions of those who were resolved to deprive us of our royal right. It having now pleased Almighty God to give us hopes of further issue, we have thought fit to require such of our Privy Council who can come, to attend us here at St. Germains, to be witnesses of the Queen's accouchement. We therefore signify our pleasure to you, that you come with all possible haste, the birth being expected to take place about the middle of next May. The King of France has given his consent that you shall have leave to come, and to return again, with all safety. Though the unquiet of the times, the tyranny of strangers, and a misled party of our own subjects have brought us under the necessity of using this unusual way ; yet we hope it will convince the world of the truth and candour of our proceedings, to the confusion of our enemies. Dated at our castle of St. Germains, 2nd April, 1692, in the eighth year of our reign.

(State Papers, William and Mary. 4, No. 36.)

Note 98.

It seems probable that it was during his time that the castle of Berry was burnt down. The following story may not seem out of place here, in connection with an alleged ghost that was supposed to appear immediately before the death of any one in the castle. About a century ago, Dr. Walter Farquhar, who was created a baronet in 1796, and who was a man of unimpeachable veracity, was staying for a time at Torquay, and was one day summoned to Berry Pomeroy professionally. Although a ruin, there still remained two or three rooms in which the steward resided with his wife. It was the latter who was ill. On the doctor's arrival he was asked to remain in the outer apartment while the steward went to see if his wife was prepared. "This apartment was large and ill-proportioned; around it ran richly carved panels of oak that age had changed to the hue of ebony. The only light in the room was admitted through the chequered panes of a gorgeously stained window, in which were emblazoned the arms of the former Lords of Berry Pomeroy. In one corner, to the right of the wide fireplace, was a flight of dark oaken steps, forming part of a staircase leading apparently to some chamber above." Whilst the Doctor was waiting, the door opened, and a richly dressed lady entered the room. The doctor, thinking it was some visitor, rose and made a step forward, but the lady paid no attention to him, but hurried across the room, wringing her hands, and evidently in the greatest distress. Arriving at the foot of the stairs, she paused a moment and then hurried up them. As she reached the highest stair the light fell strongly on her features, and displayed a young and beautiful countenance, but, to use the doctor's own words, "if ever human face exhibited agony and remorse; if ever eye, that index of the soul, portrayed anguish uncheered by hope, and suffering without interval; if ever features betrayed that within the wearer's bosom there dwelt a hell, those features and that being were then present to me." Almost immediately afterwards he was called to see the patient, whom he found so ill, that he had to give his undivided attention to her case. The next day, however, finding her much better, he inquired of the steward as to the lady he had seen, and described her appearance. The steward became greatly agitated, exclaiming repeatedly "My poor wife!" But eventually, becoming calmer, he told the doctor that he was sure she would now die, and enlightened him as to the history of the apparition so far as he knew it. It appears that it was the daughter of a former baron of Berry Pomeroy, who had borne a child to her own father and strangled it in the room above. He added that he had lived about the castle for 30 years, and had never known the omen fail and that it had been last seen the day his son was drowned. Although the doctor considered his patient much better and pronounced that all danger was over, the omen had been no mistake and the poor woman died that day.

Many years afterwards Sir Walter was called upon by a lady who came to consult him about her sister who was suffering from a severe shock. She explained that during the summer she had accompanied her brother and sister to Torquay, whence they had driven over one morning to inspect the ruins at Berry Pomeroy. The steward they found was ill, and there was some difficulty in getting the keys. She herself and her brother had, therefore, gone in search of them, leaving their sister in a large outer room (apparently, from her description, the same as that in which the doctor had before been put). When they returned they found their sister in a terrible state of alarm and distress, declaring she had seen an apparition (the description of which tallied exactly with that formerly seen by Sir Walter). They had endeavoured to rally her out of it by expressing their disbelief and laughing at her fears, but their sister only grew worse and her state now occasioned them the gravest alarm. In reply to a question of Sir Walter's she said that the steward had died whilst they were still in the castle. The doctor then said, "Madam, I will make a point of seeing your sister immediately, but it is no delusion. This I think it proper to state most positively and previous to any interview. I, myself, saw the same figure under somewhat similar circumstances, and about the same hour of the day; and I should decidedly oppose any raillery or incredulity being expressed on the subject in your sister's presence." The lady recovered and the apparition was never seen again for the old steward was the last person to inhabit the castle.

(A full account of this story is given in "Haunted Homes and Family Legends," by J. H. Ingram.)

NOTE 99.

Epitaph of Sir Edward Seymour on the monument at Maiden Bradley :—

Under this marble are deposited the remains
of Sir Edward Seymour, baronet, late
of Bury Pomeroy, in the county of
Devon, and of this place,
A man of such endowments
as added lustre to his noble ancestry,
commanded reverence from his contemporaries,
and stands the fairest pattern to posterity :
Being often called to Council, and always chosen in
Parliament.
(A friend to his Prince, a servant to his country)
He advised the King with freedom,
The senate with dignity;
That senate, the bulwark of the English liberty,
In which he presided for several years,
Found his eloquence an advocate,
His integrity a guardian,
His vigour a champion for its privileges :
Nor can any Englishman rejoice
In that envied portion of his birthright,
The Habeas-Corpus Act,

Without gratitude to the ashes of this patriot
under whose influence
it became his heritage,
Born in the year 1633,
His childhood felt not the calamities,
Which, in the succeeding years,
The spirit of anarchy and schism
Spread over the nation.
His manhood saw the church and monarchy restored,
And he lived in dutiful obedience to both :
Loaden with honour, full of years,
(Amidst the triumph of his country)
Raised to the highest point of glory,
By that immortal Princess, Queen Anne,
he died
it the year
1707.
Francis Seymour, Esquire, in just veneration
For the memory of his illustrious grandfather,
And in due obedience to the last will and testament
Of Lieutenant General William Seymour,
Second son of the deceased Sir Edward,
Hath caused this monument
To be erected,
1730.

NOTE 100.

The following report is of some interest as throwing a curious
light upon the times :—Dec. 18, 1712. Report of Sir William
Wyndham to the Lord High Treasurer on a memorial of
Lieutenant General Seymour, praying for payment of £800 for
"trophy money" for the Queen's own regiment of foot, from the
beginning of the reign. In the year 1702, the office of Great
Wardrobe delivered for the use of the regiment 12 colours, with
ensign, stave, etc. At the Union there was a warrant for a new
set of colours, and there was a warrant for two years trophy money
to General Webb on 7th August last. Dated Whitehall, Dec. 8,
1712.

MINUTED —"Ordered out of the 500,000 li. for civil list,
but the Queen will not be at this charge for the future."

NOTE 101.

Lord Aylesbury to Sir Edward Seymour, October 22, 1744.

"Dear Sir,

"Upon some enquiry that I have made, I am informed that the

Piercy estate, after Lord Hertford, is to go between Sir Charles Wyndham, and Lady B. Smithson, and the Seymour estate where the Duke of Somerset pleases, I having lately forced from the Duke of Somerset the Seymour's pedigree, I should not I fear, be a proper person to be assisting to you in this matter, though I would willingly undertake it, and as yet I cannot think upon a proper person to help in it. The Duke has two daughters by this Duchess, the eldest I believe about seventeen, and a fine young woman she is, brought up by a very good mother. The Duke has acquired about £4,000 a year in Cambridgeshire, and his personal estate in money, plate, and reversion leases, which here and in the north are very considerable, will probably be left between his daughters. Now my thought upon this is, that probably the Duke might like of a match between your son and his eldest daughter, considering your son after you will now certainly be Duke of Somerset. Were the Duke dead I should have no difficulty in moving the affair to the Duchess, who is, by my first marriage, my near relation, and one that I have been upon very good terms with several years, but as it may be proper to do something in this affair during the Duke's life, the question comes by whom it may be most properly put, and I think you will do well to advise with your neighbour, Lord Orrery, who, I think, has some acquaintance with the Duke. You were saying, when here, that Lord O. had thoughts of coming to town this way and so we to come together thither. Now if you and Lord O. would come together hither the Thursday morning or night before the Parliament meeting, my wife and we three might come to London together in my coach, and then we might at leisure talk over this affair, and which, if you think proper, you may talk over with Lord O. now upon your receipt of this, and let me know your thoughts by the bearer. If he be back thither on Thursday night will do. Should you like of my thought as to the match, which seems to me a right and a probable thing, I may be doing something towards it between this and our going to London.

" I am, Sir,
" Your affectionate humble servant,
" AYLESBURY."

(Corresp. of the Seymours, coll. by 11th Duke of Somerset.)

NOTE 102.

The Duke of Somerset to the Earl of Hertford.

" December 4, 1767.

" My dear lord,
" I should indeed be very happy to pay my duty to His Majesty, and to show my respect to your lordship and the Duke of Grafton,

by appearing next Tuesday in the House of Lords and giving my approbation to the measures of Government; nor should my present state of health, which is but indifferent (being indisposed with a cold that has brought on another complaint) prevent a journey to town for that purpose; but your lordship knows there is an invincible obstacle in my way, which however weak it may seem, my consitution will not suffer me to get over, sensible I am, that it deprives me of most of the comforts of life, as well as the advantages of my rank and situation; for whilst houses for inoculation are open to the great avenues to the town, and people with the small pox on them are suffered to walk about the street it is scarce possible in my apprehension, to escape infection; nay in the House of Lords itself, filled as it is generally with strangers on days of great debate. I should be afraid of meeting some of Mr. Sutton's patients, who may be hardy enough to venture even thither. This practice cannot I hope continue long (for if the law does not sooner interpose to prevent it there must be wanting subjects to inoculate very soon, I should imagine) but whilst it does continue I must be considered to solicit a retirement. Was it possible to persuade me out of my fears, you lordship would have power to do it, and my own inclinations on occasions like these would strongly second your arguments; but there is no getting the better of nature, and this particular sort of dread is so deeply rooted in me, that I despair of its ever being eradicated. I hope a single *content* or *not content* whichever goes with administration will not be essential if the question be agitated in a committee, and if it be in the House your lordship will make my proxy as much use as my personal presence.

"I must therefore beg your lordship to make my excuses for me, to whom ever it may be necessary, and as my apology is founded in truth, I am certain you will have no objection to take upon you the charge.

"I am, my dear lord, with the greatest
respect and esteem,
"Your lordship's truly affectionate
Cousin,
"SOMERSET."

The Duke of Somerset to the Earl of Hertford, Feb. 9, 1771.

"My Dear Lord,—I am this day favoured with your commands of the 7th instant, and should be very happy to pay my duty to His Majesty, by appearing next Thursday in the House of Lords, and giving my approbation to the measures of Government, could I think it wanted my support, but as numbers for administration are so great, and opposition so weak, I conceive you will have at least three, if not five, to one for peace, therefore I must beg your

Lordship to make my excuse to whomever it may concern, that I may not take so unnecessary a journey at this severe season, and especially too as inoculations are so ripe. My best respects attend your family and I remain, My Dear Lord, with the greatest esteem and regard, your Lordship's affectionate cousin and faithful servant,

"SOMERSET."

(Corresp. of the Seymours, coll. by 11th Duke of Somerset.)

NOTE 103.

Lord Shelburne to the Duke of Somerset.

Lord Shelburne presents his compliments to the Duke of Somerset, and has the pleasure to acquaint His Grace that His Majesty has been pleased to confirm to His Grace a pension of £1,200 a year, notwithstanding the great difficulties necessarily occasioned by the reform of the Civil List expenditure.

Feb. 25th, 1783.

The Duke of Somerset to Lord Shelburne.

The Duke of Somerset presents his most respectful compliments to Lord Shelburne, is greatly obliged to His Lordship for his polite card of the 25th instant (which is this moment come to hand) and hopes His Lordship will communicate to His Majesty his Grace's humble duty and thanks for his great goodness in confirming to him a pension. And that Lord Shelburne will be pleased to accept of his Grace's best thanks for the good offices he makes no doubt but his Lordship has done him on the occasion. When his Grace's health will permit he will take the first opportunity of paying his respects in person.

Feb. 27th, 1783.

(Corresp. of the Seymours, coll. by 11th Duke of Somerset.)

2 G

APPENDICES.

APPENDIX A.

Articles of High Treason and other misdemeanors against the King's Majesty and his Crown, objected to Sir Thomas Seymour, knight, Lord Seymour of Sudley and High Admiral of England:—

1. Whereas the Duke of Somerset was made Governor of the King's Majesty's person and the Protector of all his realms and Dominions, and subject to the which you yourself did agree, and gave your consent in writing, it is objected and laid unto your charge. That this notwithstanding you have attempted and gone about, by indirect means, to undo this order, and to get into your hands the Government of the King's Majesty, to the great danger of his Highness's person, and the subversion of the state of the realm.

2. That by corrupting with gifts and fair promises, divers of the Privy chamber, you went about to allure his Highness to condescend and agree to the same your most heinous and perilous purposes, to the great danger of his Highness's person, and of the subversion of the state of the realm.

3. That you wrote a letter with your own hand, which letter the King's Majesty should have subscribed or written again after that copy to the Parliament House, and that you delivered the same to his Highness for that intent, with the which so written by his Highness, or subscribed you have determined to have come into the Commons house yourself; and there with your factors and adherents before prepared, to have made a broil or tumult, or uproar, to the great danger of the King's Majesty's person and subversion of the state of this realm.

4. That you yourself spake to divers of the Council, and laboured with divers of the nobility of the realm, to stick and adhere unto you for the alteration of the state and order of the realm, and to attain your other purposes, to the danger of the King's Majesty's person now in his tender years and subversion of the state of the realm.

5. That you did say openly and plainly, that you would make the blackest Parliament that ever was in England.

6. That being sent for by the authority, to answer to such things as were thought meet to be reformed in you, you refused to come; to a very evil example of disobedience, and danger thereby, of the subversion of the state of the realm.

7. That since the last session of this Parliament, notwithstanding much clemency shewed unto you, you have still continued in your former mischievous purposes; and continually, by yourself and others, studied and laboured to put into the King's Majesty's head and mind, a misliking of the Government of the realm, and of the Lord Protector's doings, to the danger of his person and the great peril of the realm.

8. That the King's Majesty being of these tender years, and as yet by age unable to direct his own things, you have gone about to instil into his Grace's head and as much as lieth in you, persuaded him, to take upon himself the Government and management of his own affairs to the danger of His Highness's person and great peril of the whole of the realm.

9. That you had fully intended and appointed, to have taken the King's Majesty's person into your own hands and custody to the danger of his subjects and peril of the realm.

10. That you have corrupted with money certain of the Privy chamber, to persuade the King unjustly to have a credit towards you, and so to insinuate you to his Grace that when he lacked anything, he should have it of you, and none other body, to the intent he should mislike his ordering, and that you might the better, when you saw time, use the King's Highness for an Instrument to this purpose, to the danger of his royal person and subversion of the state of the realm.

11. That you promised the marriage of the King's Majesty at your will and pleasure.

12. That you have laboured, and gone about to combine and confederate yourself with some persons, and especially moved those noblemen, whom you thought not to be contented, to depart into their countries and make themselves strong; and otherwise to allure them to serve your purposes by gentle promises and offers to have a party and faction in readiness to all your purposes, to the danger of the King's Majesty and person and peril of the state of the realm.

13. That you parted, as it were, in your imagination and interest, the realm to set noblemen to countervail such other noble-

men, as you thought would let your devilish purposes, and so laboured to be strong to all your devices ; to the great danger of the King's Majesty's person and great peril of the state of the realm.

14. That you had advised certain men to entertain and win the favour and good will of the head yeomen and ringleaders of certain countries to the intent that they might bring the multitude and commons when you should think meet to the furtherance of your purposes.

15. That you have not only studied and imagined how to have the rule of a number 'of men in your hands, but that you have attempted to get, also gotten divers stewardships of noblemen's lands and their mannoreds to make your party stronger for your purposes aforesaid ; to the danger of your King's Majesty's person and great peril of the state of the realm.

16. That you have retained young gentlemen and hired yeomen, to a great multitude and far above such number as is permitted by the Laws and Statutes of the realm or where otherwise necessary or convenient for your service, place or estate, to the fortifying of yourself towards all your evil intents and purposes ; to the great danger of the King's Majesty and peril of the state of the realm.

17. That you had so travailed in that matter, that you had made yourself able to make, out of your own men, out of your lands and rules and other your adherents ten thousand men besides your friends to the advancement of all your intents and purposes ; to the danger of the King's Majesty's person and the great peril of the state of the realm.

18. That you had conferred, cast, and weighed so much money as would find the said ten thousand men for a month ; and that you knew how and where to have the same sum ; and that you had given warning to have and prepare the said mass of money in readiness, to the danger of the King's Majesty's person ; and great peril to the state of the realm.

19. That you have not only before you married the Queen attempted and gone about to marry the King's Majesty's sister, the Lady Elizabeth, second Inheritor in remainder to the Crown, but also being then lett by the Lord Protector, and others of the Council since that time, both in the life of the Queen continued your own labour and love and after her death by secret and crafty means practised to achieve the said purpose of marrying the said Lady Elizabeth to the danger of the King's Majesty's person ; and great peril to the state of the same.

20. That you married the late Queen so soon after the late King's death that if she had conceived straight after it should have been great doubt whether the child born should have been accounted the late King's or yours, whereupon a marvellous danger and peril might, and was like to have ensued to the King's Majesty's succession and quiet of the realm.

21. That you first married the Queen privately and did dissemble and keep close the same insomuch that a good space after you had married her, you made labour to the King's Majesty and obtained a letter of his Majesty's hand to move and require the said Queen to marry with you; and likewise required the Lord Protector to speak to the Queen to bear her your favour towards marriage; by which colouring not only your evil and dissembling nature may be known, but also it is to be feared that at this present you did intend to use the same practice in the marriage of the Lady Elizabeth's grace.

22. That you not only, so much as lay in you, did stop and lett all such things as either by Parliament or otherwise, should tend to the advancement of the King's Majesty's affairs but did withdraw yourself from the King's Majesty's service; and being moved and spoken unto for your own honour, and for the ability that was in you to serve and aid the King's Majesty's affairs and the Lord Protector's, you would always draw back and feign excuses and declare plainly that you would not do it. Wherefore upon the discourse of all these aforesaid things and of divers others, it must needs be intended that all these preparations of men and money, the attempts and secret practices of the said marriage: the abusing and persuading the King's Majesty to mislike the Government, state, and order of the realm that now is, and to take the Government into his own hands, and to credit you and to none other end and purpose but after a little gotten to the Crown and your party made strong both by sea and land with furniture of men and money sufficient to have aspired to the Dignity Royal by some heinous enterprise against the King's Majesty's person, to the subversion of the whole state of the realm.

23. That you not only had gotten into your hands the strong and dangerous Isles of Scilly bought of divers men; but that so much as lay in your power you travailed also to have Londay, and under pretence to have victualled the ships therewith, not only went about, but also moved the Lord Protector, and whole Council, that you might by publick authority, have that, which by private fraud and falsehood, and confederating with Sharington you had gotten; that is the Mint of Bristol to be yours only and to serve your purposes, casting, as may appear, that if these traitorous purposes had no good success, yet you might thither convey

a good mass of money ; where being aided with ships and conspiring at all evil events with pirates you might at all times have a sure and safe refuge if any thing for your demerits should have been attempted against you.

24. That having notice that Sir Wm. Sharington, knight, had committed treason and otherwise wonderfully defrauded and deceived the King's Majesty, nevertheless you both by yourself and by seeking counsel for him and by all means you could, did aid, assist, and bear him contrary to your allegiance and duty to the King's Majesty and the good laws and orders of the realm.

25. That where you owed to Sir Wm. Sharington, knight, a good sum of money yet to abet bear and cloak the great falsehood of the said Sharington, and to defraud the King's Majesty, you were not afraid to say and affirm before the Lord Protector and the Council that the same Sharington did owe unto you a great sum of money, viz., two thousand eight hundred pounds, and to conspire with him in that falsehood and take a bill of that feigned debt into your custody.

26. That you by yourself and ministers have not only extorted and bribed great sums of money of all such ships as should go into Island, but also as should go any other where in merchandize contrary to the liberty of this realm, and to the great discouragement and destruction of the Navy of the same to the great danger of the King's Majesty and the state of the realm.

27. That when divers merchants as well strangers as Englishmen have had their goods piratously robbed and taken, you have had their goods in your hands and custody daily seen in your house and distributed amongst your servants and friends without any restitution to the parties so injured and spoiled, so that thereby foreign Princes have in a manner been weary of the King's Majesty's unity and by their Ambassadors divers times complained ; to the great slander of the King's Majesty and danger of the state of the realm.

28. That where certain men have taken certain pirates, you have not only taken from the takers of the said pirates all the goods and ships so taken without any reward, but have cast said takers for their good service done to the King's Majesty into prison, and there detained them a good time ; some eight weeks, some more, some less, to the discouraging of such as truly should serve the King's Majesty against his pirates and enemies.

29. That divers of the head pirates being brought in to you, you have let the same pirates go again free unto the seas, and taken away from the takers of them not only all their commodity and

profit, but from the true owners of the ships and goods all such that ever came into the pirates hands as though you were authorized to be the chief pirate, and to have had all the advantages they could bring unto you.

30. That where order hath been taken by the Lord Protector and the whole Council that certain goods particularly taken upon the seas and otherwise known not to be wreck nor forfeited should be restored to the true owners, and letters thereupon written by the Lord Protector and the Council, to the which letters you yourself among the other did set to your hand, yet you this notwithstanding have given commandment to your officers that no such letters should be obeyed; and written your private letters to the contrary commanding the said goods not to be restored, but kept to your own use and profit, contrary to your own hand before in the Council chamber written, and contrary to your duty and allegiance and to the perilous example of others and great slander and danger of the realm.

31. That where certain strangers which were friends and allies to the King's Majesty had their ships with the wind and weather broken and yet came unwrecked to the shore; when the Lord Protector in Council had written for the restitution of the said goods as might, you yourself subscribing and consenting thereto, yet notwithstanding you have not only given contrary commandment to your officers but as a pirate have written letters to some of your friends to help, that as much of these goods as they could should be conveyed away secretly by night farther off upon hope that if the said goods were assured the owners would make no further labour for them, and then you might have enjoyed them, contrary to justice and your honour, and to the great slander of this realm.

32. That you have not only disclosed the King's Majesty's secret Council, but also where you yourself, among the rest, have consented and agreed to certain things for the advancement of the King's affairs, you have spoken and laboured against the same.

33. That your Deputy Steward and other your ministers of the Holt, in the county of Denbigh, have now against Christmas last past at the said Holt made such provision of the wheat, malt, beefs and other such things as be necessary for the sustenance of a great number of men, making also by all means possible a great mass of money insomuch that all the country doth marvel at it, and the more because your servants have spread rumours abroad that the King's Majesty was dead, whereupon the country is in a great maze, doubt, and expectation, looking for some broil, and would have been more if at this present by your apprehension it had not been staied.

APPENDIX B.

The names of the fortresses, abbeys, frere-houses, market towns, villages, towres, and places brent, raced, and cast downe by the commandment of Therll of Hertforde, the King's Majestie's Lieutenant Generall in the North partes, in the invasion into the realm of Scotland, between the 8th of Sept. and the 23d of the same 1545, the 37th yeare of the King's Royall Majestie's moste prousperous and victorious reigne.

On the River of Twede.

First the abbey of Kelso, raced and cast down ; the towne of Kelso brent ; the abbey of Melrosse alias Mewrose, Darnyck, Gawtenside, Danyelton, Overton, Heildon, Newton of Heildon, Maxton, Lafeddon, Marton, Beamondside, Loughefeatte, Bateshele, the abbey of Drybrughe, the town of Drybrughe, the towre of Dawcowe raced. The towne of Dawcowe, Rotherford, Stockstrother, Newtowne, Trowes, Makerston, the Manorhill, Charterhouse, Lugton Lawe, Stotherike towre raced ; East Meredean, West Meredean, Flowres, Gallowe Lawe, Broxe Lawe, Broxe Mylne, the Water-mill of Kelso. Sum 33.

On the River of Tiviot.

The Freers nere Kelso, the Larde Hog's House, the Barnes of Old Rockesborough, Towne, the towre of Rockesborough raced, the towre of Ormeston raced, the towne of Ormeston, Neyther Nesebett, Over Nesbet, Angeram Spittell, Bune, Jedworth, the two towres of Bune Jedworth raced, the Lard of Bune Jedworth's dwellinghouse, Over Angeram, Neyther Angeram, East Barnehill, Mynto Crag, Mynto Towne and Place, West Mynto, the Cragge End, Whitrick, Hessington, Bankhessington, Overhassington, Cotes, Esshebanke, Cavers, Bryeryards, Densome, Rowcastle, Newtowne, Whitchester-house, Tympinton. Sum 36.

On the Water of Rowle.

Rowle Spittel, Bedrowle, Rowlewood. The Wolles, Crossebewghe, Donnerles, Fotton, Weast Leas. Two Walke Mylnes, Tromyhill, Dupligis. Sum 12.

On the Ryver of Jedde.

The abbey of Jedworthe, the Freers there ; the towne of Jed-
worthe, Hundylee, Bungate ; the Banke End, the Neyther Mylnes,
Houston, Over Craling, the Wells, Neyther Craling, Over
Wodden, Neyther Wodden.   Sum 13.

On the Ryver of Kealle in East Tividale.

Over-Hownam, Neyther Hownam, Hownam Kyrke, Newe
Gateshaughe ; the towre of Gateshaughe, Over Grobet, Neyther
Grobet ; Grobet Mylne, Wydeopen, Crewkedshawes, Prymside,
Mylne Rigge, Marbottell, Otterburne, Cesforthe, Overwhitton,
Neyther Whitton, Hatherlands, Cesforth Borne, Cesforth, Maynes,
Mowe-house ; the Cowe Bogge, Lynton, Caverton, Sharpesrige,
Throgdon, Pringle Stede, the Maynehouse, Eckeforde, Mosse
house, Westerbarnes, Grymesley, Synles, Heyton on the Hill,
Newe Hawe, Massendewe ; the Brig End, St. Thomas Chap-
pell, Maxwell Hughe, East-Woddon, West-Woddon, Howden.
Sum 45.

On the Ryver of Bowbent in East Tividale.

Mowe, Mowe Meusles, Clifton Cote, Coleroste, Elshenghe,
Awton Barne, Cowe, Woodside, Owesnopside, Feltershawes,
Clifton, Hailhope, Kirke Yettam, Towne Yettam, Cherytres,
Barears ; the Bogge, Longhouse, Fowmerden.   Sum 19.

Heales Parish.   In the Marsse.

Long Ednam, Little Newton, Newton Mylne, Naynethorne,
Naynethorne Mylne, Over Stytchell, Nether Stichell, Cownge-
carle, Lagers Morre, Oxemoure, Kenetside, Myckell Harle, Lytell
Harle, Hassyngton, Hassyngton Maynes, Landen, Hardacres,
Stanefawde ; the abbey of Hecles, the towne there ; Newtowne,
Heclesheales, Grafton Rig, Pittelesheugh, Overplewland, Nether
Plewland, Over Tofts, Nether Tofts, Clerkeleas, Headrigge, Pud-
dingran, Howden, Marsington, and the towre raced, Letam, Bel-
clester, Boughtrige, Newbigging, Wranghame, Wester Peles ; the
Kemes, the Burnehouse, Thankles, Rowyngston, Grymeley Rigge,
Cowys, Werke, Whinkerstanes, Fowge Rigge, Foge Banke, Sir
James Trennate's House, Ryseley, Bettrikside, Elbank.   Sum 57.

Donce Parish.

Fowge Towne, Susterpethe, Susterpethe Mylne, Fowge Mylne,
the walke Myle there, the Hill, the new Mylne, Sleghden, Easte-

feld, Hardames, Stanemore Lawe; the Biers, Wodehede, Cawdeside, Lownesdale; the towre of Red Brayes raced, the towre of Pollerd raced, Pollerd Towne, Pollerwood, the Bow-House, Selburne Rigge, Stocke Fote; the towres and barmekyn of Nesbed raced, the towre of Nesbed, Nesbed Hill, Crongle, Cawedrawe, the Brigend, Gretrig, Growell Dikes; the towre of Dunce raced, Dounce Lawe, Knocke; the towne of Dounce, Hare Lawe, Borticke, East Bortick, Parkehed, Cawdefide, Black Dikes, Brykenside, Kaydesheale, Redheughe, Manderston, Nanewarre, Elfoyle, Cromersteyn, Kawkey Lawe, Sampson's Walles; the Brigg end, the Check Lawe, Dounce Mylne, the East Maynes. Sum 52.

The castell of Wetherburne, Mongouse Towre, Pele Rigge, Kemergeyme, Kemergeyme Maynes, Redheughe, Redes House, Godds Malisone; the East Mylne, the Kellawe, Edrame; the newe Towne, Blackoter Castell raced; the Twyne of Blacketer, White Lawe, East Lawes, West Lawes, Swynton, and Whitsonne. Sum 20.

Sum Total .... 287.

APPENDIX C.

Articles objected to the Duke of Somerset.

1. That he took upon himself the office of Protector upon express condition that he should do nothing in the King's affair but by assent of the late King's executors or the greatest part of them.

2. That contrary to this condition he did hinder justice and subvert laws of his own authority as well by letters as by other command.

3. That he caused divers persons, arrested and imprisoned for treason, murder, manslaughter, and felony, to be discharged against the laws and statutes of the realm.

4. That he appointed Lieutenants for armies, and other officers for the weighty affairs of the King under his own writing and seal.

5. That he communed with Ambassadors of other realms alone of the weighty matters of the realm.

6. That he would taunt and reprove divers of the King's most honourable Councillors for declaring their advice in the King's weighty affairs against his opinion, sometimes telling them that they were not worthy to sit in Council, and sometimes that he need not to open weighty matters to them, and that if they were not agreeable to his opinion, he would discharge them.

7. That against law he held a court of request in his own house, and did force divers to answer there for their freehold and goods and did determine of the same.

8. That being no officer without the advice of the Council or most part of them, he did dispose offices of the King's gift for money, grant leases and wards and presentations of Benefices pertaining to the King; gave Bishopricks and made sale of the King's lands.

9. That he commanded alchymy and multiplication to be practised, thereby to abase the King's coin.

10. That divers times he openly said, the nobility and gentry

were the only cause of dearth, whereupon the people rose to reform matters of themselves.

11. That against the minds of the whole Council he caused Proclamation to be made concerning inclosures, whereupon the people made divers insurrections and destroyed many of the King's subjects.

12. That he sent forth a commission with articles annexed, concerning inclosures, commons, highways, cottages, and such like matters, giving the Commissioners authority to bear and determine those causes whereby the laws and statutes of the realm were subverted and much rebellion raised.

13. That he suffered rebels to assemble and lie armed in camp against the nobility and gentry of the realm, without speedy repressing of them.

14. That he did comfort and encourage divers rebels by giving them money and by promising them fees, rewards, and services.

15. That he caused a Proclamation to be made against law and in favour of the rebels, that none of them should be vexed or sued by any for their offences in their rebellion.

16. That in time of rebellion he said that he liked well the actions of the rebels; and that the avarice of gentlemen gave occasion for the people to rise, and that it was better for them to die than to perish for want.

17. That he said the Lords of the Parliament were loth to reform inclosures and other things, therefore the people had a good cause to reform them themselves.

18. That after declaration of the defaults of Bulloign (Bologne), and the pieces there, by such as did survey them, he would never amend the same.

19. That he would not suffer the King's pieces of Newhaven and Blackness, to be furnished with men and provision; albeit he was advertized of the defaults and advised thereto by the King's Council; whereby the French King was emboldened to attempt upon them.

20. That he would neither attempt authority nor suffer noblemen and gentlemen to suppress rebels in time convenient; but wrote to them to speak the rebels fair, and use them gently.

21. That upon the 5th of October, the present year, at Hampton Court for defence of his own private causes he procured seditious bills to be written in counterfeit hands, and secretly to be

dispersed into divers parts of the realm; beginning thus: "Good people," intending thereby to raise the King's subjects to rebellion and open war.

22. That the King's Privy Council did consult at London to come to him and move him to reform his government; but he, hearing of their assembly, declared by his letters in divers places that they were high traitors to the King.

23. That he declared untruly as well to the King, as to the other young Lords attending his person; that the Lords at London intended to destroy the King; and desired the King never to forget but to revenge it; and he desired the young Lords to put the King in remembrance thereof with intent to make sedition and discord between the King and his nobles.

24. That at divers times and places, he said "The Lords of the Council at London intended to kill me; but if I die, the King shall die; and if they famish me, they shall famish him."

25. That of his own head he removed the King so suddenly from Hampton Court to Windsor, without any provision there made that he was thereby not only in great fear, but cast thereby into a dangerous disease.

26. That by his letters he caused the King's people to assemble in great numbers in armour, after the manner of war, to his aid and defence.

27. That he caused his servants and friends at Hampton Court and Windsor to be apparelled in the King's armour, when the King's servants and guards went unarmed.

28. That he caused at Windsor, his own person in the night-time to be guarded in harness by many persons leaving the King's Majesty's person unguarded and would not suffer his own guard and servants to be next the King's person, but appointed his servants and friends to keep the gates.

29. That he intended to fly to Jersey or Wales and laid post horses, and men, and a boat to that purpose.

APPENDIX D.

The Honourable Entertainment given to the Queen's Majesty in Progress, at Elvetham, Hampshire, by the Right Honorable the Earl of Hertford, 1591.

(London, Printed by John Wolfe, and are to be sold at the little shop over against the great South door of Paules, 1591.)

The Proeme.

Before I declare the inst time or manner of Her Majesty's arrival and entertainment at Elvetham, it is needful (for the Reader's better understanding of every part and process of my discourse) that I set down as well the convenience of the place, as also the suffising, by art and labour, of what the place in itself could not afford on the suddain, for receipt of so great a Majesty, and so honorable a train.

Elvetham House being situated in a park but of two miles in compass or thereabouts, and of no great receipt, as being none of the Earl's chief mansion houses; yet for the desire he had to show his unfained love, and loyal duty, to her most gracious Highness, purposing to visit him in this her late progress, whereof he had to understand by the ordinary Gesse, as also by his honorable good friends in Court, near to Her Majesty: his Honour with all expedition set artificers to work to the number of three hundred many days before Her Majesty's arrival, to enlarge his house with new rooms and offices. Whereof I omit to speak how many were destined to the offices of the Queen's household, and will only make mention of other such buildings, as were raised on the sudden, fourteen score off from the house on a hillside, within the said park, for entertainment of nobles, gentlemen, and others whatsoever.

First there was made a room of Estate for the nobles, and at the end thereof a withdrawing room for Her Majesty. The outsides of the walls were all covered with boughs, and clusters of ripe hazel nuts, the insides with Arras, the roofs of the place with works of ivy leaves, the floor with sweet herbs and green rushes.

Near adjoining unto this, were many offices new builded; as namely, Spicerie, Larderie, Chaundrie, Wine-seller, Ewery, and Panterie: all of which were tiled.

Not far off, was erected a large hall, for the entertainment of knights, ladies and gentlemen of chief account.

· There was also a several place for Her Majesty's footmen and their friends.

Then there was a long Bower for Her Majesty's guard; another for other officers of Her Majesty's house; another to entertain all comers, suitors, and such like; another for my Lord's Steward to keep his table in; another for his gentlemen that waited.

Most of these aforesaid rooms were furnished with tables, and the tables carried 23 yards in length.

Moreover on the same hill, there was raised a great common buttery; a pitcher house; a large pastery, with five ovens new built, some of them fourteen foot deep; a great kitchen with four ranges, and a boiling place for small boiled meats; another kitchen with a very long range, for the roast, to serve all comers; a boiling house for the great boiler; a room for the scullery; another room for the cook's lodgings.

Some of these were covered with canvass and some with boards. Between my Lord's house and the foresaid hill, where these rooms were raised, there had been made in the bottom by handy labour, a goodly pond, cut to the perfect figure of a half moon. In this pond were three notable grounds (islands?), where hence to present H. Majesty with sports and pastimes. The first was a ship isle of 100 feet in length, and 40 feet broad, bearing three trees orderly set for 3 masts. The second was a fort 20 feet square every way, and overgrown with willows. The third and last was a Snayl mount, rising to four circles of green privet hedges, the whole in height 20 feet, and 40 feet broad at the bottom. These three places were equally distant from the sides of the pond, and every one by an inst measured proportion distant from the others. In the said water were divers boats prepared for musick; but especially there was a pinnace, full furnished with masts, yards, sails, anchors, cables, and all other ordinary tackling; and with iron pieces; & lastly with flags, streamers, and pendants, to the number of twelve, all painted with divers colours and sundry devices. To what use these particulars served, it shall evidently appear by that which followeth.

The first day's entertainment.

On the 20th day of Sept. being Monday, my Lord of Hertford joyfully expecting Her Majesty's coming to Elvetham to supper, as Her Highness had promised: after dinner, when every other needful place or point of offernice was established and set in order, for so great an entertainment, about three of the clock his Honor, seeing all his retinue well mounted and ready to attend his pleasure, he drew them secretly into a chief thicket of the park, where in few words, but well couched to the purpose, he put them in mind what quietness, and what diligence, or other duty they were to use at that present :

This done, my Lord with his train (amounting to the number of 300 and most of them wearing chains of gold about their necks, and in their hats yellow and black feathers) met with Her Majesty two miles off, then coming to Elvetham from her own house of Odiham, four miles from thence. As my Lord in this first action shewed himself dutiful, so Her Majesty was to him and his most gracious, as also in the sequel between 5 and 6 of the clock, when her Highness, being most honorably attended, entered into Elvetham park, and was more than half way between the park gate and the house, a Poet saluted her with a Latin oration in heroical verse, I mean *veridicus vates*, a sooth-saying poet, nothing inferior for truth, and little for dilineary of his mind, to an ordinary orator. This Poet was clad in green, to signify the joy of his thoughts at her entrance, a laurel garland on his head to express that Apollo was ¦patron of his studies : an olive branch in his hand to declare what continual peace and plenty he did both wish and assure Her Majesty : and lastly booted to betoken that he was *vates cottiurnatus*, and not a loose and love creeping Prophet, as poets are interpreted by some idle or envious ignorants.

This Poet's boy offered him a cushion at his first kneeling to Her Majesty, but he refused it, saying as followeth (this oration being entirely in Latin, I put forward a very fair English translation of it, in place of the original) :—

The Poet to his boy offering him a cushion.

" Now let us use no cushions but fair hearts :
For now we kneel to more than usual Saints."

The Poet's speech to Her Majesty.

" While at the fountain of the sacred hill
Under Apollo's lute, I sweetly slept,
'Mongst prophets full posse'd of holy fury,
And with true virtue, void of all disdain
The Muses sung, and wak'd me withese words.
' Seest thou that English nymph, in face and shape
Resembling some great Goddess, and whose beams
Do sprinkle heav'n with unacquainted light,
While she doth visit Seymour's friendless house,
As Jupiter did honour with his presence
The poor thatch'd cottage where Philamon dwelt ?
See thou salute her with an humble voice ;
Phœbus, and we, will let thee lack no verses.

But dare not once aspire to touch her praise,
Who like the sun for show, to God's for virtue,
Fills all with majesty, and holy fear.
More learned than ourselves, she ruleth us :
More rich than seas, she doth command the seas :
More fair than Nymphs, she governs all the Nymphs,
More worthy than the Gods, she wins the Gods.
  'Behold (Augusta) thy poor suppliant
Is here, at their desire, but they desert.
O sweet Elisa, grace me with a look
Or from my brows this laurel wreath will fall,
And I unhappy die amidst my song.
Under my person Seymour hides himself,
His mouth yields prayers, his eye the olive branch ;
His prayers betoken duty, th' olive peace ;
His duty argues love, his peace fair rest ;
His love will smooth your mind, fair rest your body,
This is your Seymour's heart and quality :
To whom all things are joys, while thou art present,
To whom nothing is pleasing, in thine absence.
Behold on thee how each thing sweetly smiles
To see thy brightness glad our hemisphere :
Night only envies : whom fair stars do cross :
All other creatures strive to shew their joys.
The crooked-winding kid trips o'er the lawns ;
The milk-white heifer wantons with the bull ;
The trees shew pleasure with their quivering leaves,
The meadow with new grass, the vine with grapes,
The running brooks with sweet and silver sound.
Thee, thee, (sweet Princess) heav'n, and earth, and floods,
And plants, and beasts, salute with one accord :
And while they gaze on thy perfections,
Their eye's desire is never satisfied.
Thy presence frees each thing that liv'd in doubt,
No seeds now fear the biting of the worm,
Nor deer the toils, nor glass the parching heat,
Nor birds the snare, nor corn the storm of hail.
O Empress, O draw forth these days to years,
Years to an age, ages to eternity :
That such as lately joyed to see our sorrows,
May sorrow now, to see our perfect joys.
  'Behold where all the Graces, virtue's maids,
And lightfoot Hours, the guardians of heav'ns gate,
With joined forces do remove those blocks,
Which Envy laid in Majesty's highway.
  'Come therefore, come under our humble roof,
And with a beck command what it contains :

2 H

For all is thine : each part obeys thy will ;
Did not each part obey, the whole should perish.
　‘ Sing songs, fair nymphs, sing sweet triumphal songs,
Fill ways with flowers, and th’ air with harmony.’ ”

While the poet was pronouncing this oration, six virgins were
behind him, busily removing blocks out of Her Majesty’s way ;
which blocks were supposed to be laid there by the person of
Envy, whose condition is, to envy at every good thing, but
especially to malice the proceedings of virtue, and the glory of
true Majesty. Three of these virgins represented the three Graces,
and the other three the Hours, which by the poets are fained to be
the guardians of heaven’s gates. They were all attired in gowns
of taffeta sarcenet of divers colours, with flowery garlands on their
heads and baskets full of flowers and sweet herbs upon their arms.
When the Poet’s speech was happily ended, and in a scroll delivered
to Her Majesty (for such was her gracious acceptance, that she
desired to receive it with her own hands) then these six virgins,
after performance of their humble reverence to her Highness,
walked on before her towards the house, strewing the way with
flowers, and singing a sweet song of six parts to this ditty which
followeth :—

The Ditty of the Six Virgins’ Song.

“ With fragrant flowers we strew the way
And make this our chief holiday :
For though this clime were blest of yore,
Yet was it never proud before.
　　O beauteous Queen of second Troy,
　　Accept of our unfained joy.

“ Now th’ air is sweeter than sweet balm,
And satyrs dance about the palm :
Now earth with verdure newly dight,
Gives perfect sign of her delight.
　　O beauteous Queen of second Troy,
　　Accept of our unfained joy.

“ Now birds record new harmony,
And trees do whistle melody :
Now every thing that nature breeds,
Doth clad itself in pleasant weeds.
　　O beauteous Queen of second Troy,
　　Accept of our unfained joy.”

This song ended with Her Majesty’s entrance to the house :
where she had not rested her a quarter of an hour : but from the
Snail-mount and the Ship-isle in the pond (both being near under

the prospect of her gallery window) there was a long volley of Chambers discharged. After this, supper was served in, first to Her Majesty, and then to the nobles and others. . . . .

After supper was ended, Her Majesty graciously admitted into her presence a notable concert of six musicians, which my Lord of Hertford had provided to entertain Her Majesty withall, at her will and pleasure, and when it should seem good to her Highness. Their music so highly pleased her, that in grace and favour thereof, she gave a new name to one of their Pavans, made long since by Master Thomas Morley, then organist of Paule's church.

The Second Day's Entertainment.

On the next day following, being Tuesday, and St. Mathew's festival, the forenoon was so wet and stormy, that nothing of pleasure could be presented Her Majesty. Yet it held up a little before dinner time, and all the day after: where otherwise fair sports would have been buried in foul weather.

This day Her Majesty dined with her nobles about her, in the room of estate, new builded on the hill side, above the pond's head.

* * *

Presently after dinner, my Lord of Hertford caused a large canopie of estate to be set at the pond's head, for Her Majesty to sit under and to view some sports prepared in the water. The canopie was of green satin, lined with green taffeta sarcenet; every seam covered with a broad silver lace; valenced about, and fringed with green silk and silver, more than a handbreadth in depth; supported with four silver pillars, moveable; and decked above head with four white plumes, spangled with silver. This canopie being upheld by four of my Lord's chief gentlemen, and tapestry spread all about the pond's head, Her Majesty about 4 of the clock came and sat under it, to expect the issue of some device, being advertised that there was some such thing towards.

At the further end of the pond, there was a Bower, close built to the brink thereof; out of which there went a pompous array of sea persons, which waded breast high, or swam, till they approached near the seat of Her Majesty. *Nereus*, the prophet of the sea, attired in red silk and having a cornered cap on his curled head, did swim before the rest, as their pastor and guide. After him came five Tritons breast high in the water, all with grizly heads, and beards of divers colours and fashions, and all five cheerfully sounding their trumpets. After them went two other Gods of the sea *Neptune* and *Oceanus*, leading between them that pinnace whereof I spake in the beginning of this treatise.

In the pinnace were three virgins, which with their cornets played Scottish jigs, made three parts in one. There was also in the said pinnace another nymph of the sea, named Neœra, the old supposed love of Sylvanus, a god of the woods. Near to her were placed three excellent voices, to sing to one lute, and in two other boats hard by, other lutes and voices to answer by manner of echo: after the pinnace, and two other boats, which were drawn after it by other sea-gods, the rest of the train followed breast high in the water, all attired in ugly marine suits, and every one armed with a huge wooden squirt in his hand; to what end it shall appear hereafter. In their marching towards the pond, all along the middle of the current, the Tritons sounded one half of the way, and then they ceasing, the Cornets played their Scottish jigs. The melody was sweet and the show stately.

*　　*　　*　　*　　*

In the pinnace were two jewels to be presented to Her Majesty by Nereus and Neœra. The fort in the pond was crowded with armed men. The Snail-mount resembled some monster, having horns full of wild-fire continually burning. The God Silvanus was lying not far off, with his train, waiting for his opportunity to emerge from the wood and present Her Majesty with a holly scutchion, wherein Apollo had long since written her praises.

All this remembered and considered, I now return to the sea-gods, who having under the conduct of Nereus brought the pinnace near before her Majesty, Nereus made his oration as followeth; but before he began, he made a private sign unto one of his train, which was gotten up into the Ship-isle, directly before her Majesty, and he presently did cast himself down, doing a summerset from the isle into the water, and then swam to his company.

The Oration of Nereus to Her Majesty.

" Fair Cynthia the wide Ocean's Empress
I watery Nereus hovered on the coast
To greet your Majesty with this my train
Of dancing Tritons, and shrill singing nymphs.
But all in vain: Elisa was not there ;
For which our Neptune grieved, and blamed the star,
Whose thwarting influence dash'd our longing hope.
Therefore impatient, that this worthless earth
Should bear your Highness's weight, and we sea Gods,
(Whose jealous waves have swallowed up your foes,
And to your realm are walls impregnable)
With such large favour seldom time are grac'd :
I from the deeps have drawn this winding flood,
Whose crescent form figures the rich encrease
Of all that sweet Elisa holdeth dear.
And with me came gold-breasted Ludia,
Who daunted at your sight, lept to the shore,

And sprinkling endless treasure on this isle,
Left me this jewel to present your Grace,
For him, that under you doth hold this place.
See where her ship remains, who silkwoven tackling
Is turned to twigs, and threefold mast to trees,
Receiving life from verdure of your looks ;
(For what cannot your gracious looks effect ?)
Yon ugly monster creeping from the South,
To spoil these blessed fields of Albion,
By selfsame beams is chang'd into a Snail,
Whose bulrush horns are not of force to hurt.
As this Snail is, so be thine enemies.
And never yet did Nereus wish in vain.
That fort did Neptune raise, for your defence,
And in this barke, which Gods hale near the shore,
White footed Thetis sends her musick maids,
To please Elisa's ears with harmony.
Hear them fair Queen : and when their music ends,
My Triton shall awake the Sylvan Gods,
To do their homage to your Majesty."

This oration being delivered, and withall the present whereof he spake, which was hidden in a purse of green rushes, cunningly woven together : immediately the three voices in the pinnace sang a song to the Lute with excellent divisions, and the end of every verse was replied by Lutes and voices in the other boat somewhat afar off, as if they had been echoes.

The Sea Nymphs' ditty.

" How haps that now, when prime is don,
    An other spring time is begun ?
Our hemisphere is overrunne,
    With beauty of a second sunne."
       Echo.   A second sun.

" What second sun hath raies so bright,
    To cause this unacquainted light ?
'Tis faire Elisaes matchlesse Grace,
    Who with her beames doth blesse the place."
       Echo.   Doth blesse the place.

This song ended, Nereus commanded the five Tritons to sound. Then came Sylvanus with his attendants from the wood : himself attired from the middle downwards to the knee, in kid skins with the hair on, his legs, body, and face, naked but dyed over with saffron, and his head hooded with a goat skin, and two little horns over his forehead, bearing in his right hand an olive tree, and in his left a scutchion, whereof I spake somewhat before. His followers were all covered with ivy leaves, and bare in their hands bows, made like darts. At their approach near her Majesty, Sylvanus spake as followeth, and delivered up his scutchion ingraven with golden characters,—Nereus and his train still continuing near her Highness :—

The Oration of Sylvanus.

" Sylvanus comes from out the leafy groves,
To honour her, whom all the world adores,
Fair Cynthia, whom no sooner nature framed,
And decked with fortunes, and with virtue's dower,
But straight admiring what her skill had wrought,
She broke the mould : that never sun might see
The like to Albion's Queen for excellence.
'Twas not the Tritons' air-enforcing shell
As they perhaps would proudly make their vaunt,
But those fair beams, that shoot from Majesty,
Which drew our eyes to wonder at thy worth.
That worth breeds wonder ; wonder holy fear ;
And holy fear unfained reverence.
Amongst the wanton days of golden age,
Apollo playing in our pleasant shades,
And printing oracles in every leaf,
Let fall this sacred scutchion from his breast,
Wherein is writ, Detur dignissima.
O therefore hold what heaven hath made thy right,
I but in duty yield desert her due."

NEREUS.
" But see Sylvanus where thy love doth sit."

SYLVANUS.
" My sweet Necera was her ear so near ?
O set my heart's delight upon this bank,
That in compassion of old sufferance,
She may relent in sight of beauty's Queen."

NEREUS.
" On this condition shall she come on shore.
That with thy hand thou plight a solemn vow,
Not to profane her undefiled state."

SYLVANUS.
" Here take my hand, and therewith all I vow."

NEREUS.
" That water will extinguish wanton fire."

Nereus in pronouncing this last line, did pluck Sylvanus over head and ears into the water, where all the Sea Gods laughing, did insult over him. In the meanwhile her Majesty perused the verses written on the scutchion. . . . .

After that the Sea Gods had sufficiently ducked Sylvanus, they suffered him to creep to the land, where he no sooner set footing, but crying Revenge, Revenge, he and his begun a skirmish with those of the water, the one side throwing their darts, and the other using their squirts, and the Tritons sounding a point of war. At the last Nereus parted the fray with a line or two grounded on the excellence of her Majesty's presence, as being always friend to peace, and enemy to war. Then Sylvanus with his followers retired to the woods, and Necæra, his fair love in the pinnace, presenting her Majesty a sea jewel, bearing the form of a fawn, spake unto her as followeth :—

The Oration of Fair Necæra.

" When Neptune late bestowed on me this barke,
And sent by me this present to your Grace :
Thus Nereus sung, who never sings but truth.
Thine eyes (Necæra) shall in time behold
A sea-born Queen, worthy to govern Kings,
On her depends the fortune of thy boat,
If she but name it with a blissful word
And view it with her life inspiring beams.
Her beams yield gentle influence like fair stars,
Her silver sounding word is prophecy.
Speak, sacred Sybill, give some prosperous name,
That it may dare attempt a golden fleece,
Or dive for pearls and lay them in thy lap.
For wind and waves, and all the world besides
Will make her way, whom thou shalt doom to bliss,
For what is Sybill's speech but oracle ? "

Here her Majesty named the pinnace the " Bonadventure," and Necæra went on with her speech as followeth :—

" I now Necæra's barke is fortunate
And in thy service shall employ her sail,
And often make return to thy availe.
O live in endless joy, with glorious fame,
Sound trumpets, sound, in honour of her name."

Then did Nereus retire back to his Bower with all his train following him, in self same order as they came forth before, the Tritons sounding their trumpets one half of the way, and the cornets playing the other half. And here ended the second day's pastime, to the so great liking of Her Majesty that her gracious approbation thereof was to the actors more than a double reward, and yet withall, her Highness bestowed a largesse upon them the next day after before she departed.

The Third Day's Entertainment.

On Wednesday morning, about nine of the clock, as Her Majesty opened a casement of her gallery window, there were three excellent musicians, who being disguised in ancient country attire, did greet her with a pleasant song of Coridon and Phyllida, made in three parts of purpose. The song, as well for the worth of the ditty, as for the aptness of the note thereto applied, it pleased her Highness, after it had been once sung, to command it again, and highly to grace it with her cheerful acceptance and commendation.

The Ploughman's Song.

" In the merry month of May
In a morn, by break of day,
Forth I walked by the wood side
Where as May was in his pride
There I spied all alone
Phyllida and Corydon.
Much ado there was Godwot,
He would love, and she would not.
She said never man was true :
He said none was false to you.
He said he had loved her long.
She said love should have no wrong,
Corydon would kiss her then :
She said maids must kiss no men
Till they did for good and all.
Then she made the shepherd call
All the heavens to witness truth,
Never loved a truer youth.
Thus with many a pretty oath,
Yea and nay, and faith and troth,
Such as silly shepherds use,
When they will not love abuse.
Love, which had been long deluded,
Was with kisses sweet concluded :
And Phyllida with garlands gay,
Was made the lady of the May."

The same day after dinner, about three of the clock, ten of my Lord of Hertford's servants, all Somersetshire men, in a square green court, before Her Majesty's window, did hang up lines, squaring out the form of a Tennis-court and making a cross line in the middle. In this square they (being stripped out of their doublets) played five to five with the hand ball, at bord and cord, (as they term it) to so great liking of her Highness, that she graciously deigned to behold their pastime more than an hour and a half.

After supper there were two delights presented unto her Majesty : curious fire-works, and a sumptuous banquet : the first from the three islands in the pond, the second in a low gallery in her Majesty's privy garden. But I will first briefly speak of the fire-works.

First there was a peal of a hundred chambers discharged from the Snail-mount : in counter whereof a like peal was discharged from the Ship-isle, and some great ordnance withall. Then there was a Castle of fire-works of all sorts, which played in the fort. Answerable to that there was in the Snail-mount, a globe of all manner of fire-works, as big as a barrel. When these were spent on either side there were many running rockets upon lines, which passed between the Snail-mount and the castle in the fort. On either side were many fire wheels, pikes of pleasure, and balls of wild fire, which burned in the water.

During the time of these fire-works in the water, there was a banquet served all in glass and silver, into the low gallery in the garden, from a hill side fourteen score off, by two hundred of my Lord of Hertford's gentlemen, every one carrying so many dishes, that the whole number amounted to a thousand : and there were to light them on their way, a hundred torch bearers. To satisfy the curious, I will here set down some particulars in the banquet :—

Her Majesty's arms in sugar-works. The funeral arms of all our nobility in sugar-works. Many men and women in sugar-works, and some inforst (?) by hand. Castles, forts, Ordinance, Drummers, Trumpeters, and soldiers of all sorts in sugar-works. Lions, Unicorns, Bears, Horses, Camels, Bolls, Rams, Dogs, Tigers, Elephants, Antelopes, Dromadaries, Asses, and all other beasts in sugar-works. Eagles, Falcons, Cranes, Bustards, Herons, Hawks, Bitterns, Pheasants, Partridges, Quails, Larks, Sparrows, Pigeons, Cocks, owls, and all that fly, in sugar-works. Snakes, Adders, vipers, frogs, toads, and all kinds of worms, in sugar-work. Mermaids, whales, dolphins, congars, sturgeons, pike, carp, bream, and all sorts of fishes, in sugar-work.

All these were standing dishes in sugar-work. The self same devices were also there all in flat work. Moreover these particulars following and many such like, were in flat sugar work and cinamon. March-paves, grapes, oisters, muscles, cockles, periwinkles, crabs, lobsters, Apples, pears, and plums of all sorts. Preserves, suckats, jellies, leaches, marmelats, pastry, comfits, of all sorts.

The Fourth Day's Entertainment.

On Thursday morning, Her Majesty was no sooner ready, and at her gallery window, looking into the garden, but there began three cornets to play certain fantastical dances, at the measure whereof the Fairy Queen came into the garden, dancing with her maids about her. She brought with her a garland made in form of an imperial crown, within the sight of her Majesty, she fixed upon a silver staff, and sticking the staff into the ground, spake as followeth :—

The Speech of the Fairy Queen to Her Majesty.

" I that abide in places underground,
Aureola, the Queen of Fairy land,
That every night in rings of painted flowers
Turn round, and carroll out Elisa's name ;
Hearing that Nereus and the sylvan gods
Have lately welcomed your imperial grace,
Opened the earth with this enchanting wand
To do my duty to your Majesty.
And humbly to salute you with this chaplet,
Given me by Auberon, the Fairy King.
Bright shining Phœbe, that in human shape,
Hid'st heaven's perfection, vouchsafe t' accept it.
And I Aureola, belov'd in heaven,
(For amorous stars fall nightly in my lap)
Will cause that heavens enlarge thy golden days,
And cut them short, that envy at thy praise."

After this speech, the Fairy Queen and her maids danced about the garland singing a song of six part, with the music of an excellent concert, wherein was the lute, Bandora, Base, viol, citterne, treble, viol, and flute, and this was the Fairies' song :—

" Elisa is the fairest Queen,
That ever trod upon this green,
Elisa's eyes are blessed stars,
Inducing peace, subduing wars.
Elisa's hand is cristal bright,
Her words are balm, her looks are light.
Elisa's breast is that fair hill
Where virtue dwells, and sacred skill,
O blessed be each day and hour,
Where sweet Elisa builds her bower."

This spectacle and music so delighted her Majesty that she desired to see and hear it twice over, and then dismissed the actors with thanks, and with a gracious largess, which of her exceeding goodness she bestowed upon them.

Within an hour after, Her Majesty departed, with her nobles, from Elvetham. On the one side of her way as she passed through the park, there was placed, sitting on the pond side, Nereus and all the sea gods in their former attire: on her left hand, Sylvanus and his company: in the way before her the three Graces, and the three Hours: all of them on every side wringing their hands and showing sign of sorrow for her departure. While she beheld this dumb show, the Poet made her a short oration as followeth ·—

The Poet's Speech at her Majesty's Departure.

" O see, sweet Cynthia, how the watery gods,
    Which joyed of late to view thy glorious beams,
    At this retire do wail and wring their hands,
    Distilling from their eyes salt showers of tears,
    To bring in winter with their wet lament.
    For how can summer stay, when sun departs ?
    See where Sylvanus sits, and sadly mourns,
    To think that autumn with his withered wings
    Will bring in tempest, when thy beams are hence :
    For how can summer stay when sun departs ?
    See where those Graces and those Hours of heaven,
    Which at thy coming sung triumphal songs,
    And smoothed the way, and strew'd it with sweet flowers,
    Now, if they durst, would stop it with green boughs,
    Lest, by thine absence, the year's pride decay :
    For how can summer stay when sun departs ?
    Leaves fall, grass dies, beasts of the wood hang head,
    Birds cease to sing, and every creature wails,
    To see the season alter with this change :
    For how can summer stay when sun departs ?
    O, either stay, or soon return again,
    For summer's parting is the country's pain."

After this, as Her Majesty passed through the park gate, there was a concert of musicians hidden in a bower, to whose playing this ditty of "Come again" was sung, with excellent division, by two that were cunning :—

    " O come again, fair nature's treasure,
      Whose looks yield joys exceeding measure.

    " O come again, heav'ns chief delight,
      Thine absence makes eternal night.

"O come again, world's starbright eye,
　Whose presence doth adorn the sky.

"O come again, sweet beauty's sun,
　When thou art gone, our joys are done."

Her Majesty was so highly pleased with this and the rest, that she openly protested to my Lord ot Hertford that the beginning, process, and end of this his entertainment, was so honourable, as hereafter he should find the reward thereof in her especial favour.

(In this account it has been necessary to leave out certain portions of the author's text that were digressions from the subject owing to want of space, and also to render the spelling of the words into more modern English for the sake of legibility. In other respects the author's original text is unaltered.)

APPENDIX E.

Sir George Rodney to the Countesse of Hertford.

From one that languisheth in discontent,
Dear Faire, receive this greeting to thee sent ;
And still as oft as it is read by thee,
Then with some deep sad sigh remember mee ;
When bee thou sure this order I will keepe,
My harte shall bleede as fast as thine shall weepe :
So if in sheddinge tears thou dost not faine,
With drops of blood I'll pay thee tears againe ;
To make oure sorrowes somewhat like abound,
That as thy eies so may my hart be drown'd,
In which griefe shall bee full, sighes shall be plentie,
And for one sighe of thine, I'le give thee twentie ;
And to the audit of thy strange content
Pay interest for the thoughts which thou hast lent ;
For too too well my fortunes make me knowe
My hapless Love must worke my overthrowe,
Wherein not death itself can come with paine,
Were not my death made woeful by disdaine ;
By which the times may say, by what is donne,
My father had one lost degenerate sonne,
And I shall to the stocke from whence I came,
Behold a blott both to my blood and name,
Soe much to yield, where in disgrace I prove,
To femall softness, and unfruitful love.
Confess I doe shame is my best desert,
Plantinge affection on a barren hart.
'Twas nature's sinne thus to commix a mynd
With beautie died in graine so muche unkinde.
No—'twas my fortune's error to vow duty
To one that bears defiance in her beautie.
Sweete poyson ; precious wooe ; infectious jewell :
Such is a ladie that is faire and cruell.
Howe well could I with ayre, camelion like,
Live happie, and still gazeing on thy cheeke,
In which, forsaken man, mee thinke I see
How goodlie love doth threaten cares to mee.
Why dost thou frowne thus on a kneelinge soule,
Whose faults in love thou may'st as well controule.—

In love—but oh! that word, I feare,
Is hatefull still both to thy hart and eare.
Am I too meane in ranck? I knowe I am,
Nor can I raise the stocke from whence I came.
I am no Barron's sonne, nor borne so high:
Would I were lower, soe I were not I:
As lowe as envy's wishes could impart,
Soe I could sett my sighes beneath my hart.
Ladie, in breefe, my fates does so intend,
The period of my daies drawes to an end:
The thread of my mortalitie is spunne,
Cancell'd my life, my thread of frailtie runne.
Dearth stands before my eies, and says my doome
By destinie to die was not yet come;
Tells me I might have liv'd, and tells me truth,
I am not sick yett in my strength of youth;
But says in such a lamentable case
I must not live to overlive disgrace;
And yields strong reasons, for, says death most clearlie,
Such is her pleasure whom thou lov'st most dearlie.
Oh be that wish accomplished, to showe
How it shall bee; but hope alas is vayne
When all my hope is clouded with disdain.
Nor, ladie, dare I blame you, since your choice,
With whome in honour you doe now rejoice,
Is worthie in himself, or indeed rather
In beinge sonne to such a worthie father,
Of whom amidst my griefs I have confest
He was of Seymors both the great'st and best.
Oh may his sonne be like him in his life:
Heer's then a husband fitt for such a wife.
Yett had my father answered his degree,
I might have bin as worthie full as hee;
For I had then bin captive to love's might,
More guided by my hart than by my sight.
Neglect of errour and the hand of heaven
Are meerlie strangers, yett it might have given
Well parted grace to frame a perfect creature,
A constant judgment to a constant feature;
For youth had then been match'd, a goodlie thinge,
Not to the sapless autumne, but the springe.
But O! the time is past, and all too late:
I may lament, but not recall my fate.
Stricte stands the censure which report displays,
That takes from mee the honor of my daies.
Revive my hopes—I cannot sincke in fame,
My reputation lost, disgrac't my name.

In virtue I am wounded, and can have
No glory nowe but in the conqueringe grave.
Sad memory to come this doome may give,
And say hee died that had no hart to live :
Herein my greifes and I shall well agree :
I'le bury them, as they have buried mee :
Thus to thy angry beaut ., pretious deare,
A sacrifice of pittie will I reare ;
A sacrifice of peace to end all strife ;
As true a hart as ever harboured life.
I may doe't, but my frailetie may forslow't,
And, indeed, 'tis not fitt that you should know't.
No, ladie, no ; although I cannot wynne
Your love for suite, to die for love is sinne.
Yet give me leave to singe my former songe :
I am too deeplie wounded to live longe,
Though not to die in hast ; but I protest,
If death could make you thinke I lov'd you best,
Would I were dead, that you alone might knowe
How much to you I did both vowe and owe.
I strive in vaine : my miseries are such
That all I doe or write is all too much.
My wish I have, if I be understood,
Willing to seale my meaning with my blood,
Faire, doe not frett, nor yett at all be mov'd,
That I have thus unfortunatlie loved ;
Nor thinke herein report disgracefull for thee ;
Heaven knowes I ever thought myselfe unworthie.
Yett, if you have a thought to cast away,
Cast it on mee, and soe you may repay
My service with some ease, and I in mynde
Commend that pittie I could never finde.
Thus ever bee, as you are, ever fair :
Rest you in much content ; I in despaire.

THE COUNTESSE'S ANSWERE.

Divided in your sorrowes, I have strove,
To pittie that attemp I must not love,
For which your health you sent me (sith in vaine,
Because I could not keepe) returnes againe.
Soe nowe the case betweene us twoe thus stands,
My present state, and your mishappe, commands :
Wherein what should I say but what I see ?
Impute the faultes to destinee, not mee.

Poore is the part of beautie I enjoy,
If where it winnes one it must one destroy.
Small cause have I, the owner, to rejoyce,
That cannot take free passage in my choyce ;
But, for the fruitless paintinge of my cheekes,
Must still become a slave to him that seekes,
Or be term'd cruell, or, which is farre worse,
Of death or bloudshedd undergoe the curse :
Soe if one desperate in madnesse do it,
Not yieldinge, I am accessarie to it.
Is bondage then the happinesse attends
On those whome evene one for faire commends ?
Then surelie better much it is to bee,
Rather than faire, in thraldome borne and free :
But this I neede not pleade, since beautie's mirror
Occasions not your suite, but your own error ;
And some such men there are, in whome opinion
Of what doth seeme, not is, hath most dominion :
Those onlie that for excellent doe seeme
What is not soe, indeed, but in esteeme,
Which, though I will not tax for lust in any,
Yett very lest, no doubt, it is in many ;
For uncompounded love, pure and refin'd,
Is a moste-neate perfection of the mynde,
And, being suche, must evermore effect
Thinges like itself in qualitie elect ;
Which granted, love in these should seeke for grace
Which faire are in condition, not in face.
So love a virtue is.—How many then
True lovers should bee found amongst you men ?
Such as preferr, by reason's temperate fire,
Lawfull dessert before unjust desire ;
Such as with goodness, in itself pure fram'd,
Are mildie hot, not franticklie inflam'd ;
Such as with goodness doe affection measure,
Grounded on cause of motion, not of pleasure.
Hee's not fitt choice that passionatelie hovers ;
Lovers are men, but most men are not lovers ;
And this should make us froward in deniall,
Since still wee knowe our miseries by triall.
Successe and custom, to weake women foes,
Have made men wanton in our overthrowes.
What is't in their attempts men have not vaunted,
Because the worser of our sex have graunted ?
To weepe, to threaten, flatter, lie, protest,
Are but in earnest lust, and love in jest.
Myself have heard it now and then avow'd

By some whome use in follie hath made prowd,
That if by oathes one may his purpose winne,
Noe perjury in such a case is sinne :
And can we then bee blamed if, being harm'd
By sadd experience, wee bee stronglie arm'd
With resolution to defend our wrongs
Against the perjur'd falsehood of men's tongues ?
　But whither range I in this vaine dispute,
Since what you seeke for is a wicked suite,
In telling you are captive to love's mighte,
More guided by your hart than by your sight ?
I can but answer to the love you ow'd,
The love that should have thank'd you is bestow'd :
Soe I must die in debt ; my hart is gonne ;
You are not hee, and I must have but one.
To him I have engag'd my blushless truth :
Love is not wise in age ; most rash in youth ;
And I applaud my fortune, which have mett
That fate which grave discretion doth begett.
Terme age the autumne ; 'tis a better play
To singe in winter, than to weepe in May.
Somethinge I know ; content is match'd with yeares,
When to wedd younge is as to marry teares.
And whoe can choose but faithfullie affect
That wisedome that knowes wiselie to direct ?
When youth with youth their race together runne,
Both ignorant to guide, are both undone,
And therefore doe not you my choyce molest ;
My match must please you, for it likes mee best ;
Nor do you take the course to purchase love
From one by striveinge howe you may remove
My love from him whose nowe I am, for hee
That is no friend to him is none to mee.
Thus farr to satisfie the feeleing paine
Which in your letter seemes soe to complaine,
And speakes for you with pittie more than witte,
Have I an answer made, though farr unsitte ;
Unsitt, considering whoe, and whose, I am ;
Unsitt both for your comfort and my name.
Be not deceiv'd, nor take your hope by this,
For, doeing soe, in truth you doe amisse.
If fate had mark'd mee yours, full well you knowe
Your earnest suit had wonne mee long agoe :
But 'twas not soe ordain'd ; then 'twere uneven
To strive against tbe ordinance of heaven.
'Twas not the fortune of your lowe descent
Your happe in haveing mee did not prevent :

2 I

Full well I knowe report in no wise can
Deny your father's sonne a gentleman.
Both hee and you have well deserv'd the same
By ancient titles, and by worthie fame,
And such you are, but what is that to mee
To withstande destinie, or fate's decree ?
The many honnours donne unto our House
Make me not proude, nor being a new spouse
To my new Lorde : 'tis not an auncient seate
Of glorie, but of vertue makes us greate.
Then herein, to add greatness to your blood,
Conquer desire ; be greate in beinge goode ;
And you shall herein much more honor finde,
Makeinge your passions subjecte to your mynd,
Than if thou were term'd noble, which lov'd stile
Is, without virtue's dresse, accompted vile.
  In breefe, whereas you write the fatall strife,
'Twixt love and my disdaine have doom'd your life ;
Herein my minde is, I would have you knowe it,
Poorlie meethinke you strive to play the poet ;
And poets, I have heard, in such a case,
Hold flattery and lieinge the best grace ;
For they are men forsooth have wordes to peirce
And wound a stony heart with softning verse.
They can worke wonders, and to tricke will move
A marble hart : they teach the art of love :
They can write sonnetts, and with warbling rymes
Make woemen as lights as are the times ;
And, if I bee not then deceived much,
Your last lines intimate you to bee such :
If you bee such, then I beleeve with ease
That you cannot die for love, if that you please.
Then dye as poets doe, in sighes (false fee
To corrupt truth) in sonnetting aye mee ;
With such like pretie deathes, whose trimme disguise
May barter yielding hartes, and blind soft eies.
No, no, I never yett could heare or prove
That there was ever any died for love ;
Nor would I have you be the man begine
The earnest daunce for such a sportive sinne :
For what would prove a laughter for an age ;
Stuffe for a play ; fitt matter for a stage.
But, that I may not spend my time in words,
Thus much my leisure and my witte affordes,
To make you thinke the paines you did employ
Were not all spent on one both nice and coy.
In honourable meaninge nowe it restes

That you for worthe's sake graunt mee two requests :
First, to desist your suite, and give less scope
To the licentious aptness of your hope :
Next, that you dare not to attempt the passage
Of more replies, by letters, or by message.
The first suite I'll entreate it at your hand,
And for the latter of them, I'le commaunde.
In doeing which you give me cause to say
That some thoughts on you are not cast away :
Else, all my love is firmelie plac'd, therefore
Hope for no favour—I will love no more.

SIR GEORGE RODNEY, BEFORE HEE KILLED HIMSELFE.

What shall I doe that am undone ?
Where shall I flie, myselfe to shunne ?
Ah mee ! myselfe, myselfe must kill,
And yett I die against my will.
In starry letters I behold
My death in the heavens enroll'd :
There finde I, wrytt in skies above,
That I, poore I, must die for love.
'Twas not my love deserv'd to die ;
O no, it was unworthie I.
I for her love should not have dy'de,
But that I had no worth deside.
Ah mee ! that love such woes procures,
For without her no love endures.
I for her vertues her doe serve,
Does such a love a death deserve ?

APPENDIX F.

Sir Francis Seymour his honourable and worthy Speech, spoken in the High Court of Parliament, shewing what dangers doe issue by want of Priviledge of Parliament, etc., printed in London. 1641.

"This great Counsel (as Tully said of the Senate of Rome) is the Soul of the Commonwealth, wherein one may hear and see all the grievances of the subjects and in the multitude of such Councellors is safety.

"Amongst whom, the greatest priveledge is liberty of speech. And therefore I humbly offer it unto you, to take into consideration, what wrong hath been done herein, what judgments hath been against the members of this House, for speaking nothing but what concerned the good of the Commonwealth. Which said judgments hath been against Law and Reason, and without precedent.

"What Law or Reason is there, that a Parliament, which is the highest of all courts, should be questioned by inferior courts and judges: as if the Common Pleas should question the King's Bench or the Chancery be questioned by either of them.

"Perhaps the Authors of it, have nature to plead for themselves, which indeed teacheth every man to preserve himself.

"This perhaps, makes them advance that, and those members which otherwise must condemn themselves. And such things have been done, to maintain their proceedings, as not only trench upon the Liberties of Parliament, but also upon the Liberties of the whole Commonwealth : wherein I had rather suffer for speaking the truth, than the truth should suffer for want of my speaking.

"Where was ever more Piety in a Prince, and more Loyalty in subjects, and yet what Commonwealth ever suffered like this?

"His Majesty in the sun, which though it ever shines alike in itself gloriously; yet by reason of clouds, many times it doth not so appear, and if his Majesty, by reason of bad members may not appear in such splendour, let us labour to clear those clouds : what will it avail us, if the Fountain be clear, if the streams that issue therefrom be not so also. I will instance in some particulars.

"If we look into the face of Religion, that is out-faced, and such as heretofore durst not appear, come boldly into our houses, as if they had a concealed toleration, I mean the Seminary Priests, who though they have less power, yet have they not less malice, but more, so long as the Pope hath his agents amongst us. See we not how they go to Somerset House, and to St. James's, with too much countenance? These are the enemies of the Church; without the church; I wish we had none within it: who pull down churches, and I am sure they would build up none again: Amongst which are our Non-Residents, who o'er-sway all by worldly preferments, and many livings.

" Christ made it the Touch-stone of Peter's love unto him to feed his sheep and lambs; but these men look at their own private gains, not taking pains for their own double honours, which are daily gotten.

" What thing is there more against Reason and Nature, than for one man to have above one wife, and for one shepherd to have more than one sheepfold.

" There are dumb dogs, that cannot speak a word for God, of whom the people may seek spiritual food, but can find none.

" Others there that preach, but it is not the Gospel but themselves, that the King hath an unlimited power, and the subjects no propriety in their goods.

" There are bad divines, and worse, and more ignorant Statesmen; who under the name of Puritans, condemn all, who truly profess Religion. There are surely many, who under a form of Godliness, cloak impiety: but to teach, that a man can be too holy, is the Doctrine of Devils.

" And now for fear I have been over-long, I will speak of the subjects Liberties, wherein I remember, what was confirmed unto us by the word of a King, and God forbid, that I, or any other, should imagine that the King did otherwise than he granted us.

" But some there be, that have betrayed the King unto himself, and so committed worse treason than those who betray him to others who tell him his Prerogative is above all Laws, and that his subjects are but slaves: whereby the King is neither preserved in Honour, nor the Commonwealth in safety."

APPENDIX G.

During her imprisonment, the Lady Arbell sent the following verses to Lord Seymour by way of a letter :—

"My friend, my friend, where art thou ? Day by day,
  Gliding, like some dark mournful stream, away,
My silent youth flows from me. Spring, the while,
  Comes and rains beauty on the kindling boughs
Round hall and hamlet ; Summer, with her smile,
  Fills the green forest ;—young hearts breathe their vows ;
Brothers, long parted, meet ; fair children rise
Round the glad board : Hope laughs from loving eyes :
—All this is in the world !—These joys lie sown,
The dew of every path—On ONE alone
Their freshness may not fall—the stricken deer,
Dying of thirst with all the waters near.

"Ye are from dingle and fresh glade, ye flowers.
  By some kind hand to cheer my dungeon sent ;
O'er you the oak shed down the summer showers,
  And the lark's nest was where your bright cups bent,
Quivering to the breeze and rain-drop, like the sheen
Of twilight stars. On you heaven's eye hath been,
Through the leaves pouring its dark sultry blue
Into your glowing hearts ; the bee to you
Hath murmur'd, and the rill.—My soul grows faint
With passionate yearning, as its quick dreams paint
Your haunts by dell and stream,—the green, the free,
The full of all sweet sound,—the shut from me.

"There went a swift bird singing past my cell—
  O love and freedom ! ye are lovely things.
With you the peasant on the hills may dwell,
  And by the streams ; but I—the blood of kings,
A proud unmingling river, through my veins
Flows in lone brightness,—and its gifts are chains.
—Kings !—I had silent visions of deep bliss,
Leaving their thrones far distant, and for this
I am cast under their triumphal car,
An insect to be crushed.

'Thou hast forsaken me. I feel, I know,
There would be rescue if this were not so.
Thou'rt at the chase, thou'rt at the festive board,
Thou'rt where the red wine free and high is pour'd,
Thou'rt where the dancers meet—a magic glass
Is set within my soul, and proud shapes pass,
Flushing it o'er with pomp from bower and hall ;—
I see one shadow, stateliest there of all,—
THINE! What dost THOU amidst the bright and fair,
Whispering light words, and mocking my despair ?
It is not well of thee—my love was more
Than fiery song may breathe, deep thought explore ;
And there thou smilest while my heart is dying,
With all its blighted hopes around it lying ;
Ev'n thou, on whom they hung their last green leaf—
Yet smile, smile on ! too bright art thou for grief.' "

        etc.,   etc.

APPENDIX H.

Letter from Mr. T. Gape to the Dowager Duchess of Somerset, describing the funeral of her grandson William, Third Duke of Somerset, at Great Bedwyn. Xmas, 1671. Printed in Wilts Archæolog. Mag., p. 163.

E.

" May it please your Grace,"
We came safe with the Hearse to Reading the first night, having Colonel Cooke's mourning coach unto himself, Sir John Elwes (nephew to the Lady Seymour), Mr. Wingfield, the Herauld, and myself therein, draune by my Lord Marquesse of Worcester's six horses, having in all about eight or ten horsemen attending the Hearse and coach, we bayted not, nor so much as dranke by the way.

The next morning betwene five and six we sett forth from Reading towards Hungerford and came thither about one at noone, where the gentry of the country viz. Sir Francis Popham with his coach in mourning and sixe horses, and a gentleman of his kindred with him (but Sir Francis was in a light greyish suite) Sir John Elwes of Barton, Mr. Giles Hungerford, Mr. Pleydall of Mugehill, Mr. Jeoffrey Daniell, Mr. Goddard, Mr. Deane, Mr. Hungerford of Chisbury, and many other of lesser note, together with many of his late Grace's servants, tenants, farmers, Bayliffs and some others. After dinner we removed towards Bedwyn and came thither about three in the afternoone and drove into the churchyard ; the coffin was covered with blacke velvett and a silver plate nayled on it, having an inscription in a plate of silver with his Grace's Titles of honor, a black velvett cushion with a Ducal Coronett thereon. The corps being taken out of the Hearse, was carried by some of his Grace's servants ; Sir Francis Popham, the two Sir John Elwes, Mr. Daniell, Mr. Giles Hungerford and Mr. Pleydall bearing up the Pall at the four corners and the middle part.

The Chauncel was hung round with black Bayes having escutcheons with his Grace's coat armes pinned thereon.

Mr. Charlete, Parson of Collingbourne Dacio performed the funerall service in the middle of which after the corps was lett doun into the grave the Herauld rehearsed his Grace's Titles of Honour and Dignity.

Colonel Cooke was the chiefe mourner.

There was much rudenesse of the common people amongst whom none suffered that I hear of, but myselfe, I having above a yard of the cloth of my long blacke cloake cutt and rent off in the crowd at my going into the church.

I lay that night at the Great House at Bedwin being now in the possession of Sir John Elwes of Barton (who married the widow of Mr. Duke Stonehouse).

Colonel Cooke, Sir John Elwes, the younger, the Herald, Mr. Thomas (who came into our company at Hungerford), the late Duke's and the Lord Marquess's servants went that night to Marlborough : of whome I can give your Grace, noe further information save what I heare from Mr. Clotterbocke (who went with them thither) that Mr. Thomas hath displaced the woodward of Collingbourne woods, and putt his younger brother Alexander Thomas (who had runne out of his whole Estate, and left the countrey for debt) into his place.

And that Mr. Ryder (who makes all meanes imaginable to get into my Lord Duke's service) observed to Mr. Clotterbocke, how much money I had lost my Lady Marquesse, by my not agreeing with him in graunting wild estates at late Courts.

I humbly beg your Grace's pardon for this ruder relation ; beseech Almighty God to preserve your Grace in good health, with length of days here, and to send your Grace patience and comfort to beare this sad loss and eternal happiness hereafter.

This is now, and ever shalbe the hearty prayer of Madame your Grace's most dutifull and obedient servant

THO. GAPE.

" Ambrosbury St. John's Day in Christmas, 1671.
For her Grace the Lady Duchesse
Dowager of Somersett at Essex house."

APPENDIX I.

The Earl of Bath to Edward Seymour, Esq.

Good Cousin Seymour,

I think it is not unknown to you that intelligence hath been given very lately of the purpose which the King of Spain hath to place a fleet of his at Brest to the number of 60 galleys and so many warlike ships there to remain for such service as he shall appoint them to do, and that very shortly. I need not enlarge unto you how necessary it is to have the forces of this county in good and perfect readiness to withstand any attempt the enemy shall give upon this coast which by likelihood he may and doth intend to do, lying so near unto the same. But to prevent the worst upon the occasion offered I have thought it good to pray and require you with all expedition possible to give order that your whole regiment of men and arms, together with all things thereunto appurtaining, be commanded to be prepared in complete and perfect manner to repair unto such places of danger as upon the approach of the enemy shall be requisite for them to do ; especially in every of those bands which by former orders have been appointed for the defence of the town of Plymouth as you know. And because that company which was led by Mr. Fitz doth now remain destitute of a sufficient commander, I have likewise thought it good to pray you to have regard thereof in such sort as the same may be ready to be employed upon all occasions : and that by a sufficient and discreet Captain of whom you are to make choice in that behalf, whereof for some causes you may do well to acquaint Sir William Courtenay. I have already written my letters briefly to Mr. Wraye and Crymes for their readiness concerning this service. Notwithstanding I pray and require you to put them of your regiment in mind again from yourself thereof, giving them such admonition for the performance of their duties therein and of all other necessary things depending upon the same according to the tenor of my lords of the Council last letters touching those preparations, to the which I do refer you. I do to this effect intend to write unto the rest of the Colonels and their officers through the whole county, to the intent that they and their companies may be in like manner prepared with all expedition to do such service as the necessity of the time and occasions of the enemy's approach shall require. And so not forgetting to put you in mind that the Beacons be duly and circumspectly watched according to former directions; with my very hearty commendations I commit you to God. From Tawstock the 24th of July, 1599.

Your assured loving cousin and friend,

W. BATHON.

The Earl of Bath to Edward Seymour, Esq.

Cousin Seymour,

I thank you for your speedy advertisement of the fleet discovered by those at watch at Rennestock Beacon, the like I hear from the Captain of the fort at Plymouth to whom I have written that he should be assisted with all the forces that may be speedily upon the alarm or notice given.

I am of your mind that it were not good or warrantable to gather or raise any forces without special and apparent cause; but good it is, as I have formerly written unto you by my late letters, that all men be in readiness to march at an hour's warning, which I doubt not of. I pray you give present direction to the constables or otherwise as you please that all the persons charged with horses do forthwith take them up and put them in readiness to march with the foot companies, if you see the occasion hold. And further I pray you command the post horses between you and me to be in perfect readiness to convey letters to each of us with speed, and let me hear from you daily in any wise so long as this danger lasteth that I may know what is done and further to be done on my part. And if in your judgment there be cause, upon notice from you, and a place appointed for me to come first unto, I will come. And so in post haste I bid you heartily farewell. From Tawstock, 26th of July, 1599.

Your assured cousin and friend,

W. BATHON.

The Earl of Bath to Edward Seymour, Esq.

Cousin Seymour,

I have herein enclosed sent unto you the examination of one John Stone taken before the Mayor of Plymouth yesterday, immediately upon his arrival in that harbour from the coast of Spain unto the which I do refer you as touching the confirmation of other reports forepast. I perceive that the Captain of the Fort and the inhabitants of the town, by reason of these continual intelligences are very much terrified, and in a manner so far distracted that they persuade themselves the whole town will be surprised before they shall have any sufficient aid from the country, the enemy coming upon them with so full resolution to do their uttermost against the same ; for the preventing whereof they have often importuned me to give directions that such forces as are appointed to make their first repair unto that place upon first discovery of the enemy, might forthwith be commanded to resort to the town, there to remain for some time to join with them in service for the repulse of the enemy at his first encounter, which they allege will be a matter of great consequence and an exceeding encouragement to the inhabitants to persist in their best endeavours. For these considerations and to avoid all blame that may ensue either to myself or you and the rest that are partakers with me in these public matters of service, I have thought it good to pray and require you to take the pains to resort unto Plymouth immediately upon the receipt hereof: and there by conferring with Sir William Strode, Sir Richard Champernown, and such other gentlemen adjoining as you shall meet in behalf of the country of the one part, and the Mayor and Captain of the Fort of the other part, to devise of the best and readiest means to satisfy their desires in that behalf. To which effect I do presently write unto these gentlemen and in like manner to the Mayor who will expect your repair unto them for that purpose. And what you and they shall conclude of herein for the best and surest safety of the place, before more forces may be drawn from the country to second the first, I will approve as if I were present at the conference and conclusion thereof myself: praying and requiring you that I may be advertised of your proceeding herein under all your hands without any unnecessary delay of time, for my better satisfaction and contentment. And so with my very hearty commendations I commit you to God. From Tawstock the 30th of July, 1599.

Your loving cousin and friend,
W. BATHON.

If you do agree among you to have any forces presently to remain at Plymouth, then I would have you forthwith to give out your warrant for the same not staying for any further directions from me, because it will be a great loss of time in sending forth and back about the same, and touching the charges that shall grow unto those particular companies for their living there, if any question be made therein I doubt not but to procure that it shall be proportionately borne by the whole country upon your advertisement of it unto me. I doubt not but Mr. Reynell will have special regard of Dartmouth and Torbay with all other places of descent within your particular commandries, and so I pray you advertise him in my behalf.

Edward Seymour to the Earl of Bath.

My duty unto your good Lordship remembered most humbly. According to such agreement as was thought fittest by Sir Ferdinando Gorges & myself at Plymouth, whereunto your lordship was pleased to give allowance, I sent unto Sir William Courtenay that he should come with his companies to Dartmouth, a course which Sir Ferdinando best likes of signifying unto him that it was so appointed by your honour's consent. But for so much as he formerly received commandment from your honour to repair to Plymouth he does give credit to my notice, I do therefore most humbly pray your lordship that if your lordship be so pleased that you will signify so much unto Sir William Courtenay by this bearer, he is a foot & his companies to be directed according to your lordship's pleasure, how needful & expedient it is to have a good defence for Torbay & of Blackpool, two places of as great defence & as fit to charge in war time on the coast, I leave to your honourable consideration. And for my own part I have but half a company, the rest being appointed for Plymouth; if there be another half drawn about Dartmouth & Totnes of the eastern companies or only Sir William Courtenay's companies to remain for a time at Dartmouth, Sir Thomas Deny's regiment to repair to Plymouth, they will not be long marching to Plymouth to the best place as mentioned in your letter upon any direction from your lordship. Besides my honourable good lordship (I most humbly crave hereon if I be more forward than in duty it becomes me) for so much as there will be drawn all the most ablest & wealthiest men from their homes & leaving behind them a very weak & unable company, to which any attempt by evil disposed persons to your lordship, & divers others are busy & in action about Her Majesty's service. I can see no reason but that the sheriff, the justices of peace not having companies but should & ought to travel with their best endeavours from place to place as they shall see occasion to see the county in peace & quite free from such wicked disorders as will very ready be prone & apt to do mischief in absence of them, the which if your lordship think fit your lordship would be pleased to direct your command. I do assure your lordship it would lighten the hearts of a great many & make many men ready to perform their duties with a more resolute determination.

Edward Seymour to the Earl of Bath.

My duty unto your good lordship most humbly remembered. According unto your lordship's direction I repaired to Plymouth & had conference with Sir Ferdinando Gorges, Sir William Strode, & divers other gentlemen, then & there assembled together by your lordship's commandment, & we are of opinion (for that all intelligences hath so near a substance but especially from Captain Fenner who came from Brest, & Monsieur Sordiarts duty unto her Majesty) that the enemy will make the attempt to land upon our western coast, near Dartmouth, Plymouth, or Falmouth, or altogether as the wind shall best suit for their purpose. Therefore we have thought it fit ever referring ourselves to your lordship's pleasure, that it is very behoveful to have some companies forthwith in Plymouth, & your lordship to command the north division to repair thither with some speed, for that as I do conceive Sir Ferdinando Gorges intended to handle the enemy on their first landing then to annoy him in the fort, & therefore must at the first be better furnished with men. The companies of this country ordered to repair thither are Sir Richard Champernown's, Sir William Strode's, Mr. Cary's, Mr. Compton's, & Mr. Wyse's whom I have appointed in with his plans, & Plymouth become placed for the best for Cornwall's assistance, we thought it further meet to have some companies near Dartmouth as the remnant of my regiment is to be placed not far from Dartmouth (always the last), & Sir William Courtenay's do repair unto Dartmouth with some of his companies leaving order for the rest, & Sir Thomas Deny's to come towards us, except a countermand, so that all your forces are drawn to two heads, ready to defend those places the three repaired unto & near together to be drawn any where your lordship shall think fit. If this course like your lordship, I humbly pray your lordship to signify so much forthwith unto Sir William Courtenay, farther entreating your lordship that since Sir George Cary is not here that Mr. Knolles may follow such directions as Sir W. Courtenay & myself shall give him either for the defence of Torbay or to assist Dartmouth as invasion shall be offered & farther to be disposed as your lordship shall please. Sir R. Champernowne was not in Plymouth during my stay there, neither from Tuesday at ten o'clock until this day two of the clock, to which effect I think Sir Ferdinando hath or I am assured will advertise you of as much as this my letter doth report. Dated the 1st of August, 1599.

E. S.

Edward Seymour to the Mayor of Dartmouth.

Good Mr. Mayor,
The present yielding occasion to try the obedience & loyalty of each subject to his sovereign, love to his country, & unfeigned kindness to his friends, I find by the relation of Mr. Edward Giles who of late hath been with you that you, your Brethren, & townsmen are most willing to yield a true testimony of all these in very ample manner, assuring you for my part I cannot but take

it in very kind part & will not fail to acquaint my Lord Lieutenant therewith, whom I will entreat also as he shall find occasion to signify so much to her Majesty & the Lords of the Council, showing both your willingness & charge in accomplishing anything that shall be thought fit for the advancement of this Her Highness's service. The companies appointed by Mr. Giles to be with you tomorrow cannot come until the next day by reason that Sir W. Courtenay could not have notice from my Lord Lieutenant in time convenient, but on Saturday night next myself will not fail (God willing) to be with you also & not omit to take any pains & care that shall be thought meet & requisate for the safety of your town & selves & country as the necessity of the time & place shall require. I would entreat you to provide a convenient lodging for myself, & another for Sir W. Courtenay, & a stable for me for some six geldings. And so praying you to be careful for the providing of all things necessary within your town for the defeat of the enemy, which friendly hath been required of you, do in haste with my commendations commit you to the protection of the Almighty. From Berry castle, the 2nd of August, 1599.

E. S.

The Earl of Bath to Edward Seymour, Esq.

Good cousin Seymour,

I have received your letter this very minute being Thursday the second of August about two of the clock in the afternoon & have thoroughly considered of the particulars thereof which I find to be more large & effectual than those I received from Sir Ferdinando Gorges & the rest, & will for the present time leave to enlarge any more touching these affairs because I am with God's favour to take my journey towards Plymouth tomorrow next being Friday, & to be at Tavistock on Saturday at the furthest, where all the troop of horse for this part of the country do meet me & the two regiments appertaining to Sir Robert Bassett & my cousin Pollard are also appointed to be at Roughborough the same day if possibly they can. I have also sent unto Sir W. Courtenay & Mr. Drake for those regiments of the eastern to march onward to the place of rendezvous, by former orders appointed, & not to stay but to proceed on towards Plymouth until they shall have further direction from me to the contrary, all which I have done before the receipt of your letter. And touching Sir George Cary's regiment whereof Mr. Bamfield is Lieutenant Colonel, my pleasure is that the same as well by Mr. Reynell as the other Captains thereunto belonging shall follow such directions as Sir W. Courtenay & you shall or any of you shall set down for the defence & best furtherance of the service until they hear further from me to the contrary.

Wherewith I pray you to acquaint them presently having no time myself to write to them in particular by reason of my other despatches. And so with my hearty commendations commit you to God. From Towstock, the 2nd of August, 1599.

Your very loving cousin & friend,

W. BATHON.

Sir William Courtenay to Edward Seymour, Esqr.

Cousin Seymour,

I have made stay this night of Captain Drake at Chidley who is to be directed by you & me to what place he is to make his repair. I think it necessary we give him warrant to make his repair either for Dartmouth or Torbay, which of those places you think fittest. Draw the warrant & send it me with expedition & I will join with you & convey it forthwith to Chidley, where he will stay & expect our answer till eight of the clock in the morning. So I commit you to God. Newton this evening, 4th of August, 1599.

Yours as his one,

W. COURTENAY.

Edward Seymour Esqr. to the Justices.

Although I have very often required of you that the watches of the beacons & other places on the coast should be very carefully seen unto by the officers next adjoining, yet I have thought good now, upon the dismissing of the companies, to put you in mind thereof again & in her Majesty's name straightly charge you & every of you that according to former directions all the beacons within your hundred & other places now commanded be watched & warded & be duly & orderly done by men of good discretion & carefully seen unto by some constables or other officers next adjoining as you in your discretion for this purpose shall think most fit, & if default be made of any person or persons whatsoever either in not watching or neglecting his duty in watching, or by the constable or officer which is appointed to visit the same watches, that then upon notice thereof had, you do acquaint me with their several offence forthwith to the intent they may severely receive such several punishment for the same as the importunity of the service & the laws in such cases afford. Hereof fail not you, as you & every of you will answer your contempt at your uttermost Perills. Dartmouth the 19th of August, 1599.

E. S.

Sir Robert Cecil to Edward Seymour, Esqr.

Sir, I have received a letter from you dated the 14th. of June, whereby I find you have a desire to continue the same affection toward me, that it seems you have borne hitherto to my Lord my Father, which I do very thankfully accept, with this desire, that as occasion serves you would make me partaker of such material Spanish advices as come to your hands, whereof I have received some already, in your letter wherein was contained the examination of one Buggon, assuring you that your letters shall be very welcome to me, & for requital of your kindness you shall ever find me,

Your very assured friend,
RO. CECYLL.

Edward Seymour, Esqr. to the Constables.

Having at this instant received letters for the speedy preparation of all horse for service to be in readiness to repair to any place of descent upon occasion of service. These are therefore in Her Majesty's name straightly to will & require you with all possible speed to give notice to all gentlemen & others set to any horse or geldings for service within your hundred that they have them ready in their stables, together with their furnitures & men to serve with them so as they may repair to any place of service upon an hours warning. Hereof fail not as you will answer your neglect at your perils. Given this second of August at 9 o'clock in the forenoon, 1602.

2 K

APPENDIX J.

Lord Bath to Edward Seymour, Esqr.

5 September, 1595.

After our very hearty commendations. Whereas it hath pleased the Lords of Her Majesty's Privy Council to appoint unto you such numbers of men and furnitures of armour and weapons as did in times past appertain to the charge of Sir John Gilbert, Knight, one of the Colonels for this county of Devon. We have in regard to their lordships directions in that behalf thought it good to commend unto your special charge and government all and every of the said companies of men as well the trained as untrained; and so far forth as in us doth consist, do appoint and authorise you one of the Colonéls for this county of Devon and in that part of the shire to have the regiment of the same in as ample manner as the said Sir John Gilbert have in times past had and according to their lordships late letter touching the division of the said companies in all respects for the nearest and most ready convenience of all services which shall be required from time to time hereafter for the defence of the country. And so praying you to have regard to the discharge of that which in this behalf is requisite as well for your own particular band as others which do appertain to the said regiment in general, and likewise to be assistant from time to time for the mustering and viewing of all the forces of that part of the country as occasion is now and hereafter shall be required for the better advancement of her majesty's service. We committeth you to the protection of Almighty God, the 5th. of September, 1595.

Your assured loving friends,

W. BATHON,

W. COURTENAY, JOHN GILBERT,
GEORGE CARY.

for Mr. Edward Seymour, Esqr.

Edward Seymour to Lord Bath.

15th July, 1596.

My humble duty unto your good lordship. Whereas it pleased the right honble. the lords of her majesty's most honourable Privy Council, that Sir Ferdinando Gorges should view, muster and train all those trained companies which heretofore were appointed for the Guard of Plymouth. And therefore your lordship with the assistance of those of your lordships the deputy lieutenants, Sir William Courtenay, Sir George Gilbert and Mr. Cary gave direction that my cousin Champernown with his trained band of 200 should by fifties muster and train them at Plymouth before the said Sir Ferdinando Gorges and so the rest of the captains to follow in order with their trained bands. My cousin Champernown hath sent most of his trained band there, but intruding upon me in sending thither divers companies of my untrained men said lying in Tavistock and Lyston hundred and other places, and keepeth back his own trained band of 200 contrary to my lords of the council's order and contrawise unto your lordship's directions. These courses of my cousin's doth breed great confusion and are repugnant to your lordship's directions wherein I humbly pray your good lordship to write me so far that I may not be wronged in that their lordships and your goodness imposed on me, which is Sir John Gilbert's trained bands and his colonelship. I would as in duty it becometh me have waited on your lordship but the Assizes being so near at hand and some other accidents not unknown to your lordship deferreth me to forbear my coming unto you for a time, yet humbly praying your lordship to right me in those apparent wrongs that are offered me as your lordship may very well perceive, I have sent your lordship a note how my untrained companies are furnished with weapons which I could not do so safely as others by reason of those disorders that my cousin Champernown offered me, which I hope by your lordship's authority shall be restrained; and so resting at your lordship's devotion I cease to trouble your lordship any further. Berry Castle this 15th. of July, 1596.

Your lordship's at command,

EDWARD SEYMOUR.

The Earl of Bath to Edward Seymour, Esq.

Cousin Seymour,

I have at length received a letter from you and the rest of my deputies which I expected somewhat sooner. And for the composition which I made between you and my Cousin Champernown of the contrawise so long depending (and whereof now as you write unto me he misliketh of and disclaimeth) I can assure you I did forthwith acquaint my lords of the Council with my doings in that behalf, which I am persuaded their lordships do take in very good part. But howsoever it be I like not of his variable dealings with me therein. And albeit I can be content many times to bear an indifferent hand in matters of contention when the same

2 K 2

doth happen between my good friends, yet having myself once concluded a controversy, it shall be well known to him or any man else that I will rather hazard my friend than lose mine honour. And therefore I do pray and require you (whatsoever you hear from him to the contrary) to proceed and to prepare your regiment in perfect readiness according to the orders agreed upon at Oke-hampton and your doing therein I will be always ready to justify. I will take no notice from you of his dislike to obey the order I then made, but when he shall signify the same unto me I will show him a piece of my mind, which shall not be much to his liking. And I much marvel that he should so write unto you considering that according to the said orders he hath taken possession of the office of Colonel of the horse and given his warrant for the same throughout the whole county as I am informed. And so praying you to advertise me by way of post, what you shall further hear from him, or anything else that may concern the state of the country, or Her Majesty's service. I heartily commit you to God. From Tavistock the 8th. of December, 1596.

Your loving friend and kinsman,
W. BATHON.

Postscript. Since the writing hereof I have thought good to write unto my Cousin Champernown in such sort as this bringer your servant can inform you.

Arthur Champernown to the Deputy Lieutenants.

Gentlemen,
   I answered unto certain articles which you certified their lord-ships against me, and am now desirous to satisfy you in the same. In the latter end of your first article you affirm that I being to have my commission of Sergeant Major under your hands for the better executing the said office, I utterly refuse the same protesting with great vehemency not to accept of my commission, etc. To this I answer that yourselves thoroughly agreed that I should have my commission drawn after a form of commission which Sir Thomas Acton showed before you, the which agreement you can-not deny, and yet notwithstanding my commission was drawn with contrary additions, unprecedented before in any other com-mission by any that know the wars, the which I refuse but not all other commissions and therefore you have wronged me in putting your hand unto this certifying and justifying before their lordships of a known untruth. As for your other three articles, and especially for your fourth, I have sent you my answer which I presented unto their lordships which shall be justified. But gentlemen, whereas you used me with very hard, bitter and dis-graceful terms unto their lordships in writing and your title of

undutiful miscarriage and demeanor of Mr. Arthur Champernown, then in your fourth article nominating me of a very uneven and intemperant behaviour and unseemly speeches and great vehemency of choler and of a jesture of countenance far unseeming the place and presence; speaking words to the disgrace of the lord senior lieutenant etc. and that their lordships shall be made farther acquainted with my inconsiderate proceeding in that behalf: I must tell you in regard of my own reputation that though you as it seems by your proceedings with me and others would make it a higher matter of ordinary and easy discretion unto a gentleman to suffer himself on no just cause but on any your humour or fancies to be complained of unto their honours with disgraceful terms as though there were no reckoning to be made of their honours good opinion. Yet understand by these that I desire not to live longer than it may be in their honours good conceits of my well doing, and therefore whoso shall or will justify these said disgraceful speeches of me, I hold him as a robber of my reputation and a liar and will maintain the same as it shall best beseem a gentleman.

By me
ARTHUR CHAMPERNOWN.

August 1598.

Edward Seymour to the Lords of the Council.

My humble duty unto your good Lordships. Whereas it pleased your Lordships upon the special suit and information of my cousin Champernown to direct your letters unto my lord of Bath, Her Majesty's lieutenant of this county of Devon, you there said Mr. Champernown might have a full regiment in like sorts as other Deputy Lieutenants, or, as for others that are no Deputy Lieutenants, which he desires may be allotted unto him out of some hundred which lies in my division and out of such as I raise my own regiment, some time since Sir John Gilbert's and now by your good lordships assigned unto me; hereupon it hath pleased my Lord of Bath according to your lordships pleasures to call me before him and to acquaint me with Mr. Champernown's information, requiring my answer to every point thereof, which as it becomes me in duty and to the truth I have done, which I think his honour will make known unto your lordships, hoping of your lordships good and favourable acceptance thereof for this whole county being divided into three divisions and some Colonels in every division already appointed and each of them having 800 in his regiment divided into bands under several Captains with their plans of discipline, and how they are to be diffused and relieved as occasions of service shall require upon any attempt of the enemy,

as by the muster rolls of the which forms of this county is certified unto your lordships correction. If Mr. Champernown (who
is a Deputy Lieutenant as I suppose in Sir Francis Drake's room
who had neither regiment or band) should obtain of your lordships
a third regiment to be raised out of my division, there are neither
men nor arms sufficient, it would be overburdensome to the
country and disorder the forces that are settled to good purpose for
the defence of the same, and further if it shall please your good
lordships as serving by Mr. Champernown's information there, he
desireth to have a regiment out of my division and that I might
have the hundred of Haytor, which is Mr. Carey's, to make a
regiment complete. But Mr. Carey dwelling in the hundred of
Haytor, hard adjoining Torbay, a principal place of defence, and
the defence thereof heretofore by your lordships specially committed to him, under your lordships reformation is unwilling to
yield thereunto, for then as he allegeth his chiefest and only force
to defend that place are to be raised within the hundred of
Haytor. And so submitting myself and all other matters to your
lordships honourable consideration, do cease to trouble your lordships any further.

Your lordships always to command,

EDWARD SEYMOUR.

August 1598.

The Earl of Bath to the Lords of the Council.

My humble duty to your good lordships remembered. This
may be to advertise you that I have received your lordships letter
dated the 15th of July last by a servant of mine whom I commanded to wait upon your lordships, touching the information
given by me and my deputies against my cousins, Richard
Champernown and Arthur Champernown his brother, for the
miscarriage of themselves in their places to the hindrance and
impeachment of Her Majesty's service as by the same information
truly made, hath appeared unto your lordships. But I am sorry
my good lords that for the maintenance of Her Majesty's authority
committed unto me and mine own honour I shall be again
enforced to have recourse unto your lordships concerning the contents of those your letters : the which to accomplish will be in
some points both prejudicial to Her Majesty's service and contra-
dictory to divers orders made upon good consideration and general
liking of all with allowance of the same by divers from your lordships. However Mr. Champernown out of his particular doth at
this present disallow thereof, and my trust is that your lordships
will not now be pleased to persuade me for the satisfying of his
private desire to alter the same and especially touching the two

hundreds of Ernie and Plympton to be committed unto my said Cousin Champernown unless he will hold the said hundreds as parcel of the regiment now commanded by my cousin Seymour; otherwise his example will give other gentlemen of his rank a plain occasion to expect the like and so work a general confusion in the state and affairs of the country whereby your lordships shall never be out of trouble, nor we ever certain what course to hold; neither will there be any likelihood or possibility for me to make an atonement or general agreement between gentlemen of equal qualities, of public orders by common consent made for particular respects be altered.

Further how your lordships last favour extended unto some of them may appear to have been abused, I have herewith sent unto you a challenge from Mr. Arthur Champernown unto my deputies delivered at the Public Assizes, at what time they were by my directions in conference concerning Her Majesty's service depending upon the office of lieutenancy, of which I being made acquainted by my servant then present who perceived in them a disposition of private revenge, sent particularly unto every one of them requiring them upon their allegiance to forbear all in any of such proceedings in that behalf until your lordships might be well acquainted therewith, which I thought it my duty to do as also to give notice of the great inconvenience and mischief that might thereof follow if by your lordships authority and wisdom it shall not in time be prevented and have for the present time assured both them and myself that your lordships will be pleased as in consideration of me and them in our several authorities under Her Majesty's to give such satisfaction as shall be fit for the maintenance of the same. How near this challenge of his doth extend to myself I leave likewise to your honourable consideration and so do humbly take my leave of your good lordships.

From Tawstock, the 14th. of August, 1598,
Your lordships most humble to command,
W. BATHON.

I thought it likewise good to advertise your lordships that I sent for Mr. Arthur Champernown to make him repair unto me with a purpose to take bond of him for his appearance before your lordships, but he does not come unto me as I did expect he would; what the cause thereof is I do not yet know.

The Earl of Bath to his Deputy Lieutenants.

After my very hearty commendations. I have from the time of your last being with me at Tawstock expected to hear from my lords of the Council concerning the contents of my letters, written unto them by your consent in answer to theirs touching my cousin Champernown, and now I have received another letter of their lordships in answer to my former letter, a true copy whereof I do send unto you. You may perceive their lordships meaning is not to have their course to be altered touching Mr. Richard Champernown, which they had set down upon hearing the cause between me and him as you shall more largely perceive by these their same letters; and it hath likewise pleased their lordships upon knowledge taken of the respectless and undutiful behaviour of Mr. Arthur Champernown to send a message for him to answer his doings in that behalf: so have I thought it good both to acquaint you therewith and to pray and require you with all convenient speed you may to assemble yourselves and to consider of all the particulars contained in these their lordships letters, and to resolve with yourselves what is further meet and convenient for me and you to do in every these causes, and thereof to certify me that I may allow and approve the same, and as to that part which doth specially concern Mr. Richard Champernown, I take it that your cousin Seymour are chiefly interested therein by reason of your place and charge of Colonelship, whereupon this controversy began to grow. My desire is therefore that you with the advice of the rest will consider what is most fittest for yourself to do in this case and so to proceed accordingly. For Mr. Arthur Champernown I also pray that you will collect so many particulars of his latest abuses towards me and yourselves as shall be material for their lordships to know. And so looking to hear from you with all expedition I bid you heartily farewell. From Tawstock the 8th. of September 1598.

Your very loving cousin and friend,
W. BATHON.

I have also herewith sent you the copy of my former, the copy of Arthur Champernown's letter and the copy of R. Champernown's letter. I answered Mr. R. Champernown's servant by word of that I had signified my mind unto my Lords of the Council, and for Arthur Champernown I sent no answer at all.

APPENDIX K.

There is some doubt as to what became of this John Seymour. The majority of Peerages and other authorities concur in stating that he died without issue, and there seems a strong probability of this being correct. From the State Papers of the time, John Seymour appears to have become a Captain in the Navy, for on Aug. 17, 1626, we find the Duke of Buckingham writing to the Commissioners of the Navy to recommend Captain John Seymour for payment at the rate of 2s. 6d. per day, that officer having been lately employed in the fleet as Captain of the Cameleon. The following year we find Sir Edward Seymour, of Berry Pomeroy, making an application on his behalf that he should be given a good ship in the forthcoming expedition. From a certificate, dated Jan. 17, 1638–9, which he sends "from my house at Larkham," and from another, dated Jan. 19, he appears to have then been a Deputy Lieutenant of the county of Devon, while from a third, dated Jan. 30, in the same year, he appears also to have been Lieutenant Colonel of Sir Edward Seymour's regiment in Devon. (State Papers, Dom., Charles I.)

Playfair's Baronage, however (which is stated to be correct by the present Sir Michael Culme-Seymour), states that this John Seymour went to Ireland and there founded a family, of which Sir Michael Culme-Seymour, the present Bart., is a representative. We should be glad if this descent could be placed beyond the shadow of any doubt, for the fact of having so distinguished a younger branch would add greatly to the honour and credit of the Seymour family. The Crossley Seymours of Ireland, however, the same family, but the elder branch to the Culme-Seymours (according to the Dict. Nat. Biog.), claimed descent from Sir Henry Seymour, brother of Jane Seymour, wife of Henry VIII. This Sir Henry Seymour certainly had three sons, but, according to every authority we can find, none of these sons had any issue. The whole matter appears therefore to be wrapped in great doubt. It is possible, and indeed probable, that John Seymour may, as Playfair says, have settled in Ireland, and so we will start with his assumption, and, following various other authorities, trace the descent down to the present time.

John Seymour, the second son of Sir Edward Seymour, of Berry Pomeroy, settled (according to Playfair) in Ireland, and *there* married the sister of Sir Richard Slanning, knight, by whom he became the progenitor of five *grandsons*, four of whom survived

him, namely, John, William, Walter, and Richard. These served
at various times as Mayors and Sheriffs of the city of Limerick.
From John, the eldest *grandson*, descended the Rev. John Crossley
Seymour of Baggor Street, Dublin ; while from William, the
second *grandson*, there was only one heir, John, Rector of Palace,
in Limerick. From this point the account agrees with that of
other Peerages, who make mention of John and William, but
simply mention a John Seymour, of Limerick, as their father.

This John Seymour, whether he was or was not a son of the
John Seymour who married a sister of Sir Richard Slanning and
was brother to Sir Edward Seymour of Berry Pomeroy, at all
events resided in Limerick and was Alderman of that town and
afterwards Mayor (1720). He married Jane, daughter of Seymour
Wroughton, and, amongst other issue, left :—

> John Seymour, from whom descended the family of Crossley
> Seymour, of Castletown, Queen's County, who, as we have
> seen above, claimed descent from Sir Henry Seymour, the
> brother of Queen Jane.
> William Seymour, who married Jane, 2nd daughter of Mr.
> Alderman Edward Wight, of Limerick, by whom he had
> one son :—

John Seymour, Rector of Palace, co. Limerick, who became
Domestic Chaplain to Dr. Cox, the Archbishop of Cashel, and
afterwards became Rector of Abingdon and Chancellor of
Elmley. He married Grizelda, youngest daughter and coheir
of William Hobart, of High Mount, and died in 1795, leaving
issue :—

> William Hobart Seymour, who became an officer in the 60th
> Regiment, and was taken prisoner by the French, but soon
> after effected an almost miraculous escape from prison.
> He died in the West Indies, 1797.
> Michael Seymour, of whom we shall speak next.
> John Seymour, who became a clergyman.
> Frances Seymour, who died in 1805.
> Richard Seymour, who was killed in a naval action between
> the "Amazon," of which he was lieutenant, and the French
> ship "La Belle Poule," in March, 1806.

Michael Seymour, the second son, was born Nov. 8, 1768. He
entered the Navy in Nov., 1780, serving first in the "Merlin," a
sloop of war, and afterwards, amongst many other ships, in the
"Portland," the "Mediator," and the "Ganges" successively.
In 1782, while in the "Mediator," he took part in a very severe
action, in which his ship, of only 44 guns, attacked five French
ships, mounting between them 136 guns and carrving 637 men.

The "Mediator" succeeded in capturing two, the "Alexandre" and the "Meleager," and putting the rest to flight. In 1790 Seymour was promoted to the "Magnificent" as lieutenant, and, June 1, 1794, he took part in Lord Howe's memorable action, being then junior lieutenant on board the "Marlborough." In this action he had the misfortune to lose his left arm. In 1795 he was promoted to the rank of commander, and in 1800 was given post rank. In 1808 he commanded the "Amethyst," a 36-gun frigate, and, on Nov. 10, captured the French ship "Thetis," after one of the most desperate fights of the whole war, which lasted three hours. The enemy lost 236 men out of 436, while the "Amethyst" lost 70 out of 261. On his return home with his prize, Seymour received the gold medal, a hundred pounds from the Patriotic Fund, and was given the Freedom of the Cities of Cork and Limerick. February 8, 1809, he again distinguished himself by capturing the "Niemen," and on his return home was created a Baronet as a reward for his distinguished gallantry and conduct. Soon after this he was appointed to the command of the "Niemen," and in 1812 to the "Hannibal," of 74 guns, with which he captured "La Sultane" in 1814. The following year he was made a K.C.B., and the pension for the loss of his arm was increased to £300 a year. In 1818 he was appointed to the guardship "Northumberland"; in 1819 to the "Prince Regent," one of the Royal yachts; and in 1825 to the King's own yacht, the "Royal George." In 1829 he was made Commissioner of Portsmouth, and on that appointment being abolished he returned to active service as Commander-in-Chief in South America, 1832. In Feb., 1833, he sailed to take up this appointment at Rio, which was to be his headquarters, and the following year he contracted yellow fever, from which he died, July 9, 1834. He was buried at Rio. He had married Jane, daughter of Captain James Hawker, in 1798, by whom he left numerous issue:—

John Hobart, of whom we shall speak next.

James, a captain in the 38th Regiment, who died in 1827.

Sir Michael, G.C.B., who became a most distinguished man. An Admiral in the Navy, Vice-Admiral of the United Kingdom, Commander-in-Chief at the East India station and at Canton, Commander-in-Chief at Portsmouth, and M.P. for Devonport. He married Dora, daughter of Sir William Knighton, bart., by whom he had issue, and died in 1887.

Edward, who became a Captain in the Navy, and died in 1837.

Richard (Rev.), M.A., who became Rector of Kinwarton in Warwick and Canon of Worcester. He married Frances,

daughter of Charles Smith, of Suttons, Essex, and died
July 6, 1880, leaving issue.

William Hobart, who entered the 99th Regiment. He
married Sarah Mary Avons, of Sidney, N.S.W., by whom
he had one daughter, and died March 3, 1857.

Jane Ward, who died Aug. 30, 1862.

Frances Anne, who married Spencer Smith, of Brooklands,
in Hants, and died Feb. 2, 1897.

Dora, who married twice ; first the Rev. W. H. Clinton and
secondly Arthur Currie, of High Elms, Herts, and died
1888.

Mary Dorothea, who married Captain Gumming Sutton, R.N.,
and died March 31, 1900.

Caroline, who married Captain George Carr, and died in
1843.

Elizabeth, who married Colonel Howard Wyse, 2nd Life
Guards, and died Dec. 4, 1892.

Ellen, who married the Rev. H. B. Forster, M.A., Hon.
Canon of Glos.

Sir John Hobart Culme-Seymour, 2nd Baronet, M.A., entered
the Church and became Canon of Gloucester, Rector of Berk-
hampstead St. Mary, Chaplain in Ordinary to Queen Victoria, and
Prebendary of Lincoln. He was born March 24, 1800, and died
Sept. 17, 1880. He was twice married. First to Elizabeth,
elder of the two daughters and coheirs of the Rev. Thomas Culme,
of Tothill, Devon, by whom (who died March 6, 1841) he had
issue :—

Sir Michael Culme-Seymour, 3rd and present Bart., of whom
we will speak next.

John Hobart, late Lieutenant-Colonel in the Army, Clerk of
the Cheque and Adjutant H.M. Royal Bodyguard of Hon.
Corps Gentlemen-at-Arms. He was born Oct. 1, 1837, and
married, March 15, 1870, Mary Eliza, daughter of Richard
Hall, of Hillingdon Furze, Uxbridge, and died Nov. 10,
1887.

Elizabeth Culme, who married the Rev. J. Rawlinson, M.A.,
Rector of Bicton, Devon.

He married secondly, Feb. 10, 1844, Maria Louisa, youngest
daughter of Charles Smith of Suttons, Essex, by whom he had issue
one son and four daughters. (For names, see Burke's Peerage.)

Sir Michael Culme-Seymour, Bart., is a G.C.B. An Admiral
in the Navy. Was Commander-in-Chief in the Pacific, 1885-7.
Commander Channel Squadron 1890-2. Commander-in-Chief in
the Mediterranean, 1893-6. Commander-in-Chief at Portsmouth,
1897 to 1900. First and principal A.D.C. to Queen Victoria.

He married, Oct. 16, 1866, Mary Georgiana, elder daughter of the Hon. Richard Watson of Rockingham Castle, and has had issue :—

>   Michael, born Aug. 29, 1867, Commander R.N. ; married, April 8, 1896, Florence Agnes Louisa, daughter of Albert N. Nugent.
>   John Wentworth, born Oct. 13, 1876.
>   George, born March 8, 1878 ; a Captain in the King's Royal Rifle Corps.
>   Mary Elizabeth, born Feb. 10, 1871 ; married, Aug. 17, 1899, Commander T. D. W. Napier, R.N.
>   Laura Grace, born July 18, 1873 ; died Nov. 22, 1895.

[State Papers, Dom., Charles I. ; Dict. Nat. Biog. ; United Service Journal ; Marshall's Royal Naval Biog. ; Playfair's Baronetage ; Burke's Peerage and Baronetage ; James's Naval Hist. ; Naval Chronicle ; Forster's Baronetage ; Gent.'s Mag. &c., &c.]

APPENDIX L.

The following letters may seem of some interest in connection with Colonel Seymour's command and the Civil War.

Prince Maurice to Colonel Seymour.

Sir,
I received yours by Sir Edmund Fortescue and shall desire you to certify me what arms and munition you have in your magazine and not to dispose of any (notwithstanding my lord Piercy's order) without my consent first had and obtained, for they will be of much use here especially muskets, and so far rest sir, your friend

MAURICE.

Tavistock,
January 12, 1642.

Sir Bevill Grenville to Colonel Seymour.

Dearest brother,
You were gone before I was aware of it, I beseech God to send you a good journey and us a happier meeting. There was nothing concluded in Council after your departure, but that it was fit to follow Waller which way soever he went. I am in some doubts lest it may not be very safe for you to straggle far from the army when you come into Devon, you know their malice will exceed towards you. I would not for all the world that you should be any ways so exposed as to fall into their power. For God's sake be very circumspect. It is said that Sir William Waller moves towards Salisbury and we have orders to draw after him. I am ever,
Your most faithful servant,
BEVILL GRENVILLE.

Wells,
June 19, 1643.

Prince Maurice to Sir Edmund Fortescue and Edward Seymour, Esquire.

You shall demand in my name for His Majesty's use and service, the castle, town and blockhouse of Dartmouth, to be presently surrendered with all arms, ordinance, ensigns, ammunition, and all other warlike provisions, whatsoever. And that before the 14th. of this present month. The garrison to march out to some place as you shall agree, and you are to grant to them a free pardon, and a safe convoy if required. And you are to see all the prisoners set free before the garrison march forth; thus far you are to insist upon. But howsoever you are to conclude upon these or accidental conditions besides what are here specified for the best advantage of His Majesty's service. And for so doing this shall be your warrant. Given at Exon under my hand and seal at arms, this the 10th. of September, 1643.

MAURICE.

Prince Maurice to Edward Seymour, Esq.

Sir,
    You are immediately upon sight hereof to get carriages in a readiness and to send away with all speed all the powder which was in the Dunkirk frigate and match proportionable; you are likewise to send away the men you speak to me of, to be at Plympton with all haste. Hereof you are not to fail as you tender His Majesty's service. Given at Whitely the 4th. of December, 1643.

MAURICE.

To
    Edward Seymour, Esq.,
        Governor of Dartmouth.

King Charles to Colonel Edward Seymour.

Charles R.
    Trusty and well beloved we greet you well. Whereas by reason of the disorders occasioned by this unnatural rebellion, our customs and duties in the several ports have not been duly answered and paid unto us for goods exported and imported. And that the necessity of our affairs doth require the same should be duly answered unto us and exactly managed for our best advantage, which cannot be if the officers and collectors in our said ports shall be interrupted in that service, and not aided and assisted by our superior orders and governors there, or that the monies so collected should be by any means diverted from such uses as the Lord Treasurer and our under Treasurer shall from time to time direct and appoint. We have therefore thought fitting, and do hereby straightly charge and command you that upon all occasions for that our service, you be aiding and assisting unto such our servants and ministers as shall be appointed for that

our service in those ports and creeks whereof you are now Governor, and not to intermeddle in the disposing or diverting of any of those monies which shall be due and collected from the merchants for duties inward and outward. And herein we require you to be very careful as that which very nearly concerns our service. Given at our court at Oxford this day of December, 1643.

By His Majesty's command,
EDWARD NICHOLAS.

Sir R. Grenville to Colonel Seymour.

Sir,
I am very thankful for your honourable letter now received, as also for many other favours. I am very glad to understand you are willing to spare us 300 of your men against Plymouth ; I have therefore now written to Col. Digby, to engage him so much as I can, to importune the Prince by his letter to send unto you an order for the bringing of 300 of your men to join with Sir John Grenville's trained soldiers, to possess the quarters about St. Budeaux, as also to allow us the use of three brass pieces of field ordnance, which you have to spare at Dartmouth, wherein I hope to obtain my desire of your company.

Sir, I am now raising a regiment of horse for the advancement of His Majesty's service, both against Plymouth and wherever else they may be employed, and must therefore pray you will please to give present order that the bearer hereof George Balcher, my quartermaster, may have delivered unto him for His Majesty's service all the pistols and carbines that can be gotten and procured at Dartmouth, wherein you may very much advantage His Majesty's service and infinitely oblige me.

Your most humble servant,
R. GRENVILLE.

Fitzford,
April 24, 1644.

Prince Maurice to Colonel Seymour.

Sir,
I shall desire you to speed your regiments marching to me as much as possible you can, and to return to your regiment such stragglers as you may happily meet with on your march, which is all for the present from, Sir, your friend,

MAURICE.

Before Lyme,
May 7, 1644.

Prince Maurice to Colonel Seymour.

Sir,

Weymouth being taken and the rebels as I am informed intending to attempt something against your garrison, I thought good to advertise you thereof, that your care and watchfulness may timely prevent their wicked purposes. I have writ to Col. Carey to be watchful on the sea coast. This is all but that I am, sir, your loving friend,

MAURICE.

Honington,
    June 19, 1644.

Sir Ames Ameridath to Colonel Seymour.

22 June, 1644.

Brother,

The daily alarms I have here by reason of the Parliament ships, remaining at the mouth of our harbour, has prevented my waiting on you with this enclosed, and made me dispatch this bearer Captain Moss to you, earnestly entreating you would give order these 4 guns (Demi-culverin) if you cannot possibly spare six, may be sent to Tottness with all speed where there will be carts and ploughs for the bringing them hither, seeing it impossible to have them by sea, I shall entreat for a proportionable quantity of great shot, for I have not any, if no other guns and shot but what Captain Wade had, I pray let those be sent. It is doubted Essex will look this way suddenly, and Warwick, I believe, this spring, which if before these guns should be here, I doubt how this place will be kept which sure is of very great consequence, and which I hope will invite you to use power herein and it will very much oblige,

Your very faithful brother and servant,
    AMES AMERIDATH.

From the Fort this 22nd June, 1644.
    My affectionate service to my sister.

Generals Fairfax, Manchester, and others to the Earl of Warwick.

5 July, 1644.

May it please your Lordship,

That we may acquaint you with our present condition our late proceedings and our resolutions for the future. We have thought it fitting to make use of this opportunity and to let you know that on Monday last upon notice of Prince Rupert's march from Knasborough towards us, we resolved and accordingly drew out the

armies to have met him, and for that end did march the same
night to Long Marston Moor about four miles on the west side of
York, but he having notice thereof did pass with his army at
Barrow Bridge and so put the river Ouse betwixt him and us
whereby we were disabled to oppose his passage into York, the
bridge we built on the west side of the town being so weak that
we durst not adventure to transport our armies upon it.   This
made us resolve the next morning to march into Todcastle for
the stopping of his passage southwards, and the armies being so
far on their way as the van was within a mile of it, notice was
sent us by our horsemen who were upon our rear, that the Prince's
army, horse and foot, were advanced the length of Long Marston
Moor and were ready to fall upon them whereupon we recalled
the armies and drew them up on a cornhill upon the southwest
side of the moor in the best ways we could so far as the straight-
ness of the field and other disadvantages of the place would permit.
Before both armies were in readiness it was near seven o'clock at
night, about which time they advanced the one towards the other,
whereupon followed a very hot encounter for the space of three
hours, whereof by the great blessing and good providence of God
the issue was, the total routing of the enemy's army, the loss of all
their ordnance to the number of 20 pieces, their ammunition,
baggage, about 100 colours and ten thousand arms.   There were
killed upon the place about 3,000 of them, whereof many are chief
officers and 1,500 prisoners taken, among whom there are about
100 officers in which number is Sir Charles Lucas, Lieutenant
General of the Marquis of Newcastle's horse,—and General Major
Tilley, besides divers Colonels, Lieutenant Colonels, and Majors.
Our loss God be praised is not very great, being only of one
Lieutenant Colonel, some few Captains, and about two or three
hundred common soldiers.   The Prince in great distraction with a
few horsemen and almost no foot marched the next morning from
York 'northwards.   We have now lain down again in our old
leaguer before York, which we are in hopes within a few days to
gain and are resolved to send a great part of our cavalry after the
Prince.   We rest your lordship's affectionate friends and servants,

                              LEVEN   FAIRFAX
                         LINDSEY   MANCHESTER
                   THOMAS HATCHER.

From the Leaguer before York
        July 5, 1644.

                    Sir R. Grenville to Colonel Seymour.
Sir,
        His Highness hath commanded away the greatest part of the
foot from hence and hath sent in their stead only the Queen's

regiment of horse which were at the first not above 300 and since many of them run away and the rest being discontent, are expected daily to be drawn from us, and if so then we must of necessity draw off to a larger distance from the town, which will be of ill consequence for the country, unless we have a supply of more foot. Therefore I shall earnestly request you to speed hither two or three hundred of your foot, to strengthen our guard and so I rest your servant,

                                        R. GRENVILLE.

From Plympton,
    July 19, 1644.

Sir,
    The enemy being now abroad seeking their fortune gives me not leave to enlarge as I intended.

Sir Francis Fulford to Colonel Seymour.

Noble Sir,
    This unhappy news puts us into such a straight that we know not what to do. I had resolved once to have gone to Exon, but doubting the dangers we might meet with on the way, I had resolved to come under your protection. Therefore I shall desire you will be pleased to procure me a house for myself and company for which purpose I have sent this messenger, and for this and all other your favours I shall ever rest your assured friend and kinsman to serve you,

                                        FRANCIS FULFORD.

July 22, 1644.

Sir E. Fortescue to Col. Seymour.

My dearest friend,
    Presently upon the receipt of your letter, I addressed myself to His Majesty and made known to him your just, fair, and most necessary desires, his reply to me was that he wished the thing done, but now he could not possibly spare any horse or foot for the redemption of those parts from those perjured devils that now are in them. But with this I did not rest satisfied but with fury made it known to some of my friends who with zeal in the business again assaulted the King for a supply, but his answer was the same to them as he formerly gave me; after which I met with Sir Thomas Hele and then we joined forces and went at it again, but the King was semper idem; and yet we did not despair but, almost disheartened, at last we delivered all to the Lord Hopton, who was tender of it, and promised to do his utmost for our

endeavours; who after much discourse with His Majesty at last plainly told us that till this argument was thoroughly disputed with Essex, no man could have a Placet. This made me almost mad and then, having a dish of claret, I hastily chirp'd your help, and another to the fair Lady Governess, and then again to the noble Governor on top, and after some few rounds as long as the French spirits lasted, in a merry and undeniable humour, I went to Maurice, of whom I had good words and promises which again were assured me by Wagstaff, one that loves you, and I am confident I shall prevail very speedily for some horse, either Sir Thomas Hele's or Sir Henry Carey's regiment. Sir, nothing shall be neglected by me in which I may do you service, Ralph can tell you that in the prosecution of it I was near a mischance on a rotten bridge near the court where we are, and what we do I shall leave to honest Ensign Hemmerson's relation. This is the last act of the play, God grant that each man may do his part well. My most humble and ever best services shall attend you, your fair lady, and yours. This is the unalterable resolution of your ever constant and most faithful servant,

E. FORTESCUE.

From the army near the rebels,
August 23, 1644.

APPENDIX M.

Francis Seymour succeeded his brother, Popham, in the large estates which had been left to him by Edward, Earl Conway, in 1683. Succeeding thus in 1669, Francis Seymour took the name of Conway. He served in Parliament as member for Bramber in 1701 and 1702, and, in 1703, was raised to the Peerage, out of compliment to his father, by the title of Baron Conway of Ragley in Warwick, and of Kilultagh in Antrim, Ireland. In 1723 he was made a Privy Councillor for Ireland, and, 1728, was appointed Governor of Carrickfergus. He died Feb. 1736, having been married three times. By his first wife, a daughter of the Earl of Rochester, he had four daughters. By his second he had no issue. By his third, Charlotte, daughter of Sir John Shorter, Lord Mayor of London, he had two sons and one daughter. He was succeeded by his eldest son :—

Francis Seymour Conway, born in 1719. He succeeded his father as Baron Conway in 1736, and, Aug. 3, 1750, was created Viscount Beauchamp and Earl of Hertford, which titles had become extinct in the Seymour family on the death, without issue, of Algernon, 7th Duke of Somerset. In 1751 he was made a Lord of the Bedchamber, and in 1757 installed as a Knight of the Garter, and appointed Lord-Lieutenant and Custos Rotulorum of the county of Warwick. He was sworn of the Privy Council in 1763, and soon afterwards was sent to France as Ambassador Extraordinary. In 1766 he was Lord-Lieutenant of Ireland, and was appointed Master of the Horse and Lord Chamberlain of his Majesty's household. July 3, 1793, he was created Marquis of Hertford and Earl of Yarmouth in Norfolk. He died June 14, 1794. He had married, in 1741, Isabella, daughter of the 2nd Duke of Grafton, and by her had seven sons and six daughters. He was succeeded by his eldest son :—

Francis Seymour, Earl of Yarmouth (better known as Viscount Beauchamp), was born Feb. 12, 1743. He supported the King's train at the Coronation, Sept. 22, 1761. He entered Parliament as member for Lostwithiel, in Cornwall, in 1766; and from 1768 to 1794 sat in the Commons as member for Orford. On the death of his father he was called to the House of Lords as Marquis of Hertford. He was appointed a Lord of the Treasury in 1774 and held that office till 1780. In 1804 he was appointed Master of the Horse, but resigned in 1806. He was sworn of the Privy Council about this time. He died in 1822. He had married twice; first, Feb. 1, 1768, Alicia, second daughter and coheir of the late Viscount Windsor, by whom he had a daughter, who died in infancy; secondly, Isabella Anne Ingram, daughter and coheir of Charles, Viscount Irvine, of the Peerage of Scotland. On that nobleman's death he succeeded to a great deal of his property, and, by royal license, added the name and arms of Ingram to his own. Hertford's fortune at his death was computed at £90,000 a year. By his second wife he had one son, who succeeded him :—

Francis Charles Seymour Conway, born March 11, 1777. He entered Christchurch College, Oxford, in 1794 and subsequently removed to St. Mary Hall, where he took the degree of M.A., Nov. 14, 1814. In 1798 he was returned to Parliament as member for Orford, in Sussex. From 1802 to 1812 he sat for Lisburne, and from 1812 to 1820 for the county of Antrim. For the next two years he represented Camelford, and only left that constituency on being called to the House of Lords, on the death of his father, in 1822. In Sept. 1809, he was mixed up in a duel, in which he acted as second to his cousin Lord Castlereagh, who was fighting Mr. Canning. In 1810 the large possessions he already owned were increased by his succeeding to the greater part of the eccentric Duke of Queensberry's personal property—this Duke being the putative father of his wife. In 1811, during the discussion on the Regency, he strongly advocated giving a more extended power to the Prince of Wales, and was soon after appointed Vice-Chamberlain to the Royal household, his father being Lord Chamberlain. This appointment he resigned in Aug. 1812, on being appointed to the more lucrative post of Lord Warden of the Stanneries, soon after which he was made a Privy Councillor. On the visit of the Allied Sovereigns to England, he was appointed to attend the Emperor Alexander, and was in constant attendance on that monarch during his stay in this country. As a reward he received the order of St. Anne from Alexander. Nov. 22, 1822, he succeeded his father, and was made soon after a Knight of the Garter. In 1827 he went as Ambassador Extraordinary to convey the Garter to the Emperor Nicholas. On this occasion he sailed in the Briton, and made such a lavish and magnificent display that he created a sensation even in that Court, which was generally considered to outshine all others in Europe. The Marquis died March 1, 1842. He had married, May 18, 1798, Maria Fagniani, the reputed daughter of William, 4th Duke of Queensberry. By her he had two sons and one daughter, and was succeeded by the eldest :—

Richard, 4th Marquis of Hertford, who was born February 22, 1800. He began his career in the Army, in which he served as Captain, but did not remain in it after his father's death, soon after which he was made a Knight of the Garter. He died, unmarried, August 25, 1870, and was succeeded by his cousin :—

Francis George Hugh, 5th Marquis of Hertford, born February 11, 1812. He commenced his career in the Army, and rose to be a General. He was appointed Equerry to the Prince Consort, Groom-in-Waiting to Queen Victoria, Deputy Ranger of Windsor Great Park, and Lord Chamberlain from 1874–1879. He was a G.C.B., and P.C.D.L. for the county of Warwick. On May 9, 1839, he married Lady Emily Murray, daughter of William, 3rd Earl of Mansfield, by whom he had four sons and six daughters. He died January 25, 1884. His children were :—

Hugh de Grey, the present marquess.

Albert Charles, m. Sarah, d. of Capt. John Moore Napier, and died March 24, 1891, leaving issue.

Ernest James, m. Lady Georgina Seymour Fortescue, and has issue.

Victor Alexander, m. Elizabeth Margaret Cator, and has issue.

Frederica Georgina, d. Jan. 12, 1848.

Horatia Elizabeth, m. Henry David Erskine, and has issue.

Florence Catharine, m. Rev. James St. John Blunt, M.A.

Georgina Emily Lucy, m. Lt.-Col. H. E. Stirling-Home-Drummond.

Constance Adelaide, m. Lt.-Col. F. St. John Barne, and has issue.

Mary Margaret, m. Sir George John Egerton Dashwood, and has issue.

The present Marquess, Hugh de Grey Seymour, married April 16, 1868, the Hon. Mary Hood, 2nd daughter of Viscount Bridport, and has issue :—

George Francis Alexander, Earl of Yarmouth, born Oct. 20, 1871.

Henry Charles, Lieutenant Grenadier Guards, born May 18, 1878.

Edward Beauchamp, born Nov. 22, 1879.

George Frederick, R.N., born Sept. 2, 1881.

Margaret Alice, born March 22, 1869, m. James Hamsworth Ismay, and has issue.

Emily Mary, born Aug. 4, 1873, m. Rev. Reginald Walker.

Victoria Frederica Wilhelmina Georgina, born Oct. 20, 1874, m. Charles Alan Cathcart de Trafford.

Jane Edith, born April 1, 1877.

[Collins's Peerage ; Burke's Peerage ; Playfair's Baronetage ; Sharpes' Peerage ; Nicholas's Synopsis, ed. Courthorpe ; Dict. Nat. Biog. ; Gent.'s Mag. ; Annual Register, 1822, 1842 ; Bromley's Cat., engraved portraits, etc.]

APPENDIX N.

Samuel John, Esqr., to Edward Seymour, Esqr., 1749.

. . . . Your brother & I have been to our counsel this day, & I believe will satisfy you that every thing that can be done hath been so as expeditious at least as is consistent with the necessary precaution ; for however in general people may talk, & if conducted with guarding against every possibility of an objection, it is a clear & certain right, yet I believe there are some that wish too premature an application. . . . .

The Right Honourable Henry Fox to His Grace Edward, 8th Duke of Somerset.

My Lord Duke, The King, as soon as it was mentioned to him, most readily expressed His wish that your Grace might have no difficulty, & that the Attorney's report might be altered.

The Duke of Newcastle had a meeting with the Attorney-General upon it yesterday, & Mr. Stone this morning writes me word that every thing is settled to your Grace's satisfaction.

Mr. Finch tells me that the old Duke of Somerset's robes, were immediately upon his death, sent to his son the last Duke.

It is very likely that if Lord Northumberland knew your Grace's claim was allowed, & that you were to take your seat on Thursday, he would desire the Duchess to send them to your Grace.

Lady Caroline is happy in the hopes of the Duchess, Lady Mary, & Miss Castleton's company to dinner tomorrow—your dinner shall be on the table at three, I am, with the greatest respect, my Lord,

Your Grace's most obedient & humble servant,

H. Fox.

Holland house, January 12, 1750.

Samuel John, Esq., to Edward Seymour, Esq.

April 7, 1750.

Sir,

After I sent my letter, I heard one Barclay Seymour (Lieutenant of a man-of-war) had entered a Caveat claiming the title. I have been with his Solicitor, who tells me he is quite a stranger to his client's right, and that he was gone to the Herald's Office which I find by Mr. Anstis, with whom I dined yesterday, he had done ; and that he told him, what is very plain that he had no right, and his Solicitor tells me in a day or two he will let me know what he intends to do, and if he finds his client has no right, he will not give us the trouble of going before the Attorney General which will give delay and create expense too, with which view I was afraid at first that the Caveat was entered, the same thing being done in the title of Hereford, and a sum of money extorted from the right claimant. I have received from Bradley several deeds etc. which, with what I have already, completes the pedigree of the line of Catharine. I have received from Mr. Keen the inscription from Salisbury, and expect them from Bedwin etc. next post, which I doubt not will perfect the pedigree of Anne . . . . etc., etc.

The same to the same.

April 10, 1750.

Sir,

The person who has made a claim as I wrote in my last saith he cannot give me his answer, till after the holidays, as the offices cannot be opened for him to make enquiries in the interim, 'tis impossible for him I am sure or anyone else to make a claim, and as to him I am informed he hath an elder brother's son. What I have received from Marlborough, Bedwin, and Preshute, hath I think stopped up all chinks ; however I should be glad to hear from Trowbridge, the monumental inscription of Charles, Lord Seymour, Baron of Trowbridge, buried there the 7th of September, 1665, as one of the registers which I received from Preshute this post mentions . . . . etc., etc.

The same to the same.

April 24, 1750.

(Extract.)

. . . . Captain Barkley hath not yet retracted his claim, and it is thought unnecessary and improper to summons him to show cause, till we attend the Attorney-General, etc., etc.

The same to the same.

July 12, 1750.

(Extract.)

. . . . To-morrow at seven in the evening is fixed for going through the title, and think we cannot fail of doing it. Notwithstanding I hear the sailor hath prepared a petition, though at the same time he knows not from whence to deduce his claim, and the more he knows the more he will be convinced he is deceived by one of the Herald's office, who I find by Mr. Anstis hath given him encouragement which hath occasioned his taking a journey into the west, to enquire concerning the pedigree in Lord Bruce's possession .... etc., etc.

The same to the same.

July 14, 1750.

Sir,
I have now the pleasure of writing you, what I assured you by the last post, that we have gone through everything to the satisfaction of the Solicitor-General who hath delivered me up his papers as having no further occasion for them and with this satisfactory declaration that he never saw a clearer case made out, and I think altogether as much to the satisfaction of the Attorney-General, for he did not make one objection, or seemed in any instance not to have satisfactory proof, for indeed throughout the whole two pedigrees, there is not one link wanting to unite them, made by the strictest legal proof. It was the Solicitor's resolution throughout, it should be so because it will firmly bind everything, and prevent any dispute in the House of Lords by having a clear report from the Attorney who, at our parting, bid me send the deeds, etc., to him and he would make his report, which he would not say if he was not satisfied, and ordered me to make an index or schedule by way of reference to ease him, etc.

The sailor hath struck his colours and sheered off, after he did not appear. If he came innocently as being persuaded he had a right, I pity him, for he hath, I am satisfied, been put to some expense and been a journey to find out a pedigree. If, on the contrary, he thought that he could raise money by such an interruption, he is rightly served by being turned adrift. I have wrote to Bradley to the Duke, directed in the style I think I am now bound to do, though, till the Attorney's report is made I would choose to say as little as possible in the papers, etc., etc.

The same to the same.

August 11th, 1750.

Sir,
While I was in expectation according to the Attorney-General's promise of having the report forthwith finished, as he said he would last Wednesday night, the Captain, in order to throw what impediments he can in the way; and I imagine he is only a tool of greater people, who would if they could be instrumental to deprive you of the title; presented the Attorney-

General with a petition of reference of his claim, pretending that he is descended from Henry, the son of the Duke, whereas that Henry we have shown by inquisitions to have died, as I have a little more particularly stated in mine this post to the Duke, and really the post is going, have not time to be more particular in this, and I have sent His Grace a copy of their claim which I have but just got, and by that they have made John Seymour, who was a natural son of John, the first Duke's father, and married Jane, the daughter of Nicholas Poynings, and so it appears, by the Herald's entry, only with this difference, that they call him Nicholas Poyntz. I have taken out a summons to attend on Monday at seven, and then I think we can meet with no more rubs. This you will excuse me to take notice of, that, as we have lurking enemies to throw rubs in the way, which used to accompany the dukedom, it is plain we are to expect nothing but what is got by dint of right, and consequently dint of proof; and therefore I hope will excuse the tediousness which the necessary caution against enemies renders requisite. I'll stay and get the report if it is to be had before I stir away, etc., etc.

Samuel John, Esq., to His Grace the Duke of Somerset.

August 13, 1750.

My lord Duke,

Enclosed is the answer of the Post Office to which I have given an answer as to the title—I sent to Mr. Anstis on Sunday morning, who was so kind as to come to the town on purpose yesterday morning to give me his assistance in order to detect the attempt to impose the false pedigree on the Crown. It was made out by one Warburton, Somerset Herald; he is a man of very indifferent, if not bad character; one that is not at all agreeable to His Grace of Norfolk, nor to himself, and that he would be glad of having out. We attended, however, the Attorney-General at seven and as I apprehended this Warburton would be there, by Mr. Anstis's recommendation, one Mr. Pomfret, another of the Herald's office (superior in knowledge and an honest man) attended to prevent Warburton's imposing on the Attorney as to the nature or meaning of any of the books or entries of the office. This pedigree they have trumped up is, I think, a forgery, for Warburton must know it is false, and therefore wilful, and as it cannot be supported but by oath, it must be introductive of perjury. He must know it to be false, because this very Warburton, together with Pomfret, signed the copy of the Herald's books, whereby John Seymour who married Jane, the daughter of Nicholas Poynings, which this fellow has changed to Poyntz, is made and said truly to be the natural son of John Seymour, father of the said Duke, and the other John Seymour of Marwell, if they mean him, said to be the son of Henry (brother of the Duke), and consequently not within the line of the descendants from the body of the Duke.

He was asked by the Attorney-General whether it appeared by any entry in any of the Herald's books, that Henry had any son or that John was the son of Henry, the son of the Duke, he could not say there was, nor was there the least shadow of a reason given why it could be supposed, that John was the descendent of Henry. But it being said, that, they believed that they could make it out, the Attorney said as he had received so lately an order of reference from the Crown, he was obliged to give them some time which he should not have done had it stood merely on their Caveat, and he seems thoroughly satisfied of your claim.

He hath limited them to Michaelmas next to bring in their affidavits and proofs; and will I am satisfied give them no further time. Whence springs this interruption is worth while to trace out if we can. Plain it is there are some latent enemies, and it is as plain the parties do not give your Grace this trouble merely for the sake or in expectation of any right in them, for if they had any such they would have claimed it long ago, but it is merely by way of obstruction thinking to have something given them to buy them off. But instead of giving any encouragement to such proceedings by letting them have the fruits of their designs, your Grace, for the sake of the public, will when we have, as I dare say a little time will produce it, found out the iniquity, take such notice of it as will prevent any more such practices, which tend to rob people of their rights, &c., &c.

Postscript.—Since I wrote this letter, a gentleman called on me and told me that he had met with Barkley Seymour at Charing Cross, and asking him his business in town, he said the Ministry had sent for him to make his claim to the Dukedom of Somerset, but that he was a stranger to such rights—you are extremely obliged to some folks, but your proof is so clear that you may defy them and all their works.

Samuel John, Esq., to Lord Seymour.

October 20, 1750.

My lord,

All that I can add to my last is that the broadside that the sailor received from us last Tuesday night hath made him strike his colours, for his Solicitor Clerk this day told mine, they had given it up, and the Attorney-General told me to call on him (which I shall do the beginning of the week) from whence I conclude that they have left the same notice with the Attorney-General, and that he will forthwith prepare his report, etc., etc.

APPENDIX O.

Two of the letters from the Comte de St. Maur to the Duke of Somerset.

My lord Duc,

Depuis longtemps je soupçonnais que votre nom était Saint Maur, et prononcé a l'anglaise, fait Seymour, cependant je n'osais vous écrire dans la crainte de me méprendre. Aujourd'huy, étant persuadé que c'est votre nom, s'il faut en croire Monsieur le Marquis de Pa :—auteur des [illegible] il donne à votre maison une origine française, de la province de Normandie, et dit que vos ancêtres ont passé en Angleterre avec Guillaume le Conquérant, ou vous vous êtes perpetués jusqu'aujourd'huy.

En conséquence de cette instruction, permettez-moi, Mylord, de prendre la liberté de vous adresser cette lettre, au hasard qu'elle vous parvienne, pour vous prier de me donner quelques éclaircissements sinon des preuves sur ce que je vais vous expliquer.

Je suis Saint Maur de nom nom qui jouis en France, dans la province de la Marche, d'une noblesse ancienne et distinguée, et ose même avancer que la maison tient rang dans les plus anciennes de la province. Elle ne s'est regardée e devant son origine, mais bien comme une maison sortie d'Angleterre ; nos ancêtres ont toujours dit à leurs enfants que nous tenions notre origine de cet endroit, et sans autre preuve que cette tradition, nous nous sommes toujours cru d'origine anglaise. Le court examen que jais fait dans les titres ne m'a rien fait voir qui remonte plus qu'au 14me siècle sans lacunes. Celui qui fait la Souche d'où nous sortons se nommait Hugues ; il a epousé une héritière, vers 1396, de notre maison. Il se trouve que jusqu'à present aucun âiné n'a eu de mâle, nous sommes encore malgré cela trois branches, dont deux sans enfants, l'autre n'a qu'un garçon de douze ans et une demoiselle de 17.

Si nous sortions d'Angleterre, comme il y a apparence, c'est probablement cet Hugue de Saint Maur qui a passe d'Angleterre dans la province de la Marche avant l'epoque du 14me siècle ; nous n'avons trouvé aucun Saint Maur dans aucune chartre, ny fondation, d'avant ce temps. Cependant, l'on voit que les descendants de Hugue jouirent dans le 15me et 16me siècle d'une grande considération dans la province, non seulement par leurs emplois au service, mais par l'ancienneté de leur noblesse, et ont toujours pris alliance dans de bonnes maisons de la province et dans celles du Poitou et du Berry, qui avoisinent.

Si ma lettre, Mylord, vous parvient, faites-moi l'honneur de me répondre et mandez-moi, je vous prie, le blason de vos armes; celles de notre maison sont, d'argent, deux Pignons de sable, l'une sur l'autre, pattes et becquettès de Gueules.

Je serais bien aise, Mylord, si j'avais quelques détails précis sur cette recherche, et bien plus, si j'avais l'honneur d'être de votre tribu, a telle fin que ce puisse être, permettez que je sois très respectueusement, Mylord Duc,

Votre très humble et très obéissant serviteur,

LE COMTE DE SAINT MAUR.

Oct. 10, 1793.

Mylord Duc,

J'aurais répondu plus tôt a la lettre honnête et gracieuse que vous m'avez fait l'honneur de m'adresser si elle avait été écrite en français; j'ai été obligé d'envoyer le paquet à Paris, pour le faire traduire, nayant put trouver, dans la petite province que j'habite, aucune personne capable de me rendre ce petit service.   Encore n'ai-je reçu que la lettre traduite.

Je suis bien flatté, Mylord, de ce qu'après avoir rapproché toutes nos traditions réciproques, vous ne doutiez pas que nous ayons la même origine.   Je tiens à un singulier honneur celui que vous me faites et en ressens une grande satisfaction; il est vrai qu'il y a la plus grande probabilité.   Il nous est impossible de trouver nos ascendants, partant d'Hugue *ou Hugo*, dans les chartres, aucune trace de notre nom, avant ce temps; ce qui nous confirme que nos ayeux sont en Angleterre.   Nos maisons anciennes et voisines nous ont dit de tous temps que nous ne pouvions remonter à notre origine, qu'en votre pays; de là je conclus, Mylord, que j'ai l'honneur d'être votre parent: il se trouve dans l'Écu des armes, de la différence; elle peut provenir de notre côté, comme il arrive souvent aux cadets qui s'expatrient; il est certain que depuis que nous sommes dans la province, ellès ont toujours été les mêmes; il y a deux cents ans qu'elles sont à Malthes, et près de quatre cents chez le Généalogiste de France; Hugue pourrait les avoir tronquées, et nos pères ont suivi.

Je prends la liberté de vous envoyer un tableau des descendants de notre dernier ayeul, premier établi dans cette province; vous y verrez une chose très singulière et peut-être unique; depuis que nous sommes en ce pays, jusqu'à ce jour, notre maison s'est perpétuée toujours par les cadets, les aínes n'ont jamais eu de garçons, et à differents temps, trois filles de ces aínes étant héritiéres, ont fait passer les biens des Saint Maur's en d'autres maisons, ce qui a beaucoup contribué a diminuer leur fortune.   Je vois cependant qu'au 16me et 17me siècle, la maison était encore puissante et mes ancêtres tenaient un rang distingué au service du Roy. Il y a eu quatre chevaliers de L'ordre du Roy et Gentilshommes ordinaires de sa chambre ; un autre Envoyé Extraordinaire, et qui mit sur pied six cents hommes qu'il commandait ; un autre était Gouverneur de Montpensier ; ils ont eu l'honneur de recevoir directement des lettres de Sa Majesté pour Lordre de son service ; ils prenaient dans leurs actes la qualité de hauts et de puissants Seigneurs. Ce n'est donc que vers 1660 que la fortune nous a tourné le dos ; vous ne verrez dans le tableau cyinclus, ni filles ni célibataires, ce n'est pas faute d'en avoir, j'ai trouvé inutile de les y placer. Nous avons eu beaucoup de filles, qui ont passé dans de bonnes maisons, comme dans celles de Chamborant, de Ponthe de la Chartre, etc. Voilà en peu de mots l'historique de notre maison.

Si vous découvrez, Mylord Duc, quelquechose que nous puissions légitimement nous approprier, c'est une grande grâce que vous me feriez de m'en faire part. Ah! que ne sui-je à vingt lieues de Calais, je passerais avec un grand plaisir la Manche, pour aller vous présenter de vive voix mon respectueux hommage ; vous pouvez faiblement me dédommager, si vous avez la bonté d'entretenir notre correspondance. Dans cet espoir, j'ay l'honneur d'être, avec un parfait attachement et le plus grand respect, Mylord Duc,

Votre humble, obéissant serviteur, et

très affectionné cousin,

De Saint Maur.

March 25, 1784.

Mon épouse, enchantée de ma découverte, vous prie, Mylord Duc, d'agréer ses affectueux et empressés compliments. Elle désire beaucoup que vous lui fassiez hommage de votre portrait ; je le désire autant qu'elle, mais nous ne nous accordons pas. Elle le voudrait en miniature, et moi de grandeur naturelle, dans le costume de cérémonie des Ducs et Pairs.

APPENDIX P.

Extract of a letter from Sir J. Outram to the Governor-General.
Feb. 25, 1857.

The spirit and zeal which has induced Lord Seymour to join
the army, to expose himself to the dangers, hardships, and discom-
forts, attendant on war in such a country as this—truly deserves the
highest commendation and encouragement, and I hope may meet
with such from your Lordship. I know not whether it is in your
Lordship's power to confer local rank in this country to persons
not holding Her Majesty's or the E.I. Company's commissions.
If it is so, I would beg your Lordship to gazette Lord Seymour as
a local Captain or Lieutenant while serving with the army in
Persia, and that you will permit me to place his Lordship on my
Staff as an extra A.D.C. In the meantime he has tendered his
services gratuitously in any position wherein he can be useful, and
I have attached his Lordship therefore to Major Taylor, Political
Secretary . . . . Should it not be in your Lordship's power to
confer such a commission, may I beg the favour of your exerting
your high influence to effect this object through Her Majesty's
Minister of War or the Horse Guards.

(It was not in the power of Lord Canning, the Governor-
General, to accede to this request and, as his martial aspirations
were not encouraged at home, Lord Seymour had to be content
with his position as a volunteer.)

Extract of a letter from A. Baird, at Lucknow. Nov. 20, 1857.

This is what David says : " There is a very fine young fellow
(Lord Seymour) out here on his own hook, just to see the fun.
The other day when the men were hesitating, he drew his sword
and rushed to the front. Sir C. C. has been obliged to *order* him
back more than once or he would have been killed."

Extract from the Calcutta Gazette.

(Published by Authority.)   Friday, December 11, 1857.

(In a despatch signed C. Campbell, General, Commander-in-
Chief.)

"Lord Seymour was present throughout these operations and
displayed a daring gallantry at a most critical moment."

(In the same paper, signed R. J. H. Birch, Colonel, Secretary to the Government of India in the Military Department.)

"The Commander-in-Chief speaks in high terms of the daring conduct of Lord Seymour, who, as a volunteer, joined the Commander-in-Chief and was present throughout the operations before Lucknow. The thanks of the Governor-General in Council are due to Lord Seymour for the good service which he has freely rendered."

Extract from the Daily News. November 1st, 1860.

. . . . I do not know that you are aware under the name of Captain Sarsfield is disguised the eldest son of one of the noblest Dukes of the English Peerage. Lord S——, the heir of the illustrious title of the Duke of S——, by his mother's side a descendant of Sheridan, is the very soul of the regiment sent by the people of free England to fight for Italian liberty. Kind to his soldiers, untiring in the performance of his duties, Lord S—— is the model of an officer, and his courage, activity, and zeal would do honour to the best officer of any army in Europe . . . .

Extract from a letter signed W. Adam Smith, which appeared in the Newspapers. From Naples, November 23rd, 1860.

Whatever may be the faults of Captain Sarsfield, they are the errors of the noble and chivalrous spirit, which resents a wrong done to another, as a wrong done to himself, and I only wish there were more such men in this self-seeking world—but the age of chivalry is gone.

Extract from a Newspaper. 1869.

Many Italians are here; and we have been mourning over a death, which I may safely say was felt by them as much as by a small set which also chances to be here, and which lived a long time in great friendship with the deceased at Naples, when he took, perhaps, an uncalled for but most gallant, generous part in that movement of which his pattern of illustrious men, Garibaldi, was the leader. I have seen him exposed to danger, which is something, and to privation, extreme fatigue, and hunger, which is more, and I am sure that a more gallant soldier or a worthier fellow never carried a musket—as he did—than Ferdinand Earl St. Maur. I remember on one occasion his refusing food, because, he said, "None of my poor fellows have got any"; on another, his carrying, on a long march, the muskets of three privates who were footsore; and again, his giving a revolver to a volunteer interpreter, during a sharpish skirmish, saying, "Why, you can't help yourself with a pencil." A second after the interpreter fell dead, shot through the heart. When Earl St. Maur died, he left few better or braver men behind him.

APPENDIX Q.

Jan. 11, 1862.

Civil Service Commission.

Sir,

With reference to my other letter of this day's date, inclosing a Certificate of Qualification for Lord Edward St. Maur, I am directed by the Civil Service Commissioners to state that they think it right to bring under the notice of Earl Russell the marked proficiency which Lord E. St. Maur has displayed in his examination. Having on a former occasion, at his own request, been examined in German and obtained an honorary addition to his certificate for knowledge of that language, he has now been examined in Spanish, with which he appears to be very thoroughly acquainted. He has also answered very satisfactorily in International Law, and his report on Spain deserves high commendation for the ability and industry which it displays.

I have, etc.,

J. S. MAITLAND.

E. Hammond, Esqr.,
etc., etc.

From H.R.H. the Prince of Wales.

Sandringham.

Dec. 31, 1865.

My dear Duke,

I cannot tell you how shocked and deeply grieved I was to read in the papers the sad death of your son Edward. Pray accept my most sincere and heartfelt sympathy at the great loss you have sustained, and please express the same to the Duchess. You know how well I used to know your son some years ago when we were both much younger, and although of late years I have not had the opportunity of seeing so much of him as I should have wished, still I naturally took the greatest interest in his career, which has, alas! been brought to such an early close, and shall ever deplore him as a kind friend.

Not wishing at such a time to intrude further on your grief,

Believe me, my dear Duke,

Yours most sincerely,

ALBERT EDWARD.

(From Mr. Stewart.)

Yellapoor.

Dec. 17/65.

My dear Sir Bartle,

My telegram will have prepared you for an account of the accident that has happened to Lord E. St. Maur. I have deferred writing till I could give you the doctor's opinion—and as both Dr. Davies from Carwar and Dr. Langley from Dharwar arrived last night I am able to tell you they consider the knee wound to be a very serious one—but that his wonderfully good constitution gives him a chance that few men would have and has brought him through so far—and may enable the wound to heal, although they are prepared to amputate above the knee at a moment's warning of unfavourable symptoms. On Wednesday the 13th we came *en route* to Yellapoor to a Chupper (hut) that I had caused to be built on the banks of the Kala Nuddy near Lalgooly—we went out to a beat, and bison were started but not shot at. Instead of taking a second beat, Lord E. and Mr. Brand stalked through the remaining jungle, and the former saw bison and determined to return to the same jungle next morning. Accordingly he and Mr. Brand, each accompanied by a village Shikaree (huntsman), and another man started early (14th), and Mr. Brand came back, 9.15, having heard one shot fired by Lord E. We waited for his return, and about 10, the village Shikaree who accompanied him— a very good man—ran in with his belt and hunting-knife, in the sheath of which he had written that he was wounded by a bear— afraid his knee was out—and asked us to send for a surgeon. We reached the place where Lord E. was lying about half-past 11 and found that he had fired at a bear and rolled it over—followed the tracks and came suddenly on it lying or standing about 15 yards off, fired both barrels at it ; the bear charging on all fours seized him by the left knee, threw him down and both rolled down a steep hill, during which Lord E. struck him twice or thrice with his knife—stabbing him at least once. The two men came towards him with shouts and the bear left him, with one severe cut across the forehead over the right temple—how inflicted we cannot quite understand. He was very cool and told us what he wished done . . . . His patience and courage are most astonishing, and I never saw a more delightful patient to take care of . . . . Lord E. is very anxious that no news of his accident should be sent to England by telegraph. He is writing a short letter that will be sent by Madras, and will write another for the next Bombay mail . . . . I enclose a letter from Lord E. that I have written at his dictation: as you may fancy this lamentable accident has cast a sad gloom over our party. The doctors are of opinion that he will never recover the use of his knee even if his leg is

2 M 2

saved . . . . Lord E. desires me to add he regrets giving you so
much trouble . . . . I have carefully examined the two men
who were with Lord E. and am satisfied that no blame of rashness
can be imputed to him. He acted throughout with presence of
mind and skill, and no old sportsman—however experienced—could
have avoided the encounter . . . .

(Extract.)   Sir Bartle Frere to Lord John Hay.

Malabar Point, Bombay.
                                    Dec. 29, 1865.

I have half finished a letter to you on many subjects but have
no heart to finish it, while thinking of the grief you will feel at
the death of poor Lord E. St. Maur, of which you will hear about
this time . . . . I need not tell you how much I liked him, nor
how full of promise I thought him. He had so much manly
energy in entering into public questions, joined to an almost
feminine quickness and delicacy of perception and ready insight
into character and such ready wit. God comfort his poor parents
and his brother, of whom he seemed so fond . . . .

(Extract from a letter from Mr. Stewart to Earl St. Maur.)

. . . . I never met any one who so won my love and admiration
—short as our acquaintance was—and I can only the more bitterly
feel what must be the sorrow and distress of his friends and relations,
and what a void he must have left in many hearts. The natives of
this country are easily affected by events of this kind, but I never
saw such real grief and interest as they showed on this occasion.
Almost all who converse with me talk of it, and many with tears in
their eyes. They will long remember the brave young Lord who
stabbed the wounded bear at Lalgooly, and bore himself with such
courage and patience. One man who walked with me—while we
were carrying him from Lalgooly to Yellapoor—said, " His heart
was very large," and that was the general talk. . . . .

Extract from the Daily Telegraph.
Jan. 22, 1866.

Lord Edward St. Maur seemed marked out for an eminent,
happy, and lengthened career. Already initiated into public
service, and highly gifted, he would of course have become better
known to his countrymen, and possibly a foremost man of the
State. He was taking the right course to such results ; for,
following the wise example of men of his order like Lord Milton,
Lord Strangford, or Lord Dufferin, and of the Royal Princes

themselves, he was learning all he could by travel, before settling in earnest to a political "metier." He had been in the Southern States; and a keen observer—Jefferson Davis—with whom he was brought into contact, said that after a wide experience of Englishmen, he deemed Lord Edward St. Maur the most promising he had ever seen. Towards the close of last year he sailed for India to study our wonderful possessions in the East, about which the information prevailing among English statesmen is, as he must have known, but limited . . . . We regret as much as any one that a noble house should have lost a brave and able scion, and the public a promising young servant, whose idea of self-education was so wise and large. But even in our regrets we are glad for England and for her aristocracy, that the richest and poorest of her gentlemen know how to take their share of dangers alike, and, in spite of a luxurious age, still have this manly element in their blood. Strange, then, as it may seem, that a Deccan bear should end the career of a young nobleman who would assuredly have attained great distinction and high influence, his fate, however sad and distressing it may be, does not appear to us either trivial or unworthy.

LISBON.

Oct. 18 1866.

My dear Lord St. Maur,

Your very kind letter of the 9th instant has touched me deeply; it was on the other side of the Straits of Singapore that I learned your brother's death. The heroic circumstances were only known to me later, but they could not surprise me, who knew as well as I did the natural temper of his mind and character. My true affection for him was grounded on many months of intimate intercourse of the most delightful kind with one of the most highly-gifted minds I have ever known. It grew with my knowledge of him and was cemented by countless good offices of a friendship which never wearied in doing them. His loss was no common loss, and if I venture to say that I can in heart sympathize with the sorrows of those who saw a career of such brilliant promise so cruelly cut short, it is because I had been to myself the prophet of his future, and had looked forward with longing to the day when the voices of all his countrymen should hail in him what those who loved him knew him to be . . . .

Believe me to be, my dear Lord St. Maur,
Yours ever faithfully,
GEORGE BRACKENBURY.

Verses written on Lord Edward's tomb by his brother Lord
St. Maur.

I know, I understand that when men die
Back to a Parent God their spirits fly.
The soul I loved death has from pain set free.
This grave holds all that now belongs to me.

I know that death, which brings on flesh decay
Is but the dawning of a brighter day.
Yet here in thought my sorrowing soul must roam,
Here lie the hopes that made this earth its home.

Mine is a selfish grief, I miss a soul
Whose power could waken love, by love control;
I miss, I mourn a life which once combined
Chivalry's spirit and a master mind.

My Edward's worth renown can never show,
That knowledge lies hid in my lifelong woe.
His spirit lives, may mine through time and space
Find till we meet no lasting resting-place.

Edward is gone into the vast Unknown,
And I live on to labour here alone.
One only comfort shines through my distress—
Where my love's great, God's love cannot prove less.

HARRISON & SONS, Printers in Ordinary to His Majesty, St. Martin's Lane.

Lightning Source UK Ltd.
Milton Keynes UK
UKHW020608141019
351570UK00006B/541/P